CHRIST IN CHRISTIAN TRADITION

VOLUME TWO: PART FOUR

Christ in Christian Tradition

CHRIST
IN CHRISTIAN
TRADITION

VOLUME TWO

*From the Council of Chalcedon (451)
to Gregory the Great (590–604)*

PART FOUR
*The Church of Alexandria with
Nubia and Ethiopia after 451*

ALOYS GRILLMEIER SJ

in collaboration with
THERESIA HAINTHALER

translated by
O. C. DEAN Jr

MOWBRAY   WJK

Published in Great Britain by **Mowbray**, a Cassell imprint, Wellington House, 125 Strand, London WC2R 0BB

Published in the United States by **Westminster John Knox Press**, 100 Witherspoon Street, Louisville, KY 40202

German original published as *Jesus der Christus im Glauben der Kirche*, Band 2/4
© Verlag Herder, Freiburg im Breisgau 1990
English translation © O.C. Dean Jr 1996

English translation first published 1996

Imprimi potest: Jörg Dantscher SJ
Praep. Prov. Germ. Sup. SJ
Monachii, die 13 Aprilis 1990

British Library Cataloguing-in-Publication Data
A catalogue record for this book is available from the British Library.

ISBN 0–264–66018–8

Library of Congress Cataloging-in-Publication Data
(Revised for volume 2, part 4)
Grillmeier, Aloys, date.
    Christ in Christian tradition.
    Author statement varies.
    Edition statement varies.
    Includes bibliographical references and indexes.
    Contents: v. 1. From the apostolic age to Chalcedon (451) — v.
2. From the Council of Chalcedon (451) to Gregory the Great (590–604).   Pt. 1. Reception and Contradiction.   Pt. 2. The Church of Constantinople in the sixth century.   Pt. 4. The Church of Alexandrìa with Nubia and Ethiopia after 451.
    1. Jesus Christ — History of doctrines — Early church, ca. 30–600.
I. Title.
BT198.G743 1975 232'.09 75–13456
ISBN 0–664–21998–5 (v. 2, pt. 4)

The publication of this book has been assisted by a contribution from Inter Nationes, Bonn.

Typeset by York House Typographic Ltd, London
Printed and bound in Great Britain by Biddles Ltd, Guildford and King's Lynn

DEDICATED IN FRIENDSHIP TO
HANS QUECKE SJ
PONTIFICIO ISTITUTO BIBLICO
ROME

PREFACE

Probably in no other early church mission field outside the 'fertile crescent' – that land corridor used by peoples and armies of the East heading toward the Mediterranean and the West – do we find such peculiar geographical and cultural conditions for the proclaiming of the gospel of Jesus Christ as in the long stretch of the Nile valley from the Delta to the source of the Blue Nile near Lake Tana in the Ethiopian highland. Reaching south from the world-famous metropolis of Alexandria on the Mediterranean with its advanced culture was a seemingly interminable river landscape with a narrow green strip on each bank and immensely vast desert beyond; there were resident fellahin, wandering nomads and growing monastic colonies of various kinds. Millennia looked down on those first messengers of Christianity – long before the arrival of Napoleon's soldiers. Pyramids and mighty temple complexes in great number from Giza to Philae, the gateway to the Sudan, were the symbols and citadels of the ancient Egyptian religion; they were to be captured not by armies, as in the new world at the beginning of the modern period, but by itinerant apostles and thus quite peacefully, apart from intervention by Byzantine officials and isolated attacks by bands of monks armed with sticks in the fourth and fifth centuries. Beyond Egypt was Nubia with its three kingdoms, whose Christian culture first received proper attention with the building of the Aswan High Dam, only to disappear again to a large extent under the waters of the Nile. As difficult as the Blue Nile's passage from Ethiopia to Khartoum was the path of the missionaries in the opposite direction. From the Red Sea, however, there was an easier access to the Axumite Empire. Thus to an increasing extent, from the fourth century on, a tremendous stretch of land of the most varied kind was united by the one river in the one faith in Jesus Christ.

In this volume we will attempt, as a kind of a spiritual expedition, to follow the path of the gospel and explore the unity and diversity of the faith along the Nile during the period from the fourth or fifth century until the penetration of Islam. The struggle between the two religions, begun in the seventh century, still continues today.

In regard to Egypt, newly available sources can be evaluated christo-logically for the first time. For this I am indebted to the Coptic specialists Prof. Tito Orlandi and Prof. Dr Hans Quecke SJ, of Rome. With his advice and interest, the latter has accompanied the creation of this work from the beginning. It has also been influenced by personal contacts with the leading representatives of the Old Oriental Orthodox Church of Alexandria in the course of lengthy ecumenical dialogues in Vienna and Cairo. May the present work become a contribution to mutual under-standing.

I also owe a large debt of gratitude to the Deutsche Forschungs-gemeinschaft, which for years has included the work in progress in its research programme. This enabled my academic colleague Dr Theresia Hainthaler to make available also for this volume her precision in research and her technical and editorial capability with the computer. Beyond the work as a whole, her special contributions are noted at various places in the book.

Frankfurt am Main   Aloys Grillmeier SJ
11 February 1990

Remarks on the English Edition

We owe a very great debt of gratitude to O. C. Dean Jr, PhD, for the English translation of this work. He completed it skilfully and with great care, and it meets with our full satisfaction. After having read and carefully checked this translation, we consider it an authorized transla-tion. Dr Theresia Hainthaler undertook the task of final correction and up-dating of parts of the book, including the chapter about Dioscorus of Aphrodito and the literature supplements.

For generous financial support we would like to thank Dr Bernhard Duvenbeck, Bad Homburg. We express our gratitude also to the North German Province of the Jesuits, who made possible the work of Dr Hainthaler.

A. Grillmeier SJ
T. Hainthaler

CONTENTS

PART TWO
THE 'PROVINCE OF COPTIC CHRISTOLOGY'

PART THREE
THE 'CROSS OF CHRIST' OVER NUBIA

PART FOUR
CHRIST IN A NEW MESSIANIC KINGDOM
FAITH IN CHRIST IN ETHIOPIA

For maps we suggest the following:

1. *Atlas zur Kirchengeschichte. Die christlichen Kirchen in Geschichte und Gegenwart*, edited by H. Jedin, K. S. Latourette and J. Martin, compiled by J. Martin; updated revised edition compiled and edited by J. Martin, Freiburg etc. [3]1988, maps 10B, 11A, 29A, 130AB, 134B.

2. *Tübinger Atlas des Vorderen Orients*, compiled by S. Timm, 1983, map B VI 15 Ägypten. Das Christentum bis zur Araberzeit (bis zum 7. Jahrhundert).

3. Hammerschmidt, E., *Äthiopien. Christliches Reich zwischen Gestern und Morgen*, Wiesbaden 1967, map.

4. Ullendorff, E., *The Ethiopians. An Introduction to Country and People*, London [2]1965, map.

ABBREVIATIONS

AANL.M	Atti dell'accademia nazionale dei Lincei, Roma. Memorie. Classe de scienze morali, storiche e filologiche
AAWB.PH	*Philosophische und historische Abhandlungen der königlichen Akademie der Wissenschaften zu Berlin*
ABAW.PH	*Abhandlungen der bayerischen Akademie der Wissenschaften*, Munich, Philosophisch-historische Abteilung, NF 1, 1929ff.
ABAW.PP	*Abhandlungen der (königl.) bayerischen Akademie der Wissenschaften*, Munich, Philosophisch-philologische Klasse
AccNazLinc	Accademia Nazionale dei Lincei
ACIStEt	*Atti del Convegno Internazionale di Studi Etiopici* (Rome, 2–4 April 1959), ed. AccNazLinc a. CCCLVII–1960, Rome 1960
ACO	Acta Conciliorum Oecumenicorum, ed. E. Schwartz, Strasbourg, Leipzig, Berlin; T. IV, vol. 1 ss. ed. J. Straub (1971ff.); 2nd series ed. R. Riedinger (1984ff.)
ACW	Ancient Christian Writers
ADAI.K	Abhandlungen des Deutschen Archäologischen Instituts, Cairo. Koptische Reihe
AegC	Aegyptiaca Christiana. Cairo, Sezione 1: Monografie
AFA	Leontius of Byzantium, *Adversus fraudes Apollinaristarum*
AGWG.PH	*Abhandlungen der Gesellschaft der Wissenschaften zu Göttingen*, Göttingen, Philologisch-historische Klasse, NS 1, 1896/97ff.
AHAW.PH	*Abhandlungen der Heidelberger Akademie der Wissenschaften*. Philosophisch-historische Klasse 1, 1941
AHC	*Annuarium Historiae Conciliorum*, Amsterdam 1, 1969ff.
AION.L	*Annali dell'istituto universitario orientale di Napoli*, sezione linguistica 1, 1959
AIVS	*Atti del Reale Istituto Veneto di Scienze, Lettere ed Arti*
AJ	*Apocryphon of John*
AKM	Abhandlungen für die Kunde des Morgenlandes, Leipzig etc. 1, 1857
ALW	*Archiv für Liturgiewissenschaft*, Regensburg 1, 1950ff.
AnBoll	*Analecta Bollandiana*, Paris–Brussels 1, 1882ff.
AnGreg	*Analecta Gregoriana*, Rome 1, 1930ff.
APARA.R	Atti della Pontificia Accademia Romana di Archeologia, Rendiconti
APAW.PH	*Abhandlungen der preussischen Akademie der Wissenschaften*, Berlin, Philosophisch-historische Klasse
ARAccLinc	Atti della R. Accademia dei Lincei
ASAW	*Abhandlungen der sächsischen Akademie der Wissenschaften*, Leipzig
ASS	Acta Sanctorum

ÄthFor	*Äthiopistische Forschungen*
Aug	*Augustinianum*, Rome 1, 1961ff.
BBA	Berliner byzantinistische Arbeiten
BCLAB	*Bulletin de la classe des lettres et des sciences morales et politiques de l'académie r. de Belgique*
BEHE	Bibliothèque de l'École des Hautes Études, Paris
BeihTübAtl	Beihefte zum Tübinger Atlas des Vorderen Orients
BEL.S	Bibliotheca 'Ephemerides Liturgicae', Rome, Subsidia
BGAM	Beiträge zur Geschichte des alten Mönchtums und des Benediktiner-ordens, Münster 1, 1912ff.
BGrL	Bibliothek der griechischen Literatur, Stuttgart 1, 1971ff.
BHG	Bibliotheca hagiographica graeca I–III, ed. F. Halkin = SubsHag 8a, Brussels ³1957
BHO	Bibliotheca hagiographica orientalis, ed. soc. bollandiani, Brussels 1910
BHTh	Beiträge zur historischen Theologie, Tübingen 12, 1950ff.
Bib	*Biblica*, Rome 1, 1920ff.
BiblMus	Bibliothèque du Muséon, Louvain 1, 1929ff.
BiblScRel	Biblioteca di Scienze Religiose, Libreria Ateneo Salesiano, Rome
BIFAO	*Bulletin de l'Institut français d'archéologie orientale*, Cairo
BJRL	*Bulletin of the John Rylands University Library of Manchester* 1, 1903ff.
BKV²	Bibliothek der Kirchenväter, Kempten 1, ²1911ff.
BLE	*Bulletin de Littérature Ecclésiastique*, Toulouse, NS 10, 1899ff.; 20, 1899 (= 3. ser. 1) ff.; 30, 1909 (= 4. ser. 1) ff.
BO	J. S. Assemani, *Bibliotheca Orientalis Clementino-Vaticana* I–III, Rome 1719–28
BoJ.B	Bonner Jahrbücher, Beiheft
BOS	Bonner Orientalistische Studien, NS 1, Stuttgart 1954ff.
BSAC	*Bulletin de la Société d'Archéologie Copte*, Cairo 1, 1938ff.
BSHT	Breslauer Studien zur historischen Theologie, Breslau 1, 1922ff.
Byz	*Byzantion*, Brussels 1, 1924ff.
ByzSlav	*Byzantinoslavica*, Prague 1, 1929ff.
ByzZ	*Byzantinische Zeitschrift*, Leipzig–Munich 1, 1892ff.
BZ	*Biblische Zeitschrift*, NS 1, Freiburg–Paderborn 1957ff.
CA	*Collectio Avellana* = *Epistulae imperatorum pontificum aliorum* . . . I, II, ed. O. Guenther (Vienna etc. 1895, 1898) = CSEL 35/1–2
CAG	Commentaria in Aristotelem graeca, edita consilio et auctoritate Acade-miae litterarum regiae borussicae
CAp	*Constitutiones Apostolorum*
CCG	Corpus Christianorum, series graeca, Turnhout 1, 1977ff.
CCL	Corpus Christianorum, series latina, Turnhout 1, 1953ff.
CCT	A. Grillmeier, *Christ in Christian Tradition*, vol. I: *From the Apostolic Age to Chalcedon (451)*, London–Atlanta ²1975; vol. II/1, London 1987; vol. II/2, London/Louisville 1995
CE	Codex Encyclius

Chalkedon	A. Grillmeier and H. Bacht (eds.), *Das Konzil von Chalkedon. Geschichte und Gegenwart*, 3 vols., Würzburg 1951–54, ⁵1979 (reprint of 4th ed. with a new foreword)
ChrAnt	Christianisme antique, Paris 1, 1977ff.
CLCAG	Corpus Latinum commentariorum in Aristotelem Graecorum, Louvain 1, 1957ff.
CMC	Cologne Mani Codex
CMCL	Corpus dei Manuscritti Copti Letterari, ed. Unione Accademica Nazionale
CNE	Leontius of Byzantium, *Contra Nestorianos et Eutychianos*
CollCist	*Collectanea Cisterciensia*, Scourmont 1, 1939ff.
CPG	Clavis Patrum Graecorum, vols. I–V, Turnhout 1979ff.
CPL	Clavis Patrum Latinorum . . . , ed. E. Dekkers, Steenbrugge ²1961
CrSt	*Cristianesimo nella storia. Ricerche storiche esegetiche teologiche*, Bologna 1, 1980ss.
CSCO	Corpus scriptorum christianorum orientalium, Rome etc. 1903ff.
CSEL	Corpus scriptorum ecclesiasticorum latinorum, Vienna 1, 1866ff.
DACL	*Dictionnaire d'Archéologie Chrétienne et de Liturgie*, Paris 1, 1924ff.
DEC .	*Decrees of the Ecumenical Councils*, vol. I: *Nicaea I to Lateran V*, ed. N. P. Tanner, original text established by G. Alberigo, J. A. Dossetti, P.-P. Joannou, C. Leonardi and P. Prodi, in consultation with H. Jedin, London–Washington 1990
DHGE	*Dictionnaire d'Histoire et de Géographie Ecclésiastique*, Paris 1, 1912ff.
Doc. mon.	*Documenta monophysitica* = I. B. Chabot, *Documenta ad origines monophysitarum illustrandas*, CSCO 17 (T) (Louvain 1908, ²1952); 103 (V) (Louvain 1933, ²1952)
DOP	*Dumbarton Oaks Papers*, Cambridge, Mass. 1, 1941ff.
DP	*Doctrina Patrum de incarnatione verbi*, ed. F. Diekamp, Münster 1907, 2nd ed. 1981 by E. Chrysos
DPAC	*Dizionario patristico e di antichità cristiana* I–III, diretto da Angelo Di Berardino, Casale Monferrato 1983 (I, II), 1988 (III) (for ET see *EEC*)
DSp	*Dictionnaire de spiritualité, ascétique et mystique*, Paris 1, 1932ff.
DTC	*Dictionnaire de Théologie Catholique*, Paris 1903–72
EEC	*Encyclopedia of the Early Church*, trans. of *DPAC* by A. Walford, Cambridge 1991
EEuFL	E. Lodi, *Enchiridion Euchologicum Fontium Liturgicorum*, Rome 1979
EO	*Echos d'Orient*, Bucharest etc. 1, 1897/98, to 39, 1940/43
EPRO	Études préliminaires aux religions orientales dans l'empire romain, Leiden 1, 1961ff.
EstEcl	*Estudios Eclesiásticos*, Madrid 1, 1922ff.
EvTh	*Evangelische Theologie*, NS 1, Munich 1946/47ff.
FCLDG	Forschungen zur christlichen Literatur- und Dogmengeschichte, Paderborn 1, 1900, to 18, 1938
FlorCyr	*Florilegium Cyrillianum*

FrancStud	*Franciscan Studies*, New York etc. 1, 1924ff.
FS	Festschrift
GCS	Die Griechischen Christlichen Schriftsteller der ersten drei Jahrhunderte, Berlin 1, 1897ff.
GIF	*Giornale italiano di filologia*, Naples 1, 1948ff., NS 1, 1970
GOF	Göttinger Orientforschung, Wiesbaden
GOTR	*Greek Orthodox Theological Review*, Brookline, Mass. 1, 1954ff.
GRBS	*Greek, Roman and Byzantine Studies*, Cambridge, Mass. 1, 1958ff.
Greg	*Gregorianum*, Rome 1, 1920ff.
Grumel, *Regestes*	V. Grumel, *Les Regestes des Actes du Patriarcat de Constantinople* I/I, ²1932
HandAm	*Handes amsorya. Zeitschrift für armenische Philologie*, Vienna 1, 1887ff.
HDG	Handbuch der Dogmengeschichte, Freiburg–Basel–Vienna 1956ff.
HE	*Historia Ecclesiastica*
HEO	G. Fedalto, *Hierarchia Ecclesiastica Orientalis*, I. *Patriarchatus Constantinopolitanus*, II. *Patriarchatus Alexandrinus, Antiochenus, Hierosolymitanus*, Padua 1988
HO	Handbuch der Orientalistik, Leiden etc. 1948ff.
HSCP	*Harvard Studies in Classical Philology*, Cambridge Mass. 1, 1890ff.
HThR	*Harvard Theological Review*, Cambridge, Mass. 1, 1908ff.
HThS	Harvard Theological Studies, Cambridge, Mass. 1, 1916ff.
Irén	*Irénikon*, Amay, Chevetogne 1, 1926ff.
JA	*Journal asiatique*, Paris 1, 1822ff.
JAC	*Jahrbuch für Antike und Christentum*, Münster 1, 1958ff.
JARCE	*Journal of the American Research Center in Egypt*, Boston, Mass. 1, 1962ff.
JdChr	A. Grillmeier, *Jesus der Christus im Glauben der Kirche*, Band I: *Von der Apostolischen Zeit bis zum Konzil von Chalcedon (451)*, Freiburg 1979, ²1982, ³1990; Band II/1: *Das Konzil von Chalcedon (451). Rezeption und Widerspruch (415–518)*, Freiburg 1986, ²1991; Band II/2: *Die Kirche von Konstantinopel im 6. Jahrhundert*, Freiburg 1989; Band II/4: *Die Kirche von Alexandrien mit Nubien und Äthiopien nach 451*, Freiburg 1990
JEA	*Journal of Egyptian Archaeology*, London 1, 1914ff.
JEH	*Journal of Ecclesiastical History*, London 1, 1950ff.
JLH	*Jahrbuch für Liturgik und Hymnologie*, Kassel 1, 1955ff.
JLW	*Jahrbuch für Liturgiewissenschaft*, Münster 1, 1921, to 15, 1941
JNES	*Journal of Near Eastern Studies*, Chicago 1, 1929ff.
JSS	*Journal of Semitic Studies*, Manchester 1, 1956ff.
JTS	*Journal of Theological Studies*, Oxford etc. 1, 1899ff.; NS 1, 1950ff.
JW	Regesta Pontificum Romanorum, ed. P. Jaffé, ed. 2a auspiciis G. Wattenbach curaverunt S. Loewenfeld / F. Kaltenbrunner / P. Ewald, Tomus I, Leipzig 1888
KGA	*Kirchengeschichtliche Abhandlungen*, Breslau 1, 1902, to 11, 1920

Kl.Pauly	*Der Kleine Pauly. Lexikon der Antike,* 5 vols., ed. K. Ziegler and W. Sonnleitner, Stuttgart 1964–75
KlT	Kleine Texte für (theologische und philosophische) Vorlesungen und Übungen, Bonn 1, 1902ff.
KlWbChrOr	*Kleines Wörterbuch des Christlichen Orients,* ed. J. Assfalg and P. Krüger, Wiesbaden 1975
Lampe, *PatrGrLex*	*A Patristic Greek Lexicon. With Addenda and Corrigenda,* ed. G. W. H. Lampe, Oxford ²1968
LexÄg	*Lexikon der Ägyptologie,* Wiesbaden 1, 1972ff.
LO	Lex orandi, Paris 1, 1944ff.
LQF	Liturgiewissenschaftliche Quellen und Forschungen, Münster 1, 1909, to 32, 1957ff.
LThK	*Lexikon für Theologie und Kirche,* ed. J. Höfer and K. Rahner, Freiburg ²1957ff.
Mansi	*Sacrorum Conciliorum nova et amplissima Collectio,* ed. J. D. Mansi, Florence etc. 1769ff.
MGH	Monumenta Germaniae historica inde ab a. C. 500 usque ad a. 1500, Hanover–Berlin 1, 1877ff.
MIFAO	Mémoires publ. par les membres de l'Institut français d'archéologie orientale au Caire, Cairo 1, 1902ff.
MiscByzMon	Miscellanea Byzantina Monacensia
Mn	*Mnemosyne. Bibliotheca classica (philologica) Batava,* Leiden NS 1, 1873, to 60, 1933
MSR	*Mélanges de science religieuse,* Lille 1, 1944ff.
MThS.S	Münchener theologische Studien, Munich, Systematische Abteilung 1, 1950ff.
Mus	*Le Muséon,* Louvain 1, 1882ff.; 34, 1921ff.
MWSt	Missionswissenschaftliche Studien, NS 1, Gütersloh 1931ff.
NAWG.PH	*Nachrichten der Akademie der Wissenschaften in Göttingen,* Philologisch-historische Klasse
NGWG	*Nachrichten von der Gesellschaft der Wissenschaften zu Göttingen,* 1845ff.
NGWG.PH	*Nachrichten von der (Königlichen) Gesellschaft der Wissenschaften zu Göttingen,* Philologisch-historische Klasse
NHSt	Nag Hammadi Studies, Leiden 1, 1971ff.
NJKA	*Neue Jahrbücher für das klassische Altertum, Geschichte, deutsche Literatur und für Pädagogik,* Leipzig etc. 1, 1898, to 54, 1924
NovTest	*Novum Testamentum. An International Quarterly for New Testament and Related Studies,* Leiden 1, 1956ff.
NRT	*Nouvelle revue théologique,* Louvain 1, 1869ff.
NTT	*Nederlands(ch)e theologisch tijdschrift,* Wangeningen etc. 1, 1946/47
NZM	*Neue Zeitschrift für Missionswissenschaft,* Beckenried 1, 1945ff.
OC	Orientalia Christiana, Rome 1, 1923, to 100, 1934
OCA	Orientalia Christiana Analecta, Rome 101, 1935ff.
OCP	*Orientalia Christiana Periodica,* Rome 1, 1935ff.

OLA	Orientalia Lovaniensia Analecta, Louvain 1, 1975ff.
OLP	*Orientalia Lovaniensia Periodica*, Louvain 1, 1970ff.
Op. Min.	Opera Minora, Turnhout–Louvain 1976
ÖR.B	Ökumenische Rundschau, Beiheft
OrChr	*Oriens Christianus*, Rome 1, 1901ff.; 37 (= 4th series 1), Wiesbaden, 1953ff.
OrSyr	*L'Orient syrien*, Paris 1, 1956, to 12, 1967
OstKSt	*Ostkirchliche Studien*, Würzburg 1, 1952
ÖstlChr	*Das östliche Christentum*, NS 1, Würzburg 1947ff.
PA	*Peri Archon*
ParOr	*La Parole de l'Orient*, Kaslik 1, 1970ff.
PE	*Prex eucharistica*
PG	Patrologiae cursus completus. Series graeca (1–161), accurante J.-P. Migne, Paris 1857–1912
PIOL	Publications de l'Institut orientaliste de Louvain, Louvain 1, 1970
PL	Patrologiae cursus completus. Series latina (1–221), accurante J.-P. Migne, Paris 1841–64
PLS	Patrologiae latinae supplementum, Paris 1–5, 1958–70
PO	Patrologia Orientalis, ed. R. Graffin and F. Nau, Paris 1–5, 1907ff.
POC	*Proche-Orient chrétien*, Jerusalem 1, 1951ff.
PS	E. Schwartz, *Publizistische Sammlungen zum Acacianischen Schisma*, Munich 1934
PTSt	Patristische Texte und Studien, Berlin 1, 1964ff.
PWK	*Paulys Real-Encyclopädie der classischen Altertumswissenschaft*, revised ed. vols. 1–6, ed. G. Wissowa, Stuttgart 1894–1909; vols. 7–35 ed. W. Kroll, Stuttgart 1912–37; vols. 36ff. ed. K. Mittelhaus and K. Ziegler, Stuttgart–Munich 1947–72
RAC	*Reallexikon für Antike und Christentum*, Stuttgart 1, 1950ff.
RAPH	Recherches d'archéologie, de philologie et d'histoire, Cairo 1, 1930ff.
RE	*Realencyklopädie für protestantische Theologie und Kirche*, 3rd ed., Leipzig 1, 1896, to 24, 1913
RevBibl	*Revue Biblique*, Paris 1, 1892ff.; NS 1, 1904ff.
RevBibl.C	Cahiers de la Revue biblique, Paris 1, 1964ff.
RevÉtAug	*Revue des études augustiniennes*, Paris 1, 1955ff.
RevÉtByz	*Revue des études byzantines*, Paris 4, 1946ff.
RevÉtGrec	*Revue des études grecques*, Paris 1, 1888ff.
RevHistRel	*Revue de l'histoire des religions*, Paris 1, 1880ff.
RevSR	*Revue des sciences religieuses*, Strasbourg–Paris 1, 1921ff.
RHE	*Revue d'histoire ecclésiastique*, Louvain 1, 1900ff.
RivArcCr	*Rivista di Archeologia Cristiana*, Rome–Vatican City 1, 1924ff.
ROC	*Revue de l'Orient chrétien*, Paris 1, 1896ff.
RömQ	*Römische Quartalschrift für christliche Altertumskunde und für Kirchengeschichte*, Freiburg 1, 1887ff.
RSLR	*Rivista di Storia e Letteratura religiosa*, Florence 1, 1965ff.
RSPT	*Revue des sciences philosophiques et théologiques*, Paris 1, 1907ff.
RSR	*Recherches de science religieuse*, Paris 1, 1910ff.

SBAW	*Sitzungsberichte der Bayerischen Akademie der Wissenschaften*, Munich, Philosophisch-historische Abteilung
SC	Sources Chrétiennes, Paris 1, 1944ff.
SCH(L)	*Studies in Church History*, Ecclesiastical History Society, London etc. 1, 1964ff.
SE	*Sacris Erudiri*, Steenbrugge etc. 1, 1948ff.
SGV	Sammlung gemeinverständlicher Vorträge und Schriften aus dem Gebiet der Theologie und Religionsgeschichte, Tübingen 1, 1896ff.
SL	*The Sixth Book of the Select Letters of Severus*, ed. E. W. Brooks, vol. II/1, London–Oxford 1903
SOC.Ae	Studia Orientalia Christiana, Aegyptiaca
SOC.C	Studia Orientalia Christiana, Cairo, Collectanea
SPAMP	Studien zur Problemgeschichte der antiken und mittelalterlichen Philosophie, Leiden 1, 1966ff.
SPAW	*Sitzungsberichte der preussischen Akademie der Wissenschaften*, Berlin 1882–1921
SpicFrib	Spicilegium Friburgense. Texte zur Geschichte des kirchlichen Lebens, Fribourg 1, 1957ff.
SpicSLov	Spicilegium Sacrum Lovaniense, Louvain 1, 1922ff.
ST	Studi e Testi, Vatican City 1, 1900ff.
StRiOrCr	Studi e ricerche sull'oriente cristiano, Rome 1, 1978ff.
StSem	Studi semitici, Rome 1, 1958ff.
StudLit	*Studia Liturgica*, Rotterdam etc. 1, 1962ff.
StudPat	*Studia Patristica*, Berlin 1, 1957ff. (= TU 63ff.)
SubsHag	Subsidia Hagiographica (= *AnBoll* supp.), Brussels 1, 1886ff.
SWGS	Schriften der wissenschaftlichen Gesellschaft in Strasbourg
TD	Textus et Documenta (ser. theol.), Rome 1, 1932ff.
ThéolHist	*Théologie historique*, Paris 1, 1963ff.
TheolPhil	*Theologie und Philosophie*, Freiburg 41, 1966ff.
ThLZ	*Theologische Literaturzeitung*, Leipzig 1, 1876ff.
ThQ	*Theologische Quartalschrift*, Tübingen–Stuttgart 1, 1819ff.
TPL	Textus patristici et liturgici, Regensburg
TR	*Theologische Revue*, Münster 1, 1902ff.
Trad	*Traditio. Studies in Ancient and Medieval History, Thought and Religion*, New York 1, 1943ff.
TRE	*Theologische Realenzyklopädie*, Berlin 1, 1977ff.
TU	Texte und Untersuchungen zur Geschichte der altchristlichen Literatur, Leipzig 1, 1882ff.
TzF	Texte zur Forschung, Darmstadt 1, 1971ff.
VC	*Vetera Christianorum*, Bari 1, 1964ff.
VEGL	Veröffentlichungen der evangelischen Gesellschaft für Liturgieforschung, Göttingen 1, 1947ff.
VigC	*Vigiliae Christianae*, Amsterdam 1, 1947ff.
VIOF	*Veröffentlichung. Deutsche Akademie der Wissenschaften zu Berlin, Institut für Orientforschung*

WAAFLNW   Wissenschaftliche Abhandlungen der Arbeitsgemeinschaft für For-
            schung des Landes Nordrhein-Westfalen, Cologne 1, 1958ff.

WB (H)   Wissenschaftliche Beiträge der Martin-Luther-Universität Halle-
            Wittenberg, Halle

WuD   *Wort und Dienst. Jahrbuch der theologischen Schule Bethel*, Bielefeld

WZ(R)   *Wissenschaftliche Zeitschrift der Universität Rostock*, Rostock 1, 1951ff.

ZÄS   *Zeitschrift für ägyptische Sprache und Altertumskunde*, Berlin etc.

ZAss   *Zeitschrift für Assyriologie und verwandte Gebiete*, Leipzig 1, 1886ff.

ZDMG   *Zeitschrift der deutschen morgenländischen Gesellschaft*, Leipzig etc. 1,
            1847ff.

ZKG   *Zeitschrift für Kirchengeschichte*, Gotha–Stuttgart 1, 1877ff.

ZM   *Zeitschrift für Missionswissenschaft und Religionswissenschaft*, Münster 34,
            1950ff.

ZNW   *Zeitschrift für die neutestamentliche Wissenschaft und die Kunde der älteren
            Kirche*, Berlin 1, 1900ff.

ZPE   *Zeitschrift für Papyrologie und Epigraphik*, Bonn 1, 1967ff.

ZSem   *Zeitschrift für Semitistik und verwandte Gebiete*, Leipzig 1, 1922, to 10,
            1935

ZThK   *Zeitschrift für Theologie und Kirche*, Tübingen 1, 1891ff.

A CHRISTOLOGICAL NILE EXPEDITION FROM THE DELTA TO LAKE TANA (451–639/642)

In spite of the almost unanimous declaration of the bishops in favour of the Fourth General Council when asked by Emperor Leo I, the decision regarding the extent of the reception of this synod in the realm of the imperial church had not yet been made. Each council, especially when it brings new formulations, means a challenge to previously valid tradition. Chalcedon was not to be different from Nicaea. 'Reception' is no instant event, especially when there seem to be openly contradictory formulations: here 'one hypostasis in two natures', there 'the one nature (hypostasis) of the incarnate word'. Such formulas seemed to be created to lead to the formation of clearly delineated parties. Depending on the spiritual and psychological presuppositions of a theological grouping, the result could be fruitful dialogue or – sooner or later – irreconcilable opposition. Both are found in the aftermath of Chalcedon. Theological opposition led to schism in the church, especially in the realm of the Alexandrian church, which we are considering here.

In order to understand the formation of post-Chalcedonian Christology along the Nile, we must note the differences and the commonalities of the development, as well as its evolution in the limited area of Greek-speaking Alexandria and in the whole Nile valley (including Nubia and Ethiopia). Thus, even though we must not exaggerate the distinction, there was something like an Alexandrian-Greek-Hellenistic urban Christianity[1] and an Egyptian popular church, which had its roots deep in

---

1. See G. Grimm, H. Heinen and E. Winter, *Alexandrien. Kulturbegegnungen dreier Jahrtausende im Schmelztiegel einer mediterranen Großstadt* (Aegyptiaca Treverensia 1), Mainz 1981; also C. D. G. Müller, art. 'Alexandrien' (I), *TRE* 2 (1978), 248–61; idem, art. 'Ägypten' (IV), *TRE* 1 (1977), 512–33; J. Irmscher, 'Alexandria, die christusliebende Stadt', *BSAC* 19 (1967/68), 115–22; L. W. Barnard, 'The Background of Judaism and Christianity in Egypt', in idem, *Studies in Church History and Patristics* (Analekta Vlatadon 26), Thessalonica 1978, no. 2, pp. 27–51; p. 37: 'Alexandria was never typical of Egypt as a whole.' In the same vein: T. Orlandi, 'Patristica copta e patristica greca', *VC* 10 (1973), 327–41; idem, 'La cristologia nei testi catechetici copti', in S. Felici, *Cristologia e catechesi patristica* 1 (BiblScRel 31), Rome 1980 (213–29), 214–16. – On geographical questions: S. Timm, *Christliche Stätten in Ägypten* (BeihTübAtl series B, No. 36), Wiesbaden 1979, 15ff.

the old Egyptian culture and language and found its special character ultimately as the 'Coptic church',[2] with which the Nubian and Ethiopian churches were closely connected. Let us look first at Egypt. The special position of church development in this ancient culture must be seen in terms of the organization of the pagan Roman Empire, a situation that did not come to an end until the Arab invasion (639/642). The Roman emperor ruled Egypt *in persona*, even if through his prefect or temporary viceroy, a title that was considered a special honour. Also, after the reorganization of the Roman Empire by Diocletian (284–305), in which Egypt became a part of the *Dioecesis Orientis*, it was able as early as 382 to achieve again its relatively independent status as a province. It formed a *dioecesis* by itself with an imperial prefect, who had authority over the whole land.[3] In 554, under Emperor Justinian I (527–565), there was a far-reaching reform. In Edict 13 he combined civil and military power in Egypt and for the first time divided the single entity 'Egypt' into four provinces, of which three were further divided into two parts.[4] As a result

---

2. E. Lüddeckens, 'Ägypten', in *Die Sprachen im Römischen Reich der Kaiserzeit. Kolloquium v. 8. bis 10. April 1974* (BoJ.B 40), Cologne–Bonn 1980 (241–65), 241: 'Curiously, the country's largest city, Alexandria – site of the central government and thus the capital – was not regarded as belonging to Egypt: "Alexandria ad Aegyptum" was its designation.' (This essay is to be regarded as background for the following.) – In contrast to Alexandria, 'Egypt' is called a 'country' (χώρα). Cf. E. Schwartz, 'Über die Reichskonzilien von Theodosius bis Justinian', in *Ges. Schriften* 4: *Zur Geschichte der Alten Kirche und ihres Rechts* (111–58), 117–18: 'Because the position of patriarchs originally had its roots in the bishops of the χώρα dependent on him and thus in the native, uneducated population, they had to accept as given the need to look after the people: they first taught the Copts to emancipate themselves from the Greco-Roman upperclasses.' We must not, however, allow ourselves to be led too quickly into seeing the Copts in opposition to the imperial church and to the Roman West. More differentiated is the view of W. H. C. Frend, 'The Monophysites and the Transition between the Ancient World and the Middle Ages', in *Passaggio dal mondo antico al medio evo da Teodosio a San Gregorio Magno* (Atti dei Convegni Lincei 45), Rome 1980, 339–65; idem, 'Nationalism as Factor in Anti-Chalcedonian Feeling in Egypt', *SCH*(L) 18 (1982), 21–38. On the whole topic: M. Cramer, *Das christlich-koptische Ägypten einst und heute. Eine Orientierung*, Wiesbaden 1959; C. D. G. Müller, 'Die koptische Kirche zwischen Chalkedon und dem Arabereinmarsch', *ZKG* 75 (1964), 271–308; idem, 'La position de l'Égypte chrétienne dans l'Orient Ancien', *Mus* 92 (1979), 105–25; E. R. Hardy, *Christian Egypt, Church and People. Christianity and Nationalism in the Patriarchate of Alexandria*, New York 1952; A. S. Atiya, *A History of Eastern Christianity* I, London 1968; G. Grimm, H. Heinen and E. Winter, *Das römisch-byzantinische Ägypten. Akten des internationalen Symposions 26.–30. September 1978 in Trier* (Aegyptiaca Treverensia 2), Mainz 1983; B. A. Pearson and J. E. Goehring (eds.), *The Roots of Egyptian Christianity* (Studies in Antiquity and Christianity), Philadelphia 1986; T. Orlandi, art. 'Koptische Kirche', *TRE* 19 (1989), 595–607.

3. H. Idris Bell, *Egypt from Alexander the Great to the Arab Conquest*, Oxford 1948, 121.

4. Cf. N. van der Wal, *Manuale Novellarum Justiniani*, Amsterdam 1964, p. 28, no. 133, with n. 1 and reference to E. Stein, *Histoire du Bas-Empire* II, 476–80; also A. M. Demicheli, 'La politica religiosa di Giustiniano in Egitto', *Aegyptus* 63 (1983), 217–57, here pp. 236–38;

Byzantine Egypt could preserve its unity only in the *church* and its organization. The authority that encompassed the whole land was the patriarch of Alexandria, and it was not limited by metropolitan rights.

An old customary right is fixed by Canon 6 of Nicaea: 'The old custom shall apply that the bishop of Alexandria has all power (ἐξουσία) over Egypt, Libya and Pentapolis, because the same is also customary for the bishop of Rome.'[5] This creates the foundation for what we can call with W. Hagemann the 'relative (canonical) autonomy of Alexandria': 'At the head of a clearly delimited jurisdictional area stands the bishop of Alexandria, the patriarch. Under him we find about one hundred suffragan bishops and among them also a number of honorary metropolitans. The government is strongly centralized and encompasses the right to appoint and dismiss bishops, the right to oversee the purity of faith and practice in the patriarchate and the right to convene synods.'[6]

This authority is seen especially in the powerful figures of Athanasius, Theophilus, Cyril and Dioscorus. It is true that for Isidore of Pelusium the actions of Patriarch Theophilus awakened the memory of the pharaoh who opposed Moses.[7] Horsiesius, by contrast, felt differently and wrote to this patriarch:

'Are you not the king of the land? Are you not our shepherd? Are you not the representative (*diadochos*) of God? Are you not the true husband and bridegroom (*nymphios*) of his bride? Are you not the leader of our souls? Are you not the one on whom we are all dependent . . . ?'[8] 'Horsiesius said: "He who lives in solitude (*hesychazei*) has no reward like the man to whom all of Egypt has been entrusted [this is an allusion to the Joseph story (Gen 41,41)]; for more than a few are to be made blessed through him . . . all of Egypt will be saved today through your holy prayers, you friend of Christ." '[9]

Yet we must always observe the old division into northern Egypt (the Arabs' Lower Egypt) and southern Egypt (the Arabs' Upper Egypt) in order to understand the role of Christianity along the Nile. In northern (= Lower) Egypt the influence of Hellenism was especially strong. Here Christianity received a particular, unique character. From the north the

---

F. Winkelmann, 'Die Stellung Ägyptens im oströmisch-byzantinischen Reich', in P. Nagel (ed.), *Griechen und Kopten im byzantinischen Ägypten* (WB [H] 1984/48, I 29), Halle 1984, 11–35, p. 23: the country is divided into four subdioceses: Aegyptus I and II, Augustamnica I and II, Arcadia, Thebais I and II.

5. Can. VI: *DEC*, pp. 8–9.

6. W. Hagemann, 'Die rechtliche Stellung der Patriarchen von Alexandrien und Antiochien. Eine historische Untersuchung, ausgehend vom Kanon 6 des Konzils von Nizäa', *OstKSt* 13 (1964), 171–91, on Alexandria: pp. 171–80; here: p. 180.

7. Cf. Isid. Pelus., Ep. I, 152: PG 78, 285A and his judgement of the avarice and violence of Patriarch Theophilus towards John Chrysostom, whence his association with 'pharaoh'. Cf. Ep. I, 519: PG 78, 416C. On *pharaoh* as the sobriquet of Patriarch Dioscorus, see R. Schieffer, Index Generalis, ACO IV 3, 2, p. 135a.

8. Text in W. E. Crum, *Der Papyruscodex saec. VI–VII der Phillippsbibliothek in Cheltenham. Koptische theologische Schriften* (SWGS 18), Strasbourg 1915, 67.

9. Ibid., 69. Similarly, Shenoute to Patriarch Timothy I of Alexandria: 'To us you are courage and a mighty rod; to us you are a shepherd; you feed us and lead us in everything . . .' In J. Leipoldt, *Schenute von Atripe* (TU 25, 1), Leipzig 1903, 43.

Christian message penetrated further up the Nile, but not without thereby experiencing an unmistakable differentiation, namely, as 'Coptic Christianity'.[10] We will first consider the beginning of the construction of anti-Chalcedonian Alexandrian Christology at its centre, that is, in Alexandria. Basically, this is accomplished by focusing on Cyril.

10. Cf. C. D. G. Müller, *Mus* 92 (1979), 109. The terms *Copt* and *Coptic* first appeared in the seventh century in the period of Arab rule (beginning in 641). The Greek αἰγύπτιος, which the Greeks coined in the eighth century BC, spread from the Memphis temple ('palace of the soul of Ptah'), which was consecrated to the god Ptah, and in Arabic texts became *qbt* or *qft*. For the Arabs *qoft* was equivalent to *Christian* (from Egypt); cf. P. du Bourguet, *Les coptes* (Que sais-je? 2398), Paris ²1989, 5–12. Coptic writing originated in the second century BC and developed especially in the third century AD with the spread of the Christian church. See now P. du Bourguet, art. 'Copt' in *The Coptic Encyclopedia* 2 (1991), 599–601. In the following we may use *Coptic* generally in the sense of 'Egyptian (Christian)' or especially in the confessional sense, that is, in reference to the anti-Chalcedonian church in Egypt.

PART ONE
ALEXANDRIAN-GREEK CHRISTOLOGY

SECTION ONE

THE CHRISTOLOGY OF THE PATRIARCHS

CHAPTER ONE

TIMOTHY AELURUS: THE FOUNDATION OF ALEXANDRIAN-GREEK CHRISTOLOGY IN THE REJECTION OF CHALCEDON

The development of a separate Coptic path that was to lead ever further away from the imperial church and the church at large could only have succeeded on the basis of a solid foothold in Alexandria. We can observe a first phase in the growth of the anti-Chalcedonian minority, to whom the name 'Monophysites' was later given.[11] They present a textbook example of the persistence of an initially relatively small group, who opposed the majority but laid claim to the authentic tradition and blamed the Council of Chalcedon for the move towards separation. Post-Vatican (I and II) comparisons can be made. At the centre of things at that time was a figure who was unfortunately seen too simply – a situation to which, admittedly, he himself contributed – namely, Timothy Aelurus. After the murder of the Chalcedonian Proterius (451–457), Aelurus alone was patriarch of Alexandria, first from 457 to 460 and then again from 475 to 477. After the already analysed questioning of the bishops by

---

11. We use the name *Monophysite* here to designate those who, in opposition to the two-natures doctrine of Chalcedon, confess the formula of the 'one nature of the incarnate Word'. It was first used towards the end of the sixth century, whereas the term *Diphysite* or *Dyophysite* appears immediately. Both should be used sparingly for ecumenical and objective reasons. On the following sections see W. H. C. Frend, *The Rise of the Monophysite Movement*, Cambridge 1972; L. Perrone, *La chiesa di Palestina*, Brescia 1980, 89–103; F. Winkelmann, *Die östlichen Kirchen in der Epoche der christologischen Auseinandersetzungen (5.–7. Jh.)* (Kirchengeschichte in Einzeldarstellungen I/6), Berlin ³1980; idem, 'Die Stellung Ägyptens im oströmisch-byzantinischen Reich', in P. Nagel (ed.), *Griechen und Kopten im byzantinischen Ägypten* (WB [H] 1984/48, I 29), Halle 1984, 11–35.

Emperor Leo I, the latter was pressured from almost all sides in 457–458 to restore peace in Egypt and depose the 'murderer and heretic Timothy'.[12] When Emperor Leo waited until late 459 or early 460 to remove Timothy from Alexandria, the emperor's sense of the true situation and his will to find a compromise between the ecclesiastical parties, in addition to the pressure of Aspar,[13] were probably of prime importance. Patriarch Proterius had not succeeded in securing for himself and the Fourth Council a broader following among the people and the monks.[14] This he found only in the upper stratum of the nobility and officialdom, which today would lead him even more quickly to ruin than at that time. Under imperial direction, his election had been undertaken by the party of the nobility of Alexandria.[15] Proterius was unable to move Pope Leo I to a more broad-minded Chalcedonian policy. Presumably it was no more successful with the Chalcedonians than the mediation policy of Peter Mongus was later with the extreme anti-Chalcedonians of Egypt. The main reason for Pope Leo's unyielding position was the conviction that the teachings of Dioscorus and Aelurus were nothing but pure Eutychianism or even Manichaeism. Timothy makes it quite clear that there was a big difference here. How much Leo from Rome and Aelurus

---

12. Cf. Theophanes, *Chron.* A. M. 5952: de Boor I, p. 112,2–3: the bishops . . . Τιμοθέου δὲ συμφώνως καταφηφίζονταί ὡς φονέως καὶ αἱρετικοῦ. Michael Syr., *Chron.* IX 5: Chabot II, 145B, regretfully admits that even Amphilochius of Side, who was the only one in the CE to speak against Chalcedon, questioned the consecration of Timothy: 'désapprouvant, il est vrai, l'ordination de Timotheus'.

13. Cf. Theophanes, *Chron.*, A. M. 5952: de Boor I, p. 112,4–5.

14. The influence of the monks in the aftermath of Chalcedon is emphasized especially by Frend (*The Rise*, ch. 3 [pp. 104–42]: 'The Intellectuals and the Monks'; idem, 'The Monks and the Survival of the East Roman Empire in the Fifth Century', in *Past and Present* 54 (1972), 3–24). Frend (*The Rise*, 154) cites the chronicle of the year 846 (Brooks-Chabot, 163) in order to show the extent of the Monophysite following: 'After Dioscorus was sent into exile, many in the monasteries still clung to him (*proclamabant*) secretly.' Cf. F. Haase, 'Patriarch Dioskur I. von Alexandria nach monophysitischen Quellen', in *KGA*, Breslau 1908 (141–233), 192–94; K. Khella, 'Dioskoros I. von Alexandrien. Theologie und Kirchenpolitik', in *Les Coptes – The Copts – Die Kopten*, vol. 2, ed. Koptische Gemeinde e.V., Hamburg 1981, 9–282 (part 1); vol. 3, 1982, 15–111 (part 2). The presentation is from the Coptic viewpoint. – H. Bacht, 'Die Rolle des orientalischen Mönchtums in den kirchenpolitischen Auseinandersetzungen um Chalkedon', in *Chalkedon* II, 193–314.

15. Cf. Liberatus, *Breviar.* XIV: ACO II 5, pp. 123, 126–28: 'Thus the nobility (*nobiles*) of the city were called together to elect the one who in life and word (*sermone*) was worthy of the pontificate; this was commanded by imperial decrees (*sanctionibus*) also'. Cf. Zacharias Rh., *HE* III 2: Brooks, CSCO 87, p. 106; Hamilton-Brooks, p. 48; Michael Syr., *Chron.* VIII 12: Chabot II, 91.

from exile both fought on a mutually unrelinquishable front was unfortunately known to neither.

1. The secret patriarch of Alexandria

Let us reach a little further into the past. With all the ongoing attempts after the removal and death of Proterius to fill the patriarchal see of Alexandria with bishops of Chalcedonian inclination, Timothy – whether secretly or openly – was an important factor in Egypt, and even in exile he remained the secret patriarch and spiritual leader of the anti-Chalcedonian monks in the desert; he was the 'saint' of the simple people.[16] The anti-Chalcedonians along the Nile, in Palestine and in Constantinople looked to him. The Chalcedonians in the East could offer no father-figure of similar attractiveness. There Leo I of Rome could bring to bear his authority – so effective in the West – only in a limited way, if at all.[17] Timothy built the first great arch of a bridge that was to lead from Cyril and Dioscorus to Severus of Antioch, the prominent church father of the anti-Chalcedonians. Timothy also began the construction of an organization and hierarchy that set itself apart from the imperial church and that Jacob Baradai was later to complete in grand style.[18] Therefore we must present the essentials of Timothy's activities

---

16. Cf. Leont. Schol., *De sectis* (CPG 6823), Actio V, I: PG 86, 1228C: καὶ ἦν ὁ μὲν Προτέριος φανερῶς ἐν Ἀλεξανδρείᾳ ἐπίσκοπος, ὁ δὲ Τιμόθεος κρύφα (in Alexandria Proterius was bishop in public, but Timothy in secret). Theophanes, *Chron.*, A. M. 5952: de Boor, p. 112.6–8: ἔνθα ποτὲ καὶ Διόσκορος ὁ τούτου διδάσκαλος. ὁ αὐτὸς δὲ κακεῖ ἤρξατο παρασυναγωγὰς ποιεῖν καὶ ταραχάς, ἃς μαθὼν ὁ βασιλεὺς μετεξώρισεν αὐτὸν ἐν Χερσῶνι (There, in Alexandria, Dioscorus was also his teacher at one time. He himself [Timothy] began to hold rival assemblies there and [cause] trouble. When the emperor found out about it, he banished him to the Chersonese). Leo M., of course, based on a letter of Patriarch Anatolius, underestimated Timothy's influence, seeing only four bishops behind him: ep. 157: ACO II 4, pp. 109–10.

17. Cf. Frend, *The Rise*, 164. He stresses the inefficiency of West-Roman measures against Egypt. 'Leo, moreover, had made the mistake of continually interfering in purely local concerns or matters of internal administration in the eastern patriarchates.' Cf. W. de Vries, *Orient et Occident*, Paris 1974, 126–49.

18. Cf. Michael Syr., *Chron.* VIII 14: Chabot II, 122–23: 'Since the true faith was scorned at Chalcedon, the churches were split and believers divided. Therefore, wherever there were true enthusiasts, they fled the communion of heretical bishops and consecrated orthodox ones in their place; as we have shown, in place of Juvenal in Jerusalem they installed Theodosius, upon whom a synod of orthodox bishops laid their hands' (cf. Chabot, ibid., 83, 89). 'Likewise, in place of Proterius in Alexandria they consecrated St Timothy. And similar events occurred everywhere, even down to the most ordinary [episcopal] sees.'

against Chalcedon, his conception of Alexandrian Christology and his significance for later history.[19]

Taken ('by force') from the monastery by Cyril and ordained a priest,[20] Timothy was at the Synod of Ephesus in 449 with the patriarch Dioscorus and his own brother, the priest Anatolius.[21] After Dioscorus was deposed in 451 and Proterius was called to be patriarch of Alexandria, Timothy was secretly consecrated a bishop, though by only two bishops, Peter the Iberian and Eusebius of Pelusium.[22] The Chalcedonian patriarch Proterius was able to hold the throne only until the death of Emperor Marcian. Then came the revolt of the anti-Chalcedonian party

---

19. The most important study is still that of J. Lebon, 'La christologie de Timothée Aelure . . . d'après les sources syriaques inédites', *RHE* 9 (1908), 677–702; idem, *Le monophysisme sévérien*, Louvain 1909 (= Lebon I); idem, 'La christologie du monophysisme syrien', in *Chalkedon* I, 425–580 (= Lebon II). – Among the older studies see especially E. Renaudot, *Historia Patriarcharum Alexandrinorum Jacobitarum* . . ., Paris 1713, 120–22; G. Krüger, *Monophysitische Streitigkeiten im Zusammenhange mit der Reichspolitik*, Jena 1884; idem, art. 'Monophysiten', *RE* 13 (1905), 372–401; M. Jugie, art. 'Monophysisme', *DTC* 10b (1929), 2216–51; R. Devreesse, 'Les premiers années du monophysisme', *RSPT* 19 (1930), 251–65; J. Meyendorff, 'Chalcedonians and Monophysites after Chalcedon', *GOTR* 10 (1964/65), 16–36; F. M. Young, 'A Reconsideration of Alexandrian Christology', *JEH* 22 (1971), 103–14 (concerns more the pre-Chalcedonian period). – More extensive studies: F. Pericoli-Ridolfini, *Le controversie cristologiche del secolo V et le chiese d'oriente che ad esse si collegano*, Rome 1968; J. Jarry, *Hérésies et factions dans l'empire byzantin du IVe au VIe siècle* (RAPH 14), Cairo 1968; E. Stein, *Histoire du Bas-Empire* I, 284–476; II, 476–565; B. Spuler (ed.), *Religionsgeschichte des Orients in der Zeit der Weltreligionen. Die westsyrische (monophysitische/ jakobitische) Kirche* (HO I, 8: Religion, 2nd section), Leiden 1961, 170–216; F. Winkelmann, *Die östlichen Kirchen in der Epoche der christologischen Auseinandersetzungen (5.–7. Jh.)*, Berlin ³1980; B. A. Pearson and J. E. Goehring (eds.), *The Roots of Egyptian Christianity*, Philadelphia 1986. Individual studies will be cited in the appropriate context.

20. Zacharias Rh., *HE* IV 1: Hamilton-Brooks, 64; Brooks, CSCO 87, p. 118,2–6; cf. Evagrius, *HE* II 8: Bidez-Parmentier, p. 56,1–5.

21. Cf. Timothy Ael., *Histoire*: Nau, PO 13, pp. 203–7: 'Un concile se réunit plus tard à Ephèse . . . Il était dirigé par notre bienheureux père le confesseur Dioscore, avec lequel j'étais, moi et mon bienheureux frère, le prêtre Anatolius.' The last sentence is missing in the corresponding Armenian text; cf. K. Ter-Mekerttschian and E. Ter-Minassiantz, *Timotheus Älurus' des Patriarchen von Alexandrien Widerlegung der auf der Synode zu Chalcedon festgesetzten Lehre*, Leipzig 1908, 145,26. On the authenticity of this *Histoire* see Lebon I, 103–11; F. Nau, PO 13, p. 206. Anatolius accompanied his brother into exile in Gangra, where he died, as Dioscorus had earlier. Neither of the two deceased had been forgotten in Alexandria when in 475 Timothy brought the remains of both to Egypt in a silver coffin. Cf. Land, *Anecdota Syriaca* III, 172.

22. R. Raabe, *Petrus der Iberer*, Leipzig 1895, 65; Zacharias Rh., *HE* IV 1: Hamilton-Brooks, 64; Brooks, CSCO 87, p. 118; Evagrius, *HE* II 8: Bidez-Parmentier, p. 56,1–12. According to the report of Pseudo-Theopist, the deacon of Dioscorus, the latter had, in a presentiment of what was to come when he went to the Council of Chalcedon, already presented Timothy Aelurus to the people as his successor. Cf. F. Nau, 'Histoire de Dioscore, Patriarche d'Alexandrie, écrite par son disciple Théopiste', *JA* X 1 (1903), 37, 255. Cf. ibid., pp. 42, 259. Dioscorus recommended Timothy as his successor again before his death: ibid.,

and Proterius's cruel murder.[23] Even apart from party politics, this event cast a shadow over Timothy's image in the eyes of history. In the extant writings of the anti-Chalcedonians there is no word of regret over this outrage.[24] For Pope Leo I it burdened Bishop Timothy so much that his assuming the Alexandrian patriarchate was simply unthinkable. The pope often called him a *parricida sacrilegus* (sacrilegious father-murderer) or *parricida impius* (godless father-murderer), an especially serious indictment on the lips of a Roman.[25] In a letter to Emperor Leo, the pope

pp. 102, 305. It is said that he was given this commission by Cyril in a vision, in which Severus was also mentioned. Thus the whole thing is to be credited to a later editor (after 518). The succession of anti-Chalcedonian bishops is supposed to be legitimated through visions.

23. Zacharias Rh., *HE* IV 2: Brooks, CSCO 87, p. 106; Hamilton-Brooks, 66. – Evagrius, *HE* II 8: Bidez-Parmentier, p. 56; Zacharias Rh. and Michael Syr. (*Chron.* VIII 14: Chabot II, 125) write – though not convincingly – of Proterius being killed by a Roman soldier. Similar is the postscript of the *Histoire de Dioscore*: Nau, *JA* X 1, 108, 310. Theodorus Lector, *HE* II, Epit. 368: Hansen, 103–4, says briefly: 'When Timothy heard of Marcian's death, he rose against Proterius and arranged for him to be killed in the baptistery of the church and for his body to be dragged through the city and burned.'

24. The primary source for judging the Egyptian events of 457 are of course the Chalcedonian bishops and elders, who after the outrage had fled to the imperial court (see A. Grillmeier, *CCT* II/1, pp. 202–3). Their writing to Emperor Leo and Patriarch Anatolius became known to the whole empire through the emperor. Cf. CE 7: ACO II 5, esp. pp. 13–15, which says, characteristically: 'The instigator and clever planner (*sapiens architectus*) of all this was Timothy, first an adulterer [because he had robbed Proterius of the diocese, the "bride"], then also a murderer, because he almost (*paene!*) committed this outrage with his own hands' (p. 14,23–25). Cf. CE 8 *ad Anatol.*: ibid., pp. 17–21, esp. 18,32–19,36. A distinction is made here between Timothy's activity and that of the monks and the people; the murder, however, is traced back to the 'instigation' of Timothy: *suadens* [+ lacuna: Schwartz inserts: *commovit*] *aliquos, sicut rerum eventus ostendit, homicidas vere contra eum (Proterium) insurgere, qui eum commorantem in baptisterio peremerunt . . .* (p. 19,28–30). In the analysis of the CE we have already established that numerous bishops acted with reservation in regard to the reports of the Chalcedonian Egyptians (see A. Grillmeier, *CCT* II/1, p. 203, n. 33). Even Pope Leo did not want to believe the first rumours and waited for more precise reports. Cf. Ep. 144: ACO II 4, p. 138,32–34; Ep. 145 *ad Leon. aug.*: ibid., p. 95, which states that Anatolius sent a first report to Pope Leo.

25. Cf. Ep. 157 *ad Anatol.*: ACO II 4, p. 109,17; Ep. 164 *ad Leon. aug.*: ibid., p. 112,6 and 27; Leo's harsh statements about Timothy are found in letters 169–73, which are preserved in the *Collectio Avellana* I–II (= *CA*), ed. O. Guenther, CSEL 35, 1895 and 1898, nos. 51–55. In Ep. 169: 'improbus parricida depulsus'; 'praedo nefarius' (*CA*, no. 51, p. 117,14 and 15); Ep. 170: 'parricida ille' (ibid., no. 52, p. 120,1); Ep. 171: Timothy is 'antichristi . . . opprobrium', which sits with this man on the patriarchal chair of Alexandria (ibid., no. 53, p. 120,18–19); cf. also Theophanes, *Chron.* A. M. 5950: de Boor I, 110,35: [Timothy] ὁ δὲ Ἀντιχρίστου πρόδρομος. Ep. 172: 'remota procul ea bestia, quae vineam plantationis dominicae . . . singulari feritate vastabat' (*CA*, no. 54, p. 122,6–8); Ep. 173: Timothy is 'cruentissimus Alexandrinae Ecclesiae pervasor' (ibid., no. 55, p. 123,9). 'Parricida' ultimately becomes (probably only in the Latin tradition) Timothy's proper name or sobriquet, as attested by the title of Emperor Leo's circular in the Collectio Sangermanensis (CE, ACO II 5, p. 9,32).

compares Timothy with Cain, who did not respond to God's call 'but was inflamed to murder, for which vengeance is supposed to be so reserved for the judgement of the Lord that vile robbers and cruel father-murderers turn against themselves and cannot take what is ours'.[26] For Leo, finally, Timothy is the 'raging tyrant of the Alexandrian church', which finds itself in 'miserable imprisonment', from which the emperor is supposed to set it free;[27] in this way 'the dignity of the fathers and the sacerdotal right' would be re-established in all the cities of Egypt.[28] 'Man of the people',[29] 'confessor' and 'saint' on the one hand, 'murderer' and 'heretic' on the other: this is the way Timothy was branded forever by friend and foe. An overall picture of his personality cannot be sketched here. If, however, we turn away from the polemical literature around him and from his own polemics and look at his letters, we find a surprisingly distinct picture. The writings and letters of the first anti-Chalcedonian patriarch after Dioscorus are, of course, as good as lost in the original language; his final and most voluminous work[30] survives in complete form only in an Armenian translation. It was written during exile in the Crimea. In an abridged form or excerpt it appears in a Syriac translation in Br. L. Add. 12156, fol. 1ra–29vc with the title (on fol. 1), 'The Book Written by Mar Timothy, Bishop of Alexandria, against the (Godless) Synod of Chalcedon'.[31] The mutual relationship between

---

26. Leo M., Ep. 162 *ad Leon. aug.*: ibid., p. 107,11–13 (*improbus praedo et parricida crudelis*).

27. Leo M., Ep. 156 *ad Leon. aug.*: ibid., p. 104,1–2; Ep. 162: ibid., p. 107,13–15.

28. Leo M., Ep. 162: ibid., p. 107,15–16.

29. Timothy Aelurus did not lose the favour of the people even when the 'popular' and 'humble' Timothy Salophaciolus ('wobble hat') became Chalcedonian patriarch in place of Proterius – thus Zacharias Rh., *HE* IV 10: Brooks, CSCO 87, 127; here Hamilton-Brooks, 78: 'And just in proportion as the people loved Timothy the believer, so they hated this man [Tim. Sal.]. And they never ceased imploring and entreating the king that Timothy should be restored to them from banishment.'

30. Timothy Aelurus, 'Contra eos qui dicunt duas naturas' (CPG 5475): K. Ter-Mekerttschian and E. Ter-Minassiantz, *Timotheus Älurus' des Patriarchen von Alexandrien Widerlegung der auf der Synode zu Chalcedon festgesetzten Lehre*, Leipzig 1908.

31. A more precise description is given by W. Wright, *Catalogue of the Syriac Manuscripts in the British Museum*, vol. II, London 1871, no. DCCXXIX, pp. 639–48. An overview of the entire ms., as well as information on a future edition, is found in L. Abramowski, 'Zur geplanten Ausgabe von Brit. Mus. add. 12156', in *Texte und Textkritik. Eine Aufsatzsammlung*, ed. J. Dummer (TU 133), Berlin 1987, 23–28, esp. p. 23. A large part of the ms. (fol. 1–91a) consists of material that in the main comes directly from Timothy's authorship or is quoted by him. A summary of the part of the ms. published through 1970 is offered by R. Y. Ebied and L. R. Wickham, 'A Collection of Unpublished Syriac Letters of Timothy Aelurus', *JTS* 21 (1970) (321–69), 322–23; further: idem, 'Timothy Aelurus: Against the Definition of the Council of Chalcedon', in C. Laga et al. (eds.), *After Chalcedon* (OLA 18), 115–66. In general see A. Grillmeier, *CCT* II/1, pp. 63–65.

longer and shorter form has been sufficiently clarified.[32] The title of the work preserved in Armenian, translated back into Greek by E. Schwartz, gives us the intention of Timothy's writings as a whole, as will be shown below. It reads:

'On the fact that one must assert as *one* our Lord and God Jesus Christ with his flesh and must assign everything to him, what is divine and what is human, and that he became consubstantial with us according to the body but also remained God, and that it is godless to separate him into two [natures]' (with an addendum, p. 316: 'wherein also is the refutation of the blasphemies contained in Leo's *Tome* and of the godlessness of the definition of the synod held at Chalcedon').[33]

In the Syriac ms. Br. L. Add. 12156, along with the first tractate (fol. 1–29 – an abridgement of the Armenian work), there is yet another: 'Treatise of Timothy Aelurus against the Definition of the Council of Chalcedon and against the *Tome* of Leo'.[34] Between the two tractates this

---

32. We find an initial comparison in Lebon I, 100–3, and in his treatment 'Version arménienne et version syriaque de Timothée Élure', *HandAm* 11–12 (1927), 713–22; cf. also idem, *RHE* 9 (1908), 677–702. E. Schwartz has undertaken to describe 'both the Armenian and the Syriac text with special consideration of the χρήσεις . . .', in *Codex Vaticanus gr. 1431* (*ABAW.PH* XXXII 6), Munich 1927, 98–117, for the Armenian text; pp. 117–26 for Br. L. Add. 12156, fol. 1–61, 66v–80r. He refers there to the previous work of F. Cavallera, 'Le dossier patristique de Timothée Aelure', *BLE* 4/1 (1909), 342–59, beyond which he is able to verify an even greater number of patristic quotations, yet without completion.

33. E. Schwartz, *Cod. Vat. gr. 1431*, 98, on Ter-Mekerttschian and Ter-Minassiantz, p. 1, repeated on p. 316: Περὶ τοῦ ἕνα λέγειν [γενέσθαι p. 316] τὸν κύριον ἡμῶν καὶ θεὸν Ἰησοῦν Χριστὸν μετὰ τῆς σαρκὸς αὐτοῦ καὶ τῷ αὐτῷ πάντα ἀπονέμειν τὰ θεοπρεπῆ καὶ τὰ ἀνθρώπινα καὶ ὅτι ὁμοούσιος ἡμῖν γενόμενος κατὰ σῶμα ἔμεινε καὶ οὕτως θεός, καὶ ὅτι εἰς δύο [δύο φύσεις p. 316] διαιρεῖν αὐτὸν ἀσέβεια ἐστίν [p. 316 adds ἐν ᾧ καὶ ἡ ἀντίρρησις κατὰ τῶν ἐν τῷ Λέοντος τόμῳ βλασφημιῶν καὶ τῶν ἀσεβημάτων τοῦ ὅρου τῆς ἐν Χαλκηδόνι γενομένης συνόδου]. See R. Y. Ebied and L. R. Wickham, 'Timothy Aelurus: Against the Definition of the Council of Chalcedon', in C. Laga et al. (eds.), *After Chalcedon* (OLA 18), 118, n. 5.

34. Timothy Aelurus, 'Refutatio synodi Chalcedonensis et tomi Leonis' (CPG 5482): Br. L. Add. 12156, fol. 39v–61r; previously edited and translated: fol. 39v–42va by F. Nau in PO 13, pp. 218–36; fol. 42v–51v and 59v–61r by R. Y. Ebied and L. R. Wickham in OLA 18; 120–42 (Syr.); 143–66 (Engl.); still lacking are fol. 51v–59v (quotations from the acts of the Council of Ephesus 449), cf. Ebied-Wickham (OLA 18), p. 119. Individual portions are also translated in J. Lebon, *RHE* 9 (1908), 677–702. – Cf. Wright II, 642–43, nos. 10–11; E. Schwartz, *Cod. Vat. gr. 1431*, 122–26, with a Greek reverse translation of the title of this tractate. On p. 122 he describes the work: 'It is constructed like the above described work preserved in Armenian: the sections from the Chalcedonian definition are followed by ἀντιρρήσεις [counterspeeches]; only after the penultimate one are passages from Nestorius cited. According to the title one would expect this after each ἀντίρρησις; also, originally more orthodox authorities were probably cited than the one that now stands at the end of the last ἀντίρρησις. Thus the manuscript contains [even for this second tractate] only an epitome, as is expressly indicated regarding the last *antirrhesis* [PO 13, p. 232,13]. An essential difference from the large work is that no individual passage is lifted out of the second part of the definition, but rather the whole – naturally apart from the two older symbols – is cut up into individual, consecutively numbered pieces.'

ms. contains in fol. 29b–39b an interesting collection of letters and confessions of faith.[35] The first are especially important for us because they show us a more 'genuine' Timothy than the two treatises taken for themselves and the reports of friend and foe[36] that otherwise we have. It is characteristic of Timothy's way of working – as already shown[37] – that he includes himself among the authors who adduce the proof for a teaching from tradition through a florilegium of the fathers, but he does this for an ecumenical theme that is highly significant in the history of dogma.

For an exhaustive presentation of the patriarch's Christology, his patristic texts would have to be examined in detail beyond the preliminary work already completed. We must limit ourselves to the most important details.

It is noteworthy that the patristic florilegium of the tractate preserved in Armenian begins with two texts of Pseudo-Felix of Rome, which are to be included in the so-called Apollinarian forgeries, as are also the further quotations under the name of Pope Julius[38] and Vitalis, who is likewise called bishop (or patriarch according to other testimonies) of Rome. The latter is none other than the Apollinarian bishop of the same name.[39]

---

35. Timothy Aelurus, *Epistulae* (CPG 5476–81): Br. L. Add. 12156, fol. 29b–36b; Ebied-Wickham, *JTS* 21 (1970), 333–69 (Syr. and in English translation with commentary); on the content of fol. 36–39 (confessions of faith, etc.) see L. Abramowski, 'Ein Text des Johannes Chrysostomus über die Auferstehung in den Belegsammlungen des Timotheus Älurus', in C. Laga et al., *After Chalcedon* (OLA 18), 1–10. – For more literature on Timothy see also C. Moss, *Catalogue of Syriac Printed and Related Literature in the British Museum, compiled by the late C. M.*, London 1962; (s.v. 'Timotheus'). Also J. T. Clemons, 'Un supplément Américain au "Syriac Catalogue" de Cyril Moss', *OrSyr* 8 (1963), 469–84.

36. Cf. Zacharias Rh., *HE* IV and V 1–5: Hamilton-Brooks, pp. 64–100, 101–14; Brooks, CSCO 87, pp. 117–44, 145–52; Evagrius, *HE* II 8–17; III 1–11: Bidez–Parmentier, pp. 55–67, 99–109; Liberatus, *Brev.* 14–16: ACO II 5, pp. 123–25; Michael Syr., *Chron.* VIII 12 (according to Zacharias Rh.): Chabot II 91; IX, 1–6 (death of Tim.): Chabot II 126–53; Theodor. Lect.: Hansen, GCS (1972): Index 'Timotheos', p. 202.

37. E. Schwartz, *Cod. Vat. gr. 1431*, p. 97. Cf. n. 34 above and A. Grillmeier, *CCT* II/1, pp. 63–64.

38. Cf. the analysis of E. Schwartz in *Cod. Vat. gr. 1431*, pp. 99–116, nos. 12–14, 92, 114; F. Cavallera (n. 32 above) arranges the cited and excerpted fathers according to the alphabet. 'Felix': pp. 352–53, where the first quotation is from Cyril, *Apol. Anath.* 6; 'Julius', pp. 355–56.

39. Cf. F. Cavallera, ibid., p. 358, no. 26; E. Schwartz, *Cod. Vat. gr. 1431*, p. 99, no. 10; H. Lietzmann, *Apollinaris von Laodicea und seine Schule*, Tübingen 1904, 273. This same *chresis* is found under the same name in the Coptic Monophysite florilegia 'The Priceless Pearl' and 'The Confession of the Fathers'. Cf. G. Graf, 'Zwei dogmatische Florilegien der Kopten', *OCP* 3 (1937), 49–77, 345–402. Cf. pp. 77, 374, with reference to Cyril of Alex., *De recta fide*

Special attention must be given to an Apollinarian text of the writing *Ad Jovianum*, which is disguised as a 'Presentation of the Blessed Athanasius, Bishop of Alexandria, and of Our Fathers on the Divine Incarnation of the Logos . . .'[40] It contains the *mia-physis* formula. Furthermore, Cyril incorporated it into his writing *Oratio ad dominas (reginas)*,[41] which was very highly appreciated in the Armenian church. For this reason Cyril was suspected of Monophysitism. But he understood his formula correctly, as was already shown by his explanation of the incarnation in his second letter to Nestorius (*Obloquuntur* letter),[42] which was read aloud at Ephesus (431), but even more by the so-called *Laetentur* letter, which in addition to the one just mentioned was especially confirmed in Chalcedon. We have already emphasized that both letters contain discussions that were utilized by the gifted Bishop Basil of Seleucia in the finding and preparation of the Chalcedonian formula, 'in two natures'.[43] Now, it is interesting that in no. 98 (Armenian) Timothy quoted Cyril's *Obloquuntur* letter but stopped *before* the sentence interpreted by Basil: 'The natures brought together into true unity are, of course, different, yet *one* Christ and son from both . . .'[44] Thus, as the bishop of Seleucia has shown us, there could be a bridge between Cyril and the Chalcedonian 'in two natures'. We will have to see whether in anti-Chalcedonian writings in general, and not only in Timothy, there is a further interpretation of Cyril or, on the contrary, a limitation. Here there is first a narrowing in the way that such Chalcedon-like passages of the great teacher are 'passed

---

ad reginas (dominas). On pp. 372–74 are the remaining *chreseis*, which were ascribed by the Apollinarians to Roman popes. Cf. G. Graf, 'Unechte Zeugnisse römischer Päpste für den Monophysitismus im arabischen "Bekenntnis der Väter" ', *RömQ* 36 (1928), 197–233, where he makes a number of corrections in the *OCP*.

40. Cf. H. Lietzmann, *Apollinaris*, pp. 250–53; E. Schwartz, *Cod. Vat. gr. 1431*, p. 115, no. 371 (Armen.); p. 122, no. 50 (not 40) (Syr.).

41. H. Lietzmann, *Apollinaris*, pp. 250,6–252,11; PG 76, 1212–1213A. ACO I 5, pp. 65,25–66,10.

42. Cyril of Alex., Ep. 2 *ad Nestor.*: PG 77, 45B; ACO I 1, 1 26 ss.

43. Cf. A. Grillmeier, *CCT* II/1, p. 231, n. 124.

44. Cyril of Alex., Ep. 2 *ad Nestor.*: ACO I 1, 1, p. 27,1–5: διάφοροι μὲν αἱ πρὸς ἑνότητα τὴν ἀληθινὴν συνενεχθεῖσαι φύσεις εἷς δὲ ἐξ ἀμφοῖν Χριστὸς καὶ υἱός, οὐχ ὡς τῆς τῶν φύσεων διαφορᾶς ἀνῃρημένης διὰ τὴν ἕνωσιν . . . I. Rucker calls attention to this stop in his study: 'Cyrillus von Alexandrien und Timotheos Aelurus in der alten armenischen Christenheit', *HandAm* 11–12 (1927) (699–714), 712. On the other hand, Nestorius referred to this Cyril passage in *Liber Heraclidis* (ed. Bedjan 1910), 209ff., 271ff., 404ff. But Timothy is approaching the Cyril passage just cited when in Ep. ad Alexandrinos (Ebied-Wickham, p. 358, fol. 32ᵇ) he says: '. . . our Lord was consubstantial in flesh with us and . . . he was not of a different nature.' Cf. the expression, 'Jesus Christ is of an alien nature from us', ibid., p. 359; similarly p. 367, bottom. Naturally the Cyril text omitted by Timothy is presented by the *Florilegium Cyrillianum* already in no. 2: Hespel (1955), p. 112.

over' although they could have contributed to the understanding of the Chalcedonian 'innovation'.[45] We want to guard against doubting Timothy's good conscience,[46] when he made the centre of his Christology the *mia-physis* formula that he believed was so well attested in the tradition.[47] Timothy is regarded (probably with greater justification than Dioscorus) as the initiator of this development, which not only would produce a pointed, selective Cyrillism among his followers but also would force Chalcedonian theologians to interpret the council of 451 more in Cyril's spirit.

2. A christological battle on two fronts

For most of Timothy's contemporaries there were only two parties: (1) supporters of Chalcedon = the orthodox; (2) opponents of the council = supporters of the *mia-physis* formula = Eutychians = Apollinarians = Manichaeans and Docetists. Gradually, of course, it became clear to individual theologians in the West that there are distinctions to be made here.[48] Actually, it should have been remembered that Patriarch Anatolius of Constantinople – himself, of course, a creature of Dioscorus in the see of the imperial city – had emphasized at the council that Dioscorus was not condemned because of faith, that is, on account of heresy, and

---

45. Interesting is I. Rucker's comment in *Florilegium Edessenum anonymum (syriace ante 562) (SBAW 16)*, Munich 1933, in which he sets the Monophysite florilegium that immediately follows the Timothy writings in Br. L. Add. 12156, fol. 69rc–80rb, as an 'overworked tradition of monophysitism' with 'more striking dogmatic consciousness', against the 'original tradition' of Timothy. But, says Rucker, this Flor. Edessenum does not yet show the signs of the division of Monophysitism into Severanism and Julianism. It is still determined by Cyril.

46. Theophanes, *Chron.* A. M. 5950: de Boor I, p. 111,7–11, while referring to a presbyter Peter of Alexandria, accuses Timothy of forging unedited Cyril texts. But this cannot be demonstrated. Cf. I. Rucker, *HandAm* 11–12 (1927), 699.

47. Cf. the overview of the use of this formula by Timothy in Br. L. Add. 12156, which Lebon I gives after p. 308. He says simply 'passim' and indicates a few passages. That Cyril played the main role in Timothy is shown by I. Rucker in the already mentioned study in *HandAm* 11–12 (1927), 699–714; see also F. Cavallera, in *BLE* 1909, 348, n. 1, where he defines Cyril's part in the florilegium of Timothy: 'The fragments taken from St Cyril of Alexandria, still rare in the initial florilegium (*florilège initial*) (no. 4) (cf. Schwartz, *Cod. Vat. gr. 1431*, p. 101, nos. 74–77) exceed in number by far [those] in the remainder of the work and alone account for almost half the total number of quotations. Several are still unedited.'

48. E.g. Vigilius of Thapsus, *C. Eutych.* II 10: *PL* 62, 110C.

this is also confirmed by the tenor of the indictment and the condemna-tion.[49] That a clear distancing from Eutyches and all Docetic and Manichaean inclinations was already achieved with the deposed patri-arch and with Timothy became obvious only with the Eastern sources. It is true, the main reproach of the fathers of Chalcedon against Dioscorus was exactly that he rehabilitated Eutyches at Ephesus in 449. Likewise, however, later followers (after the changing of his sentence) had to defend him against the suspicion of a change of mind or even a betrayal of Eutyches. The sources show that Dioscorus had models among the holy fathers, who at first accepted certain teachers but afterwards con-demned them because they had concealed their true opinion and only later revealed their heresy. Thus also, they say, Eutyches relapsed after he had corrected himself.[50] From Dioscorus, Timothy inherited not only his opposition to Chalcedon but also the great concern that from Con-stantinople to Egypt Eutychianism and Manichaeism should live on. He

49. The indictment: ACO II, 1, 1, p. 65, no. 9; the condemnation: II 1, 2, p. 29, no. 94 (Leo's legates) and pp. 41–42, no. 99 (the synod as a whole). The most comprehensive dossier on the reasons for the deposition of Dioscorus is contained in the 'Gestorum Chalcedo-nensium versio a Rustico edita': ACO II 3, 2 (tertia cognitio Conc. Calched. of 13. Oct. 451), nos. 1–103, pp. 17–87. The fragments, which have survived only in Latin, are indicated in the indices of ACO II 3, 3, p. 123. Cf. R. Schieffer, Index generalis, ACO IV 3, 2 p. 131b ss. In the Libellus of the Presbyter Athanasius (ACO II 3, 2, no. 57, p. 35,15) Dioscorus is accused of heresy, but not in the indicated final sentence and its announcement or proclamation: the statement of the synod to the emperors Valentinian and Marcian (with the most extensive substantiation of the deposition); to the people of Constantinople and Chalcedon; to the clerics of Alexandria who were at the council (with a separate statement to a presbyter and a deacon in no. 102, ACO II 3, 2, p. 86); to Dioscorus himself and finally to Empress Pulcheria (no. 103; only here on p. 87,21 does one speak of 'errores', which does not mean 'haeresis' but his behaviour described in detail). – On the judgement of the 'Dioscorus case' by the Monophysites see J. Lebon, 'Autour du cas de Dioscore d'Alexandrie', Mus 59 (1946), 515–28. He refers to Br. L. Add. 12155, fol. 46r a–b (W. Wright II, pp. 921–55), in which a chapter is offered with the title: 'Sur ceci: que ce n'est pas à cause de la foi qu'eut lieu la déposition de saint Dioscore'. See A. Grillmeier, CCT II/1, pp. 41–42.

50. Cf. J. Lebon, in Mus 59 (1946), 518–19 according to Br. L. Add. 12155, fol. 162rB–163rA. Lebon, ibid., pp. 525–28, edits and translates a letter of Severus of Antioch to the orthodox in Tyre, in which Dioscorus is defended in the indicated sense. It states that Eutyches confessed before Flavian the right faith and therefore was unjustly condemned and likewise correctly restored by Dioscorus. For Eutyches had confessed before Flavian 'que le Seigneur est consubstantiel à nous et s'est fait homme de la Vierge . . . mais, dans la suite, ayant vu qu'il demeurait dans l'impiété, il (= Dioscore) dit que cet homme était digne du feu et non pas seulement de l'anathème, comme le font connaître les (actes) de l'action (tenue) à Chalcédoine . . .' Br. L. Add. 12155 contains a similar text of Philoxenus of Mabbug. Cf. J. Lebon, ibid., p. 519 and his article, 'Textes inédits de Philoxène de Mabboug', Mus 43 (1930), 57 (T) and 83–84 (V); see further idem, Mus 59 (1946), 520, n. 15; E. W. Brooks, 'A Collection of Letters of Severus of Antioch', PO 12 (1915), 264–69. Cf. R. Draguet, 'La christologie d'Eutychès d'après les actes du Synode de Flavien (448)', Byz 6 (1931), 441–57; at the end an indication of a changed attitude of the Monophysites towards Eutyches.

seems to have followed his master in the judgement of Eutyches himself[51] and his followers, but above all of the Manichaeans (see below).

(a) On the truth of the incarnation of Christ

From Gangra, the first place of Timothy's exile, he wrote a letter to Constantinople, where two Egyptians – Isaiah, bishop of Hermopolis, the city founded by Ikhnaton, and the presbyter Theophilus (of an unknown Theophilus church in Alexandria) – were spreading their errors and misusing Timothy's name for their own purposes.[52] Indeed, according to the report of Zacharias, which is taken up by Evagrius Scholasticus, there was still around 475 a strong Eutychian party in the imperial city, which hoped to get help from Timothy as the inspirator of the *Encyclion* of Basiliscus in the year 475.[53]

---

51. Leont. Schol., *De sectis*, Actio V, I: PG 86, 1228C, reports: Οὗτος δὲ ὁ Τιμόθεος ἀνεθεμάτιζε καὶ τὴν σύνοδον, καὶ τὸν μὲν Εὐτυχῆ, ἐπειδὴ μὴ ἔλεγεν ὁμοούσιον ἡμῖν τὸ σῶμα τοῦ Χριστοῦ τὴν δὲ ἐν Χαλκηδόνι σύνοδον, ὅτι δύο φύσεις ἔλεγε τοῦ Χριστοῦ. Similarly Severus of Antioch in the letter to John the Tribune, in E. W. Brooks, *The Sixth Book of the Select Letters of Severus* I/2, p. 316 (Syr.), II/2, p. 281 (trans.).

52. Timothy Ael., *Ep. ad C'politanos* (CPG 5476): Ebied-Wickham, 351–57 (trans.): 'The Letter written to the city of Constantinople . . . against the heretics who do not confess that God the Word who is consubstantial in his Godhead with the Father, is consubstantial in flesh with us, and against those who talk of "two natures"'. On the text and parallels see ibid., pp. 323–24. Letters I and II in Ebied-Wickham (= CPG 5476, 5477) are also preserved in Ethiopian translation. – In Alexandria, however, John the Rhetor, at the time of Patriarch Proterius and under the name of Theodosius of Jerusalem and Peter the Iberian, spread extreme teachings that meant a denial of the true incarnation through Mary. This is reported in Zacharias Rh., *HE* III 10: CSCO 83, pp. 163,1–164,19; 87, pp. 112,5–113,4; Ahrens-Krüger, pp. 17–18. Cf. L. Perrone, *La chiesa di Palestina*, 115–16. He refers to Severus of Antioch, *SL* V 6, p. 315, who repeats in intensified form the teachings of John the Rhetor: '. . . John the Rhetor, who said that it was in His essence that the Word of God endured the saving cross and took upon Himself the passion on our behalf, and would not consent to call the one Lord and our God and Saviour Jesus Christ of one essence with us in the flesh'. But Severus himself then rejects the term μία οὐσία in the discussion with Sergius Grammaticus. See A. Grillmeier, *CCT* II/2, pp. 122–26.

53. Zacharias Rh., *HE* V 4: Hamilton-Brooks, p. 109: 'When the purport of the king's Encyclical letters became generally known, certain monks holding opinions similar to those of Eutyches, who happened to be in the Royal City, came in a body to Timothy, supposing him to be of their way of thinking, and disputed with him about the terms of the Encyclical; because it anathematized everyone who affirmed that Christ was incarnate in semblance. But when he said to them, "What then is your opinion respecting the Incarnation?" then they brought up to him the illustration of the signet-ring which, after the impression, leaves no part of its substance upon the wax or the clay.' Where these monks came from is not said; in any case, from the continuation we can gather that it was not from Alexandria (p. 110): 'Then Timothy, having learned by the whole tenor of the conversation of those who came to him what their mind was, made a written statement, declaring that Christ was like unto us in everything belonging to humanity. Whereupon the monks of the place separated themselves

Isaiah and Theophilus travelled to Constantinople, apparently in order to make contact with the Eutychian group. This can be assumed from the title of the named letter in Zacharias the Rhetor (*HE* IV 12).[54] This writing is also directed against the 'Eutychians'. The testimonies of many fathers are included in order to explain the true doctrine of the incarnation:

> I have written this upon hearing that certain persons are opposed to obeying the tradition of the holy fathers who taught Christ's fleshly consubstantiality with us. Such persons the fathers also anathematized. For we believe, in accordance with the tradition of the fathers, that our Lord Jesus Christ was consubstantial in flesh with us . . . and one with his own flesh.[55]

The concern about the continued existence of Eutychianism is also the main tenor of the second letter, which went from Gangra to Alexandria. The excommunication of Isaiah and Theophilus was due. The two had even threatened the bearer of Timothy's first letter in Constantinople and stirred up the people with the assertion that it was a forgery. A letter (not extant) tried to move the two stubborn men to repentance:

> I promised that if they refrained from heterodoxy and confessed that our Lord was consubstantial in flesh with us and that he was not of a different nature, I would maintain them in their former honour [position] and would grasp them with the same love [as before].[56]

Against the command of their banished patriarch, the two Egyptians remained in the capital. For there they had connections with 'important persons', which he interpreted for them as earthly greed.[57] Now the Monophysite church of Alexandria was given the declaration of excommunication against the two:

---

from him, saying, "We will have no communion with the Alexandrians." But the others, having discovered that he had no tendency to the Eutychian doctrine, attached themselves to him.' The disappointed group of Eutychians then sought through Zenonis, the wife of Basiliscus, to have Timothy again deposed and banished. Thus the split in the anti-Chalcedonians began very early.

54. Cf. Brooks, CSCO 87, p. 129; Hamilton-Brooks, p. 81.

55. Timothy Ael., *Ep. ad C'politanos* (CPG 5476): Ebied-Wickham, p. 352: here with consideration of their textual corrections. On the patristic florilegium see below.

56. Timothy Ael., *Ep. ad Alexandrinos* (CPG 5477): Ebied-Wickham, p. 358. For four years Timothy waited with the excommunication, although his second (lost) letter bore no fruit either. Severus of Antioch, in his controversy with Julian of Halicarnassus, also referred back to the letters of Timothy Aelurus in matters of Bishop Isaiah (and of Theophilus, or Timothy). Severus speaks of a presbyter Timothy and regards the teaching of Julian as Manichaeism and Eutychianism. See his writing *Contra Additiones Juliani*, ed. R. Hespel, CSCO 296 (V), Louvain 1968, pp. 135,21–136,2. Cf. with Ebied-Wickham, *JTS* 21 (1970), 352,29–33 and Zacharias Rh., *HE* IV 12: Hamilton-Brooks, 81, and Index, s. n. Isaiah, bp. of Hermopolis. See A. Grillmeier, *CCT* II/2, p. 81, n. 193.

57. Timothy Ael., *Ep. ad Alexandrin.*: Ebied-Wickham, p. 359. We recall the reproaches against Proterius.

> ... to inform everyone, naming the above mentioned Isaiah and Theophilus as persons
> who, by asserting that our Lord and God Jesus Christ is of an alien nature from us and that
> he was not consubstantial in flesh with men and that he was not really human, have
> alienated themselves from communion with the holy fathers and with me and give
> warning that no man henceforth should hold communion with them.[58]

He bases this procedure on apostolic church discipline (1 Jn 4,1–3; 2 Jn
7.10–11; Gal 1,8–9; Titus 3,10–11) but also on the councils of 325 and
381, which formulated God's law for us.[59] Whoever holds to this remains
on the 'rock of Peter'. Two things are to be noted here: (1) The Council
of Constantinople in 381 is recognized here, and this is not invalidated
even in Timothy's *Refutation of the Council of Chalcedon*.[60] On the other
hand, the Alexandrians of his party, who in 457 took their case to
Emperor Leo I, acted differently. They expressly said: 'We do not know
a synod of the 150.'[61] (2) The reference to Mt 16,18 is interesting.
Intended here is not, say, communion with Rome and the see of Peter as
the guarantee of the true faith, but simply the 'orthodox faith' that has its
measure in the testimony of the fathers. Whoever keeps this faith, which
is anchored in tradition, is built on the rock of Peter; whoever does not
keep it falls under the power of hell.[62]

The noticeable concern about the spread of Eutychianism also moves
Timothy in letters V and VI. Letter V is still written from Gangra and
goes to Palestine.[63] It expands the picture of the spread of Eutychian or

---

58. Ibid.

59. Cf. Ebied-Wickham, p. 361, where the excommunication is substantiated once
again.

60. Cf. Timothy Ael., *Refutatio synodi Chalcedonensis et tomi Leonis* (CPG 5482): F. Nau,
PO 13, p. 226, where Timothy emphasizes that Chalcedon refers to the council of the 150
fathers, but not to that of Ephesus. This does not mean a rejection of the council of 381 by
Timothy. Therefore it is not entirely understandable when Ebied-Wickham, *JTS* 21 (1970),
329, n. 1, speak of an 'apparent inconsistency between Timothy's appeal here to the authority
of the Council of Constantinople and what he says in his treatise against the Synod of
Chalcedon'. The reference to PO 13, pp. 23–24 must mean pp. 223–24. The council of 381
found reception in the *Encyclion* of Emperor Basiliscus, which is addressed to Timothy. Cf.
Zacharias Rh., *HE* V 2: Brooks, CSCO 87, pp. 146–47; Hamilton-Brooks, pp. 105–7; also
the host of 700 bishops gathered around Timothy in Ephesus, ibid. V 3: Brooks, CSCO 87,
pp. 148–49; Hamilton-Brooks, p. 107. Cf. other bishops such as Timothy Salophaciolus and
Martyrius of Jerusalem, ibid. V 5 and 6: Hamilton-Brooks, pp. 114, 115; Peter Mongus: ibid.
V 7: Hamilton-Brooks, p. 115. Finally in the *Henoticon* of Zeno: ibid. V 8: Hamilton-Brooks,
pp. 121, 122; Brooks CSCO 87, pp. 151–59.

61. ACO II 5, p. 22,18. Only Nicaea and the two Ephesian councils are recognized by this
group. Cf. E. Schwartz (n. 24 above) regarding a lacuna.

62. Timothy Ael., *Ep. ad C'politanos*: Ebied-Wickham, pp. 351–52. Cf. ibid., p. 351, n. 4,
the addendum of Zacharias Rh., *HE* IV 12: Hamilton-Brooks, p. 82; Brooks, CSCO 87, p.
130.

63. Timothy Ael., *Ep. ad Faustin. diac.* (CPG 5480): Ebied-Wickham, pp. 364–66, with
pp. 331–32.

even Manichaean views. Previously Constantinople and Alexandria were more prominent as the centres of these heresies:

> Inasmuch as I have heard that Palestine is full of schisms arising out of the teaching of many roving antichrists, who confess neither that our Lord was truly made man while remaining also God, nor that the unchangeable God the Word was consubstantial with us and of the same fleshly stock as us, by divine providence, and inasmuch as I have heard, while in exile for Christ's sake, of their dreadful blasphemies, which I did not even venture to commit to writing, I exhort you, dear friends, to be diligent, in so far as you are able, in saving those who are seduced.[64]

Letter VI is supposed to have been written from the Chersonese, if we may believe the heading, but this is not otherwise confirmed in the letter.[65] Again, it is against the Eutychians. Where they are to be found cannot be determined, since the addressees, the 'godly priest Claudianus and his brethren', are unknown. Presumably we must seek them in Egypt, since they form a group around Timothy that remains loyal to him, though he is in exile. But at work around them are 'dogs' and 'enemies of the cross of Christ' (Phil 1,27–30), who harm the flock of Christ no less than the Diphysites. The Antichrist is at work in them.

> These antichrists neither acknowledge that Jesus Christ has come into the world in human flesh, nor believe that God the Word became man while remaining God unchanged.[66] Their heresy is an ancient and many-headed monster, which gained confidence from the wicked Synod of the Nestorians at Chalcedon. Some of them say that our Lord's incarnation was illusion, imagination and unreal.[67]

Thus it is a question of Docetic groups. How their heresy is supposed to have been promoted by Chalcedon, as Timothy asserts, remains an unsubstantiated reproach. From these 'Docetists' he distinguishes yet another group, which he censures as worldly and uneducated; nevertheless, they think themselves wiser than the holy fathers and thus have become true fools:

> For they are now preaching the evil doctrines of the Phantasiasts' heresy (things which the followers of the blessed Athanasius, Julius, the older Gregory and Cyril anathematized) by saying that the body of our Lord and God Jesus Christ is uncreated, that body which was

---

64. Ibid., Ebied-Wickham, p. 365. Cf. also p. 331.

65. Timothy Ael., *Ep. ad Claudian. presb.* (CPG 5481): Ebied-Wickham, pp. 366–69; further ibid., pp. 331–32. This letter was perhaps written shortly before the death of Timothy (477).

66. Ebied-Wickham, p. 367, refer to letter V, p. 365 (fol. 35[a]).

67. Ibid., p. 367 (fol. 36[a]). L. Abramowski, 'Ein Text des Johannes Chrysostomus über die Auferstehung in den Belegsammllungen des Timotheus Älurus', in *After Chalcedon* (OLA 18), pp. 1–10, points out 'that the christological disagreement with the Eutychians over the problem of the human *homoousia* of Christ also involved the problem of the real bodily death and the identity of the resurrection body' (ibid., pp. 9–10). This emphasizes the humanity of Christ not only in its static reality but also in its entire history.

constituted of created manhood. They are asserting that God the Word was not ineffably incarnate from the Virgin, Mother of God, sharing blood and flesh in our likeness – so as to be made wholly like us, sin excepted [cf. Heb 2,17 and 4,15], and so that in becoming truly man, he could be seen by earthly men revealed in human flesh for our salvation, and so that 'he should also suffer in the flesh for our sake', according to the divine Scriptures [1 Pt 4,1] . . .

[Timothy's opponents say: Christ's body is uncreated, not really human and not consubstantial with Mary and with us, his brothers. But Timothy says:] Was he not consubstantial with the holy Virgin and with us by the providence of God, while remaining immutable God and consubstantial with the Father, not to be divided or separated into two natures, essences, hypostases, or persons? . . . Whoever refuse to confess that our Lord's flesh is created, and that it was of created manhood must needs blaspheme with the Arians . . .[68]

The same words could have been written by Leo I against the Eutychians – among whom, indeed, he also included Timothy. Although the banished patriarch retains his bad feelings regarding the Diphysites, his actual concerns and entreaties are for the sympathizers of Eutyches, who has (again) fallen away from the traditional faith. For by 'Docetists', 'Manichaeans' and 'Phantasiasts' he means primarily them.[69]

Speaking in this letter is a different Timothy from the one known to us from his tractates or the Chalcedonian polemics. Even though the letters make no concessions to Chalcedon, they allow – if we disregard the *miaphysis* formula – the construction of a Christology that is more Chalcedonian than Monophysite, at least in regard to the way they 'explain' the incarnation. The fear of 'Docetists and Phantasiasts' could not be greater for Leo of Rome. The letters show Timothy as a bishop

---

68. Timothy Ael., *Ep. ad Claud. presb.*: Ebied-Wickham, pp. 367–68 (fol. 36ᵃ). Here in the first part of his text, in clarification of the double consubstantiality of Christ, Timothy takes up a formula that is also found in Chalcedon: 'like us in every respect, except for sin'. He would hardly have borrowed it from the council, but rather from the Alexandrian tradition, in which the key phrases from Heb 2,17 and 4,15 were combined. We find a somewhat modified form in Theophilus of Alex., *Sixth Easter Letter*, read at the Council of Ephesus in 431: τὴν δὲ κατὰ πάντα πρὸς ἡμᾶς χωρὶς ἁμαρτίας οὐκ ἐκφεύγειν κρίνας ὁμοίωσιν (ACO I 7, p. 91,35–36).

69. For the equating of 'Phantasiasts' and 'Eutychians' Ebied-Wickham p. 367, refer to Br. L. Add. 12156, fol. 61ᵃ, that is, to the text that follows the close of the *Refutation of the Definition of Chalcedon*. F. Nau, PO 13, no. XIII, p. 237, gives this text (fol. 61ᵃ), which, however, probably does not come from Timothy but rather is a heading for the anathema that was demanded of converts to Monophysitism: '. . . à tous ceux qui voulaient se convertir de toutes les hérésies: c'est-à-dire de ceux qui disent deux natures et des Nestoriens ou des *Phantasiastes*, qui sont encore les *Eutychiens* [emphasis added] ou de toutes les hérésies . . .' At the close of letter VI Timothy simply sets the two groups of heretics over against each other: 'the heretical Diphysites and Phantasiasts' (Ebied-Wickham, 369).

concerned about the church.[70] If we found such sharp language against the 'Phantasiasts' or 'Eutychians' only in Chalcedonian sources, then we would have to surmise behind it polemical exaggerations and unjustified generalizations. In this regard Timothy is an impartial witness. Through his letters he contributes a great deal to the religious picture of this period and of the imperial church of the fifth century. Interesting is the parallel between Nestorius and Timothy (together with Dioscorus): as the former dissociates himself from 'genuine Nestorians', so also does the latter from the wrong representatives of the Alexandrian *mia-physis* Christology. Both could have used the same words – even if in opposing directions – regarding their radicalized, out-of-control followers: 'Leur enseignement et le nôtre n'est pas le même'![71]

Even the personal picture of the banished man, distorted by polemic, receives milder, more human characteristics. In the letters Timothy shows a certain *moderatio*, which was so often recommended also by Pope Leo.[72] He practised it especially with regard to 'converts' from the followers of Chalcedon and other 'heretics' – even though this may have had a certain partisan political motivation.

Timothy's attitude towards the Chalcedonian Christians is characterized by moderation. As we have seen before in the previous letter to the City of Alexandria [Ep. II], the penance imposed on clerical converts [to Monophysitism] is light and is limited to a written anathematization of the Council of Chalcedon and the Tome of Leo, and a year of suspension from priestly functions.[73] Laymen are to be received into communion apparently immediately upon anathematizing heretics in general. In the case of foreign religious, Timothy appears to envisage that they should be informed of the harm involved in the Diphysite heresy, invited to anathematize the Council of Chalcedon and the Tome of Leo, and then received into

---

70. Cf. Timothy Ael., *Ep. ad Aegyptum, Thebaidem et Pentapolim* (CPG 5479): Ebied-Wickham, 364 (fol. 34[b]): 'A mighty storm has come upon the church of God, dear brethren, and we must suffer in company with one another.'

71. Thus Nestorius in *Ep. ad C'politanos* (CPG 5680): trans. by F. Nau, *Nestorius. Le livre d'Héraclide de Damas*, Paris 1910, 373–75, here p. 374,8.

72. Cf. Leo M., Ep. 95, 2: ACO II 4, p. 50,33: *moderationem volui custodiri*, a saying that H. Rahner made the motto of his contribution in *Chalkedon* I, pp. 323–39: 'Leo der Große, der Papst des Konzils (von Chalkedon)'.

73. According to Severus of Antioch, *Ep. ad Ioann. Tribunum*: Brooks, *SL* II, pp. 280–1, Timothy vacillated. In the beginning he did not recognize the consecration of the Proterians when they confessed against Chalcedon, but later when they had done church penance. This letter comes from the period 489–508. In letter 60 to the presbyters Photius and Andrew and the archimandrites of Caria from the period 519–538 (Brooks, ibid., pp. 179–91) Severus again refers to this practice of Timothy. – Leo I also allowed church penance for converted 'Eutychians' (*legitima satisfactione correctis paenitentiae remedium non negetur*, Ep. 164: ACO II 4, p. 112,35). But a reinstallation of Timothy as bishop was unthinkable for Leo.

communion *in sanctis* on the sole condition that they do not communicate also with the Diphysites. If they do, they are to be allowed to go freely and peacefully.[74]

(b) The polemic against the 'Nestorianism' of Leo I's Tome to Flavian and of the Council of Chalcedon[75]

The direction of theological thrust now turns 180 degrees. The targeted 'heretic' is Leo I of Rome with his *Tomus ad Flavianum*. For easier refutation Timothy divides the text into twenty-eight sections and supplies them with just as many answers, which in some cases produce several sections.[76] It is not necessary to follow the individual numbers altogether. Rather it is sufficient to give the basic direction of Timothy's remarks and point out only those particularities that illuminate the patriarch's position.

Throughout Timothy makes the reproach of heresy against Leo, who is designated simply as the crony of Nestorius. Leo is in conflict with the 'teachers of the church' (cf. sections 1–2, 6–9 [pp. 143–44, 146–48]). This aim is sometimes served by the juxtaposition of Leo's statements and

---

74. Ebied-Wickham, pp. 330–31; cf. Timothy Ael., *Ep. ad Alexandr.* (CPG 5477): Ebied-Wickham, p. 361; *Ep. ad Aegypt., Thebaid. et Pentapol.* (CPG 5479): ibid., pp. 362–63. See also *Preces* (CPG 5483): Br. L. Add. 12156, fol. 61va–b; Nau, PO 13, pp. 238–39, where we find the short prayer that Timothy ordered to be said over the converts. Certain information is also in Michael Syr., *Chron.* IX 1: Chabot II, 135b. According to the proceedings of Cyril and Dioscorus, Timothy prescribed a year's penance for bishops, priests and deacons at 'conversion' and then allowed the resumption of official functions. One hundred years later, two or three years' penance was imposed (cf. F. Nau, PO 13, p. 238, n. 1).

75. Here we follow R. Y. Ebied and L. R. Wickham, 'Timothy Aelurus: Against the Definition of the Council of Chalcedon', in *After Chalcedon* (OLA 18), pp. 115–66. As already mentioned, the two editors present the first publication of Br. L. Add. 12156, fol. 42v–51v and 59v–61r: on pp. 120–42 (in photocopy) the Syriac text and on pp. 143–66 the English translation. The Syriac translation of the *Tome* edited here is based on a Greek text, which was present at the Council of Chalcedon in 451 (ed. E. Schwartz, ACO II 1, 1, pp. 10–20).

76. We follow the numeration (in *stichoi*) of the edition of C. Silva-Tarouca, *S. Leonis Magni Tomus ad Flavianum Episc. Constantinopolitanum* (TD 9), Rome 1959. Timothy's text follows exactly Leo's text in Greek translation with the exception of no. 6 (TD 9, vv. 43–56a). There the famous vv. 54–55: *Salva igitur proprietate utriusque naturae, et in unam coeunte personam* are expanded in the Syriac with *et hypostasim* (qnomā). Syr. Text: p. 123 = fol. 44r, lin. 28/29; cf. translation on p. 146 with n. 22: 'This addition, no doubt erroneous, of "and one hypostasis" makes the passage precisely resemble the definition of the Council of Chalcedon. Elsewhere in the Armenian work [K. Ter-Mekerttschian and E. Ter-Minassiantz, *Timotheus Älurus' des Patriarchen von Alexandrien, Widerlegung der auf der Synode zu Chalcedon festgesetzten Lehre*, 1908, 64] Timothy represents Leo's text unaltered. Curiously, Schwartz [ACO II 1, 1, p. 13,11] fails to notice the variant.' The same is true of the edition by Silva-Tarouca, v. 55.

those (allegedly) of Nestorius, which, however, in individual cases cannot be documented.

(aa) The different concept of nature

The contrast between the Alexandrian-Cyrillian and the Leonine-Roman traditions found actual expression in different concepts of nature. Now, because Leo's Tome talks especially often about natura (duae naturae), his opponent is provoked more and more as the exposition progresses. A particularly rich section in Leo (vv. 177–85) forms no. 27 in Timothy.

In allusion to the interrogation of Eutyches at Flavian's synod of Constantinople in 448, Leo says, with an obvious reproach against Flavian himself:

> As an answer to your judicial cross-examination, Eutyches responded: 'I confess that our Lord was *from two natures* before the union; after the union, however, I confess only *one nature*.' I am astonished that such an absurd and perverse confession was not rebuked by a critique (*increpatione*) from the judges and that this all too foolish manner of speaking was passed over as if nothing offensive had been heard. Yet as the only-begotten Son is designated in so godless a way as being of two natures before the incarnation, how evil (*nefarie*) it is then to assert a single nature in him after the Word has become flesh.[77]

Thus in the confession of one nature Leo sees the assertion of a 'mixed nature' in the strict sense. Leo always presupposed that what the Word received from Mary (a true body with a human soul) merits the designation *nature*.

But even this was already decisively rejected by Timothy in his ninth answer to vv. 63–68 of the *Tome* in reference to an Apollinarian forgery. He cites Pseudo-Julius, *Letter to Dionysius*:

> Those who confess that the God who comes from heaven was incarnate of the Virgin also vainly disturb [the idea] that he is one along with his flesh, falling into their impious statements. For they speak also, I learn, of two natures, although John has plainly shown our Lord to be one by saying 'the Word became flesh' [Jn 1,14] . . . For if he who was born of the Virgin was called 'one', and it is he through whom everything was made, the nature is one because the person is one, having no division into two because *the body is not a nature on its own* nor is the Godhead in the incarnation a nature on its own, but just as a man is one nature so also is Christ who was made in the likeness of men.[78]

Timothy does not recognize that from the incarnate Logos, Pseudo-Julius in the strict sense makes a 'nature unity' out of Logos and *sarx*. His eleventh answer to Leo's Tome (vv. 77–90) also follows this track when it says: 'He [Leo] again makes the man a nature [*kyanā*] (45r, lin. 13) on

---

77. Vv. 177–85: Silva-Tarouca, p. 32.

78. Ps.-Julius, *Ep. ad Dionys.* § 2: Lietzmann, *Apollinaris*, p. 257,7–19; cf. OLA 18, pp. 147–48.

its own in what he says.' That is, Timothy does not confer the term *nature* on the humanity of the incarnate One,[79] although he holds to the completeness of that humanity.[80]

(bb) A questionable argument for the divinity of the incarnate One

In addition to the numerous Apollinarian forgeries, the source of the *miaphysis* Christology, Timothy also presents the text of a Bishop Erechtius of Antioch in Pisidia, who does not belong among these forgers but whose authority as a church father was doubted.[81] This Erechtius offers a substantiation of the divinity of Christ and a rejection of the two-natures doctrine, as it certainly does not correspond to the conception of Proclus:

> For he [Christ] is not two natures, but the Virgin, receiving the overshadowing of the Spirit, gave birth in mysterious fashion to God incarnate. For if Christ is a growth of human seed I should have agreed that fruit must resemble root in nature, but if he is of the Holy Ghost, in accordance with the Archangel's words, he who is born is God because God is the cause of his birth.[82]

Timothy himself seems here perhaps to have been suspicious of this interpretation and substantiation of the divinity of Christ and the manner of his bodily reality. For immediately after these words of 'Erechtius' comes a section from the two letters of Patriarch Dioscorus of Alexandria,[83] who in a few lines seems to represent the opposite viewpoint:

> My declaration is that no man shall assert that the flesh, which our Lord took from holy Mary, through the Holy Spirit, in a manner known only to himself, is different from or alien to our body.[84]

Based on these comments of Timothy Aelurus, which now have been made accessible in Syriac and in English translation, we can make various observations:

---

79. Cf. also the 15th answer to the *Tome* vv. 103–6.

80. Cf. the 25th answer to the *Tome* vv. 163–65 (OLA 18), p. 156: 'complete man'. On the confession of the 'soul of Christ' see the 27th answer to the *Tome* vv. 177–85, OLA 18, p. 157.

81. G. Fedalto, *HEO* I, names Erechtius under no. 25.1.15, p. 256, yet with uncertain dates of office (elected before 434–447), that is, for the period under Proclus of Constantinople; cf. M. Le Quien I, p. 1038, IX. Patr. Ephraem of Antioch (Photius, *Bibl. cod.* 229: Henry IV, p. 155) considers him a Eutychian; Leont. Schol., *De sectis*, Act. VIII, V: PG 86, 1257B: 'He was never heard among the fathers.' Cf. F. Nau, PO 13, pp. 162–63.

82. Greek text in Schwartz, *Cod. Vat. gr. 1431*, p. 28; Syriac with French translation: F. Nau, PO 13, p. 170; cf. Photius, *Bibl. cod.* 229: Henry IV, p. 155; here according to OLA 18, p. 159.

83. See OLA 18, pp. 159–62.

84. Timothy's 27th answer to the *Tome*, vv. 174–85: OLA 18, p. 160. This is then further discussed. Later in this volume an Ethiopian text is given, which closely resembles the teaching rejected by Dioscorus.

(1) The main difference between the Alexandrians and Leo I of Rome depends on terminological presuppositions, which especially concern the words *nature, kyana, physis, natura*.

(2) The difference is clearly traceable to the role of the Apollinarian forgeries that invaded Alexandrian theology and were especially promoted and employed in polemics by Timothy Aelurus. In comparison with them the genuine teachings of Cyril receded.

3. The Christology of Timothy and its aporias

For modern Christologists, who want to grant the Council of Chalcedon only historical validity, Timothy – in spite of his decisive rejection of Chalcedon – remains within the scope of precisely this Chalcedonian problematic, and indeed even under the influence of its essential assertions. In spite of his rejection of the *language* of the *two natures*, the recognition of the unmixed reality of divinity and humanity in Christ is decisive for him. Nowhere is this shown more clearly than in his teaching of the 'twofold consubstantiality' of Christ with God and with humankind. No theologian before him expressed it as often as he did – and always in dispute with the Eutychians and their Docetic-Manichaean sympathizers. What has always echoed in his letters will now be briefly summarized because of its significance.

(a) Appeal to tradition

In his first letter (to the city of Constantinople) Timothy placed in service to this theme of the double consubstantiality of Christ the possibility of presenting his proofs through patristic florilegia. Thus in this respect we have a collection of testimonies from the fathers that are unique in the patristic literature.[85] His other voluminous florilegia are devoted to combating the formula of the two natures. There he had no occasion to emphasize the double *homoousios*. According to M. Wiles the impulse for the introduction of the *homoousios* into the Logos doctrine (and thus into

---

85. As the purpose of Timothy's letters, Michael Syrus, *Chron.* IX 1: Chabot II, 128 A states: 'Thimotheus n'écrivait pas seulement contre Nestorius, pendant qu'il était en exil, mais aussi contre les Eutychéens. Cela est manifeste par les choses qu'il écrivit à Alexandrie et en Palestine, contre ceux qui pensaient comme Eutychès, et ne confessaient pas que le Christ nous est consubstantiel dans la chair, tout en étant consubstantiel au Père dans la divinité.' – The historical development of the doctrine of the double consubstantiality of Christ (without considering Monophysitism) is traced by M. Wiles, 'ΟΜΟΟΥΣΙΟΣ ΗΜΙΝ', *JTS* 16 (1965), 454–61; B. Studer, 'Consubstantialis Patri, Consubstantialis Matri. Une antithèse christologique chez Léon le Grand', *RevÉtAug* 18 (1972), 87–115 (with additional literature). See A. Grillmeier, *CCT* II/1, p. 53 (C) I.1.).

trinitarian theology) originated with Arius, even if the effect was not desired by him. In Christology Apollinarius was the first to introduce the double *homoousios* with regard to Christ. Here too this way of speaking was subsequently maintained and elaborated, while the Apollinarian content was overcome. Its harmful effects, however, are still recognizable a long time afterwards, not least of all in Eutyches and the Eutychians fought by Timothy. Now, in adducing his proof against them, Timothy reaches back extensively to the fourth century but works in part with minor text corrections[86] or with the so-called Apollinarian forgeries and other spurious texts. The most significant text of the florilegium is masked with the name of Pope Julius and in reality belongs to Apollinarius's writing *De Unione*. Here Timothy probably went back to the oldest text that sets the consubstantiality of Christ with God over against the consubstantiality with humanity, yet in a linking of anti-Arian and Apollinarian understandings. 'Thus he [Christ] is consubstantial with God according to the invisible *pneuma* [i.e., divinity]. The name he bears includes his flesh, because it is united to the consubstantial one with God. And on the other hand he is consubstantial with human beings.'[87]

The next text is ascribed to Gregory Thaumaturgos but is not genuine. It is interesting in that it contains within it a deterrent against the conclusions that had been drawn from the basic Apollinarian conception: the flesh of Christ, because of its physical *synousia* with the Logos, is to be

---

86. Even the first testimony, Athanasius, *C. Arian. or.* II 74: PG 26, 304B does not use *homoousios* but reads *homoios*, although semantically the intention is the same: as Logos Christ has no peers. He is *unigenitus*. 'At factus homo similes habet, quorum videlicet similem carnem assumpsit.' Timothy understands: 'But having become man, he has beings *consubstantial* with him' (*bar kyana*; Ebied-Wickham, *JTS* 21 (1970), 352; Br. L. Add. 12156, fol. 30ᵇ). Thus he inserts *homoousios*. The second testimony from Epictetus (PG 26, 1064B) has a different opposition from that which Timothy presupposes. It indeed proves that Christ's body came from Mary, but the role of the term *consubstantial* in this quotation cannot be transferred to Timothy's problem (cf. Ebied-Wickham, p. 353).

87. Apollinarius, *De unione* § 8: Lietzmann, p. 188,9–18; cf. Ebied-Wickham, *JTS* 21 (1970), 354. Cf. Wiles, 'ΟΜΟΟΥΣΙΟΣ ΗΜΙΝ', 456: Apollinarius sees in Christ only the unity of Logos and *sarx* (without the soul); thus frag. 45 in Lietzmann, p. 214: οὐκ ἀλλ' ὡς ἄνθρωπος, διότι οὐχ ὁμοούσιος τῷ ἀνθρώπῳ κατὰ τὸ κυριώτατον; therefore Logos and *sarx* produce a 'natural' symbiosis but not a 'human being'. Cf. A. Grillmeier, *JdChr* I³, pp. 483–90; *CCT* I², pp. 330–40; further passages in R. Hübner, *TheolPhil* 56 (1981), 271. M. Wiles says correctly: 'For Apollinarius insists that the relationship of the flesh to the Godhead is in no sense adventitious but rather συνουσιωμένη καὶ σύμφυτος (Lietzmann, frag. 36). Such language was open to very obvious objection. If the Son is ὁμοούσιος with the Father and the flesh and the divinity in Christ constitute a single οὐσία, then it is being regarded as heavenly in nature and ὁμοούσιος with the Father.' This seems to be the root of Eutyches' error, which had its full effect only in his extreme followers. Apollinarius himself, in spite of his teaching of the symbiosis of Logos and *sarx*, rejected the consubstantiality of the 'flesh' of Christ with the divinity. Cf. Wiles, p. 456; A. Grillmeier, *JdChr* I³, pp. 483–86; *CCT* I², pp. 330–33.

designated as 'consubstantial' with the divinity. But Pseudo-Gregory asks: 'How can flesh, which is in time, be called consubstantial with nontemporal Deity? For *consubstantial* designates what is the same nature, immutably and eternally.'[88] Unfortunately, in all his florilegia Timothy overlooks Didymus of Alexandria, who was probably considered a suspicious Origenist by Timothy. Precisely there he would have found the double *homoousios* of Christ and yet the clearest rejection of Apollinarius: the human consubstantiality of Christ with us requires a total humanity, body and soul. The *homoousios* is expressly applied to the 'soul' of Christ.[89] Cyril of Alexandria, Timothy's chief witness, also stresses the double consubstantiality of Christ with God and with us, and, regarding the humanity of Christ, Cyril in his later works often expressly emphasizes its totality (body and soul). The text quoted in the first letter brings this to expression: 'For thus you worship one Son who is both consubstantial in Godhead with the Father and consubstantial with us in his humanity.'[90] Another Cyril text from the second letter to Succensus would be clearer vis-à-vis the Eutychians:

> But even if the body, which is joined to the Word springing from God the Father and in which is a rational soul, is not consubstantial with the Word, even if intellectual consideration perceives that the united [i.e., divinity and humanity] are of different natures, we still confess one Son and Christ and Lord, since the Word became flesh; but when we speak of flesh, we mean 'human being'.[91]

When Timothy repeatedly – even more than Leo I – emphasizes the double consubstantiality of Christ with God and with us, then it is still a special concern of his to depict this ontological fellow humanity of

---

88. Ebied-Wickham, *JTS* 21 (1970), 354, no. 5: PO 10, 1028A; ACO I 1, 6, pp. 147,23–148,2. The last sentence reads: ὁμοούσιον γὰρ λέγεται τὸ ταυτὸν τῇ φύσει καί τῇ ἀιδιότητι ἀπαραλλάκτως. In this conceptual determination, consubstantiality is seen as 'static', whereas the Syriac *bar kyana* derives consubstantiality from the descent of the one from another, as the etymology of *kyana* indicates. Cf. R. Payne Smith, *Thesaurus Syriacus* I, 1703; B. Studer, *RevÉtAug* 18 (1972), 101: 'En outre, il faut tenir compte du fait que le terme de "consubstantiel" comporte en filigrane l'idée d'origine, de production naturelle d'un être. Bien que souvent négligé par les historiens des dogmes, cette connotation s'est avérée fondamentale dans toute l'histoire du mot.' Ibid., 102: 'Il ne fait donc aucun doute que d'après les auteurs des premières siècles chrétiens, les individus et les choses sont consubstantiels en vertu de leur rapport d'origine, soit de génération, soit de production, soit d'émanation.' Ps.-Gregory Thaum. does not fit into this history of concepts; he comes later.

89. Cf. A. Grillmeier, *JdChr* I³, pp. 529–35, esp. 531; *CCT* I², pp. 361–67, esp. 363. For *consubstantialis* in Didymus all texts edited since 1965 are to be considered. Cf. Wiles (n. 85 above), p. 459.

90. Cyril of Alex., *Fragmenta ex libro II contra Theodorum*, CPG 5229 (2): ed. Pusey, III, Oxford 1872, 525,14–16; Ebied-Wickham, *JTS* 21 (1970), 356.

91. Cyril of Alex., *Ep. 46 ad Succens.* II: ACO I 4, 2, p. 237,21–25 (Lat.). Greek in I 6, no. 172, p. 158,21–25; PG 77, 240BC.

Christ. He does this in his first letter (to the Alexandrians) with the words of Dioscorus, which can hardly be exceeded in clarity. Beginning with the main biblical text for the human consubstantiality of Jesus (Heb 2,17: 'Therefore . . . it was right that he should become like his brothers in all things'), he says:

> The phrase is 'in everything'. It does not exclude any part of our nature at all. It includes nerves, hair, bones, veins, belly, heart, kidneys, liver, and lungs. That flesh of our Saviour, which was born of Mary and which was ensouled with a rational soul, was constituted of every element of which we are composed, but not through male seed, sleep, and sensual gratification . . . For he was with us, like us and for us.[92]

Timothy also has a similar analysis of Christ's humanity *per partes*. It represents the end-point of a special development in the history of dogma. Thus, in the first tractate against the Diphysites, he says regarding the death of Jesus:

> He gave up his spirit when he committed it, that is, his soul, into the hands of the Father, when he wanted to do this. He proved thereby that the precious body of Christ was endowed with a rational soul; he really became a human being and truly died through the separation, the parting of the soul from the body. In this way he indeed tasted death for us, he who was immortal and 'free among the dead' [*inter mortuos liber*, cf. Ps 87,6 (V)]. In the economy [the incarnation], however, he [as God] was not separable from his body and his soul, in accordance with the kind and the inexplicable and incomprehensible manner of divine incarnation. For he was not united with one part and separated (not united) from another. No one among the saints said that he had a soul without the body or a body without soul; rather, he was united with flesh in which there is a rational soul.[93]

In short, Dioscorus, Timothy and Leo agree completely in this interpretation of the humanity of Christ. All three can summarize their Christology in the sentence that Cyril wrote to Succensus: 'Christ exists

---

92. Dioscorus of Alex., *Ep. ad Secundinum*, cited by Timothy Aelurus, *Ep. II ad Alexand.*: Ebied-Wickham, 360. A more lengthy excerpt from the letter of Patriarch Dioscorus to Secundinus is found in Timothy Aelurus in his writing *Against Chalcedon*: Ebied-Wickham, OLA 18, pp. 159–60 (according to Br. L. Add. 12156, fol. 49v–50r). M. Le Quien, *Oriens Christianus* II, Paris 1740, Graz 1958, p. 411, therefore judges incorrectly when he says of Dioscorus: 'Negabat igitur ille, perinde atque Eutyches Christum consubstantialem nobis esse secundum carnem et humanitatem.' In Le Quien's view, it was not until Timothy and Severus that the Copts and Jacobites distanced themselves from Eutyches.

93. Timothy Ael., *Contra eos qui dicunt duas naturas* (CPG 5475): Br. L. Add. 12156, fol. 23rb, translated according to the French text in J. Lebon, *RHE* 9 (1908), 691. Here Timothy rejects the doctrine of the separation of the Logos from the body and soul of Jesus and the interpretation of Jesus' death on the basis of this separation of the Logos from the body, which after Athanasius and Hilary had assumed a long and persistent tradition. The rejection of the separation of the Logos from the humanity is in an alleged letter of Pope Liberius, referred to by Dioscorus, in 'Histoire de Dioscore', *JA* X 1 (1903), 264. Cf. A. Grillmeier, *CCT* II/1, p. 157, n. 124, and the interpretation of Jesus' death by the Anonymus c. Eutychen and the correct teaching of Leo himself. Cf. A. Grillmeier, *CCT* I²², pp. 315–17 and my study mentioned there, 'Der Gottessohn im Totenreich', in idem, *Mit ihm und in ihm*, Freiburg ²1978, 76–174.

as one and only Son, one and the same is God and man, as perfect in divinity as perfect in humanity.'[94] Over against this confession stands another with equal validity: *consubstantialis Patri consubstantialis matri*, which the two Alexandrians repeat even more often than Leo.

(b) The aporia of the mia-physis formula

After such statements, how can one still confess *mia physis* in Christ? Cyril discussed this tormenting problem above all in the second letter to Succensus. This letter will accompany the history of the pro- and anti-Chalcedonian discussion, as already attested by the famous *Florilegium Cyrillianum* before 500 (see *CCT* II/2, p. 34) and even later by Photius, *Bibl.* 228, 230. In Timothy's first letter, he adopted Cyril's decisive statement of the problem and his solution. Zacharias Rhetor adopted this *chresis*, which Br. L. Add. 12156 omitted. Therefore we follow Zacharias. Cyril's text is not quite literally reproduced:

> They say, if Christ be perfect God and perfect man, and the same is of the Nature of the Father in the Godhead and of our nature in the manhood, how is He perfect if his human nature is not seen? and how is He of our nature if that actual and self-same nature which is ours be not seen? The answer which we have given at the beginning should suffice to enlighten them. For if, when speaking of *one* nature of the Word, we refrained from saying 'incarnate', rejecting the dispensation, their word would be plausible when they ask, 'How can He be perfect in manhood and in nature?' But since our word indeed testifies that He is perfect in manhood and nature by saying that He became flesh, therefore let them cease from these objections, and not lean upon a broken reed.[95]

Thus up to this point Timothy and Leo, the Alexandrians and the followers of Chalcedon could go along entirely together. The parting begins with 'in two natures', which, however, is nothing but the consequence of the Cyrillian 'perfect in divinity', '*the very same one* also perfect in humanity' or 'one and the same consubstantial with the Father according to divinity' and 'consubstantial with us according to humanity'. Why does Timothy energetically reject the application of the word and concept *physis* to the 'complete humanity' of Christ? He seems to have various reasons for this, and they cannot all be reduced to a common denominator:

---

94. Cyril of Alex., *Ep. II ad Succens.*: ACO I 1, 6, no. 172, p. 161,2–3; PG 77, 244B; cf. Wickham, *Select Letters*, 90–91.

95. Zacharias Rh., *HE* IV 12: Brooks, CSCO 87, p. 139; Hamilton-Brooks, p. 95. Hamilton's translation does not reveal the peculiar character of the Cyril text, which the Syriac translation preserves. Better is the Latin translation of E. W. Brooks in CSCO 87, p. 139, where *bar kyana* is rendered as *connaturalis*. Cf. Land, *Anecdota Syriaca* III, pp. 158,26–159,10. Cf. Cyril of Alex., *Ep. II ad Succens.*: ACO I 1, 6, no. 172, p. 160,14–24; PG 77, 241D–244A. Cf. the *chreseis* in Michael Syr., *Chron.* IX 1: Chabot II, pp. 136B–137B. On the Cyril text see T. Šagi-Bunić, *'Deus perfectus et homo perfectus' a concilio Ephesino (a. 431) ad Chalcedonense (a. 451)*, Rome 1965, 55, 62, 87.

(1) To speak of *nature* means to assert of a subject what belongs to it necessarily and unrelinquishably from birth. To the divine Logos, however, belongs from eternity necessarily and unrelinquishably only the divine essence. To assert of him a second 'nature' would mean that being human belongs to the one and only Son of God just as originally and necessarily as being divine. The incarnation is rather a deed of the '*oikonomia*', that is, of the free assumption of human form in time:

> He is not that which he was not through a metamorphosis or a transformation (conversion); rather, he remained entirely God, consubstantial with the Father who begot him; because of the *oikonomia* [God's free arrangement of salvation] and not because of his nature, he became human for us and our salvation.[96]

(2) If one must apply to the humanity of Christ the designation 'second nature of the God Logos', then one would have to make the same assertions about it as about the divine essence of Christ; what cannot be said of the divine nature must also be withheld from the human nature:

> It is impossible to call the life-giving flesh of our Lord the second nature of the God Logos or his second essence. Indeed, it is written that he who was crucified, the Lord of glory [cf. 1 Cor 2,8], suffered in his flesh. No one can say that the Lord of glory suffered in his nature or essence [i.e., in his divinity]. But if the God Logos appropriated himself another nature, that is, united himself with a perfect human being, and if Christ is of two natures, as he seems to be for those who speak of two natures, then it follows that they say that he suffered in his nature [i.e., in his divinity] – which is a godless assertion – and that they assert that the divine nature is capable of suffering. For the nature of Christ is only divinity, which also became flesh without transformation for our salvation and so that he might appear in the flesh, according to the scriptures [cf. 1 Tim 3,16b] . . .[97]

It was precisely this consequence that Chalcedon sought to avoid through its distinction between hypostasis and nature. With the text just quoted, Timothy shows that he did not understand this basic idea. As long as he kept his concept of nature, he was right in rejecting the two-natures formula. But his two objections against the application of the nature concept to the humanity of Jesus are contradictory. (1) To assert the 'nature' of the incarnate Logos can mean only what belongs to him from eternity as the Son of the Father. To have humanity as a 'second nature' would mean that Christ would also have to have been pre-existent as a human being, and indeed in the form of God. This,

---

96. Timothy Ael., *Contra eos qui dicunt duas naturas* (CPG 5475): Br. L. Add. 12156, fol. 25vb; French translation by J. Lebon, *RHE* 9 (1908), 691. Again we note that the Antiochenes rejected ἕνωσις κατὰ φύσιν or a ἕνωσις φυσική (a 'union according to nature' or a 'natural union') for the very same reason that Timothy rejected the term *nature* for the humanity of Christ.

97. Timothy Ael., op. cit., fol. 19vb; French translation by J. Lebon, *RHE* 9 (1908), 691–92.

however, would make humbling and exalting, as described in Phil 2, impossible:

> If those who assume two natures say that the voluntary *kenosis*, the humbling and the exalting belong to the human nature [of Christ], then how can it be that he was in the form of God [Phil 2,6] and renounced his greatness, he who is worshipped by all in the glory appropriate to God [cf. Phil 2,11]? How can one say that he took on the form of a slave if he already was one? How has he become like human beings and been found in human form [Phil 2,7], this human being who was already this by nature, according to the statements of those who speak of two natures? Then he would have become like God through robbery. But he humbled himself [Phil 2,8] . . .[98]

This original meaning of *physis*, which the Syriac *kyana* also contains, is thus to be considered: it means 'innate essence'. For the Logos of the Father, creaturely humanity can never be 'innate', that is, 'nature'. There is absolutely no place for a 'duality', for the nature of the Logos is simple. And to a 'simple' being one cannot accord a 'natural duality'.[99] Timothy's rejection of the nature concept for the humanity of Christ is best understood on the basis of this fundamental idea of his. (2) Following this immediately, yet secondarily, is a further determination of nature: it is entirely, completely, with all its characteristics, what Timothy interprets with the words *hypostasis* (*qenōmā*) and *person*:

> There is no nature that is not also hypostasis and no hypostasis that is not person (*parṣōpā*). Thus if there are two natures, there are also with all necessity two persons and even two Christs, as the new teachers proclaim.[100]

In order thus to escape the Nestorian division into two natures or persons, Timothy reserves the term *nature* solely for the God Logos, the μία φύσις τοῦ θεοῦ λόγου, and expresses the humanity only with the word σεσαρκωμένη. He wants to hold exclusively to the Nicaean schema, in which for him the entire doctrine of the incarnation is expressed – not in a static view, as seems to be characteristic of Chalcedon, but in the spectacle of the historical event. We will summarize his teaching again with a section of the petition that he sent to Emperor Leo:

> But I believe that God has put it into the mind of your Serenity to set right the statements in this letter, which are a cause of stumbling to the believers; for these statements are in accord, and agreement, and conjunction with the doctrine of Nestorius, who was condemned for cleaving asunder and dividing the Incarnation of our Lord Jesus Christ, in respect of natures, and persons, and properties, and names, and operations; who also

---

98. Ibid., fol. 18vc, quoted by Lebon, p. 689.

99. Cf. ibid., fol. 19rb, where Timothy declares it impossible to accord 'two natures to simple beings' (see Lebon, p. 692).

100. Thus in the 9th refutation of the definition of Chalcedon, fol. 41rc; Lebon, p. 693. Note here n. 1 with its reference to fol. 24rb.

interpreted the words of Scripture to mean two, which are not contained in the Confession of Faith of the 318. For they declared that the only-begotten Son of God, Who is of the same Nature [*homoousios*] with the Father, came down, and became incarnate, and was made man; and suffered, and rose again, and ascended to Heaven; and shall come to judge the quick and the dead. And natures, and persons, and properties were not mentioned by them, nor did they divide them. But they confessed the divine and the human properties to be of One by the dispensation.

Accordingly, I do not agree with the transactions of Chalcedon, because I find in them divisions and cleavage of the dispensation.[101]

Thus the number 'two' cannot be applied at all to Christ as long as the assertion concerns Christ himself. One cannot speak of two natures or persons or characteristics or names or activities. Similar formulations are found in the *History of Dioscorus*, but there they exhibit a more advanced form, which belongs to the time of Severus. Thus Dioscorus is supposed to have written to Emperor Marcian:

How can the rebellious Leo have dared to open his mouth and blaspheme the Most High by saying: we must confess in the Messiah two natures and two characteristics and [two] activities, since the holy church confesses one nature of the incarnate God without mixing or change; [even in death] the divinity of my master was not separated from his humanity, not even for a moment; but this horrible, this stupid, this accursed Leo, who wanted to separate the soul from the body of our Lord, must immediately and without delay be thrown into utter darkness.[102]

Similarly, Dioscorus is supposed to have written to Juvenal of Jerusalem, still at Chalcedon:

Cursed be anyone who assumes two natures in the Messiah after the indivisible unity . . .! Cursed be anyone who assumes in the Messiah two properties and two activities.[103]

In this connection Dioscorus again emphasizes (probably against Pope Leo) that on the cross Christ's divinity did not separate from his humanity.[104]

This introduces the main themes of the Monophysite controversy with the followers of Chalcedon. The basis for understanding would

---

101. Zacharias Rh., *HE* IV 6: Brooks, CSCO 87, p. 123,2–15; (here according to) Hamilton-Brooks, p. 72; Land, *Anecdota Syriaca* III, p. 141, fol. 81va, lin. 14–15; cf. Michael Syr., *Chron.* IX 1: Chabot II, 120B.

102. F. Nau, *JA* X 1, p. 254 (with Syr. text on p. 36) esp. lines 2–3.

103. Ibid., 278 (Syr. p. 64).

104. Ibid., 279 (Syr. p. 65): 'Et quand il fut pendu sur le bois et supporta tous les coups pour nous, sa divinité ne se sépara pas de son humanité, il monta au ciel avec le même corps qu'il avait pris de Marie, mère de Dieu, et il siège à la droite de son père.' The above-mentioned Logos separation is, however, also expressly rejected by Leo (cf. A. Grillmeier, *CCT* II/1, pp. 136–37).

have still been broad enough if the two sides had perceived and appreciated their mutual intentions. Leo of Rome could have recognized from the letters of Timothy that the latter's confrontation with Eutychianism and Manichaeism was much sharper even than his own. Timothy fought primarily against them; Leo fought from an angle of vision in which Alexandrian and Eutychian doctrine coincided.

CHAPTER TWO

THE STRUGGLE BETWEEN CHALCEDONIANS AND ANTI-CHALCEDONIANS

(by T. Hainthaler)

1. The peaceful Chalcedonian, Timothy 'Wobble–Cap'

We have no written testimonies from the very peaceful patriarch Timothy Salophaciolus,[1] who was beloved among the people, 'soft in his manners and feeble in his actions'.[2] His *synodicae* to Pope Leo (460) and Pope Simplicius have not survived.[3] He was elected patriarch in 460 after Timothy Aelurus was deposed and remained until Timothy's triumphal return in 475 under Basiliscus.[4] Without resisting, he retreated and moved back into the monastery of Canopus, a suburb of Alexandria, from which he had come.[5] This Tabennesiote cloister seems to have

---

1. On Timothy Salophaciolus, including information on the sources, see E. Schwartz, *PS*, pp. 178, 186–87, 190–91, 195–96. Cf. also H. Bacht, 'Die Rolle des orientalischen Mönchtums in den kirchenpolitischen Auseinandersetzungen um Chalkedon (431–519)', in *Chalkedon* II, pp. 259–60, 262, 264–65; now W. H. C. Frend, art. 'Timothy Salofaciolus', in *The Coptic Encyclopedia* 7 (1991), 2268–69.

2. Zacharias Rh., *HE* IV 10: Hamilton-Brooks, p. 78; Brooks, CSCO 87, p. 127,6–7: *moribus humilis erat et factis debilis.*

3. Cf. Leo I, *Ep. ad Tim.* of 18 Aug. 460: *CA* ep. 53, pp. 120–21. Also *PS*, no. 24, p. 163; the *synodica* to Pope Simplicius was delivered by Bishop Esaias and two Alexandrian clerics in Rome. On its content cf. Simplic. *Ad Acac.*: *CA* ep. 63, pp. 142–44. Also extant are two letters of Zeno to him (*PS*, nos. 14 and 15), by which Timothy Salophaciolus is called back to the patriarchal see, as well as a letter (*PS*, no. 33) in which Emperor Zeno grants the petition of Timothy Sal. regarding a Chalcedonian successor.

4. E. Schwartz, *PS*, p. 186.

5. According to Theophanes, *Chron.* A. M. 5967: de Boor I, p. 121,14–17: '... ὑπεχώρησεν ἐν τοῖς μοναστηρίοις τοῦ Κανώπου, ὧν ἐγεγόνει καὶ τῆς ἀσκήσεως'. Cf. Liberatus, *Brev.* 16: ACO II 5, p. 125,11–12: *in Canopi castellum et in monasterio latuit.* Cf. H. Bacht, art. cit., p. 259 with n. 28.

been a 'stronghold of Chalcedonian orthodoxy'.[6] From there, after the death of Timothy Aelurus (presumably on 30 July 477), he was recalled on imperial order by the prefect Anthemius.[7] He tried to ensure that a Chalcedonian patriarch would become his successor, and to this end sent the monk John Talaia from the Tabennesiote monastery to Constantinople. Because of the latter's relations with Illus, however, this attempt ultimately failed. John Talaia was indeed elected patriarch after Timothy Salophaciolus's death (February 482), but then was dropped by the emperor.[8]

Timothy Salophaciolus occupied the patriarchal see in peace for almost twenty years (460–475 and 477–482, interrupted by the two-year reign of Timothy Aelurus) and thus nominally far longer than Timothy Aelurus, in whose shadow he nonetheless stood.

He acted so charitably (*mansuete*) that the Alexandrians said, 'Even if we do not have communion with you, we love you.'[9] Even Acacius presented him as an example of 'Davidic gentleness' and praised his patience.[10]

All of his efforts to draw the people to himself and even to include the name of Dioscorus in the diptychs were not enough to win the Alexandrians to Chalcedon.[11] Instead, this co-operation brought him into conflict with the popes.[12] After his return to office, Timothy strove to conform to the hopes of Rome: he asked forgiveness for including, out of fear, the name of Dioscorus in the diptychs,[13] confessed to the definition of Chalcedon in writing and presented a submission formula that the clerics of Timothy Aelurus and Peter Mongus were supposed to sign. In this way Rome's mistrust was demolished.

His championing of Chalcedon, to be sure, did not concern the determination of Constantinople's pre-eminence over Alexandria. Zacharias Rhetor reports that he argued before

---

6. H. Bacht, art. cit., 259 with n. 29; cf. D. J. Chitty, *The Desert a City*, Oxford 1966, 92.

7. Liberatus, *Brev*. 16: ACO II 5, p. 125,19–24; E. Stein, *Histoire du Bas-Empire* II, p. 22.

8. Cf. in detail E. Schwartz, *PS*, pp. 195–97. On John Talaia: A. Malaspina, *DPAC* II, 1578. John Talaia brought the so-called *Florilegium Cyrillianum* to Rome (cf. *CCT* II/2). Later he was appointed bishop of Nola.

9. Liberatus, *Brev*. 16: ACO II 5, p. 126,9–11.

10. Acacius, *Ep. 8 ad Simplic.*, before March 478: Thiel, p. 194.

11. Zacharias Rh., *HE* V 5 and IV 10: Brooks, CSCO 87, p. 152,29–34 and p. 127; Hamilton-Brooks, pp. 114 and 78–79.

12. Pope Leo I forbade this co-operation when he heard about it, cf. Zacharias Rh., *HE* IV 10: Brooks, CSCO 87, p. 127; Hamilton-Brooks, p. 79. Pope Simplicius mentions in his letter of 8 March 478 to Acacius that Timothy Sal. had been obliged to include the name of Dioscorus in the diptychs and expressed the hope that he would henceforth prove himself blameless: *CA* ep. 61, CSEL 35, p. 139,10–15.

13. Simplicius, *Ep. ad Acac.* (Oct. 478): *CA* ep. 63, pp. 142–44, esp. 142.

the emperor with Gennadius about that and said, 'I do not accept the synod which would make your see next in importance to Rome and cast contempt upon the honour of my see.'[14]

All the same, he did not succeed in making lasting peace, and this was 'due above all to Peter Mongus'.[15]

2. Peter Mongus, anti-Chalcedonian patriarch 'by *Henoticon*'s grace'

Perhaps Peter Mongus[16] was already present at the Council of Chalcedon as one of the deacons of Dioscorus.[17] Certainly he, along with Timothy Aelurus, headed the opposition against the Chalcedonian patriarch Proterius, who banished both of them (before 454)[18] after his futile attempts to incorporate them into the Alexandrian imperial church. Peter Mongus, the 'most significant follower' of Timothy Aelurus, was secretly consecrated as his successor after his death[19] but had to flee before Timothy Salophaciolus and go into hiding. Ultimately, however, the unfortunate politics of John Talaia did not prevent Peter's reign as anti-Chalcedonian patriarch of Alexandria (482–489). Emperor Zeno installed him in order to create unity in the Alexandrian church within the framework and conditions of the *Henoticon*.[20] Although his position vis-à-vis the Council of Chalcedon and the *Tome* of Leo was indeed one of rejection, it was not as uncompromisingly stringent as that demanded of him by the 'ultras' among the monks, who during his time in office separated from him (as ἀποσχισταί, 'separatists'[21]); one of their spokesmen was the monk Nephalius, who later appeared as a Chalcedonian

---

14. Zacharias Rh., *HE* IV 10: Hamilton-Brooks, p. 79; Brooks, CSCO 87, p. 127,27–31.

15. H. Bacht, art. cit., p. 260.

16. E. Schwartz, *PS*, p. 172: 'the Stammerer' (from μογιλάλος). On Peter Mongus see F. Hofmann, 'Der Kampf der Päpste um Chalkedon', in *Chalkedon* II, 39–60; H. Bacht, art. cit., pp. 257–69; G. Fritz, art. 'Pierre Monge', *DTC* 12, Paris 1935, 2029–31; W. H. C. Frend, *The Rise of the Monophysite Movement*, Cambridge 1972, pp. 174–83; T. Orlandi, art. 'Pietro Mongo', *DPAC* II (1983), 2796.

17. G. Fritz, art. cit., 2030, according to the 'récits de Dioscore exilés à Gangres'. H. Bacht, art. cit., p. 257.

18. Cf. Gesta de nomine Acacii, 13 and 19: *CA* ep. 99, pp. 445,3–7; 447,16; also E. Schwartz, *PS*, p. 172 with document no. 1, ibid., p. 161.

19. E. Schwartz, *PS*, p. 190 with n. 4.

20. In the treatment of this imperial edict in vol. II/1 we have already discussed repeatedly the figure of Peter Mongus: A. Grillmeier, *CCT* II/1, pp. 249–50, 258–60, 263–64, 289–90.

21. Their origin is described by Zacharias Rh., *HE* VI 1–2: Brooks, CSCO 88, pp. 1–4; Hamilton-Brooks, pp. 133–36.

against Severus of Antioch.[22] Peter Mongus was not inclined to break off canonical relations.[23] He had been installed by the emperor 'with the object of uniting the people together, and not keeping them divided into two parts'.[24] Severus took offence against Peter Mongus because he 'embraced the communion of those who did not write the same things as he did'.[25] He reproached him, however, not because his condemnation of Chalcedon and Leo's *Tome* was too mild, but because he acquiesced in the *Henoticon* without also expressly demanding that the 'impious things done at Chalcedon or the impious Tome of Leo'[26] be addressed.

Tradition records an address of Peter Mongus[27] that he delivered to the people in order to win them over to the *Henoticon*. In it he says that Zeno wanted to destroy what was introduced in Chalcedon as innovations and additions. He says that in this writing Zeno confesses the true faith, the twelve *capita* of Cyril, condemns Nestorius and Eutyches, proclaims that the incarnate God-Logos was *one* nature in suffering and miracles, and rejects the opinion of the Diphysites, since their teaching and the *Tome* were opposed to this; and that Dioscorus and Timothy fought against them as martyrs. Thus Peter asserted before the people that the *Henoticon* rejected (*respuit*) Chalcedon.

In the letter to Acacius,[28] however, which he wrote after Acacius demanded an examination of Peter's faith,[29] he approved the Council of Chalcedon three times and said that it

---

22. Cf. A. Grillmeier, *CCT* II/2, pp. 47–52. Also C. Moeller, 'Un représentant de la christologie néochalcédonienne au début du sixième siècle en orient: Nephalius d'Alexandrie', *RHE* 40 (1944–45), 73–106, on the report of Zacharias Rhetor: pp. 83–89. Zacharias Rh., who is the main source, reports that Peter hesitated to sign the *Henoticon*, since 'there was no clear and express anathema of the Synod and the Tome in it, and consequently he feared that it might prove a stumbling-block to the people' (*HE* V 7: Hamilton-Brooks, p. 119). Some separated from him 'because there was no clear and decided anathema of the Synod and the Tome, either in the Henotikon or in the letters of the chief priests to Peter' (*HE* VI 1: Hamilton-Brooks, p. 133). Peter berated (*vituperaverat*) the council in justification. Thereupon Acacius had the matter investigated. The verdict of the proceedings was that Peter had not expressly condemned the council ('non expresse anathematizatam'). Afterwards Peter, upon examination by Peter the Iberian and others, finally signed something in which he condemned the council and the *Tome* (ibid., p. 134). Under pressure of the separatist monks he condemned the council publicly in the presence of the imperial envoy Cosmas and the leaders of the separatists (*HE* VI 2: Hamilton-Brooks, p. 135) and declared that the *Henoticon* had nullified Chalcedon (ibid., p. 136).

23. Cf. C. Moeller, art. cit., p. 86.

24. Zacharias Rh., *HE* VI 2: Hamilton-Brooks, p. 135; Brooks, CSCO 88, p. 2,28–29.

25. Severus Ant., *Ep. ad Ammon. presb. Alex.*: Brooks, *SL*, p. 254.

26. Ibid., p. 255.

27. Peter Mongus, *Allocutio* (CPG 5497): Zacharias Rh., *HE* V 7: Brooks, CSCO 87, pp. 156–57; Hamilton-Brooks, pp. 119–21.

28. Peter Mongus, *Epistula ad Acacium* (CPG 5495): Evagrius, *HE* III 17: Bidez-Parmentier, pp. 115–16; PG 86, 2629–34.

29. Zacharias Rh., *HE* VI 1: Brooks, CSCO 88, pp. 1–2; Hamilton-Brooks, pp. 133–34.

brought nothing new and was in harmony with Nicaea.[30] Evagrius is the only source of this writing.

In the last extant written witness,[31] the response to the *synodica* of the newly elected patriarch Fravitta of Constantinople (490),[32] he finally interprets the *Henoticon* clearly as a condemnation of Chalcedon and of Leo's *Tome*. There he also expresses himself clearly against Eutyches, as he had already done earlier.[33]

On the whole, we can certainly say that Peter Mongus represented a moderate 'Monophysitism', condemned the Council of Chalcedon[34] but supported the compromise of the *Henoticon*, which 'teaches the true faith'[35] and at the price of which he also gained imperial recognition of his patriarchal dignity.[36] Nonetheless, the popes Simplicius, Felix III,[37] Gelasius I, Symmachus and Hormisdas considered him a heretic and one of the exponents of Monophysitism. They equated him with Eutyches and repeatedly made the demand that his name be removed from the diptychs and that communion with him be terminated.[38]

3. The successors of Peter Mongus

Athanasius II, who became patriarch of Alexandria after the death of Peter Mongus (489), continued his ecclesiastical policies 'with undiminished energy';[39] in particular, he expressed his satisfaction with the *Henoticon* as a formula for unification.[40] This fact was used later by

---

30. Evagrius, *HE* III 17: Bidez-Parmentier, pp. 115,23–28; 116,6–7; 116,12–17; cf. P. Allen, *Evagrius Scholasticus the Church Historian* (SpicSLov 41), Louvain 1981, 134.

31. On the unauthentic *Epistulae ad Acacium* (CPG 5499) see M. Cramer and H. Bacht, 'Antichalkedonisches im koptisch-monophysitischen Schrifttum', in *Chalkedon* II, p. 324; and V. Inglisian, 'Chalkedon und die armenische Kirche', in *Chalkedon* II, p. 369 with n. 32; pp. 377/78, n. 65.

32. Peter Mongus, *Epistula ad Fravitam* (CPG 5496): Zacharias Rh., *HE* VI 6: Brooks, CSCO 88, pp. 7–9; Hamilton-Brooks, 142–45.

33. Zacharias Rh., *HE* VI 6 and V 7: Brooks, CSCO 88, p. 8 and CSCO 87, pp. 156–57; Hamilton-Brooks, pp. 143–44.

34. Zacharias Rh., *HE* VI 1, 2, 4: Brooks, CSCO 88, pp. 2–3, 5; Hamilton-Brooks, pp. 133–36, 138–40. The *Libellus synodicus* reports that right after the appointment of Peter Mongus he called a synod and anathematized Chalcedon (Hardouin, Coll. concil. V, 1527; Mansi VII, 1023, 1178); cf. Hefele-Leclercq, II/2, p. 919.

35. Zacharias Rh., *HE* VI 4: Hamilton-Brooks, p. 138; Brooks, CSCO 88, p. 5,11–12.

36. Whether such a position deserves the judgement of Damaskios in Photius, *Bibl. cod.* 242: Henry VI, p. 39,37; PG 103, 1288A, that he was an audacious and very evil man (ἰταμὸς ... καὶ περιπόνηρος) may be left as an open question.

37. Under Felix III Peter Mongus was anathematized by the Roman synods of 484 and 485; cf. L. Salaville, art. 'Hénotique', *DTC* VI (1920), 2167–68.

38. Cf. A. Grillmeier, *CCT* II/1, pp. 288–90, 296–97, 307, 310, 312–13, 331.

39. H. Bacht, art. cit., p. 275.

40. Even if Zacharias Rh., *HE* VII 1: Hamilton-Brooks, p. 150 notes that Athanasius 'more openly and authoritatively anathematised the Synod and the Tome'.

Emperor Anastasius[41] to frustrate the desire of John Nicaiotes to condemn Chalcedon expressly. Also, at the Synod of Sidon this example
played an important role, so that Severus (justly) speaks of the disgrace
that such behaviour brought to their cause. In Alexandria the quarrel
with the separatists continued under Athanasius as with his predecessor.

Athanasius II found his position shared by Palladius of Antioch and
Sallustius of Jerusalem,[42] and a close relationship developed among the
three patriarchates. With Sallustius he carried out the deposition of
Euphemius of Constantinople: they passed on to the emperor the *synodica* of Euphemius to Pope Felix and wanted to prove in this way that
Euphemius was a heretic.[43] The later deposition of the patriarch of
Constantinople (two years after the death of Sallustius in 494) was,
however, ultimately justified by the emperor politically (because of 'high
treason' since Euphemius had contacts with the rebellious Isaurians).

After the death of Athanasius in 496 his policies were continued by
John II Hemula (496–505), that is, John endorsed the *Henoticon* without
express rejection of Chalcedon.[44]

John III Nicaiotes (505–516) seems to have gone somewhat further in
the condemnation of Chalcedon.[45] From Timothy of Constantinople
(511–518) he demanded the formal condemnation of Chalcedon as a
prerequisite to ecclesiastical communion, a demand to which Timothy
ultimately acceded. This re-established the *communio* between Constantinople and Alexandria, which was interrupted during the time of
Macedonius.[46]

---

41. According to Severus Ant., *Ep. ad Ammon. presb. Alex.*: Brooks, *SL*, p. 255.
42. Cf. Liberatus, *Brev.* 18: ACO II 5, p. 132,9–12; Zacharias Rh., *HE* VI 6 and VII 1:
Hamilton-Brooks, pp. 144, 150. Therefore, J. Lebon, *Le monophysisme sévérien*, p. 39, speaks
of a union between Palladius, Athanasius and Sallustius.
43. Zacharias Rh., *HE* VII 1: Hamilton-Brooks, p. 150. According to Zacharias Rh. this
was, of course, preceded by the 'hatred' of Euphemius against Athanasius II, since the latter
is said to 'condemn the council and the *Tome* even more openly [than Peter Mongus]' (ibid.),
and therefore Euphemius wanted to depose the Alexandrian with the help of Rome. Cf. R.
Haacke, 'Die kaiserliche Politik in den Auseinandersetzungen um Chalkedon (451–553)', in
Chalkedon II, 95–177, here p. 128.
44. Thus Severus Ant., op. cit.: Brooks, *SL*, 255; cf. Liberatus, *Brev.* 18: ACO II 5, p. 132.
By contrast, Zacharias Rh., in speaking of the Alexandrian patriarchs Peter Mongus,
Athanasius II and John Hemula, tries to emphasize their condemnation of the *Tome* and the
council. He reports of John Hemula that he demanded from Flavianus of Antioch a written
statement 'in which there would be an anathema of the Synod and the Tome' (*HE* VI 6, p.
145), and that otherwise there was no agreement in the faith.
45. E. Schwartz, *PS*, p. 238, n. 1. Cf. R. Haacke, art. cit., p. 129.
46. R. Haacke, art. cit., pp. 129, 132.

The successor to John Nicaiotes, Dioscorus II (516–517), assumed his office during great troubles. Although his election was equally accepted by the people and by the imperial officials, 'the fact that the authorities proceeded immediately with his installation . . . was enough to bring the people to revolt . . . The crowd forced Dioscorus to let himself be consecrated a second time in the absence of the representatives of the secular power'.[47] Then, however, when Theodosius, the son of the imperial prefect, took part in the first pontifical mass, he was killed. Dioscorus travelled to Constantinople in order to appease the emperor, who was demanding exemplary punitive measures, and was successful. Soon afterwards Dioscorus died. This event was one of many insurrections in the seething metropolis of Alexandria[48] and possibly also signalized the hate that the Alexandrian population had for Byzantine foreign rule, since in this case there were no dogmatic differences.

There are no known writings of Dioscorus, about whose anti-Chalcedonian position there is no doubt. Avitus of Vienna seems to have written to him.[49]

On the whole, the line that Peter Mongus took did not essentially change under his successors. In the dispute between Rome and Constantinople, Alexandria hardly played a role.[50]

4. Timothy IV (III), Patriarch of Alexandria at the time of the controversy between Julian and Severus

Discorus II (June 516 until his death on 14 October 517)[51] was followed by Timothy IV,[52] who from October 517 until 7 February 535 was patriarch of the Copts. Towards the end of his life he received an invitation from the emperor to a unification dialogue, which, however,

---

47. Cf. the presentation of events in E. Stein, *Histoire* II, p. 164. Source: Theophanes, *Chron.* A. M. 6009: de Boor, pp. 162–63.

48. Cf., e.g., J. Maspero, *Histoire*, pp. 43–46.

49. G. Bardy, 'La répercussion des controverses christologiques en Occident . . .', in *Chalkedon* II, p. 782. The letter is not extant, only the title of the writing. A letter of Severus of Ant. to Dioscorus is found in Brooks, *SL*, pp. 257–60; cf. also ibid., p. 133.

50. E. Schwartz, *PS*, p. 214: 'In publicizing reports, whose coverage leaves nothing to be desired, the successors of Peter Mongus do not appear at all.' E. Stein, *Histoire du Bas-Empire* II, pp. 161–62, states that the successors of Peter Mongus 'appear to have been very insignificant personalities'.

51. This corresponds to the dating of E. W. Brooks, 'The Dates of the Alexandrine Patriarchs Dioskoros II, Timothy IV, and Theodosius', *ByzZ* 12 (1903), 494–97, which is also supported by A. Fortescue in J. Maspero, *Histoire des patriarches d'Alexandrie*, Paris 1923, 346, n. 3, as opposed to Maspero, pp. 343–46.

52. A. Fortescue, in J. Maspero, *Histoire*, p. 79, n. 1: the Copts call him Timothy III, since they do not count Timothy Salophaciolus; the Melkites say Timothy IV.

he could no longer pursue.[53] He did not interfere in the dispute between Julian of Halicarnassus and Severus of Antioch.[54] For many people Severus was the real patriarch.[55] Timothy could not dissuade the deacon Themistius, who founded the Agnoetes, from his convictions.[56] The patriarch was considered a 'writer';[57] 'in spite of his mediocrity', 'he was loved and recognized as representative of the "true" faith' and represented a power in the land.[58]

From Timothy we have only a few fragments of homilies,[59] possibly an anaphora (CPG 7098) and parts of an *ordo baptismatis* (CPG 7099). The fragments reveal an orthodox Severan theology.

Timothy twice presents an opposition, a 'partition' of Christ's ways of acting into divinity and humanity, for example, when he says that Christ is God according to nature, as the works and signs (σημείων) reveal (making lepers clean, giving light to the blind, strengthening the lame, giving life to the dead) but most strongly through the words, 'I and the Father are one.' As true man (ὡς φύσει καὶ ἀληθείᾳ καὶ οὐ δοκήσει γέγονεν ἄνθρωπος) he proves himself by undergoing sufferings, but only those that come from the weakness of the human body (like hunger, thirst, fatigue, sleepiness) and do not lead to sin (ἀναμαρτήτοις πάθεσιν),[60] that is, the

---

53. Cf. J. Maspero, *Histoire*, pp. 99–100, 348. It was a new imperial attempt, after the failure of the *Collatio cum Severianis* of 532, to achieve a unification of Chalcedonians and anti-Chalcedonians, this time with the heads of the anti-Chalcedonian movement. The dialogue took place in 536 in Constantinople with the participation of Severus.

54. J. Maspero, *Histoire*, p. 80. According to Leont. Schol., *De sectis* V, IV (PG 86, 1232A) he supported first the one then the other side. The *Hist. Patr.*, PO 1, p. 455, presents Timothy as a fighter for the 'orthodox' – that is, Severan – faith against Julian.

55. Cf. J. Maspero, *Histoire*, pp. 86–88: 'Severus is a personality of the Coptic church, which he profoundly shaped.' A similar assertion is found in W. E. Crum, 'Sévère d'Antioche en Égypte', *ROC* 23 (1922/23), 97, n. 5: 'For his Egyptian admirers he always remained the patriarch κατ᾽ ἐξοχήν.'

56. Cf. J. Maspero, *Histoire*, p. 96; A. Grillmeier, *CCT* II/2, pp. 362–64.

57. J. Maspero, *Histoire*, p. 79. K. Krumbacher, *Geschichte der Byzant. Litteratur*, Munich 1897, 53, adds: Ἀντιρρητικά in several books, and the συγγράμματα κατὰ τῆς συνόδου Χαλκηδόνος καὶ τοῦ Τόμου Λέοντος, which Anastasius Sin., *Viae dux*, VI, 1, 17–18 (ed. Uthemann), gives in addition to the homilies (cf. CPG 7090–7101).

58. J. Maspero, *Histoire*, p. 123.

59. *Homiliae*, CPG 7090–7096: PG 86, 265–69. These fragments (in a different order) are also found in Cosmas Indicopl., *Topograph. christ.* X, 68–73: Wolska-Conus, III, SC 197 (Paris 1973), 307–13 (in CPG III erroneously written: SC 159), except for part of *Hom.* (CPG 7090), which is given only in Latin.

60. *Hom.* (CPG 7090): PG 86, 265C–268A. Similarly in *Hom.* (CPG 7095): PG 86, 268D–269A: It is proper to God to work miracles, to command the elements, to foretell the future; it is human, however, to live in community, show respect to parents, live together with brothers and have human relations with the disciples.

πάθη ἀδιάβλητά. In this way Christ shows the power of divinity (δύναμις τῆς θεότητος) and preserves the laws of humanity (νόμους τῆς ἀνθρωπότητος).[61] Timothy gives special emphasis to the soteriological dimension of the incarnation: for our sake (δι' ἡμᾶς, διὰ τὴν ὑμῶν σωτηρίαν),[62] in order to point out to human beings an entrance, a path to heaven.[63] Through passion and resurrection he assumed immortality and the renewal of nature (διὰ τοῦ πάθους καὶ τῆς ἀναστάσεως ἀφθαρσίαν καὶ ἀνακαινισμὸν φύσεως λαμβάνοντα) (ibid.). With him we are to be made pure.[64] In the extant fragments the *mia-physis* formula never appears.

The author of the 'Anaphora Sancti Timothei patriarchae Alexandrini' was 'probably' Timothy IV.[65]

First, it is striking that the consubstantiality of the Holy Spirit is clearly emphasized (five times in doxologies: 11,11; 13,2; 13,12–13; 25,2; 27,13) especially at the beginning of the anaphora. The Logos, 'who created us after your image and likeness' (13,26–15,1), is called the maker and creator of everything (*opifex et creator omnium*, 15,3). The soteriological view is seen clearly in the terms: *salvator* (extremely frequent), *liberator animarum et corporum nostrorum* (17,23). The rejection of any duality in Christ is alluded to in the formulation of the '*Vere sanctus*' that the God-Logos 'became perfect flesh and man, but not so that there are two; rather, one [single] King, one Christ, one Lord, one incarnate God-Logos appeared to us, lived among the people . . .' (19,8–11). Shortly before, there is a confession to hypostatic union: 'The Word became flesh without change or modification; rather, it was conceived by the Holy Spirit and the holy bearer of God and ever virgin Mary with a body having a rational soul (*animam rationabilem et intelligibilem*) in true and personal unity (*in unitate vera et personali*)' (19,1–4); 'He truly assumed a body and a human soul and everything of which a human being consists . . . except sin' (19,5–7). The words after the formula of consecration, 'Remember your true and life-giving burial, which did not see corruption' (21,18–19), echo the dispute about the *aphtharsia* of Christ's body. In praise of Christ at the end he emphasizes his inability as God to suffer (*passus est in carne, et permansit impassibilis ut Deus*, 47,4–5). All these statements fit well into Severan theology.

Whether the *ordo baptismatis* (CPG 7099) can be ascribed to Timothy IV is a question best left open, according to Brock.[66] The passages in the

---

61. *Hom.* (CPG 7095): PG 86, 269A.
62. *Hom.* (CPG 7095: 7096): PG 86, 269A.AB.
63. *Hom.* (CPG 7096): PG 86, 269B.
64. *Hom.* (CPG 7093): συμπεριτμηθῶμεν, Χριστῷ, ἵνα καὶ συγκαθαρθῶμεν αὐτῷ (268B).
65. A. Rücker, 'Anaphora Syriaca Timothei Alexandrini', in *Anaphorae Syriacae* I, Rome 1939, p. 3. We are citing according to this edition.
66. S. Brock, 'A New Syrian Baptismal Ordo Attributed to Timothy of Alexandria', *Mus* 83 (1970), 367–431, here 397–98 and 431: 'Whether the attribution can stand, however, and if so, to which Timothy it should apply, are questions which it does not seem possible to answer with any certainty.' If texts do come from Timothy (which Timothy?), they certainly include the prayers numbered 29 and 32–34, which exhibit parallels with Egyptian texts.

consecratory prayer of the water, which could perhaps have come from Timothy, emphasize deliverance from evil through Christ and purification through his expiatory death.

5. Gaianus and the Gaianites[67]

The controversy between Julian of Halicarnassus and Severus of Antioch between 518 and 528 in Egypt has already been presented in vol. II/2 in both its external events and its content.[68]

The followers of Julian became very strong in Egypt in the last years of Patriarch Timothy IV (517–535).[69] In particular the monks followed Julianism in droves, and with them the rural population and the lower classes in Alexandria.[70]

Only the high-ranking clergy of the city and a few followers remained loyal to Severus, who himself had to leave Alexandria and hide in the country.[71] Moreover, Julian's teaching spread in the Roman Empire, among the Persians, Indians(?), Cushites, Himyarites, Armenians.[72] In

---

67. On the following see M. Jugie, art. 'Gaianites' and art. 'Gaianite (la controverse) et la possibilité du corps de Jésus-Christ', *DTC* 6 (1915), 999–1002 and 1002–23. On the term: Timothy of Constant., *De iis qui ad ecclesiam accedunt* (CPG 7016): PG 86, 58, calls them Gaianites of Gaianus, who was their patriarch in Alexandria and had accepted Julian and his teaching. Their opponents called them Phantasiasts, Manichaeans. They themselves called their opponents phthartolatrites, ktistolatrites, or *corrupticolae, creaticolae*. Anastasius Sin., *Viae Dux*, 23: ed. Uthemann, CCG 8, 305: Gaianites or Julianists or Agranites (Nagranites). The last-named designation, which Jugie (*DTC* 6, p. 999) could not explain, can be traced back to the Christians of the southern Arabian city of Najrān (cf. our presentation of the Christianization of southern Arabia below, under Ethiopia, part IV, chap. 3). Nicephorus Callist., *HE* 29: PG 147, 293B also speaks of Gaianites.

68. A. Grillmeier, *CCT* II/2, pp. 25–26, 79–111.

69. *Hist. Patr.*: PO 1, p. 454, reports that all but seven had fallen in with Julian's *Tomus*, which he spread in all Egypt, even among the monks in the desert. From this we can conclude that almost all churches, at least in Lower Egypt, had fallen into the hands of the Julianists; cf. J. Maspero, *Histoire*, pp. 94–95.

70. J. Maspero, *Histoire*, p. 95.

71. *Hist. Patr.*: PO 1, 457. W. E. Crum, 'Sévère d'Antioche en Égypte', *ROC* 23 (1922/23), 92–104, esp. 92–96, has gathered the small amount of extant information on the life of Severus in Egyptian exile.

72. Michael Syr., *Chron.* IX 30: Chabot II, p. 251. On Armenia cf. V. Inglisian, *Chalkedon* II, p. 404.

the theological circles of Constantinople Julianism was ignored for a rather long time.[73]

Around 538, however, there were also monasteries and churches in Constantinople itself.[74]

When Patriarch Timothy IV died, the Severans (at the instigation of Empress Theodora[75]) elected the deacon Theodosius patriarch, which led to a revolt among the people.[76] Apparently even before the funeral ceremonies for Timothy had ended, Theodosius was deposed from his patriarchal throne and had to leave the city.[77] The Julianists elected the archdeacon (under Timothy) Gaianus, and he was consecrated (by Julian of Halicarnassus[78]). Gaianus was able to maintain his position as patriarch for 103 days.[79] After an investigation of the election by the imperial envoy Narses, Theodosius was declared the legitimate patriarch and reinstalled, and Gaianus was banished by imperial officials (Liberatus: *a iudicibus*) to Carthage (on 23 or 25 May 535) and finally to Sardinia, where he died.[80] Alexandria was split: 'The magnates of the city were with Theodosius; the demes with Gaianus.'[81] The people fought for

---

73. A discreet allusion is found in Hypatius of Ephesus (in 532), ACO IV 2, p. 173; by contrast, there is no mention at the Council of Constantinople in 536, nor does Justinian mention Julianism in his letter to the monks of Egypt (542 or 543) (PG 86, 1104–52; Schwartz, *Drei dogmatische Schriften Justinians*, Munich 1939, 7–43). Theodore of Raithu in the *Praeparatio* (CPG 7600) goes into the dispute between Julian and Severus (Diekamp, *Anal. Patristica*, OCA 117, p. 197). Yet the writing could not have been composed before the end of the sixth or beginning of the seventh century; cf. Diekamp, op. cit., p. 174 (between 580 and 620), versus M. Richard, *RHE* 35 (1939), 790–91 (before 553).

74. Victor Ton., *Chron.*, a. 540: MGH 11, p. 199; PL 68, 956B; cf. J. Maspero, *Histoire*, p. 95.

75. Liberatus, *Brev.* 20: ACO II 5, p. 134.

76. According to J. Maspero, *Histoire*, p. 114, the causes were, on the one hand, the antipathy of the Egyptian population towards Byzantine rule and, on the other, the fact that the poor (Levantines) distrusted the rich, so that the result was open revolt when the secret election of a Severan to the patriarchate became known to the people.

77. Leont. Schol., *De sectis* V, IV: PG 86, 1232AB.

78. A. Fortescue, in J. Maspero, p. 115, n. 1: according to Alexandrian law, Julian himself, as bishop of Halicarnassus, could not become bishop/patriarch of Alexandria. In the dating of events we are following E. W. Brooks, *ByzZ* 12 (1903), 494–97, according to which the consecration of Gaianus occurred on 9 or 11 February 535.

79. Liberatus, *Brev.* 20: ACO II 5, p. 135,11.

80. It hardly seems likely that a reconciliation between Gaianus and Theodosius occurred, as *Hist. Patr.*, PO 1, 461–62, asserts, for the Gaianites remained separated from the Theodosians, cf. J. Maspero, *Histoire*, p. 127.

81. Leont. Schol., *De sectis* V, IV: PG 86, 1232B. A. M. Demicheli, 'La politica religiosa di Giustiniano in Egitto. Riflessi sulla chiesa egiziana della legislazione ecclesiastica giustinianea', *Aegyptus* 63 (1983) (217–57), 229–33: Theodosius and the followers of Severus were considered 'imperial'; the Gaianites were regarded as representatives of the Coptic national spirit ('ai gaianiti esponenti dello spirito nazionale copto', ibid., 233).

Gaianus, and Theodosius was apparently able to keep his position only with the help of the imperial troops (2,000 of the 6,000 men under Narses protected him);[82] he remained unpopular.[83] After one year and four months (Liberatus) as patriarch, while riots raged around him, Theodosius left the city and went to Constantinople, where he remained until the end of his life (22 June 566).[84]

In 564/565 the Gaianite party was still the strongest in Alexandria. It elected as patriarch Elpidius, whom, however, Justinian I had arrested in 565 and brought to Constantinople. On the trip there, he died in Lesbos (Sigris).[85] Afterwards Dorotheus was the patriarch of the Julianists for many years (until 580).[86]

When the Severan church was reorganized, the influence of the Gaianites began to diminish. After Emperor Justin II (565–578) they seem to have no longer played the principal role in the Monophysite church.[87] In 581, however, they still represented a considerable factor, and there occurred a short-lived union of Theodosians and Gaianites.[88]

Towards the end of the sixth century there appeared in Rome an aphthartodocetic monk Andrew, whom Eusebius of Thessalonica refuted.[89] In the West, Fulgentius had already expressed himself in writing earlier, in response to an inquiry of the *comes* Reginus, on the question whether the body of Christ was incorruptible (*incorruptibile*) from conception or first corruptible (*corruptibile*) before the passion and incorruptible only after the resurrection,[90] apparently the positions of the

---

82. According to Michael Syr., *Chron.* IX 21: Chabot, II, p. 194, 3,000 residents of the city died during the riots after the banishment of Gaianus.

83. J. Maspero, *Histoire*, pp. 124–25.

84. G. Fedalto, *HEO*, p. 587; cf. A. Fortescue, in J. Maspero, *Histoire*, p. 350, n. 3.

85. Theophanes, *Chron.* A. M. 6057: de Boor, p. 241. Cf. J. Maspero, *Histoire*, p. 214.

86. Joh. Eph., *HE* I 40: Brooks, CSCO 106, p. 34. The temporary union (570–573) between Theodosians and Gaianites under the patriarch John Monachus, of which Theophanes (ibid.) reports, is considered a 'confusing note' by A. Jülicher, 'Die Liste der alexandrinischen Patriarchen im 6. und 7. Jahrhundert', in *Festgabe Karl Müller*, Tübingen 1922, 22; versus J. Maspero, *Histoire*, pp. 216–22.

87. J. Maspero, *Histoire*, p. 244. For Patriarch Theodore (from 575) the Julianists are still arch-enemies with whom he battles in his synodical letter; cf. below, pp. 73–74.

88. The Chalcedonian patriarch Eulogius of Alexandria (581–608) took a position against it in a writing *Contra Theodosianos et Gaianitas*: cf. Photius, *Bibl. cod.* 227: Henry IV, 111–14; PG 103, 953–56. J. Maspero, *Histoire*, pp. 294–95.

89. The work of Eusebius is not extant. A summary of his comments is found in Photius, *Bibl. cod.* 162: Henry II, pp. 129–35; PG 103, 452–57. Cf. G. Bareille, art. 'Eusèbe de Thessalonique', *DTC* 5, 1551–53; M. Jugie, art. 'Gaianite (controverse)', *DTC* 6, 1012.

90. Fulgent. Rusp., *Ep. 18 ad Reginum*: CCL 91A, pp. 619–24; PL 65, 493–98; cf. also B. Nisters, *Die Christologie des hl. Fulgentius von Ruspe* (MBT 16), Münster 1930, pp. 79–80.

Julianists and Gaianites on the one hand and the Severans on the other! These came to the attention of the *comes*.

Sophronius of Jerusalem (634–638) mentions Gaianites (and Julianists).[91] Followers of Gaianus are apparently also to be found in Ephesus.[92] Towards the end of the seventh century Anastasius Sinaita dealt with them as an important sect.[93] The *History of the Patriarchs* mentions Gaianites into the ninth century.[94]

At the time of the Coptic patriarch Simon I (693–700), the patriarch of the Gaianites was Theodore (*c.* 695), and he sent a Gaianite bishop to India.[95] His successor Patriarch Alexander II (704–729) succeeded in bringing Gaianites back under his jurisdiction, especially in the Wadî Habîb, where they had existed for 170 years.[96] There were still Gaianites, however, even in the time of the patriarch Jacob (819–830), who in the sermon at his installation anathematized the Council of Chalcedon and the Phantasiasts or Gaianites, 'who deny the life-giving Passion of God the Word, which he accepted in the flesh'.[97]

On the doctrine of the Gaianites

Timothy of Constantinople reports on three groups among the Gaianites:[98] those who call the body of the Lord from the union on incorruptible in every respect (κατὰ πάντα τρόπον); second, those who do not hold the body of Christ to be incorruptible in every respect but believe that he was upheld by the power of the Logos (ἐπικράτεια) from ruin; third, those – also called actistites – who are of the opinion that the body of Christ was not only incorruptible after the union but was even uncreated (ἄκτιστον).[99]

For the author of *De sectis*, the textbook on heresies, the Gaianites represent a considerable group,[100] which he treats individually along with

---

91. Sophronius Hier., *Narratio miraculorum ss. Cyri et Iohanni* (CPG 7646), mirac. 12: PG 87, 3460B (Julianists: 3458B; mirac. 36: 3549D); A. Mai, Spicileg. III, p. 179 (Julianists: pp. 174, 386).

92. Fedalto, *HEO*, no. 15.1.15: in 549 the Julianist Procopius was bishop of Ephesus; cf. Assemani, BO III/2, 455–59: there was a bishop of the 'Phantasiasts' named Procopius.

93. Anastasius Sin., *Viae dux* (CPG 7745): K.-H. Uthemann, CCG 8 (Turnhout–Louvain 1981), esp. chap. 23; in more detail below!

94. J. Maspero, *Histoire*, p. 341: into the eighth century.

95. *Hist. Patr.*: PO 5, pp. 34, 36–37.

96. *Hist. Patr.*: PO 5, p. 63.

97. *Hist. Patr.*: PO 10, pp. 447–48.

98. Timothy of Constant., *De iis qui ad ecclesiam accedunt* (CPG 7016), *De Theodosianis*, 7–9: PG 86, 44B–C. At another point (ibid., 57A) he divides into only two subgroups: those who teach the body of Christ as created but incorruptible from the virginal conception (ἄχραντος) and those who confess him as not merely incorruptible but uncreated.

99. Cf. Michael Syr., *Chron.* IX 31: Chabot II, p. 265.

100. Yet not at all in the sense formulated by M. van Esbroeck, 'La date et l'auteur du *De sectis* attribué à Léonce de Byzance', in *After Chalcedon*, FS A. Van Roey (OLA 18), Louvain 1985, 422: 'Ce sont les Gaianites qui sont surtout l'objectif de l'exposé.'

the Agnoetes, Origenists and Theodosians. In actio X, I–II exclusively, as well as in actio VII, VI, he deals with their doctrine and presents it as follows.

After the union of the Logos with the body one can in no case speak of two or of a distinction, although the union is without mixing.[101]

The God-Logos assumed a perfect and true human nature from the Virgin Mary. But after the union they confess the body to be incorruptible. Christ suffered all sorts of evil, but not as we do. He endured everything voluntarily. He was not a slave to the laws of nature; otherwise we would be saying that these sufferings happened to him involuntarily, which would be foolish.[102]

– Against this the author of De sectis objects that Christ suffered afflictions and tribulations voluntarily, but nonetheless we do not say that he suffered them out of necessity (ἐξ ἀνάγκης). Rather, he voluntarily subjected himself to the laws of nature. A short florilegium (Gregory of Nazianzus, Cyril of Alexandria, Athanasius) serves as patristic proof.

If he suffered in the same way as we, we cannot attribute to him an incorruptible body.

– Against this the author of De sectis replies that if you call the body of Christ incorruptible, he is not consubstantial with us.

– If they say that before the resurrection he was incorruptible out of grace, we say that this does not accord with what is said about Christ. Before the resurrection he was hungry etc.; after the resurrection nothing of this kind is reported. If he ate, then it was δι' οἰκονομίαν – not because he was hungry but in order to show the disciples that he had really risen from the dead.

Besides the author of De sectis, Anastasius Sinaita probably discusses the doctrine of the Gaianites in the most detail.

In his Viae dux (CPG 7745)[103] he classifies the Gaianites with the 'ten-horned orchestra'[104] of heretics, among whom he includes the followers of Eutyches, Dioscorus, Timothy, Julian, Jacob, Peter Knapheus, Barsanuphius, Theodosius and Severus (as exarch!). He names them among the heretics who set aside the incarnate oikonomia (ἔνσαρκον οἰκονομίαν, XIII 1, 4). Otherwise he often mentions Theodosians and Gaianites together,[105] occasionally also Severans and Gaianites,[106] until in chapter 23 he finally turns especially to the Gaianites, after he describes the reason for the split between Severus and Gaianus: when Severus declared that before the resurrection the body of Christ was corruptible (φθαρτός), Gaianus immediately turned away from him, since one would then necessarily have to say that there were two natures in Christ.

---

101. Leont. Schol., De sectis VII, VI: PG 86, 1245.

102. Ibid., X, I: PG 86, 1260BC.

103. According to K.-H. Uthemann, CCG 8 (Turnhout–Louvain 1981), p. CCXVIII, the individual parts of the work originated in 686/689 at the latest and were composed into one whole work between 686 and 689. We cite from this edition and according to chapter, section and line.

104. Anastas. Sin., Viae dux, VI 2, 14: τὸ δεκακέρατον τῆς πλάνης; VII 1, 51: δεκακέρατον ταύτης ὀρχήστρας; X 5, 68: ὅλον τὸ δεκακέρατον.

105. He takes common elements at the following points: Theodosians and Gaianites take φύσις and πρόσωπον as the same in the incarnation (IX 2, 90; X 1, 3, 24); both teach mia physis (X 5, 68/69) and present patristic testimonies for the capacity of the divinity to suffer (XII 2, 2; 3, 3); they understand Cyril as a confessor of mia physis (XXII 4, 5).

106. Anastas. Sin., Viae dux, XIII 1, 7; 6, 12; 7, 31; all three (together with Theodosians): VII 1, 49; X 1, 1, 14; XII 3, 3.

It is peculiar to the Gaianites that for them the body of Christ is in every respect incorruptible and divine from the union on and possesses one (single) property (ἰδιότης), namely, the divine and impassible. For them the nature of the human body is something impure, especially the natural weaknesses of the flesh, to which we are drawn because of disobedience.[107]

In chapter 23 Anastasius offers in the form of a dialogue a very strange-sounding argumentation, which he seems to regard as especially cogent: the Gaianite dialogue partner can save himself only by turning to the testimony of the Fathers, who (at least in part), however, teach incorruptibility! Since the Gaianite confesses the real presence of Christ in the eucharistic elements of bread and wine, he suggests that he take the holy body and the blood of Christ and store it. If after a period of time it has not changed, then the Gaianites are right. If it has indeed changed, then either it is not the body of Christ or the body of Christ was also corruptible before the resurrection. As Jugie says,[108] behind this assertion is probably the idea that the body of Christ in the Eucharist as in earthly life is capable of suffering (Anastasius: it can be sacrificed, penetrated, broken, eaten).

Anastasius says that the Gaianites, through a different (clever!) reading, changed the text of Proclus of Constantinople: whereas Proclus wrote that Christ was born ἀφθάρτως, they read that he was born ἄφθαρτος. When Proclus says that Thomas saw Christ in this conjunction of natures (οὗ τὴν συζυγίαν), they turn it into a negation: οὐ τὴν συζυγίαν, that is, Thomas did *not* perceive the conjunction of the natures![109]

John of Damascus, in his *Expositio fidei* (CPG 8043), presents a short summary position against the teaching of Julian and the Gaianites:[110] if the body of Christ had been incorruptible before the resurrection, then he would certainly not have been consubstantial with us. The mystery of the assumed humanity (οἰκονομία) would be deception and theatre, and true salvation would not have been obtained for us.

Thus, we can point to the following characteristics of Gaianite doctrine. They are definite confessors of *mia physis* and strong opponents of the two-natures doctrine, more uncompromising than the Severans and so strict that they recognize only one characteristic in Christ. They adopt Julian's teaching that Christ was incorruptible from the union on, but in distinction to Julian they regard the natural weaknesses of the human body (in Julian: πάθη ἀδιάβλητα!) as the consequence of sin. The substantiation for the acceptance of the *aphtharsia* of Christ's body is the following: the voluntary acceptance of suffering would not be preserved if Christ were subject to the laws of nature; furthermore, the nature of human suffering is abhorred as unclean.

---

107. Anastas. Sin., *Viae dux*, XIV 2, 67.

108. M. Jugie, art. 'Gaianite (controverse)', *DTC* 6, 1011.

109. Anastas. Sin., *Viae dux*, X 2, 7, 199 and 1, 2, 104–8. The text here is Proclus Const., *Hom. De laudibus s. Mariae* (CPG 5800), 2: ACO I 1, 1, p. 104,4–6.

110. John of Damasc., *Expositio fidei* (CPG 8043), III 28: Otter II, p. 171,12–14; PG 94, 1100.

When Julianists and Gaianites appealed to the Fathers, it was not always done in error. There were Fathers who spoke of a certain deification of Christ's flesh through hypostatic union.[111] With Jugie, we can demonstrate this in individual passages from Gregory of Nyssa, Clement of Alexandria and Hilary of Poitiers.

Gregory of Nyssa:[112] 'If the mortal through its union with the immortal achieves immortality, as also the corruptible was changed into incorruptibility and all that is [human] was changed into the impassible and the divine, what pretext is left for those who split the one into the diversity of two?' Yet this statement serves the polemic against the Apollinarian reproach that he, Gregory, would introduce two sons.

Clement of Alexandria: 'For he ate not in order [to sustain] his body, which a holy power sustained, but so that those who were with him would not get the wrong idea, like those who later held him to be a phantom. He was, however, absolutely incapable of suffering, to the extent that not the least motion of passion, neither pleasure nor sadness, could slip up on him.'[113] With Clement the ideal of (Stoic?) self-control was overly dominant.

Hilary of Poitiers offers somewhat different assertions in his treatise De trinitate (esp. in X, 23) and in his commentary on Psalms.[114] He writes: 'Even if a blow struck [him] or a wound penetrated or knots tied [him] or hanging lifted him up, then this would, of course, lead to an attack of suffering (impetum passionis) but would not bring the pain of suffering (dolorem passionis).'[115] To help visualize this, Hilary offers a comparison with a weapon that penetrates water, fire or air. But these can nevertheless not be (permanently) injured by the weapon, although it is the nature of a weapon to injure. It is the same with Christ. He indeed had a

---

111. M. Jugie, art. cit., 1012.

112. Greg. Nyss., Ad Theophil. adv. Apoll. (CPG 3143), II: Jaeger-Müller, III/1, p. 125,6–10: εἰ δὲ τὸ θνητὸν ἐν τῷ ἀθανάτῳ γενόμενον ἀθανασία ἐγένετο, ὁμοίως < δὲ > καὶ τὸ φθαρτὸν εἰς ἀφθαρσίαν μετέβαλε καὶ τὰ ἄλλα πάντα ὡσαύτως πρὸς τὸ ἀπαθές τε καὶ θεῖον μετεποιήθη, τίς ὑπολείπεται λόγος ἔτι τοῖς εἰς δυικὴν διαφορὰν τὸ ἓν διασχίζουσιν; PG 45, 1273D–1276A.

113. Clem. Alex., Strom. (CPG 1377), VI 9, 71, 2: GCS 15 (Leipzig 1906), p. 467,13–15; PG 9, 292C: αὐτὸς δὲ ἀπαξαπλῶς ἀπαθὴς ὄν, εἰς ὃν οὐδὲν παρεισδύεται κίνημα παθητικὸν οὔτε ἡδονὴ οὔτε λύπη. Cf. Strom. III 7, 59, 3: GCS 15, p. 223 with the quotation from Valentinus that in Christ there was no true digestion and excretion of food. See A. Grillmeier, CCT I², pp. 136–38, esp. p. 138; JdChr I³, pp. 264–66, esp. p. 266.

114. On the passages, Hilary of Poitiers, In ps 53,12; 138,3; 141,8, cf. M.-J. Rondeau, OCA 220 (1985), p. 347. Cf. here G. Rauschen, 'Die Lehre des hl. Hilarius von Poitiers über die Leidensfähigkeit Christi', ThQ 87 (1905), 424–39. Rauschen is of the view that Hilary nonetheless remained the same in both works, that is, that it was impossible for Christ to feel pain. Only in his substantiation, Rauschen says, did he waver: in De trin. this was effected by the conception by the Holy Spirit; in the commentary on Psalms he traces it back to the divinity of the Redeemer, which is immutable. A presentation of the various interpretations is found in C. F. A. Borchardt, Hilary of Poitiers' Role in the Arian Struggle (Kerkhistor. Studien 12), The Hague 1966, pp. 117–30; J. W. Jacobs, 'The Western Roots of the Christology of St Hilary of Poitiers: A Heritage of Textual Interpretation', in StudPat 13/II (= TU 116), Berlin 1975, p. 202, n. 3. Cf. A. Grillmeier, CCT I², p. 397; JdChr I³, pp. 584–85: there is (against the Arians) a theology of glorification.

115. Hilary of Poitiers, De Trinitate X, 23: CCL 62A, p. 477,4–7; PL 10, 361A. Cf. A. Grillmeier, loc. cit.

body that was destined to suffer, and he did suffer; but it was not his nature to suffer.[116] The body (more precisely: *virtus corporis*) caught the force of the punishment that gave vent in him, without feeling the punishment.[117]

The text of Hilary then formed the starting-point for a 'new edition' of the dispute between Julian of Halicarnassus and Severus of Antioch in the twelfth century between the two Latin monks Philip of Harveng (Premonstratensian abbot) and John. Probably without any knowledge of the dispute in the sixth century, they dealt with the same problem, Philip in Julian's role and John in that of Severus, and they came to a similar solution.[118]

116. Hilary of Poitiers, CCL 62A, p. 478,28–30; PL 10, 363A: *habens ad patiendum quidem corpus, et passus est; sed naturam non habens ad dolendum.*

117. Ibid., p. 478,18–19; PL 10, 362A: *sine sensu poenae vim poenae . . . excepit.*

118. Philip of Harveng, *Ep. 5–7 ad Joann.*: PL 203, 34D–66C; John, *Ep. 22–24 ad Philipp.*: PL 203, 170A–174C; Hunald., *Ep. 25 ad Joann.*: PL 203, 174–80. See M. Jugie, art. 'Gaianite (controverse)', *DTC* 6, 1014–17.

CHAPTER THREE

THEODOSIUS, PATRIARCH OF ALEXANDRIA, SPIRITUAL HEIR OF SEVERUS OF ANTIOCH

---

1. *Sollicitudo omnium Ecclesiarum*

If Cyril of Alexandria was for Severus of Antioch the 'father of the dogmas', then Severus himself assumed this role for the last great theological figure of anti-Chalcedonian Christology in the sixth century, Theodosius of Alexandria.[1] In all three, patriarchal authority and theological power of expression were bound together in an impressive unity. Theodosius[2] claimed the patriarchal dignity of Alexandria until his death (566), although he was able to exercise it there only briefly.[3] His followers often designated him the 'ecumenical patriarch' and meant by this his universal responsibility for the church.[4] In any case, for him the office of patriarch meant a general responsibility going beyond Alexandria for

---

1. Theodosius speaks with highest praise of Severus already in the *Epist. synod. ad Severum* (CPG 7134): CSCO 103, pp. 1,27–2,8, probably addressed to Constantinople in the summer of 535; beginning in winter 534/535 Severus lived in the capital at the invitation of Justinian. Cf. the *Ep. synod.* that Theodosius himself directed from Constantinople to Severus, who had fled to Egypt (CPG 7148): Zacharias Rh. cont., *HE* IX 24, CSCO 88, pp. 107–11; also Theodos. Al., *Ep. ad eppos orthod. Orient.* (CPG 7141): CSCO 103, p. 68,16–17, in which Severus, who died in 538, is called 'our father' and 'ecumenical light'.

2. On the sources: Liberat., *Brev.* XX: ACO II 5, nos. 142–44; pp. 134–35; Zacharias Rh. cont., *HE* IX 19, 23, 26: Brooks, CSCO 88, pp. 93–94, 105–7, 114–17; Michael Syr., *Chron.*: Chabot II, pp. 211–19; Leont. Schol., *De sectis* V, IV–VI: PG 86, 1232–33; Severus of Ashmunein, *Hist. Patr. Eccl. Alex.*, chap. XIII: PO 1, pp. 455–72.

3. So he says in *Ep. canon.* (CPG 7138): CSCO 103, p. 57,4: *dum sumus extra sedem nostram.*

4. On the term: Iacob. (Barad.), Eugen. et Eunom., *Ep. ad Theodos.* (CPG 7170): CSCO 103, p. 63,8–9; Iacob., *Ep. ad Theodos.* (CPG 7171): ibid., p. 91,24; Archim. Orient., *Ep. ad eppos orth. Constant.* (CPG 7192): ibid., p. 128,2. The universal care of Theodosius for the church is emphasized by: Paul. Ant., *Ep. synod. ad Theodos.* (CPG 7203): CSCO 103, p. 72,20–22: 'God has now entrusted to you deservedly the guidance of the whole holy church'; Theodore of Bostra, *Ep. ad Patr. Paul. Ant.* (CPG 7201): CSCO 103, p. 66,17–23: he speaks

those anti-Chalcedonian churches that had no bishop of their own. When the Monophysite patriarch Anthimus of Constantinople was deposed, the care of his followers was taken over by Theodosius; similarly, he saw to the naming of a successor to his friend the patriarch Sergius of Antioch (558–561?). With great cunning he succeeded in manoeuvring the monk Paul into this position (564–577).[5] Yet his main concern was the *sedes evangelica Alexandriae*[6] and the occupation of vacant episcopal chairs in Egypt,[7] for which he felt responsible.

2. '*Causa multiplicis certaminis*'

These 'hierarchical' efforts, however, served the proclamation of right doctrine, not so much vis-à-vis the Chalcedonians as within the divided anti-Chalcedonian churches and monasteries. In a 'Letter on the Differences in Belief Among His Followers'[8] Theodosius led an agitated complaint about the 'mutual dispute' among brothers.[9] For this there were many occasions. As the Gaianites had driven him out of Alexandria, so the dispute over the knowledge and ignorance of Christ, which was begun by Themistius, followed him to Constantinople.[10] There was added the tritheist dispute, which, however, was taking place especially in Syria and Alexandria. In a letter to the Alexandrians he speaks of the 'inner betrayal of those who seemed to belong to us'.[11]

---

of Theodosius as one 'who leads the holy church of God everywhere' and who after God is 'our lord'. The title 'ecumenical patriarch', on the other hand, claimed by the bishop of Constantinople after John IV the Faster (and his synod of 587), has an 'imperial church' character. Cf. *CCT* II/2, p. 5; Grumel, *Regestes* I², N. 264 (Joh. IV Nesteutes); V. Laurent, 'Le titre de patriarche oecuménique et la signature patriarcale', *RevÉtByz* 6 (1948), 5–26.

   5. Cf. Theodos. Al., *Ep. synod. ad Paul. Ant.* (CPG 7142); *Mandator. primum ad Paul. patr.* (CPG 7143) and *Mandator. alterum ad eundem* (CPG 7144). Important is E. W. Brooks, 'The Patriarch Paul of Antioch and the Alexandrine Schism of 575', *ByzZ* 30 (1929), 468–76.

   6. This designation is used by Theodos. Al. in *Ep. synod. ad Sever. Ant.* (CPG 7134): CSCO 103, p. 5,18. For him this chair is '*sedes nostra*' (*Ep. canon.* [CPG 7138]: CSCO 103, p. 57,4).

   7. Cf. Theodos. Al., *Ep. ad Alexandrinos* (CPG 7147), CSCO 103, pp. 96–99, esp. 97,18–31. Cf. T. Orlandi, 'Teodosio di Alessandria nella letteratura copta', *GIF* 23 (1971), 175–85.

   8. Theodos. Al., *Ep. propter var. fid. inter eius asseclas exortam* (CPG 7135): CSCO 103, pp. 22–24, esp. p. 23,10–11; idem, *Tract. theol. ratio et scopus* (CPG 7136): CSCO 103, pp. 24–26.

   9. In ibid., pp. 23,22, 25–26, Theodosius speaks of the 'open' and 'manifold struggle' (*aperta pugna . . . multiplex certamen*) in the Monophysite church.

   10. Cf. Leont. Schol., *De sectis* V, VI: PG 86, 1232. See A. Grillmeier, *CCT* II/2, pp. 362–64.

   11. CSCO 103, p. 97,34–35. We discuss the contribution of Theodosius in the struggle against tritheism especially in vol. II/3.

In such confusions and intertwinings it is impossible to sort out the christological and theological significance of the patriarch Theodosius especially for the church of Alexandria. And yet with the unmistakable greatness of this bishop and theologian, we must have an interest in determining his part in the further development of the specifically Alexandrian tradition. Is the theology there not as 'Theodosian' as it is 'Severan' and ultimately 'Cyrillian'? It may be in this very triad that the attraction and far-reaching influence of Egyptian anti-Chalcedonian Christology lies. With it the shrill, forced tones of Julianist-Gaianist voices were ultimately covered. For we cannot forget the threat to Egyptian Christ-piety, as it has already been presented in part and must yet be made apparent. The talk of the 'earthly Jesus', the Jesus of the *kenosis*, always seemed to the lower classes to mean a denial of his divinity. We need only think of the extremists with whom Dioscorus I, Timothy Aelurus, Peter Mongus, Severus and finally Theodosius himself had to fight. The dangerous disintegrative phenomena with which Shenoute in Upper Egypt had to struggle will be treated in detail below. If the Old Oriental Orthodox church of Alexandria ultimately found a balanced image of Christ, it is indebted to its choice of the Severan-Theodosian way. Yet even after Theodosius the anti-Chalcedonian church of the East faced turbulent times. In maintaining the uniformity of the anti-Chalcedonian church he did not even shrink from the use of excommunication.[12]

3. The basic traits of Theodosian Christology[13]

(a) His authorities

The series of *normative* christological *documents* that are repeatedly named is quickly presented: it contains the first three general councils of 325, 381 and 431. Ephesus II (449) is not included. Then follow the twelve

---

12. Cf. his *Ep. canonica* (in questions of tritheism) (CPG 7138): CSCO 103, pp. 56,22–36; 57,9–26.

13. The reader is referred to the presentation of the teaching of Theodosius on the knowledge of Christ in A. Grillmeier, *CCT* II/2, pp. 362, 369–74. On the theological writings of Theodosius see CPG 7130–7159 and A. Van Roey, *Théodose d'Alexandrie dans les manuscrits syriaques de la British Library*, OLA 13 (1982), 287–99. The most significant texts of Theodosius are contained in the *Documenta monophysitica*, CSCO 17 (T), 103 (V). We cite according to V.

anathemas of Cyril and the *Henoticon* of Zeno, which at this time seems to celebrate its happy appearance, though interpreted differently from what Emperor Anastasius I wanted to allow – namely, as condemnation and rejection of Chalcedon.[14]

The number of patristic authorities that Theodosius adduces is greatest in his *Oratio theologica*. He appeals mostly to the three Cappadocians, Athanasius and Cyril of Alexandria. Naturally, the Apollinarian forgeries are also not missing.[15] Noteworthy are his multiple references to Pseudo-Dionysius Areopagita.

(b) His confession of faith

It is only natural for Theodosius that in the *confession-like* ('confiteor') *exposition* of his faith the disagreement with Gaianus is prominent: the passibility of Christ and his actual death are – against the background of the story of Adam's fall – emphasized in detail in their absolute soteriological significance.[16] The Christian faith in redemption stands or falls with the idea that Christ became like us in every respect (Heb 2,14–17). Here Theodosius could know that he was in full communion with the Chalcedonians.

(c) His heresiology

Severus could declare himself in complete agreement with the list of heretics that condemned all opponents of *una persona et una hypostasis Verbi Dei incarnata* on the left (Apollinarian, Eutychian, Gaianite[17]) and on the right (Diodore, Theodore of Mopsuestia, Nestorius until Chalcedon and Leo's *Tome*), as Theodosius assumes:

---

14. Cf. Theodos. Al., *Ep. synod. ad Sever. Ant.* (535) (CPG 7134): CSCO 103, p. 2,20–33; see *Ep. synod. ad Paul. Ant.* (564) (CPG 7142): CSCO 103, p. 85,24–25: *Henoticon . . . et illud ad eversionem synodi Chalcedonensis.* Cf. A. Grillmeier, *CCT* II/2, p. 348, with n. 139. Even Severus can now confess to the *Henoticon* understood as an anti-Chalcedonian document. Cf. CPG 7070 (8): CSCO 103, p. 20,18–20.

15. Cf. Theodos. Al., *Or. theol.* (CPG 7137): CSCO 103, p. 51,9–21 = Apollinar., *Quod unus sit Christus*, no. 3: Lietzmann, p. 296,3–15, added as Athanasius, *De fide* (PG 28, 123). Athanasius, however, is also discussed with genuine passages.

16. Theodos. Al., *Ep. syn. ad Sever. Ant.*: CSCO 103, pp. 3,7–5,4.

17. Directed especially against the Gaianites is p. 4,25–31: 'Because he was capable of suffering, he endured the natural, voluntary and blameless passions, and even death on the cross. Only through the God-befitting miracle of the resurrection did he make this flesh impassible, immortal and in every way incorruptible.' Cf. pp. 4,36–5,4.

In these apostolic, patristic, divine, faultless doctrines, our holy brother, I and all churches that depend on the *evangelical see of Alexandria* extend to you the right hand of *communio*.[18]

(d) Connections with Severan terminology

All this is authentic Severus.[19] Somewhat striking is just the fact that the 'two natures' of Chalcedon are not (always) rejected by the *mia-physis* formula preferred in Severus, but by the somewhat modified form: 'one incarnate person (*parṣopā*) and one hypostasis (*qenōmā*) of the God-Logos'.[20] But Theodosius is able to use variation, as his *Epistula synodica* to Patriarch Paul of Antioch shows:[21]

The hypostatic union did not falsify the distinction of natures that marks the united and also left no place for division and separation; rather, for us it created from two the one and indivisible Emmanuel; one is his nature or composite hypostasis; this means the same as when we say: the nature of the God-Logos himself and his hypostasis has become flesh and perfectly human being . . .

Thus *physis* and *hypostasis* continue to be synonymous also for the *oikonomia*. In this Severus and Theodosius are one.

What is new vis-à-vis the old Severus is indeed the formula, 'One out of the Trinity, the hypostatic Word of God the Father'.[22] We still find it at the end of Theodosius's life in the synodical letter to Paul of Antioch (564).[23] Even Severus seems to have adopted it, as his synodical letter to Patriarch Theodosius in 535 shows.[24]

The term *synthesis*, on the other hand, is employed by Theodosius entirely in the Severan usage.[25] 'Composite' (*compositus, synthetos*), applied to the hypostatic Word of the Father, means nothing other than

---

18. Idem, ibid. p. 5,16–19. Cf. p. 2,18–19. The actual extent of agreement within his own camp was considerably overestimated by Theodosius, as he would soon learn.

19. See his answer to Theodosius (CPG 7070 [8]): CSCO 103, pp. 6–22 (in 535).

20. Theodos. Al., *Ep. syn. ad Sever.*, p. 5,14–15.

21. Theodos. Al., *Ep. synod. ad Paul. Patr.* (CPG 7142): CSCO 103, pp. 84,35–85,4.

22. Theodos. Al., *Ep. synod. ad Sever.* (CPG 7134): CSCO 103, p. 4,20–21. The whole section p. 4,20–25 is powerfully formulated.

23. Theodos. Al., *Ep. synod. ad Paul. Ant.* (CPG 7142): CSCO 103, p. 84,22.

24. Severus Ant., *Ep. synod. ad Theodos. Al.* (CPG 7070 [8]), CSCO 103, p. 17,27–28: of Christ he says: *et sic unus e Trinitate mansit, etiam cum in carne pateretur;* cf. ibid., p. 12,32–33; also Theodos. Al., *Or. theol.*: CSCO 103, p. 41,19–22 (the Severus passage is not identified in Chabot).

25. Severus's position is explained in A. Grillmeier, *CCT* II/2, pp. 126–28.

inhumanatus, incarnate. The two terms are synonymous.[26] Since Theodosius must in this connection reject a false tritheistic determination of the subject of the incarnation, he notes that this is done incorrectly by referring to Pseudo-Dionysius. The intention of the opponents is to assert the incarnation of the whole Trinity.[27] The patriarch correctly rejects the conclusion that according to Pseudo-Dionysius the 'general natures' of divinity and humanity have entered a *union* and *composition* and emphasizes, on the contrary, that Severus had appealed precisely to Pseudo-Dionysius, whom he had well read, in rejecting such ideas. The just-mentioned passage is adduced twice in differing lengths.[28]

> [The basic principle of the divinity . . .], however, was finally [designated] in a quite special way as philanthropic, because in a truly unrestricted way *in one of his hypostases* he entered into fellowship with us and thereby summoned to himself and established the uttermost human separation from God of which in an inexpressible way *the simple Jesus was composed* (ὁ ἁπλοῦς Ἰησοῦς συνετέθη).[29]

(e) The one energeia

As we have already seen in the interpretation of the knowledge of Christ in the *Tractatus ad Theodoram,* Theodosius connects this concept of the synthesis of divinity and humanity with the idea of the unity of *energeia,* activity, *operatio.* In Severus also, this concept played a special role in Christology in his discussion with Julian of Halicarnassus. Surveying the history of the substantiation of the unity in Christ, one sees that efforts

---

26. Cf. *Exemplar subscriptionis,* which Theodosius had signed by the bishops *(sacerdotes)* present in Constantinople: CSCO 103, p. 59,17–25: *solam hypostasim Dei Verbi . . . compositam esse et inhumanatam, cum neque Pater neque Spiritus sanctus compositus est cum carne aut inhumanatus est.* Cf. Theodos. Al., *Or. theol.* (CPG 7137): CSCO 103, p. 29,10–12: 'We believe that Christ our Lord is *composed* out of two natures, the divine and the human; not of generic and general [natures]' (but of the concrete natures of the Son and his own flesh). Result (ibid., l. 18–19): *et unius itaque compositi est eius natura et eius hypostasis.* Likewise p. 51,4–7; used in parallel here are *compositus, inhumanatus, incarnatus.*

27. Theodos. Al., *Or. theol.* (CPG 7137): CSCO 103, p. 52,3–20. Cf. Ps.-Dionys., *De div. nom.* I 4: PG 3, 592A8–10. Theodosius quotes Ps.-Dionys. as saying on the whole Trinity: 'Appellata est autem et philanthropa excellenter, quia nostris, vere et integre, per unam ex suis hypostasibus, participavit'; trans. by B. R. Suchla, *Pseudo Dionysius Areopagita, Die Namen Gottes,* Stuttgart 1988, p. 24,8–11.

28. Ps.-Dionys., *De div. nom.* I 4: PG 3, 592A8–12, in CSCO 103, p. 52,9–11; 592A8–B2: ibid., p. 53,2–9. We cite the longer passage in the translation of B. R. Suchla, op. cit., 24,8–13.

29. The Latin translation in CSCO 103, p. 53,5–6 has inexactly . . . *ex qua simplex Iesus ineffabili modo consistit,* with which PG 3, 591A agrees. We see from the above text that the incarnation is asserted of only one divine hypostasis. This hypostasis is the ἁπλοῦς Ἰησοῦς, that is, the Son in his divinity, who enters a synthesis with our finitude. Theodosius: *per hypostasim facta Unigeniti, quem, 'simplicem Iesum' appellat propter simplicitatem quae antecedit incarnationem* (p. 53,12–14). The teaching of Ps.-Dionys. is thereby summarized with PG 3, 644A = Suchla, p. 34,31–40.

first concerned the idea of deification and the exchange of characteristics (*communicatio idiomatum*). In the discussion with Julian of Halicarnassus, whom he certainly judged too harshly, Severus recognized the danger of understanding the unity in Christ from the idea of the qualitative assimilation of the humanity of Christ to the divinity; the *kenosis* would be abolished. Thus he shifted to emphasis on the μία ἐνέργεια, the *one* activity in Christ. The one *energeia* becomes the strongest expression of the *mia physis* and the guarantor that Christ is really one – in contrast to the 'Nestorianism' of the two activities of Leo I.[30]

Theodosius advanced this development decisively, as we have seen in his interpretation of the knowledge of Christ.[31] *Mia energeia* gets the better of *mia physis*. The way is already prepared for the era of the *energeia* doctrine of the seventh century.[32] We close with a Theodosian text from his *Epistula synodica* to Patriarch Paul of Antioch, whom he wanted to make the heir of his own ideas. The reference is to Chalcedon and Leo I.[33]

This perfidious and damnable synod taught unlawfully among its other blasphemies that Christ is to be known in two natures, and against the best valid *canones* it set up a different definition of faith and called the *Tome* of Leo a pillar of orthodoxy, which openly affirmed the godless teachings of Nestorius and two natures and hypostases, as well as [two] forms (*agit enim utraque forma!*) and activities and characteristics . . .

Your Holiness in your wisdom has fallen into a state of agitation about the damnation of those who assert that our Lord Jesus Christ, the wisdom and power of the Father, suffered ignorance. A truly wise man of humanity cannot reach the conclusion that he [Christ] did not know the day of consummation or anything else from the realm of being, even if he took on our ignorance on account of the economy of salvation. How then can this holy and life-giving flesh – which from the beginning of the union, that is, from formation in the womb of the holy Virgin, was equipped with soul and understanding and *with every activity befitting God* – not know something that is or was or will be?

---

30. On this transformation of ideas cf. A. Grillmeier, *CCT* II/2, pp. 162–73.
31. Cf. *CCT* II/2, pp. 368–74.
32. Further examples of this are found in the *Documenta monophysitica*.
33. Theodos. Al., *Ep. synod. ad Paul. Patr.* (CPG 7142): CSCO 103, pp. 85,26–86,7.

CHAPTER FOUR

THE DEVELOPMENT OF TWO HIERARCHIES

(by T. Hainthaler)

I. THE CHALCEDONIAN HIERARCHY: THE MELKITES

1. The Melkite patriarchs of 538–580

After Theodosius had to leave Alexandria and Justinian was not able to convert him to Chalcedonianism, the emperor took decisive action. Between September 537 and August 538[1] (and thus still during Theodosius's lifetime) he had the Tabennesiote monk Paul – on recommendation of the papal legate Pelagius[2] – consecrated patriarch of Alexandria; this was done in Constantinople by Menas, the patriarch of Constantinople. This gave a signal:

> So this custom began for the patriarchs of the Melkites, that [from that time on] they should be ordained at Constantinople, and then proceed to Alexandria.[3]

The pre-eminence had ultimately passed to Constantinople, and in Egypt there were now two hierarchies side by side! Paul arrived in Alexandria escorted by soldiers.[4] In addition, the emperor provided the Alexandrian patriarch with secular power[5] and thereby created the basis for the 'soldier-patriarchs'.[6] Paul took vigorous action: he obtained an order from Justinian to close all Monophysite churches.[7] After a year the

---

1. Cf. A. Schönmetzer's chronology in *Chalkedon* II, p. 964.
2. E. Stein, *Histoire* II, p. 389.
3. *Hist. Patr.*: PO 1, p. 469.
4. *Hist. Patr.*: PO 1, p. 466; J. Maspero, *Histoire*, p. 138.
5. Liberatus, *Brev.* 23: ACO II 5, p. 139,2–4; E. Stein, *Histoire du Bas-Empire* II, p. 389: he 'was provided with the powers of a true viceroy'. Cf. A. M. Demicheli, 'La politica religiosa di Giustiniano in Egitto', pp. 235–36: beginning with Paul of Tabennesi the Melkite patriarch became the representative of the emperor.
6. Cf. J. Maspero, *Histoire*, pp. 45, 283.
7. *Hist. Patr.*: PO 1, p. 466.

Monophysites dared to build two new churches, but the old ones were reserved for Chalcedonians – one reason for the growing bitterness. Paul could hold his seat only two years; then he was deposed by the Synod of Gaza because of his involvement in the death of the deacon Psois.[8] In his place Zoilus, a Palestinian monk, was elected.

Zoilus, the addressee of Justinian's dogmatic letter on the double activity of Christ (539/540), which we have already analysed,[9] carried out a more peaceful reign than his predecessor, yet also remained in need of military protection.[10] After seven years in office (546) he had to flee to Constantinople because of an insurrection.[11] He remained true to the Chalcedonian confession. His opposition to imperial policy in the 'Three Chapters' controversy led to his deposition (551).[12]

Named as successor was Apollinaris, who favoured condemnation of the 'Three Chapters'.[13] He was from a military background and presumably still a layman at his election.[14] His succession was at first rejected by Pope Vigilius, who called him '*pervasor*' and '*adulter ecclesiae*'.[15] A year and a half later, however, he accepted the *professio* of the patriarch Eutychius of Constantinople (553) that was countersigned by Apollinaris

---

8. See A. Grillmeier, *CCT* II/2, pp. 355–56.

9. See A. Grillmeier, *CCT* II/2, pp. 361–62, 382–83.

10. Zacharias Rh., *HE* X 1: Brooks, CSCO 88, p. 120,7; Hamilton-Brooks, p. 300, who speak of a chiliarch, who was assigned to protect Zoilus 'from the violence [of] the people of the city'.

11. On dating cf. J. Maspero, *Histoire*, pp. 154–55.

12. In 543 Zoilus received the first decree of the emperor against the Origenists with the order to sign it, which he did, together with Menas of Constantinople, Ephraem of Antioch and Peter of Jerusalem (Liberatus, *Brev.* 23: ACO II 5, p. 140,8–10). Against a second decree in 544/545, which anathematized the 'Three Chapters' (Iustinian. imp., *In damnationem trium capitulorum* [CPG 6881], extant only in excerpts, cf. *CCT* II/2, pp. 421–22!), he offered resistance. Finally Zoilus signed under pressure (*compulsum*) (cf. Facundus of Hermiane, *Pro def. tr. cap.* IV, IV, 8: CCL 90A, p. 124,53–58; PL 67, 626AB). Then, however, he turned with a delegation to the pope (546), in order to excuse himself for this weakness, and ultimately paid for his resistance with deposition. Cf. J. Maspero, *Histoire*, pp. 153–54; E. Stein, *Histoire du Bas-Empire* II, pp. 637, 640. Cf. also Facundus Herm., *C. Mocianum Scholasticum* (CPL 867), 37: CCL 90A, p. 409; PL 67, 861CD.

13. Victor Ton., *Chron. a. 551*: MGH auct. ant. 11, p. 202. On Apollinaris see R. Aigrain, art. 'Apollinaire', *DHGE* 3 (1924), pp. 992–93.

14. Eutych. Al., *Annal.*: PG 111, 1069B: *dux*; cf. Breydy, CSCO 472, p. 86; Severus of Ashm., *Refutatio Eut.*: PO 3, p. 203: one of Justinian's friends, accompanied by an armed escort. He acted like a patrician and resided in the palace of the military governor. The background of Apoll. is discussed in detail in J. Maspero, *Histoire*, pp. 156–61. Cf. E. Stein, *Histoire du Bas-Empire* II, p. 629 with n. 1.

15. Vigilius, Ep. of 14 Aug. 551 (CPL 1694): Schwartz, *Vigiliusbriefe*, p. 13,22–23; PL 69, 62A. In this letter he excommunicated Theodore Askidas, who had struck the name of Zoilus from the diptychs and inserted that of Apollinaris.

and thereby tacitly recognized his legitimacy[16] – indeed, he seems even to have sent a cordial reply.[17] Apollinaris participated in the council of 553 as one of the four patriarchs of the East and also bore its decisions. On the other hand, he resisted the last 'aphthartic' action of Emperor Justinian.[18]

Apollinaris violently persecuted the supporters of *mia physis* in Egypt and thereby achieved superficial success.[19] Not another Monophysite bishop came to Alexandria. The Makarios monastery became all the more the centre for the oppressed adherents of the *mia-physis* formula.[20] Among the people, however, there was indeed hardly a confession to Chalcedon to be found.

Already at the beginning of his time in office a massacre provided extremely impressive signs. Apollinaris was pelted with stones at his first mass. On the following Sunday, when he read aloud an imperial letter and threateningly demanded Chalcedonian confession, stones were again thrown at him, but the troops standing by began a bloodbath in the churches and in the streets.[21] Even if we probably cannot credit this entirely to the patriarch, it was nonetheless successful: 'The city became quiet.'[22]

The picture of Apollinaris that Eutychius sketches is that of a brutal military man installed by the emperor to establish order, that is, to get the Chalcedonian confession adopted by force. For this, the robe of the patriarch appears only as a practical form of dress. Then comes the description of the feast that Apollinaris held to celebrate the news of the death of the exiled patriarch Theodosius, as reported by Severus of Al-Ashmunein. By contrast, however, his private life seems to have been blameless, as presented, for example, by the legendary edification story of the patriarch's generosity in the *Pratum spirituale*, a work that was nevertheless composed scarcely fifty years later.[23]

---

16. That is to be concluded from the *Constitutum de tribus Capitulis* (CPL 1694) of Pope Vigilius: *CA* ep. 83, no. 19, p. 234.

17. According to JW 933*.

18. J. Maspero, *Histoire*, p. 165.

19. Cf. the presentation of the situation in J. Maspero, *Histoire*, pp. 264–65.

20. Cf. Eutych. Al., *Annal.*: PG 111, 1069.

21. Cf. the detailed presentation in Eutychius Al., *Annal.*: PG 111, 1069; M. Breydy, CSCO 471 (T) and 472 (German trans.), Louvain 1985, pp. 86–87; also Severus of Ashm., *Ref. Eutych.*: PO 3, 203–4; cf. for comments J. Maspero, *Histoire*, pp. 162–64; E. Stein, *Histoire* II, pp. 630–32; A. M. Demicheli, 'La politica religiosa di Giustiniano in Egitto', p. 244. Eutychius, Melkite patriarch of Alexandria in the first half of the tenth century, offers here a broad description that one will not immediately dismiss as invention, since he as a Melkite would more likely be interested in suppressing such reports. The information in Peter Ibn Rahib, *Chron. orientale*: ed. Cheikho, CSCO Script. Arab. III, 1 (Beirut 1903), p. 128 (Lat. trans.), which includes 200,000 Jacobite men, women and children who were killed under Apollinaris, is simply to be understood as the imagination of the *homines innumeri* in Eutychius. Peter Ibn Rahib, moreover, is rather inexact in his presentation (he reports this story twice, the first time connected with Timothy Aelurus!).

22. Eutychius Al., *Annal.* [251]: Breydy, CSCO 472 (V), p. 87; PG 111, 1070A.

23. John Moschus, *Pratum spirituale* (CPG 7376): PG 87, 3072–3076; also J. Maspero, *Histoire*, p. 157. John Moschus may have come to Alexandria in 608; cf. P. Pattenden, art. 'Johannes Moschus', *TRE* 17 (1987), pp. 140–44, here: p. 141.

Apollinaris died in 570. His successor, John IV (570–581), likewise from a military background, had a peaceful reign.

John of Nikiu characterized him with these words: 'John, an ex-military man, was appointed in [Apollinaris's] stead. And he had a goodly presence and forced none to forsake his faith. But he glorified God in His Church in the midst of all the assembled people, and they gave thanks to the emperor for the noble acts he had done.'[24] Also one can hardly call John IV a persecutor of Monophysites. Against that, above all, is the silence of the chroniclers about him. Nor can one speak of evidence of a persecution in the report of John of Ephesus.[25] According to it, he repeatedly complained about Monophysite clerics from Alexandria in Constantinople, until they were taken by imperial command to Constantinople. After Patriarch Eutychius was unable to move them to accept Chalcedon, they were held in various monasteries. There Theodosius, archpriest of the Alexandrian church, also died; he was the first instigator of the illegal election of Theodore in 575. Finally, Mundhir effected their liberation in 580. They returned to Alexandria, which leads to the conclusion that they did not feel very threatened there.

His synodical letter (not extant) was attacked by Anastasius of Antioch.[26] The patriarch of Constantinople, John, consecrated him.[27] His time of office fell in a period of great divisions among the Monophysites in Egypt. There were at times three patriarchs(!): Theodore, Damian and Dorotheus (the patriarch elected by the Gaianites), in addition to John IV.[28]

When we look back at this series of the first four Melkite[29] patriarchs, certain characteristics emerge:

Dependence on the emperor (not incorrectly already announced in name) was in fact given in all cases (also later with Eulogius). From the emperor they received at times great secular powers, by which they more and more turned into imperial functionaries.[30] Their appearance was

---

24. John Nik., *Chron.* 94, 24: Charles, p. 151.

25. John Eph., *HE* IV 37–38.42: Brooks, CSCO 106, pp. 163, 168; Schönfelder, pp. 168–69, 173. Cf. J. Maspero, *Histoire*, pp. 257–58.

26. Theophanes, *Chronogr.* A. M. 6062: de Boor I, p. 243. J. Maspero, *Histoire*, p. 257 traces this rejection back to his secular background.

27. This continued the tradition that the Melkite patriarchs received their ordination from either Rome or Constantinople.

28. Cf. John Eph., *HE* IV 44: Brooks, CSCO 106, pp. 170–71.

29. The 'Monophysites' called adherents to Chalcedon 'Melkites', from Syriac *malkânyia*, 'imperial' (from Syriac *malka*, 'emperor, king'). Thus already Niceph. Callist., *HE* 18, 52: PG 147, 437D: 'Those, however, who remained with right doctrine were named Melkites because they followed the holy fourth council and the emperor, for Melchi is among Syrians the emperor.' Cf. R. Janin, art. 'Melchite', *DTC* 10 (1928), 516–20; W. de Vries, art. 'Melchiten', *LThK* 7 (1962), 253–56.

30. See A. M. Demicheli, 'La politica religiosa in Egitto', p. 247. This also included the bishops who, provided with great powers, became to some extent imperial officials; cf. the evidence in ibid., pp. 248–49. J. Maspero, p. 139: the bishop as 'préfet religieux' who was responsible to the emperor for the conscience of his people and announced the theological decisions of the ruler.

connected with military power (Paul, Apollinaris) or at least could not dispense with military protection (Zoilus); some were of military background (Apollinaris, John IV). The catchword *soldier-patriarch* represents this development.

Consecration occurred in Constantinople through the patriarch of Constantinople (Apollinaris, John IV) or through the papal nuncio (Paul, Zoilus). The Alexandrian clergy were excluded.[31]

A pacification in and around Alexandria was achieved only by force, but was admittedly 'successful' there; the influence of the Melkite patriarchs remained limited to this area.

> The catholic patriarchate was an artificial power. In the highlands [Upper Egypt] it was ignored; in Lower Egypt it had some adherents; only in Alexandria was it a party.[32]

By origin, none except presumably Paul (a monk from the Canopus monastery) came from Egypt,[33] so that from this side a close attachment to the people was not promoted.

Theologically hardly anything is held against miaphysitism. That does not come until Eulogius, except perhaps for some attempts by John IV. But even in view of the untiring work of Eulogius there finally remains on balance Maspero's judgement that he still 'achieved almost nothing'.

> Nothing shows better how much the cause of orthodoxy in Egypt was lost than the life of this man [Eulogius], highly gifted, educated, intelligent, farsighted, full of ideas, active, zealous, who was one of the most notable bishops of his time, and who after almost thirty years of uninterrupted efforts achieved almost nothing. His history and that of his first two successors transpired in a small, limited, self-contained world, completely indifferent and foreign to the true Egypt.[34]

When, however, the patriarchal history of Severus of Al-Ashmunein speaks of martyrs and suffering and persecutions, then that is to be considered critically.

Apart from the massacre under Apollinaris, prior to which the patriarch was pelted with stones, no further cruel interventions are known that accompanied the takeover of power by

---

31. J. Maspero, *Histoire*, p. 136 with n. 2: 'That was against the *canones* and against custom.'

32. J. Maspero, *Histoire*, p. 265.

33. It is true that of the Coptic patriarchs Damian was Syrian, and Theodosius, Anastasius and Andronicus were Greek Alexandrians, not Copts (J. Maspero, *Histoire*, p. 18). Almost an identification of being anti-Chalcedonian and being a Copt can be perceived in the *Hist. Patr.* (on Benjamin: PO 1, 498) when it says that the Metras monastery – precisely because all inhabitants were Egyptian by race and included no foreigners – was unusually strong vis-à-vis Emperor Heraclius, who wanted to force them to accept the Chalcedonian faith.

34. J. Maspero, *Histoire*, pp. 274–75.

the Melkites. Bishops were deposed but often not banished; instead, they were allowed to flee to Upper Egypt.[35]

In summary, Maspero's view may well be accurate:[36]

The policies of Byzantium did not succeed in establishing an Egyptian Catholic church, but only a Byzantine enclave in the middle of the Copts. Without authority or moral influence in the land that he claimed to rule, the Melkite archbishop remained the servant of the prince, obliged to cater to all his whims in order to get in return the necessary support for his own existence.

2. Eulogius, a neo-Chalcedonian theologian of mediation?

The Syrian Eulogius led the Melkite church of Alexandria as patriarch in the years 581 (or 580) to 608 (or 607).[37]

He seems to have been a monk,[38] was a priest in Antioch and headed the monastery of the Mother of God, that is, the Justinian monastery.[39] He was the leader of the ξενοδοχεῖον in Antioch.[40]

In Alexandria he rebuilt the church of the martyr Julian[41] and had a church built in honour of the Mother of God, which was named the Dorotheus church.[42] Of special significance is his lifelong friendship with Pope Gregory the Great,[43] which presumably began in Constantinople when Eulogius was consecrated patriarch and Gregory was still working there as nuncio of Pope Pelagius II.[44] An extensive correspondence attests to this relationship.[45]

---

35. J. Maspero, *Histoire*, p. 178.

36. J. Maspero, *Histoire*, p. 183.

37. On Eulogius: S. Helmer, *Der Neuchalkedonismus*, Bonn 1962, 236–41; J. Darrouzès, art. 'Euloge', *DHGE* 15 (1980), 1388–89; P. Goubert, 'Patriarches d'Antioche et d'Alexandrie contemporains de S. Grégoire le Grand. Notes de prosopographie byzantine', *RevÉtByz* 25 (1967) (65–76), pp. 71–74: 'Vie et oeuvres'. J. Maspero, *Histoire*, Index, esp. pp. 258–59. On dating: A. Jülicher, 'Die Liste der alexandrinischen Patriarchen im 6. und 7. Jahrhundert', in *Festgabe Karl Müller*, Tübingen 1922, 19; cf. V. Grumel, *La chronologie*, Paris 1958, 443.

38. Photius, *Bibl. cod.* 230: Henry V, 53–54; PG 103, 1076D.

39. Photius, *Bibl. cod.* 226: Henry IV, 111; PG 103, 953A.

40. John Eph., *HE* I, 40: Brooks, CSCO 106, p. 34,25.

41. John Mosch., *Pratum spir.* 146: PG 87, 3009–12; cf. SC 12, pp. 197–98.

42. Ibid., 77: PG 87, 2929D; SC 12, p. 119.

43. On this cf. J. Maspero, *Histoire*, pp. 268–74.

44. Cf. J. Maspero, *Histoire*, p. 259. Presumably the reaction of the pope to the synodical letter of Eulogius also goes back to Gregory. The pope reproached Eulogius with a list of deficiencies, in consequence of which Eulogius actually would have represented a very pronounced theology of mediation à la *Henoticon* (Maspero, p. 273). Eulogius answered in an apologia (Photius, *Bibl. cod.* 230: Henry V, 8–10) and from then on proved himself an ardent defender of Leo's *Tome*.

45. Cf. P. Goubert, art. cit., p. 72. We cite according to *S. Gregorii Magni. Registrum epistularum, libri* I–VII.VIII–XIV, Appendix, ed. D. Norberg (CCL 140 and 140A), Turnhout 1982; in < > are the differing numbers in MGH, Epistulae I–II, ed. P. Ewald, L. Hartmann, Berlin 1891–99.

There are ten extant letters of Gregory to Eulogius personally (from the years 596–603),[46] plus two that are addressed to Eulogius and Anastasius of Antioch together (V, 41 of 1 June 595 and VII, 31 of June 597), as well as Gregory's synodical letter of February 591 to the four patriarchs (John of Constantinople, Eulogius of Alexandria, Gregory of Antioch, John of Jerusalem) and Anastasius of Antioch. Some letters are connected with the dispute over the title 'ecumenical patriarch', which the patriarch of Constantinople claimed.[47] The answers from Eulogius have not survived.

As defender of Leo's *Tome* Eulogius had legendary fame.[48] He took sides even in quarrels within the Monophysite groupings.[49] Besides the miaphysites, he also fought the Samaritans and the Novatians.[50]

Of the extensive work of the Alexandrian patriarch that is attested by the detailed description of Photius,[51] only a few fragments have come down to us. When six (of eight) texts ascribed to Eulogius in the *DP* were assigned by M. Richard (1977)[52] to John the Grammarian of Caesarea, this also removed large parts that had previously shaped the

---

46. The ten personal letters: VI, 61 < 58 > (July 596); VII, 37 (July 597); VIII, 28 and 29 (from July 598); IX, 176 < 175 > (July 599); X, 14 (July 600); X, 21 (August 600); XII, 16 (August 602); XIII, 42 < 44 > and 43 < 45 > (July 603).

47. Cf. S. Vailhé, 'Saint Grégoire le Grand et le titre de patriarche oecuménique', *EO* 11 (1908), 161–71. The letters to Eulogius and his reaction to them: ibid., pp. 164–65, 166–67. Eulogius did not go into the first common letter of Gregory (V, 41) and was therefore criticized by Gregory (VI, 61 < 60 >). Finally Eulogius gave in; he deprived the patriarch of Constantinople of this title and gave it to Gregory, who, however, also rejected it (VIII, 29). The dispute that Gregory had 'inherited' from his predecessor lasted through his whole pontificate, and he achieved nothing. According to S. Vailhé the title (for Constantinople) was recognized in the East but was not regarded as a depreciation of Rome. On the spread of the title cf. idem, 'Le titre de patriarche oecuménique avant saint Grégoire le Grand', *EO* 11 (1908), 65–69.

48. Cf. here the following works of Eulogius: Against Severus and Timothy, in Photius, *Bibl. cod.* 225: Henry IV, 99–108; Against Theodosius and Severus (cod. 226): Henry IV, 108–11; as well as the dream in John Mosch., *Pratum spir.*, 148: SC 12, pp. 199–200, according to which Pope Leo himself appeared to Eulogius to thank him for his intervention.

49. Cf. *Contra Theodosianos et Gaianitas*: Henry IV, 111–14 (cod. 227); *Contra Severum et Timotheum*: Henry IV, 99–108 (cod. 225); *Contra Theodosium et Severum*: Henry IV, 108–11 (cod. 226). His position on the Agnoetes issue has already been treated in *CCT* II/2, pp. 379–81.

50. Samaritans: *Adversus Samaritas Dositheanos*: Henry V, 60–64; cf. J. Maspero, *Histoire*, p. 261, n. 1; five books against the Novatians: *Contra Novatianos*, cod. 182, 208, 280: Henry II, 192–95; III, 105–6; VIII, 188–214; cf. here H. J. Vogt, *Coetus Sanctorum. Der Kirchenbegriff des Novatian und die Geschichte seiner Sonderkirche* (Theophaneia), Bonn 1968, 284–87.

51. Cf. CPG 6976. Photius describes four tractates and eleven orations (in the cod. 182, 208, 225–27, 230, 280).

52. M. Richard, *Iohannis Caesariensis presbyteri et grammatici opera quae supersunt* (CCG 1), Turnhout–Louvain 1977, p. XVIII.

image of Eulogius's theology.[53] Not in doubt are the extant fragments 'Dubitationes orthodoxi' (CPG 6972; *DP*, 152–55) and the fragments of 'Defensiones' or Συνηγορίαι (CPG 6971; *DP*, 209–10, 211–13), as well as three short fragments of scripture interpretation (CPG 6973–75). What sort of Christology can we know from this?

In the *Dubitationes orthodoxi* Eulogius works above all against the pure *mia physis* with the indication that one would then have to accept a consubstantiality of God (Father, Logos) and flesh (nos. 3, 4, 5, 6). The *mia-physis* formula in itself seems for Eulogius to be a part of orthodox teaching, but he demands in it the confession to the two natures.[54] The formula of the 'one composite nature' that results (*apotelesthai*) from the two natures faces the problem of how one can thereby preserve the consubstantiality of Christ after the union with the Father (nos. 1 and 9). Throughout these objections confession to the two natures is demanded (in no. 7 also through the indication that the union between Father and Logos in the Trinity is unsurpassable; how then does one claim not to distinguish two in Christ?). Yet the confession to 'from two natures' would also have to move directly to 'in two natures' (no. 12). These objections never speak of hypostasis or of the hypostatic union.

The first fragment of the *Synegoriai* (only in *DP*, pp. 209–10)[55] provides an insight into Eulogius's concept of the incarnation:

In no way has a plain human being, consisting of body and soul, first been shaped for himself and then the Logos hypostasis attached to him (209,1–18). It was no human being with his own hypostasis who was united to the God-Logos; rather, Christ is from two natures and in two natures, which he has perfectly (209,21–24). Hence, we find here both formulas 'from two' and 'in two' side by side with equal right.

Thereupon Eulogius explains that the nature of a human being designates a whole composed of body and soul and represents an example of a species. One *physis* becomes a hypostasis through the *idiomata* that distinguish it from another individual of its species (*eidos*)

---

53. Thus part 3, 'Das Inkarnationsschema', in S. Helmer, *Der Neuchalkedonismus*, pp. 240–41, is based on evidence in the *DP* that does not come from Eulogius (nn. 710, 712–16, in part n. 718). Also in C. Moeller, 'Le chalcédonisme et le néo-chalcédonisme', in *Chalkedon* I, 691–93, p. 692 is cancelled down to the last four lines as a presentation of the theology of Eulogius, since the references are to texts of John the Grammarian. Only a reference in n. 157 remains valid; those references in nn. 151–159 are all to unauthentic texts; cf. CPG 6972 and 6979. Likewise p. 698, n. 9. Only the statements about the use of the anthropological argument (p. 692) and about Christ's ignorance (pp. 693, 712) are based on authentic Eulogius texts.

54. *DP*, p. 153,16–22, no. 4: 'You teach one incarnate nature of the God-Logos in the same manner. But if you want us therefore to think that God and the flesh are one being, how can the created be like the uncreated and the eternal like what is subjected to time? But if he as one has one other nature or is of one other, what makes one and one be not two but one?'

55. M. Richard, CCG 1, p. XXI, points out that this fragment cannot come from John of Caesarea.

(209,29–210,4). In the incarnation the Logos hypostasis has united to himself a human nature, without thereby assuming another hypostasis – a process that is without comparison (210,4–7). The 'miaphysites', however, understand by nature the independent hypostasis and must therefore actually confess a nature union from three.

The second fragment from these *Synegoriai* is attested several times: in addition to being handed down in PG 86, according to Richard we can even give the passage in Photius, where it is repeated in summary fashion.[56] The extant text is the answer to the reproach of the 'miaphysites', who use the body–soul analogy as support for the assertion of the 'one nature':

> [According to Photius] Just as one says that a human being is composed of two natures, since he has one [single] nature after the union, why does one not confess one nature in Christ if one says that he is from two natures? We know that the composite is one single nature, and we know in an analytical way the two natures that have come together.

The comparison of texts in the *DP* and in Photius undertaken by Richard shows clearly that Photius offers a shorter and somewhat modified text vis-à-vis the *DP*.[57] What tendencies can be detected here?

Both begin with the idea that in a *compositum* one can speak of 'one nature' when the name of a single component is not sufficient to designate the whole. The text in the *DP* illustrates this with three examples: of a house of wood and stone one does not say simply 'wood' or 'stone'; a body consisting of the four elements cannot be called by the name of one of these elements (fire, water, earth, air). The third example in the *DP*, the only one that Photius also gives, is that of man out of body and soul: although composed of body and soul, he is still not body or soul and cannot be designated by one of the two (except in an imprecise manner of speaking). Now, according to Photius there is no more fitting paradigm than this for the inexpressible union in Christ. Diametrically opposite is the statement of the author of the *DP* text: on the whole earth no example can be found! Now, whereas the point of the author of the *DP* text is that one cannot simply assert 'one nature' of Christ, the argumentation in Photius moves towards the expression 'union according to the hypostasis' in Christ, a term that never appears in any of the texts that are indisputably attributed to Eulogius.

After a brief transition in Photius there are two quotations from Cyril (from the first letter to Succensus and from the letter to Valerian of Iconium), from which he concludes: 'What does this mean except that the same one is at the same time God and man?' (Henry V, p. 30,8–9). The *DP* text contains the same references, yet they are impressively interpreted as proof of the two natures in Christ: 'What does this mean except that Christ is two natures?' (*DP*, p. 212,27–28). These differences in the structure of the argumentation are underscored by the choice of words. Photius uses the word *physis* quite sparingly (only in two places), but in the *DP* text it is frequent (ten times!). The 'two natures' occur in Photius only in connection with the 'hypostatic union'; in the *DP*, they appear many times.

The formula 'from two' is the only formula in this fragment of the *DP*; Christ *is* two natures; the phrase 'in two natures' is not used.

---

56. PG 86, 2956C–2957B; Photius, *Bibl. cod.* 230: Henry V, pp. 29,22–30,9. M. Richard, CCG 1, pp. XIX–XXI gives an exact comparison of the two texts!

57. In particular the lines Henry V, p. 29,38–41, which deal with union according to the hypostasis and the anthropological paradigm, bear their own imprint, which is found only in Photius.

The answer to the question posed at the beginning reads in the *DP*: Christ is two natures and not a *compositum* about which one can simply assert one (single) nature (212,12). He is from two unseparated natures (212,12–16). The body–soul model is fundamentally disavowed, here not because of ontological considerations but for linguistic and logical reasons. The clearly formulated two-natures terminology in the text of the *DP* is lost in Photius.[58] He is concerned with the phrase 'union according to the hypostasis'[59] and the high estimation of the body–soul analogy.

The fragments of scripture interpretation are very brief. Only the fragment on Jn 21,16 touches somewhat on the Agnoete issue:

> 'When the Lord asked Peter . . . the one who knows everything did not want to learn something through questions; rather, the one to whom he then trusted the flock was supposed to show how great his concern was for the flock.' Therefore he asked him three times, so that he might show his great solicitude (ἐπιμέλεια) for the sheep.[60]

Thus the passage is interpreted in the spirit of the *oikonomia*: for Peter's salvation he is asked by the Lord, who because of his omniscience would not have had to ask him at all. Here, however, it is a question of an encounter with the risen Christ.

One the whole, Eulogius proves himself an energetic defender of the 'two natures' against the mere *mia physis*; the formula 'from two' stands on a par with 'in two' or is even used exclusively. He affirms the *mia-physis* formula to the extent that he finds the two natures expressed in it. He stresses that the humanity of Christ did not exist in itself before the union and rejects the body–soul analogy as an explanation for the union in Christ.

An evaluation of the writings of Eulogius that are preserved only by the summary in Photius seems to us nonetheless difficult. The differences we have observed in the one piece available to us for comparison (see above) warn us to be very cautious; yet on the other hand the comparative material is not extensive enough for us to be able to draw conclusions that are to some degree certain. It is only possible here to sketch the picture that Photius draws of Eulogius's theology.

The *sesarkomene* in the *mia-physis* formula designates for Eulogius the assumed second nature (V, 9,36–37). After the incarnation the one nature of the Logos no longer reveals itself alone but with the flesh, and both remain preserved without change (V, 9,3–7).

---

58. M. Richard, CCG 1, p. XXI notes that Photius is interested in the dialectic and the patristic arguments of Eulogius but not in his theological conclusions.

59. Cf. here M. Richard, CCG 1, p. XXII with n. 57.

60. Eulogius Al., *Fragmentum in Ioh. 21,16* (CPG 6975): PG 86, 2961BC.

Mia-physis formula, 'piously spoken',[61] and two-natures formula (which means here 'two natures unmixed in hypostatic union') are compatible with each other (V, 10,10–15); indeed, they are practically equivalent (V, 10,27–29, διαφορὰν οὐδεμίαν). This position in the answer to the objections of the pope against his synodical letter is carried further in the 'Apologia for Chalcedon'. There we find explicit neo-Chalcedonianism, at least in the presentation in Photius. Each of the two formulas by itself alone is incomplete, insofar as with subtle interpretation it justly draws condemnation.

For Eulogius the *mia-physis* formula was above all a specification of the union (V, 19,44–2); taken by itself it is inadequate (cf. V, 12,41–4). In order to protect it from misinterpretations one must add: 'animated with a rational and intelligent soul' and that what has come together does not mix.[62] But even to speak of 'two unseparated natures' is not enough. In order to prevent a misuse à la Nestorius we must add either:

- bound in hypostatic union, or
- the *mia-physis* formula, or
- the same one is God and man.

Otherwise the formula remains misunderstandable.[63]

On the whole, we find repeatedly as the essential formula for Eulogius (according to Photius!): two unseparated natures in hypostatic union.[64]

Cyril is untouched as the great model, and this is underscored by the wealth of titles – always in the presentation according to Photius! – such as protector, model, teacher of precision, the ardent lover of precision and truth.[65]

As head of the body, Christ has accepted everything that affects us: sin, curse, lack of knowledge, *as if* (ὡς) it belonged to him (V, 11,13–22).

Thus we can make the following observation. The strong emphasis on the *mia-physis* formula and its equivalence with the (correspondingly expanded) statement about the two natures, that is, the very clearly marked theology of mediation, is found only in the works of Eulogius

---

61. An addition that is often found: V, 10,11 (εὐσεβεῖν); 14,17 (εὐσεβῶς); cf. V, 48,43; 50,12.
62. More exactly: συνεπιθεωροῦντα τὸ ἀσύγχυτον; V, 39,21–28.
63. V, 39,31–38; cf. 22,40ff.
64. V, 14,7.13–14; 19,1–2. It is attested by Cyril; cf. V, 17–19. It was confessed by Chalcedon: V, 27,24–26.
65. In *DP*, p. 212, Cyril is only called the one 'among saints', but Photius offers a multitude of honorary titles: θεσπέσιος: IV, 109,40; 110,30; ἁγιώτατος: 110,27; μακάριος: V, 11,26; 49,32; 59,2; θεῖος: 12,15; 26,16; μέγας: 13,22; ἱερός: 13,1; 23,27; 34,13; 37,7; ὁ φύλαξ τῆς ἀκριβείας: 14,19; ὁ θερμὸς τῆς ἀκριβείας ἐραστής: 14,31; ὁ τῆς ἀληθείας θερμὸς ἐραστής: 16,22–23; σοφός: 21,10; 24,41; 24,14; 30,25; ἀδίστακτος τῆς εὐσέβειαν: 24,14–15; ὁ θαυμάσιος: 34,22; γνώμων τῆς ἀκριβείας: 35,30–31; ὁ διαιτᾶν σοφός: 36,36; τῆς ἀκριβείας διδάσκαλος: 38,43; τὰ θεῖα σοφός: 39,25–26.

summarized by Photius, even if the rudiments are not to be denied.[66] Even the respectful mention of Cyril is not found thus in the fragments preserved in the *DP*, although Cyril clearly appears there as an (or the) authority.

II. THE ANTI-CHALCEDONIAN HIERARCHY: THE COPTS

1. The Coptic hierarchy after 575

After a (chaotic) vacancy of a good nine years[67] after the death of Theodosius without a recognized patriarch, the effort to elect an anti-Chalcedonian patriarch of Alexandria led to a schism in Egypt. Between 23 June and 25 August 575 Longinus, the bishop of the Nobatae, together with two other bishops, John of Chalcis and George Urtāyā, consecrated as patriarch the Syrian Theodore, the Archimandrite of one of the monasteries in the Scetis.[68] Paul of Antioch agreed though he was not present.[69] Naturally, the consecration did not take place without the agreement of Alexandria,[70] but some of the Alexandrian clergy felt left out and, vexed on that account, six weeks later elected their own patriarch, Peter IV, a former deacon of Patriarch Theodosius.[71]

Peter, who reigned only two years, tried to use his power to build up the Monophysite episcopacy (he consecrated seventy bishops) and consolidate the throne. He banned Paul of Antioch. Jacob Baradai, who first called him a 'new Gaianus', was finally won over to him and recognized Peter as legitimate.

---

66. For example, the use of 'in two natures' and 'from two natures' side by side (*DP*, p. 209,21–24), or 'we say from two natures' (*DP*, p. 212,13).

67. John Eph., *HE* IV, 12: Brooks, CSCO 103, p. 146,17–18. The Coptic *History of the Patriarchs* (PO 1, p. 470) has Peter IV immediately following Theodosius; cf. J. Maspero, *Histoire*, pp. 212–33, who offers an attempted reconstruction of this period ('anarchie monophysite') of 566–575.

68. A list of documents connected with the consecration of Theodore is found in P. Allen, 'Overview of the Documenta Monophysitica', in A. Van Roey and P. Allen, *Monophysite Texts of the Sixth Century* (OLA 56), Louvain 1994, pp. 267–303. Cf. the presentation in E. Honigmann, *Évêques et Évêchés*, pp. 200–202, 226–27; J. Maspero, *Histoire*, pp. 236–37. Also John Eph., *HE* IV 9–11: Brooks, CSCO 103, pp. 140–45.

69. On Paul of Antioch cf. E. W. Brooks, 'The Patriarch Paul of Antioch and the Alexandrine Schism of 575', *ByzZ* 30 (1929), 468–76.

70. Longinus was written to by the Alexandrian presbyter Theodosius (CPG 7223) and by a deacon, Theodore Copris (CPG 7225). Theodore of Philae asked Longinus to consecrate a bishop (CPG 7227) but retracted this later. John of the Kellia did not want to participate in the consecration because he had quarrelled with Joseph of Metellis (according to Theodore Copris), but he showed his agreement with Longinus in a letter to him after the consecration.

71. Cf. the presentation in J. Maspero, *Histoire*, pp. 238–40, with evaluation, pp. 242–46; E. Honigmann, op. cit., pp. 227, 229.

Theodore, who lived until 587 and continued his monastic life, exerted little offensive effort towards the recognition of his patriarchate and had few followers in Egypt, for he was considered the favourite of Paul of Antioch.

From the synodical letter of Peter IV to Jacob Baradai we have only a short fragment that expresses joy and satisfaction over Jacob's rejection of Paul.[72] By contrast, the synodical writing of Theodore (575) to Paul of Antioch is extant and exhibits remarkable parallels to the synodical letter of his later rival Damian (578), but especially to that of Theodosius (535), whom both considered a model. A synodical writing[73] of the anti-Chalcedonians apparently includes certain elements:

(1) introduction with description of the special situation of the consecration,
(2) confession to the three councils of Nicaea, Constantinople and Ephesus (perhaps also the twelve anathemas of Cyril and Zeno's *Henoticon* understood as condemnation of Chalcedon),
(3) beginning with a symbol, development first of the theology of the Trinity and then of Christology,
(4) a catalogue of heretics,
(5) closing.

In view of the threat of tritheism, in Theodore and Damian the part on trinitarian theology is about as broadly developed as the christological part; in Theodosius, however, there is (still!) no explicit declaration of trinitarian theology. Yet both Theodore and Damian refer to him or to his tractate as a basis against the tritheists.[74] The targeted opponent is John Grammaticus (= Philoponus) with his tractate on the Trinity, with

---

72. Peter Al., *Epistula synodica ad Iacobum Baradaeum* (CPG 7238): Chabot, *Documenta ad origines monophysitarum*, CSCO 17 (T); 103 (V) (Louvain 1908; 1933), p. 161,5–11.

73. Theodos. Al., *Ep. syn. ad Severum* (CPG 7134): Chabot, CSCO 103, pp. 1–5; Theodor. Al., *Ep. syn. ad Paul. Ant.* (CPG 7236): CSCO 103, pp. 208–15; Damian Al., *Ep. syn. ad Iacob. Baradaeum* (CPG 7240): Mich. Syr., *Chron.* X 14, Chabot II, 325–34.

74. Theodore Al., CSCO 103, p. 211,17–22: *amplectimur tractatum compositum ab eo qui cum sanctis est, patre nostro Theodosio, adversus eos qui dividunt unam sublimem deitatem et excogitant substantias et naturas, quod idem est ac dicere deos et deitates, et adversus eos qui balbutiant totam Trinitatem sanctam incorporatam esse per unam e suis personis.* Damian Al., op. cit., p. 333: 'Si quelques-uns détournent . . . les expressions des Pères . . . et s'efforcent d'en déduire . . . des divinités, ou la pluralité d'essences ou de natures, pour nous, nous suivons Theodosius qui a travaillé apostoliquement, comme pas un autre, et qui connut le sentiment des Pères, et nous nous refusons à admettre un nombre quelconque de natures ou d'essences, de dieux ou de divinités.'

detailed quotations in Damian, which now offer valuable fragments of the lost work.[75]

Similar to Theodosius, Theodore begins the christological part with echoes of the *Nicaeno-Constantinopolitanum*, and he inserts here already the formula 'unus e trinitate' that Theodosius uses only later.[76] Theodore especially stresses the soteriological aspect of the incarnation.[77] Whereas the hypostatic union is the centre of interest for Theodosius, Theodore especially emphasizes the 'like us without sin'. Both adduce the same scripture references,[78] but Theodore explains in more detail than Theodosius Jesus' participation in blameless human suffering (with reference to Jn 19,30 and the servant song of Is 53,4–5) in an appealing Christology. In the name *Emmanuel* in particular, the whole mystery becomes clear: 'our God with us', and thus Theodore can successfully summarize:[79]

> ... who is like us and at the same time over us, since he is one from two, divinity and humanity, which are perfect in their respects, consubstantial with the Father in the divinity and the same one consubstantial with us in the humanity, who is not divided into those of which he consists and not separated into the duality of natures or mixed through any kind of transformation or metamorphosis of natures; rather, after he was hypostatically united to an animated body, he was born as man from woman, and without having abandoned his nature, he became like us, but the same one is God and man, that is, God has become man ...

The front against Julian of Halicarnassus becomes clear in both authors in the detailed emphasis on the passibility and the mortality of Jesus before the resurrection, yet Theodore, in contrast to Theodosius, expressly calls the opponent by name.[80] For Theodore, too, the Julianists or Gaianites are still a very significant group! The body–soul analogy, which Theodosius often uses against those who 'divide the one Christ into two

---

75. Theodore Al., CSCO 103, p. 212,4–9 (Iohannem, ματαιοπόνον Grammaticum . . . et librum ab eo conscriptum, quem appellavit Theologiam [Sermo de divinis]). Damian Al., op. cit., p. 330a (Grammaticus); p. 331a (Tractate on the Trinity). Cf. below on John Philoponus!

76. Theodos. Al., CSCO 103, p. 4,20.

77. Theodore Al., CSCO 103, p. 212,21–31: '. . . for our salvation became human . . . for our sake; . . . to save us from the weakness and misery that were added to our nature through Adam's trespass, the Logos became human.'

78. 1 Pt 2,22; Heb 2,14–15; Theodore already draws Heb 2,16–17 to Heb 2,14–15.

79. Theodore Al., CSCO 103, pp. 213,33–214,6.

80. Julian is directly addressed (and rejected) on p. 213,27–28 and in detail on p. 214,13–17: *Iulianum halicarnassensem, qui blateravit ab ipsa unione cum Verbo Deo impassibile et immortale fuisse corpus quod ex nobis assumpsit et sibi univit hypostatice, et qui introduxit phantasiam et fictionem in mysterium incarnationis verae et immutabilis.* Cf. also p. 213,9–10: *in corpore passibili in similitudinem nostram et passionis capace*; p. 213,19–21: *toto enim tempore oeconomiae reliquit illud passibile et mortale: ut mors . . . non in fictione sit, sed vera et non in phantasia appareat.*

natures', is not adduced by Theodore – perhaps also because the rejection of the two-natures doctrine has already become formulaic for him.

Theodore adopts literally from Theodosius, however, the long catalogue of heretics,[81] including the condemnation of Chalcedon and the *Tome* of Leo. But he expands the *mia-persona* formula of Theodosius to a confession of *mia physis* and *mia energeia!*[82] The recognition of Zeno's *Henoticon* 'in destruction of the forenamed Chalcedonian synod and *Tome* of Leo'[83] is mentioned by Theodore only at this point, not like Theodosius already at the beginning after the confession to the three councils and the twelve anathemas of Cyril, the latter appearing in Theodore only implicitly in the condemnation of those who have written against them. The last heresy that is described is that of the Agnoetes. Thus, in Theodore's view the chief enemies of orthodoxy are tritheists, Gaianites and Agnoetes. Finally, Theodore stresses with two quotations from the letters of Severus how important it is to preserve the tradition of the Fathers unabridged.[84]

Since Theodore did not fight for the recognition of his patriarchal dignity, the schism had little effect in Egypt itself, but it perhaps increased tensions with Syria. In 576 came negotiations with Jacob Baradai, and as a consequence recognition of Peter of Alexandria and deposition of Paul of Antioch. Yet there was no real union with Syria, and indeed would not be until 616.[85]

---

81. Theodore Al., CSCO 103, p. 214,9–24: 'Valentinus, Marcion, Mani, Arius, Macedonius, Eunomius, Apollinarius, Eutyches, Julian of Halicarnassus . . ., Paul of Samosata, Diodore, Theodore, Nestorius, Theodoret, Andrew, Ibas, Eutherius, Alexander of Hierapolis, Irenaeus Bigamus, Cyrus, John of Aegea and all who dared to speak against the twelve chapters of our father Cyril and the Persian Barsauma with his shameful Canones.' The only difference is that Julian of Halicarnassus is called by name, while Theodosius speaks only of 'those who . . .'

82. E. Honigmann, *Évêques et Évêchés*, p. 201, n. 1, points out that the two synodical letters (of Theodore and Paul) are quoted at the Sixth Ecumenical Council of Constantinople (680/681): Mansi XI, p. 448DE (Theodore); p. 449AB (Paul). Probably because of this confession to '*mia energeia*' (p. 214,29: 'unam operationem') in Christ, the council adopted into its acts the whole final section on the condemnation of Chalcedon. Also the rejection of the two natures is somewhat broadened. Theodore adds: 'those who define him "in two natures"' (cf. the similar formulation in Damian, Chabot II, p. 328b).

83. Theodore Al., CSCO 103, p. 214,31–32: 'in destructionem praedictae synodi chalcedonensis et Tomi Leonis'.

84. Idem, CSCO 103, p. 215,5–14; he quotes from Severus Ant., Brooks, *SL* II, p. 349 (V. 14) and p. 109 (I. 38).

85. John Eph., *HE* IV 12: Brooks, CSCO 106, pp. 145–47, ascribes the separation of the churches of Alexandria and Antioch to Peter IV. J. Maspero, *Histoire*, p. 239: 'The pacification of the Jacobite churches was delayed forty-five years.'

2. Damian, head of the 'Monophysite' world

Damian,[86] who for a long time was the Coptic patriarch of Alexandria (578–607), was by origin not from Egypt but from Syria,[87] presumably from Osrhoene, since his brother was prefect in Edessa.[88] He soon moved to Egypt into the desert and to Scetis, entered the monastery of St John the Small, where he was ordained deacon and remained sixteen or seventeen years.[89] From there he went into the monastery 'of the Fathers' (also called Enaton monastery, since it lay nine miles west of Alexandria), where Peter IV made him his secretary in 575.[90] One year after the death of Peter (577) Damian was elected his successor (578).

The synodical letter with which Damian introduced himself to Jacob Baradai after his ordination as patriarch[91] exhibits the same basic structural traits as the writing of Theodore (as whose opposite he was consecrated in succeeding Peter IV). Yet even in the introduction Damian shows the verbose, picturesque language that we find in his letters to Peter of Callinicum and that also reveals in its humble designations the self-consciousness of one who knows that he is called 'to the throne of this primatial chair of the theologian Mark, the blessed apostle'.[92]

Like Theodore, Damian begins the christological part with the soteriological idea, which he develops thus: out of merciful love for human beings, who had lost the likeness of God and immortality, and in order to make them participants in heaven, the 'one out of the Trinity' became man. If Theodore stressed the full humanity of Christ (against Julian), Damian first gave strong emphasis to the unity with the Father ('whose womb he did not leave'[93]). The two births (from the Father above, from the Virgin Mary in the flesh) have the same subject: 'Thus was God born.' Whence also the significance of the *theotokos* title, which Damian

---

86. A detailed presentation of his life and work is offered by J. Maspero, *Histoire*, pp. 278–317; from the Coptic viewpoint: C. D. G. Müller, 'Damian, Papst und Patriarch von Alexandrien', *OrChr* 70 (1986), 118–42. Cf. also S. Vailhé, art. 'Damien', *DTC* 4a, pp. 39–40. On the writings of Damian: CPG 7240–45.

87. John Eph., *HE* I 40: CSCO 106, p. 35; Michael Syr., *Chron.* X 13: Chabot, p. 325.

88. Michael Syr., *Chron.* X 17: Chabot, p. 344; J. Maspero, *Histoire*, p. 278.

89. *Hist. Patr.*: PO 1, 473; J. Maspero, *Histoire*, p. 279.

90. Cf. *Hist. Patr.* I 14: PO 1, p. 471; Synaxaire arabe jacobite (17th of Baounah): PO 17, pp. 575–76.

91. Damian Al., *Epistula synodica ad Iacobum Baradaeum* (CPG 7240): Mich. Syr., *Chron.* X 14, Chabot II (325–34), 325b–32b.

92. Damian Al., op. cit., p. 327a: '. . . le trône de ce siège primatial du théologien Marcus, le bienheureux apôtre. Considérant la sublimité du trône de l'Évangéliste et méditant la grandeur de la fonction du souverain pontificat . . .'

93. Damian Al., op. cit., p. 326b.

expressly emphasizes just like the *virginitas Mariae ante et post partum.*
Immediately following are the *mia-physis* formula – which he especially
stresses later, just like the ἐκ δύο – and the confession to *mia energeia.*

> We proclaim not two Christs nor two sons nor two natures nor two activities (*opérations*)
> but one single Son and one single nature of the incarnate Word, one single hypostasis, one
> single person, one single activity.[94]

The incarnation is presented by Damian in detail:

> He was not transformed into the nature of flesh but remained what he was and assumed
> what he did not have; . . . one single [nature] formed from two, perfect in itself, that is, he
> is composed out of divinity, which was before the worlds and brought everything into
> existence out of nothing, and out of humanity, which was formed by the Logos itself and
> was assumed by him from the first moment.[95]

In Damian the polemic flared up again against the two-natures doctrine,
against Chalcedon and against the *Tome* of Leo, which in Theodore
appeared more as an exercise in duty. The 'out of two' and the *mia-physis*
formula are stressed again, yet without new arguments. Thus in the
condemnation of heresies Damian begins with the anathema over Chalcedon, which in his rival comes only at the end. He offers no list of
heretics but goes into the individual heresies by groups (against those
who destroy the unity, against the 'Phantasiasts'). He also clearly points
out the capacity of Jesus to suffer and (against Julian without expressly
naming him) the *corruptibilitas* of Jesus' flesh before the resurrection,[96] as
well as emphasizing the voluntariness with which Jesus accepted suffering. At the end he turns against the Agnoetes: whoever asserts Christ's
ignorance fails to appreciate that through the union the flesh of Christ
was enriched by the divinity – an argument that follows Theodosius![97]
Thus the front against Chalcedon, Leo's *Tome* and Julian of Halicarnassus, against the tritheists and the Agnoetes, can be seen as Damian's main

94. Ibid., p. 327b.

95. Ibid., with reference to Ps.-Athan., *Ad imp. Iovianum* (CPG 2253): PG 28, 532, a text
that the *DP* (p. 133 IV) also knows and which represents an anti-Chalcedonian reworking of
Dial. IV (CPG 2284) (from Ps.-Athanasian dialogues). Cf. C. Bizer, 'Studien zu pseud-
athanasianischen Dialogen', diss. Bonn 1970, esp. pp. 299–305.

96. Damian Al., op. cit., pp. 330b–31b. The passage p. 330b: '. . . il s'est uni notre chair
débile, sans le peché et en dehors de la corruption' – if the text is correctly reported – cannot,
in any case, be understood in Julian's sense, for soon thereafter Damian specifically explains
(p. 331b): 'The flesh in which the God-Logos became human for us was before the
resurrection passible, mortal, subject to corruption, to blameless passions . . . But after the
resurrection he became . . . incorruptible . . .'

97. Chabot II, p. 331b: 'If after these words one imputes or ascribes ignorance to him in
whom the sources of knowledge and wisdom originate, he despises this knowledge and does
not consider that the ensouled and rational flesh of our Lord was enriched by the union with
the divine glory and with every activity (*opération*) that befits the divinity.' Cf. on Theodosius:
A. Grillmeier, *CCT* II/2, p. 372.

concern – also in the fragment from the letter of consolation on the occasion of the death of Jacob Baradai in the same year 578.[98]

Damian succeeded in assuming the legacy of Theodosius: he became the head of the Jacobite East.[99] Yet although he himself was a Syrian by birth, he achieved no unification with the Syrian Jacobite church; indeed, his quarrel with the patriarch of Antioch, Peter of Callinicum, resulted in a schism that lasted until 616, almost ten years after his death.

Damian was doubtless a very strong personality, full of courage and energy, even if his selection of means to achieve his goals was such that doubt could at least be cast upon his integrity.[100]

In 579 he travelled to Syria under the pretext of wanting to visit his brother, who was prefect in Edessa. But then he declared that he had come out of 'sollicitude ecclésiastique'.[101] Secretly he made his way to Antioch to install a Syrian patriarch and thus carry out the deposition of Paul of Antioch pronounced by Damian's predecessor Peter IV. This attempt failed in an adventurous way.[102] From Antioch Damian fled to Constantinople, where he consecrated some bishops and participated in a uniting council under the Ghassanid prince Mundhir.[103] After his return to Alexandria he nevertheless revoked his assent of Constantinople (under the pressure of his followers?) and sent circulars against Paul of Antioch to Syria and Arabia, about which even Mundhir could no longer do anything.[104]

In 581 Peter of Callinicum was elected the Jacobite patriarch of Antioch,[105] with the agreement of the Alexandrians,[106] and that still during the

---

98. Damian Al., *Ep. consolatoria* (CPG 7241): Mich. Syr., *Chron.* X 16: Chabot, pp. 339–42.

99. Cf. J. Maspero, *Histoire*, p. 281.

100. J. Maspero, *Histoire*, p. 282: 'Il retrouvait sa supériorité dans la politique secrète d'intrigue, qu'il préférait de beaucoup.' There are many examples of his cunning and disloyal politics.

101. Michael Syr., *Chron.* X 22: Chabot II, p. 366b.

102. The story is described by John Eph. in *HE* IV 41. Damian's invitation was not followed at first by all Syrian bishops, since some said that Paul had not been canonically condemned and deposed. The rest came together, and after they had proposed this candidate and that in vain, they finally elected Severus. Damian wanted to consecrate him with two bishops secretly in Antioch itself in the Cassian church. The Chalcedonian patriarch, however, learned what was planned and had the house where they were staying surrounded and stormed. Damian, the two bishops and Severus could only escape through the house's latrine and the city's sewer system (*cloacae*).

103. John Eph., *HE* IV, 40–41: Brooks, CSCO 106, pp. 165–68; Michael Syr., *Chron.* X 17: Chabot II, p. 345; J. Maspero, *Histoire*, p. 302. The council began on 2 March 580; W. H. C. Frend, *The Rise of the Monophysite Movement*, Cambridge 1972, p. 328.

104. Cf. John Eph., *HE* IV 43: Brooks, CSCO 106, pp. 169–71.

105. John Eph., *HE* IV 45: Brooks, pp. 171–72. Michael Syr., *Chron.* X 17: Chabot II, pp. 345–46.

106. Michael Syr., *Chron.* X 21: Chabot, p. 361. The report of John Eph., *HE* IV 45, that Peter was ordained in Alexandria (and thus by Damian! – which J. Maspero, *Histoire*, p. 304, also assumes) is with good reason doubted by R. Y. Ebied, A. Van Roey and L. R. Wickham, *Peter of Callinicum* (OLA 10), Louvain 1981, pp. 4–5.

lifetime of Paul of Antioch, who did not die until 584, abandoned and alone, near Constantinople.

The friendly relationship between the two patriarchs Damian and Peter[107] was severely disturbed and finally changed into open animosity when Damian sent a paper written by him against tritheism to Peter (c. 586) and Peter ventured a critique of it, even if a very polite and carefully formulated one.[108]

Damian's paper – perhaps the tractate (CPG 7245) – is not extant and can only be deduced from the quotations in Peter of Callinicum, *Contra Damianum* (CPG 7252). This work by Peter, however, has not yet been edited.[109]

In the quarrel, in the course of which Damian was accused of Sabellianism and Peter of tritheism, there was never a reconciliation during the lifetimes of the two opponents. Rather, the two parties even fought each other still later.[110]

An impression of the manifold attempts of Peter of Callinicum to have discussions with Damian is conveyed by the presentation in Michael the Syrian as well as in the letter given there (in excerpts) of Peter to the Syrians living in Alexandria.[111] At first three meetings with Damian fell through because agreement was not possible on either the participants or the place of a synod. When Peter followed Damian to Egypt, the latter avoided a meeting by travelling from monastery to monastery. Finally Peter wrote his work *Contra Damianum* in three volumes.

Damian had asserted that the characteristic properties of the hypostases (unbegottenness, begottenness, *processio*) of the holy Trinity are the hypostases themselves.[112] He said, further, that the general *ousia* of the holy Trinity (which is different from the hypostases) is truly God; the

---

107. Testimonies of this are the letters of Damian to Peter (CPG 7242–44), which at the time exuberantly praised Peter. Damian in *Ep. I* of 581 (CPG 7242) approves Peter's synodical letter with the words: 'as though I had found an *alter ego* for succour' (Ebied, Van Roey and Wickham, OLA 10, p. 55,1–2). His *Ep. II* (CPG 7243) of 582 reads: '. . . the confession of the faith as put forward to the men by you . . . is exact, finely polished, without deficiency, as it were hedged round with fences and secured everywhere by the walls of truth. For how should anything be indited amiss or fall short of perfection, when once you had taken the business in hand, you trusty, prudent and priestly steward of God's mysteries?' (ibid., p. 57,12–19).

108. This quarrel is presented in detail in Ebied, Van Roey and Wickham, OLA 10, pp. 34–43.

109. Cf. Ebied, Van Roey and Wickham, OLA 10, pp. 12–14, as well as the detailed chapter headings in Appendix II, pp. 104–21. Part I has now been edited by Ebied, Van Boey and Wickham: CCG 29 (Louvain 1994).

110. Cf. the presentation in Timothy Const., *De iis qui ad eccl. accedunt* (CPG 7016), 8–9: PG 86, 60: the Angelites or Damianites were called by their opponents Sabellianists or Tetradites. The Petrites on the other hand were vilified by their opponents as tritheists.

111. Michael Syr., *Chron.* X 22: Chabot II, pp. 364–71; the letter: pp. 367a–71. Michael Syr. depends on the report of Dionys. of Tell Maḥrē, which is not extant.

112. Peter Call. deals with this concept in his whole work *Contra Damianum*; cf. OLA 10 (1981), pp. 104–21, esp. chap. II 6; III 1, 5, 8, 17, 22, etc.

three hypostases (or persons), on the other hand, he recognized as God only in a metaphorical sense and through participation.[113]

Damian's position can be lifted from the detailed headings of Peter's tractate *Contra Damianum*. We will only sketch it briefly. Peter repeatedly discusses the view that the characteristic properties of the hypostases (or of the *ousia*) are the hypostases themselves (or the *ousia* itself). As evidence Damian adduces passages from Fathers (III 5, 14) such as Severus (III 7, 8, 10), Amphilochius, Damasus and John of Jerusalem (III 16), as well as Basil (III 17) and Cyril (III 29, 30). Peter quotes some of Damian's sentences word for word:[114] 'The persons of the divinity do not mean the divinity' (III 40). 'It is polytheistic to recognize each person of the holy Trinity as God' (III 37). 'The hypostases and the divine *ousia* are in concept different things' (III 46). The hypostases of the Trinity appear as a metaphorical concept (III 36) without real existence (cf. II 21). Damian calls the hypostases Father, Son and Spirit as names and titles (II 18) and seems to accept them only 'en theoria' (II 7).

We can find these positions already laid down in the synodical letter to Jacob Baradai (578), for example, when he writes: 'Each person [of the holy Trinity] exists precisely in its property without being mixed or mingled with another . . . The three persons of Father, Son and Holy Spirit subsist without mixture or separation in their properties.'[115] Also the temporal independence and unseparatedness, which he later adduces as characteristic of a hypostasis (III 28), is especially emphasized here. It is also noteworthy already in the synodical letter how the single *ousia* of the Trinity is placed unconnected beside the persons and properties: 'It admits the number in the persons but in a single and same *ousia*, which is the divinity, it subsists apart from any number.'[116]

The battle against heretics and heresies kept Damian busy in many ways, and the one against tritheism, out of which he formed his trinitarian doctrine, probably made the most intensive demands on him.

Already in his synodical letter of 578 he documented his study of the writings of John Philoponus through six fragments (four from the latter's *De trinitate* and two others from an undetermined work of the Grammarian).[117] After having broadly rendered these, he then appealed to the patristic authorities Basil, Athanasius and Severus; he also esteemed Gregory of Nazianzus highly. In particular, however, he stood behind the views of Theodosius. His own position is substantiated primarily by referring to the unity of the *ousia*, since it is the indivisible divinity. It is not contradicted by the distinction of persons or hypostases.[118]

Besides the opposition to Julian of Halicarnassus (and with it against the Gaianites), against the Agnoetes and especially against Paul of Beth Ukame, there was interaction with other groups. This was symptomatic

---

113. Cf. *Contra Damianum*, III 36, 37, 40. In view of the obvious deficiencies in the doctrine of the Trinity that Damian apparently advocated, it still seems like minimizing too much when C. D. G. Müller, art. cit., p. 132, characterizes Peter's resistance to this conception as unmerciful and uncompromising, 'relentless' (*unerbittlich*).

114. Peter complains about Damian's unclear mode of expression and his contradictory statements in III 32; cf. III 7.

115. Mich. Syr., *Chron.* X 14: Chabot II, p. 329.

116. Ibid.

117. A. Van Roey, 'Les fragments trithéites de Jean Philopon', *OLP* 11 (1980), 135–36.

118. Damian Al., *Ep. synodica*: Mich. Syr., X 14, Chabot II, pp. 325–34, the fragments: pp. 330–32, the patristic quotations and his own position: pp. 333–34.

of the splintering of the anti-Chalcedonians at the end of the sixth century.

It is possible that Damian even succeeded in temporarily winning the Gaianites, so that they accepted him as patriarch[119] – just as the tritheists apparently also accepted him as authority.[120] He intervened against the Meletians in the monasteries with such success that part of them withdrew while the remaining were banished.[121] The few remaining Acephali split up among themselves again: when one of the four priests in eastern Egypt, Barsanuphius, was elected bishop, the Acephali in the West felt left out and elected their own bishop.[122]

Damian also took effective action against the 'Stephenites': he proceeded against the teaching of the 'sophist' Stephen of Alexandria with many admonitions, and when these availed nothing, Damian condemned him.[123] Stephen σοφιστής, presumably a philosophy professor in Alexandria, represented the view:

> We cannot say that the distinction of the natural significance of those natures of which Christ is composed is preserved after the union.[124]

We do not know what conclusions Stephen drew from this sentence.[125] Two theologians from the following of Peter of Callinicum, Proba and the archimandrite John Barbour, of whom one (Proba) at first rejected Stephen in writing, finally became followers of Stephen.[126] Damian drove Proba out of Alexandria.[127]

---

119. Cf. the polemic of Eulogius against the temporary union of Theodosians and Gaianites (Contra Theodosianos et Gaianitas: Henry IV, pp. 111–14).

120. Cf. the Cononite group, who laid a summary of the tritheist confession (libellus, capitula) before Damian for his approval: John Eph., HE V 9, CSCO 106, p. 197,9 (libellum); Mich. Syr., Chabot II, p. 382 (capitula).

121. Hist. Patr.: PO 1, p. 473; further PO 17, p. 576.

122. Hist. Patr.: PO 1, pp. 474–75.

123. Dionys. Telmahr., HE Fragm.: Chabot, CSCO 88, p. 151,4–15. Cf. the presentation in Ebied, Van Roey and Wickham, op. cit., pp. 6–8.

124. Dionys. Telmahr., op. cit., p. 151,5–7. Cf. Mich. Syr., Chabot II, p. 361b: 'Il n'est pas possible que la distinction de la signification naturelle des [natures] dont le Christ est [composé] existe en dehors de la division des natures.'

125. J. Maspero, Histoire, p. 292, thinks that he possibly adopted the ideas from Julian.

126. Michael Syr., Chron. X 21: Chabot II, p. 362b, asserts that they hoped that for their zeal Peter would reward them with the office of bishop, but disappointed afterwards, they turned to Stephen and joined his sect.

127. In Antioch both were ultimately condemned by a synod in Gubba Barraya (584/585) after John Barbour also confessed openly to the teaching of Stephen. After that the two joined the Chalcedonian church of Antioch. We treat the figure of Proba, his writings and the discussions about him in vol. II/3.

Under the patriarchate of Damian there developed a school of Coptic writers,[128] whose most significant representative is perhaps John of Parallos, who excelled especially in the defence against heresy.[129] From Damian himself there are extant fragments of a Coptic sermon that he preached at the Christmas celebration in Alexandria.[130]

3. Benjamin, Coptic patriarch and leader under Persian, Byzantine and Islamic rule

Under the two peace-loving anti-Chalcedonian patriarchs Anastasius of Alexandria (607–619), Damian's successor, and Athanasius of Antioch (595–631) the very difficult task[131] of reconciling the two churches began and reached its conclusion in 616.[132] After six years with Andronicus in office (619–626)[133] Benjamin was elected patriarch and for almost forty years was to be the dominant personality, the 'Coptic key figure of the time'.[134] His patriarchate falls in the closing years of Persian occupation

---

128. Cf. T. Orlandi, art. 'Damiano di Alessandria', *DPAC* I, 886.

129. A. van Lantschoot, 'Fragments coptes d'une homélie de Jean de Parallos contre les livres hérétiques', in *Misc. G. Mercati* I, Vatican City 1946, pp. 296–326, offers the Coptic fragments of a homily of this bishop on the archangel Michael and against heretical writings, with introduction and French translation. Also C. D. G. Müller, 'Die alte koptische Predigt', diss. Heidelberg 1954, pp. 102–3, 150–56.

130. The text appears with English translation in W. E. Crum, *Theological Texts from Coptic Papyri* (= Anecdota Oxoniensia), Oxford 1913, 21–33. Cf. also C. D. G. Müller, 'Damian, Papst und Patriarch von Alexandrien', *OrChr* 70 (1986), 139 with n. 75. Damian preached the homily in the presence of the imperial ambassador Constantine; there had been an earthquake in Syria shortly before. Damian spoke of the unchanged divinity in Christ, praised Mary with chosen words and addressed himself against heretics, especially those who name three divinities and thus separate the Father from the Son and Holy Spirit. Thus the tritheists were still strong.

131. J. Maspero, *Histoire*, p. 329: 'la tâche . . . des plus ardues'.

132. Cf. J. Maspero, *Histoire*, pp. 318–42.

133. Andronicus, from a rich Alexandrian family, was apparently the first Jacobite patriarch who was able to live in Alexandria itself – probably because of his background – according to *Hist. Patr.*: PO 1, p. 484.

134. C. D. G. Müller, *Der Stand der Forschungen über Benjamin I., den 38. Patriarchen von Alexandrien* (*ZDMG* Supp. 1, 2), Wiesbaden 1969, 404–10, here p. 404. Also on Benjamin: A. van Lantschoot, art. 'Benjamin I', *DHGE* 7 (1934), 1341–42. Based on *Hist. Patr.*: PO 1, pp. 487–518, there is a biographical outline of Benjamin's life in C. D. G. Müller, 'Benjamin I. 38. Patriarch von Alexandrien', *Mus* 69 (1956) (313–40), 322–40; idem, 'Neues über Benjamin I, 38. und Agathon, 39. Patriarch von Alexandrien', *Mus* 72 (1959), 323–47; cf. also H. Brakmann, 'Zum Pariser Fragment angeblich des koptischen Patriarchen Agathon. Ein neues Blatt der Vita Benjamins I', *Mus* 93 (1980), 299–309. The fragment (Paris, copt. 129[14], f. 125) of a 'church consecration homily', which is ascribed by C. D. G. Müller to Benjamin's successor, Agathon, is credited by Brakmann, however, to the Sahidic 'life' of Benjamin, which is extant only in fragments. For the idea that Agathon is the author of this life, 'there is so far not the least bit of evidence' (ibid., 307).

(619–628/629) and the beginning of Arab rule over Egypt (starting in 639/642).[135]

In connection with the presentation of Benjamin, the Coptic history of patriarchs strikes a more intensely anti-Chalcedonian note: the Arab attack is interpreted as punishment because of Chalcedon.[136] In addition it expresses a connection between Egyptian self-consciousness and anti-Chalcedonianism: only the monastery of Metras is said to have resisted the efforts of Heraclius to adopt the faith of Chalcedon, and for this reason: 'For the inmates of it were exceedingly powerful, being Egyptians by race and all of them natives, without a stranger among them.'[137]

Benjamin was probably born around 590[138] in the western Delta as the child of well-to-do parents.[139] Around 620 he became a monk in the Canopus monastery (otherwise a stronghold of Chalcedonian confession!) as a pupil of Theonas. He came to the attention of Patriarch Andronicus, who ordained him a priest, introduced him to administrative duties and designated him as successor. In 626 Benjamin became patriarch. At the beginning of the reign of Cyrus as Melkite patriarch and prefect (631–642) Benjamin fled to Upper Egypt, where he remained in hiding for ten years. Then he returned to Alexandria (643/644) under the protection of the Islamic leader ʿAmr.[140] He died on 3 January 665.

---

135. Cf. the short outline of Egypt's political history in C. D. G. Müller, 'Benjamin I', *Mus* 69 (1956), 314–22. The issues raised here are reserved for a thorough presentation of this period in vol. III of this work; they must be discussed against the background of the monenergism controversy. Here we will mention only the two important papers of F. Winkelmann: 'Ägypten und Byzanz vor der arabischen Eroberung', *ByzSlav* 40 (1979), 161–82; and 'Die Stellung Ägyptens im oströmisch-byzantinischen Reich', in *Graeco-Coptica*, ed. P. Nagel (WB [H] 48), Halle 1984, 11–35; also J. Moorhead, 'The Monophysite Response to the Arab Invasion', *Byz* 51 (1981), 579–91.

136. *Hist. Patr.*: PO 1, pp. 492–93: 'The Lord abandoned the army of the Romans before him [Muhammad], as punishment for their corrupt faith, and because of the anathemas uttered against them, on account of the council of Chalcedon, by the ancient Fathers.'

137. *Hist. Patr.*: PO 1, p. 498. Similarly, Müller, art. cit., p. 314: 'Deadly hate against everything Greek filled the Copts' because of economic exploitation by Byzantium and the Chalcedonians' attempts at conversion. Winkelmann and Moorhead, on the other hand, support a more differentiated judgement with regard to the anti-Byzantine attitude of the Copts, as well as to the separatist trend of the Monophysites in general. Winkelmann, art. cit., *Graeco-Coptica*, p. 18: 'We must . . . begin with a much more differentiated attitude of the Coptic Monophysites towards Byzantium than has long been assumed.' Moorhead, art. cit., p. 591, asks for an 'abandonment of the national-religious hypothesis'.

138. On the dates see the chronology in C. D. G. Müller, *Die Homilie über die Hochzeit zu Kana und weitere Schriften des Patriarchen Benjamin I. von Alexandrien (AHAW.PH* 1968, 1), Heidelberg 1968, pp. 35–36.

139. This membership in the Coptic *dynatoi* causes Winkelmann, *ByzSlav* 40 (1979), 175, to ask: 'Could Benjamin's anti-Byzantine attitude perhaps have its roots in the separatism of circles of the Egyptian upper class, and could Benjamin's family itself – including him – have been especially conscious representatives of such an attitude?'

140. ʿAmr issued a letter of protection for him; *Hist. Patr.*: PO 1, 495–96. The date of the return is according to A. Jülicher, 'Die Liste der alexandrinischen Patriarchen im 6. und 7. Jahrhundert', in *Festgabe Karl Müller*, Tübingen 1922, 12. A panegyric presentation of the position of the Coptic patriarchs in the seventh century is found in C. D. G. Müller, 'Stellung und Haltung der koptischen Patriarchen des 7. Jahrhunderts gegenüber islamischer Obrigkeit und Islam', in *Acts of the Second International Congress of Coptic Studies, Rome, 22–26 September 1980*, ed. by T. Orlandi and F. Wisse, Rome 1985, 203–13.

Benjamin made fundamental changes towards the rebuilding of eccle-siastical organization. He built monasteries and churches and strengthened church discipline through orders (*canones*) and visitation trips. His high esteem was underlined by miracle stories; he was seen as the successor to St Mark. Those who under the rule of Cyrus had 'fallen away' to the Chalcedonian faith – presumably through the special attrac-tion exercised by the emerging monotheletism under Cyrus[141] – were brought back by Benjamin through intelligence and without force, if we may believe the presentation of the *History of the Patriarchs*.[142]

Excerpts of Benjamin's sermons have been preserved,[143] in particular the homily (probably his) on the wedding at Cana.[144] Of the annual Easter festal letters that he wrote[145] only a fragment of the sixteenth letter is extant.

In the *Sermon on the Wedding at Cana* 'Benjamin' clearly emphasizes the divinity of Jesus:

He has him say to his mother Mary: 'I will announce to everyone the power of my divinity' (p. 98) or 'I have revealed the glory of my divinity' (p. 104).

The miraculous character is strongly emphasized.

Thus already in Mary's announcement: 'My son . . . will accomplish a great miracle with you' (p. 92). 'This miracle that has occurred is mine and my Father's' (pp. 104–6). The stress on miracles in general is also seen in other passages (p. 150).

The 'miracle' of God (especially as Creator) and man in Jesus is empha-sized through four paradoxes: he who invites everyone to his true

---

141. Cf. J. Maspero, *Histoire*, p. 339.

142. *Hist. Patr.*: PO 1, p. 497: 'He induced them to return to the right faith by his gentleness, exhorting them with courtesy and consolation.' This presentation of Benjamin appears, to be sure, exactly as the type vis-à-vis the picture sketched of Heraclius (as antitype), 'the misbelieving Roman' (p. 496) and 'heretic', who through persecution and torture compelled confession to Chalcedon (pp. 491, 498).

143. Cf. C. D. G. Müller, 'Neues über Benjamin I, 38. und Agathon, 39. Patriarch von Alexandrien', *Mus* 72 (1959), 323–47, with a fragment that contains three sermon excerpts allegedly from Benjamin: one from the homily on the wedding at Cana and two from sermons on Shenoute. Also a homily on Theodore the Anatolian (preserved in Arabic) is ascribed to Benjamin, along with some other fragments; cf. C. D. G. Müller, *Der Stand der Forschungen*, p. 410.

144. Edited and with German translation by C. D. G. Müller, *Die Homilie über die Hochzeit zu Kana*, pp. 52–285. In the following we cite for abbreviation only according to the Bohairic version (homily) or according to the Berlin ms. (Easter festal letter). Concerning Benjamin's authorship, which Müller decisively affirms, H. Brakmann is not fully convinced: idem, 'Zum Pariser Fragment angeblich des koptischen Patriarchen Agathon. Ein neues Blatt der Vita Benjamins I', *Mus* 93 (1980), 299–309, here p. 308: 'yet without all doubt being removed by the argumentation [by Müller] supporting such a claim'.

145. Possibly he collected them in one volume; cf. Benjamin, 16. Osterfestbrief: C. D. G. Müller, *Homilie*, pp. 306/7, who speaks of 'the volume of letters that comprises 12/15 chapters'.

marriage is invited; he who creates human beings in his own image is himself at table with them; he who created wine drinks it himself; he who created bread eats it himself with everyone (pp. 86–88).

Benjamin stressed the real humanity of Jesus expressly against the reproach of the heretics, who are offended by this humanity, and confessed:

'I believe that everything that human beings do, my Saviour himself did, except only sin' (p. 118). In particular he confessed his belief in Jesus' real hunger and thirst and in his genuine joy with those who celebrate. All that happened in reality and not in appearance (pp. 118–20).

There is a catalogue of heretics already at the beginning of the sermon.

As new 'Judases' he designated Arius, Nestorius, Macedonius, Leo, Ibas, Theodore (of Mopsuestia), Theodoret, Leontius (of Byzantium), Julian (of Halicarnassus), George, Gregory (both rival bishops to Athanasius of Alexandria), also Cyrus, the opponent of Benjamin, Victor of Fayyum and Melitios of Lykopolis (pp. 82–84).

The patristic knowledge of Benjamin can be seen especially in the sixteenth Easter festal letter (end of 643/beginning of 644).[146] In addition to the Cappadocians, he refers there above all to the Alexandrian patriarchs Athanasius, Cyril and Dioscorus.[147]

According to Graf,[148] Benjamin's sixteenth Easter letter appears in two Coptic florilegia, namely, in the 'Priceless Pearl' in the seventh section ('On the Sufferings on the Cross that Give Life'),[149] and in the 'Confession of the Fathers',[150] where there is an 'abbreviated version'.[151]

The theme of the letter is given at the beginning: it is directed against 'the heresy of the Arians and the Apollinarians', who say that the God–Logos is mortal (like angels, according to text B). After the confession to the Trinity (three hypostases, alike in work and way of acting, one God, one will), Benjamin comes to speak of the incarnation of 'one from the Trinity'. He became flesh 'in his own hypostasis' (p. 304). In the addition

---

146. In excerpt in C. D. G. Müller, *Die Homilie über die Hochzeit zu Kana*, pp. 302–51, according to the Ethiopian version in the 'Confessions of the Fathers'.

147. C. D. G. Müller, *Homilie über die Hochzeit zu Kana*, pp. 30–31: Cyril of Alexandria (pp. 306, 314, 316, 334, 346, 350), Athanasius of Alexandria (pp. 310, 332, 342, 348), Gregory of Nazianzus (pp. 306, 320, 340), Basil of Caesarea (pp. 322, 336), Dioscorus of Alexandria (p. 342), Severus of Antioch (p. 322), Gregory of Nyssa (p. 330), Epiphanius of Salamis (p. 312), Theodotus of Ancyra (p. 332), Felix of Rome (p. 326), John Chrysostom (p. 322). Müller, ibid., p. 31: 'The quotations are as a rule very vague . . . and are never found word for word in the Greek original text.' Of course, that does not apply to all quotations (at least not for Epiphanius or Pseudo-Felix).

148. G. Graf, 'Zwei dogmatische Florilegien der Kopten', *OCP* 3 (1937), 49–77, 345–402. Renaudot, *Hist. Patr. Alex. Iacobit.*, p. 172, already mentions this letter.

149. In G. Graf, art. cit., p. 68, named under no. 30.

150. G. Graf, art. cit., p. 394, no. 208.

151. G. Graf, art. cit., p. 68.

'without separation' one can probably assume the confession of one nature. The incarnate Logos from the Virgin Mary (nothing is said of the role of the Holy Spirit) is without sin, capable of suffering, with a rational soul.

Benjamin then goes into the resistances evoked by the twelve- or fifteen-chapter comprehensive volume of letters written by him. In this compendium, he says, he cited Gregory of Nazianzus and Cyril of Alexandria as witnesses that 'the Son of God suffered in the flesh and not in the divine nature'.

For clarification he offers the image of the iron in the fire (= divinity): a hammer can strike the iron, of course, but it does not hit the fire – an interpretation that in its point is astonishingly 'un-Monophysite'![152] The opponents, however, who hold that 'God the Word suffered and died in the divinity as in the flesh' (p. 308) follow the Arians, Apollinarians (and 'Nestorians'[153]), whose error he has already shown to them.

Now follows a renewed proof for the statement that Christ suffered in the flesh, not in his divinity.

For this purpose Benjamin starts first with the scriptures, specifically with Peter (1 Pt 3,18; 4,1, 6), and then for authority turns to the 'apostolic' Athanasius of Alexandria,[154] as well as Epiphanius of Cyprus.[155] Then comes the rational basis: 'because this [the divinity] is not mortal and does not change' (p. 314).

How does the suffering of the Lord happen? The question is not asked, but the answer is given: intentionally, 'through the grace of God he tasted death . . . for all' (p. 316). Thus spoke Paul (Heb 2,9) and Peter (probably again with 1 Pt 3,18).[156]

God did not die because he was not flesh. If something was added to the flesh, it was not to the soul (p. 318).

Again, a number of patristic authorities are adduced for the assertion that Christ suffered in the flesh and not in his divinity: Gregory of Nazianzus (Homily on Baptism), Basil, Chrysostom (Homily on the Apostle Thomas), as well as Severus of Antioch, with regard to whom the comment is made that Christ is not split into two hypostases or two prosopa (p. 324).

---

152. The coal–fire analogy of Cyril is different; cf. A. Grillmeier, CCT II/2, p. 82.

153. Müller uses Nestorianer (pp. 310, 346) to translate an Ethiopian word that should be correctly rendered as 'Gennadius' according to Prof. M. Kropp, to whom we are indeed grateful for this information. If this should be a question of Patriarch Gennadius of Constantinople, then possibly a statement of communicatio idiomatum has been misunderstood here, since Benjamin writes: 'And the Nestorians . . . said: the divinity suffered along with the human nature' (ibid., p. 346).

154. Here it was probably a matter of Marcell. Ancyr., De incarnatione et contra Arianos (CPG 2806), 21: PG 26, 1021C–1024A. In the Pseudo-Athanasian (Apollinarist) Oratio IV contra Arianos (CPG 2230), to which the reference in the text, 'in his fourth homily, while he contradicted them, the Arians' (p. 310), seems to point, no basis for the quotation can be found.

155. Epiphan. Const., Panarion (CPG 3745), 77, 32,5: GCS 37 (1933), p. 444,27–30.

156. Versus Müller, who assumes here Peter I of Alexandria (p. 316, n. 3).

He suffered his passion not as (a mere) human 'but while he was God' (p. 326). Evidence: 'Felix of Rome', that is, one of the Apollinarian forgeries.[157]

Christ was not divided into two when he lived on earth (pp. 330–32; evidence: Gregory of Nyssa, Theodotus of Ancyra). The soteriology is broadly developed, especially with Athanasius.

The parable of the iron in the fire is repeatedly used to show that only the flesh of Christ suffered. But during the suffering the divinity did not separate from the human nature (p. 338).

It was also especially emphasized that Christ had a soul (pp. 338ff.).

Benjamin's opponents[158] apparently accused him of following the Council of Chalcedon by saying that Christ suffered in the flesh and not in his divinity (p. 346). To this Benjamin replied, with support from Cyril, that one could not reject a formulation merely because it was used by heretics, since heretics certainly believe 'much that is right'.[159] In this case, he said, he actually did agree with the Council of Chalcedon that the Logos suffered in the flesh but not in the divinity (pp. 346–48), but he did not share the council's opinion when it spoke of two natures and divided the only-begotten One into two hypostases (which it also did not do!).

Benjamin ends with confession to *mia physis, mia hypostasis* and *mia energeia* and with the statement that in many things there is a separation from the heretics.

Thus Benjamin's position produces a very clear confession to the true humanity of Christ and to the soul of Christ, challenged especially by the theopaschite inclinations of a strong group within his anti-Chalcedonian church,[160] whom he confronts with all desirable energy. He supports his views with the recognized patristic authorities, among whom are only a few Apollinarian forgeries, certainly induced also by the problem itself. By the way, the rejection of Chalcedon is not further substantiated.

---

157. The text is in Lietzmann, *Apollinaris*, p. 319,16–20.

158. K. N. Khella, 'Ein Dioskoros-Zitat beim Patriarchen Benjamin. Ein Beitrag zur Klärung der griechischen christologischen Termini im ägyptischen Verständnis (4.–7. Jahrhundert)', in *Probleme der koptischen Literaturwissenschaft* (WB [H] 1968/1 [K 2]), Halle 1968, begins with the Arabic version of the sixteenth Easter festal letter (in it: 'fifteenth pastoral letter') in the 'Confession of the Fathers'. He adopts the whole text beginning with 'And second said the holy Dioskoros, the confessor, the archbishop of Alexandria' (here according to Müller, p. 342) to the end of the Easter festal letter as a fragment of a letter of Dioscorus of Alex. (cf. CPG 5459).

159. Cf. Cyril of Alex., *Ep. 44 ad Eulog.*: ACO I 1, 4, p. 35; PG 77, 225A; see A. Grillmeier, *CCT* I², p. 480 with n. 23.

160. The fear of otherwise accepting Chalcedon (p. 346) apparently plays a large role in this group. The members are presumably to be found in monastic circles.

Summary

In reviewing the theology of the 'Coptic' patriarchs examined here, we can state the following:

- The *unus ex trinitate* is a constituent part of anti-Chalcedonian theology.

- The confession to the true humanity of Christ with a rational soul and a truly human (corruptible) body is expressed again and again, especially against Julian of Halicarnassus.

- *Mia energeia* in Christ is confessed together with *mia physis* and *mia hypostasis*.

- The first three councils are seen as the foundation of faith, to which the twelve anathemas of Cyril are more or less clearly added. The *Henoticon* of Zeno, understood as a rejection of Chalcedon, still gains a certain significance, especially in the late sixth century.

- The battle against Chalcedon and the *Tome* of Leo loses its topicality – except in Damian, where polemics receives new life – and rejection becomes a formality.

The Patriarchs of Alexandria Beginning with Cyril (according to Fedalto[161])

Cyril 17 Oct. 412–27 June 444
Dioscorus 444–13 Oct. 451
Proterius Nov. 451–28 Mar. 457
Timothy Aelurus 14 Mar. 457–Jan. 460; 475–31 July 477
Timothy Salophaciolus June 460–Dec. 475; Sept. 477–June 482
Peter Mongus 31 July 477–Sept. 477; Dec. 482–29 Oct. 489
John Talaia June 482–Dec. 482
Athanasius Celites 489–17 Oct. 496

Reconstructed List for the Period 500–700 (according to Jülicher[162])

John I Hemula 496–29 Apr. 505 (504)
John II Nicaiotes 505 (504)–22 May 516 (515)
Dioscorus II 516 (515)–14 Oct. 517
Timothy III 517–7 Feb. 535
Theodosius 9 Feb. 535, again June 535–22 June 566

Chalcedonians:	Monophysites:
Paul Tabennesiota 538–spring 540	(Julianist bishop Gaianus Feb. 535 (11?) to May? (24?))
Zoilus 540–551	(Julianist Elpidius ?–565)
Apollinaris 551–570(569)	(Julianist Dorotheus [565]–after 580)
John III 570(569)–580	Theodore 575–after 587, not recognized by the majority; Peter IV 576–19 June 578(577)
Eulogius 581–(13) Feb. 608(607)	Damian 578(577)–12 June 607(606)
Theodore Scribon 608–609; John Eleemon, late 610–11 Nov. 619	Anastasius Apozygarius 607(606)–19(18) Dec. 619(618)
Georgius 620(?)–630?	Andronicus 619–3 Jan. 626
Cyrus 631–late 643 or early 644	Benjamin (Jan.) 626–3 Jan. 665 (634 Julianist bishop Menas)
(Peter 643–651)	Agathon 665–13 Oct. 681

---

161. G. Fedalto, *Hierarchia Ecclesiastica Orientalis. Series episcoporum ecclesiarum christianarum orientalium II. Patriarchatus alexandrinus, antiochenus, hierosolymitanus*, Padua 1988. Cf. also A. Furioli, 'I Patriarchi di Alessandria', *Nicolaus* 13 (1986), 179–241 (not accessible to us).

162. A. Jülicher, 'Die Liste der alexandrinischen Patriarchen im 6. und 7. Jahrhundert', in *Festgabe Karl Müller*, Tübingen 1922, 7–23, here: p. 23.

SECTION TWO

THE CHRISTOLOGY OF THE SCHOLARS

Even if the influence of the great figures of the patriarchal see influenced the shaping of Alexandrian Christology in a special way, the contribution of the Greek-speaking intellectuals of Egypt still must be given particular attention and evaluation. Among them we find poets, exegetes and philosophers. Here, too, Alexandria is naturally the most important centre, but the view towards Upper Egypt represents a significant expansion of the overall picture, at least for the fifth century.

CHAPTER ONE

THE POET NONNUS OF PANOPOLIS AND HIS FELLOW COUNTRYMEN

Testifying to the flourishing Greek culture not only in Alexandria but also in the interior of Egypt, in the Chora, are the names of Greek-writing poets, who wandered as far as Constantinople and Rome, offering their services to princes and notables.[1] One can even with a

---

1. A detailed presentation of this literary activity is offered by Alan Cameron, 'Wandering Poets. A Literary Movement in Byzantine Egypt', *Historia* 14 (1965), 470–509. He speaks of a 'regular school of poets' and, using many examples, shows some of the traits of this 'school': they were almost always professed pagans who in their poetic art went into current topics, travelled freely and often were scholars (many also had a certain familiarity with Latin literature) or were involved in political life (p. 471). Cameron precisely characterizes the propaganda significance of such professional poets: 'To capture a clever and able poet like Claudian was like gaining control of a leading newspaper' (p. 502). In terms of social background, they all came, with few exceptions, from well-to-do, propertied families.

certain justification speak of an 'Egyptian hegemony in poetry' in the fifth century.[2] The city and vicinity of Panopolis or Akhmim in Upper Egypt apparently offered an especially lively cultural milieu, which was, to be sure, primarily borne by paganism.[3]

Paganism in Egypt around 400 was in retreat, to be sure, but still organized and strong enough to undertake the struggle against Christianity. Around 450 this struggle was decided: the pagans had become the minority. Certain places, however, were still held: the school of Alexandria, the shrines of Isis and a few places in Upper Egypt. Possibly the pagan resistance was strengthened by the fact that paganism understood itself as the bearer of national tradition in the sense that: 'Being truly an Egyptian means being a pagan.'[4] From Justinian on, paganism presented itself only as a remnant – even if a stubborn one – that sustained itself in individuals or small groups until the Arab invasion.[5]

In the fifth century there were among the Egyptian poets only a few who became Christians, such as Cyrus, Nonnus and Horapollon.[6]

1. Cyrus of Panopolis

Cyrus[7] is the author of panegyric poems and epigrams. Through Empress Eudocia he came into contact with Emperor Theodosius II and between 435 (438?) and 441 became *praefectus urbi(s Constantinopolitanae)* and at times also *praefectus praetorio Orientis*. Since he became too influential for his lord, the latter deposed him. After he became a priest, the emperor had him sent as bishop to Kotyaion in Phrygia, but not without ulterior motives, for the citizens of this city were rumoured to have killed four previous bishops. This seemed an inconspicuous means to get rid of a rival. The new bishop was received with open distrust, since he was suspected of secret paganism. On his arrival at a Christmas feast in the

2. E. Wipszycka, 'La christianisation de l'Égypte aux IVe–VIe siècles. Aspects sociaux et ethniques', *Aegyptus* 68 (1988) (117–65), 144. The majority of the Greek-writing poets in the 4th and 5th centuries were Egyptians or had at least studied in Alexandria. Cf. also the often quoted statement of Eunapius of Sardis (*c.* 400): 'The Egyptians are exceedingly mad on poetry' (cf. Al. Cameron, art. cit., 470).

3. Panopolis was the bastion of Hellenistic culture and the centre of paganism; cf. Al. Cameron, art. cit., 472; also R. Rémondon, 'L'Égypte et la suprême résistance au christianisme (V^e–VIIe siècles)', *BIFAO* 51 (1952) (63–78), 67: 'Les intellectuels paiens . . . se recrutent dans l'aristocratie de Panopolis et de Thèbes.'

.4. Thus R. Rémondon, art. cit., 66–67, with reference to the comments of J. Maspero, *Histoire*, pp. 34–35.

5. Cf. R. Rémondon, art. cit., p. 72 (summary).

6. Cf. E. Wipszycka, art. cit., 145.

7. See CPG 5646–47; *Kl.Pauly* 3, Kyros 4; T. C. Gregory, 'The Remarkable Christmas Homily of Kyros Panopolites', *GRBS* 16 (1975), 317–24; cf. Evagrius Schol., *HE* I 19: Bidez-Parmentier, 28; in addition P. Allen, *Evagrius Scholasticus* (SpicSLov 41), pp. 89–90. Also Al. Cameron, art. cit., 473–74, 497–98; D. J. Constantelos, 'Kyros Panopolites, Rebuilder of Constantinople', *GRBS* 12 (1971), 451–64.

years between 440 and 450, the people immediately demanded of him a speech by which they wanted to test his orthodoxy. Undisconcerted, Cyrus gave what is probably the shortest Christmas sermon in recorded tradition:

> Brethren, let the birth of God our Saviour Jesus Christ be honoured with silence, because the Word of God was conceived in the holy Virgin through hearing (ἀκοῇ) alone. To him be glory for ever! Amen.[8]

The people were won. For in this short address was everything they wished to hear: confession to Jesus Christ as God and his incarnation in the holy Virgin. Here Cyrus follows the patriarch Proclus of Constantinople, who seems also to be the ultimate source of a saying that he included in a poem for the pillars of St Daniel the Stylite after he had returned to Constantinople: 'proclaiming the Son of a mother without marital experience'.[9]

2. Pamprepius

Before we turn to Nonnus, we must first mention the pagan Neoplatonist Pamprepius of Panopolis, who caused a stir as poet, politician and administrator.[10] Born in 440 in Panopolis, and at first a professional poet, he went to Athens for further studies and became a teacher of grammar there. In Constantinople (after 476) he gained great influence on Illus,[11] became a quaestor and patricius and served as advisor in the uprising of Illus against Emperor Zeno. He is credited with the plan to proceed against the 'Monophysites' through an alliance with paganism under the leadership of Illus.[12] Yet he failed in his attempt to support John Talaia in Alexandria, as well as to secure for his plans the support of the pagan Alexandrians – who apparently still existed as a party.[13] 'The conspiracy

---

8. T. C. Gregory, art. cit., 318; Theophanes, *Chron.* A. M. 5937: de Boor I, 97,10–15.

9. T. C. Gregory, art. cit., 322–24; Proclus, *Or. 4 de incarn.*: PG 65, 712: Ὦ, παρθένε, κόρη ἀπειρόγαμε, καὶ μήτηρ ἀλόχευτε. – By contrast, in Cyrus Pan., added to the short biography of Daniel (*Vitae Epitome*): H. Delehaye, *Les saints stylites* (SubsHag 14), Brussels–Paris 1923, 97,19: υἱέα κηρύττων μητρὸς ἀπειρογάμου(-οιο); idem, 'Une épigramme de l'Anthologie Grecque (I,99)', *RevÉtGrec* 9 (1896), 216–24.

10. Cf. the analysis of R. Asmus, 'Pamprepios, ein byzantinischer Gelehrter und Staatsmann des 5. Jahrhunderts', *ByzZ* 22 (1913), 320–47; in detail: R. Keydell, art. 'Pamprepios', in *PWK* 18,3 (1949), 409–15; also Al. Cameron, art. cit., 473, 486, 491, 499–500, as well as the presentation in R. von Haehling, 'Heiden im griechischen Osten des 5. Jahrhunderts nach Christus', *RömQ* 77 (1982) (52–85), 60–61.

11. E. Stein, *Histoire du Bas-Empire* II, p. 9: 'the Seni of the Isaurian Wallenstein'.

12. Ibid., 23.

13. Ibid., 24–25. On the mission of Pamprepius in Alexandria cf. R. Asmus, art. cit., 332–35.

of Illus is perhaps the last attempt of paganism to regain power.'[14] In late November 484 Pamprepius died a violent death during the siege in Papirius.[15]

3. Nonnus of Panopolis

Compared to either of the two Panopolitans named above, Nonnus is by far the more famous poet.

(a) Preliminary questions

For good reasons Nonnus is today considered the author of both the *Dionysiaca* and the *Paraphrase of John*. The issue is whether he wrote both works as a Christian, since they stand opposed to each other in terms of their object.[16] After an exposition of the whole problem and the history of research, E. Livrea (1989) reaches the conclusion that the *Dionysiaca* and the *Paraphrase of John* were written between 444 and 451, both by Nonnus and probably as a Christian, for this name was borne by Christians in the Syrian region.[17] Nonnus, writes Livrea, attended the famous law school of Beirut and had contact there with famous pagan jurists but also with Eustathius, who between 448 and 451 was bishop of the city.[18] These contacts had left tracks behind not only in the Christology of the

---

14. R. Rémondon, art. cit., 66.

15. E. Stein, *Histoire*, p. 30. R. Asmus, art. cit., 337–47, on the basis of his analysis of the sources, comes to the conclusion that behind the death of Pamprepius there was not a betrayal but a failure of his political calculations that was interpreted as his 'deception' (by the troops of Illus). Against Asmus cf. R. Keydell, art. cit., 414.

16. Cf. CPG 5641–42; *Paraphrasis in Johannem*: PG 43, 749–922; here according to A. Scheindler, *Nonni Panopolitani paraphrasis s. Evangelii Ioannei*, Leipzig 1881; also J. Golega, *Studien über die Evangeliendichtung des Nonnos von Panopolis* (BSHT 15), Breslau 1930; P. Peeters, *AnBoll* 49 (1931), 160–63; J. Golega, 'Zum Text der Johannesmetabole des Nonnos', *ByzZ* 59 (1966), 9–36; for a new edition of the John paraphrase see E. Livrea, 'Per una nuova edizione della Parafrasi del Vangelo di S. Giovanni di Nonno', in *The 17th Internat. Byz. Congress, Abstracts of Short Papers*, Washington DC, Aug. 3–8, 1986, pp. 198–99; idem, *Nonno di Panopoli. Parafrasi del Vangelo di S. Giovanni. Canto XVIII, Introduzione, testo critico, traduzione e commentario*, Naples 1989. Also R. Keydell, *PWK* 17 (1936), 904–20; *Kl.Pauly* 4, 154–55. Keydell holds that it is improbable that Nonnus wrote the *Dionysiaca* as a Christian, since a positive evaluation of the (pagan) mysteries is to be found there; opposed is J. Golega, *Studien*, 79–88, with considerable reasons. See Nonnus Pan., *Dionysiaca* (CPG 5642): ed. R. Keydell I–II, Berlin 1959.

17. E. Livrea, op. cit. (1989), p. 20, n. 4.

18. G. Fedalto, *HEO* II, no. 67.6.2. E. Livrea, op. cit., pp. 28–29; he presents Eustathius incorrectly as an adherent 'dell'eresia monofisita di Eutiche' (p. 29). See, however, the information on his person and his role between 448 and 451 in *CCT* II/1, p. 99, n. 16; p. 232, n. 127; vol. II/2, p. 416. According to all reports Eustathius proved himself in difficult times as the moderate representative of a Christology that followed Cyril. Cf. A. Van Roey, art. 'Eustathe', *DHGE* 16 (1967), 23.

John paraphrase but also in the juristic interest that is evident in the presentation of Jesus' trial before Pilate in the paraphrase of Jn 18–19, according to Livrea. He also sees here an evident sympathy with the representative of *auctoritas Romana*, the procurator Pontius Pilate.[19]

At the same time, Livrea continues, Nonnus, with the mobility typical of 'wandering poets', maintained close relations with the Neoplatonist Alexandrian circles – especially with the ruling figure Hierocles[20] but also with the patriarchate of Alexandria. The result of such varied contacts was not an 'ideological indifference'. Rather, Nonnus strove, in Livrea's view, 'for a bold and heroic cultural-syncretistic synthesis', which made him two things simultaneously: (1) the enthusiastic paladin of a soterio-logical Dionysian mystery cult ('di un dionisismo misterico e soteriologico'),[21] in which the immense manifold heritage of the Alex-andrian past lived on, and (2) the Christian, permeated with Neoplatonist elements but deeply impressed by the wondrous, polymorphic divinity of the (Johannine) Logos-Christ. Perhaps this – certainly not unproblem-atic – interpretation of Nonnus by Livrea does justice to the monstrous tension that comes to expression in the struggles of late antiquity under Plotinus, Porphyry, Iamblichus, Proclus, Isidore and others with Chris-tianity. The exegetical effort that Nonnus devoted to the Gospel of John fits in well, in Livrea's view, with analogous initiatives towards the revision and resurrection of holy texts of the past, such as *De antro Nympharum* of Porphyrius,[22] the commentary on the *Carmen aureum* of the Pythagoreans, written by Hierocles,[23] the various Plato commen-taries of Proclus,[24] and later in the sixth century the commentaries on Aristotle and Epictetus by Simplicius.[25] At the same time the difference from the *De martyrio s. Cypriani* of Empress Eudocia (CPG 6020)[26] and the *Metaphrasis psalmorum*, which is ascribed to Apollinarius of Laodicea (CPG 3700), would become clear. Perhaps after this bold intellectual-historical classification of Nonnus by Livrea one expects an indecipherable mixture of religious and especially christological views.

---

19. Cf. Nonnus Pan., *Paraphras. in Ioh.* XVIII, 29–40: E. Livrea, pp. 98–103 with commentary pp. 178–205.

20. E. Livrea, op. cit., pp. 29–30, n. 27. On Hierocles: *Kl.Pauly* 2, col. 1133, no. 6.

21. E. Livrea, op. cit., p. 31.

22. *Kl.Pauly* 4, col. 1064–69.

23. Cf. I. Hadot, *Le problème du néoplatonisme alexandrin. Hiéroclès et Simplicius*, Paris 1978, pp. 17–20.

24. *Kl.Pauly* 4, col. 1160–62.

25. *Kl.Pauly* 5, col. 205–6. Cf. I. Hadot, op. cit., pp. 20–32.

26. *Kl.Pauly* 2, col. 405–6.

We must not forget, however, that for us it is primarily a question of evaluating the *Paraphrase of John*, which exhibits a relative uniformity.

The addressees, according to Livrea, were probably in the first instance pagans of the higher cultivated and more pretentious class; one cannot, however, rule out the possibility that the readers of the paraphrase also included the educated Christian elite, who relished contact between pagan and Christian culture and were perhaps not indifferent to the mystical currents of the dying paganism.[27] That Nonnus was controversial is also expressed in the divided, antithetical judgements on his paraphrase in the course of history.[28] Genuine attempts at serious evaluation of the exegesis of John in the paraphrase did not come until 1918.[29] Then in 1930 J. Golega successfully and definitively demonstrated that the John paraphrase belongs to Nonnus.[30] Yet the tasks of research into the John paraphrase are by no means completed. According to Livrea we lack, in the first place, its evaluation as an 'independent creative work' and with that also a judgement of the poet as a John exegete.[31] Livrea sees

---

27. E. Livrea, *Parafrasi*, pp. 31–35. D. Ebener, *Nonnos. Werke in zwei Bänden. Leben und Taten des Dionysos I–XXXII* (vol. 1), *Leben und Taten des Dionysos XXXIII–XLVIII. Nachdichtung des Johannesevangeliums* (vol. 2) (Bibl. d. Antike. Griech. Reihe), Berlin–Weimar 1985, sees the opposition between paganism and Christianity at work in both writings by Nonnus. Ebener bases the tension between the two writings on the two saviour figures described therein, Dionysius and Jesus of Nazareth. Let us limit ourselves to the John paraphrase. Ebener deals with the possibility that Nonnus used his retelling (of the Fourth Gospel) 'as a not unskilled, carefully camouflaged rejection of the Christian redeemer concept, as he understood it: the expectation of a materially visible and comprehensible redemption of troubled and burdened people accomplished in this world. The scarcity and unproductivity of the sources prevents us from giving such an unrestricted yes. The two works we have before us allow us to know only one thing: the redemption envisioned by the author in the *Dionysiaca* can only relate to earthly existence . . . The conclusion that the poet reaches is this: neither the pleasure-seeking, cheerful and at the same time inhumanly cruel master of the grapes, who gave his tears, nor the unassuming, upright Nazarene, who gave his blood for the redemption of humanity, could overcome the limits of reality' (vol. 1, pp. XXXIIf.). D. Ebener is a long way from grasping the theological content of the John paraphrase; one important reason: he knows nothing of the dependence of the paraphrase on the John commentary of Cyril of Alex. and of the dependence on Cyril in general, who guarantees a theological depth in spite of certain restrictions that we also make here. Moreover, some serious translation errors falsify the content of the paraphrase (see below).

28. E. Livrea, op. cit., pp. 43–47. Also the accusation of heresy and semi-Pelagianism is not lacking in the series of different evaluations (ibid., p. 46).

29. With the article by K. Kuiper, 'De Nonno Evangelii Johannei interprete', *Mn* 46 (1918), 223–70, and the dissertation of his student A. H. Preller, *Quaestiones Nonnianae desumptae e Paraphrasi Sancti Evangelii Johannei cap. XVIII–XIX*, Noviomagi 1918 (not available).

30. See n. 16 above. J. Golega also wanted to edit the paraphrase again but was prevented by death. Apart from Cantus Σ, we are dependent on the edition by Scheindler (Leipzig 1881).

31. E. Livrea is now undertaking this task for Cantus Σ, which is devoted to Jn 18.

the goal of the paraphrase of Nonnus in establishing a connection between the Jewish-Christian biblical poetry in the Greek language (Philo), with the great poetic tradition of the Homeric-Alexandrian kind, and the Neoplatonism of educated pagan circles. He finds three motifs at work in Nonnus:[32]

(1) Knowledge of the greater public effectiveness of the poetic form in comparison to prose. The poetic 'paraphrase' was supposed to make the gospel or the Christian message far more acceptable to the pagan class, which took offence at the inadequate stylistic form and the development, in ignorance of grammar, prosody and metrics, of individual Christian products.

(2) With this Nonnus tried to connect an *interpretatio theologica* and to make the most refined instruments of rhetoric serviceable to an exegesis that could bring a certain prestige to Alexandrian Christian dogmatics and *realpolitik* in the dress of late antiquity.

(3) Nonnus wanted, in any case, to bring his poetic genius to Christian proclamation.

These motifs presumed by Livrea for good reasons in the John paraphrase of Nonnus are above all, however, of cultural-historical and also religious significance. His partial commentary on the paraphrase of Jn 18[33] leads one to expect rich ideas for the evaluation of the work as a whole, yet in the main only within the view just presented. We will not attempt to trace these perspectives or even to verify them. Our interest is a partial one that results from the goal of the work as a whole. We will merely ask about the significance of the John paraphrase for the history of christological dogma, and for the other questions we point to the already published (or still forthcoming) commentary of E. Livrea.

(b) The christological standpoint of Nonnus's paraphrase of John
(aa) General characterization

The poet shows a striking reticence regarding the theological discussions and agitations of the period between 431 (428) and 451, during which, according to Livrea, the work was composed. It is true that Nonnus lets his 'Alexandrian' standpoint be known. His picture of Christ can be

---

32. E. Livrea, op. cit., pp. 40–42.

33. E. Livrea, op. cit., pp. 107–205; indeed, this partial commentary provides the justification for a much higher assessment of the significance of Nonnus for cultural history than, for example, that of the great Nonnus scholar R. Keydell (cf. E. Livrea, op. cit., p. 22, n. 9).

classified as Cyrillian Logos Christology.[34] Yet we see at first glance that the heated Cyril–Nestorius struggle plays no role. Nonnus seems rather to be dependent on the Cyril of the great John commentary, which was written in the period between 425 and 428 and thus in the years still immediately before the Nestorian controversy.[35] One can hardly venture an explanation of why Nonnus, if he wrote between 428 and 451,[36] did not mention in his work the anti-Nestorian polemic of Cyril and of Alexandria. But the question is justified: Did the aforementioned controversies have to be considered by the poet? Were not the interest in the Gospel of John as such and making it accessible to the circle of readers described above sufficient explanation of the origin of the paraphrase? Since, on the other hand, the extensive use of Cyril's commentary on John has been demonstrated as fact, we have a solid *terminus post quem*, and the *terminus ante quem* can remain indefinite until research produces further fixed points. The discovery of traces of Cyrilliana after 428 must be kept open as a possibility.

(bb) The christological statement of Nonnus's paraphrase of John

As alienating as the poetic dress of the John paraphrase may be in comparison to the Fourth Gospel, it still lets the author's orthodoxy be sufficiently known. One must grant Nonnus a certain poetic licence in his choice of words. Thus right at the beginning of the prologue of John he expresses the consubstantiality and coeternity of the Son with the Father as a paraphrase of Jn 1,1–2 (A 1–2). Here, to be sure, as elsewhere in the whole poem, he avoids the word *homoousios* but replaces it with expressions that sufficiently assert the Nicaean faith in the divinity of the Son. Faith in the God-Logos, the light from light, the uncreated Son

---

34. Cf. E. Livrea, op. cit., p. 31, n. 29: '. . . la cristologia nonniana sembra dipendere interamente da Cirillo'.

35. E. Livrea, op. cit., p. 25, emphasizes this dependence in reference to numerous exegetical solutions. He mentions the prior work of A. H. Preller, *Quaestiones Nonnianae desumptae e Paraphrasi Sancti Evangelii Johannei cap. XVIII–XIX*, Noviomagi 1918. For Livrea's part he adds in n. 17: 'Numerosi nuovi riscontri cirilliani sono offerti nel mio comm.' (op. cit., pp. 107–205, but only for chap. 18).

36. Cf. E. Livrea, op. cit., p. 25: 'Sull' altro versante, il terminus ante quem è rappresentato dal Concilio di Calcedonia che nel 451, con la condanna delle tesi monofisite, segnerà il definitivo distacco della Chiesa di Alessandria dal Patriarcato di Costantinopoli . . .' This chronological limitation is unsatisfactory. If Nonnus wrote to Alexandria after 431, he would have to have betrayed knowledge of the Cyrillian–Nestorian points of disagreement (*mia physis, synapheia* etc.). If Chalcedon was supposed to play the role of the *terminus ante quem*, a knowledge of Eutyches would have to betray itself somehow. Neither is the case.

who is himself creator – these and other things are clearly reproduced in the paraphrase of the prologue (A 1–11).

Like the divinity of the Son, the consubstantiality of the Holy Spirit with God is also made clear in similar terms. The time of the Pneumatomachians has already passed. Contrary to the assumption of J. Golega,[37] however, the *Symbolum Nicaeno-Constantinopolitanum* is not quoted or included. If this were the case, we would have at Alexandria a testimony to the knowledge of this symbol and indeed during the period before Chalcedon. The verses for Jn 1,14, however, betray that Nonnus also assumes the *homoousios* for the Paraclete, but only in equivalent expressions. The Paraclete, whom the Father will send (Jn 14,16), is designated as Christ's σύγγονος ἄλλος, ὁμοίιος, ἀρχέγονον φῶς, πνεῦμα θεοῦ γενετῆρος.[38] That Nonnus recognized the divinity of the *pneuma* is seen in the strong anti-Pneumatomachian emphasis on the procession of the Spirit from the Father.[39]

More interesting for us is his position on the Alexandrian-Cyrillian Christology and its language. Possibly the Nestorian controversy is brought to mind by the often repeated designation of the mother of Jesus as *theotokos*.[40] There he joins with Cyril as well as with his fellow countryman Shenoute (see below). Only with a shaking of the head, however, would the patriarch of Alexandria read the paraphrase of Jn 1,14:

κaὶ λόγος αὐτοτέλεστος ἐσαρκώθη, θεὸς ἀνὴρ
ὀψίγονος προγένεθλος, ἐν ἀρρήτῳ τινὶ θεσμῷ
ξυνώσας ζαθέην βροτοειδέι σύζυγα μορφήν.

And the Logos perfect in himself [absolute] became flesh, God-man,
born afterwards [and yet] born before [pre-existent], through an indescribable bond
uniting the divine to the mortal human form as companion.[41]

---

37. J. Golega, *Studien*, pp. 106, 110–11.
38. Nonnus Pan., *Paraphr. in Ioh. XIV*, 63 and 66–67: Scheindler, 159.
39. Cf. J. Golega, op. cit., pp. 112–15.
40. For passages cf. ibid., 107–9; *Paraphr. in Ioh.*, B 9.66; T 135 (θεητόκος). But there was already *theotokos* in the fourth century; see Lampe, *PatrGrLex*, p. 639. Nonnus, however, says each time Χριστοῖο θεητόκος, which creates a certain distance from any current controversy on the significance of the Nestorian strife. Or is the Nestorian 'Christotokos' thus corrected?
41. Nonnus Pan., *Paraphr. in Ioh.*, A 39–41: Scheindler, pp. 5–6. D. Ebener (II, p. 286) translates A 39–41 thus: 'But the Word assumed human form, a divine young man, timely born. In a mysterious-holy way it accommodated itself to a noble human body.' θεὸς ἀνήρ means God-man, not divine young man. The Johannine idea of incarnation, which Nonnus clearly expresses, does not come to light in Ebener's translation.

This sounds more Antiochene than Alexandrian. Perhaps for the first time in christological usage the phrase θεὸς ἀνήρ, 'God-man', appears as a variant of *theos anthropos*, and indeed twice.[42] The main reason for this choice is probably poetic metre. Certainly this designation of Christ is consciously distinguished from the term θεῖος ἀνήρ, 'divine man', which is applied to John the Baptist (A 129) and Moses (E 179). Would Cyril be satisfied with the description of the union offered in the third line? Would the designation of the humanity of Christ as *syzygos* not be highly suspicious to him? One could even think of Mani – no doubt unjustly. Cyril would more likely have suspected him of Nestorianism.

Let us look for further christological peculiarities. E. Livrea correctly emphasizes the heavy stress on the divinity of Christ in the paraphrase.

Christ is the 'Logos God' (A 202), which amplified in this passage reads: 'Son and Logos of the eternally living God' (A 201–202: υἱὸς ἀειζώοιο θεοῦ λόγος). Linked with this, as interpretation of Jn 1,50, are the titles 'Shepherd of the heavenly ones', 'God-king of the children of Israel', 'Messiah (*Christos*)' (A 200–204). Jesus can rightly boast of God as his 'genuine Procreator' (θεὸν αὐτογένεθλον . . . τοκῆα) and thus in spite of his human appearance claim true likeness with the heavenly King (E 69–70 on Jn 5,18). The union with God 'his Father' (E 83 on Jn 5,22, which has only the simple πατήρ) and in K 10 on Jn 10,30 ('I and my Father are one') appears on the one hand quite unproblematic in terms of Nicaea, yet on the other hand Hellenistically loosened when it says: 'I and my Lord and Father are of one race, from the root of one stock, from which come thousands of living beings of the world' (K 106–107 on Jn 10,30: αὐτὸς ἐγὼ μεδέων τε πατὴρ ἐμὸς ἓν γένος ἐσμέν, ἔμφυτον, αὐτόπρεμνον, ὅθεν φυτὰ μυρία κόσμου). The genuine sonship vis-à-vis God the Father, the transcendence (ξεῖνος) vis-à-vis this world and his true affiliation with the other-worldly ethereal cosmos also determine Christ's virginal conception. He knows no human father (Θ 53–54 on Jn 8,23: ξεῖνος ἔφυν κόσμοιο καὶ οὐ βροτὸν οἶδα τοκῆα). Typically Hellenistic-Alexandrian is the exchange of the predicate ἀγαθός, 'good', for Jesus with σοφός, 'wise' (H 42 and 44 on Jn 7,12). Unusual sounding is the formulation in M 94 (on Jn 12,23): ἀνθρώπου σοφὸς υἱός: the *wise* Son of Man, whose exaltation is now imminent, and indeed on the cross. The poetic rhythm may have insinuated such connections. Typical is the reproduction of the famous confession of doubting Thomas: ὁ κύριός μου καὶ ὁ θεός μου (Jn 20,28) as: κοίρανος[43] ἡμέτερος καὶ ἐμὸς θεός (Y 131).

If we look at the unfolding of the christological difficulties *circa* 431, two things are striking: (1) the lack of an anti-Nestorian emphasis on the *henosis* of God and humanity in Christ; (2) the introduction of the verb συνάπτειν, 'join together', rejected by Cyril in this controversy precisely as the expression of the union of God and humanity in Christ. Out of Jn 3,13 ('No

---

42. Ibid. on Jn 1,14 and 42, A 39 and 157–58: Scheindler, pp. 5 and 12–13. Cf. A. Grillmeier, art. 'Gottmensch', *RAC* 12 (1983), 330–31, where these passages are missing.

43. Nonnus has an affinity for the Homeric κοίρανος (21 times). Also the famous Homeric ἀγκυλομήτις, 'crafty', appears often associatively in Nonnus, not applied to God, but only to people.

one has ascended into heaven except the one who descended from heaven, the Son of Man') Nonnus makes an assertion about the incarnation that after 431 Cyril no longer wanted to make: 'Only the Son of Man left the form of immortality [cf. Phil 2,6] and descended from heaven and *united* with foreign [unfamiliar] flesh.'[44]

From these short references we may conclude that Nonnus is inspired mainly by the John text itself and does not include the violent Cyrillian–Nestorian conflict in his paraphrase. If he had been in close contact with it, we could have expected passionate negative adjectives also against Nestorius (or even Eutyches), such as we find in regard to the high priests and Pharisees.[45] For the poet it is not important to develop the theological content of the gospel in a substantially new dimension and thus also contribute to the christological controversy of his time. He seeks his development for his time in the modernization of the linguistic dress of the Fourth Gospel. This means an increased Hellenization of the Christian message, even if nothing essential is sacrificed. Indeed, one can certify for Nonnus a good theological understanding of Christology around 430. But one can scarcely avoid the impression that the religious power of the gospel is scattered in an enchanting verbosity.[46]

---

44. Nonnus, Par. Γ 67–69: . . . ὃς ἀθανάτην ἕο μορφὴν οὐρανόθεν κατέβαινεν ἀήθεϊ σαρκὶ συνάπτων, ἀνθρώπου μόνος υἱός . . . The fact that Cyril first used the verb συνάπτειν to represent the connection of divinity and humanity in Christ and after the appearance of Nestorius rejected it as unsuitable has already been mentioned in this work (*CCT* II/2, pp. 40–45). Cf. on Jn 3,13: Cyril of Alex., *Comm. in Jo.* (CPG 5208): PG 73, 249BD, where the problem of the union in Christ is taken up. This section also supports the writing of the paraphrase before the height of the Nestorian strife.

45. In Par. Λ 185–90 they are qualified as 'godless priests', 'completely unbelieving Pharisees', 'unreasonable high priests'; Caiaphas is 'lawless' and 'cunning' (Λ 199).

46. Since D. Ebener accords to chaps. 14–17 of the paraphrase a special significance, we add a few comments on his translation:

(1) On Jn 14,1: Scheindler, p. 156,2–3, θεσπεσίη τιμή, which the poet claims for the Father and Jesus, is rendered with 'honour befitting the gods' (meaning: divine adoration) (II, p. 371).

(2) The promise of the Spirit in the paraphrase of Jn 14,16–17 is very misleadingly expressed; XIV 67: πνεῦμα θεοῦ γενετῆρος, 'the Spirit of God the Father' is translated (II, p. 373) as: 'the soul of God, of the Father'! It is a question of the 'Spirit of truth that the world cannot receive'.

(3) Jn 14,22: 'How is it that you will reveal yourself to us, and not to the world?' reads in Nonnos XIV 86: Scheindler, p. 161,86–87: πῶς τεὸν εἶδος ὁμοφρονέων ἀναφαίνεις μούνοις σοῖς ἑτάροισι καὶ οὐ θηήτορι κόσμῳ ; in translation according to Ebener (II, p. 374): 'Lord, how can you reveal yourself willingly in a form like God's to your disciples alone, not also to the seeing eyes of the world?' The possessive pronoun τεόν is exchanged with θεόν. Thus it would be correct to say: 'your form'.

4. Dioscorus of Aphrodito
(by T. Hainthaler)

Through accidental discoveries of papyri[47] with the literary legacy of the jurist and poet Dioscorus of Aphrodito, it has become possible for us 'to watch a lawyer at work, in an Egyptian provincial capital of the sixth century'.[48] According to the translation by L. S. B. MacCoull, this reveals 'the high level of civilization attained by the Coptic leisured class', which attests to the compatibility of classical and Coptic culture.[49] The bilingual Dioscorus, a representative of the Coptic *dynatoi*, probably influenced also by the works of the great Nonnus, reveals in his occasional works, in MacCoull's view, the extent to which Coptic culture (of the fourth to seventh centuries) was a 'culture founded . . . on praise'.[50]

The panegyric on Emperor Justin II[51] could perhaps contain an indication of an anti-Chalcedonian conviction of the lawyer: Justin is called φιλόχριστος (8); and in the mention of 'Theodosius' we would more likely see an allusion to the 'rehabilitation', by Justinian's successor, of the Alexandrian patriarch who died in exile in 566, the 'head of the Monophysite world', than a reference to Emperor Theodosius, as Mac-Coull assumes.[52] On the whole, however, hardly anything of the religious convictions of the poet is revealed.[53] The allusions that Mac-Coull finds – to Cyril, for example[54] – are so general in nature that in our view they are lacking in cogency. Also, the presumed relationship to John Philoponus in Alexandria,[55] while certainly not to be excluded, still remains in the realm of speculation. In particular, the use of the word μονοειδής for the Trinity in the period 570–575 points precisely not to the followers of Philoponus, who designated the three trinitarian persons as *heteroeideis* (see below, p. 134).

---

47. Cf. the report in L. S. B. MacCoull, *Dioscorus of Aphrodito. His Work and His World* (The Transformation of the Classical Heritage 16), Berkeley–Los Angeles 1988, 2–5.

48. Ibid., p. 151.

49. Ibid., p. 152.

50. Ibid., p. 159. The poetic qualities of Dioscorus were judged negatively by J. Maspero and H. I. Bell (cf. p. xvi).

51. Ibid., pp. 72–73; English translation: pp. 73–74.

52. Ibid., p. 74.

53. Thus also MacCoull, p. 144.

54. MacCoull gives: ψυχωφελῆ (p. 25), διασαφήσῃ μοι (p. 32), ἀκαρπία (p. 48), ἀδιαστρόφως καὶ ἀταραχῶς (p. 49), ὀρθὴ πίστις (p. 65), ἀδάμας (p. 116, n. 74), Solon (p. 106, on 5), Νεῖλος ἀρουροβάτης (p. 143, on 43).

55. On this: L. S. B. MacCoull, 'Dioscorus of Aphrodito and John Philoponus', *StudPat* 18/1 (Kalamazoo 1985), 163–68.

CHAPTER TWO

TWO ALEXANDRIAN EXEGETES

Although we lack indications of an exegetical school in Alexandria, we do have documents from two Alexandrian clerics of the fifth and sixth centuries who wrote commentaries on biblical texts. They are preserved above all (or exclusively) through the catena tradition. On the whole it cannot be denied that the written documentation for this period is meagre.[1]

1. The presbyter Ammonius

We stand on relatively solid ground with the presbyter Ammonius and his writings, even if his person cannot be clearly identified.[2] For us, his commentary on John is especially important, because in it his position on Chalcedon is clearly expressed and his Christology is well developed.

J. Reuss has reproduced this commentary in an excellent edition,[3] yet he is too quick to find there a reference to the text of the Chalcedonian definition and therefore to make the author unjustly a Chalcedonian. The passage in question is the scholium on Jn 3,6, which contains the sentences: 'Now, Christ is consubstantial (*homoousios*) with the Father as

---

1. See CPG 5500 ss. The concern here, however, is really only Ammonius of Alexandria (CPG 5500–5508). We cannot claim 'Eusebius of Alexandria' for the Alexandrian church. See G. Lafontaine, *Les homélies d'Eusèbe d'Alexandrie. Mémoire . . . de Licencié en Philosophie et Lettres (dactylographié)*, Louvain, Université Catholique, 1966; J. Leroy and F. Glorie, '"Eusèbe d'Alexandrie" source d' "Eusèbe de Gaule"', *SE* 19 (1969/70), 33–70. Ibid., 47: 'G. Lafontaine [who is preparing an edition of Ps.-Eusebius] détermine le terminus a quo: pas avant le début du IVᵉ siècle, et le terminus ad quem: pas après le VI–VIIᵉ siècle, et date le recueil "de la fin du Vᵉ, ou du VIᵉ siècle"; il rejette l'hypothèse d'un milieu alexandrin.'
2. See the literature on this in CPG III, p. 66, esp. J. Reuss, 'Der Presbyter Ammonius von Alexandrien und sein Kommentar zum Johannes-Evangelium', *Bib* 44 (1963), 159–70; idem, 'Der Exeget Ammonius und die Fragmente seines Matthäus- und Johannes-Kommentars', *Bib* 22 (1941), 13–20; Reuss has shown the Matthew commentary to be not genuine.
3. We will follow the edition of the John commentary by J. Reuss, *Johanneskommentare aus der griechischen Kirche* (TU 89), Berlin 1966, 196–358, with a total of 649 bits of text.

to divinity and consubstantial (*homoousios*) with the mother as to the flesh, even if Christ is one from both, unchanged and unmixed.'[4] J. Reuss places this alongside the text of the Chalcedonian definition, and here we must pay attention to the exact wording. The definition reads: 'consubstantial with the *Father* as to divinity, and the Same consubstantial also with *us* as to humanity; in all things like unto *us* (*hemin*), sin only excepted'. We have here the famous assertion about Christ's twofold consubstantiality with the Father and with us, which through the Antiochene Symbol and the *laetentur* letter of Cyril from the year 433 finally went into the definition of Chalcedon. Yet in frag. 75 there is no direct quotation from this definition, as Reuss assumes. Rather, it is a question of one of the various current forms of this double assertion.[5] The difference between the Ammonius fragment and the definition of 451 lies in the fact that the former, as was predominant in Western tradition, speaks of being 'consubstantial with the *mother* (*consubstantialis matri*)' (thus Leo M.), while the latter, with the Eastern tradition (Symbol of Antioch, Union of 433, Chalcedon), speaks of being 'consubstantial with *us*'. Ammonius further interprets his words of frag. 75 in frag. 76. It is to be noted that this still does not give a *formal* statement on the 'two natures', even if (in the view of the Chalcedonians) it is given *in essence*. We also learn this from the text of Emperor Zeno's *Henoticon* adopted at Alexandria.[6] In it, on the one hand, the Eastern form of the double *homoousios* is cited, but, on the other hand, an express rejection of Chalcedon is added with regard to the two natures. Thus acceptance of the double *homoousios* in essence and rejection of the express two-natures formula – this is the position of Ammonius as derived from frag. 266 of the John commentary. He equates this formula with confession of two sons in Christ and calls this blasphemy.[7] Thus *physis* here amounts to 'a concrete subject'. In substance there is agreement between Ammonius and the *Henoticon*. Yet

---

4. Cf. J. Reuss, *Bib* 44 (1963), 162; idem, TU 89 (1966), p. XXIX, where he states that Ammonius 'places a special emphasis on the defence of the doctrines of Christology, for example, when he formulates his statement no. 23 on [Jn] 1,14 on the incarnation and no. 75 on [Jn] 3,6, with the terminology of the Council of Chalcedon, on the two natures and their union in Christ'.

5. On this see B. Studer, 'Consubstantialis Patri, Consubstantialis Matri. Une antithèse christologique chez Léon le Grand', *RevÉtAug* 18 (1972), 87–115.

6. E. Schwartz, *Codex Vaticanus gr. 1431 (ABAW.PH* XXXII 6), Munich 1927, 52–54; see the English translation in *CCT* II/1, pp. 252–53, esp. p. 253.

7. Ammonius the Presbyter, John Commentary frag. 266 on Jn 8,12: Reuss, TU 89, p. 263: '. . . to divide Christ after the incarnation into two sons or into two natures (this is the same thing) is blasphemous.' On the other hand, frag. 201 (Reuss, 247) speaks of the 'one *prosopon* and of the one hypostasis', which, however, contains a distinction between soul and divinity in Christ.

he, by contrast, chooses the form: 'consubstantial with the mother'. This then allows him, moreover, to deduce the assumption of a human soul in Christ (frag. 76 on Jn 3,6; Reuss, p. 216). Otherwise such argumentation can hardly be substantiated.

In any case, Ammonius can be counted among the moderate anti-Chalcedonian theologians of Alexandria. He also cites Severus of Antioch, though with a non-christological passage, as attested by frag. 630 on Jn 20,22–23 (Reuss, p. 353). According to Ammonius, Eutyches is correctly condemned; he gives his own substantiation: because of the errors of his followers after Ephesus II (449) (thus frag. 111 on Jn 4,3; Reuss, p. 225). Ammonius shows a strong dogmatic interest, as Reuss elaborates in his summary.[8] The bracketing of a doctrine of the Trinity based on the three hypostases in the one *ousia* of God with the order of the incarnation, that is, the *oikonomia*, gives his theology a solid framework. Sabellianism and Arianism are still fought as heresies,[9] without giving the impression that they represent an acute danger for the church. The pneumatology of the Alexandrian exegete is noteworthy. *Pneuma* is both an assertion about the nature of God, as in early Alexandria, and a designation for the hypostasis of the Holy Spirit (frag. 133 on Jn 4,24; Reuss, p. 230). Faith in the Trinity is the 'realization of the true worship of God' (*theosebeia*).[10] Thus, apart from the opposition of Ammonius to the two-natures formula of Chalcedon, an adherent to the council can affirm everything that Ammonius says on Christology. In the commentary on Acts 14,10–11 the uniqueness of Jesus is concisely emphasized: 'Only in reference to Jesus is this given: he was God and human being in one, according to the teaching (*logos*) of the union.' The antithesis of this is to see in Jesus a 'mere human being' (*psilos anthropos*).[11] Everything in Ammonius moves towards the Cyrillian conception of the incarnation. If Leo I could have read the John commentary, he would have had to be astonished at how little his picture of the Alexandrian church agreed with reality. We are reminded again of the confession to the humanity of Christ with body and soul, in which Ammonius agrees with Dioscoros and Timothy Aelurus. Also, the death of Jesus is understood as separation

---

8. J. Reuss, TU 89, pp. XXVI–XXX.

9. Ibid., p. XXIX bottom, with a reference to the evidence.

10. Interesting in regard to pneumatology is frag. 631 on Jn 20,22–23, J. Reuss, 353: 'By breathing on them [the disciples] and giving them the *pneuma*, he showed that the *pneuma* is consubstantial with and not foreign to him and through him goes out from the Father . . .' A *filioque* would no longer be far away. – On the cited passage for the Trinity see frag. on Acts 10,13: PG 85, 1537A and frag. 509 on Jn 15,1: Reuss, 323.

11. Ammonius the Presbyter, Commentary Acts 14,10–11: PG 85, 1545B.

of soul and body.[12] Older traditions in the *descensus* teaching are still visible. The descent of Christ into hell is painted with the colours of the Gospel of Nicodemus.[13] Here it is emphasized that Jesus as the God-Logos preached in Hades. This can also be valid, according to the law of communication of idioms, if for Ammonius the instrument of the descent is the soul of Christ. Whoever believes this preaching and calls on Christ can be led out of hell with him. Thus a decision for salvation is still possible there for the people of earlier times. For the Redeemer has not been preached to them until now.[14]

On the whole, Ammonius knows how to develop in close connection with the scripture a relatively well-rounded dogmatics. It is trinitarian and Christocentric, with a strong emphasis on the universality of salvation, but also on human freedom vis-à-vis God's offer, and further on the necessity of proclamation and baptism. High demands are placed on one's knowledge of God (PG 85, 1529C). Finally, the goal of history is the return of Christ. Thus Ammonius is a prominent representative of Alexandrian Christology and theology in the period of the fifth and sixth centuries. In the exegesis of scripture he follows more the Antiochene than the Alexandrian allegorization, which, however, is not completely missing. Echoes of Origen are scarce.[15] Ammonius attests to the ecclesiastical nature of the Alexandrian Christology of his time.[16]

12. John Commentary, frag. 600 on Jn 19,30: Reuss, pp. 344–45. On the early Alexandrian Christology in this question see A. Grillmeier, *Mit ihm und in ihm*, 118–19.

13. Ammonius the Presbyter, Commentary on Acts 16,29–30: PG 85, 1560C–1562A. A detailed *descensus* teaching is developed in the frag. on 1 Pt 3,19: PG 85, 1608B–1609B, where the obstinacy of Judas is emphasized.

14. In the just-mentioned text Ammonius especially develops the preaching motif for the descent of Christ.

15. Cf. the introduction by J. Reuss, in TU 89, pp. XXIXf.; idem, *Bib* 22 (1941), 13–20; 44 (1963) 159–70. – In frag. 55 on Jn 1,51; Reuss, 211, Origen's formula 'kat'eikona' is adopted for our likeness to God. On this cf. A. Grillmeier, *JdChr* I³, pp. 106–10.

16. Ammonius announces his interest in Antioch with a peculiar reference to the substantiation of the prominence of the see of this city, which is a 'thronos archontikos' (thus in the frag. on Acts 11,26: PG 85, 1540A).

2. The deacon Olympiodore
(by T. Hainthaler)

Also active as an exegete in Alexandria in the sixth century was the deacon Olympiodore, who was ordained by Patriarch John II Nicaiotes (505–516).[17] In regard to additional personal information we know only that Olympiodore wrote his Ecclesiastes and Job commentaries under commission from 'Julian' and 'John' – presumably ecclesiastical dignitaries in sixth-century Alexandria who nonetheless cannot be further identified.[18] A high appreciation of Olympiodore in later time is attested by Ps. Anastasius Sinaita, who calls him a great philosopher and scholar.[19]

Of his exegetical works, only the Job commentary has been critically edited so far; the commentaries on Ecclesiastes and on Jeremiah, Lamentations and Baruch are available only in Migne.[20] Hence the textual foundation for a treatment of Olympiodore's theology does not yet exist,[21] and thus we must content ourselves with a few comments.

The effort in his Job commentary to take the pure Septuagint text as a basis – that is, to assemble it from the various manuscripts[22] – identifies Olympiodore as a scholarly exegete of his time who moreover also 'exhaustively' used the aids at his disposal.[23]

---

17. This is according to the postscript under the Jeremiah commentary of Olympiodore: PG 93, 11f. Cf. U. and D. Hagedorn (eds.), *Olympiodor, Diakon von Alexandria. Kommentar zu Hiob* (PTSt 24), Berlin–New York 1984, p. XLIV.

18. U. and D. Hagedorn, PTSt 24, p. XLV.

19. Ps. Anastas. Sin., *In hexaemeron* (CPG 7770), l. VI: PG 93, 936–37; idem, *Contra Monophysitas* (CPG 7771): PG 93, 1189AB. Olympiodore was regarded 'for centuries as an especially important author' (Hagedorn, PTSt 24, p. XLV). Yet whether he was wrongly identified with the Alexandrian philosopher of the same name remains an open question.

20. Olympiodore, Deacon of Alex., *Commentarii in Iob* (CPG 7453): ed. Hagedorn (PTSt 24), Berlin–New York 1984; *Commentarii in Ecclesiasten* (CPG 7454): PG 93, 477–628. A Jeremiah commentary (incl. Baruch, Lamentations, Letter of Jeremiah) (CPG 7455–58) is found in PG 93, 628–780. Beyond this a commentary on the book of Ezra is attested but not extant: Hagedorn, PTSt 24, pp. XLI–XLII.

21. According to U. and D. Hagedorn, PTSt 24, pp. XXXIX–XLII, for the Ecclesiastes commentary (and also the Jeremiah commentary) there are still many open questions regarding tradition. In the Job commentary 'the unreliability of the text printed in Migne goes so far that it is virtually unusable as a basis for knowledge of Olympiodore's Job commentary: hardly more than half of the text printed in PG 93, 13–470 really comes from Olympiodore' (Hagedorn, PTSt 24, p. XII, n. 6).

22. Hagedorn, PTSt 24, pp. XLVIIs, LIII–LVI.

23. Ibid., pp. LVII–LXXXII.

The designation of Christ as σωτήρ[24] (almost as frequent as the title *kyrios*) underlines his soteriological view. The incarnation of Christ is especially emphasized with some expressions.[25] Striking is the conjoining (perhaps coined in Alexandria) of the Logos with wisdom in the explanation of the song on wisdom (Job 28), for example, in the designation σοφία οὐσιώδης for Christ.[26] Olympiodore often speaks of the 'only begotten Son of God' (ὁ μονογενὴς υἱὸς τοῦ θεοῦ).[27] The expression ἐνυποστάτου λόγου (p. 219,7.16) shows the use of ἐνυπόστατος in the sense of 'really existing' (not in the sense of the insubsistence of the humanity of Christ in the Logos hypostasis). He uses the words ὁμοούσιος and ὑπόστασις in reference to the Trinity[28] or in general, but not christologically.

Of special interest would be his writing 'Against Severus of Antioch', which, however, is attested only in a short fragment (CPG 7459). Presumably in this text Severus's doctrine of the one will is refuted with an appeal to Athanasius,[29] particularly with reference to the Athanasian interpretation of Christ's suffering on the Mount of Olives.[30]

---

24. Cf. 'our God and redeemer': p. 23,21; 40,8; 378,17; the incarnation of the God-Logos 'for us' is expressed in p. 40,18–19. The name σωτήρ is found twenty times.

25. ὁ σαρκωθεὶς λόγος, p. 226,9; ἐνανθρωπήσας λόγος, p. 235,2; 364,13; ἐνανθρωπήσας ὁ κύριος, p. 363,20; ἐνανθρώπησις τοῦ λόγου/μονογενοῦς, p. 92,16; 333,1; 383,14.

26. pp. 219,14; 241,21. Cf. also p. 238,7–9: 'Without participation in the true wisdom of the paternal Logos it is impossible to attain the wisdom of the fear of God.' The essential ideas appear already in the *protheoria* to the chapter on p. 219,7–19: Olympiodore is concerned here with human wisdom as it is made possible through participation in the wisdom of the Logos through the Holy Spirit, not with the wisdom of the divine Logos himself. Thus in this connection he places the accent on the doctrine of grace, not on Christology.

27. pp. 219,8, 15; 241,21; 280,1–2; 342,13.

28. p. 226,2–3, 10–11. The emphasis of the one will and one essence of the Trinity (p. 335,24–25), as well as the inseparable (ἀχώριστος) conjoining of the only begotten Son with the Father (p. 170,18), is orthodox trinitarian theology.

29. Perhaps Athanasius of Alex., *Orat. c. Arianos* (CPG 2093) III, 57: PG 26, 441B.

30. See A. Grillmeier, *JdChr* I³, p. 466f.; *CCT* I², p. 313f.; the fragment: PG 89, 1189B.

CHAPTER THREE

JOHN PHILOPONUS, PHILOSOPHER AND THEOLOGIAN IN ALEXANDRIA

—————

(by T. Hainthaler)

I. THE MAN AND HIS WORK

With John Philoponus[1] we come into contact with the milieu of the philosophical school of Alexandria,[2] which in the fifth century was borne by an influential pagan elite. With its academy, Alexandria proved to be

---

1. R. R. K. Sorabji, art. 'Johannes Philoponus', *TRE* 17 (1987), 144–50, whose comprehensive source information and bibliography are especially recommended; a detailed presentation of the content of the *TRE* article is found in idem, 'John Philoponus', in idem (ed.), *Philoponus and the Rejection of Aristotelian Science*, London 1987, 1–40. Also J. R. Martindale, art. 'Ioannes Philoponus 76', in *The Prosopography of the Later Roman Empire* II, Cambridge etc. 1980, 615–16. Earlier: A. Gudeman and W. Kroll, art. no. 21, 'Ioannes Philoponus', *PWK* 9 (1916), 1764–95, in which, however, Philoponus is incorrectly identified with John the Grammarian, the opponent of Severus; also, he is supposed to have become bishop of Alexandria, an assumption that was already rejected by T. Hermann, 'Johannes Philoponus als Monophysit', *ZNW* 29 (1930), 209–64, here: p. 210, n. 9. Besides this work of T. Hermann, which is especially important for our purposes, we also mention: H.-D. Saffrey, 'Le chrétien Jean Philopon et la survivance de l'école d'Alexandrie au VIᵉ siècle', *RevÉtGrec* 67 (1954), 396–410; H. Martin, 'La controverse trithéite dans l'Empire Byzantin au VIᵉ siècle', diss. Louvain, esp. pp. 32–50.161–183.207–213; W. Böhm, *Johannes Philoponus. Grammatikos von Alexandrien (6. Jh. n. Chr.). Christliche Naturwissenschaft im Ausklang der Antike, Vorläufer der modernen Physik, Wissenschaft und Bibel. Ausgewählte Schriften*, Munich–Paderborn–Vienna 1967, with numerous German translations of texts of John Philop.; M. Lutz-Bachmann, 'Das Verhältnis von Philosophie und Theologie in den "Opuscula Sacra" des A. M. S. Boethius. Eine Studie zur Entwicklung der nachchalcedonischen Theologie', diss. Münster 1983, 116–55; H. Chadwick, 'Philoponus the Christian Theologian', in R. Sorabji (ed.), op. cit., 41–56.

2. A detailed description of school life is found in F. Schemmel, 'Die Hochschule von Alexandria im IV. und V. Jahrhundert p. Ch. n.', *NJKA* 24 (1909), 438–57. On the difficulties of the concept of a 'school of Alexandria' cf. I. Hadot, *Le problème du néoplatonisme alexandrin. Hiéroclès et Simplicius*, Paris 1978, Introd., pp. 9–14.

an educational centre for the whole Orient.[3] Between the schools of
Alexandria and Athens there were close connections, also of the familial
kind.[4] But whereas in Athens, after the death of Proclus (485), there was
a decline and the academy was finally closed by an edict of Justinian
(529), in Alexandria the school successfully continued to operate even
into the time of Islam.[5] This was probably due not least of all to the skill
of the pagan philosopher Ammonius Hermeiou[6] (a student of Proclus in
Athens), whose interpretation of Aristotelianism was attractive to many.
Regarding Christianity, he was at least open enough to admit Christian
students, presumably on the basis of a contract with the current Alexandrian patriarch.[7] In this way John Philoponus, who was probably a
Christian from the beginning, was able to become the editor of his
writings.

The question whether John Philoponus was already a Christian when he wrote his Aristotle
commentaries is repeatedly discussed. The categorical judgement of Gudeman, who held that
Philoponus was 'without doubt himself still a pagan when he joined the pagan Ammonius',[8]
which was widely adopted, was rejected especially by E. Evrard for good reasons (similarly
Saffrey).[9] But Verbeke reservedly established that in his study of Philoponus's commentary on
the *De anima* of Aristotle he hardly encountered actually Christian elements. 'To the extent
that he admits the teaching of the pre-existence of the soul and reincarnation, one would
have to ask, rather, whether in his sense these theories are compatible with the Christian faith.
That is not out of the question . . . That is, it is not impossible for an educated Christian of
the sixth century to assume that the pre-existence of the soul and reincarnation are not in
contradiction with his faith. We acknowledge, however, that this question is extremely
delicate . . .'[10] The assumption that John Philoponus was a Christian from birth, however, is

---

3. On the significance of the pagan intellectual elite in Alexandria cf. E. Wipszycka, 'La
christianisation de l'Égypte aux IVe–VIe siècles', *Aegyptus* 68 (1988), 125–27.

4. See H.-D. Saffrey, art. cit., pp. 396–98.

5. See the noteworthy article of M. Meyerhof, 'Von Alexandrien nach Bagdad. Ein
Beitrag zur Geschichte des philosophischen und medizinischen Unterrichts bei den Arabern',
SPAW (1930), pp. 389–429.

6. Cf. J. R. Martindale, art. 'Ammonius 6', in idem, *Prosopography* (op. cit.), 71–72.

7. Cf. H.-D. Saffrey, art. cit., pp. 400–1.

8. Gudeman/Kroll, *PWK* 9 (1916), 1769.

9. E. Evrard, 'Les convictions religieuses de Jean Philopon et la date de son Commentaire
aux "Météorologiques"', *BCLAB* 5 Ser., 34 (1953), 299–357, summary: pp. 356–57. H.-D.
Saffrey, art. cit., p. 402; cf. R. R. K. Sorabji, *TRE* 17, p. 144.

10. G. Verbeke, Introduction to: *Jean Philopon. Commentaire sur le De anima d'Aristote.
Traduction de Guillaume de Moerbeke, édition critique* (CLCAG 3), Louvain–Paris 1966, p. LXX.
Cf. also idem, 'Levels of Human Thinking in Philoponus', in *After Chalcedon*, FS A. Van
Roey (OLA 18), Louvain 1985, p. 499, n. 47: 'This viewpoint of Philoponus is hardly
compatible with christian teaching on eschatology. If Philoponus, when he wrote his *De
anima*, was already a christian, he probably did not realize there to be a lack of conformity and
coherence.'

supported by the following considerations. He already had the Christian name John when he wrote the Aristotle commentaries. In his writings there is no perceptible break.[11] None of his later opponents makes an allusion to his earlier paganism. If such a thing had been known, his anti-tritheistic opponents or those who opposed his resurrection teaching, for example, would doubtless have accused him of backsliding into his past. To be mentioned in particular here is Cosmas Indicopleustes, the earliest known foe[12] of Philoponus, who is alleged by his opponent to be a baptized Christian. Moreover, in the evaluation of the statements in the early *De anima* commentary (before 517) we must consider the Origenist currents (beginning of the sixth century in Palestine and Byzantium [cf. *CCT* II/2] and already in the fifth century; cf. below on Shenoute), as well as the fact that it was not until the generation of John Philoponus that Christians could play a role in the academy of Alexandria. In particular, however, we must note that the views in the *De anima* commentary can already be coherently explained within Neoplatonism.[13] In sum, compelling reasons are lacking for the assumption of an original paganism of John Philoponus.

John the Grammarian, with the sobriquet Philoponus, may have been born at the end of the fifth century (*c.* 490) and died perhaps around 575.[14] The nickname 'Philoponus' – gladly corrupted by his opponents to 'Mataioponus' (one who strives in vain)[15] – could be an allusion to his

---

11. H. Blumenthal, 'John Philoponus and Stephanus of Alexandria: Two Neoplatonic Christian Commentators on Aristotle?', in D. J. O'Meara (ed.), *Neoplatonism and Christian Thought*, Norfolk, Va. 1982, 54–63, 244–46, p. 60: 'If however one is trying to show that he held pagan views in the commentaries, and Christian views elsewhere, one has to show that there is a clear measure of inconsistency between the commentaries and those works which are indisputably part of Philoponus' writings *qua* Christian. Now when one looks at some of his views on the soul in this light, the opposite turns out to be the case.' Even in vocabulary Blumenthal can ascertain no Christian elements, and this, he claims, is also true to a large extent for another Alexandrian commentator, Stephen, who was certainly a Christian. Therefore, says B., in the writing of this commentary the Christian faith played little or no role.

12. This is with the presupposition that the thesis of W. Wolska-Conus is correct, namely, that as polemics the text *De opificio mundi* of John Philoponus and the *Topographia christiana* of Cosmas Indicopleustes refer to each other. For details see the following chapter. The quarrel may have been still carried on before the Second Council of Constantinople (553).

13. See especially H. Blumenthal, art. cit., esp. pp. 58–61, 62.

14. For bibliography (Philoponus as philosopher): C. M. K. Macleod, 'Jean Philopon, commentateur d'Aristote', in CLCAG 3, pp. XI–XIX; for dating cf. R. R. K. Sorabji, art. cit., p. 147; differently T. Hermann, art. cit., pp. 210–11, with n. 3, p. 211, who assumes a year of death 'soon after 565'. Nonetheless, the text *De trinitate* is for good reasons placed at the end of 567 and *De resurrectione* around 570 (cf. below).

15. Cf. Theodore of Alex., *Epistula synodica ad Paulum Antiochenum*: Chabot, CSCO 103, p. 212,4–9: Iohannem, ματαιοπόνον Grammaticum. In the list of heretics of the Third Council of Constantinople (680/681) the sobriquet is added with the comment: Φιλόπονον, μᾶλλον δὲ Ματαιόπονον (Mansi XI, 501). Cf. also Photius, *Bibl. cod.* 55: PG 103, 97B; Henry I, p. 13. – Origen was also bestowed with this sobriquet by Epiphan. of Salam., *Haer.* 64, 63,8: Holl (GCS 31), Leipzig 1922, p. 501,8!

zeal for work[16] or a reference to the fact that John belonged to a fellowship[17] of especially committed Christians in Egypt, the φιλόπονοι. They are reported on by Zacharias the Rhetor, who even joined them himself, together with Severus of Antioch, during their common time of study in Alexandria.[18] They were lay people who undertook a variety of services: in the care for the poor, the building of churches, in the worship service, and who were also prepared for militant discussion with non-believers.[19]

John Philoponus could have been a student of the academy with Ammonius around 510.[20] In 517 his Aristotle commentary on the *Physica* appeared. Beyond that he wrote commentaries for Aristotle works on the categories and on meteorology. Three further Aristotle commentaries carry the note that they come from the classes of Ammonius Hermeiou, mostly with the addition of 'personal comments'.[21] John Philoponus is thus one of the 'official editors' of the school director Ammonius of Alexandria.[22] In 529 he published the polemic *De aeternitate mundi contra*

---

16. Cf. here the lovely Arabian legend 'according to which John Philoponos was a poor mariner who used to transport the professors of the school of Alexandria to the island where the "house of knowledge" was located. While listening to their conversations, the ferryman received an indomitable inclination towards the study of philosophy. An ant that strove the whole day long in vain to drag a date pit up a hill but in the evening was successful taught him persistence, and so he sold his boat and became a student', according to M. Meyerhof, 'Von Alexandrien nach Bagdad', p. 398.

17. John Beth-Aphth., *Vita Sev.*: PO 2, p. 214: 'la sainte association'. For details and discussion of the sources in Egypt in the 4th through 9th centuries: E. Wipszycka, 'Les confréries dans la vie religieuse de l'Égypte chrétienne', in *Proc. of the XIIth Internat. Congress of Papyrology*, Toronto 1970, 511–25. E. W. speaks of 'religious fraternities (confrérie religieuse)' and understands by this a group of people who have united in a certain organizational form in order to lead a common religious life, without breaking off relations with the 'world' (ibid., 511). Such organizations arose in the fourth century (in Syria they are called σπουδαῖοι).

18. That may have been around 485–487 according to M. Minniti Colonna, *Zacaria Scolastico. Ammonio*, Naples 1973, Introd., p. 23.

19. Cf. Zachar. Schol., *Vit. Sev.*: ed. Kugener, PO 2, pp. 12,9; 24,3; 26,9; 33,1. Also the presentation in H.-D. Saffrey, art. cit., pp. 403–4; more recently: L. S. B. MacCoull, 'Dioscorus of Aphrodito and John Philoponus', *StudPat* 18,1 [Oxford 1983] (Kalamazoo, Mich. 1985) (163–68), 164. A thorough description of the qualities and activities of the *philoponoi* based on the sources is found in E. Wipszycka, art. cit. (1970), esp. pp. 513–17.

20. H.-D. Saffrey, art. cit., p. 403.

21. The Commentaria in Aristotelem graeca (= CAG), vols. XIII–XVII offer the Aristotle commentaries of John Philoponus. CAG XIII/2–3 (*Analytica* I–II), XIV/2 (*De generatione et corruptione*), XV (*De anima*) carry the addition ἐκ τῶν συνουσιῶν Ἀμμονίου τοῦ Ἑρμείου with the addendum (except in XIII/2, that is, the commentary on the first analysis): μετὰ τινῶν ἰδίων ἐπιστάσεων.

22. H.-D. Saffrey, art. cit., p. 405.

Proclum (CPG 7266) against the spiritual head of Athenian Neoplatonism, Proclus (410–485), this in the year of the closing of the academy in Athens.[23] This paper could have played a supporting role in the action of the emperor.[24] In it Philoponus opposed the Neoplatonic axiom of the perpetuity and indestructibility of the world and strove to prove the Christian teaching that the world was, a certain time ago, created by God out of nothing.

This event was qualified by R. R. K. Sorabji as the first Christian attack against the pagan concept that the world had no beginning. Until 529 Christians limited themselves to a defensive position. Here Philoponus could turn to arguments that he had already developed in the earlier Aristotle commentaries. In all, he dealt intensively with this issue in three (or four) works: in addition to *De aeternitate mundi*, these include the writing *Contra Aristotelem* (six books) and *De opificio mundi* (CPG 7265).[25]

The works of John Philoponus exhibit an enormous breadth of scientific themes. Our task here is not to evaluate his philosophical works,[26] to go into his Aristotle commentaries, his critique of Aristotle and his significance for modern physics (space theory, impetus theory)[27] or his influence on the Middle Ages.[28] In the next chapter we will go into his

---

23. On the controversy on the significance of the closing of the Athens academy cf. R. R. K. Sorabji, *Time, Creation and the Continuum. Theories in Antiquity and the Early Middle Ages*, London 1983, 199–200.

24. W. Böhm, op. cit., p. 24, speaks of a 'justification document for the closing of the Athens school'.

25. S. Pines believed that he had found an Arabic summary of a lost additional writing; cf. *De aeternitate mundi (summarium)* (CPG 7274); yet this may be a question of fragments from *Contra Aristotelem*, according to R. R. K. Sorabji, op. cit., pp. 198–99, who, however, excludes the possibility that Philoponus composed a further, non-polemical work against the perpetuity of the universe.

26. Cf. the overview of his writings in R. R. K. Sorabji, art. cit., p. 148 (evaluation: ibid., 144–46); W. Böhm, op. cit., pp. 459–62.

27. Cf. W. Böhm, op. cit., who wants to show with his work that Philoponus represents 'the connecting link between Aristotle's teaching on nature and modern physics' (ibid., p. 5) and assumes a 'key position as the evoker of dynamics' (p. 11). See also S. Sambursky, *Das physikalische Weltbild der Antike*, Zurich–Stuttgart 1965, p. 641 (index); more recent: R. Sorabji (ed.), *Philoponus and the Rejection of Aristotelian Science*, London 1987, esp. pp. 121–53; on the concept of time and on the doctrine of creation cf. idem, *Time, Creation and the Continuum*, London 1983, p. 467 (index).

28. See C. M. K. Macleod, 'Le "De intellectu" de Philopon et la pensée du XIIIᵉ siècle', in CLCAG 3, pp. LXXI–LXXXVI. According to Macleod one cannot assume that Thomas Aquinas used the commentary on Aristotle's *De anima* by John Philoponus, as was often assumed. Yet this commentary was cited by Henri Bate de Malines (b. 1246) and Radulphus Brito, Gilles de Rome and an anonymous Averroist appeal to John Philoponus as an authority. W. Böhm, op. cit., pp. 337–87, devotes his whole chap. 7 to the effect of John Phil. on posterity. Cf. also R. R. K. Sorabji, art. cit., *TRE* 17, pp. 147–48, among others, on Bonaventure's use of the arguments of Philoponus for the beginning of the world.

disagreement with Cosmas Indicopleustes, which (according to Wolska) was reflected in *De opificio mundi* (CPG 7265) and the *Topographia christiana* (CPG 7468) of Indicopleustes and represents the two schools in Alexandria.[29] First, and of greater priority, we will turn our attention to his christological writings.[30]

II. THE CHRISTOLOGY OF JOHN PHILOPONUS

In the centre of the Christology of John Philoponus stands the formula μία φύσις σύνθετος.[31] He repeats it almost like a refrain again and again in his *Diaetetes*. Most of the deliberations serve to demonstrate the philosophical basis of this formula and its rooting in tradition. He thinks through the *mia-physis* Christology of the Severan type given to him above all in regard to the manner of the union in Christ, which for him is clearly to be conceived as a synthesis (*compositio*) and indeed one of natures. The basic axiom of his thought lies in his almost total equation of nature and hypostasis.[32] In an individual they come together as the

---

29. W. Wolska, *La topographie chrétienne de Cosmas Indicopleustès. Théologie et Science au VIe siècle*, Paris 1962, 147–92, esp. pp. 161–83; note also on pp. 297–99 the collected accusations of Philoponus against Theodore of Mopsuestia.

30. Cf. CPG 7260–82, esp. the main work *Diaetetes* (CPG 7260) with the supplements *Epitome* and *Dubiorum quorundam in Diaetete solutio duplex* (CPG 7261–62), also the *Tractatus de totalitate et partibus* (CPG 7263), all in Syriac with Latin translation in A. Sanda, *Opuscula Monophysitica Ioannis Philoponi*, Beirut 1930; in addition the *Tomi quattuor contra synodum quartam* (CPG 7271), which are extant in fragments in Syriac: Mich. Syr., *Chron.* VIII 13, trans. in Chabot II, 92–121. The *Tractatus de differentia, numero ac divisione* (CPG 7277), also preserved in Sanda, who divides it into 37 sections, is not from Philoponus, according to Sanda, p. 7, yet for reasons that according to A. Van Roey, 'Fragments antiariens de Jean Philopon', *OLP* 10 (1979), 238, n. 7, are not entirely correct; yet even Van Roey assumes a time of composition around 580: that is the time when the problem of the Stephenites was current. The treatise begins, namely, by speaking of those who say that it is impossible 'after the inexpressible union to preserve the essential distinction of the natures that are joined in the Redeemer of us all, Christ, without at the same time also preserving their number and separation' (translation follows Van Roey, loc. cit.). This view, however, corresponds exactly to the thesis of Stephen of Alexandria, who followed Probus after 580.

31. The *Diaetetes* is entirely in line with the confession to 'una natura composita Christi', as is already clear in the Prooemium no. 2: Sanda, p. 36.

32. Cf. *Tmemata*, chaps. IV and VII: p. 103 ('. . . dans la nature, puisque celle-ci est la même chose que l'hypostase') and p. 107; chap. V: p. 105 ('chacune de ces deux natures existe nécessairement avec sa propre hypostase').

same thing. Therefore even the Fathers used nature and hypostasis synonymously in regard to Christ.[33]

1. The basic traits of Philoponian Christology in the polemic *Tmemata*

We now turn to his polemic against Chalcedon, the Τμήματα or *Tomi quattuor contra synodum quartam* (CPG 7269), preserved in Syriac in excerpts[34] in Michael the Syrian and written at the time of the Second Council of Constantinople (553).[35]

Philoponus even quotes literally canons III, IV, V, VII, IX, XII, XIII and XIV of the council and is therefore a textual witness for these sections.[36] Noteworthy is the fact that here an Alexandrian 'Monophysite' accepts the Second Council of Constantinople. In citing the anathemas he wants to show that these imply a condemnation of the Chalcedonians and the Council of Chalcedon. In the named canons the topics include the rejection of a union only according to grace or *schesis*, etc. (IV), and the negation of two hypostases (V) – both aimed at Theodore of Mopsuestia and the Nestorians – as well as the correct understanding of 'in two natures' (not in the sense of a separation) (VII) and worship (not two acts of worship) (IX), also the prohibition of a separation of Christ into two (*allos kai allos*) (III), to say nothing of the condemnation of the 'three names' Theodore, Theodoret and Ibas (XII–XIV). The point of attack is Leo's *Tome*, especially for canons III, IV, V. He sees the Council of Chalcedon itself condemned by canons XII–XIV and IX.

Philoponus works on various levels for his attack on Chalcedon.[37] Apart from the external, more formal view, which concerns the participation of imperial judges in Chalcedon as well as criticism of the pre-eminence of the bishop of Rome (which one can plainly call an anti-Roman

---

33. Ibid., chap. VI (vol. III): p. 106 ('conformément au sentiment des Pères de l'Église, que, surtout dans le Christ, nature et hypostase signifient la même chose'); cf. chap. I: p. 97.

34. Michael Syr., pursuant to his closing word (Chabot, p. 121), offers excerpts from the four volumes of the work of John Philoponus. He says that he has put the arguments in order and left out those that prove to be without significance 'pour conduire au choix de la vérité'.

35. *Tmemata*, chap. I: Chabot II, pp. 97–98: 'Le synode qui s'est réuni de nos jours à Constantinople ...'; chap. IV, p. 102: '... nos jours, dans le synode qui se réunit à Constantinople pour l'examen des Trois chapitres'.

36. *Tmemata*, chap. XI, pp. 117–21. On the canons (translation, commentary) cf. A. Grillmeier, *CCT* II/2, pp. 446–53.

37. The characterization of his procedure against the Aristotelian and Neoplatonic dogma of the perpetuity of the world, given by Sambursky, op. cit., p. 575, seems enlightening here also: 'P.'s attack was a concentric one; he attempted to refute every aspect of the dogma of the bipartition ... He sought to expose contradictions ... indeed, he did not even shy away from sophistries and mutually contradictory assertions. Since he was convinced of the total perversity of the Aristotelian position, he laid no great worth on the consistency of his own. For him it was simply and solely a question of undermining Aristotle's teaching from every conceivable viewpoint.'

feeling),[38] it is his aim again and again to show the followers of Chalcedon to be Nestorians in disguise (cf. chap. V, VI, VIII), who ultimately separate Christ into two persons, confess no hypostatic union and in their views are not distinguishable from the condemned heretics Nestorius and Theodore of Mopsuestia.

That becomes clear already in chap. I, which presents an attack on Leo and his *Tome*: Philoponus shows with quotations from the *Tome* that Leo sees in Christ only one person by name and concedes only a moral union, but not a hypostatic union, which he never confesses. If Leo says much that is correct, that is no hindrance to classifying him among the followers of Nestorius, since he has mixed what is right with things that imply a separation.

The Fathers proclaim 'the nature union that is in the hypostasis', and they ascribe 'to one single nature or hypostasis the divine and human things'.[39]

If the Council of Chalcedon asserts that there is only one hypostasis, then it must necessarily be simple or composite. If it is simple, then one must say that Christ is God in the flesh. If composite, then the composition is necessarily in the nature, since this is the same as the hypostasis (*sic!*). Thus there remains either an incarnate nature of the God-Logos or a composite nature and hypostasis of the one composite Christ. Those who reject this alternative (i.e., the Chalcedonians) can only assume multiple hypostases, which leads to Nestorius. If they then still want to speak of union, then it is one in name only. Hence it follows that those who assert two natures in Christ after union cannot mean a hypostatic union but only a moral one.[40] Thus again and again Philoponus works through to this conclusion, which essentially depends on his equation of

---

38. The sharp questioning, indeed rejection, of the Roman primacy is found in chap. IV: Chabot II, pp. 101–2. Philoponus alleges that the primacy of the bishop of Rome is mere custom, supported by the greatness of the city of Rome as well as imperial authority, and that it is anchored neither by ecclesiastical nor imperial law. He maintains that only the emperor, not the pope, can convoke a synod. He also stresses the 'arrogance' of the Romans (esp. Pope Vigilius). Cf. M. Jugie, 'La primauté romaine d'après les premiers théologiens monophysites (V^e–VIe siècles)', *EO* 33 (1934) (181–89), 187–89 (on Philoponus). – It is noteworthy that here with John Philoponus an Alexandrian affirms the principle of the imperial church! On the comment that Ephesus, 'adorned with the apostolic halo', is in the meantime guided by Constantinople 'because the seat of the empire was moved there' (Chabot II, p. 101), cf. E. Herman, 'Chalkedon und die Ausgestaltung des konstantinopolitanischen Primats', in *Chalkedon* II, p. 486: 'But in the following century the Monophysite John Philoponus in his work against the Council of Chalcedon makes the assertion that Constantine the Great transferred the imperial dominion as a whole to the new capital . . . Theories of the renewal . . . of the Roman Empire in the West were cut off at the roots if the whole empire was transferred to the East.' On this see A. Michel, 'Der Kampf um das politische oder petrinische Prinzip der Kirchenführung', in ibid., pp. 491–562.

39. *Tmemata*, chap. I: Chabot II, p. 97.

40. Thus also in chap. V, pp. 104–5.

nature and hypostasis. Yet at least twice he challenges the Chalcedonians to a conceptual clarification, that is, to say what the hypostasis (which he describes as the essence of an individual nature) in their opinion designates beyond the essence,[41] if it is not the same thing as the nature. This justifiable question, especially in connection with the question how two natures can be joined in such a way that the result is not a composite nature, was answered at the time by Leontius of Jerusalem, a solution that seems unknown to Philoponus: no nature union but an *enhypostasis* as the subject union of two natures. The synthesis is achieved in the hypostases; the natures remain intact. For Leontius and Philoponus the focus is on the concept of synthesis, and Philoponus also considers the *idiotetes* (*proprietates*) of the natures, which in his concept of synthesis are left unchanged and in a sense gathered up from the one composite nature that results from the union. But because of his conceptuality of nature and hypostasis, which he places so close to each other, he is still denied access to the solution of Leontius, namely, that the union occurs in such a way that the human nature of Christ has its hypostasis in the Logos hypostasis. For Philoponus (therefore) there is only composition in the natures, and if not there, then not at all. Immediately he has then arrived at two persons, two beings, and the union in Christ is destroyed.

Within the framework of a nature union Philoponus can make quite clear how the two natures remain preserved. The concept of composition ensures (even in purely logical terms) the 'unmixed' and 'unchanged' of the definition of Chalcedon.[42] Therefore Philoponus vehemently resists the idea of emphasizing the duality of natures after the joining – only out of fear of confusing them[43] – so that the union in Christ is jeopardized. He declares true real Monophysitism to be a fiction of the Chalcedonians that no one conceives in that way.[44] Philoponus can also explain well how with a composite one can speak of certain parts

---

41. Chap. VII, p. 107: 'S'ils disent que l'hypostase signifie autre chose et la nature autre chose, qu'ils disent d'abord ce que signifie hypostase en dehors de l'essence soit de l'homme, soit de Dieu, soit de quelque autre des choses qui existent.' Chap. VIII, ibid.: 'S'ils veulent que l'hypostase ne signifie pas seulement l'essence, mais quelque chose autre que la nature, qu'ils disent (d'abord), comme j'ai dit, ce que c'est . . .'

42. Philoponus explains this in detail in the *Diaetetes*, to which he also refers in the *Tmemata*, chap. XI, Chabot II, p. 110: just as in a human being the body is preserved by the soul, so also in Christ the lesser is preserved by the greater, the humanity by the divinity.

43. Cf. *Diaetetes*, Prooemium no. 2, Sanda, p. 37: *mero timore confusionis duas naturas se appellare dicunt.*

44. *Tmemata*, chap. IV, p. 103: 'Personne de ceux qui méditent les choses du Christ n'a jamais dit qu'il y avait une seule nature de la chair et de la divinité . . .'; cf. chap. XI, p. 110: 'Nous disons pas qu'il y a une nature ou une hypostase de la divinité et de l'humanité . . .'

of which it is composed, without thereby asserting that the composite has the nature of a part. As a human being does not have an incorporeal nature because of the soul or a corporeal nature because of the body, so also with Christ the nature of the composite Christ is not simply the divinity or the humanity but that which is composed of both. Thus, if one says that Christ suffered in his earthly nature or he did not suffer in his divine nature, that does not mean that Christ has two natures but that he suffered in the one part and not in the other.[45] Again and again Philoponus employs, as here, the body–soul analogy as *the* example by which he explains the union in Christ.[46]

Philoponus delivers an exposition of his patristic argumentation especially in his position[47] on two often cited and very much discussed patristic passages, which were the object of forgeries: *De fide* II 9, 77 of Ambrose of Milan and the closing chapter (§ 17) of *De unione*, which was ascribed to Pope Julius I. Both can be called classical components of the (Diphysite) florilegia.[48]

The Ambrose text from *De fide* reads: 'Unus *in utraque* loquitur dei filius, quia in eodem utraque natura est; etsi idem loquitur, non uno semper loquitur modo.'[49] The quarrel revolved around whether it is supposed to read 'in utraque' (referring to 'natura') or 'in utroque' (referring to 'modo'). The passage was quoted[50] already at the Council of Ephesus, as well as by Pope Leo I (*utroque*), Theodoret, Nestorius, at the Council of Chalcedon (both readings!), much discussed by Severus of Antioch, quoted by Leontius of Jerusalem[51] and Justinian (ἐν ἑκατέραι),[52] and also discussed by John Scythopolis and Eulogius of Alexandria.[53]

---

45. *Tmemata*, chap. XV: Chabot, p. 113.

46. Cf. on this also *Tmemata*, p. 97: the things of the soul and of the body are ascribed to a single human being; chap. VI, p. 106: composition of two natures; XI, p. 110: in human beings (and in Christ) the lesser, that is, the body, is preserved by the greater, that is, the soul; XV, p. 111: human beings can be described according to their corporeal as well as their spiritual characteristics or according to their corporeal-spiritual ones; they do not, however, therefore have two natures; XVII, p. 114.

47. *Tmemata*, chap. XVII: Chabot II, pp. 113–16.

48. Cf. on this M. Richard, 'Les florilèges diphysites du Vᵉ et du VIᵉ siècle', in *Chalkedon* I, 721–48 (published also in Op. Min. I as no. 3), esp. pp. 725, 736 (on Ambrose); 746 (on Julius).

49. Ambrose, *De fide* (CPL 150), II 9, 77: O. Faller (CSEL 78), Vienna 1962, pp. 84,33–85,35; on the two readings at the councils of Ephesus and Chalcedon see the information in the apparatus on the passage.

50. Cf. the information in G. Bardy, 'Sur une citation de saint Ambroise dans les controverses christologiques', *RHE* 40 (1944/45), 171–76.

51. Leont. of Jer., *Contra Monoph.*: PG 86, 1829BC.

52. Justinian, *Contra Monophysitas* (CPG 6878): Schwartz, *Drei dogm. Schriften*, p. 32,30–35.

53. Eulogius of Alex., *Apologiae pro synodo Chalcedonensi*: Photius, *Bibl. cod.* 230, Henry V, pp. 21–22.

The second passage, the closing chapter of *De unione* (§ 17) (CPG 3646),[54] is found already in Cyril, Ephraem of Amida[55] and Leontius of Jerusalem.[56]

In regard to the Ambrose text Philoponus demanded the reading 'in utroque'; that is, Christ, the Son of God, speaks in two ways, as God and as a human being, and not 'in utraque', that is, in two natures – which in fact represents here an unnecessarily forced interpretation referring to the two natures. Also, the reading 'in utroque' (*modo*) is likewise often attested, even with the Chalcedonians, and fits well the structure of the sentence.

In the treatment of the so-called Julius text we encounter the problem of the Apollinarian forgeries. Philoponus begins with the reading 'the natures' (which he also chooses for reasons of content), through which the sentence can be interpreted as an assertion of the two natures. But he interprets it in the sense of the *mia physis* and for support refers to § 5 of the same treatise, in which the one nature is clearly confessed. Now, against the position that these words come not from Julius but from Apollinarius, he offers three arguments. (1) No proof for this could be produced; also, in the tradition they are always handed down under the name of Julius. (2) At the Council of Chalcedon itself it would have been adduced as a Julius quotation (yet nowhere in the documents of Chalcedon is *De unione* 17 or 5 quoted;[57] perhaps Philoponus had Leontius of Jerusalem in mind here). (3) Apollinarius supported a union of *sarx* and *Logos* without a soul; the present treatise, by contrast, clearly states that the body of the Lord is endowed with a soul. Finally, he explains that if the topic here is natures in the plural, then the natures *before* the union are meant, not perchance two natures in *Christ* after the union. With this interpretation he also rejects the two quotations (Cyril and Gregory)[58] from the Chalcedon florilegium as proof of the two natures.

---

54. Lietzmann, *Apollinaris*, pp. 192,14–193,2: 'Therefore one must necessarily assert both the corporeal and the divine according to the whole; and those who cannot see in the different united ones what is peculiar to each of the two will fall into absurd contradictions; but those who perceive the peculiarities and preserve the union will neither deceive themselves about the nature [Philoponus: change the natures] nor ignore the union.'

55. Photius, *Bibl. cod.* 229: Henry IV, p. 173,31–36.

56. Leont. of Jer. offers the same text twice in *Contra Monophysitas*: PG 86, 1828A and 1842B, as a quotation from Cyril and from Severus. Cf. H. Lietzmann, *Apollinaris*, pp. 116–17.

57. On this see ACO IV 3, 1, pp. 119–21.

58. In the *Adlocutio* (προσφωνητικός) *ad Marcianum*: Cyril of Alex., *Ep. I ad Succ.*: ACO II 1, 3, pp. 115,33–116,2, and Greg. of Naz., *Ep. 101 ad Cledon.*: ibid., p. 114,15–16.

Recently the thesis has been presented[59] that *De unione* originally came, nevertheless, from Julius but was falsified through Apollinarian interpolations and then in this form ascribed to Apollinarius by the Apollinarians as well as the Chalcedonians.[60] According to Richard's (complicated) thesis,[61] on the other hand, this work arose first as a pseudepigraphical forgery of the Apollinarians and was then falsified again by the Chalcedonians.

For Philoponus the patristic argumentation is only one of the various means that he employs to attack the two-natures doctrine and thereby support his assertion that 'none of the holy scholars has said that Christ had two natures or was in two natures after the union'.[62] We cannot detect a particular knowledge of the Fathers beyond the well-known quotations. That in his comments he may have had Severus or Leontius of Jerusalem[63] in mind is very possible, but we cannot offer proof for that. He applies all means, be they historical knowledge, familiarity with the council texts (Chalcedon, Constantinople II), philosophical argumentation and even patristic, for the 'concentric' attack on Chalcedon and in the *Tmemata* proves himself a sharp polemicist, in contrast to the rather moderate tone in the *Diaetetes*. Yet philosophical conceptual analysis is his real domain. With his Aristotelian, grammatical schooling, he has taken his anti-Chalcedonian confession, as he found it and adopted it, and given it a philosophical justification.

2. The *Diaetetes* and its conceptuality

After this overview of the basic traits of the christological position of John Philoponus based on the Τμήματα, we now turn to his writing (in ten chapters) called the *Diaetetes*, which is wrongly introduced by Nicephorus Callistus as the chief tritheistic work.[64] Nonetheless, it is a

---

59. A. Tuilier, 'Remarques sur les fraudes des Apollinaristes et des Monophysites. Notes de critique textuelle', in TU 133, Berlin 1987, 581–90, esp. pp. 586–88. T. supports his thesis especially through his thorough investigation of the manuscript tradition of *De unione* § 8 and § 15. He explains the *mia-physis* statement in § 5 by stating that *physis* here means *hypostasis*.

60. On this see Leont. of Byz., *AFA*: PG 86, 1961AB, where he cites texts from *De unione* 1–2 and 8 as Apollinarian.

61. M. Richard, art. cit., p. 746.

62. John Phil., *Tmemata*, chap. XV: Chabot II, p. 116.

63. Severus Ant., *C. imp. Gram. Or.* III 40: CSCO 102, p. 196,7–11, discusses *De unione* § 17 and then § 5; *Or.* III 17: CSCO 94, pp. 196–97, adds *De unione* § 5, then the Ambrose text, and discusses both. Leont. of Jer., *C. Mon.*: PG 86, 1865B contains *De unione* § 5, 1829BC the Ambrose text, 1827A and 1842B *De unione* § 17.

64. Niceph. Call., *HE* 47: PG 147, 423CD.

question here of philosophical foundations that are applied to Christo-logy,[65] even if it also reveals 'seeds' of the later tritheism.[66] The *Diaetetes* was written before 553[67] and except for parts of chapters IV and VII, which are found in Greek in the *Doctrina Patrum* and in John of Dam-ascus,[68] is preserved only in Syriac. The introduction expresses the tranquil rest of a philosopher who especially emphasizes the love of truth[69] but at the same time knows very well the human weaknesses that stand over against the search for truth. With his writing he would like to answer questions regarding the christological dispute, whether after the union in Christ one is to speak of one nature or two, to explain correct doctrine and defend it through arguments and to examine what the opponents present as to whether it contains a correct meaning.[70]

The starting-point for Philoponus is a short credo on the incarnation, in agreement with the holy scriptures, 'that the eternal Son, the only begotten Word of the Father, true God of true God, consubstantial with his Begetter, at the end of the ages, truly became flesh out of the blessed Mary, Mother of God, and came forth as a perfect human being, without suffering a variation or change in his own being but uniting himself hypostatically to a human body, animated with a rational and spiritual soul'.

Even if he leaves no doubt as to what for him is correct doctrine – the confession to one composite nature of Christ – he later found it necessary for explanation to compose three more short writings (*Epitome libri diaetetis, Dubiorum quorundam in Diaetete solutio duplex*) in order to prove his anti-Chalcedonian orthodoxy.[71]

They reproached him in this way: 'You are not allowed to say that those who have thrown the world into confusion and have appeared as the cause of such great vexation and division of the church of God, namely, those who celebrated the Chalcedonian synod, have the same

---

65. Cf. already the Prooemium nos. 2 and 3, pp. 36–37, in which it is clearly asserted that *de Incarnatione divina Verbi/Salvatoris nostri* is treated.

66. Cf. *Diaetetes*, VII 23; X 46; *Epitome*, 22; *Epist. ad Iust.*, 4: Sanda, pp. 58, 86, 103, 175–76; also H. Martin, 'Jean Philopon et la controverse trithéite du VI° siècle', *StudPat* 5 (1962) (= TU 80), 519–25, esp. 520–22, 525.

67. The *Diaetetes* was already there when the Τμήματα was written, for in the latter, chap. I and XI: Chabot II, pp. 97 and 110, refer to the *Diaetetes*. The Τμήματα, however, according to information in ibid., chap. I, pp. 97–98, was written at the time of the Second Council of Constantinople (553). Cf. H. Martin, art. cit., p. 520.

68. John of Damascus, *De haeresibus* 83 addit.: ed. Kotter IV (1981), pp. 50–55. It is a question of large parts of no. 16 of chap. IV, and of chap. VII, in which large parts of no. 27 and half of no. 28 are omitted (in Sanda: pp. 61,2–63,2). The *Doctrina Patrum* has the text on pp. 272,20–283,16. According to Kotter, *Einleitung*, p. 6 (cf. Diekamp, *DP*, p. LXXII s.) the addition in John of Dam. may not have been in the original text but was 'the elaboration of a copyist'. In what follows we cite the Greek text according to Kotter's edition.

69. No. 2, p. 37: *amatorum veritatis*; no. 3, p. 37: *veritatis amore freti*. No. 1, p. 35: *Veritas sibimetipsi ad sui defensionem sufficiens iis videntur, qui acute oculo mentis cernere valent.*

70. No. 3: Sanda, p. 37.

71. Cf. T. Hermann, art. cit., p. 242.

assertions (*sententia*) with us.' Philoponus, however, was quite amazed that they 'have not ascertained the exact sense of our words'.[72] The tone of the argumentation becomes much more polemical in the two writings *Dubiorum quorundam* and has similarities with the later *Tmemata*, which possibly originated soon afterwards.

Perhaps there was already confusion because of his openness to 'misled' Chalcedonians, whom he wanted on a rational basis to help to the right way.

We now turn to the conceptuality of John Philoponus, which he explains and substantiates in detail in the *Diaetetes*.[73]

First he presents the teaching of the church on what the terms *nature*, *prosopon* and *hypostasis* mean (no. 21). *Nature* is the general *ratio* of being of those who participate in the same essence (e.g., a *human being* is a rational, mortal living being with reason and knowledge). Essence and nature, however, are considered the same thing (οὐσίαν δὲ καὶ φύσιν εἰς ταυτὸν ἄγει[74]).

Hypostasis or *person* is the individual existence (ἰδιοσύστατον ὕπαρξιν) of each of the natures, and the summary (περιγραφὴν συγκειμένην, *collectio*, composite) of their characteristics, in which those who share the same nature are different – the peripatetics say: atoms (ἄτομα), in which the division into genus and kind finally ends. Individual living beings are called in ecclesiastical terminology *hypostases*, since they have genus and kind, and outside of these individuals do not exist.

In φύσις Philoponus now distinguishes

(1) the common *ratio* (κοινὸς λόγος) of a nature that is actualized in no atom (no. 21),

(2) the actualization in an individual and μερικωτάτην in each ὕπαρξις taken by him (no. 22).

(The realization of a nature in a particular individual, however, occurs only once) (no. 22).

Hypostasis designates the indivisible ὕπαρξις peculiar to an individual. Often *prosopon* is distinguished from *hypostasis*: the relationship (σχέσις) of some to one another is called *prosopon* (no. 25).

(a) The manner of the union

Yet the possibility that a solution like that of Leontius of Jerusalem could have been known to Philoponus can be deduced from his question (no. 27) to those who confess the two natures and one hypostasis after the union:

Did the union happen in the same degree (*in aequali gradu*, ὁμοτίμως, of equal honour, of equal value) in natures and hypostases, or do you mean rather that the hypostases were united

---

72. *Dubiorum quorundam*, no. 2: Sanda, p. 105. How hard he had to fight is seen perhaps in no. 22, p. 121.

73. On this see especially the outstanding presentation in T. Hermann, art. cit., 215–18. Cf. H. Martin, diss. cit., pp. 162–73.

74. John of Dam., *De haer.*, 83: Kotter, p. 51,33.

and *one* hypostasis came from the two, but [the union was] less in the natures, and therefore two also remained after the union?[75]

The 'lesser' union in the natures is indeed, according to Leontius of Jerusalem, to be conceived in such a way that the human nature of Christ has its hypostasis in the Logos and thus no nature union occurs. Such a solution, however, is rejected by Philoponus for two reasons: (1) The *ousia* (which is to be equated with the *physis*[76]) admits no 'more' or 'less'. The union results not through any accidents[77] but through them (the natures or essences) themselves. (2) But since the particular nature of individuals is the same thing as the hypostasis with its adherent characteristics (as Philoponus has demonstrated[78]) and the union of particular natures belongs to the individual, one cannot say that the hypostases are more united than the natures (namely, 'one hypostasis, two natures').

It becomes even clearer in no. 29 that Philoponus might have known the solution of Leontius of Jerusalem when he formulates the following as the objection of the Chalcedonians:

Since the humanity (τὸ ἀνθρώπινον) of Christ had hypostasis in the Logos and did not exist before the union with the Logos, we say that the hypostasis of Christ is *one*.

Here too we see that because of his close coupling of hypostasis and (particular) nature he cannot be open to this solution.

If, however, the term *nature* means something different from the term *hypostasis*, but they allege, as the reason that the hypostasis of Christ is one, that the hypostasis or person of the human being did not exist (μὴ προυπάρξαι) before the union, then the reason that there are two natures in Christ is also that the human nature existed before the union. But if the particular nature (ἡ μερικὴ φύσις) existed before the union with the Logos, then the hypostasis must also have existed (προυποστῆναι). For one cannot be without the other [particular nature without hypostasis, particular hypostasis without nature]. For both are one according to the subject (ὑποκείμενον), even if in many ways they come together in the same, as we have already shown. Thus if the hypostasis, as also the nature united to the Logos, did not exist before the union with him, and therefore precisely they require one hypostasis of Christ, then they should also require one nature. For since they are not distinguished insofar as having been united, they are also not to be distinguished therein [on the basis of nature].[79]

The model of the union according to Philoponus appears further developed and thus clearer in the Pseudo-Philoponian writing *Tractatus de*

---

75. Here John of Dam. omits the answer (cf. p. 54,155–156) and continues in the middle of no. 28 (cf. Sanda, p. 63,2: *Unam enim naturam . . .*).

76. Thus in no. 21, Sanda, p. 56: *Essentia vero et natura idem enuntiant.* John of Dam., *De haer.*, 83: Kotter, p. 51,33: οὐσίαν δὲ καὶ φύσιν εἰς ταυτὸν ἄγει.

77. No. 27, Sanda, p. 61: *per aliud eorum quae illis adhaerent.*

78. Cf. *Diaetetes*, VII 21.22 and 27: Sanda, pp. 56, 57, 62; *Epitome*, 8: Sanda, p. 94.

79. No. 29, Sanda, pp. 63–64; Kotter, p. 55,181–195.

differentia, numero ac divisione (CPG 7277): a combination of characteristics (*coadunatio proprietatum*) and a union of natures (*unio naturarum*).[80]

'We do not confess a union of characteristics but believe that it is produced from natures, without detriment to the multiplicity of characteristics that are representative of one [single] thing. At the same time we say that many characteristics are both like one another and with one another, and a pure *combination (coadunatio) of characteristics* is present.' But no one, says the treatise, dares to assert that 'a union of characteristics has occurred, as if *one* characteristic were effected. For this would obviously introduce a confusion. For as we even assert at times many characteristics of the simple nature, how can we [then] assert only one characteristic of the composite?' It is correct only to speak of a *combination of characteristics and a union of natures!* Then the multiplicity of characteristics or differences is also preserved after the union, but the multiplicity of natures is suppressed by the union.

Unproblematic for Philoponus is the question how the non-mixing of the united is to be preserved. For there is no mixture when the things to be united do not belong to the same genus.

A mixing or destruction is experienced by natural predicates like black and white, hot and cold, but not, say, sweet and red and heavy, etc.[81] Therefore no change is to be feared in the union of divinity and humanity in Christ, since divinity and humanity belong to foreign genera, just like soul and body.

If, however, the natures remained without mixture in the union because neither of them has experienced a change or mixing by virtue of the union, how then is one not to speak of two natures after the union? To this question Philoponus gives various answers and especially develops his ideas about the teleological arrangement of divinity and humanity in Christ.

First he presents the logical argument (in many variations already explored and especially developed in chap. 1 of the *Diaetetes*): If there is a *union*, how can one then claim to speak of *two* (natures)?! Because of the union one is forced to speak of *one* nature.[82] One can, however, also offer 'infinitely many' (*infinite multa*) examples: No one will say of human beings who are composed of body and soul that they have two natures. Illuminated air and shining bodies are unmixed entities that are not separated and are thus 'one from two',[83] and neither of the two is harmed in any way. This is shown when the light recedes from the air. The shine that is potentially in the light is consummated through the access of the light and actually changes into light.[84] It is the same when a person acquires education: what was potentially in him or her is consummated. For the incarnation there is a corresponding state of affairs: 'For the humanity of the Word of God proceeds more completely through union with him, or rather:

---

80. Ps. John Philoponus, *Tractatus de differentia, numero ac divisione* (CPG 7277), no. 33: Sanda, p. 167. That this is also the opinion of Philoponus is shown by, e.g., *Diaetetes*, X 41: Sanda, p. 79 (about the characteristics): the (many) characteristics of the two natures of which Christ consists are preserved, but the nature of his totality is one. He is one composite nature and hypostasis.

81. *Diaetetes*, X 38: Sanda, pp. 73–75.

82. *Diaetetes*, X 36: Sanda, p. 70.

83. *Diaetetes*, X 37: Sanda, p. 72: *unus . . . ex duobus.*

84. Ibid., pp. 72–73.

it is deemed worthy of the things that are over nature [i.e., supernatural grace]. In regard to human beings, soul and body remain what they are, since their ground of being (*ratio essentiae*) was in no way changed by what happened to the soul and body out of the union of God's Word.'[85]

Does the divinity of Christ thus know imperfection (before its union with the humanity)? Yet here Philoponus expresses only the determination of the humanity of Christ to perfection through the divinity of the Logos, which he understands as parallel to the perfection of the body through endowment with a soul.

In another passage Philoponus expressly goes into the persistent idea that the divinity is incomplete, namely, where he explains that the divinity of the Logos with regard to the economy of salvation is a part of the composite Christ, since our redemption was effected only through the incarnation of the God-Logos.[86] As a part it would be incomplete. Here, however, it is a question of a quite definite functional consideration, just as one can say of a helmsman that he is a part of the ship and incomplete as a part. In view of the strong orientation of Philoponus's manner of expression towards the logic of language, great caution is suggested when one removes statements from the immediate context and course of argumentation.

Incidentally, we find in Leontius of Byzantium the quite similar assertion that the Logos is not the complete Christ (τέλειος Χριστός); only after union with the humanity is he complete in this regard, although he is complete as God.[87]

(b) The number 'two'

Again and again Philoponus demonstrates that one cannot speak of two natures in Christ *after* the union. For the most part it is a question of logical conclusions.

– The name *Christ* cannot designate two natures, for that would happen only analogously or univocally. If analogously, then there would be a union in name only; if univocally, then there would again be two individual Christs present in contradiction to the union.[88]

– Yet in a pure *cohaesio* or *coaptatio* the number remains. Now if, however, the name *Christ* designates neither the divinity alone nor the humanity alone but what is effected out of both, and that is supposed to designate not the essence or nature but the accidents, then it can only be a question of a coherence of natures for which precisely the number remains applicable.[89]

---

85. Ibid., p. 73.

86. *Diaetetes*, X 43: Sanda, p. 82: *respectu necessitatis oeconomiae divinitas Verbi pars est compositi Christi, si quidem non aliter redemptio nostra nisi per Incarnationem Verbi Dei procurata est. Imperfectum igitur respectu huius est utrumque eorum, quae in unionem venerunt.* Cf. *Epitome*, 21: Sanda, pp. 101–2.

87. Leont. of Byz., *CNE* 2: PG 86, 1281CD; cf. A. Grillmeier, *CCT* II/2, p. 189.

88. John Phil., *Diaetetes*, I 9: Sanda, pp. 44–45.

89. Ibid., III 14: Sanda, pp. 48–49.

– In a kind there are many individuals who according to kind are one but as individuals are many. Conversely, one can also apply numbers to something that is continuous (e.g., two yards of wood), but this then happens only potentially (δυνάμει), not actually.[90] Now, the two natures of Christ, however, insofar as they are natures, are two and separated, and not merely as two individuals of the same kind but separated in everything, since they have in common neither genus nor kind. For divine nature as such is higher than all others, which have indeed come into existence through it. Thus if Christ is undividedly united (*indivisibiliter unita*) and the natures themselves are united and the union is caused not through accidents, then one can no longer speak of twoness in this undivided united One (for twoness means division).[91]

– The composition of two simple natures can produce only a composite nature.[92] Philoponus proves this through correct syllogisms, yet with the presupposition that one nature is either simple or composite, which does not apply to a nature coming from a hypostatic union in the manner of Leontius of Jerusalem.

The close binding of nature and hypostasis, which Philoponus anchored in his system, is again responsible for the fact that in his opinion it is impossible for two natures to effect one hypostasis and preserve their double number.[93] 'For it is impossible that a nature subsists (ὑποστῆναι)[94] for itself and does not appear in an individual.' Individual and hypostasis, however, are the same thing.

The *Tractatus de totalitate et partibus*, dedicated to Sergius, discusses numbers in a special manner. In it Philoponus distinguishes parts and elements.[95] Elements are of such a kind that they penetrate that which is composed of them and each other (examples: the four elements earth, fire, water, air; material and form; body and soul; characteristics that complete the substance, for example, fire is perfected by warmth, dryness, lightness, etc.).[96] That which is composed of elements is actually one and not many. Elements suffer no change through the mutual penetration.[97] Elements of a whole cannot be counted. What is continuous is only potentially divisible into (infinitely many) numbers.

---

90. Ibid., IV 16: Sanda, pp. 51–52; John of Dam., *De haeresibus*, ed. Kotter IV, pp. 50,5–51,21.

91. Ibid., IV 17: Sanda, pp. 52–53.

92. Ibid., V 19: Sanda, pp. 54–55.

93. Ibid., VII 28: Sanda, pp. 62–63; Kotter, p. 55,161–162: Δύο δὲ φύσεις σῴζούσας κατ' ἀριθμὸν τὴν δυάδα μίαν ἀποτελέσαι ὑπόστασιν ἀδύνατον.

94. Ibid., Kotter, p. 55,168.

95. *Tractatus de totalitate et partibus* (CPG 7263), 3: Sanda, pp. 129–30, esp. p. 130: 'Parts in the real sense are all things that penetrate neither the whole, which is composed out of them, nor each other', e.g., with a house, the walls, the roof, the door, stones, wood, etc., with a living being, the quasi-parts like nerves, bones, veins and organs, and the things that consist of them, such as hand, head, etc.

96. Ibid., p. 129.

97. Ibid., no. 7: Sanda, p. 135.

In no. 4 Philoponus presents a detailed discussion of the division of continuous wood. We are reminded of the deliberations in Leontius of Byzantium regarding numbers.[98] Through the distinction of division, actual or potential, Philoponus is more precise here than Leontius: the same example of the wood that is ten yards long[99] is now explained as a continuum, which can potentially be divided by the number ten but not actually, for then one would have destroyed the wood (into ten parts).

We have a clearly different view with Leontius of Byzantium and Philoponus. In consequence of the latter, in a whole composed of elements (and Christ is surely one such whole) numbers are, to be sure, possible in the act of analysis; when I do that, however, I have already destroyed the unity. With parts of a whole one can probably consider one separated from the others, without destroying the whole, since nature itself distinguishes them.[100] But with elements that is not possible:

> Since nature does not distinguish such things individually for itself but mixes their number into one, those who later attempt to divide them according to number, even if it happens only in deliberation, dissolve the whole and destroy it, since plurality . . . is alien to a continuum and to the one.[101]

Leontius, however, vehemently rejects ascribing to numbers such a power to separate.[102] Then one would also be forced to separate as soon as one speaks of two characteristics (ἰδιότητες).[103]

The treatise *Tractatus de differentia, numero ac divisione* from the Philoponus school is devoted to the question how one can speak of difference, number and division. Here much is developed even more distinctly. Thus it clearly states: 'Whoever talks of difference is not therefore forced also to count.'[104] Things or natures that are united *hypostatically* receive no number, for here a composite thing or a composite nature comes into being. Discrete quantities cannot be united

---

98. Cf. A. Grillmeier, *CCT* II/2, pp. 198–200.

99. *Tractatus de totalitate et partibus*, no. 4: Sanda, pp. 131–32: *de ligno decem cubitorum*.

100. No. 8, p. 135: *ipsa enim natura creatrix ita eas disposuit*.

101. No. 8, p. 136.

102. Leont. of Byz., *Epap.* 8: PG 86, 1904B: the number would be the cause of the separation (τῆς διαιρέσεως αἴτιος).

103. Leont. of Byz., *Epap.* 10: PG 86, 1904C: if the number separates what is counted, then not only does the number of natures separate the natures but then the number of characteristics (*proprietates*) will separate in general. Cf. *Diaetetes*, X 41, pp. 77–79: to the objection, 'If union did not draw together the plurality of characteristics (*proprietates*), then it also did not draw together the duality of the natures', Philoponus answers (after a definition of *proprietates* as: *essentiales differentiae seu distinctiones cuiusvis naturae, quae intrinsecus et specialiter in iis cernuntur*) that there is a plurality of characteristics (*proprietates*) that distinguishes one nature from another. The nature of Christ is (a composite) one; the characteristics (*proprietates*) of the divine and human nature are maintained.

104. Ps.-John Philop., *Tractatus de differentia, numero ac divisione*, no. 7: Sanda, p. 147.

hypostatically but only through combination (*coadunatio*).[105] With a composition (*compositio*) one can distinguish, to be sure, but not count, for
then one would undertake a loosening (of the composition).[106]

> The composite does not include division or discrete quantity – what a number is – even
> if it does include the difference of those that have come together.[107]

(c) On the intellectual division

While the *Diaetetes* does not speak explicitly of separation '*in consider-
atione*', this is a theme in nos. 7 and 8 of the *Tractatus ad Sergium* and even
more in the *Tractatus de differentia, numero ac divisione*. The first treatise
represents the act of the intellectual analysis of a composite in its separating function. If one, for example, considers souls and bodies in
themselves and explores their nature, this deliberation immediately dis-
solves the composite, for the *compositio* is not in either of the two in itself
but only in the composite.[108] The Pseudo-Philoponian treatise seems to
see the processes further (and more precisely) developed, when in the
intellectual analysis it speaks of mutual separation and seeing together.
From the composite the view moves to the components, and it shapes
the concept of the composite and potentially divides it. In this way it
perceives the differences but then moves again to consideration of the
union, which is real and natural, and thus grasps the composite – provided that it is a question of a natural and hypostatic union.[109]

The thus perceived differences are not, like the division and the number, a product of
deliberation (*opus cogitationis*); rather, we see and recognize them in the analysis.[110] The
(intellectual) division, however, is completely dispelled by the hypostatic union.[111] If we
divide in the mind, then that comes from the fact that our mind cannot consider different
objects at the same time.[112] Since our view cannot encompass something large and compact

---

105. Ibid., no. 17: Sanda, pp. 153–54.

106. On this see ibid., no. 22: Sanda, pp. 158–59.

107. Ibid., p. 159.

108. John Philop., *Tractatus de totalitate et partibus*, 7: Sanda, p. 135. The same is true of fire:
'If I in consideration look at the warmth of fire in itself, and the dryness and lightness, then
I have destroyed the substance of fire through consideration. For fire is nothing from them in
itself.' Thus it is a question here of essential characteristics; cf. the definition of *proprietates* in
Diaetetes, X 41.

109. Ps.-John Philop., *Tractatus de differentia, numero ac divisione*, no. 21: Sanda, p. 158.
Similarly already in nos. 4, 5, 8, 9, 15, 18, 19.

110. Ibid., no. 8, p. 147: *Non enim sicut divisionem et numerum ita et eorum differentiam opus
cogitationis esse dicimus neque eam, cum non esset, formavimus neque omnino creatores obiectorum
sumus, sed dum eam ope analysis videmus, eam agnoscimus, sicuti antea dictum est.*

111. Ibid., no. 9, p. 148.

112. Ibid., no. 18, p. 154: *Non enim est possibile menti nostrae, ut uno actu eodem tempore
diversa obiecta attingat.*

at one time, it adopts it through many acts – in which division occurs again and again[113] – and thus it wanders around.

(d) On the picture of Christ of John Philoponus

In the foreground, certainly, is the dialectical securing of the formula of the *mia physis synthetos*. Somewhat more plastic, however, is the picture of Christ of Philoponus revealed in the proem to his *Diaetetes*. There he gives to the predominance of the Logos over the human (comprising body and soul) a certain, even if moderate, superiority.

> The divine nature of the Logos and the human were united, and thereby *one* Christ came forth out of two, not in a usual union of natures, as one says that God is united to the human, or the human to the human, while their natures remain separated, nor is a single reality mutually effected through them, for example, *one* human, or *one* living being. Rather, in the same way that in us the soul rules the body, whose inner strengths it moves, so also with regard to our Lord Christ it is true of the whole human composite that it, out of the part of the divinity united to it, assumes the movement as the latter wants, in that the rational soul, because of the union with the divinity, that I say thus, was moved by God, and that it subjected all its rational capabilities of movement as an instrument (*ad modum organi*, ὀργανικῶς[114]) to the divine activities of the Logos united with it – since the body is indeed also naturally (φυσικῶς) serviceable to the soul as its own instrument – so that by virtue of the whole composition there is an activity that is initiated, however, primarily by the divinity of Christ our Lord, as an instrument (*ad modum organi*) but through the rational soul united with it steps forward and is carried out in the capability for movement of the divine body.[115]

Thus by virtue of the composition *one operatio* is effected, which takes its outcome from the divinity but is accomplished *through* the soul and in the movement of the body! This confession to *mia energeia* grants an instrumental participation to soul and body, and the limiting additions – *principaliter* (initiated by the divinity), *ad modum organi* (brought forth by the rational soul) – reveal the conception of composition as the foundation.

If we now consider at this point how much Philoponus in his early *De anima* commentary (before 517!) employed the union of matter and form as a model,[116] then here we will also envision the composition accordingly. The particularity of the components is preserved in such a composition.

---

113. Ibid., no. 19, pp. 155–56.
114. According to T. Hermann, art. cit., p. 236, n. 4.
115. John Philop., *Diaetetes*, 3: Sanda, p. 38.
116. Philoponus explains there (*Ioannis Philoponi in Aristotelis de anima libros Commentaria*, ed. M. Hayduck [CAG XV], Berlin 1897) how one can speak of one soul although he distinguishes rational, irrational and vegetative souls: the three souls form a unity like matter and form in such a way that the lower souls, like matter, relate to the higher soul, which is their form. Cf. G. Verbeke, 'Psychologie et noétique', in idem (ed.), *Jean Philopon. Commentaire sur le De anima d'Aristote. Traduction de Guillaume de Moerbeke* (CLCAG 3), Louvain–Paris 1966, pp. XXXVII–XXXIX and XLV.

In addition, there is still a 'more' with Christ: namely, that the body's own actions, which are given no impulse by the soul and which it cannot guide as it wants, are ruled and guided in him by the divinity.

> With regard to our Lord Christ, however, since the almighty divinity draws to every action (*effectus*), no natural capability of movement either of the soul or of the body simply acts according to nature, but rather is guided by the divinity united to him, as it pleases. Apparently it [the divinity] voluntarily transmitted the divine will into the body by means of the soul (*mediante anima*). And as of us living beings, actions of the composite One who is from two (e.g., walking, speaking, smelling, seeing, hearing) can be asserted neither of the body alone nor of the soul alone but in common of the whole because, namely, they begin from the soul and are carried out in the body, so one must also speak of our Lord Christ: since indeed the whole natural power of the soul and of the body or of that composite One, because he is from both, is harnessed by the divinity united to him and obeyed at its signal, it is not possible to distinguish in him something in the activities of those things of which the composite One consists. For example, we do not say that 'walking' belongs only to the body nor 'to fulfil all righteousness' only to the soul or simply to the human nature of Christ; rather, it is fitting to say that every activity is carried out by the whole composite One, by the divinity, as it were, as the main cause that begins, and by means of the soul (*mediante anima*) in the divine body, which is united to it.[117]

Of special interest is the formulation *mediante anima*: the divinity, by means of the soul, transmitted the divine will into the body. Here too the instrumental participation of the human soul is not excluded; it is rather a question of asserting the unhindered action of the highest, most excellent one (the divinity) on the lower ones (soul, body); the powers are thereby activated in accordance with their correct ordering.

Here again it may be useful for understanding to refer to the anthropology of Philoponus in his *De anima* commentary. Through its conjunction with the body, the interweaving (διαπλοκή, συμπλοκή), the rational soul is faced with a choice; it must decide for the good, towards which its will was previously addressed from the beginning. The body represents a hindrance to the free development of its perfection; earthly life is a test. When the soul follows the intellect, a person is in harmony with his or her nature.[118] The perfection of Christ is indicated by the fact that in him there are no such bodily stirrings on which the soul has no influence.

The sufferings that stem from the weakness of human nature were voluntarily assumed by Christ in order thereby to prove his true incarnation. This is Severan doctrine. Philoponus does not speak of an explicit Logos permission to suffer; he is concerned first of all with the subject union when he suggests that the sufferings of Christ can be asserted with greater justification, since they did not occur against the will of the Logos.[119] This union (ἀποτέλεσμα) can properly be called 'God', and the

---

117. Ibid., no. 4: Sanda, p. 39.
118. Cf. the presentation of the body–soul union (according to Philoponus in the *De anima* commentary) in G. Verbeke, op. cit., pp. XL–XLV, esp. p. XLIII.
119. *Diaetetes*, 5: Sanda, p. 39.

human sufferings can be asserted of it; but it is also not astonishing when the scripture calls Christ a human being. Philoponus closes conciliatorily: When I hear 'God', I also think of humanity, and in the designation as human I perceive at the same time the divine nature.[120]

The formula of the one composite nature of Christ also does not contradict the double *homoousios*:[121]

It is possible to have '*partialiter communio*' with various others, but that still does not require two natures in the wholeness of being. Example: water is consubstantial with the air with respect to its dampness and consubstantial with the earth with respect to cold. Thus there is partial communion with air or water, but by no means does water therefore have two natures! Christ has consubstantiality with the Father or with us only *in part*.[122] By reason (*ratione*) we divide him into that of which he is composed and thereby perceive his consubstantiality with the Father and with us. These comments seem to correspond to Leontius of Byzantium: in the *Epaporemata* no. 19[123] such an idea is rejected.

Philoponus was certainly an opponent of the *aphtharsia* teaching of Julian of Halicarnassus. That is shown, among other places, in some fragments on the resurrection newly edited by A. Van Roey. At least until the resurrection the body of Christ was not transformed into incorruptibility.[124] Philoponus is indeed aware of the significance for our salvation of the crucifixion of the Son of God.[125]

Philoponus has occasionally been charged with Origenism in connection with his resurrection doctrine (Germanus of Constantinople)[126] or

---

120. Ibid., p. 41: *Nunc vero sicuti Deum audiens cum hoc humanitatem quoque eius vere intellego, ita etiam in appellatione hominis simul intellegi naturam divinam cognosco.*

121. *Diaetetes*, X 34: Sanda, pp. 68–69.

122. Ibid., p. 69: *Ergo partialiter est ei respectu Patris et respectu nostri consubstantialitas, et non per totalitatem . . .*

123. Leont. of Byz., *Epaporemata* no. 19: PG 86, 1908BC. Cf. also T. Hermann, art. cit., p. 239, n. 2.

124. Fragm. 25 in A. Van Roey, 'Un traité cononite contre la doctrine de Jean Philopon sur la résurrection', in ΑΝΤΙΔΩΡΟΝ I, FS M. Geerard, Wetteren 1984 (123–39), 133.

125. Fragm. 29: Van Roey, p. 135.

126. Germanus I Const., *De haeresibus et synodis* (CPG 8020), 33: PG 98, 69D. According to L. Lamza, *ÖstlChr* 27, Würzburg 1975, 161, this treatise was written between 730 and 733. When Patriarch Germanus of Constantinople (d. 733) reports (PG 98, 72A) that the monk Leontius (ὁ τῆς ἐρήμου μοναχός) wrote a book *Leontia* (against Philoponus?) on the 'language of twoness' (δυϊκῆς φωνῆς), then Leontius of Byzantium is not possible, since Germanus has the time of Patriarch Anastasius of Antioch in mind here. For one, it could be a question of Leontius Presb. Constantinopolitanus; cf. CPG 7888–7900. According to C. Datema and P. Allen, *Leontii presbyteri Constantinopolitani Homiliae* (CCG 17), Turnhout–Louvain 1987, 37, this Leontius may have lived in the middle of the sixth century. Another possibility, however, is Leontius Scholasticus, author of the *Liber de sectis* (CPG 6823), cf. Act. V, VI: PG 86, 1232–33.

his doctrine of the abolition of the spherical heaven (Cosmas Indico-pleustes).[127] With regard to the latter topic these accusations seem 'peu fondées',[128] yet on the whole not all suspicion has been wiped out.

3. The letter to Justinian

In advanced age Philoponus seems to have received an invitation to come to Constantinople to Emperor Justinian. In his *Epistula ad Iustinia-num*[129] he excuses himself with his age and his health[130] for not accepting this invitation (also in winter). The whole letter seeks to move Justinian to remove the tessera of the 'two natures' and of 'in two' from the church in order finally to establish unity in the church.[131] Here he mostly employs the argumentation from him that we are already otherwise familiar with. As a human being, who consists of soul and body, is one single nature, so also Christ is one single nature out of divinity and humanity, unmixed and unchanged. If a union has taken place, one can no longer speak of two. Now, since Justinian confesses one composite hypostasis, it necessarily follows that the nature of Christ is also one single composite one.

Philoponus substantiates this in two ways. Since we confess the consubstantiality of the Trinity and something cannot be consubstantial with itself, it is true that each of the hypostases of the Trinity is consubstantial with the other two. But that which constitutes the essence of God is Father, Son and Holy Spirit, since each of them is God. Hence each of their hypostases can be nothing other than their nature. Second, since Justinian confesses and teaches with the Fathers the one incarnate nature of the God-Logos (*mia-physis* formula), it is to be noted that this (one nature) is not that of the whole Trinity but only the nature peculiar to the Logos, which is distinguished (by everyone who confesses the Trinity) from those of the Father and of the Spirit. So each of the three hypostases is also a nature. Thus the one

---

127. If the hypothesis of Wolska is correct that Cosmas Indicopleustes in *Top. chr.* VII in the 'alleged Christian' is attacking Philoponus, then *Top. chr.* VII, 95: ed. Wolska, SC 197, p. 165, is also a proof of the charge of Origenism. Cf. W. Wolska, *La topographie chrétienne de Cosmas Indicopleustès*, Paris 1962, 191–92.

128. W. Wolska, *La topographie chrétienne*, 191.

129. CPG 7264. Besides the Latin translation in Sanda, pp. 172–80, there is a further one in G. Furlani, 'Una lettera di Giovanni Filopono all'imperatore Giustiniano', *AIVS* 79 (1919–20), 1248–57, with commentary, ibid., pp. 1257–65. The letter is also transmitted in the (not yet evaluated) collection Harvard Syr. 22, f. 31[b] (no. 15) referred to by S. P. Brock, 'Some New Letters of the Patriarch Severos', *StudPat* 12/1 (= TU 115), Berlin 1975 (17–24), 21.

130. *senectus et magna corporis debilitas*: Sanda, p. 172.

131. Thus already at the beginning in no. 2: 'The assertion of two natures in Christ contradicts correct ideas and teachings that your majesty earlier recalled' (Sanda, p. 175). Unless they are condemned, says Philoponus, there will be no unity in the church. Finally he says in summary in no. 7: Sanda, p. 180: *ut tesseram illam 'duarum naturarum', quae causa scandali et divisionis ecclesiae Dei exstitit, et illam 'in duabus', altera quoad divisionis opinationem non inferiorem, . . . ex ecclesia Dei eiciatis.*

composite hypostasis is only the composite nature of Christ.[132] These deliberations already give expression to essential substantiations for tritheism (cf. below).

Then in no. 5 he refutes three (simple) objections:

(1) 'The nature of the divinity and humanity cannot be one.' That is correct, but it is not a question of a simple nature but of a composite nature (as also of its hypostasis).

(2) 'The hypostasis of Christ must be one, since the flesh of Christ did not exist before the union.' But if there are two natures after the union, then the nature of the flesh must have existed before the union, which leads to the heresy of Paul of Samosata and Nestorius. But if one claims to say that the nature was without hypostasis before the union, then that means as much as to be and not to be, which is absurd.

(3) 'The two natures of Christ are universal divinity and universal humanity.' But there is a union only of particular natures, not of universal natures. Particular natures, however, are the same as hypostases. Thus one can speak only of one nature and one hypostasis, or with two natures one also asserts two hypostases, which is Nestorianism.

Finally Philoponus shows (no. 6) that the expression *in duabus* is allowed only if one speaks of parts of a whole that are locally distinguished from each other. But with parts that penetrate each other, like body and soul, and divinity and humanity in Christ, one can only say *ex duabus*. *In* points to separation,[133] *ex* to composition.

In this writing, which may be one of his last documents, we again see in abbreviated form the method as well as the essential ideas of this miaphysite thinker.

III. JOHN PHILOPONUS AND TRITHEISM

In the literature, however, John Philoponus is less known for his philosophical substantiation of the formula of *mia physis synthetos* than for the fact that soon after his death he was considered the 'heresiarch of the tritheists'.[134] Through the work of A. Van Roey[135] we have a certain insight into the tritheistic opus of Philoponus. Of the four works that Van Roey could discern here we can regard as the main work *De trinitate* (CPG 7268) or *De theologia* (CPG 7270), of which only eleven or six

132. No. 4: Sanda, pp. 175–76.

133. Cf. also the expression: The person of the king appears in his noblemen.

134. Thus was he called by Leont. Schol., *De sectis* VI, VI: PG 86, 1232D. *De sectis* presents the tritheist teaching of Philoponus as the consequence of his Aristotelianism: 'because he took his point of departure from the Aristotelians'. Furthermore, we continue to hold to the dating given in the writing itself (during the rule of Eulogius of Alexandria, 580–608), versus the thesis of M. van Esbroeck, who wants to date *De sectis* as early as 543–51 (on this T. Hainthaler, in *JdChr* II/2, p. 523, n. 91a; *CCT* II/2, p. 494, n. 68). At this time, however, tritheism still could not be found – even Theodosius (d. 566) saw in the beginning of the movement no heresy threatening the church, to say nothing of the later involvement of John Philoponus and his rise to leadership.

135. A. Van Roey, 'Les fragments trithéites de Jean Philopon', *OLP* 11 (1980), 135–63, was able to establish thirty different fragments in all, which he edits here anew with Latin translations; four of them cannot be more closely determined (cf. 5. Incertae originis: pp. 157–58 [Syr.]; pp. 162–63 [Lat.]).

fragments, respectively, can be made out; with great probability the two names designate the same work.[136] In addition, a writing *Contra Themistium* (CPG 7269)[137] is attested, as well as a letter to a follower (*Epistula ad consentaneum quemdam*).[138]

The espousal of the tritheistic concept did not occur until late, in the so-called second phase of tritheism.[139] It appears that Philoponus was moved to involvement through Athanasius, who was a glowing admirer of the founder of the sect, John Askotzanges.[140] Perhaps the main work *De trinitate* arose as an answer to a catechetical talk of Patriarch John Scholasticus of Constantinople.[141] In any case, its appearance can be dated in the last month of 567;[142] at this time the work circulated in Syria.[143] 'Probably 567, perhaps even before the publication of this work',[144] Philoponus and all his writings were anathematized by Bishop John of the Kellia (*cellarum*) and the whole Alexandrian (miaphysite) clergy.[145] We read of a condemnation of Philoponus by oriental bishops in 569.[146]

---

136. Text of the fragments in A. Van Roey, art. cit., pp. 148–54 (Syr.); 158–61 (Lat.); ibid., pp. 146–47, a substantiation for the identification of the two works.

137. Eight (different) fragments are edited by A. Van Roey, art. cit., pp. 154–56 (Syr.); pp. 161–62 (Lat.).

138. From the *Scripta antitritheistica* (CPG 7282): frag. in A. Van Roey, art. cit., p. 157 (Syr.); p. 162 (Lat.).

139. Preceding it was the so-called 'archaic phase', which comprises the period from the appearance of John Askotzanges in 557 until the intervention of Patriarch Theodosius (563/564). Cf. A. Van Roey, 'La controverse trithéite jusqu'à l'excommunication de Conon et d'Eugène (557–569)', *OLP* 16 (1985), 141–65, esp. p. 143. The development of tritheism is presented in vol. II/3 of this work.

140. Michael Syr., *Chron.* IX 30: Chabot II, p. 255.

141. According to Photius, *Bibl. cod.* 75: Henry I, p. 153, John Philoponus wrote a βιβλιδάριον ('booklet') against this *logos katechetikos*. Does this refer to *De trinitate*? If so, the diminutive must be understood as adverse criticism. The talk of the patriarch took place in the period 1 Sept. 567 to 31 Aug. 568. Events must have followed each other in very short order if *De trinitate* was really the reply to John Scholasticus; cf. the following note.

142. This is substantiated by H. Martin, 'Jean Philopon et la controverse trithéite du VIᵉ siècle', *StudPat* 5 (= TU 80) (1962), 519–25; summary, p. 525. *De trinitate* must have appeared after 17 May 567, the first condemnation of tritheism by the oriental archimandrites in the monastery of Mar Bassus in Bitabō (the centre of the Antitritheists), and before 3 Jan. 568, the second meeting at the same place.

143. *Syndocticum alterum factum ab archimandritis Orientis* (CPG 7190): *Doc. mon.*, pp. 116–20, esp. p. 117.

144. E. Honigmann, *Évêques et Évêchés*, p. 183.

145. *Doc. mon.*: CSCO 103, pp. 111–12; John of the Kellia, one of the bishops consecrated by Jacob Baradai (Honigmann, p. 175), consecrated Peter patriarch of Alexandria (*Doc. mon.*, p. 195,20). Thus he was one of the leaders of the church of Alexandria.

146. *Ep. epporum orthodoxorum Orientis ad eppos orthodoxos Cpoli* (CPG 7193): CSCO 103, p. 135.

Basic to the tritheistic doctrine of John Philoponus is the nominalistic base: the general (κοινόν) has no existence of its own.[147]

'Every κοινόν is inferred from the ἰδικά only through our intellect' (no. 1). 'None of the things that one calls κοινός has its own existence, nor does it exist before the ἰδικά; but on the contrary: out of these [individual things] the mind inferred that [the general], and only in it [the mind] does it have existence' (no. 2). In the *Diaetetes* Philoponus writes that the concept, for example, of living being and human being (i.e., genus and kind) has being only in the individual and outside of this does not subsist.[148] It does not expressly say that Philoponus will also apply the same deliberation to the Trinity. But already in *Diaet.*, VII 23 he uses the same conceptuality for the doctrine of the Trinity also when he adduces the Trinity to illustrate that one nature (general nature is meant) can have many (here: three) hypostases. Appearing there is the noteworthy assertion: 'What would be the one nature of the divinity (μία φύσις θεότητος) other than the κοινὸς λόγος of the divine nature, considered for itself (καθ᾽ ἑαυτόν) and separated in thought (ἐπινοίᾳ) from the particularity of each hypostasis?'[149]

The general is inferred from the particular individual things by the intellect. The κοινόν is divisible; otherwise it would not be common to the particular individuals (no. 2). Therefore it is countable in those in which it exists.[150]

Already in the *Diaetetes* Philoponus wrote that the common *ratio* (κοινὸς λόγος) of human nature is, to be sure, one in itself but copies itself in many subjects in which it is in each case completely inherent.[151] As further examples of this state of affairs he adds: the idea of the ship that is realized in many copies, knowledge that the teacher has and that is copied in the pupils, or the seal in a signet ring and in the impressions.

In the transference to the doctrine of the Trinity this leads in Philoponus to the idea that union in God is given only in abstraction:

Divinity and substance, which are in the venerable Trinity, are not one in reality (πράγματι) but only in the mind and in the reason. And thus we understand God as one. But there are three substances of God and of nature, since they are separated into hypostases. And thus one is God the Father, one God the Son and one God the Holy Spirit (no. 29).

He confesses three consubstantial divinities (no. 5), yet the *homoousios* is not found in the properties (*idiomata*), namely, Father, Son and Holy Spirit, nor in the *koinon* (no. 6). For as the kind is determined by adding

147. Fragment no. 1 (*De trinitate*); no. 18a (*Contra Themistium*): 'For we have shown that the nature called the general one has no existence of its own in any of those that are, but either is nothing at all – which is also true – or is constituted out of the individual ones in our intellect alone.' No. 22 (*Contra Themistium*): 'For none of what is called "general" has its own existence beyond the particular.' We quote the fragments according to A. Van Roey, OLP 11 (1980), 148–63. Cf. on the following the detailed presentation in H. Martin, diss. cit., pp. 173–83 (tritheist works after 567–70); pp. 161–73 (*Diaetetes, Ep. ad Iustinian.*).
148. *Diaetetes*, VII 21: Sanda, p. 56; Kotter IV, pp. 51,48–52,50.
149. *Diaetetes*, VII 23: Sanda, p. 57; Kotter IV, p. 52,71–73.
150. Fragment no. 3: 'In this way the general is therefore countable in those things in which it subsists, while it [itself] has no existence of its own.'
151. *Diaetetes*, IV 16: Sanda, p. 51; Kotter IV, p. 50,5–8.

'rational' or 'irrational' to 'animal', so it is also in the Trinity: through the addition of 'Father', 'Son' and 'Holy Spirit' to 'God' the various species are designated (no. 6). The three consubstantial substances are not foreign according to genus (no. 7) but according to kind; one can call Father, Son and Holy Spirit ἑτεροειδεῖς and ἑτεροούσιοι (no. 14). Consubstantiality can be predicated in principle only of several![152] The unity in God is thus found only in the οὐσία δευτέρα, in the general substance (which has no real existence), but not in a singular *ousia*.

According to nature there is no difference in God:

> Thus if people say that the divinities are of a different nature (ἑτεροφυεῖς), their talk is pagan and Arian. If, however, they say one (divinity) according to number and in one hypostasis, they become Sabellians (no. 20).

John Philoponus holds throughout that with his explanation he is in agreement with the Fathers. Thus he says that Gregory was against three non-consubstantial and by nature alien *ousiai* in the Trinity, but not against three consubstantial substances (no. 7).

If we ignore the characteristics, then the abstraction process does indeed lead to a common (abstract) nature, the general nature or genus 'God'. The three divine hypostases are thus, according to Philoponus, to be understood as concrete copies of this genus.

These elements of Philoponian tritheism that we can discern in the fragments are in part already to be discovered in the *Diaetetes* – we have already noted them at the relevant places. In these (few) passages Philoponus goes into the doctrine of the Trinity only *en passant* in this his main *christological* writing. Nevertheless, the later explicit tritheism of the fragments appears to be a natural development of the 'seeds' in the *Diaetetes*.

How can one explain this phenomenon? Martin holds that Philoponus understood the *mia-physis* formula and Christology with a view that was schooled by his Aristotle commentaries and thus moved logically to his theology of the Trinity. We also have here again a remarkably close interweaving of theological and philosophical conception; an already present theological doctrine (miaphysitism or tritheism) comes together with philosophical theory. One probably cannot say that 'Monophysitism' necessarily led Philoponus to tritheism, as Severus of Antioch and other 'Monophysites' show. Yet his system offers itself as a

---

152. Fragment no. 16: *etenim consubstantialitas non habetur in uno sed in pluribus.* Cf. on this the earlier *Ep. ad Iustinian.* 4: Sanda, p. 175: 'Something is not consubstantial with itself; one is necessarily consubstantial with another or with others, as Peter and Paul and all people are consubstantial with each other.' Cf. H. Martin, diss. cit., pp. 169–70.

logical, coherent further development, which unfortunately does not do justice to trinitarian theological dogma. The concepts and assertions are applied even to God without further testing and without Philoponus giving an accounting of the legitimacy of this process. In particular, the doctrine of relation, already going back to the Cappadocians, seems to be outside his field of vision.

While at this point we do not want to go into attempts from the 'Monophysite' side to refute the tritheism of Philoponus,[153] we shall briefly present a Chalcedonian initiative.

The anti-tritheistic initiative of Patriarch Eutychius of Constantinople

We have an anti-tritheistic writing of a Chalcedonian in the *Opusculum* of Patriarch Eutychius on the difference between nature and hypostasis,[154] written during 568–577,[155] whose Christology we have already presented and recognized as pure Chalcedonian (cf. *CCT* II/2, pp. 490–93).

The work has two parts. Nos. 1–12 deal with the difference between nature and hypostasis in regard to trinitarian theology and Christology. Nos. 13–16 go into the doctrine of characteristics from the christological standpoint. In support of his conception Eutychius offers several long patristic testimonies, in particular the Cappadocians Basil, Gregory of

---

153. H. Martin, diss. cit., pp. 220–28, in his detailed presentation mentions especially Patr. Theodosius of Alexandria (*Oratio theologica*, CPG 7137) and the monk Thomas of Mar Bassus (*Scripta antitritheistica*, CPG 7282, PO 14). While in the first (archaic) phase of tritheism the refutation was purely patristic and put forward again and again the idea that the 'tritheistic' initiative must necessarily have as its consequence the confession of three gods, the task of refutation became more difficult after the appearance of the writings of Philoponus. Yet the central theme of the teaching of Philoponus, the doctrine of the double *ousia*, was never attacked.

Positively, it was argued that when one names the divine hypostases *ousia*, *physis*, *theotes*, *theos*, one may do that only *en theoria* or when one considers each hypostasis in itself. Moreover, consubstantiality of the divine hypostases was not explained in the Aristotelian sense as Philoponus did but in the Basilian (or Platonic) sense of a participation of the hypostases in the same, real divine *ousia*. The three hypostases are thus only one single divine *ousia*, which really exists in itself and through itself (ibid., pp. 244–46).

154. Eutychius of Const., *De differentia naturae et hypostaseos* (CPG 6940): P. Ananian, 'L'opuscolo di Eutichio patriarca di Costantinopoli sulla "Distinzione della natura e persona"', in *Armeniaca*, Venice 1969, 316–54 (Armenian); 364–82 (Ital.).

155. According to John of Eph., *HE* II 35: Brooks, CSCO 106, pp. 73–74, Eutychius, during his exile in Amaseia, wrote papers with patristic arguments in which he 'in the manner of the synod of Chalcedon and the *Tome* of the impious Leo taught a quaternity for the holy Trinity . . . for he taught: "there are two natures in Christ even after the union. All the Fathers also confess this."' The work *De differentia naturae et hypostaseos* (CPG 6940) may (also) be meant here; cf. P. Ananian, art. cit., pp. 355–57.

Nazianzus and Gregory of Nyssa, also Pseudo-Justin (= Theodoret) and from the second
Succensus letter of Cyril.

The anti-tritheistic character is expressed clearly in the closing sentence
of the first part of the treatise (no. 12): 'If nature were the same thing as
hypostasis, there would be three natures and three substances (*ousiai*),
since there are three hypostases. That is the blasphemy of those who
drivel . . .'[156] The theme of dealing with the difference between nature
and hypostasis may be inspired by the current concern to oppose tritheism, but it is naturally likewise useful for the second, christological aim of
guaranteeing the two-natures doctrine.

Eutychius begins with a clarification of terms that bears a great resem-
blance to the beginning of the seventh chapter in the *Diaetetes* of John
Philoponus and at the same time distances itself from the latter at some
points. First, he states that 'those who have been taught by worldly
scholarship and glorify it' – one may easily see an allusion to Philoponus
– have said erroneous things about nature and hypostasis and thus led
many astray: namely, that nature, essence and hypostasis are the same.
The consequence of this, he says, is great linguistic confusion. Against
this the church sets forth the truth: 'Nature, essence and form (*morphe*)
are and designate the same thing', while hypostasis is different from these
and refers to individual things. The individual (ἰδικόν) participates in the
κοινόν. Nature and essence are in the order of the κοινόν, whereas
hypostases are particular (nos. 1–2).

Eutychius circumvents the distinction of Philoponus between φύσις
κοινή and φύσις μερικωτάτη by understanding *physis* from the beginning
only as the φύσις κοινή. What Philoponus calls 'particular nature' is
hypostasis in Eutychius. Likewise, as one distinguishes κοινόν and ἰδικόν,
so also nature and hypostasis. *Ousia* is a general term and therefore a
unity[157] – Philoponus, on the other hand, expressly states that the *koinon*
can be counted in the particular individuals in which it subsists.

Now, Eutychius stresses individuality so much that he says: strictly
speaking, one could not say that the human being Paul and the human
being Peter are two human beings, although they are complete as human
beings, for they do not represent being human in its generality (no. 2).

    156. Ananian, p. 378 (Ital.); p. 349,558–563 (Arm.). Cf. also A. Van Roey, 'La con-
troverse trithéite depuis la condamnation de Conon et Eugène jusqu'à la conversion de
l'évêque Elie', in *Von Kanaan bis Kerala*, FS J. P. M. van der Ploeg, Kevelaer, Neukirchen–
Vluyn 1982, p. 490, n. 1.
    157. Cf. no. 3: Ananian, p. 339, resp. 371: 'Quindi è unica la natura umana e l'essenza e
la forma, molte sono invece le ipostasi degli uomini.'

Carried over to *theologia* this means: the individuality of the three hypostases Father, Son and Holy Spirit, who are all three alike God, forbids speaking of three gods (in the plural). Thus, while inexact speech is not harmful in the case of human beings, with the Trinity it destroys the correct confession (no. 3).[158] Hence with God one can speak neither of number ('three gods') nor of difference ('three *different* gods'):

> Therefore the holy and *consubstantial*[!] Trinity is not three gods, although each divine and adorable hypostasis is perfect God. Nor are there three different gods, because the three holy hypostases are one divinity. Now, since there is no difference between God and God regarding being God, so there is only one God but three hypostases, but not three gods, since each of these hypostases is perfect God, nor are there three different gods, as individuals unsoundly say.[159]

Besides this logical argument Eutychius also offers this consideration: when the distinction (of the individual hypostases in God) already has as a consequence a plurality (in essence), then there would be a more or less in being God. But that is already nonsense with human beings – how much more with God.[160] At this point an extensive substantiation would be desirable. Then Eutychius presents a long excerpt from Ep. 38 of Ps.-Basil = Gregory of Nyssa.[161] Thus his solution consists primarily of an appeal to the Cappadocian hypostasis teaching! Moreover, by stressing individuality he seems to want to loosen the close relationship between abstract concept and the single individual (in Philoponus) as far as possible, so that one actually may no longer use the abstract concept for a plural of individual copies.

> One must connect the *koinon* with the individual, but the individual is not then perchance the *koinon* itself, and the *koinon* receives no plural.

Applied to the doctrine of the Trinity this means: the individual divine hypostases cannot be called gods. Here Eutychius carries over his conceptual system, which he found in the creaturely (finite) order, to the doctrine of the Trinity, just as Philoponus did. He does not go into the

---

158. Ananian, p. 336 (Arm.); p. 368 (Ital.). Quite similarly at the close of no. 12 in the summary (p. 378): 'But also in sublime and uncreated nature you say, although you add the ἰδικόν to the κοινόν, God Father and God Son and God Holy Spirit, and God and God and God; but the three holy hypostases are not three gods but one God. And since there is no difference between God and God, so also the plural is superfluous. In similar fashion we speak among ourselves of the human being Peter, the human being Paul and the human being Timothy by adding the κοινόν to the ἰδικόν and saying human and human and human; but one really should not say three human beings, since in being human there is no difference of name.'

159. No. 3: Ananian, p. 368 (Ital.).

160. Ibid. Quite similarly in John Philop., *Diaetetes*, VII 27: Sanda, p. 61: *cum essentia plus et minus omnino non admittat*; Kotter IV, p. 54,155–156.

161. Cf. here A. Grillmeier, *JdChr* I³, pp. 542–45; *CCT* I², pp. 373–75, 378.

doctrine of relation either, just as neither reflects on the difference between finite and infinite nature.

IV. JOHN PHILOPONUS AND HIS TEACHING ON THE RESURRECTION

A third split in the miaphysites through Philoponus came about through his teaching on the resurrection. This doctrine, which is laid down in at least two writings: *De resurrectione* (CPG 7272) and *Contre la lettre de Dosithée*,[162] divided the tritheists into two groups: the 'Philoponians' or 'Athanasians' (followers of Philoponus), named after Theodora's grandson Athanasius, and the 'Cononites' (against Philoponus), from Bishop Conon, who in practice probably represented the head of the tritheists (*princeps haeresis*).[163]

John of Ephesus (and also Photius and Timothy) report that both groupings held fast to the first writing of Philoponus: they carried it around like gospel and took great pride in it.[164] The second on the resurrection, however, was accepted only by the Athanasians, not by the Cononites.

Several writings were composed against the resurrection teaching of Philoponus – which said among other things that there is no resurrection of *these* bodies, but that other bodies are created and the latter come to the resurrection from (the house of) the dead.[165] Photius knows two of these writings, namely, the refutation of the monk Theodosius, Ἀνατροπή, and that of Conon, Eugenius and Themistius; both of these were lost. Van Roey reproduces a patristic florilegium from 'the treatise that the tritheists wrote against John the Grammarian', possibly a 'quasi official refutation of the teaching of Philoponus'.[166] Of these nos. 25, 29, 30, 32, 33 are from works of Philoponus. From *De resurrectione* (at least six books, since we have fragments from the fourth and sixth books) there are now about fifteen fragments.

---

162. This discussion of the letter of Dositheus, who was obviously an opponent of the teaching of Philoponus, is not extant and not contained in the CPG; two fragments of this work are in A. Van Roey, 'Un traité cononite contre la doctrine de Jean Philopon sur la résurrection', in ANTIΔΩΡΟΝ I, FS M. Geerard, Wetteren 1984 (123–39), 134–35, no. 29. T. Hermann, art. cit., p. 211, n. 7, has already called attention to this writing.

163. John of Eph., *HE* I, 31: Brooks, CSCO 106, p. 28.

164. John of Eph., *HE* V, V: CSCO 106, p. 194.

165. Ibid.

166. A. Van Roey, art. cit., p. 138. The florilegium is found in Br. L. Add. 14532 (8th cent.) and 14538 (10th cent.). It may come from the refutation of Conon, Eugenius and Themistius mentioned by Photius.

From the fragments, which Van Roey has edited,[167] the resurrection doctrine of Philoponus can be presented as follows. Christ is the first of those who have fallen asleep to be resurrected to incorruptibility – no other before him. This means, however, that he has a new nature; *per definitionem* the resurrected One can no longer have a human body, since an essential part of being human is to be mortal. The mortal body that Christ received from his mother had to be transformed into incorruptibility. That means that the mortal perished and a new incorruptible body arose. Philoponus expressly says (against the Gaianites without naming them): before the resurrection he was corruptible. Strongly criticized are Cyril and Gregory of Nyssa, the latter without substantial reasons being discernible from the present fragments.

He reproaches Cyril: 'You destroyed the definition of a human being by saying "incorruptible and immortal". For humans are rational and mortal living beings. When you take "mortal" away, you take away human beings, and you change their *ousia* into another in which you have not preserved mortality.'[168]

For the philosopher it was unacceptable that φθαρτός and ἄφθαρτος, as well as mortal and immortal, could be asserted of the same nature. This did indeed contradict the elementary conceptual system as it was also taught at the academy, for example, by the teacher of Philoponus, Ammonius Hermeiou.

Ammonius, in his commentary on the *Isagoge* of Porphyry, states that to the definition of human being as a rational, *mortal* living being, one must add that this completes the *ousia* of human beings – in distinction to the accidents.[169]

Thus he cannot conceive the transformation of a mortal body into an immortal one without the destruction of the old and the new creation of a new body, whereby the identity of the earthly with the resurrection body is, of course, lost. Philoponus expressly strengthens the difference

---

167. T. Hermann, art. cit., pp. 261–62, n. 1, had already reported their essential content, in part in literal translation; yet he seems to have used only one of the two Syr. mss. (Add. 14538, = B in Van Roey, not Add. 14532 = A).

168. No. 32, Van Roey, pp. 135–36; further: 'When you say "incomparably better, incorruptible and imperishable", you have shown that the resurrected ones are of a different nature. In each [of these assertions] you condemn yourself, for you assert neither what is true nor what agrees with reality; rather, you present what pleases you alone.' The Cyril saying quoted by Philoponus (which recalls 1 Jn 3,2): 'we will be what we are, namely, human beings, but incomparably better, incorruptible and imperishable and moreover glorified' could not be identified.

169. Ammonius, *In Porphyrii Isagogen sive V voces (zu 2,15)*, ed. A. Busse (CAG IV 3), Berlin 1891, p. 54,18–24; cf. esp. op. cit. (on 9,24), p. 100,1–20!

between the two not only according to number but also according to kind:

> Consequently human bodies will become in the resurrection what they had not been before. For the previous bodies will not rise; they have perished, and no bodies similar to them will be given. They not only will be different from the present ones according to number but will not be of the same kind as they. The bodies in the resurrection are indeed actually incorruptible and immortal. And all who do not follow Christ, who taught this through Paul, set themselves against God.[170]

The presentation that Timothy of Constantinople[171] gives of the teaching of Philoponus is an interesting supplement,[172] which also indicates the framework of his eschatology. According to this, the Alexandrian maintained:

> All these perceivable and visible bodies were brought by God out of non-being into being. They are created corruptible and do perish according to matter and form, and instead of these God creates other bodies, better than these visible ones, incorruptible and eternal. Completion of the visible cosmos or transition and creation of the new cosmos. Resurrection of the dead is defined as the indissoluble union of the rational soul with an incorruptible body.[173]

As we have already seen above, resurrection from the dead includes first the demise of the visible body, which is φθαρτός, and second the new creation of *another* body. Added is the demise according to matter *and* form, from which the Cononites expressly distance themselves. According to their concept only the form perishes; the matter is only reformed and remains eternal.[174] The criticism of Philoponus regarding the conceptual difficulty produced by the (alleged) words of Cyril seems completely justified. Yet his conception, which we admittedly can only weakly surmise, raises the problem of where Philoponus sees the identity of the resurrected ones given. Perchance in the speculative spirit (νοῦς

---

170. No. 32: Van Roey, pp. 136–37.

171. Timothy Presb. of Const., *De iis qui ad ecclesiam accedunt* (CPG 7016): PG 86, 61–64.

172. Cf. J. M. Schönfelder, 'Die Tritheiten', in idem, *Die Kirchen-Geschichte des Johannes von Ephesus. Aus dem Syrischen übersetzt*, Munich 1862, pp. 267–311, here: pp. 301–9.

173. Timothy Presb., op. cit., PG 86, 61C5–14.

174. Op. cit., 61D7–64A5: 'These perceivable and visible bodies, to be sure, do not perish in regard to matter, but they remain always the same and visible and do not perish. Only in regard to form do they perish. The same matter is again transformed, they say, and receives a better, imperishable and eternal form. The creation of the visible cosmos [happened] according to matter and form, perishing or passing away only in regard to form. For they confess, as we say, that the matter always remains the same. But they define resurrection from the dead as a second indissoluble union of this body with the rational soul.'

θεωρητικός), on which he comments in his early *De anima* commentary[175] that it remains with the separation from soul and body alone? The question is not treated in the few fragments that have come down from him. Origenist echoes, which this commentary still reveals, might in the meantime, however, have no longer been attractive. In any case, it was considered disgraceful even among the tritheists to be Origenist.[176]

The resurrection teaching of Patriarch Eutychius

According to John of Ephesus the Chalcedonian patriarch Eutychius of Constantinople is supposed to have become a follower of the Athanasians as soon as he heard of them.[177] This probably means his view of the resurrection, which Gregory the Great reproduces in his *Moralia*.[178] At that time Gregory was papal apocrisarius in Constantinople and fell into violent disagreement with Eutychius. Emperor Tiberius decided that the book that Eutychius had written on the resurrection was to be burned. This controversy happened before the death of Eutychius (5 April 582) and in this way came to an end.

Since the work did not survive, its content can be inferred only from Gregory's report. According to it the patriarch wrote: 'In the glory of the resurrection our body will be intangible (*impalpabile*) and finer than wind and air.'[179] He had also referred to Paul (1 Cor 15,36) as evidence, in order to show that the flesh would be either tangible or not at all.[180]

From the presentation that Gregory gives one cannot perceive that Eutychius followed the eschatological idea of Philoponus and adopted his whole system; for him it seems to be only a question of the quality of the resurrection body.[181] For the rest, we have already indicated above that the patriarch of Constantinople was not a follower of tritheism.

---

175. John Philop., *Comm. in Arist. De anima* II 2: CAG XV, p. 241,7–9. Cf. G. Verbeke, 'Levels of Human Thinking in Philoponus', in *After Chalcedon* (= OLA 18), Louvain 1985, 465.

176. According to Timothy Presb., op. cit., 64C, the Cononites and 'Philoponians' (Φιλοπονιακοί) called each other Origenists.

177. John of Eph., *HE* II 51: CSCO 106, pp. 85–86: 'he became one of them'; also in II 36; Eutychius, according to John, not only did not give up this opinion but also openly proclaimed it vocally and in writing. That Eutychius stood fast in his view is likewise reported by Gregory the Great (see below).

178. Gregory the Great, *Moralia sive Expositio in Iob* (CPL 1708), 14,72–74 (on Job 19,26): CCL 143A, pp. 743–45; SC 212, pp. 432–38; PL 75, 1077–79.

179. CCL 143A, p. 743,4–5.

180. CCL 143A, pp. 744,55–745,61.

181. This has already been worked out by J. M. Schönfelder, op. cit., pp. 304–8.

V. FINAL EVALUATION

At the close of our overview of the theological works of the Alexandrian philosopher we want to ascertain several characteristics – with all due caution in view of the meagre sources and the fragmentary tradition.

John Philoponus certainly begins with the Severan *mia-physis* doctrine that he inherited; he expounded the confession to *mia energeia* with new substantiation. The *mia-physis* formula itself, however, plays a notably small role in his *Diaetetes*.[182] It serves him solely as evidence that there is a 'union of natures or hypostases',[183] as well as that with the *mia physis* not the general nature of the divinity but that of a particular nature of the God-Logos became flesh. *The* formula for Philoponus, however, is *mia physis synthetos*. He seeks to prove it in the *Diaetetes*, that is, the unity of the natures, as well as the singularity and composite quality of the nature of the resulting subject.

He tries to substantiate the synonymity of *nature* and *hypostasis* with Aristotelian conceptuality by understanding *nature* here as φύσις μερική (particular nature) and *hypostasis* as an individual (ἄτομον) that realizes the corresponding φύσις κοινή through the acquisition of individualizing characteristics; more precisely, *hypostasis* is comprehended as the individual state (ἰδιοσύστατον) of the nature concerned and outline (περιγραφή) of all individualizing characteristics (*Diaetetes* VII, 22). Through the distinction of the *physis* concept on the one hand in the abstract concept of the φύσις κοινή, which exists only in mind and becomes real only in the particular individual, and on the other hand in that of the particular nature, which is practically the same thing as the hypostasis with its adherent characteristics,[184] he gains an effective instrument through which in his interpretation the distance from the Chalcedonian view is considerably diminished at some points. This will be made clear in the following paragraphs.

– In the formula *mia physis tou theou logou sesarkomene*, *physis* can only mean the particular nature of the second divine person and thus the Logos hypostasis. Therefore Philoponus understands this formula as simply: the one incarnate hypostasis of the God-Logos, a formulation that is also fully correct for Chalcedonians.

---

182. The formula is mentioned one single time: *Diaetetes*, VII 23; Sanda, p. 58; Kotter IV, pp. 52,86–53,87. In the first apologia of the *Diaetetes*, the epitome (CPG 7261), it does not appear at all; in the *Dubiorum quorundam . . .* (CPG 7262) it appears twice: nos. 4 and 6, Sanda, pp. 106, 108. In the *Tmemata*, chap. XI: p. 110, Philoponus quotes it as a 'sentence' of St Athanasius and Cyril!

183. *Dubiorum quorundam*, 4: Sanda, p. 106.

184. *Diaetetes*, VII 27: Sanda, p. 62; the text is missing in John of Dam.

– This one particular nature or hypostasis, however, is composite: *mia physis synthetos* is, of course, the favourite formula of the Alexandrian, which he untiringly repeats and exhibits. Yet through Justinian *mia hypostasis synthetos* was adopted into church doctrine, while Leontius of Jerusalem provided the speculative reasoning. It is interesting that Leontius of Jerusalem and Philoponus think quite similarly of this synthesis as a gathering up of the characteristics (divine and human) – if one also includes the Pseudo-Philoponian writing *Tractatus de differentia, numero ac divisione*! In this way, then, the new composite hypostasis or nature comes into being. While Leontius emphasizes so strongly here the newness of the hypostasis that he falls into trinitarian problems (the properties assumed through the incarnation become what is to be distinguished even vis-à-vis the other two divine hypostases!), there is in Philoponus, so far as we know, no statement of this sort. Did he consider this problem?

– Philoponus emphasized that even after the union the human and divine characteristics remain preserved:[185]

> For the natures themselves did not remain without mixing; indeed even the hypostases of the natures are mixed; the characteristics of the hypostasis of the God-Logos, however, through which it is distinguished from the Father and the Holy Spirit, are preserved even after the union, and also its characteristics are not mixed with the characteristics of the human nature united with it, through which it is distinguished from the remainder of humanity.

He only turns against the confession of two natures in order not to endanger the subject unity, which in this close contact of the concepts of nature and hypostasis in his terminology must indeed immediately be called into question.

> Even if the differences of divinity and humanity show up in him (*cernuntur*, cf. the γνωριζόμενος at Chalcedon!), it is still not permissible to speak of two natures ... For Christ is not one of them ... but that which is effected out of the two, a single being.[186]

– The starting-point for Philoponus is that a *union of natures* ('out of two one [composite one]') takes place; that is seen already in the proem of the *Diaetetes*.[187] The union in Christ is in reality (no. 8); it is not a *cohaesio* (no. 14). Two particular natures – even the humanity of Christ, although with its existence it is immediately united to the Logos, is to be confessed

---

185. *Diaetetes*, VII 28: Sanda, p. 62 (the passage is missing in John of Dam.).

186. *Diaetetes*, II 13: Sanda, p. 48.

187. No. 2: after the union of the Logos with humanity one must confess Christ as *one composite nature*. No. 3: the description of the kind of (hypostatic) union succeeds immediately with the help of the body–soul model.

as nature and hypostasis![188] – are united in one composite nature, which corresponds to a hypostasis (no. 27, not in John of Damascus!).

– The union in Christ is (presumably) conceived as one that is called forth by the natures or *ousiai* themselves, not by something that adheres to them (no. 26); we have not encountered any statement in Philoponus as to whether it was by a creative act of God. Christ is a composite whole of the kind in which the two natures have penetrated each other (no. 45, p. 85); therefore the appropriate expression is *ex duabus* and not *in duabus*.

One of the main traits of Philoponian Christology is the prominent significance given the body–soul comparison. Again and again this model is employed for clarification.

This is seen programmatically already in the proem; immediately after the reproduction of a christological credo comes: 'and as of us as human beings one must think, namely, that from two natures a unification (*coadunatio*) has come, namely, out of rational soul and body, out of mixed elements one composite, because from them this rational, living "human being" is completed, so also with Christ.'[189]

With the example of human beings Philoponus indicates how in this *coadunatio* from two natures one part serves the other as *organon* (the body serves the soul); movements go out from the higher part but are completed in the body; suffering is asserted of the whole combination (applied as substantiation for the communication of idioms!) and we are more human because of the soul than because of the body (is Christ thus more God?). The balance is thus shifted clearly in favour of the divinity. In Christ there has occurred no *cohaesio* but a *unio in natura et secundum naturam*,[190] as in human beings. A human being is *one* composite nature from body and soul (no. 19), in which the natures of body and soul have remained without mixing (no. 30). Humans can be called 'consubstantial' with bodies as also with incorporeal things (no. 34), since their generic nature is both corporeal and incorporeal. In this, however, they are by no means two natures (no. 34), for neither the body in itself nor

---

188. *Diaetetes*, VII 26: Sanda, p. 60; Kotter IV, p. 54,136–147: The humanity of Christ was not ἀνυπόστατος before the union, since it had the ἰδιοσύστατον beyond all other human beings, and the ἰδιοπερίγραφον in the *idiomata*, through which it was distinguished from all other human beings. One must confess nature and hypostasis of the humanity of Christ so that one cannot be forced to confess a non-hypostatic nature! For one of the *atoma* that realizes the common nature is present in the human part of the Redeemer (τὴν κοινὴν φύσιν τελούντων ἀτόμων τὸ τοῦ σωτῆρος ὑπῆρχεν ἀνθρώπινον).

189. *Diaetetes*, 3: Sanda, p. 38.

190. *Diaetetes*, III 14, Sanda, p. 49: *non mera cohaesione tantum unionem naturarum in Christo factam esse, sed in quantum sunt naturae vel essentiae.*

the soul in itself makes up their nature as human beings. Through ensoulment the body (of a living being) is completed. They remain, however, bodies according to the *ratio* of their being, just as they are. Whether ensouled or unensouled, they remain bodies. So is it with the incarnation. The humanity of the God-Logos comes forth more completely, but the human body and soul remain what they are (no. 37). With regard to the soul, it is considered in itself alone more complete and exquisite than a living, composite being. For the rational and unbodily life of the soul stands above that of earthly living beings joined with bodies (no. 43). But in view of any usefulness it is a part and as such incomplete. This consideration then forms a support for the idea that the divinity of Christ is, considered in itself, indeed above all perfection and all comparison, but in regard to the redemptive work, it is a part of the composite Christ and as such imperfect (no. 43). Finally, it is also to be noted that a totality that comes forth from two natures (and this includes human beings from body and soul) represents not a mere connection of essences but nature and essence (no. 45).

– We want to emphasize especially that Philoponus does not shy away from ascribing nature and hypostasis to the humanity of Christ. It is not an anhypostatic nature that is united with the divine nature of the Logos. A composite whole arises from the two natures, and the characteristics of both natures are maintained.

– The very great significance that the body–soul model has in Philoponus is to be considered especially in regard to his picture of Christ. The uniting of body and soul is not so close that a mixture, *krasis*, comes about, but rather an interweaving, *diaploke*; the uniting of matter and form is for Philoponus in his *De anima* commentary an important model for this kind of union. In this way he also explains how one can speak of a single soul in human beings, although he distinguishes rational, irrational and vegetative souls: the lower of each pair is related to the higher as matter is to form. The result is not a single substance but a single whole that appears as a unit.

– The Logos hegemony: just as the soul moves the inner forces of the body, so in Christ the *anima rationalis* is moved by the divinity, which is the higher here, and the body is moved *mediante anima*.

– Doctrine of characteristics: Philoponus understands by characteristics (*proprietates*) of the natures the essential differences (*differentiae seu distinctiones*) of one nature from the other natures in itself and according to kind. Now, however, he is above all concerned that individual characteristics are not already a nature (and thus he can absolutely concede that in Christ various – human as well as divine – characteristics are to be observed but without therefore requiring one to speak of two natures). Nature is thus that subject which is both completed and perfected out of all.[191]

The legacy of such an explosive speculation of great consequence was limited by the condemnation of Philoponus by both sides.[192]

---

191. *Diaetetes*, X 41: Sanda, p. 78; cf. here Hermann, art. cit., p. 218, n. 7.

192. As one example of this among others, Ethiopian documents that show Philoponus as a heretic: *Vie de Georges de Saglā*, ed. G. Colin (CSCO 493), Louvain 1987, p. 35,22; *Storia dei quattro concili*, Cerulli (ST 204), Vatican City 1960, p. 99.

CHAPTER FOUR

'COSMAS INDICOPLEUSTES'

(by T. Hainthaler)

An impressive description of the *orbis christologicus* – from India through Persia, Armenia, Palestine, Antioch, Ethiopia, Egypt, Asia Minor, Greece and Africa to the Franks and Goths – reads:

> On the island Taprobana [Ceylon] in the interior of India, there where the Indian Ocean is, there is also a church of Christians and clerics and believers; I don't know whether there are even more. Likewise also on the [islands] that are called Male, there where pepper grows, and in Kalliana is a bishop who was consecrated by the Persians. Likewise also on the island of the Dioskorides [Socotra] in the Indian Ocean; there the inhabitants speak Greek, foreigners according to the Ptolemies, who came after Alexander of Macedon; also there are clerics, who were ordained by Persians and sent into these regions, and many Christians. I sailed to this island but did not land there. But I have conversed with people from there who speak Greek and came to Ethiopia. Also among the Bactrians, the Huns, Persians, the other Indians, Persarmenians, Medes, Elamites and in the whole Persian land: innumerable churches and bishops, many Christian people, many martyrs and hesychast monks. Likewise also in Ethiopia, Axum and in the entire vicinity, among the felicitous Arabs who are now called Himyarites, in all Arabia and Palestine, Phoenicia and all Syria and Antioch to Mesopotamia, Nobatae and Garamants, Egypt and Libya and Pentapolis, Africa and Mauritania to Gadeira towards the south [Tangier?]. Everywhere there are churches of Christians and bishops, martyrs, hesychast monks, wherever the gospel of Christ is proclaimed. Likewise again in Cilicia, Asia, Cappadocia, Lazikia and Pontus and the hyperborean parts of the Scythians and Hyrcanians, among the Herulians, Bulgars, Greeks (*helladikoi*), Illyrians, Dalmatians, Goths, Spaniards, Romans, Franks and the other peoples as far as Gadeira on the ocean going to the north, the people believe and proclaim the gospel of Christ and confess the resurrection of the dead.[1]

---

1. Cosmas Indicopleustes, *Top. chr.* III, 65–66: SC 141, pp. 503–7.

The author of these lines from the Χριστιανικὴ Τοπογραφία[2] was a well-travelled Alexandrian businessman (πραγματεύτης).[3] He knew the Red Sea and the Ethiopian harbours in particular; he went as far as the Nile sources, was familiar with Palestine and was in Sinai; he travelled as far as the Persian Gulf and Somalia. But he does not seem to have seen India with his own eyes,[4] in spite of his sobriquet 'Indicopleustes', which was not bestowed until the eleventh or twelfth century.[5]

According to his own information he wrote a book on geography (which was dedicated to the 'friend of Christ' Constantine) (Prol. 1) and a book on astronomy (dedicated to the deacon Homologus) (Prol. 2). In addition he wrote a commentary on the Song of Songs,[6] at the request of his friend Theophilus. These three works have not survived.

His main work, the *Topographia christiana*, may have been written during 547–549. This dating can be inferred from the passage: 'about 25 years ago . . . at the beginning of the reign of Justin . . . when the king of the Axumites, Ellatzbaas, went into war against the Himyarites'.[7] The work appeared anonymously, and the name of the author was even unknown to Photius.[8]

---

2. Idem, *Topographia christiana* (CPG 7468): W. Wolska-Conus, *Cosmas Indicopleustès. Topographie chrétienne (Livres I–IV, V, VI–XII)* (SC 141, 159, 197), Paris 1968, 1970, 1973. We cite according to book and paragraph. The title is mentioned in II, 5: Wolska-Conus, SC 141, p. 311,16. On the person, work and theology of Cosmas the editor goes into detail in W. Wolska, *La Topographie Chrétienne de Cosmas Indicopleustès. Théologie et Science au VIe siècle*, Paris 1962 (abbreviated: *Topographie Chrétienne*). On Cosmas cf. also: H. Leclercq, art. 'Kosmas Indicopleustès', *DACL* 8, 1, Paris 1928, 820–49; N. Pigulewskaja, *Byzanz auf den Wegen nach Indien*, Berlin–Amsterdam 1969, 110–29; H. Hunger, *Die hochsprachliche profane Literatur der Byzantiner* I (Byzant. Handbuch XII, 5, 1), Munich 1978, 520–22; A. De Nicola, art. 'Cosma Indicopleuste', *DPAC* I, 1983, 792–94. On the significance of the numerous illustrations in the *Topographia christiana*: W. Wolska-Conus, SC 141, pp. 124–231; cf. for iconographic analysis L. Brubaker, 'The Relationship of Text and Image in the Byzantine Mss. of Cosmas Indicopleustes', *ByzZ* 70 (1977), 42–55.

3. Cosmas Ind., *Top. chr.* II, 56: SC 141, p. 369,8–9. He included himself among 'those from Alexandria and Ela who carry on trade' (II, 54: p. 365,5–6). On Alexandria as the home of Cosmas see M. V. Anastos, 'The Alexandrian Origin of the *Christian Topography* of Cosmas Indicopleustes', *DOP* 3 (1946), 75–80.

4. W. Wolska, *Topographie Chrétienne*, pp. 4–9, substantiates the improbability of this assumption.

5. In catenas that preserve fragments from the *Top. chr.*: W. Wolska-Conus, SC 141, pp. 110–12, with reference to E. O. Winstedt, *The Christian Topography of Cosmas Indicopleustes, ed. with geographical notes*, Cambridge 1909, Introduction, pp. 21–22. None of the three mss. of the *Top. chr.* call him 'Indicopleustes'.

6. Cosmas Ind., *Top. chr.* VIII, 3: SC 197, p. 171.

7. Idem, *Top. chr.* II, 56: SC 141, p. 369; also W. Wolska-Conus, SC 141, p. 16.

8. Cf. Photius, *Bibl. cod.* 36: Henry I, pp. 21–22. On the anonymity: Wolska, SC 141, pp. 60–61. The name Cosmas is attested in a single ms. from the eleventh century (Laur. Plut. IX.

The *Topographia* comprises twelve books, of which the first five represent a closed unit; the following books VI–XII are to be regarded as an appendix.[9] According to the analysis of W. Wolska-Conus, the work, soon after its completion around 553 (before or after the Second Council of Constantinople), underwent a theological reworking, which accentuated the Diphysite standpoint. Ascribed to this redactor are books XI (excerpts from the geographical work of Cosmas) and XII and additions in book X (X, 42–75) and V (V, 176).[10]

According to W. Wolska-Conus we have in this writing a testimony for the presence of Nestorian ideas in Alexandria and for resistance to the penetration of philosophy into the Christian faith.

Judgements on the christological position of Cosmas vary considerably,[11] yet the reproach of Nestorianism is widespread and old; H. Leclercq,[12] for example, reports that La Croze had already reached this judgement in 1724 for the following reasons:
– Cosmas presented himself as a disciple (Patricius, Diodore, Theodore of Mopsuestia) and friend (Thomas of Edessa) of Nestorians;
– he uses formulations that cater to the Nestorians when he speaks about Christ and the incarnation;
– he does not name Nestorians among heretics;
– he praises the extension of the church eastwards and by this indirectly shows the zeal of the Nestorian missionaries.

It is true that in one passage he turns to Mary as mother of God, but this passage is missing in the best manuscripts (*Top. chr.* V, 244,2; cf. the apparatus).

In particular, the cosmographical teaching of Cosmas and the pronounced catastasis teaching are often called Nestorian.[13]

W. Wolska-Conus concedes that this 'Nestorianism', exported to Alexandria in the version of the school of Nisibis of the sixth century, can hardly be distinguished from 'Constantinopolitan orthodoxy'.[14] She says that it is also quite distant from the Nestorianism of Narsai in Persia in the preceding period.

But if we take Nestorianism in the strict christological, dogmatic sense, then it means that in Jesus Christ there are two hypostases or persons who are bound together through the so-called *synapheia*, that is, by God through goodwill (*eudokia*) and by Jesus of Nazareth through good moral conduct (*hexis*), whereby an accidental *schesis* is founded and no substantial *henosis*. The question whether one can speak of a christological, dogmatic Nestorianism in the strict sense in the *Topographia christiana* will be discussed below (under 2).

The polemic of Cosmas is directed against 'would-be Christians who think not like the holy scripture but like the philosophers on the outside'[15] and assume that the sky has a spherical shape, because they were led astray by eclipses of the sun and moon. They want 'to be Christians

---

28) in an addition by a different hand: Wolska, ibid., p. 61. Otherwise it is found in catenas. The tradition of the name 'Cosmas Indicopleustes' goes back only to the tenth or eleventh century.
9. An analysis of the work is offered by W. Wolska-Conus, SC 141, pp. 19–36.
10. W. Wolska-Conus, SC 141, pp. 53–58.
11. W. Wolska, *Topographie Chrétienne*, pp. 28–29.
12. H. Leclercq, art. cit., 821.
13. Cf. N. Pigulewskaja, op. cit., pp. 113–14.
14. W. Wolska-Conus, SC 141, pp. 38–40.
15. Cosmas Ind., Hypothesis 4: SC 141, p. 265, and title of lib. I: p. 273.

and at the same time they adorn themselves with the words, wisdom and trinkets of the madness of this world'; they are correctly called 'dimorphos'; 'they undo the rejection of Satan that they made in baptism and return to him'. They are like 'empty houses in the air', without foundation; 'such people cannot belong to us'.[16]

Does this refer to John Philoponus, the representative of the whole movement? In book VII Cosmas attacks an individual, 'one of those who boast of being a Christian and wants to speak against the pagans [Greeks]', a man with great erudition and wisdom (τὴν οὕτω πολυμαθῆ τοῦ ἀνδρὸς σοφίαν), a scholar (σοφός, λογιώτατος). He follows the teaching of the people from the outside and not the spiritual tradition from within; in that way he falls into contradictions.[17] He builds his chatter not on rock but on sand (VII, 2). Cosmas is working against one who asserts a spherical sky in constant rotation, although he calls it destructible. He follows Origen rather than Christian teachings (VII, 95). We cannot deny that these characterizations are in harmony with what we know about John Philoponus. Wolska succeeds, moreover, in composing a lengthy 'dialogue' between the two 'opponents' on nineteen different cosmological themes.[18]

This context also results in a serious inquiry into the previous dating of *De opificio mundi* as 557–560, which is probably to be regarded as too late.[19]

Cosmas apparently goes into objections or earlier discussions, whereas Philoponus treats theses as formulated by Cosmas in the *Topographia*. Both refer to questions brought up by the dispute about Theodore of Mopsuestia, whose fate, however, is still not decided. This suggests a composition before 553, that is, before Theodore's condemnation at the Second Council of Constantinople. Against this *terminus ante quem* is the fact that Sergius, to whom the work *De opificio mundi* is dedicated, is called there *archiereus*, but according to Brooks[20] Sergius was not Patriarch of Antioch until 557.

Wolska-Conus, however, points out that *De opificio mundi* is, to be sure, directed entirely against Theodore[21] and details much for which one could reproach Theodore but says

---

16. Idem, *Top. chr.* I, 3: SC 141, p. 275,1–3; I, 4: p. 277,4–10.
17. Idem, *Top. chr.* VII, 1–3: SC 197, pp. 57–61.
18. W. Wolska, *Topographie Chrétienne*, pp. 167–79.
19. Cf. W. Wolska, *Topographie Chrétienne*, pp. 163–65. On the previous dating see E. Evrard, 'Les convictions religieuses de Jean Philopon et la date de son Commentaire aux "Météorologiques"', *BCLAB* 5 Ser., 34 (1953), 299, n. 3.
20. E. W. Brooks, 'The Patriarch Paul of Antioch and the Alexandrine Schism of 575', *ByzZ* 30 (1929), 469.
21. Cf. the numerous quotations of Theodore pointed out by the *Index nominum*, ed. Reichardt (*Joannis Philoponi De opificio mundi libri VII*, Leipzig 1897), pp. 314–15. Also Photius, *Bibl. cod.* 43: Henry I, p. 27, knows that Philoponus holds the position counter to Theodore of Mopsuestia.

nothing about his being condemned by the council. Yet in the *Tmemata* Philoponus presents the full wording of the anathema against Theodore.[22] It would be incomprehensible that in this polemic against Theodore of Mopsuestia he would include no reference to the conciliar condemnation.

The polemic that was carried out here on cosmological questions brings to expression, according to W. Wolska,[23] a conflict of two schools that flourished at the same time in Alexandria, but which can also be pursued further. The attempt of Philoponus at reconciliation was taken up by the Syrians and via the Arabs reached the Middle Ages (and Galileo). The system of Cosmas won the masses in the Middle Ages and experienced a renaissance in Russia in the fifteenth to eighteenth centuries in reaction to Western ideas.[24] The two works in which this conflict crystallized both begin with Genesis in the Old Testament and the entire holy scripture, with the one author also considering Greek physics and astronomy and the other borrowing from popular science with Oriental reminiscences.[25]

The struggle here, however, is in the first instance about Theodore of Mopsuestia, whom Philoponus openly attacks and whom Cosmas does not call by name, but whose views he largely represents. Since it is primarily a question of issues in the realm of cosmology and the teaching of angels, we will not go into it further here.[26]

1. On the Christology of the *Topographia Christiana*

The Christology of Cosmas exhibits some striking characteristics that we want to sketch.[27]

---

22. John Philop., *Tmemata*, chap. XI: Chabot II, pp. 119–20, contains the text of Anath. XII of the Second Council of Constantinople.

23. W. Wolska, *Topographie Chrétienne*, pp. 182–83.

24. An overview of the Slavic translations of the *Topographia christiana* is given by A. Jacobs, 'Kosmas Indikopleustes, Die Christliche Topographie in slavischer Übersetzung', *ByzSlav* 40 (1979), 183–98.

25. W. Wolska, op. cit., p. 182. Also the presentation of B. Schleissheimer, 'Zum Problem Glauben und Wissenschaft im sechsten Jahrhundert', in *Polychordia*, FS F. Dölger, edited by P. Wirth (Byz. Forsch. 2), 1967, 318–44.

26. Cf. here the accusations of John Philoponus against Theodore of Mopsuestia gathered by W. Wolska, *Topographie Chrétienne*, appendix V, pp. 297–99.

27. Cf. on Christology esp. W. Wolska, *Topographie Chrétienne*, pp. 87–111; idem, SC 141, pp. 36–43. Also *Index*, SC 197, pp. 411–14.

(a) A christological rereading of the Old Testament

First we find long and impressive stretches of consistent interpretation of the Old Testament in the light of Christ, which are untiringly carried through. 'The whole scope of the holy scripture is directed towards him.'[28] In order to document this assertion, Cosmas follows the Old Testament in detail in book V and presents as *prefigurements* of Christ a long series of persons – Adam, Abel, Enoch, Noah, Melchizedek, Abraham, Isaac, Moses, Jonah – in an interesting, biblically based interpretation.

Broadly developed here in reference to Paul is the comparison of Adam and Christ as the *second Adam* (II, 90–95; V, 68, 192; VII, 37). Christ conquered death and prepared a new way through the resurrection. Just as Adam sinned on the sixth day, so the Lord on the sixth day endured the salvation-bringing cross. In the ninth hour Adam and Eve were driven from paradise; in the ninth hour the Lord, according to the soul, and the thief entered paradise (II, 90–95).

Cosmas sees the overcoming of death and the resurrection modelled in the figures of Abel (V, 75), Enoch (V, 82), Noah (V, 94), often while appealing to the Letter to the Hebrews.

With the priest figure of Melchizedek[29] the extraordinary nature of the *priesthood of Christ* becomes clear in advance: a priest who does not stand in succession to others and does not pass his priesthood on to others(!). He performs divine worship not according to the law of Moses but on the basis of other, better symbols(!). He was blessed by Abraham; he had neither father nor mother; he was king and priest. So also is Christ without father according to the flesh, without mother according to divinity; he has no genealogy: he has no beginning according to his divinity and no end of life again according to his divinity but also according to his humanity, for (through the resurrection) he has become immortal and immutable.

The *typos* of the *offering of Christ* is represented in a particular way by Isaac (V, 104). Cosmas makes the parallels clear: both carried their sacrificial wood themselves; their fathers did not spare them; interesting here, however, is the following explanation: the flesh of Christ alone was given for the Son of God as ransom and substitute (like the ram of Isaac?), since the divinity cannot die.

Moses, finally, prefigured in word and deed what is involved in the *salvific work* (*oikonomia*) *of Christ* (V, 111–12), such as the Passover (exodus from Egypt), baptism (passage through the sea), the giving of the law, the Holy Spirit and the church (sojourn in the wilderness), cross (exaltation of the bronze serpent). He prophesied Christ as the coming prophet.

He also comprehends the place of atonement or mercy seat (τὸ ἱλαστήριον) and the high priest as *typos* of Christ according to the flesh (V, 36), supported by Paul (Rom 3,25; Heb 9,7.11–12). He sees prophecies about Christ and his coming given in a number of Old Testament figures.[30]

---

28. Cosmas Ind., *Top. chr.* V, 105: SC 159, p. 159,12: πρός ὃν πᾶς ὁ σκοπὸς τῆς θείας Γραφῆς ἀφορᾶ.

29. Cosmas Ind., *Top. chr.* V, 95 and 98: SC 159, pp. 143–45, 147.

30. He names Noah, Abraham, Isaac, Moses, David, Elijah, the minor prophets, Isaiah, Jeremiah, Ezekiel, Daniel, John the Baptist, Zechariah, Elizabeth, Hannah, Simeon. Cf. also the information in the *Index*, SC 197, pp. 412–13.

(b) An optimistic anthropology

Also to be stressed, however, is the rather high estimation of humanity, to which angels and the whole world are subordinate. Men and women are equal.[31] Human beings are the image of God and the bond of creation;[32] they are the coregents of Christ.[33] The whole creation is orientated towards them. Humankind is 'king of all on earth and coregent of Christ in heaven', as the writer says truly majestically at the end of a description:[34]

> ... human beings, who are the bond of friendship of the whole creation, who walk on the earth but fly in spirit and explore everything, upright of form, who easily see heaven, their home, king of all on the earth and coregent of the Lord Christ in heaven and fellow citizens of the heavenly, at whose service is all of creation – as image of God – since it is subject to God and wants to preserve the good will of the Creator.[35]

This anthropology corresponds to the unique position of Christ. Both spring from the plan of salvation of God, who from the beginning wanted to give others a share in his perfection. Hence he created the cosmos (with the two catastases); this is served by the preparation of human beings in this first catastasis, all upbringing that is experienced here; in the incarnate Lord Christ, however, the plan of salvation of God is realized and perfected.[36]

The strikingly strong emphasis on the *paideia* of God,[37] the education, is to be understood as part of this plan. Through joy and sorrow we learn and are tested until we receive the good things of the future, all that is good for us (V, 64). From beginning to end God has led human beings

---

31. Cosmas Ind., *Top. chr.* III, 47: SC 141, p. 483.

32. Idem, *Top. chr.* III, 35: SC 141, p. 473,20: σύνδεσμος φιλίας πάσης τῆς κτίσεως; bond of the cosmos: II, 101, SC 141, p. 421,10.

33. Cf. idem, *Top. chr.* V, 254: SC 159, p. 371,14 (συμβασιλεύουσιν).

34. Idem, *Top. chr.* III, 35: SC 141, pp. 471–73, offers an impressive description. The angels serve human beings and the entire creation: sun, moon and stars light the way and serve the traveller as markers on the sea and in the wilderness. Air, fire, water and earth serve each in their own way (breath, refreshment; cooking, warming, light; quenching thirst, washing, pouring; dwelling, letting trees grow). Four-footed animals serve as joy (of the table) and clothing; domestic animals assist and aid in rest; wild animals bring pleasure (of the hunt).

35. Ibid., p. 473,19–27.

36. Idem, *Top. chr.* V, 58–61: SC 159, pp. 93–97.

37. There are numerous, even unusual examples of this. Cf., e.g., the assertion that God accomplished the creation in six days in order to teach the angels (cf. V, 74). Through the creation of the woman after the man, human beings should learn to recognize that God also created them (III, 36–38 or 48–49).

step by step through education and instruction to better things and does not stop leading them.[38] Here we find a very optimistic view of humanity!

It is the destiny of all humans to rise from the dead, to become incorruptible, immortal and immutable,[39] gifts that God gives to the whole cosmos.

(c) The eschatological viewpoint

Therefore the idea of hope receives a central significance. So its lack is also made a reproach against the opponents: only pagans without hope,[40] who count on no better catastasis, like these theories (namely, eternity of the world, multiplicity of spheres).[41] But the hope of Christians is for the resurrection of the dead and the kingdom of heaven, which from the beginning of the world has been prepared for humankind.[42] In a very impressive summary Cosmas describes this Christian hope, which is aimed at a comprehensive being with and ruling with Christ:

> First provided with *immortality, incorruptibility and immutability* . . . they will inherit with Christ the kingdom of heaven, rule with Christ, receive with Christ heaven as a dwelling . . . rejoice with Christ, be exalted with Christ, crowned with Christ, glorified with Christ, rejoice with Christ . . . over all eternal and inexpressible goods. What nation or heresy draws in its faith on such hopes as Christians?[43]

The rather pronounced eschatological viewpoint is also seen in two confessions of faith, which in different conceptualities exhibit a strong orientation towards what is to come (future catastasis or the image of the wedding hall).[44]

Of an especially peculiar nature also are Cosmas's initiatives in the theology of history, which accord a unique significance to the Roman (or Byzantine) Empire. Since the Christian message was first believed in the Roman Empire and proclaimed there, God will leave it invincible until the end of the world! In second place is the Persian Empire, for the Magi from

---

38. Cf., e.g., *Top. chr.* V, 93: SC 159, p. 139,8–12, etc.
39. *Top. chr.* V, 180–81, SC 159: p. 279,5–7. This trio appears strikingly often: cf. *Top. chr.* III, 61; V, 187.221.251; VII, 36–37.64.67; IX, 20.22, etc.
40. *Top. chr.* V, 252: SC 159, p. 369,1.
41. *Top. chr.* IV, 20: SC 141, p. 565,8–10.
42. *Top. chr.* V, 248–51.
43. *Top. chr.* V, 251: SC 159, p. 367.
44. *Top. chr.* V, 254: SC 159, p. 371,11–17; and VI, 28: SC 197, p. 45,14–21. For the text, see below under 2 (b).

there venerated Christ, and the gospel was proclaimed among them (by the apostle Thaddeus). The Roman Empire is the 'servant of the salvific dispositions of Christ'![45]

2. A brief synthesis of the Christology of the *Topographia Christiana*
(by A. Grillmeier)

(a) The question of 'Nestorianism'

What consideration should be given to the statement of W. Wolska, the best expert on the *Topographia christiana*, which she wrote on the Christology of Cosmas as a 'system'?[46] She warns: 'If we assume that the major part of book V was not conceived by Cosmas, we find ourselves confronted with a curious fact: there is, so to speak, no Christology of Cosmas'; what he otherwise offers by way of christological arguments in the course of his work would not suffice to substantiate a doctrine. An overall picture, Wolska continues, becomes visible only against the background of the Nestorian Christology of his epoch, which was inspired by the treatise of Thomas of Edessa[47] on the birth of Christ and the confession of faith of Mar Aba of 540.[48] Without our being able to go into source analysis here, we take the *Topographia christiana* the way it presents itself in the sixth century (*c.* 553) after all the *remaniements* that W. Wolska-Conus provides.[49] From the outset, however, we cannot expect much for a synthesis of the Christology of the *Topographie chrétienne*. For W. Wolska correctly says:

> Cosmas systematically avoids dealing with the real christological problems. Even when the text cited by him offers an opportunity for this, he withdraws into the anecdotal, the

---

45. *Top. chr.* II, 74–77: SC 141, pp. 389–95; ὑπηρέτις . . . τῶν τοῦ Χριστοῦ οἰκονομιῶν (II, 74: 389,11–12; II, 75: 391,16–17). On this theology of history of Cosmas and its significance in the Byzantinism of the sixth century cf. S. MacCormack, 'Christ and Empire, Time and Ceremonial in Sixth Century Byzantium and Beyond', *Byz* 52 (1982), 287–309.

46. W. Wolska, *Topographie Chrétienne*, pp. 105–11, esp. p. 105.

47. See S. J. Carr, *Thomas Edessenus tractatus de Nativitate Domini Nostri Jesu Christi*, Rome 1898; I. Ortiz de Urbina, *Patrologia Syriaca*, Rome 1965, p. 127; W. Wolska, op. cit., pp. 72–85.

48. See J. B. Chabot, *Synodicon Orientale*, Paris 1902, pp. 551–53. New English translation from the Aramaic by M. J. Birnie, *The Eastern Synods* (prepared for publication in San José 1991), pp. 62–63. Bishop Ashur Mar Bawai of the Holy Apostolic Catholic Assyrian Church of the East graciously made the ms. available in advance. We deal with these sources in detail in vol. II/3. W. Wolska, op. cit., p. 105: 'Ainsi, un *Traité sur les deux catastases*, composé par Mar Aba, ou Thomas d'Édesse, qui l'avait accompagné à Alexandrie, doit être à l'origine du Vᵉ livre de la *Topographie Chrétienne*.' See also ibid., n. 2.

49. W. Wolska-Conus, SC 141, pp. 53–58.

marvellous, the picturesque, or he returns once again to the resurrection of Christ, which leads the human race into the second catastasis.[50]

Only book V offers a 'christological substance'.[51] Here the comments are ruled by the theme of the two natures. Yet Cosmas does not use the technical terminology of the Greek two-natures doctrine; the formula of the one hypostasis in two natures does not appear at all, nor does that of the 'one incarnate nature of the God-Logos'.[52] The author talks simply of the 'divinity' and the 'humanity' of Christ. Cosmas shows how he does Christology in the interpretation of the (according to him only) four messianic psalms (Pss 2, 8[!], 44 and 109).[53] They are interpreted according to the 'divinity' and the 'humanity' of Christ.[54] Especially important is the interpretation of Ps 109 (110):[55] the expression 'his Lord' clearly designates Christ as God. By contrast, the words 'Sit at my right hand' evidently apply only to his humanity. One says 'Sit' to someone who is not sitting (that is, who is capable of a change that can be asserted only of a creature). Now, divinity and humanity are in the one Christ in the status of their own glory and blessedness. It is the humanity of Christ that is addressed in this psalm in consequence of its inseparable union with the divinity.[56] In general, the divinity and humanity of Christ are so clearly drawn that it is sufficient to point to a few special passages:

50. W. Wolska, *Topographie Chrétienne*, p. 90.

51. Ibid., p. 92. This Christology is sketched on pp. 92–98. Also to be considered therefore are II, 87–95; III, 18–24, and end of VI.

52. Ibid., pp. 93–95.

53. Cosmas emphasizes expressly that these four are the only psalms that 'alone speak of the Lord Christ' (V, 134). The apostles quoted the other psalms because some passages were appropriate to the particular content, but not because the whole psalm referred to Christ (V, 135). The classification of Ps 8 among the so-called messianic psalms is unusual; cf. P. van Imschoot and H. Haag, art. 'Psalmen' (V E), *Bibel-Lexikon*, edited by H. Haag, Tübingen ²1968, 1424. W. Wolska, *Topographie Chrétienne*, pp. 51–52.93–94, shows that in this view Cosmas comes close to Theodore of Mopsuestia. In the interpretation there is partly strong agreement, which has been indicated already by R. Devreesse, *Le commentaire de Théodore de Mopsueste sur les psaumes (I–LXXX)* (ST 93), Vatican City 1939, pp. 45, 288, 290, in the apparatus on Pss 8 and 44. Yet in contrast to Theodore, Cosmas does not speak at all of 'homo assumptus' but of the 'humanity of the Lord Christ'.

54. See Cosmas Ind., *Top. chr.* V, 123–34: SC 159, pp. 183–95.

55. Ibid., 131–34: SC 159, pp. 191–95.

56. Ibid., V, 131: SC 159, pp. 191,12–193,1: ἡ ἀνθρωπότης τοῦ Χριστοῦ ὑπὸ τῆς ἡνωμένης αὐτῇ ἀχωρίστως θεότητος ἐπιτρέπεται, ἀκούουσα· 'Κάθου ἐξ δεξιῶν μου'. The statement in V, 132, p. 193,6: ἐκ γαστρός . . . ἐγέννησά σε is interpreted in terms of the *homoousios*! And there is also here the allusion to a technical language: ἐκ τῆς ἡμετέρας οὐσίας σε ἐξεγέννησα (p. 193,11).

In the introduction to the Gospel of John in V, 202–5 (SC 159, pp. 303–5) Cosmas stresses that the fourth evangelist 'proclaims clearly and in a special way the divinity of Christ and makes it the foundation of his writing'.[57]

With regard to the humanity of Christ attention is called to two things: (1) to the soul of Christ, which is addressed in book VI.[58] Much more than otherwise usual, the characteristics of the soul of Christ are emphasized. In this way the humanity of Christ receives a clear accent. Its destiny and its circumstances in the two catastases are clearly visible.[59] (2) Attention is then directed to the functions of the humanity of Christ in the context of the teaching of the catastases. In V, 133 the topic is the priesthood of Christ. It is asserted of his humanity,[60] not of his divinity or of the Logos. From the position of the Old Testament covenant God and of the service of the priest (of the high priest) therein, the title of 'high priest' for Christ receives a special assertive power. This would in general be the place to look more closely at the 'functional Christology' of Cosmas, which results from his teaching of the catastases and the offices of Christ therein. It meets us at every turn.[61] As the 'second Adam', Christ stands over against the first.[62] From the position of eschatology in the *Topographia christiana* also comes the emphasis on Christ's office as judge (V, 254; VII, 38–40).[63]

On the whole, Cosmas probably gives the functions of Christ, the incarnate One, the most peculiar framework to be found in the teachings of the Fathers. The conjunction of the idea of the two spaces and the two catastases, which is present from the beginning of his work but in book V built into the overall picture of the divine *oikonomia*,[64] gives the person and work of Christ a particular and unique horizon. In Christ, the new

---

57. *Top. chr.* V, 202: p. 303,28–30.

58. Cf. *Top. chr.* VI, 27: SC 197, p. 43.

59. Cf. *Top. chr.* VI, 28: SC 197, pp. 43–45. W. Wolska-Conus probably judges too harshly when she states that in II, 101–2 and VI, 27–28 the 'divinity' of Christ is now drawn too weakly. She finds that in VI, 28: SC 197, pp. 43–45, and also in VII, 35 (ibid., p. 93), the subject of the action is God the Father, at whose disposal is the humanity of Christ as instrument. The result is that 'Dieu le Verbe est partout étrangement écarté' (idem, *Topographie Chrétienne*, p. 90). In VI, 28 (end) this is certainly not the case. In VII, 35 Cosmas simply speaks like Paul in interpretation of 1 Cor 15,57 and uses the designation θεός for the 'Father' (of Christ), from which no denial of the divinity of Christ may be derived.

60. Cosmas Ind., *Top. chr.* V, 133: SC 159, p. 193,4–5: Ps 109(110),4 is thus interpreted: οὐ γὰρ ἡ θεότης ἱερατεύει ἢ λατρεύει, ἀλλὰ μᾶλλον αὐτὴ λατρεύεται καὶ ἱερεῖα προσδέχεται. In Heb 5,4–6 also Ps 2,7 and 109(110),4 are related to the humanity of Christ. Here Cosmas agrees with Cyril of Alex., *Or. ad Augustas* 23 and 32: ACO I 1, 5, p. 40,4–8.11; pp. 50,36–51,1. This is an important development against the background of the Philonian-Origenist logos priesthood (cf. A. Grillmeier, *Chalkedon* I, p. 64 with n. 43).

61. See W. Wolska, *Topographie Chrétienne*, Index général: 'conditions', p. 309; 'Christ', pp. 307–8. Relatively frequent are the designations Δεσπότης Χριστὸς κατὰ σάρκα and Κύριος Ἰησοῦς.

62. Cf. W. Wolska, *Topographie Chrétienne*, p. 305, index 'Adam'.

63. Cf. op. cit., pp. 23, 97.

64. Influenced here by Thomas of Edessa, *Tractatus de Nativitate Domini Nostri Christi*, as W. Wolska, *Topographie Chrétienne*, pp. 73–85, shows. Included in the development of the whole are Theodore of Mopsuestia, Thomas of Edessa, Mar Aba, Cosmas and finally Giwargis (*c.* 680 *katholikos*). We will discuss this context in the presentation of the Christology of the so-called Nestorian church.

Adam, however, it is a question of human beings in general and their being led to knowledge of God and to God himself.[65]

(b) The trinitarian-christological credo of Cosmas and its orthodoxy

After attempting to make visible some basic outlines of the Christology of Cosmas and determine at least in a preliminary way his 'christological place', we must deal even more precisely with the question of his orthodoxy and his closeness to or distance from Nestorianism. For this purpose we begin with a relatively detailed credo in V, 253–54:

> one God in three hypostases, without beginning, eternal, uncircumscribed, invisible, intangible, incorruptible, immortal, impassible, incorporeal, unlimited, not composite, indivisible, Creator of heaven and earth, of visible and invisible things, known and adored in Father, Son and Holy Spirit, who at the end of days wanted to re-create the cosmos in the incarnation. Taken from our dough, from the holy Virgin Mary, without semen, the God-Logos with the Father and the Holy Spirit restores the microcosmos, the bond of the whole creation, namely, humankind, and unites with it from this short moment on in an outstanding and indestructible union [note the play on words: ἐξαιρέτος καὶ ἀναφαιρέτος], so that one cannot imagine assumption before the union, but formation, assumption and union as simultaneous. He [the God-Logos] accepted to suffer, be killed, and after being brought to perfection through resurrection, brought up to heaven, honoured with the seat on his right and made judge of the cosmos. With him, with the bridegroom, people who live well enter the wedding room, who mutilate neither the divinity nor the humanity. They form a single choir with Christ and will rule with him in heaven . . .

Here the assumption of a previously existing human being at the event of the incarnation is clearly rejected, and the incarnation of Christ is understood as a new creation (*anaktizo*) of the whole cosmos and restoration of the microcosmos (i.e., of humankind, the connecting link of creation). The confession of faith[66] in book VI, however, which is completely committed to the teaching of the catastases, sees in the incarnation a revelation of the future catastasis – both catastases were indeed already created from the beginning!

> Creator of all, the one God in three hypostases of Father, Son and Holy Spirit, the holy consubstantial Trinity, of equal power and equal strength, equal honour and equal glory and at the same time without beginning, and the great and wise and almighty order of salvation, cause of all, as wise and fitting he created the two catastases from the beginning, this one and the other one; and through the perfect humanity of the Lord, which is consubstantial with us in everything according to the soul and the body except for sin, he

---

65. See W. Wolska, *Topographie Chrétienne*, pp. 73–85.

66. A short credo that shows some echoes of the *apostolicum* is found in VII, 96, SC 197, p. 165: 'I believe in the one God, that is, the Father and Son and Holy Spirit, the consubstantial Trinity, and in the resurrection of the flesh, in the one holy, catholic and apostolic church, as the symbol also says. I believe that there will be a resurrection from the dead and life in the coming age.' Since a christological assertion is lacking here, we can disregard this text from now on.

lived in the last time, showed and revealed the future catastasis and preserved faith for all by awakening it [i.e., the humanity] from the dead. Thus all the perfect ones in accordance with this rule – peace over them and mercy over the Israel of God – will rightly hear in the future catastasis through the Lord Christ from heaven: Come, you blessed ones of my Father . . . To him be honour with the Father and the Holy Spirit in all eternity. Amen[67]

Here in VI, 28 one will look in vain for an express statement about the identity of Jesus Christ and the second divine person. Yet preceding this credo is a rejection of christological heresies. Immediately before (VI, 27) a stand is taken both against any denial of the perfect humanity of Christ (i.e., a rational, intelligent soul and a body with all the *idiomata* of the soul and the body) and against any denial or diminution of the divinity of Christ and subordination under the Father. Thus the credo can be interpreted as orthodox.

But let us now look at the first-named confession in V, 253–54. W. Wolska holds that this credo has 'une saveur nestorienne prononcée',[68] both (1) through the statement about the simple 'assumption' of the flesh and of the human soul in the moment of incarnation and (2) through the assignment of suffering and death to 'the human alone'. In addition, (3) the capability of Christ for perfection through the resurrection and the honouring of his humanity in heaven at the ascension point in the direction of this 'Nestorianism'.

These considerations, however, are overdrawn. It is crucial that in the credo of V, 254 the 'Theos-Logos' is given as the subject of the incarnation (SC 159, p. 371,3). It would be 'Nestorian' if the 'emphasis' of the incarnation were the to-be-assumed human being, who through moral testing made himself worthy of assumption (*assumptio*) as son. But there can be no talk of this in V, 254. The terms of the Antiochenes that were suspect to the Alexandrians, (1) *assume* = ἀνα-προς-λαβεῖν, *assumere*,[69] and (2) *conjoin*, συνάπτειν, συνάφεια, are not found. On the contrary, from the terminological viewpoint, the greatest demand of a Cyril of Alexandria and Severus of Antioch is fulfilled when even the verb ἑνόω is chosen with the noun ἕνωσις to express the 'outstanding and indestructible union', which coincides with the moment of creation of the humanity of Christ.[70]

---

67. Cosmas Ind., *Top. chr.* VI, 28: SC 197, pp. 43–45.

68. W. Wolska, *Topographie Chrétienne*, pp. 96–97, here p. 97; likewise in SC 159, p. 370, note on no. 254.

69. In *Top. chr.* V, 254, p. 371,1 we find λαβών, which, however, is given in Phil 2,7.

70. On this discussion of the union terminology between Cyril and Nestorius see: A. Grillmeier, *JdChr* I³, p. 681; in Cyril and Severus: *CCT* II/2, pp. 40–46.

It is also incomprehensible when in W. Wolska 'Nestorianism' is seen in the fact that the suffering and death are ascribed to 'the human alone'. Even the Alexandrians assume that the instrument of suffering is the human being, that is, the human nature, in Christ. The concrete term *human being* need not frighten. The subject and bearer is the God-Logos himself. And of *him* it is said that he volunteered to suffer and be killed.[71] That is so Alexandrian that one can even concede that too little expression is given to the freedom of the acceptance of suffering by the human will of Christ, which belongs to the divine subject.[72] The centring of the whole event of the *oikonomia* from the conception in Mary to the exaltation of the human Jesus on the throne of God in the Theos-Logos is unambiguous, and in the sense of the general tradition any diminution, be it of divinity or of humanity, is likewise rejected,[73] as is any separation. Therefore it is quite incomprehensible when W. Wolska says: 'Mais on peut affirmer que la divinité et l'humanité du Christ se séparent toutes les fois qu'on voit le Christ engagé dans son oeuvre salvatrice.'[74] They are 'distinguished' but not 'separated'; the 'natures' are distinguished (θεότης, ἀνθρωπότης!) (p. 371,13), not the persons separated. In order to understand the procedure of Cosmas, we will recall Leo I's *Tome* to Flavian and the both famous and controversial verse 94:

> Agit enim utraque forma cum alterius communione quod proprium est, Verbo scilicet operante, quod Verbi est et carne exsequente quod carnis est (Each of the two natures does its own thing in communion with the other: the Word does what is of the Word; the flesh carries out what belongs to the flesh).[75]

The Cyrillians would probably find the reproach of W. Wolska against Cosmas that we just cited more likely confirmed in Leo than in the credo that is contained in book V of Cosmas.

---

71. Cosmas Ind., *Top. chr.* V, 254: SC 159, p. 371,3.8. The grammatical subject of συνεχώρησε is still Θεὸς Λόγος of line 3. In general, it is theologically quite correct if the incarnation event is regarded as the work of the trinitarian God *ad extra* and is ascribed to all three persons in common (SC 159, p. 371,3). The 'aim' of the union of the human nature is, to be sure, the God-Logos alone. Similarly, also in the confession of faith of *Top. chr.* VI, 28 (SC 197, pp. 43–45) the creation of the two catastases is correctly ascribed to the three persons of the Trinity, and yet the special role of the 'perfect humanity of the Lord' (διὰ τῆς τελείας ἀνθρωπότητος τοῦ Κυρίου) in this is emphasized.

72. These problems are developed in connection with Leontius of Byzantium in A. Grillmeier, *CCT* II/2, pp. 222–26.

73. Cosmas Ind., *Top. chr.* V, 254: SC 159, p. 371,13.

74. W. Wolska, *Topographie Chrétienne*, p. 97.

75. Cf. A. Grillmeier, *JdChr* I³, pp. 743–44.

(c) Cosmas and tradition

The position of Cosmas on the Christian faith tradition as a whole is to some extent clearly revealed in book X.[76] His cosmological, anthropological, eschatological views, which he sees very well confirmed by the holy scripture – this evidence is indeed served by the foregoing books – were apparently attacked with the reproach that they were not supported by patristic exegesis.[77] Therefore he feels compelled to present an extensive patristic argumentation. Cosmas wants to prove his work as a 'genuine product' of ecclesiastical tradition (γνήσιον τῆς ἐκκλησιαστικῆς παραδόσεως γέννημα)[78] and furnish the proof that the prophets, apostles, evangelists, Jesus Christ himself, and the entire holy scripture, together with the Fathers and teachers, attest to his view.[79]

Notable are the many excerpts from the Easter festal letters of St Athanasius of Alexandria[80] and from Alexandrians in general. The main witness, however, is not an Alexandrian but Severian of Gabala.[81] While Athanasius, Gregory of Nazianzus and Theophilus of Alexandria offer the traditional explanations of the Christian faith, Cosmas derives his cosmology from Severian alone (*In Cosmogoniam* 1–6) (CPG 4194). At the end of the quotations Cosmas summarizes his proofs in his *Commentaries*, but in so doing always goes into the graded, two-part worldview (teaching of the catastases) and 'dogma', that is, the history of salvation in Christ, or ecclesiology.[82] Christ is the high priest who steps from the outside into the inner sanctuary as the new Moses.[83] The connection of outer worldview (σχῆμα), theologically historical typology and dogmatic Christology (δόγμα) is unique to Cosmas.[84]

---

76. Cosmas Ind., *Top. chr.* X: SC 197, pp. 239–313.

77. Ibid., X, 1, p. 239.

78. *Top. chr.* X, 75, p. 313,7–8.

79. *Top. chr.* X, 40–41: SC 197, pp. 279–81.

80. On this see A. Camplani, *Le lettere festali di Atanasio di Alessandria. Studio storico-critico*, Rome 1989, 41–43; cf. index s.v. Cosma Indicopleuste, p. 324.

81. The passages (commented on by Cosmas) are taken from Athanasius (nos. 3–14), Gregory of Nazianzus (nos. 15–16), Theophilus of Alexandria (nos. 17–19), Severian of Gabala (nos. 20–41!), Epiphanius of Salamis (nos. 43–45), John Chrysostom (nos. 46–56), Philo of Carpathus (nos. 57–62), Theodosius of Alexandria (nos. 63–67) and Timothy of Alexandria (nos. 68–75).

82. See Cosmas Ind., *Top. chr.* X, 14: SC 197, p. 253: σχῆμα τοῦ κόσμου – δόγμα); X, 16: p. 255 (ἡ συμφωνία τῆς Ἐκκλησίας).

83. Ibid., X, 19, p. 259.

84. Especially clear in X, 52–56, pp. 291–95 (on John Chrysostom). He sets out the religious view of a total, comprehensive unity of world and history (of both testaments), which is given in the church (συμφωνία τῆς Ἐκκλησίας – ὁμοφωνία μυστηρίων Θεοῦ) (X, 55: p. 293,6–7).

PART TWO

THE 'PROVINCE OF COPTIC CHRISTOLOGY'

Today it is no longer permissible to see the pre- and post-Chalcedonian Christology of Egypt as located only in Alexandria and its immediate vicinity. A walk into the desert and a trip up the Nile let us discover the christological 'province' according to new finds in the sands of the Nile and with the initial evaluation of texts that in the course of our century and even earlier disappeared into the great libraries of the world. The discovery and deciphering of the first Coptic christological texts are to be deemed a significant event for us. Their interpretation is also possible, at least in part, only if we take into consideration the Nag Hammadi codices discovered just a few decades ago. Yet for the present we must be satisfied with only a few texts, which, however, already strikingly illuminate the beginning of the actual *Coptic* proclamation about Christ. The hope is justified, however, that in a few decades this journey of discovery up the Nile – through Nubia to Ethiopia – will be accorded greater success.

CHAPTER ONE

SHENOUTE AS THE FOUNDER OF COPTIC CHRISTOLOGY

First we must pause on the middle Nile in the region where the Pachomius monasteries were founded and also where the Nag Hammadi discoveries were made. If we look beyond Pachomius himself and his second successor, Abbot Horsiesius,[1] we encounter a great figure who links the fourth century with the fifth, including the Chalcedonian and post-Chalcedonian period: the archimandrite Shenoute the Great, the real founder of Coptic theological literature and head of the 'White Monastery' at Sūhāg.[2] Born in a little village of Thebaid as a peasant's son, by 371 at the latest he had entered the monastery founded by his uncle on his mother's side, Pgōl. After the latter's death in 385 he took over the leadership of the new foundation, which under him acquired very great

---

1. On the Christology of the Pachomian movement cf. H. Bacht, 'Christusgemeinschaft. Der theologische Gehalt der frühesten ägyptischen Mönchsdokumente', in *Praesentia Christi*, FS J. Betz, ed. by L. Lies, Düsseldorf 1984, 444–55.

2. On the 'White Monastery' of Atripe as a foundation by Shenoute see P. Cherix, *Étude de lexicographie copte. Chenouté, Le discours en présence de Flavien* (RevBibl.C 18), Paris 1929, 2–3; H.-G. Evers and R. Romeo, 'Rotes und Weißes Kloster bei Sohag. Probleme der Rekonstruktion', in K. Wessel (ed.), *Christentum am Nil*, Recklinghausen 1964, 175–94; O. F. A. Meinardus, *Christian Egypt Ancient and Modern*, Cairo 1965, 290–93; D. W. Young, 'The Milieu of Nag Hammadi: Some Historical Considerations', *VigC* 24 (1970), 127–37; M. Cramer, *Das christlich-koptische Ägypten einst und heute. Eine Orientierung*, Wiesbaden 1959, 5–6; C. D. G. Müller, art. 'Schenute der Große von Atripe', in *KlWbChrOr*, 316–18 (with lit.). – On the extensive, largely still unedited writings of Shenoute in the main dialect of Coptic see D. W. Young, op. cit. It is to be placed between 388 and 466. Included according to Young are 'the expository epistle, the apocalypse, the homily and the diatribe'. On the critique of previous editions (before T. Orlandi) see ibid., p. 128, n. 4; on J. Leipoldt, *Schenute von Atripe und die Entstehung des national ägyptischen Christentums* (TU 25), Leipzig 1903, see ibid., p. 130 with n. 10. An excellent bibliography on Shenoute is offered in P. J. Frandsen and E. Richter Aerøe, 'Shenoute: A Bibliography', in D. W. Young (ed.), *Studies in Honour of J. J. Polotsky*, East Gloucester, Mass., 1981, 147–76. Cf. now Unione Academica Nazionale, *Coptic Bibliography* 2 (CMCL), Rome 1985, pp. 54–56. Good information is offered by J. Timbie, 'The State of Research on the Career of Shenoute of Atripe', in B. A.

importance. In 431 he accompanied Patriarch Cyril of Alexandria to Ephesus. He was also supposed to participate in the Council of Chalcedon but was prevented from doing so by illness. Would he have been on the side of Dioscorus there? We have some indications of a positive answer, which may not have been without significance for the basic orientation of the Christology in the province, although we will later discover zealous adherents of Chalcedon precisely among the Pachomians.

Shenoute is considered the father of Coptic literature above all because of his sermons, letters and theological works, to which he sometimes refers. Everything that is still available to us today was copied in the 'White Monastery' but is now divided among more than twenty libraries of the world and must be tediously gathered together and edited.[3] In the meantime, from this extensive material – as far as it can be attributed to Shenoute – we can evaluate only two longer christological texts. If both are authentic, they alone will suffice to invalidate the harsh judgement of J. Leipoldt on the Christless piety of Shenoute and the enormous damage it allegedly caused.[4] Both texts mention Nestorius,

---

Pearson and J. E. Goehring (eds.), *The Roots of Egyptian Christianity*, Philadelphia 1986, 258–70. – General introductions: A. Guillaumont, art., 'Copte (Littérature spirituelle)', in *DSp* 2 (1953), 2266–78; M. Krause, 'Koptische Literatur', in *LexÄg* III (1980), 694–728; P. Nagel (ed.), *Probleme der koptischen Literatur* (WB [H]), 1968/1 (K 2), Halle/S. 1968. On the editions see *Sinuthii Archimandritae vita et opera omnia*, ed. by J. Leipoldt and W. Crum, I. *Sinuthii vita boharice*: CSCO 41 (1906) (T); III: CSCO 42 (1908) (T); IV: CSCO 73 (1913) (T); V: CSCO 129.96.108. E. Chassinat, *Le quatrième livre des entretiens et épîtres de Shenouti* (MIFAO 23), Cairo 1911. Further edited texts are named below.

3. See T. Orlandi, 'Un projet milanais concernant les manuscrits du Monastère Blanc', *Mus* 85 (1972), 403–13; A. Campagnano, 'Monaci egiziani fra V e VI secolo', *VC* 15 (1978), 223–46. The Orlandi project is incorporated into Unione Acad. Naz., *Coptic Bibliography* 1–4 (= CMCL), Rome 1989 (and is ongoing).

4. J. Leipoldt, *Schenute* (TU 25), pp. 81–82, speaks of a 'barren Christology', which is also qualified as inadequate. For 'he adopted the christological formulas of the Greek church, which naturally did not go with his view of religious duties or with his whole piety. So this automatically resulted in the necessity that the person of the Lord remained meaningless for him.' Further negative judgements are added by H.-F. Weiss, 'Zur Christologie des Schenute von Atripe', *BSAC* 20 (1969/70) (177–209), 179–80. Ibid. from A. v. Harnack, *Lehrbuch der Dogmengeschichte* II, Tübingen [5]1931, 373, n. 1: '. . . almost nowhere did this man, totally caught up in the monastic and in magic, bring his own Christology to expression. In truth he had none but was satisfied with a superstitious view that naturally could cope theologically only with Monophysitism.' Following this harsh judgement of Leipoldt is A. Veilleux, 'Chénouté ou les écueils du monachisme', *CollCist* 45 (1983), 124–31. The new texts that L. T. Lefort and T. Orlandi have edited will show how inappropriate these judgements are. Even his personality was or is characterized negatively, say, in G. G. Stroumsa, 'The Manichaean Challenge to Egyptian Christianity', in Pearson and Goehring, *The Roots of Egyptian Christianity*, Philadelphia 1986, p. 315: 'Shenoute boasts of once having burned two

and one of them even his death. Thus they must have been written after 431 or 451. For Nestorius, as we shall see, also endured the last part of his exile not far from the 'White Monastery'. Shenoute himself did not die before 451; indeed, since he is supposed to have reached 118 years of age, he could have lived until 466.

I. A NEW SOURCE FOR SHENOUTE'S CHRISTOLOGY AND FOR COPTIC THEOLOGY IN GENERAL

The research of T. Orlandi has offered us an extensive Coptic text, whose manuscripts come from the 'White Monastery' and which he ascribes to Shenoute. In a first announcement he gave it the title, 'A Catechesis against apocryphal texts by Shenoute and the Gnostic Texts of Nag Hammadi'.[5] If this authorship is accepted definitively, we have an extraordinarily rich document for the pastoral and theological situation

---

Manichaean priests – the man was no doubt capable of such a deed . . .' Stroumsa is referring at this point to the homily on the wedding at Cana by Patr. Benjamin: idem, 'Monachisme et marranisme chez les manichéens d'Égypte', *Numen* 29 (1982), 201, n. 54. But there it is a question of the like-named *Duke* Shenoute, the military and civil head of Thebaid, to whom Patriarch Benjamin turns and hands over the two sinners, and this is around 643 and thus about 200 years later: cf. C. D. G. Müller, *Die Homilie über die Hochzeit zu Kana und weitere Schriften des Patriarchen Benjamin I. von Alexandrien* (*AHAW.PH* 1968, 1), Heidelberg 1968, pp. 20–23.

5. T. Orlandi in *HThR* 75 (1982), 85–95; (already earlier) idem, 'La cristologia nei testi catechetici copti', in S. Felici (ed.), *Cristologia e catechesi patristica* I (BiblScRel 32), Rome 1980, 213–29; T. Orlandi made available to me in Italian translation and before publication the new text compiled by him, for which I am grateful to him. I was able to discuss questions on the Coptic text with Hans Quecke of Rome. Information on the reconstruction of the text is found in the diagram offered by T. Orlandi in *HThR* 75 (1982), 87, which states: 'The treatise we present here is reconstructed from fragments of three codexes and one folio of a fourth. The evidence constitutes several blocks of text, which partly overlap with one another and which, on the whole, have enough shared elements to demonstrate that they are from one and the same work.' Only a few fragments had been previously published (cf. ibid., n. 9); see also B. Layton, 'The "Missing" Fragments of a Shenoute Homily. (Brit. Lib. Or. 7561 [72][81][83][96])', *Orientalia* 52 (1983), 424–25. A few christological texts are also found in the works of G. Giamberardini: (1) *La teologia assunzionista nella Chiesa Egiziana* (AegC 1, 2), Jerusalem 1951; (2) *La mediazione di Maria nella Chiesa Egiziana*, Cairo 1952; (3) *L'Immacolata Concezione di Maria nella Chiesa Egiziana*, Cairo 1953; (4) *La consecrazione Eucaristica nella Chiesa Copta* (AegC 1, 8), Cairo 1957; (5) 'La doctrine christologique des Coptes', *POC* 13 (1963), 211–20.

in Upper Egypt at the beginning of ecclesiastical Coptic writing and for the role of Shenoute himself. The content does indeed show contacts with individual Nag Hammadi codices (NHC). But not only 'gnosis' is fought here but also – in more or less clear connection with it – 'Origen' and ultimately also Nestorius. In regard to the name *Origen*, it is not a question only of historical teachings of the master that we designate *Origenist* but also of further developments that we must call *Origenistic*. They are so prominent in the new text that T. Orlandi has given it in a second, still preliminary treatment the title 'Contra Origenistas'.[6] The nexus to the Gnostics and the distinction between 'Origen' and 'apocrypha' remain to be clarified in further discussion.

While it must be left to the Coptologists to carry out comparative linguistic examinations of the relationship of the new text to the previously known writings, some indications of its situation can be given.

1. The Nag Hammadi tractates and the monastic movement in Upper Egypt (Thebaid)

After the NHC were found in the vicinity of the Pachomius monasteries and pieces of Greek and Coptic papyri were discovered in the bindings of certain codices, it was concluded that the codices were produced in the Pachomian monasteries. With the presupposition that no gnostic groups would have been tolerated in these monasteries, the motive for this preservation was sought. It seemed obvious that someone was occupied with the writings for the purpose of refuting heresies and buried the books after carrying out this task.[7] This indulgent interpretation could be supported by the fact that our sources (the Pachomius lives, the *Historia Lausiaca*, etc.) at first glance yield no indication that gnosticizing ideas were represented in the Pachomian movement. Before the discovery of the NHC, in any case, this suspicion had occurred to no researcher. A closer examination, nonetheless, seemed to produce a somewhat different picture. Several researchers pointed

---

6. T. Orlandi, *Shenute. Contra Origenistas. Testo con introduzione e traduzione* (= CMCL), Rome 1985.

7. On these questions see the contributions of J. W. B. Barns, NHSt 6, Leiden 1975, 9–17; T. Säve-Söderbergh, NHSt 7 (1975), 3–14. The problem has been recently investigated by A. Veilleux, 'Monachisme et Gnose. Première partie: Le cénobitisme pachômien et la Bibliothèque Copte de Nag Hammadi', *CollCist* 46 (1984), 239–58.

out that some Pachomian monks liked to gather and read such writings in good faith, and indeed that some letters of Pachomius himself could be interpreted in the spirit of the Nag Hammadi texts.[8]

Despite all purifying tendencies, the Greek and Coptic Pachomius lives reveal that in the monasteries of Thebaid there were actually monks who came in contact with 'dangerous' books. Here the name of 'Origen' also played a special role. Yet at this point there is a special difficulty. With the original Greek language of the writings of Origen and then of Evagrius – in case one wants to bring this name into consideration here – what opportunity was there to read these writings in Thebaid? T. Orlandi would like to prove, through a new interpretation and new arrangement of the Coptic dossier of 'Agathonicus of Tarsus', that there is here a

---

8. See C. W. Hedrick, 'Gnostic Proclivities in the *Greek Life of Pachomius* and the *Sitz im Leben* of the Nag Hammadi Library', *NovTest* 22 (1980), 78–94. – All indications needed to be collected, both in the Pachomius life and in other writings that report the penetration of heretical groups or tendencies in the region of Thebaid. Here are a few:
(1) For the history of the calling according to the *Epistula Ammonis* (recruitment by Melitians, Marcionites) see below, p. 219. – (2) According to the *Histoire de Saint Pacôme*, ed. J. Bousquet and F. Nau (PO 4), p. 499, Pachomius admonished his monks two days before his death to make no acquaintance with the heresies of Origen, Melitios, Arius or other enemies of Christ. Cf. K. Heussi, *Der Ursprung des Mönchtums*, Tübingen 1936, IV, 3: *Pachomius und die Klöster der Melitianer*, pp. 129–81; ibid., 287–98; G. Ghedini, 'Luci nuove dai papiri sullo scisma meleziano e il monachismo in Egitto', in *La Scuola Catt.* 6th ser. vol. 6 (1925), 261–80. Among the schismatic Melitians there was a Hellenistic and a larger Coptic group. There was 'una larga famiglia di monaci, tutti scismatici, disciplinati, con regole precise' and indeed of the Pachomian type (ibid. 269, 277). See L. W. Barnard, 'Athanasius and the Meletian Schism in Egypt', *JEA* 59 (1973), 181–89. Even more important is the Manichaean mission in Egypt: K. S. Frank, ΑΓΓΕΛΙΚΟΣ ΒΙΟΣ (BGAM 26), Münster 1964, 158–61; J. Jarry, 'Le manichéisme en Égypte Byzantine', *BIFAO* 66 (1968), 121–37; A. Henrichs and L. Koenen, 'Der Kölner Mani-Kodex . . . Edition d. SS. 72,8–99,9', *ZPE* 32 (1978), 168–69: 'A few years after Mani had freed himself of the baptists, the Manichaean Adda missionized in the Roman Empire and reached Alexandria (*c.* AD 242). In this way "he founded many monasteries".' Besides Adda an abbot Mani missionized in the West. On this see L. Koenen, 'Manichäische Mission und Klöster in Ägypten', in G. Grimm, H. Heinen and E. Winter (eds.), *Das römisch-byzantinische Ägypten* (Aegyptiaca Treverensia 2), Mainz 1983, 93–108; also: J. Vergote, 'L'expansion du manichéisme en Égypte', in *After Chalcedon*, FS A. Van Roey (OLA 18), Louvain 1985, 471–78; G. G. Stroumsa, 'Monachisme et marranisme chez les manichéens d'Égypte', *Numen* 29 (1982), 184–201, esp. pp. 186–88; idem, 'The Manichaean Challenge to Egyptian Christianity', in B. A. Pearson and J. E. Goehring (eds.), *The Roots of Egyptian Christianity*, Philadelphia 1986, 307–19; D. W. Johnson, 'Coptic Reactions to Gnosticism and Manichaeism', *Mus* 100 (1987), 199–209. – On Mani and Egypt see also P. Nagel, *Die Thomaspsalmen des koptisch-manichäischen Psalmenbuches* (Quellen, NF 1), Berlin 1980, 11–15.

connection and a linguistic bridge to the relatively far distant Nitrian desert.[9]

First, with regard to the 'gnosis', C. W. Hedrick attempted to discover in the *Vita Graeca*[10] of Pachomius traces of 'gnostic proclivities'.[11] He stresses that in this regard not all the Pachomian monasteries would have followed the same line. Especially the monastery of Monchosis was more liberal in practical matters than Pachomius could have liked (art. cit., 81). After the death of the monastic father 'there was a general dissolution of concord among the brothers and a breakdown in the coenobitic way of life' (ibid., 83). Accordingly, the Pachomius monasteries would have encompassed people of all kinds. This must in no way mean, according to Hedrick, that 'Gnostics' belonged to the monastic *system* of Pachomius, but individuals with gnostic leanings and positions would have been able to find a place in it (ibid., 83). Yet here we are working in the realm of hypotheses.

The reference to 'dreams' and 'visions' and their influence in the Pachomian movement (ibid., 85–88) does not lead very much further. Thus the visionary element plays a large role in the life of Shenoute (especially according to the *Vita Bohairica*). But he is anything but a Gnostic. C. W. Hedrick unjustly points to the unexplained phenomenon of the 'secret writing' as 'gnostic proclivities'.[12]

More important and more certain, however, are the references to the dangers that threaten from 'Origen'. The appearance of an angel teaches Pachomius about the 'godless dogmas of Origen' that allegedly were read *secretly* by monks in the monastery. They should be thrown into the Nile (Halkin, pp. 131,11–132,6). Therefore the monastic father warns earnestly against either reading the silliness of the Alexandrians oneself or letting it be read aloud to oneself (ibid., 195,10–16; cf. p. 281,11–24). With reference to God Pachomius affirms to the brothers that the reading and recognition of the writings (*syntagmata*) of the Alexandrians brings damnation (pp. 240,24–241,10; 307,25–308,12). No communion is allowed with Origen, Melitios, Arius and other opponents of Christ (p. 268,9–11). We encounter the same names or heresies also in the new exhortation, yet with the addition of Nestorius! In any case, even in Thebaid the familiarity of Pachomius with writings that went under the name of Origen must be recognized as possible and given.

We can assume the following as given for the new exhortation: (1) We have a text from Thebaid. (2) We can assume in it certain traces of familiarity with Nag Hammadi writings, which must be made more precise. (3) Besides Origen, Nestorius is also named and refuted, which places the text in the period after Ephesus (431). (4) The text is full of laments over 'gnostic proclivities' in the monastic realm and speaks of the acute dangers of the dissolution of the life of faith. So we can ask what further indications there are for the authorship of Shenoute.

---

9. See excursus below. Important on the classification of the Orlandi exhortation is idem, 'Gli Apocrifi copti', *Aug* 23 (1983), 57–71; also A. Orbe, 'Gli Apocrifi cristiani a Nag Hammadi', ibid., 83–109.

10. Cf. F. Halkin, *Sancti Pachomii vitae graecae* (SubsHag 19), Brussels 1932.

11. C. W. Hedrick, art. cit. In the evaluation of the 'visions' as 'gnostic proclivity' one must naturally be careful. The whole 'visionary' phenomenon and its judgement, say, in Pachomius and in monasticism in general must also be considered especially from the viewpoint of discernment of the spirits. Excellent help is offered by A. Guillaumont, *Aux origines du monachisme chrétien* (Spiritualité orientale 30), Bégrolles en Mauges 1979, 136–47: 'Les visions mystiques dans le monachisme oriental chrétien'.

12. See H. Quecke, *Die Briefe Pachoms* (TPL 11), Regensburg 1975, 18–40.

2. Special indications of Shenoute as the author of the new exhortation

As a more exact analysis of the text shows us, we have before us an admonitory talk that was held in a larger monastic community. The speaker, however, also has a broader vision. Without doubt he is a man of great authority who in his own circle is involved in an almost hopeless battle against numerous invading abuses and heresies. 'Among us' are those who spread the teachings of the apocrypha! The heretics are not fought theoretically – in the manner of the apologists. The prevailing relationship between the various groups seems still to be that which can also be established in the NHC:[13] they feel that they are together in one community. We do not still have separate communities standing over against each other as 'denominations'. Rather, the fundamental tradition is recognizable as the common point of departure. But it is already – under foreign influences – interpreted quite antithetically. It is a matter of the fundamental, originally common kerygma that is threatened by numerous speculations of the gnostic and 'Origenistic' kind. The whole order of salvation in Christ is sacrificed to them. It is ultimately a question of the divinity of Christ, against which Nestorius finally appears as the main opponent.

Thus we have a unique situation report on the state of faith in the Coptic monastic province after 431. On the other hand, there is no mention yet of the problems around the Council of Chalcedon, although the christological problem permeates the whole exhortation. We are between 431 and 451. If we seek in this period a leading figure in or around the White Monastery, from which the manuscript comes, there is none other than Shenoute, its archimandrite.

---

13. See esp. the studies of K. Koschorke, *Die Polemik der Gnostiker gegen das kirchliche Christentum* (NHSt 12), Leiden 1978; idem, ' "Suchen und Finden" in der Auseinandersetzung zwischen gnostischem und kirchlichem Christentum', *WuD* NF 14 (1977), 51–65; idem, 'Eine gnostische Pfingstpredigt', *ZThK* 74 (1977), 323–43; idem, 'Der gnostische Traktat "Testimonium Veritatis" aus dem Nag-Hammadi-Codex IX. Eine Übersetzung', *ZNW* 69 (1978), 91–117; idem, 'Eine gnostische Paraphrase des Johanneischen Prologs. Zur Interpretation von "Epistula Petri ad Philippum" (NHC VIII,2) . . .', *VigC* 33 (1979), 383–92; idem, 'Eine neugefundene gnostische Gemeindeordnung. Zum Thema Geist und Amt im frühen Christentum', *ZThK* 76 (1979), 30–60. Also of Koschorke's view is M. Krause, 'Christlich-Gnostische Texte als Quellen für die Auseinandersetzung von Gnosis und Christentum', in idem (ed.), *Gnosis and Gnosticism. Papers read at the Eighth Internat. Conference on Patr. Studies, Oxford 1979* (NHSt 17), Leiden 1981, 47–65. – Koschorke refers to J. Kunze, *Glaubensregel, Heilige Schrift und Taufbekenntnis*, Leipzig 1899, 313–442 (rule of faith, Gnosticism, Marcionitism).

To this argumentation from within we must yet add three groups of outside testimonies, which speak more or less clearly for Shenoute as the author of this exhortation. We will order them according to the strength of their evidence.

(a) A call for help from Patriarch Dioscorus (444–451/454) to Shenoute
Word of serious irregularities in Upper Egypt had reached Alexandria. Fortunately we now have a letter of Patriarch Dioscorus to the archimandrite of the White Monastery, which undoubtedly fits the described situation and forms the missing link between the Orlandi exhortation and Shenoute himself.[14]

The patriarch came to the throne of Alexandria in 444. At the time of the writing of the letter he was still in office. The deposition by the fathers of Chalcedon in 451 has not yet occurred. Between 444 and 451, but probably between 444 and 449 – that is, before the turbulent synod of Ephesus (449) – he sent a letter to the White Monastery together with a memorandum (*hypomnestikon*) for the three bishops of Thebaid (Sabinus, Gennadius and Hermogenes), both in Greek. Shenoute was instructed to translate this *hypomnestikon*, or have it translated, into the Egyptian language. Then it was supposed to be read aloud publicly before clergy, monks and the entire people, probably in Shmin and in the other dioceses. In the patriarch's letter Shenoute is first informed of the relapse of the priest Helias into Origenism, which he had renounced. In the memorandum to the three bishops the case was explained more precisely. Strict instructions were given for the total isolation of the lapsed priest. The three bishops were to turn the contents into regulations for the monasteries of Panopolis (Shmin). Shenoute, however, is supposed to initiate inquiries in the cities and monasteries of these dioceses, visit them and take care of everything, especially with regard to the execution of the given instructions within monasticism. Especially affected is a monastery of Shmin that is called *Parembole*, which probably means that it is accommodated in a *colonia militaris* or in an old garrison.[15]

The letter was not written to Shenoute without reason. For Dioscorus can boast of him as a proven fighter against all enemies of God, together

14. Dioscorus of Alex., *Ep. ad Sinuthium* (CPG 5461): H. Thompson, 'Dioscorus and Shenoute', in *Recueil . . . J.-Fr. Champollion* (BEHE 234), Paris 1922, 367–76. Cf. A. Grillmeier, 'La "peste d'Origène". Soucis du patriarche d'Alexandrie dus à l'apparition d'origénistes en Haute Égypte (444–451)', in ΑΛΕΞΑΝΔΡΙΝΑ, Mél. Cl. Mondésert, Paris 1987, 221–37.

15. Cf. E. Carpentier, ASS Oct. XII, 1867, § 25, p. 742.

with a few other monks and the priest Psenthaesius. Although the patriarch himself wants to take care of the monasteries that are causing him concern, the archimandrite is nonetheless entrusted with the performance of the tasks to be done:

> For we will also care specially for those convents, searching into everything. Meanwhile the presence of your Reverence and the care which you will exercise daily for them will greatly benefit the business. It is on this account that I have written to you . . . May your Reverence make speed to have the entire Memorandum translated into the Egyptian tongue, so that it may be read in that form and none may be ignorant of the authority (*dynamis*) of the things that are written therein.[16]

The most interesting sentence, however, stands at the close of the long fragment of the memorandum:

> But since I have heard moreover that there are *books and numerous treatises (syntagmata) of the pest (loimos) named Origenes and other heretics* in that convent [namely, Parembole] and in the former temple of Shmin and elsewhere, let your Reverences inquire after them carefully and collect them and write their *kathema* and send them to us; for if God has given us power to bind . . .[17]

These inquiries into the dangerous books in the whole district of the three dioceses and especially in Shmin are to proceed in three ways: the bishops, the patriarch and especially Shenoute are supposed to and will be concerned about them. The words to Shenoute are especially noteworthy:

> And do thou moreover inquire earnestly also concerning the cities and monasteries of that diocese [Panopolis, Shmin] and convene them, and further do thy best not to let any insolence assail the beloved priest Psenthaesius and the worthy monks who are with him.[18]

Thus Dioscorus places great confidence in Shenoute in this affair, which concerns both the priest Helias and the Origenistic writings and other heretical books. If Origen stands in the foreground for Dioscorus, then it is precisely because of the named lapsed priest. But the other *haeretica* are not to be underestimated either. Now, apparently this refers especially to apocryphal and gnostic works. In brief, we are *in situ* with regard to the Orlandi exhortation. It can with complete certainty be credited to Shenoute. As we shall see, the exhortation corresponds exactly to the situation described by Dioscorus. It sounds almost like the carrying out of

---

16. Dioscorus of Alex., *Ep. ad Sinuth.*: H. Thompson, p. 374.
17. Ibid., H. Thompson, p. 376.
18. Ibid., H. Thompson, p. 374.

the entrusted mission. Certainly, Shenoute's proceeding against the pagan temples in the vicinity of the White Monastery, redolent of the prophet Elijah, was also known to the patriarch.[19] The inner testimony of the exhortation and the external, the letter of Dioscorus, correspond exactly.[20]

(b) Shenoute and Nestorius in Upper Egypt

The Orlandi exhortation presents a lengthy section on Nestorius. The two came close together, even if not face to face, not only in Ephesus but also in Egypt itself. That is not without significance for the new text and its authenticity. Severus ibn al-Muqaffaʿ, bishop of Al-Ashmunain, reports in his patriarchal history on the banishment of Nestorius by Emperor Theodosius II: 'So Nestorius was exiled in company with a chamberlain who conducted him to Egypt.'[21] Before this trip into exile began, the bishops (of Ephesus) again sent a letter with the admonition: 'Confess that the Crucified is God Incarnate, and we will receive thee again and obtain the repeal of thy sentence of banishment' (ibid.). Now, Severus apparently has the *Coptic Church History* itself (edited and translated by T. Orlandi) as source (or both a common third source?) when he reproduces the dialogue between Nestorius and the imperial guard, now already on Egyptian soil:

> And when he [Nestorius] said to the chamberlain: 'Let us rest here, for I am tired,' the chamberlain replied: 'Thy Lord also was weary when he walked until the sixth hour [cf. Jn 4,6], and he is God. What sayest thou?' And Nestorius answered: 'Two hundred bishops assembled to make me confess that Jesus is God incarnate, but I would not do so. Shall I then say to thee that God suffered fatigue?'[22]

In some now edited fragments of the same 'Coptic church history of Alexandria'[23] the dialogue just quoted is adopted almost word for word but then extended. In it the Coptic interpretation of 'Nestorianism' is reproduced. The further report of the fragments, however,

---

19. Cf. J. Leipoldt, TU 25, pp. 175–82.

20. Versus E. Lucchesi, 'Chénouté a-t-il écrit en grec?', in *Mél. A. Guillaumont. Contribution à l'étude des christianismes orientaux* (Cah. d'Orientalisme 20), Geneva 1988, 201–10, esp. pp. 206–7, n. 10.

21. Thus according to *Hist. Patr.*: PO 1, pp. 432–41; the English translation is also in T. Orlandi, *Storia della Chiesa di Alessandria* II, Milan–Varese 1970, pp. 80–87; here p. 87.

22. *Hist. Patr.*: PO 1, p. 441; T. Orlandi, *Storia della Chiesa di Aless.* II, p. 87.

23. See D. W. Johnson, 'Further Fragments of a Coptic History of the Church', *Enchoria* 6 (1976), 7–17. Also H. Brakmann, 'Eine oder zwei koptische Kirchengeschichten?', *Mus* 87 (1974), 129–42. Johnson and Brakmann hold, versus Orlandi, that in these named texts it is a question of parts of *one* Coptic church history.

contains some details that are of interest for the relationship between Nestorius and Shenoute and agree in part with Evagrius Scholasticus.

(1) The way into the oasis according to the Johnson fragment of the church history: When the court official (*pallatinos*) with the help of the *dux* of Thebaid (Caesarius; see below) wanted to lead the exile further into the oasis, he heard from the *Sakko* of the oasis through the *Mazices*.[24] There was nothing left for him to do but leave Nestorius behind in the fortress of *Simbelǧe*[25] with a guard. Here began a lengthy stay for Nestorius, and in a place that was not far from the White Monastery. There he became seriously ill ('he became all swollen and dried up. And he continued under the torment a great many years'). Thus the exile was granted a long life after 434, which agrees with other reports.[26]

Naturally Nestorius must have learned that he was not far from Shenoute and his monastery. He sends to the archimandrite and challenges him: 'Take my possessions and give them to the poor.' Remembering Ephesus, however, Shenoute takes this offer as pretence and refuses to come. Nevertheless, according to the Johnson fragment he met with Nestorius. During the visit the discussion turns to the theopaschite question. It is determined that Nestorius has not changed his opinion: 'I will never say that God died.' Based on this information, Shenoute will have nothing to do with a turning over of the exile's possessions: 'You are anathema together with your possessions.' Then the archimandrite left him and returned to his monastery.

---

24. D. W. Johnson, op. cit., 15. The *Mazices* are also mentioned: (1) in John Rufus, *Pleroph.* 36: PO 8, p. 82,9: the arrest of Nestorius is ascribed to the *Mazices* themselves. Released by them for money, he came to Panopolis, the city of Pan (Shmin), the symbol of the 'two natures' (Pan = a human figure with the feet of a he-goat); (2) in Evagrius, *HE* I 7: Bidez-Parmentier, p. 14,33, this in an excerpt from a letter of Nestorius to the *dux* of Thebaid. According to it, the threatening invasion by the *Mazices* will be preceded by the great attack by the barbarians (Blemmyes), who capture Nestorius but then release him. Because of the new danger he then also comes to Panopolis but reports to the imperial Comes in Antinoe. On Shenoute and a Blemmyes attack see *Sin. Vit. Boh.*, 89–90: CSCO 129, pp. 24–25. On Evagrius see P. Allen, *Evagrius Scholasticus*, pp. 80–81. The testimonies about Blemmyes, Mazices and Nobatae are considered in detail in U. Monneret de Villard, *Storia della Nubia Cristiana* (OCA 118), Rome 1938, 36–60; ibid., pp. 48–49, on Nestorius. The Blemmyes invasion was between 440 and 450.

25. Since the caravan route went off into the *Great Oasis* (El Charge) of Abydos, Nestorius remained either from the beginning on or after a temporary stay in the oasis (until the invasion by the Blemmyes) in the monastic realm of Shenoute. The fortress (*kastron*) *Simbelǧe* is mentioned as the place of the last stay and the death of Nestorius (1) in the Johnson fragment of the Coptic church history, p. 15; (2) in H. Thompson, 'Dioscorus und Shenoute', in *Recueil . . . Champollion* (BEHE 234, 1922), 367–76, where the above-mentioned letter of Patr. Dioscorus to Shenoute is reproduced from a volume with the correspondence of the archimandrite. The talk is, to be sure, only of a *kastron* near Shmin (Panopolis), which according to O. von Lemm is precisely Simbelǧe (ibid., p. 370). (3) In A. van Lantschoot, 'Allocution de Timothée d'Alexandrie prononcée à l'occasion de la dédicace de l'Église de Pacôme à Pbou', *Mus* 47 (1934) (13–56), 43: 'Psūmbeleǧ', where Nestorius remained until his death. (4) According to Eutychius, *Annales* II 12: PG 111, 1033BC, Nestorius was brought to Echmin (Shmin = Panopolis), where he died seven years later and was buried in a place called Saklan.

26. See J. F. Bethune-Baker, 'The Date of the Death of Nestorius: Shenoute, Zacharias, Evagrius', *JTS* 9 (1908), 601–5; idem, *Nestorius and his Teaching*, Cambridge 1908, 36, n. 1. Nestorius was still living around 451.

(2) According to the fragment, however, Nestorius made an appeal to the Comes Caesarius, who sat in Antinoe and was responsible for Thebaid (if not for all Egypt?).[27] From him as the 'friend of our father' – an expression by which the Johnson fragment is transposed into Shenoutian circles – he probably hoped to get a (new) meeting with him. Because of damage to the ms., however, the content of the appeal is not clearly determinable. The 'miserable death' of the exile and the distribution of his estate are now briefly described.

Evagrius Scholasticus also reports on two letters to the governor (without name).[28] Here there is not a word about Shenoute. The (neo-)Chalcedonian historian offers only negative judgements of Nestorius: through all his illness he did not become wiser and finally died a miserable death, since his tongue was eaten away by worms and 'he wandered to even heavier and eternal judgement'.[29] From all of this it is certain that Nestorius was in Thebaid for a lengthy period and that Simbelǧe was the place of his imprisonment and death. Thus Shenoute could learn very quickly of his death, as the Lefort catechesis confirms. The Orlandi exhortation still knows nothing of this but would certainly have mentioned it. This is an indication that it falls before 451. As we shall see, it speaks of Nestorius on the basis of relatively good information. The letters to Caesarius are also to be accepted as genuine. But a meeting between Shenoute and Nestorius cannot be demonstrated. Also, the offer that Shenoute be permitted to dispose of the estate of the exile and the concomitant dialogue belong in the realm of legend.

---

27. On Comes Caesarius see J. R. Martindale, *The Prosopography of the Later Roman Empire*, vol. 2 (Cambridge Univ. Press ¹1980), 249–50, s. nom. Caesarius 2 comes (?Aegypti): 'He was a *comes* ("the comēs") in Egypt and an acquaintance of Senuthis of Athribis.' Sin. Opera III: CSCO 96 (V) § 12, pp. 11–13. According to Martindale this Caesarius is identical with the addressee of Isidore of Pelusium in Ep. I 66: PG 78, 225CD: 'Presumably also with Caesarius, ὁ μεγαλοπρ(ἐπέστατος) κόμες, son of Candidianus, who built the monastery'; *Sammelbuch Griech. Urkunden aus Ägypt.* (ed. F. Preisigke . . . 1915), 6311, 'inscription in a monastic building at Dêr-el-Abiod [the White Monastery] (assigned a fifth century date by the editors)'. Reference to U. Monneret de Villard, 'La fondazione del Deyr el-Abiad', in *Aegyptus* 4 (1923), 156–62: 'The author relates the foundation of the White Monastery and identifies the Komes Caesarios (mentioned in CSCO 96, nos. 12 and 13) with the man by the same name, son of Kondidianos, mentioned in an inscription in the monastery.' See P. J. Frandsen and E. Richter Aerøe, *Shenoute: A Bibliography* (s.nom.). This confirms the Johnson fragment, which designates Caesarius as a friend of Shenoute. See the detailed texts in J. Leipoldt, *Schenute von Atripe* (TU 25), pp. 162–65, 175.

28. Evagrius Schol., *HE* I 7: Bidez-Parmentier, pp. 14,19–16,26. These are only excerpts, which P. Allen, *Evagrius Scholasticus*, p. 80 calls 'a correspondence which is otherwise unattested'. From the Johnson fragment of the Coptic church history of Alexandria we can probably now infer two letters of Nestorius to the comes of Antinoe.

29. Shenoute's report of the 'swollen tongue' of Nestorius is probably only to be taken as a legendary interpretation of the alleged blasphemies of Nestorius against Christ. Evagrius, *HE* I 7: Bidez-Parmentier, p. 16,21–25, with the indication of a suffering from cancer, is probably an exaggeration. See John Rufus, *Pleroph.* 36: PO 8, pp. 83–85, with the description of this suffering by Timothy Ael. during his stay in Gangra (between 460 and 475); likewise *Pleroph.* 33: PO 8, p. 76; *Pleroph.* 45: PO 8, p. 97 with reference to PO 2, p. 288 (death of the pope Agapetus). Thus, it is a question of a topos. J. F. Bethune-Baker, *Nestorius and his Teaching*, Cambridge 1908, p. 36, n. 1, holds that the transfer from the oasis to Panopolis exposed Nestorius 'to further persecution from Schenute'.

(c) The Annals of Patriarch Eutychius of Alexandria
as background description

In the *Annals* of Eutychius (877–940, patriarch 933–940)[30] we find a relatively detailed description of the historical situation with regard to heresy during the time of Patriarch Timothy I (380–385).[31] In Egypt Manichaeism is widespread. Eutychius also mentions Nicaea in 325 and Constantinople in 381 and then continues:

> Moreover, the Alexandrian patriarch Timothy allowed the patriarchs, bishops and monks the consumption of meat at the festivals of the Lord, and that because of the Manichaeans, who were called Sadikini (*ṣiddīqūn*). One was thus supposed to be able to perceive who among the patriarchs and bishops were Manichaeans. By this manner of eating meat their religion and their laws were to be made invalid. For the Manichaeans believe it is not permissible to slaughter an animal; they feed themselves neither with meat nor with anything else that comes from an animal. *The majority of the metropolitans and bishops were Manichaeans.* Thus the orthodox patriarchs with their bishops and monks ate pork at the festivals of the Lord; the metropolitans of the Manichaeans, on the other hand, with the bishops and monks, abstained from this [eating of meat] and fed themselves instead with fish (*piscibus*), which they set in place of meat [i.e., with which they replace the meat], since fish belong among living things. This was observed during the time of Mani, the unbelieving heretic. But when he and his followers stepped down, the orthodox patriarchs with their bishops and monks returned to the old order and abstained from the consumption of meat at the festivals of the Lord.[32]

It is not our task to verify the historical reliability of these reports in detail. From the analysis of Shenoute's exhortation we can see that there

---

30. On the following see J. Jarry, 'Le manichéisme en Égypte Byzantine', *BIFAO* 66 (1968), 121–37. He analyses the Greek and Arabic sources known before the work of T. Orlandi: (a) Serapion of Thmuis, *Lib. adv. Manich.* (CPG 2485): PG 40, 900–924; the whole text is in R. P. Casey, *Serapion of Thmuis against the Manichees* (HThS 15), Cambridge 1931. (b) Didymus of Alex., *C. Manichaeos* (CPG 2545): PG 39, 1085–1110; Eutychius, *Annales*: ed. L. Cheikho 1 (CSCO 50), pp. 146,8–148,7; PG 111, 1023–24. See also G. Graf, *Geschichte der christlichen arabischen Literatur* 2, Vatican City 1947, 32–35: Eut. offers numerous otherwise unattested reports, whose reliability cannot be simply rejected. Cf. M. Breydy, 'Über die älteste Vorlage der "Annales Eutychii" in der identifizierten Handschrift Sinait. Arab. 580', *OrChr* 59 (1975), 165–68. Especially important is C. Colpe, 'Häretische Patriarchen bei Eutychios', *JAC* 14 (1971), 48–60. On Patr. Timothy I (380–385) cf. Philostorg., *HE* III 15: Bidez, pp. 46–47 (meeting of the Arian Aetius with the Manichaean Aphthonius). – Among the early non-Christian testimonies of Manichaeism in Egypt is Alexander Lycopolitanus, *Contra Manichaei opiniones disputatio*, ed. A. Brinkmann, Leipzig 1895; French translation: A. Villey, *Alexandre de Lycopolis. Contre la doctrine de Mani* (Sources gnostiques et manichéennes 2), Paris 1985; also H.-M. Schenke, *JAC* 30 (1987), 213–17.

31. J. Jarry, art. cit., 128; C. Colpe, art. cit., 51.

32. Eutychius, *Ann.*: PG 111, 1023A–B. Ibid., 1023C gives as the motive for the abstinence from meat among the Samakini (*sammākūn*) that they thereby avoided the consumption of sacrificial meat, which did not have to be feared with fish. It is a strange way to separate oneself from heresy through the consumption of meat instead of through abstinence: 'It is the necessary responsibility of all to consume meat at least once a year according to the example of our Lord Christ. They are thereby to free themselves from doubts and make known to all that they are against the godless sect of the Manichaeans . . .'

is hardly another text that can serve as background to the strong words of Eutychius as clearly as precisely the alarm cry of the abbot of the White Monastery. One thing is especially highlighted by the new text: the penetration of gnostic and Origenistic teachings into the episcopacy, the presbytery and the cloister. Thus that was also towards 450 as well as at the time of Patriarch Timothy I. Eutychius makes this a little more precise:

> There are, as said, two kinds of Manichaeans: the first [are] the Samakini, that is, those who eat fish (*piscarii*); the others [are] the Sadikini. The Samakini fast on certain days of individual months; the Sadikini, however, fast their whole lives in that they eat nothing but what the earth has brought forth [vegetarians]. (PG 111, 1021B)

According to this, one can regard only the Sadikini as true Manichaeans. Those who, like the Samakini, did not preserve the 'seal of the mouth' could not belong to the purebred followers of Mani, the *electi*. Now it is the Marcionites, who were also in Egypt, who attest that they value the 'frutti del mare'.[33] J. Jarry is probably correct when he sees here Marcionites instead of 'Manichaeans', who are according to Eutychius supposed to be the majority of the Egyptian episcopacy. This they could be – if Eutychius's assertion is at all correct[34] – without leaving the Alexandrian hierarchy. This agrees with the picture that the Orlandi exhortation draws of the situation in Upper Egypt.

Thus we shall proceed on the basis that the exhortation edited by T. Orlandi against the apocrypha, Origenists, Nestorius and other groups of heretics actually comes from Shenoute, even if the Coptologists must give the final verdict.

II. SHENOUTE'S EXHORTATION AS A MIRROR OF THE FAITH SITUATION OF THE COPTIC CHURCH BETWEEN 431 AND 451

The archimandrite had to wage a difficult defensive battle in his monastery and in his surroundings. The catalogue of censured errors ranged from superstition and paganism to gnostic rationalism. The following discussion of these events will combine the heresiological presentation with the abbot's positive proclamation of faith.

(reference to Acts 10,13ff.). The absolute rejection of the consumption of meat was thus in contradiction with the Christian religion and a confession to Manichaeism (1021AB). Cf. C. Colpe, art. cit., 51–53, who points to the contradictions of this report; also: G. G. Stroumsa, 'The Manichaean Challenge to Egyptian Christianity', in B. A. Pearson and J. E. Goehring (eds.), *The Roots of Egyptian Christianity*, Philadelphia 1986, 312–14.

33. Cf. Tertullian, *Adv. Marcion.* I 14: CCL 1, p. 455,29–30: *Reprobas et mare, sed usque ad copias eius, quas sanctiorem cibum deputas.* – On the Zandīks see R. C. Zaehner, *Zurvan*, Oxford 1955, 38 (semantic change of the designation!).

34. Eutychius, *Ann.*: PG 111, 1024B, also points to the large number of Manichaeans among the 'Greeks', recognizable by their refusal to wash their things with water, which is made extremely clear and graphic for us now by the CMC. Cf. L. Koenen and R. Merkelbach, ' "Vorbericht" ', *ZPE* 5 (1970), 141–60.

1. The spread of superstition

Shenoute laments that Christians in suffering and testing 'forget God and seek refuge in magic and [pagan] shrines', which he with the fire of an Elijah has more than once attacked and destroyed:[35]

> Thus I myself have seen the head of a snake tied to the hand of many a person or another person with a crocodile tooth on the arm or yet another with fox claws around the leg. This was especially bad when, say, a 'man of influence[?]' [Coptic in § 0257: ἀϱχων] had fallen into such practices. When I took him to task and expressed my doubt whether the claws of a fox could heal him, he said to me: 'It was an old monk who gave them to me with the words: Tie them on and you will find relief.'[36]

The archimandrite was little pleased with all kinds of anointments with oil, with washings, with incantations, medicines and other fraudulent means of relief. That is 'paganism', which Elijah had pursued with the Israelites (1 Kings 18,21). We are reminded of the admonitory sermons of Caesarius of Arles against Gallic superstition and of his recommendation of the *medicina ecclesiae*, the consecrated oil of the church.[37] But Shenoute does not bring himself to such a recommendation. Yet all this is only the harbinger of more serious complaints. At stake among his monks and in the monastic realm is the substance of the Christian faith.

2. The threat to the Nicene faith in God and Christ

'Jesus Christ' is, as we shall see, the main theme of Shenoute's exhortation. Although the great heresies that shook the fourth century have stepped into the background, they are still alive in various groups, who make Christ into a mere creature and thereby destroy the Christ-piety of the believers. The means of creating such confusion are the 'apocrypha', in the sense of the festal letter of Apa Athanasius of 367.[38] Yet we will go

---

35. On the actions of Shenoute against the pagan cult see: E. Wipszycka, 'La christianisation de l'Égypte aux IVe–VIe siècles. Aspects sociaux et ethniques', *Aegyptus* 68 (1988) (117–65), 147–55; cf. J. Leipoldt, TU 25, pp. 175–82.

36. §§ 0256–58: P 129(12)66.P.161; DS,K 9199.P.59; *HThR* 75 (1982), 96. – On Shenoute as opponent of superstition see *Sin. Vit. Boh.*: CSCO 129 (V), §§ 151–53, pp. 38–39.

37. Caesar. Arel., *Sermo* 52, 5: CCL 103, p. 232; similarly Eligius of Noyons (d. 660): PL 87, 529AB. See G. Viaud, *Magie et coutumes populaires chez les Coptes d'Égypte*, Sisteron 1978; but also *Irén* 53 (1980), 46–60.

38. It is the Easter festal letter of Athanasius of the year 367 (thus Lefort); cf. CPG 2102 (2); L.-T. Lefort, *S. Athanase. Lettres festales et pastorales en copte*, CSCO 150 (V), Louvain 1955; letter XXXI (AD 367), pp. 31–40; also M. Tetz, art. 'Athanasius', *TRE* 4, pp. 344–45. See now A. Camplani, *Le lettere festali di Atanasio di Alessandria. Studio storico-critico* (= CMCL), Rome 1989, 275–79; also R.-G. Coquin, 'Les lettres festales d'Athanase (CPG 2102). Un nouveau complément: Le manuscrit IFAO, copte 25', *OLP* 15 (1984), 133–58.

beyond his catalogue. For Shenoute's anger also applies just as much to the scriptural interpretation of Origen, which is, to be sure, already seen and condemned in the refraction of 'Origenism'. From there it seems to be only a short distance to Arianism and Nestorianism. Shenoute takes up an old theme of early Christology, the theme of angel Christology. It is provoked by the apocryphal work that bears the title: 'Gospel of Jesus, the Son of God, Begotten by the Angels' (§ 0309).

(a) Angel Christology and the creatureliness of the Son

If, said Shenoute, one were to take the just given apocryphal title seriously, then Christ would be like one of the angels that God created (an allusion to Ps 104,4, quoted in Heb 1,7) (thus in §§ 0308/09). This would make the Son a creature. After a section on the apocryphal writings of the Meletians, which Athanasius mentions in his Easter festal letter of the year 367 on the canon of holy scripture and the apocrypha (CSCO 150, p. 39,27–30), there are words which in part are taken word for word from the excerpt of Apa Athanasius from the *Thaleia* of Arius in *De Synodis* 15[39] or are reproduced in essence (§§ 0325–28). In this text Christ's sonship of God is expressly denied. In truth – thus Shenoute – Jesus Christ is the true Son of God, who always was and is with the Father, and as such also becomes the mediator for creation of the universe. For these questions, he says, it is sufficient to refer to Apa Athanasius, the archbishop (§§ 0329–30).

(b) The two seraphim of Is 6,2

Shenoute knows a special interpretation of these two 'seraphim', 'who have six wings on one side and six on the other'. They are interpreted (allegorically) in the sense that 'those that stand are the Son and the Holy Spirit. Since their [i.e., the apocryphal writers'] thoughts became hazy, they did not understand that the seraphim are servants who wait upon God' (cf. Heb 1,7 with Ps 104,4). Shenoute has in mind here Origen's exegesis of this famous Isaiah vision, but probably presents it in a form that is already further developed in an 'Origenistic' way.[40]

In his *Homily on Is 1,2*, which he gave in Caesarea, Origen says: 'Who are these two seraphim? My Lord Jesus and the Holy Spirit . . . They covered the face of God, for the origin of God is unknown. But also the feet. For what would be the last thing comprehended in our God? Only the middle is visible; what was before I do not know. From what now is I know God; what will be after this in the future I do not know.'[41] Of special interest are the two passages from Origen, *Peri Archon* [= *PA*] I 3, 4 and IV 3, 14.[42] In the first passage he refers to the 'Hebrew', by which is meant, according to G. Bardy,[43] a convert to Christianity who wanted to find trinitarian ideas expressed in it: 'The Hebrew said the two six-winged

---

39. See the text in A. Grillmeier, *JdChr* I[3], pp. 372–77.

40. Cf. G. Kretschmar, *Studien zur frühchristlichen Trinitätstheologie* (BHTh 21), Tübingen 1956, index: Is 6, esp. pp. 64–71, 92–94. Kretschmar refers on p. 64, n. 2, to Origen, *Hom. in Isa. 1,2* on Is 6: GCS, Or. W. VIII, 244 ff.; German in H. U. von Balthasar, *Geist und Feuer* ([2]1951), no. 870, p. 447; also *Hom. in Isa. 1,5*: p. 247; 4,1: pp. 257ff.; *Hom. in Ezek. 14,2*: pp. 452ff.

41. According to the translation of H. U. von Balthasar, loc. cit. For further proof passages see Biblia Patristica 3 (1980), 118 col. a.

42. See H. Görgemanns and H. Karpp, *Origenes. Vier Bücher von den Prinzipien* (TzF 24), Darmstadt 1976, 165–68, 777–79.

43. G. Bardy, 'Les traditions juives dans l'oeuvre d'Origène', *RevBibl* 34 (1925) (217–52), 221ff.

seraphim in Isaiah [Is 6,3] . . . are the only begotten Son of God and the Holy Spirit. But we hold that in the song of Habakkuk [Hab 3,2] the sentence, "In the middle of two living beings you will be known", is also said of Christ and the Holy Spirit.'[44]

Origen himself did not think of putting the Son (and the Holy Spirit: on this see *PA* I 3) into the creaturely order, even if his subordinationism is unmistakable. In *PA* IV 3, 14 he ascribes to Christ and the Holy Spirit the comprehension of 'beginning and end of all things' (thus divine knowledge; cf. 1 Cor 2,11), while 'the hosts of holy angels' and the 'thrones, dominions, kingdoms and powers' (cf. Lk 2,13 and Col 1,16) cannot know perfectly 'the beginning of all things and the end of the universe'.[45] Accordingly, Shenoute has before him already a refined, genuinely *Origenistic* further development of the old, admittedly hypothetical teaching of Origen. For he finds in his addressees or hearers already the same offence against faith in the divinity of Christ and of the Holy Spirit as that expressed by Justinian in the edict against Origen, that is, in the letter of the emperor to Menas.[46] This is a significant indication of the spread of Origenistic teachings in the area of the White Monastery around the year 431.

(c) Injury to the Nicene and Nicene-Constantinopolitan faith

Thus the Origenistic interpretation of the two seraphim already becomes Arianism and means the denial of the Nicene *homoousios*! 'On the contrary, the Son and the Holy Spirit have the same essence of the Father, as the scriptures attest' (§§ 0331–32). Shenoute speaks already of the 'consubstantial Trinity' (§ 0803). Here the old objection (of the Arians) is not overlooked: 'Show us this word *homoousios* where it is written in the scriptures!' But it will be raised this time – as we shall see – by the Origenists (§§ 0803–5). The archimandrite counters with the challenge: 'You show me, rather, from where, from which scripture you know that the Son is different from the Father in substance, that he, as you say, is of another essence (*heteroousios*), that is, different in essence. But you have no answer.' In this context there is a reference to Jn 10,30: 'I and the Father are one.' In the first part of this saying, according to Shenoute, Christ shows the hypostases (of 'Father and Son'); in the second, however, the union of nature, which is one single essence, that is, the '*homoousios*' (§ 0806).

Shenoute is, as we see, already familiar with the application of *homoousios* to the Holy Spirit. This presupposes that he accepts the standpoint of the temporary president of the Council of Constantinople in 381, Gregory of Nazianzus, who came to the council supporting the adoption of this formula, at first without having any success. Also, the formula '[three] hypostases in the union of nature or essence' (§ 0806) is adopted. In this way the abbot differentiated himself from Athanasius and the old Nicaeans and joined the Cappadocians.[47] This formula is already adopted in Egypt. But there are still opponents of the trinitarian-christological dogma understood according to the meaning in the universal church in Shenoute's surroundings. He must still take a position on Jn 14,28 ('the Father is greater than

44. H. Görgemanns and H. Karpp, pp. 165–67.

45. Ibid., p. 779.

46. Iustinian. aug., *Ep. ad Menam*: ACO III, Coll. Sabb., p. 210,10–14.

47. M. Simonetti, *Studi sull arianesimo*, Rome 1965, 455–58; idem, 'All'origene della formula teologica una essenza/tre ipostasi', *Aug* 14 (1974), 173–75 (Marius Victorinus, Didymus [Porphyry], Basil). 'The first official document that contains this solution is the declaration of the Meletians [followers of Meletius of Antioch] about their understanding of the three-hypostases Trinity, made before the committee that the Synod of Alexandria of 362 had formed under the leadership of Athanasius for resolving the Antiochene schism. The Meletian declaration, as well as that of the opposition party, is contained in the *Tomus ad Antiochenos*, which Athanasius wrote.' Thus L. Abramowski, 'Trinitarische und christologische Hypostasenformeln', *TheolPhil* 54 (1979) (38–49), 42, cf. also pp. 41–47. Thus Shenoute could have arrived at the three-hypostases formula with Alexandrian help.

I'). The Father is, namely – so say the deniers of *homoousios* – greater in the praise of his glory and thus also in his nature (§ 0807: 'forse è più grande nella lode della gloria ed è diverso da lui nella sua natura'). Also, says Shenoute, it is impossible to declare how the Father begot the Son (§ 0809). In the answer Shenoute distinguishes between birth in the flesh and the birth of the Son in God. The first can be known by all intelligent people (*sapienti*) and the whole church of Christ and is proclaimed from the beginning by the angels and the Gospels (cf. 1 Tim 3,16) and is already 'signalized' by the great patriarchs. Yet begetting from the Father is known by none of the angels, none of the prophets and apostles, but only by the Father alone (cf. Is 53,8; Acts 8,33; Mt 11,27b). Thus there is only one revelation in Jesus Christ, which is accessible to all creatures, from angels to human beings (§§ 0812–20).

(d) The dispute over prayer to Jesus

The monastic community of the White Monastery and even Christians in the vicinity were aroused and divided by the discussion of the question, May one pray only *through* Jesus, and naturally to the Father, or is prayer *to* Jesus himself also permitted? The 'Hellenizers among us' (§ 0423) assert that one may not pray to Jesus because he himself prays (cf. §§ 0655–56). Unfortunately, at this point eight pages are missing from the codex DQ in its supposed form.

The problem comes from Origen and was formulated in his writing *On Prayer*.[48] In chap. XIV he distinguishes according to 1 Tim 2,1 four kinds of prayer: προσευχή, δέησις, ἔντευξις, εὐχαριστία. Petition, intercession and thanksgiving, the last three kinds named, can also be directed towards people, but above all to Christ. Prayer in the narrower sense, the προσευχή, should only go to God, because it wants to attain great goods and is linked with adoration. Origen's reasons for this are that when one wants to pray correctly, one may not pray (a) to one who himself prays (XV 2), (b) to one whom the Father has made high priest and intercessor, (c) to one who has called us his brothers. No difficulties are created here by Heb 1,6 (with Dt 32,43): all the angels of God have to worship him! For Origen understands these passages 'from a mere greeting of Christ' (Jungmann, p. 139). 'Thus let us pray to God through him and all talk in the same way without division in the kind of prayer. Or are we not divided when some pray to the Father, others to the Son? A sin of ignorance (ἰδιωτῶν ἁμαρτίαν) is committed by those who in exaggerated simplicity pray without testing and reflection to the Son, whether with the Father or without the Father' (XVI 1: Jungmann, pp. 139–40).

In the discussion of this passage J. A. Jungmann (p. 140) distinguishes between private and public, liturgical prayer. For the first, according to him, prayer to Jesus is already found in the oldest Fathers (p. 140 with n. 59). But in the writing *On Prayer* Origen, according to Jungmann, speaks of *solemn* and also of *corporate* prayer: 'Are we not divided?' Corporate prayer is expressly recommended in many passages (XX 1; XXXI). Yet Jungmann would like to understand by this the 'corporate prayer of the people' that according to Justin (*Apol.* I 65) precedes the prayer of thanksgiving spoken by the προεστώς and which also in later Eastern liturgies as richly developed antiphonal prayer was directed preferably to Christ or simply to the 'Lord'. If the sin of ignorance is seen in this among the *idiōtai*, that is, the simple people, who 'pray without testing and reflection to the Son' (cf. above), then Origen's criticism also reaches into private prayer and does not concern only the corporate, public prayer of the people. Origen also embarrasses us by simply presupposing prayer *to* Jesus in a number of

---

48. Origen, *De orat.* 15,1–16,1 (after 232): GCS, Or. W. II, Koetschau, pp. 333–36; English: E. G. Jay, *Origen's Treatise on Prayer*, London 1954, 126–31, and J. J. O'Meara, in ACW 19 (London 1954), 57–61. Cf. J. A. Jungmann, *Die Stellung Jesu im liturgischen Gebet* (LQF 19/20), Münster ²1962, 137–51; K. Baus, 'Das Nachwirken des Origenes in der Christusfrömmigkeit des heiligen Ambrosius', *RömQ* 49 (1954), 21–55, esp. § 5, pp. 50–53.

statements, especially in his homilies.[49] He speaks here once – without distinguishing between private and corporate prayer – of devout prayer as a sacrificial gift, which through the angel is presented to the true high priest Jesus (*In Num. hom.* 11,9: Or. W. 7, 93B). It is even more important that he prays to Jesus in the doxologies with which he closes almost all homilies. The basic form of the doxology, which changes only rarely, reads in Origen: . . . *Jesus Christus, cui est gloria et imperium in saecula saeculorum.*[50] With all this one cannot simply speak of something inconsequential in Origen. For ultimately Jesus Christ is for him 'God' (*theos*), even if not *ho theos*, that is, the Father, the God without origin. Thus this allows him to pray *to* Christ, while his subordinationism and his unsystematic way of treating such problems give him the freedom to demand prayer *through* Jesus. Above all, however, he takes Jesus seriously as a human being who is God incarnate. Thus in this way both the *through* and the *to* are justified in his christological spirituality.[51]

Yet from Origen's alternative Shenoute's opponents selected only the one side: basically there is only 'prayer through Jesus to the Father'. Shenoute countered: 'Thus those who do not want to pray to the Son should hold their tongues and not name the Father [either]' (§ 0655).

---

49. On this question see also 'Disputation des Origenes mit Heraklides und seinen Mitbischöfen über den Vater und den Sohn und die Seele', ed. J. Scherer, *Entretien d'Origène avec Héraclide et les évêques ses collègues, sur le Père, le Fils, et l'âme*, Cairo 1949 (= SC 67 with minor changes), Paris 1960, p. 62,17–64; English: R. J. Daly, in ACW 54 (1992), 60–61. Italian: G. Lomiento, *Il dialogo di Origene con Eraclide ed i vescovi suoi colleghi sul Padre, il Figlio e l'anima*, Bari 1971. This text comprises the minutes of a synod between 244 and 249. Cf. H. J. Sieben, *Konzilsidee*, pp. 469–76. The divinity of Christ and prayer are the first two areas of discussion. Perhaps under Jewish influence, Heraclides wanted to pray only to the Father, without giving the Son his proper place. Versus Origen, *Dialogus* 4, 24–27: Scherer, p. 62: 'The sacrifice of prayer (προσφορά) is always directed to God, the Almighty, through Jesus Christ . . . the sacrifice of prayer is supposed to be directed not in two ways but to God through God.' The προσευχή, however, may be directed only to the Father (through Christ!); cf. *De orat.* 15, 1. See also *C. Cels.* VIII 12, 13: GCS Or. W. II, pp. 229–31. *In Rom.* VIII 4: according to Lommatzsch t. VII, pp. 207–17. Cf. Scherer, *Entretien*, pp. 31–32.

50. H. Crouzel, 'Les doxologies finales des homélies d'Origène selon le texte grec et les versions latines', *Aug* 20 (1980) (95–107), 100. Crouzel investigates specially the closing doxologies of the homilies of Origen and refers there to (a) the homilies extant in Greek and (b) those that Jerome translated. Then come the *Tractatus sive homiliae in Psalmos*, which Dom G. Morin edited under Jerome's name, but which belong to Origen (apart from some insertions of Jerome), as was demonstrated by V. Peri, *Omelie Origeniane sui Salmi. Contributo all'identificazione del testo latino* (ST 289), Vatican City 1980; see also H. Crouzel, op. cit., 98; M.-J. Rondeau, *Les commentaires patristiques du Psautier (IIIe–Ve siècles)*, vol. I: *Les travaux des pères grecs et latins sur le Psautier. Recherches et Bilan* (OCA 219), Rome 1982, 44–63; '*Hieronymus', Tractatus in Psalmos*, ed. G. Morin, Maredsous 1903 and 1913, now in CCL 78. Also these Latin texts offer on the whole the same picture as given in Crouzel; CCL 78, pp. 429, 439 (*gloria et imperium*); otherwise cf. pp. 142, 167, 175, 230, 234, 261, 403, 424, 446; esp. p. 222,1–3. – (c) Crouzel also studies the translation of Rufinus; (d) three doxologies in *PA*. In this way he can distinguish the various types.

51. On this problem cf. B. Neunheuser, 'Les fêtes de l'année liturgique, fêtes du Christ? (Comment expliquer l'absence de fêtes du Père?)', in A. M. Triacca and A. Pistoia (eds.), *Le Christ dans la liturgie*, Rome 1981, 143–49; A. Grillmeier, *JdChr* I³, pp. 266–80; N. Brox, '"Gott" – Mit und ohne Artikel', *Biblische Notizen* 66 (1993), 32–39.

Shenoute's solution: Prayer *to* Jesus, the incarnate Son of God, is for him based on the Nicene *homoousios*. It guarantees the commonality of the name and of the adoration of Father and Son. He summarizes this in a hymn-like doxology:

(§§ 0800–03): 'Glory be to you and to your blessed Son from the heavens of the heavens and from that which is therein. Be praised, O God. Glory be to you and to your blessed Son from the *oikumene* and from all that is therein. Be praised, O God; glory be to you from all your things, to you and to your blessed Son, from whom are all your things, and all his things are yours. Be praised, O God, you and your blessed Son, whose name together with yours are one and the same in the mouth of the one who struggles against those who support this new ungodliness. For this is his wealth and his hope:
"when entering [the house to say]: God,
and when leaving: Jesus,
and when resting: God,
and when rising: Jesus,
and when blessing: God,
and when petitioning: Jesus".
'In order not to stop any longer here: it is clear that we are naming the consubstantial Trinity when we say Jesus.'

Thus with the name Jesus the 'holy Trinity' is named (§§ 0803, 0818–19). This is attested by the commandment to baptize (Mt 28,19), Paul's words about baptism in Christ (Jesus): e.g., Rom 6,3; Gal 3,27; or Acts 8,16b: 'They had been baptized only in the name of the Lord Jesus.' 'Thus it is clear: when we name Jesus, we name the holy Trinity, yet the Father as Father, the Son as Son and the Holy Spirit as Holy Spirit. But let us not further investigate these things' (§§ 0819–20). In any case, we have here a trinitarian explanation of baptism in the name of Jesus and finally – in express opposition to the Origenists – an instruction to put the name of Jesus over the whole of human life with all its joys and sorrows:

'Seek the meaning of these words and you will have them in your mouth and find them on the lips of your sons:
If you celebrate a feast and are joyful [say]: Jesus;
if you have worry and suffering: Jesus;
if the sons and daughters laugh: Jesus;
those who touch water: Jesus;
those who must flee from barbarians: Jesus;
those who see monsters or other frightening things: Jesus;
those who have pain or illness: Jesus;
those who have been taken captive: Jesus;
those who were unjustly judged and suffer injustice: Jesus.
The name of Jesus alone is on their lips and is their salvation and their life: he and his Father' (§ 0821).

'Thus if only one is our God and only one is the Lord, why should you not pray to him, O you hearts of unbelieving Jews and other heretics of that ilk, who resemble one another in one and the same deceitful spirit? Hear the holy apostle John: "He is the true God and eternal life" [1 Jn 5,20b]; and the apostle Thomas says: "My God and my Lord" [Jn 20,28]. If he is also your Lord and your God, why should you not pray to him?' (K 9206, p. 164). Shortly, the fragment breaks off: the unbelief of the Jews according to Jn 10,33 also resides in those who reject prayer to Jesus (§§ 0823–26).

Certainly Origen personally stood closer to the words and ideas of Shenoute than did his later interpreters, the 'Origenists' against whom the archimandrite has to fight. Indeed, one can presume that the monastic father received his pronounced Jesus-piety directly from the inspirations of Origen. *Jesus* in Shenoute is the actual name of the *kyrios*, while *Christ* – in him as well as in the Coptic in general – always connected with the article, reveals the original meaning of 'anointed'.[52] Our exhortation also exhibits this linguistic usage.

Shenoute as witness to prayer to Jesus

These beautiful texts of prayer to Jesus are among the first significant testimonies of a spiritual practice that is familiar to us under the name 'Jesus prayer'. Their significance becomes visible only in juxtaposition with a newly discovered Coptic parallel text that sounds like a summary of Shenoute's comments.[53] It is found as an inscription on the wall of a prayer room in a hermitage of the Kellia monastery, which was discovered only a few decades ago and partially excavated. In its preserved form it is placed in the period from the middle of the seventh to the middle of the eighth century.[54] It is worth presenting in its structure and its main assertions:[55]

The text begins with an objection that is ascribed to the blandishments of demons: If you constantly call only 'Lord Jesus', you pray neither to the Father nor to the Holy Spirit. The inscription attests that the practice of Jesus prayer became the occasion for mockery, specifically about those 'who [are] in the name of Jesus in order to bring to ruin those who believe in his name'. But the ignorance of these mockers is striking: 'For we, we know that if we pray to Jesus, we pray with him to the Father, together with him [Jesus] and the Holy Spirit of the Father. For it is not true that we divide the holy Trinity! Rather, it is fitting to pray thus: if

---

52. In our text cf., e.g., §§ 0307–48 (Copt.) (cf. the variant translation of T. Orlandi!); cf. also 'le Christ' in P. Cherix, *Étude de lexicographie copte. Chenouté. Le discours en présence de Flavien* (RevBibl.C 18), Paris 1979, 21–36. But can as much be gained from this usage as J. Leipoldt (TU 25), pp. 348–75, believes?

53. See A. Guillaumont, 'Une inscription copte sur la "Prière de Jésus" ', in idem, *Aux origines du monachisme chrétien*, Bégrolles en Mauge 1979, no. 11, pp. 168–83 (Copt. and French: pp. 174–75). First edition: *Kellia I Kom 219 Fouilles exécutées en 1964 et 1965* (fasc. I), Cairo 1969, 99. Cf. A. Grillmeier, 'Das "Gebet zu Jesus" und das "Jesus-Gebet". Eine neue Quelle zum "Jesus-Gebet" aus dem Weißen Kloster', in *After Chalcedon*. FS A. Van Roey (OLA 18), Louvain 1984, 187–202. For further attestation see E. Lanne, 'La "prière de Jésus" dans la tradition égyptienne', *Irén* 50 (1977), 163–203. – On the more recent archaeological discoveries it would be good to consider: *EK 8184. Mission suisse d'archéologie copte de l'Université de Genève, Survey archéologique de Kellia (Basse Égypte). Rapport de la campagne 1981*, Louvain 1983, fasc. I–II.

54. A. Guillaumont, op. cit., p. 178.

55. A. Guillaumont, op. cit., pp. 174/175,1–28.

we say, "You, Christ Jesus", we say, "You Son of God the Father", and we say: "the Father of Christ Jesus". And when we close each prayer with him, we say: "through your only Son our Lord Jesus Christ".'

So far there is not a more exact parallel to this Coptic inscription than Shenoute's words on prayer to Jesus.[56] In both cases it is a question of one and the same battle within Coptic monasticism and Coptic believers. In both cases prayer to Jesus is attacked with the same motive: 'Those who indeed want to pray to the Son, dare not name the Father' (Shenoute); 'The cry "Lord Jesus" is not a prayer to the Father and to the Holy Spirit' (Kellia). But in Shenoute the Origenistic background is more clearly evident, and this as it was present at the beginning of the fifth century. As the objection is the same in both cases, namely, Origenistic, so also is the answer: praying to Jesus means praying to the Father and to the Holy Spirit. But in the Shenoute text we see the instructions for Jesus prayer are inserted into quite concrete situations, and at the same time a valuable biblical substantiation is given. Yet one has the impression that the archimandrite's exhortation is directed not only at monks but at the believers who live in the vicinity of the White Monastery and within its broad territory — as it is presented to us by Shenoute's disciple Besa. If incursions of barbarians, imprisonment and animal attacks are named, this fits in exactly with Thebaid, as we likewise shall soon see (cf. below on Nestorius). Shenoute's text is more original, richer and more concrete than the necessarily short text of an inscription in a small monastic prayer room. The similarity, however, is so striking that one would like to assume a familiarity with the exhortation from the White Monastery.

---

56. A. Guillaumont, op. cit., p. 182: 'Nous ne connaissons pas de critique à la "prière de Jésus" avant la grande controverse hésychaste du XIVe siècle, et les critiques qui lui furent faites alors paraissent assez différentes de celle qui est ici [i.e., in the Kellia inscription] formulée.' Through the Orlandi exhortation our attention is now called to the connecting link that leads directly to Origen. We see again what effect the writings of Origen had not only in the Kellia but also above in Thebes. First, however, the positive influence of Origen on the origination of the Jesus prayer is not to be overlooked, and indeed not least of all on his (already mentioned, newly attributed) homilies on Psalms!

We mention only briefly the peculiar version of the 'prayer to Jesus' in the *Manichaean Psalms* preserved in Coptic, which, however, are completely permeated with the typical teachings of Mani. They contain doxologies in which Jesus (Christ) is frequently addressed, but also the 'Paraclete' and 'our Lord Mani'! See C. R. C. Allberry (ed.), *A Manichaean Psalmbook*, part II, Stuttgart 1938. Jesus, however, is not the 'incarnate one', as Ps. CCXLV, pp. 52–54, esp. 52,22–24, shows: 'Jesus the new God. . . . He was not born in a womb corrupted . . .' This agrees well with the deniers of the incarnation, also out of the Virgin, whom Shenoute was fighting (see below).

This would have to be verified through a linguistic analysis, in which the use of 'Christ Jesus' would have to be considered!

3. Gnostic-Origenistic infiltration of 'apocryphal' origin

From the whole of the newly assembled exhortation of Shenoute we feel a hotter wind than from the previously described 'classical' special opinions or heresies. Shenoute sees it shimmering in the brains of many a monk. Typically gnostic and Origenistic, mythological and rational things are pictured for us in a colourful mixture. To bring all this into a system, as it were, and give it a coherent interpretation might be a futile undertaking. Also one probably may not assume that it is a question of the White Monastery alone. Shenoute has wider circles of monasticism and the Coptic church in mind, but on a very different intellectual level. The fault that encompasses all is that they rely on *apocryphal* writings. Whether everything is covered by the catalogue of Nag Hammadi writings found in the vicinity of the White Monastery can hardly be answered with a yes. Naturally it is also uncertain how much the monks or Christians of the Nile valley understood these writings or gnostic and Origenistic teachings in general, and whether Shenoute himself reproduces them correctly or can himself arrange them correctly. He often refers to further writings of his own. Also we may not forget that we are a good bit beyond the fourth century, long after the various systems combined, as was usual among the Gnostics. Thus one can perceive certain echoes of various Nag Hammadi writings, without being able thereby to grasp the whole. Certain indications seem to point to Manichaean dualism but still do not reveal the typical division into *electi* and *auditores* that enabled us to make an easier decision with Augustine and to a certain extent also with Leo the Great. Nevertheless, there are some starting-points from which we can ascertain tendencies of a more comprehensive kind. With appropriate caution we can already attempt a more systematic commentary, as is appropriate to a history of faith in Christ.[57]

---

57. On the following see U. Bianchi, 'Polemiche gnostiche e anti-gnostiche sul Dio dell'Antico Testamento', *Aug* 22 (1982), 35–51; idem, 'Le gnosticisme et les origines du Christianisme', in J. Ries et al. (eds.), *Gnosticisme et monde hellénistique*, Louvain-la-Neuve 1982, 211–35; K. Müller, 'Beiträge zum Verständnis der valentinianischen Gnosis I–IV', *NGWG.PH* 1920, no. 2, pp. 179–204; no. 3, pp. 205–42; M. Simonetti, 'Variazioni gnostiche e origeniane sul tema della storia della salvezza', *Aug* 16 (1976), 7–21; see also the sections on the Valentinian gnosis in A. Orbe, *Cristología gnóstica* II, Madrid 1976, with bibl.

(a) Double creation

'For the Gnostics, creation and history begin long before what is told in Genesis, but for them the story contained in the book of Genesis is decisively and generally interpreted because it concerns the history of *this* world and *these* human beings.'[58] Belonging here is a text that Shenoute reproduces as an apocryphal statement:

> (The author of an apocryphal work) 'also says: "The Son said there was a time when the Father completed *twelve* worlds that the angels did not know; and then he created *seven* worlds"; and "within the twelve [worlds] stand the inexpressible goodnesses"; and "apart from the seven [worlds] he created *five* other worlds"; and "in them stand the mighty spirits; and apart from the five [worlds] he created *three* other worlds. These – so they say – are the residence of the angels"; and "the twenty-seven worlds are all outside of this heaven and this earth"' (§ 0102).

To be noted here is the distinction between *this* heaven and *this* earth on the one hand and the twenty-seven graduated *external* worlds on the other. Between the two is a deep trench, even if this is expressed only indirectly. For the scandal in Shenoute's view lies in the fact that special *revelations* are necessary to have knowledge of these other worlds, knowledge that is not even granted to the angels. The creation report of Genesis is superseded. But this is against the expressed revelatory will of God and Christ: 'The Lord does nothing without showing it to his servants, the prophets [cf. Jn 15,15; 5,20]; thus how much more will he show it to the angels. How do you [the false recipients of revelation] know these things?' (§ 0103). They take the argument for the plurality of worlds besides our visible one from Jn 17,5 ('now, Father, glorify me with the glory that I had before the world was with you') and Jn 5,17 ('my Father is still working, and I also am working'). The reference to Jn 5,17 is apparently otherwise found seldom or not at all among the Gnostics, but rather among the Manichaeans, as Augustine reports.[59] They wanted to prove that the New Testament works against the Old.[60]

We are reminded of a discussion in Origen, *PA* III 5, 3, where the subject is an objection to the assumption of a temporal beginning of the world (cf. I 4, 3–5):

> Yet one usually replies to us: if the world began at a point in time, then what did God do before the world began? For it is just as godless as it is nonsensical to designate God's nature as idle and motionless or to believe that at some time his goodness did not effect good and at some time his omnipotence did not exercise power (Görgemanns/Karpp, pp. 625–27). The answer: We say that God did not begin to work only when he created this

---

58. U. Bianchi, *Aug* 22 (1982), 37.
59. Augustine, *De Genesi c. Manich.* (CPL 265) I, chap. XXII: PL 34, 189.
60. Cf. ibid., chap. II: PL 34, 174.

visible world; rather, just as there will be another world after the end of this one, so other worlds, in our opinion, existed before this one (ibid., p. 627).

Thus Origen assumes a *successive* origination of various worlds. According to Is 66,22 and Eccl 1,9–10, 'two things are simultaneously demonstrated: that there were earlier worlds and will be later worlds. Yet it is not to be assumed that several worlds exist simultaneously but that after this one, until further notice, there will be another.'[61]

One must concede that with these words Origen could have built for the opponents of Shenoute a bridge to their assumption of the creation of other worlds, but that they go beyond him and now assume a *simultaneous* existence of various worlds. The common argument, however, could still be Jn 5,17, even if Origen alludes to it only remotely. Shenoute denies its cogency in the sense of the Gnostics. He wants to have it understood in the sense of the constant working of God for our *salvation* in this one world. This working continues forever and is accomplished for us in Jesus Christ, namely, in the healing of our sicknesses and sufferings. This is the context of the already mentioned admonition to take refuge in this always available help instead of in magicians and their means (§§ 0256–58).

Thus the new revelations distinguish between a higher, great world and a lower, small one. The most obvious source seems to be the *Apocryphon of John*. The analogies are very clear and will be briefly indicated:[62]

(1) It is a matter of revelations of the 'Son' on the question of the relationship of the lower to the higher world, which places itself 'in John's heart': 'How then was the Redeemer installed and why was he sent into the world by his Father, who sent him? And who is his Father? And of what kind is that aeon (*aiōn*) to which we will go? He said to us: "This aeon (*aiōn*) has assumed the form (*typos*) of that imperishable aeon (*aiōn*)." But he has not taught us about that

---

61. *PA* III 5, 3: Görgemanns/Karpp, pp. 627–29.

62. See W. Till, *Die gnostischen Schriften des Papyrus Berolinensis 8502* (TU 60), Berlin 1955 (this edition is cited here). On NHC III, II and IV see M. Krause and P. Labib, *Die drei Versionen des Apokryphon des Johannes* (ADAI.K 1), Wiesbaden 1962. In *AJ* III, 16 (Krause/Labib, pp. 70–71) we find the numbers 12, 7, 3; cf. F. Siegert, *Nag-Hammadi-Register*, Tübingen 1982, s.v. *aion* (thus spatially considered); also s.v. *kosmos* (plur. *worlds*). On the origin and significance of the *Apocryphon of John* see G. Quispel, 'Gnosis', in *Die Orientalischen Religionen im Römerreich*, ed. M. J. Vermaseren, Leiden 1981 (413–35), esp. 422–23: 'The *Apocryphon of John* contains, contrary to its name, no Christian elements if one disregards the introduction and a very few interpolations. But the work contains all the Jewish elements that we sketched above [the unknown God and the Demiurge, etc.] . . . The mythos of the *Apocryphon of John* is a linking of the *sophia* model and the *anthropos* model . . . [It is] of great significance because it underlies Christian *gnosis*, Mandaeism and the orthodox Jewish throne mysticism of Palestine.' Quispel holds 'that the Jewish heterodoxy of Alexandria underlies all later gnostic formations'. All the more understandable is the reaction of Shenoute, who apparently has the ideas of the *AJ* in mind.

one, of what kind it is' (*AJ* 20,8–18: p. 81). Immediately now begins the revelation through him 'who is with you always' (*AJ* 21,18–19: p. 83). Above all, an answer is given to the question: Who is the Father? (*AJ* 22,19ff.: p. 85ff.) and in a way that sketches a picture of God, which distinguishes itself as an answer to the God concept of Zervanism with its teaching of the temporal and spatial limitedness of the highest Being. We have here a presentation of the positive infinity of God, which perhaps belongs to the oldest and most beautiful texts of this kind (*AJ* 22,1–26,19: p. 85,1–93,19). Then begins the revelation of the origin of the higher and lower worlds.

(2) The 'Father' is the creator of the aeons of the *higher* world and remains their head (*AJ* 26,9–10: p. 93; 26,21–27,1: pp. 93–4). We find some numbers for these aeons, even if not in Shenoute's specific order; named are (a) the 'fiveness of the aeons' (*AJ* 29,7–15: p. 99,7–15); (b) three aeons (*AJ* 34,5: p. 109,5); (c) twelve aeons that belong to the Son (*AJ* 34,10: p. 109).

(3) The creator of the *lower* world is Yaldabaoth, the first archon (*archōn*). The distinction of the world leads necessarily to the assumption of different creation principles. Actually we find corresponding statements both in Shenoute and in the *AJ*. The archimandrite speaks (in §§ 0423–24) of 'Hellenizers who are among us' and assert: 'God has sustained this world until now and was able to provide it with power through the *archon*, as though Satan, this *archon*, had disputed with God [cf. Job 1,6–12]. These words make one's hair stand on end. For there is no other earth and no other place in the heavens of heavens and in the whole world even into the roots of the earth and the underworld that is not in the hand of God, the almighty Lord, as also to the smallest things and even to this *archidaemon*, who is not the lord or sustainer of any place apart from the hearts of people who give him room to blaspheme against God and are unbelieving in regard to his things [the world].'

Corresponding to this are statements of the *AJ* about Yaldabaoth, the first *archōn* (38,14–15: p. 117), who is understood both as anti-god (*AJ* 44,14–18: p. 129) and as the principle 'of the creation found under him and the host of angels under him, who originated out of him' (*AJ* 44,9–18: p. 129). This lower world is presented strictly as a copy and antitype of the higher creation (*AJ* 44,5–13: p. 129) and this again with the same graduation of numbers that the higher world exhibits. We meet the 'twelveness' (namely, of the zodiac) (*AJ* 39,7–40,18: pp. 119–21), the ruler of the *seven* planets (*AJ* 39,11–42,10: pp. 119–23) (sevenness of the week), the *five* kings over the *chaos* of the underworld (*AJ* 41,12–42,10: pp. 123–25).

The similarity of the brief information from Shenoute on the higher as well as the lower world to the statements of the *AJ* is striking. Appearing are all number systems and above all the gnostic distinction between the 'Father' as the creator of the higher world and the *archontes* over the lower world. Shenoute emphasizes that against this teaching of 'other worlds that are under this one' he has written a separate book. Whether or not this survived cannot be investigated here. But he points to his concept of the *one* world in his *Discussion on Problems of Church Discipline and Cosmology*.[63] Three things are most important to Shenoute: first, the uniqueness of God and his creator power and dominion over the whole world, including the deepest underworld; second, the unity of the

---

63. P. du Bourguet, *Entretien de Chenouté sur des problèmes de discipline ecclésiastique et de cosmologie* (BIFAO 57), 1958, 99–142, esp. 122–23. He expects no revelation about the world: 'Dieu seul le Tout-Puissant est celui qui connaît ses oeuvres; nous, il nous appartient d'examiner les choses qu'il nous a montrées.' Further research is pointless.

revelation that was enacted in Christ and recorded in the holy scriptures; and third, its sufficiency for the faith that leads us to salvation.

(b) 'Large' and 'small' history

Corresponding to the two cosmic realms, which were brought forth by two different principles, there is also a double history. Now, taking part in this distinction each in its own way are various gnostic systems but also Origen and Gregory of Nyssa.[64] Thus in the following, the actual gnostic version is in each case to be distinguished from Origen's or the Origenistic version! Both are clearly recognizable in T. Orlandi's text. Again we are referred to a special source of revelation, to *a new* gospel, indeed even to *twelve* gospels. Naturally, these revelations are valid only for the 'higher' history.

(aa) The 'gospel of Jesus the Son of God, generated by the angels' (generazione degli angeli)

With this title the tempters designate an apocryphon of which they assert 'that there [is] another gospel beyond the four Gospels, which the church has not condemned as heretical'. The issue here is not the presence of such a piece of writing but the antithesis the title opens up between the beginning of the Matthean Gospel with the earthly lineage of Jesus and the true genesis of the one who is to come from Abraham. He comes instead from the *angels*. The 'Son of God', whom Shenoute here equates with Jesus of Nazareth, had his beginning, according to the apocryphon, in the 'higher world'. Hence he also has a 'higher history'. Against this Shenoute places the known saying from Gal 1,7–8 and charges the proclaimers of this apocryphon with 'changing the gospel of Christ' (§ 0307).

Another group, which we have already met as representatives of the doctrine of an anti-god (*archōn* of this world), asserts according to Shenoute even the existence of twelve gospels, as they also assume forty aeons (worlds). Again he asks these dreamers how they know this (§§ 0423–26). The four Gospels, however, are sufficient to 'give light to the whole world' (§ 0425). It is vain knowledge that wants to establish whether there are forty or ten thousand worlds. Christ clearly said that there will be only this world (age) and the one to come (cf. Mk 10,30). The starting-point of our salvation, however, is this world, in which we prepare ourselves for the coming one, and indeed differently from 'the sons of this aeon' (cf. §§ 0428–29). Yet Shenoute takes the gnostic 'knowledge' too much as only material. It is in reality knowledge of salvation. Because the origin of the world is traced back to an act of 'ignorance', only 'insight' (K. Rudolph) can lead to the abolition of this apostasy. 'Basically the gnostic mythos is a union of cosmogony, anthropogony and soteriology, which is, to be sure, presented variously and often is only reminiscent, but represents a closely meshed system of adaptation by the Gnostic, who assures his liberation from the world. He gives the redeeming answer to the questions that stir people, as they are contained in a gnostic excerpt of Clement of Alexandria: "Who were we? What did we become? Where were we? Into

---

64. See U. Bianchi, *Aug* 22 (1982), 38.

what were we thrown? Where are we hurrying to? From what are we liberated?"[65] How small, by contrast, does the salvation faith of church Christians look, who build the *soteria* precisely on the 'small history'!

(bb) The denial of the 'small history' of Jesus on earth

It is no great distance from the transposition of the genesis of Jesus – that is (ecclesiastically speaking), of the incarnate One – into the higher world to the denial of the whole 'small history' of the earthly Jesus. In the case of the Egyptian Gnostics around Shenoute one does not even need to presume 'Docetism'. The conception of Christ in Mary as such is drawn into doubt. The archimandrite reports:

> Others blaspheme that Mary did not conceive the Christ, and if she became pregnant [with Christ], [they ask:] did her body then not swell up and shrink again? (§§ 0345–46).[66]

Does Shenoute correctly reproduce the Gnostics' question here? As it reads, it sounds banal. With requisite care, perhaps we can come somewhat closer, based on the underlying idea of the tractate 'Exegesis on the Soul' (NHC II 127,18–137,28). The 'soul', as long as it remains with the Father, is virginal and masculine-feminine. In its 'fall' into the body there is a separation into the masculine and feminine parts of the soul. Apparently only the feminine part 'falls' and loses thereby its virginity. In this case the MHTPA turns outward and submits itself carnally to defilement. But if the fallen soul calls to the Father, he will have mercy on it. Now the reversal of this turning outward can occur: 'If, however, it [the soul] perceives the pain in which it is [through turning outward and falling into the body] and cries to the Father and does penance, then the Father will have mercy on it and turn its MHTPA; he will turn it from the outside again towards the inside, and the soul will receive its individuality.'[67]

Even a virginal conception of Jesus would be in the sense of the Gnostics a 'lustful turning outward'. Even in the incarnation there is a fall into the body. Even a reference to Is 7,14 and Lk 1,35 (§ 0346) avails nothing with these Gnostics. The incarnation as fall would have to be

---

65. See Clement of Alex., *Exc. Theod.* 78, 2; cited according to K. Rudolph, *Die Gnosis*, Göttingen 1977, 78–79. The possibility of positive and negative relationships between the gnosis and Zoroastrianism is addressed in the important chapters III–V in R. C. Zaehner, *Zurvan. A Zoroastrian Dilemma*, Oxford 1955, 54–146. It is to be noted that Zoroaster is mentioned in the *AJ* twice: Cod. II, p. 19,10 and Cod. IV, p. 29,19: Krause/Labib, pp. 160, 229. Yet the name is lacking in the older version of the *AJ*, in Pap. Berol. 8502 (Till). The 'Book of Zoroaster' must not be confused with the 'Tractate of Zostrianos' (= NHC VIII), 1. See J. H. Sieber, 'An Introduction to the Tractate Zostrianos from Nag Hammadi', *NovTest* 15 (1973) (233–40), 235. See also L. Abramowski, 'Nag Hammadi 8, 1 "Zostrianus", das Anonymum Brucianum, Plotin Enn. 2, 9 (33)', in FS H. Dörrie (*JAC* Erg. Bd. 10), 1983, 1–10; on the whole: R. Haardt, *Die Gnosis. Wesen und Zeugnisse*, Salzburg 1967, 154–72, with nn. 319–21. J. Duchesne-Guillemin, 'Gnosticisme et dualisme', in J. Ries et al., *Gnosticisme et monde hellénistique. Actes du Colloque de Louvain-la-Neuve (11–14 mars 1980)* (Publication de l'Institut Orientaliste de Louvain 27), Louvain 1982, 89–101.

66. Thus according to the recommendation of H. Quecke, with his reference to Crum, *Coptic Dictionary* 102 b, s.v. ⲕⲱⲱⲗⲉ.

67. Following the translation of M. Krause and K. Rudolph, in W. Foerster (ed.), *Die Gnosis* II, Zurich 1971, 130. – The most detailed expression in the NHC on the virgin birth of Jesus is in the *Testim. Truth* (NHC IX). See K. Koschorke, 'Der gnostische Traktat "Testimonium Veritatis" aus dem Nag-Hammadi-Codex IX. Eine Übersetzung (mit Kommentar)', *ZNW* 69 (1978), 91–117. Yet 'disparate elements of tradition' are used, e.g.: 'according to 30,18–30 Jesus came directly from heaven to earth; yet according to 45,6ff. he was born [of a virgin]. For the *Testim. Truth* the sense of both traditions is the same: Jesus

reversed again on the way to a turning inward. For Shenoute, however, this means that the whole 'small history' of Jesus is from the beginning thereby denied and abolished:

> But if he was not conceived, he was also not born; and if he was not born, he did not become human; and if he did not become human, he was not crucified; and if he was not crucified, he did not rise on the third day and did not ascend to his former holy dwelling (cf. Jn 17,5), before the Father sent him, that he might be born by a woman, by her herself, the holy virgin Mary (§ 0347).

The radicality of the rejection of the incarnation goes beyond the presuppositions that are familiar to us, say, from the Valentinian system, which represents genuine Docetism. We must face a decidedly flesh-hostile dualism. Here one can imagine Marcionite or even Manichaean influences. Pointing to the latter is the relatedness of our statement to a document that Epiphanius preserved, the letter of Mani to Marcellus.[68] It emphasizes that the Son of God, who goes forth from the bosom of the Father, could only have been born in this way as Son of God. It is unthinkable that the Son of the Father is also 'Son of Mary and thus from a woman, formed of blood and flesh and the ugliness of women in regard to these things'.[69] According to the *Acta Archelai*[70] Mani says: 'Absit ut dominum nostrum Iesum Christum per naturalia pudenda mulieris descendisse confitear . . .' We are reminded that Augustine had to devote himself to the same problem vis-à-vis the difficulties coming from Neoplatonism, but even more vis-à-vis the Manichaeans.[71] The latter know, in his words, only the *spiritualis saluator*, which could not be penetrated by a lance, and the *Iesus patibilis*, namely, the light bound in heaven, in the stars, on the earth and in all that is born (*confixum et conligatum atque concretum Christum*).[72] Thus it is probably Photius's own interpretation when in his *Bibl. Cod.* 114 he ascribes 'Docetism' to the Manichaeans (cf. C. Riggi, p. 124, n. 1). In any case, the Manichaean hostility to the incarnation fits the decided denial of the conception in Mary in Shenoute's surroundings.[73]

Quite worthy of note is what Shenoute says interrogatively a few pages later: 'Is it perhaps a question here of a new godlessness that has appeared among the *pagans*? Their activity indeed consists in always slandering the scriptures; no, it is a question of a new godlessness *among us* (Orlandi: *fra noi*), namely, that Mary did not conceive the Redeemer . . .' (§ 0367; cf. § 0423: 'Hellenizers among us'). All the mysteries of Jesus' life are affected by this, even his miracles, which otherwise could have suited the Gnostics. Thus Shenoute's Gnostics are

---

remained far from the sphere of "fleshly procreation" (30,30)' (ibid., 95). K. calls the first named sentence that of the Marcionites (ibid., p. 96; importantly, p. 98 with n. 13). That the church Christians do not imitate this denial of marriage and procreation, which lies in the mystery of the virgin birth, is the reason why they, in spite of baptism and martyrdom, do not come to salvation, and incidentally some of the Gnostics also.

68. Epiphanius, *Panar.* (CPG 3745), 66, 6: C. Riggi, *Epifanio contro Mani*, Rome 1967, 32–35 (Greek-Ital.), who is inclined here to assume a 'documento autentico del primo Manicheismo' (ibid., 32, n. 1).

69. See also the *Acta Archelai* 38–43: GCS 16, pp. 55–64: 'Archelaus' shows vis-à-vis the Manichaeans that Jesus is really the Son of Mary, although he is also consubstantial (*homoousios*) with the Father. The use of *theotokos* is according to Riggi, pp. 46–47, note, probably a later insertion.

70. *Acta Archelai*, 54, 11: GCS 16, p. 80,16–17.

71. Cf. A. Grillmeier, *JdChr* [3]I, pp. 602–3.

72. See the good evidence in F. Decret, *L'Afrique manichéenne (IVe–Ve siècles)*, Paris 1978, I, 284–86 and II, 215–18; here, with reference to the research of A. Böhlig, there is a discussion of the relationship of North African to the older Manichaeism, and the CMC – evaluated here – is also brought into the discussion (II, p. 218, n. 83). See also C. Riggi, *Epifanio contro Mani*, pp. 124–25 with n. 1.

73. See A. Grillmeier, *CCT* II/1, p. 183, n. 207.

radical (cf. §§ 0420–24). Even the awaking of Lazarus is reinterpreted (§ 0419). It is a question of the liberation of the human *nous*. Martha and Mary, by contrast, are the *aretai* that come from the four elements. The gnostic hermeneutic is thus applied consistently to the kerygma of the mysteries of Jesus' life, which are thereby fully denied.

(cc) The Pascha in heaven and on earth (§§ 0312–16)

In his commentary on Jn 2,13 ('the Pascha of the Jews was near') Origen distinguishes a threefold Pascha:[74] 'The first is a human Pascha, namely, of those who do not celebrate it according to the will of the scripture' (Is 1,13–14), and the 'divine, the true Pascha that is celebrated in spirit and in truth by those who worship God in spirit and in truth [cf. Jn 4,24]; set over against the divine is the one that is called [the Pascha] of the Jews'.[75] In the John commentary X, the 'divine Pascha' is especially interpreted in connection with 1 Cor 5,7 and Jn 6, and in the framework of a spiritual-allegorical exegesis. Underlying the word *Pascha* is the Hebrew etymology: Pascha in the sense of a passing over (passover) of the Lord.

In the John commentary X 19 (pp. 190–91) Origen deals with the interpretation of 'Pascha' by Heracleon, who (like Melito of Sardis and Hippolytus) begins with the etymology *pascha = paschein*. Here we see a gnostic interpretation, namely, the distinction between the act of the slaughter of the lamb and the act of eating. The first is done on earth; the second, the eating, is interpreted according to the rest in the coming wedding.[76] Here we already have a distinction between a heavenly and an earthly Pascha, although – as also elsewhere with the Gnostics – the phrase *heavenly Pascha* does not occur. In reality, however, we have in Philo, Origen and the Gnostics a Pascha celebration on different levels; with the Gnostics, naturally, it corresponds to their cosmos soteriology. Hence: (1) in the *pleroma*, (2) in the realm of the planets over which the archons reign, (3) on earth.[77] Shenoute deals with such 'demonic teachings' of the apocrypha but explains them on the basis of his presuppositions:

> These are words that human beings have spoken: the Father proclaims the Pascha *in the heavens* and in *all worlds*, so that they celebrated the Pascha in six days; they understand [by this] the Pascha that *we celebrate on earth* and equate it with the completion of what God created in them [i.e., these days] as the whole creation: 'When they come to this day every year, the Father and the angels and the spirits celebrate it' (§ 0312). Can there be a greater blasphemy than to say that God celebrated a Pascha and suffered pain? Indeed, even the other twelve worlds celebrate it also at the same moment each year, and they will continue to celebrate it until the world passes away, because it [Pascha] has come for them with the suffering (§ 0313) . . . When does the Lord in fact celebrate Pascha if not when he became human with human beings and suffered for us and fasted and prayed and had all the experiences we had, except for sin [cf. Heb 4,15] (§ 0315)? Whoever says that God, the almighty King, felt pain, or that he celebrated a Pascha, does not understand the meaning of these sounds. For the eternal God cannot be hungry or suffer; rather, he gives

---

74. Origen, *Com. i. Io.* (from the years 235–236), XIII(11)–XIX(14): GCS Or. W. IV, pp. 183–91 (§§ 67–118).

75. Ibid., § 68. On the understanding of Pascha (passover) in Origen see Origène, *Sur la Pâque. Traité inédit publié d'après un papyrus de Toura par O. Guéraud et P. Nautin* (ChrAnt 2), Paris 1979, comm.: 112–50; text and trans.: 154–253; M. Naldini, 'Note sul De Pascha di Origene e la tradizione Origeniana in Egitto', *Aug* 26 (1986), 63–71.

76. See GCS Or. W. IV, pp. 190–91 (§§ 117–18): τὴν ἀνάπαυσιν τὴν ἐν γάμῳ. 'Rest in the wedding' is for the Gnostics a technical expression for the reuniting of the pneumatic elements in human beings with the original *pleroma*. See E. Corsini, *Commento al Vangelo di Giovanni di Origene*, Turin 1968, 407; M. Simonetti, 'Eracleone e Origene', *VC* 3 (1966), 3–75.

77. The Gnostics do not speak expressly of a heavenly Pascha but transpose it logically into the *pleroma*. Cf. A. Orbe, *Cristología gnóstica* II, pp. 141–74, 263–93.

strength to those who hunger and relief to those who take up suffering for him (§ 0316).

The etymology of *Pascha* that Shenoute presupposes is similar to that of Melito and Hippolytus.[78] In this way, to be sure, the archimandrite misses the idea of the Gnostics. But he wants to keep any 'suffering' far from God. The true Pascha takes place on earth in the suffering and death of Jesus Christ, the true Easter Lamb. This means the celebration of Holy Week from Palm Sunday to Good Friday. Shenoute believes the Gnostics would ascribe such a suffering Pascha to the Father, the angels and the spirits (archons). But he indicates, nonetheless, that the 'six days' in the Gnostics mean the hexaemeron and refer to the earthly, material creation. In reference to the 'Father' *Pascha* might mean God's rest from creation (*anapausis*).[79] Thus there can be no talk of a 'suffering' (*paschein*) of God, a theopaschitism, however difficult the other idea is to explain. But in the White Monastery or in its vicinity there is apparently a disagreement regarding the liturgical celebration of Holy Week and its content. This assumption can be supported by distinctions in the understanding of the sacraments to be discussed below.

(dd) Human beings in this 'large' and 'small' history: Origenism

Anthropology and soteriology among the Gnostics in Shenoute's vicinity correspond in general to the views on the incarnation of Christ. Here Origenistic influences are especially at work, above all in the doctrine of the pre-existence of the soul and the assumption of a prehistoric fall. Human beings begin in the 'large history' with their higher part.

The special teachers Shenoute addresses do not want to make God a *vasaio*, a potter, who every moment must continually make new souls. 'Rather, he created them all in the beginning and gathered them in certain places and in certain chambers (ταμειον) for the purpose of birth' (§ 0435).[80] This birth occurred as punishment for a guilt in the period of existence before union with a body (§§ 0409, 0412). Shenoute, however, cannot accommodate a prehistoric guilt and call it a genuine *actus humanus*. *Where* then are these (pure – i.e., not yet bound to a body) souls supposed to have sinned? *From where* did they come into a body? Perhaps from heaven, which belongs to this (in the sense of the Gnostics, 'lower') world? From heaven, which for Shenoute, however, is the place of sinlessness? From a heaven that belongs to other worlds? But these do not exist!

How can a soul without bodily existence sin at all? What happens to the freedom of decision? Are we to assume, asks the archimandrite, a temporal difference between the creation of the soul and that of the body, or rather a simultaneous creation of both in the

78. See on this R. J. Daly, 'The Peri Pascha: Hermeneutics and Sacrifice', in *Origeniana Tertia: Third Intern. Colloquium for Origen Studies, Manchester 1981*, Rome 1985, 109–17. Also idem, 'The Hermeneutics of Origen: Existential Interpretation in the Third Century', in *The Word in the World*, Cambridge, Mass. 1973, 135–43.

79. See A. Orbe, *Cristología gnóstica* II, 115–16: The 'six days' acquire a special meaning: 'El mistero de la economía afecta al hombre sensible en general, sin excluir al Salvador. Hubo de realizarse, en consecuencia, el día sexto o Parasceve. Cristo hombre fue "hecho hombre perfecto" (τέλειος ἄνθρωπος) mediante la pasión.'
The six days in Shenoute refer in any case to the earthly world. One would need to pursue the symbolism of the number six, which the Chiliasts especially emphasize, in reference to Rev 13,18: '666'. Cf. Iren., *Adv. haer.* V 30,1–3; Lactantius, *Div. inst.* VII 14: CSEL 19, 627–30; V. Loi, *Lattanzio. Nella storia del linguaggio e del pensiero teologico pre-niceno*, Zurich 1970, 237; K.-H. Schwarte, *Die Vorgeschichte der augustinischen Weltalterlehre* (Antiquitas I, 12), Bonn 1926, 23–32. Augustine compares the six *aetates* of the world with the *requies aeterna* of the seventh day of creation in Sermo 216, VIII,8: PL 38, 1081 to the six life stages of each human being, with the *septima aetas* as eternal rest.

80. Cf. Plato, *Tim.* 41e, 42aff.

womb? If a fall of the soul before union with the body is to be assumed, then can there ever still be 'righteous and godly people' out of body and soul, which the scripture nevertheless attests? If righteousness and godliness are possible even in this world, why should it not be easier to realize both in that world of pre-existence?

Shenoute also finds that the Gospel report of the last judgement would be cancelled by this teaching of the fall of souls and their punishment by embodiment. Indeed, judgement would have already been accomplished in the beginning and would happen continually (§ 0412).

Moreover, every soul that left a dying body would immediately be banished into another. Thus in Shenoute's surroundings the teaching of *metempsychosis*[81] is also present. This has far-reaching consequences. The souls of people remain exiles into 'small history': 'And the souls of those who die go out of them and enter the bodies of those who are begot, as I have already said once before. Truly a foolish and twisted spirit lives in those who say such things' (§§ 0435–36).

Thus the doctrine of the transmigration of souls seems to hang on stubbornly in Egypt. By what means did it come to the monks? According to a text that is admittedly uncertain as belonging to Origen, Basilides is supposed to have supported this teaching in Alexandria.[82] 'The speeches of Basilides, which depreciate those who strive to the death for truth [i.e., martyrs] in order to confess Jesus before humankind [cf. Mt 10,32], and which teach that it is indifferent to deny alien gods or sacrifice to them [indeed, that "martyrdom" is also a sign of guilt], also pollute and ruin their hearers no less by teaching in the same speeches that there is no punishment for sins other than the re-embodiment (*transcorporationes*) of souls after death.'

It is striking that both 'Origen' and Shenoute (§ 0408) speak of deception here. The destructiveness of such teachings for the Christian churches is obvious. Redemption through Jesus Christ is called into question. That is why Shenoute goes into such detail on all these views (§§ 0335, 0340–44). His anthropology is sound: body and soul together form the 'human being', 'because the human being does not exist without soul, nor the soul without the human being [i.e., the body] . . . Neither the body exists before the soul nor the soul before the body, but it and the body were created together in the womb by God' (§ 0340). Here the archimandrite is more correct than Origen, who in discipleship to the Platonists in *PA* developed his theory of the pre-existence of souls, though 'not as doctrine . . . but as an object of explanation and research' (*PA* II 8, 4: Görgemanns/Karpp, pp. 396–97). According

---

81. In A. Orbe, *Cristología gnóstica* II, Madrid 1976, 573–97 (chap. 34: 'Ascensión y reincorporaciones'), the terminology and the doctrine of metensomatosis, etc., in all the individual forms of the gnostic families are explained. Irenaeus, *Adv. haer.* II 32, 2, blames Plato as the first to introduce this teaching (see n. 80). According to Clement of Alexandria (*Strom.* III 3, 16, 4ff.) and Jerome (*Adv. Rufin.* III 39 fin.) it is to be traced back to Pythagoras. See also A. Orbe, 'Textos y pasajes de la Escritura interesados en la teoría de la Reincorporación', *EstEcl* 33 (1959), 77–91. Very informative is: J. W. Sedlar, *India and the Greek World*, Totowa, New Jersey 1980, chap. V, pp. 22–32 (with nn. pp. 306–8): Soul-Wandering.

82. A. Orbe, *Cristología gnóstica* II, 583: Origen, *Ser. in Matth.* 38 post medium. Cf. Plato, *Tim* 42c.46c; K. Rudolph, *Die Gnosis*, Göttingen 1977 (97–130), 120, 126ff.; R. van den Broek, 'The Creation of Adam's Psychic Body in the Apocryphon of John', in R. van den Broek and M. J. Vermaseren (eds.), *Studies in Gnosticism and Hellenistic Religions presented to G. Quispel* (EPRO 81), Leiden 1981, 38–57. An interesting variation on our problem is presented by Origen, *Dial. c. Heraclide* 12–16: Scherer, SC 67, pp. 80–88, esp. 82–84 (§§ 13–14).

to H. Crouzel[83] there are allusions to this anthropology in his entire work. The spiritual part of the human being exists first as *nous* and not as *psyche*. At first this *nous* lived entirely as 'spirit' (*pneuma*) (*PA* II 8, 3) and completely resembled the angels in their nature. But these *noes* were negligent in their zeal, and this led to their becoming *souls*, *psychai* (derived from *psychos*, 'cold') and being bound to bodies. Thus in *PA* IV 2, 7 Origen can say: 'I now call "human beings" the souls that make use of the body.'[84] The *psyche* is subject to all the limitations of the earthly body, which for it is the place of testing (and thus of joylessness, as Shenoute concludes). Certainly the *nous* is maintained as the higher part of the soul, as Origen comments in fragment 11 on Luke (GCS Or. W. IX, p. 237,23). Thus human beings preserve their identity between the time before and after the fall, in that the *nous*, as what human beings were created in pre-existence, is also maintained in the fallen soul as its contemplative ability: '. . . the *nous*, which is in them, in possession of the nature according to which the Creator made them'.[85] There is also the possibility that the purified *psyche* will become the *nous* again and return to the original view, and for those who depend on the flesh to build in metempsychosis or the assumption of a successive reincarnation of souls. It should not be overlooked that Origen's opinion of this view is in dispute. Plato seems to be the source of the idea that the reincarnation corresponds to the degree of guilt and could go so far as souls being banished into animal bodies (*Tim.* 42c). Origenists in or around the White Monastery would not have needed any inhibitions here, at least not when Shenoute correctly interpreted them.

Actually, Origen is on the whole more reserved here than his 'followers'. He assumes that there are also righteous people on earth, who are thus 'spirit', whereas the sinner is 'flesh' (*PA* III 4: Görgemanns/Karpp, pp. 602–20). When a soul has become entirely flesh, it goes to hell. The spirit, however, will return to God, who gave it (*Ser. In Matt.* 62: GCS, Or. W. XI, p. 144,9ss.). Thus hell consists, in a certain respect, in the separation of the inner person. The righteous, by contrast, with their three parts – their *nous*, their soul, which has become completely pneumatic, and their flesh, which has also assimilated to the order of the spirit – will go to heaven. They are again integrated into the 'large history'.

Thus, although with the doctrinal opinion of the pre-existence of souls adopted from the Platonists – 'l'élément le plus aberrant de l'origénisme'[86] – Origen left Christian anthropology a heavy burden, one still must not load on him personally the typical refinements that we find in his followers at the time of Shenoute. On the basis of the presuppositions presented above, we no longer marvel that resurrection of the body is decidedly rejected by them. Yet they do not hark back here to Origen alone, as their reasoning shows: the human body is mixed and formed of the four elements; it is composed of water, earth, air and fire. Hence the complete

---

83. Cf. H. Crouzel, *Théologie de l'image de Dieu chez Origène*, Paris 1955, 130–33 (on Origen's anthropology); p. 130, n. 8: 'La ψυχή était dans la préexistence un νοῦς et non un πνεῦμα. Le pneuma exprime une certaine participation de ce noûs à la nature divine, qui subsiste dans la psyché déchue.'

84. Cf. U. Bianchi, *Aug* 22 (1982), 46. But when Bianchi assumes a second definition of human being in Origen (*nos homines animal sumus compositum ex corporis animaeque concursu, in quanto esseri terrestri*) and refers to *PA* I 6, 6, then this proof is not correct. On this matter, however, see H. Crouzel, *Théologie de l'image*, 130–33. It is correct that Origen sometimes presupposes a dichotomous anthropology according to Platonic usage. But mostly he finds, with the scripture, three parts in a human being: spirit, soul, body. Cf. M.-J. Pierre, 'L'âme dans l'anthropologie d'Origène', *POC* 34 (1984), 21–65.

85. Text provided in H. Crouzel, op. cit., p. 132, n. 24.

86. H. Crouzel, op. cit., p. 132.

dissolution of the body is permanently pre-programmed. At death it immediately disintegrates into these components (§ 0401).[87] Shenoute's aversion to such teachings must not be judged according to modern chemistry. He reacts 'theologically', as a reader of the Old Testament, which he exegetes *ad litteram*, specifically, the passage in Gen 1,27. Human beings are made of 'earth', and God has breathed into them the breath of life. Correspondingly, he will also resurrect them and will do it once and for all (§ 0402). The Greek nature philosophers (Empedocles) have nothing to say here. Years later, in a christological catechesis probably of the post-Chalcedonian era, Shenoute will support the same interpretation of Gen 1,27 in application to the creation of human beings in general and of the body of Christ in the Virgin in particular.[88]

The idea of the 'resurrection' is reinterpreted in the heads of those in error. It takes place in the reincarnation of souls. The behaviour of the newborn is supposedly a proof of this. Since new bodies are formed out of the disintegrating old ones, the 'identity' of the reincarnated ones is transferred into this very matter. This is allegedly seen in the behaviour of the newborn. Why else would they turn after birth immediately to the (mother's) breast (§ 0405)? The bearer of this 'memory' is the matter! And because the body formed therefrom is basically the prison for the *nous* (§§ 0409–10), that would also be the case after the resurrection. Thus there is no reawakening of the body. The archimandrite finds that this teaching of the body as the prison of the soul is nonsense and contradicts experience. In a prison, he argues, there can be only sadness. But in people composed of body and soul there is the experience of joy, which the soul shares over the body! This indication may suffice for the crude opinions of the Origenists around Shenoute. The master of Alexandria – as we saw above – made specifications that in part would have invalidated the objections of the abbot. Still, his critique of Origenism gives us an insight into the Christian understanding of life in the White Monastery and its surroundings: joy is its basic tone, not the mentality of 'prisoners'. The ultimate source of this joy is, of course, Christ and the celebration of his 'festivals'. As there is festal celebration in heaven, so also in the 'church of the firstborn [ones]' (Heb 12,23) (§ 0411).

Marcion or Mani?

Yet the denial of the resurrection among the false teachers around Shenoute is not to be explained only by Origenism. They despise the body out of genuinely dualistic motives. The body is fundamentally so bad that it is not capable of resurrection:

> Some despise the body [by saying] that it is the flesh of swine and is thrown away because they do not believe that it will rise again. Well, if it is swinish, who made it so, and indeed worse than swine? Is it not you yourselves? Even more like this animal body are those who say that the soul was banished into the body after it had sinned; such people are justified in despising their own flesh (§§ 0356–57).

It is true that in the second part of this text Shenoute traces the contempt of the body back

---

87. On the teaching of the elements in the disagreement with the Gnostics and Manichaeans see E. Beck, 'Bardaisan und seine Schule bei Ephräm', *Mus* 91 (1978) (271–333), 271–80. The tetrad of elements in our text is found 'in Greek philosophical and semi-philosophical literature': *pyr, aēr, hydōr* and *gē*. 'The rarer fifth (Aristotelian) element of *aithēr* (the heavenly element) is included by the Stoa, who maintained the tetrad by dividing the *pyr* into an earthly and a heavenly fire (= *aithēr, pneuma*)' (p. 271). Numerous references to the teaching of the elements are offered by R. C. Zaehner, *Zurvan*, Oxford 1955, 411. See Index p. 482. – The Manichaean sources, in Epiphan., *Panar.*, 66, 2: Riggi, p. 114 (with n. 1), ascribe a pentad of elements to the first human being: wind, light, water, fire, ethereal matter. Cf. Augustine, *De haer.* 46; cf. E. Beck, *Mus* 91 (1978), 292–95.
88. Cf. L. T. Lefort, 'Catéchèse Christologique de Chenoute', *ZÄS* 80 (1955), 44.

to Origenism. But the beginning of the text points to Marcionite-Manichaean ideas. In Manichaeism we have the ultimate conclusions of Marcionite dualism in regard to the estimation of the body. The cosmology and especially the anthropology of Mani are based on the idea of the fusion of the pentad of light with the pentad of darkness.[89] In the proclamation of the Manichaeans this finds its expression in the repeated description, violating all good taste, of the 'swinish' nature of the human body and the emphasis on its impurity. Now in NHC II 2, pp. 138,1–145,19, in the so-called *Book of Thomas*,[90] we have very clear echoes of this in the wording and conception, which K. Koschorke calls 'proto-Manichaean elements': 'For the *Book of Thomas* the body – of disgusting origin, seat of the passions, destined for destruction – is the source of all evil.'[91] The typical sayings are briefly given: 'All bodies [come into being like] the animals that reproduce them [or themselves] . . . [they are] apparently like [the creat]ion, which [. . .] this itself' (NHC II 2, p. 138,40). – '. . . for the body is animal-like. Now, as the bodies of animals perish, so also these realities will perish. Does it [i.e. the body] not come from copulation, like that of animals? If it also comes from there, how will it produce a greater difference than they?' (ibid., p. 139,5–10) . . . 'The saviour spoke: . . . If, however, all the elect take off the animal nature, then the light will withdraw to his true essence above. And it will take its true essence to itself, because it is a good servant' (ibid., p. 139,25–30) . . . 'The saviour spoke: "Truly, consider those not as human beings but count them among the animals, for as the animals devour one another, so it is also with these thus constituted people; they devour one another, but they are excluded from the [truth]"' (ibid., p. 141,25) . . . 'Then the saviour continued and spoke: ". . . Woe to you who hope in the flesh and prison(!) that will perish"' (ibid., p. 143,10). Those who do not live as Gnostics 'vegetate in the flesh' (ibid., p. 145,5). In the quoted text of Shenoute we need only replace the expression 'swine' with the genus 'animal' and we have all the essential statements as in the *Book of Thomas*. The CMC offers further genuine Manichaean illustrations, which cannot be exceeded in clarity.[92] Thus what Shenoute reproduces as the body-hostile theses of a section of his hearers or readers can be corroborated in detail from Marcionite-Manichaean sources.

This classification is also true for the following: Shenoute alludes to the meaning of *sun* and *moon* in a way that betrays Mazdean-Manichaean ideas. Again it is a question of apocrypha:

89. See C. Riggi, *Epifanio contro Mani*, Rome 1967, 114–15, with n. 1; S. N. C. Lieu, 'Some Themes in Later Roman Anti-Manichaean Polemics' I, *BJRL* 68 (1985/86) (434–69), 450–51; II, *BJRL* 69 (1986/87) (235–75), 235; idem, *Manichaeism in the Later Roman Empire and Medieval China. A Historical Survey*, Manchester 1988 (reprinted), 8–24.

90. Cf. *Die Gnosis* II: 'Koptische und Mandäische Quellen', Zurich 1971, 139–48 (trans. M. Krause, with introduction 136–38).

91. According to K. Koschorke, *Die Polemik der Gnostiker gegen das kirchliche Christentum*, Leiden 1978, 125.

92. From the relatively numerous references in the text and commentary, the following are given: CMC 81, 1, *ZPE* 32 (1978), 101: '[Mani:] For this body is impure and the formation of an impure creation', which is explained more precisely in what follows, esp. in vv. 8–20 (commentary, ibid., 138–39 = nn. 188–89). In Hom. 6, 8 the (first) shaper of human beings (cf. Gen 2,7) is cursed. The *miarotēs* of this creation and of the body (cf. Keph. 89,35) results from the already mentioned mixture of particles of light and of darkness according to Keph. 95,13ff. This establishes the fundamental impossibility of purifying the body, which the Baptist sect strove to do. 'For Mani, purification was a cosmic process, the separation of spirit and matter in which man as a microcosmos participated': A. Henrichs, 'Mani and the Babylonian Baptists', *HSCP* 77 (1973) (23–59), 58, which says in n. 137: 'In a Manichaean cosmogony the human body is said to be created "from the dirt of the male demons and the faeces of the female demons".' Thus every bearer of a human body must be ashamed of it. What Porphyry says about Plotinus (*Vita Plot.* 1): 'he was like one who was

'They say of the almighty God that it is he who moves in the sun's orbit, and that the light of the moon makes the trees and animals grow. Oh, what godlessness! Is it not perhaps godless to say that the God of the universe moves in the sun and is ignited in the moon? Is it not he who by his order makes the sun move as in his service, and does the moon not also shine at his command? And can the moon make the plants and the animals grow? Does not all of this grow through the work of God? Does he not make the stars shine in their various positions . . . ?' (§§ 0385–87). Thus, God does not let himself be borne by the sun, and the moon does not bring forth plants and animals; rather, he moves everything without moving himself (with reference to Acts 17,28) (ibid., 41).

What is being alluded to here can be discerned as the Mazdean sun and moon myth, which is also represented in a few hints in the *Book of Thomas* (cf. 144,1–25): 'Woe to you who are in error in that you do not look to the light of the sun, which judges the universe, which looks at the universe, for it shall surround all works in order to serve the enemies! And furthermore you do not know the moon, how it is made up by night and by day, when it looks down and sees the bodies of your killed ones . . . The sun and the moon will give you a good aroma with the air, the spirit, the earth and the water.' As background we can give the 'Song of the Magians', which Dio Chrysostomus preserved and which is thoroughly researched by the historians of religion.[93]

According to the myth, Zeus (i.e. the highest God, Zurvān) is the 'perfect charioteer of the perfect chariot. This chariot, which is the Cosmos, is guided by the one charioteer and proceeds on its course throughout "unceasing periods of eternity". Men can only see the courses of the Sun and Moon but cannot grasp the movement of the whole.'[94] It is interesting

---

ashamed to be in the body' (*ZPE* 32 [1978], 138) sounds harmless compared to the Manichaean texts. Mani actually speaks of his earthly life as a 'wandering in this disgusting flesh' (CMC 22, 12: *ZPE* 19 [1975], 25). With the body one puts on 'drunkenness' (ibid.). The result of the first *plasis* of human beings is passed on in sexual activity, which was therefore forbidden to the *electi*. In this way human beings beget an 'amazing structure of terror', a 'castle of death', a 'figure of poison'. In this context also belong the food taboos, as formulated by Epiphanius, *Panar.*, 66, 9: Riggi, p. 41: 'dice che chi mangia la carne mangia anche l'anima e deve anche lui diventare come quel che mangia, se ha mangiato del maiale diventare anche lui un maiale, e cosí pure se si tratta di bue, di volatile o di altro comestibile. Perciò si astengono dai viventi.'

The commentary in *ZPE* 32 (1978), 138–39, points to 'fundamental connections between Gnosis and Platonism, particularly between middle Platonism and Valentinianism' (p. 138). Yet the dualism of Mani is so negative that one must not confuse it with Plato. Cf. C. Parma, *Pronoia und Providentia. Der Vorsehungsbegriff Plotins und Augustins* (SPAMP VI), Leiden 1971; S. Pétrement, *Le dualisme chez Platon, les Gnostiques et les manichéens*, Brionne 1982.

93. See R. C. Zaehner, *Zurvan. A Zoroastrian Dilemma*, Oxford 1955, 226–27; J. Duchesne-Guillemin, *Symbolik des Parsismus* (Symbolik d. Religionen VIII), Stuttgart 1961: (a) pp. 83–84: 'Der Gott mit dem Wagen'; (b) pp. 66, 93–94: astral symbols and the vegetable world.

94. R. C. Zaehner, op. cit., 226; also Index: 'Moon'. On sun and moon we have two more important references: (1) Photius, *Bibl.*, cod. 179: Henry II, 185–86. Here the lost work of Agapius, a follower of Mani (with 23 books and 202 other *capita*), is analysed. Sun and moon are regarded as divinities consubstantial with God. Their light is unsensory, only intelligible. – (2) In the *Great Anathemas against the Manichaeans*, which contain good information. Cf. A. Adam, KlT 175, p. 99: 'I reject those who say that Christ is the sun and pray to the sun or the moon or the stars and behave towards them entirely as towards gods and call them the most visible gods.' Hence they would also constantly change their direction of prayer with the movement of the sun. Also to be renounced are those who declare that Zarades (Zurvān), Buddha, Christ, Mani and the sun are one and the same.

that in this hymn, as in the *Book of Thomas*, the four elements, fire, air, water and earth, are mentioned; they are the four horses (of Zeus, of Hera, of Poseidon and of Hestia). Here we still do not have the Manichaean world-machine in its final form, but probably early stages on which Mani could build.

We also have evidence for the significance of the moon for the growth of plants and animals. It is a question of an aspect of light symbolism in Mazdaism and Manichaeism. That to which Shenoute alludes can only have been present in Manichaean circles that were equally influenced by one of the most important concepts of Iranian civilization. The concept of X^{v}AR∃NAH contains, according to its most recent interpreters, the elements that are addressed in our text. X^{v}AR∃NAH is to be understood as a *fluidum* that comes out of the sun but also out of the moon and the stars like an emanation and awakens life everywhere. It is at the same time 'un fluide igné' and 'une semence vitale'.[95] Similarly, the concept χ^{v}arrah, applied to God, simply means 'sa semence'. These are the *logoi spermatikoi* of the Manichaeans. What Shenoute is fighting is perhaps best expressed with the words of J. Duchesne-Guillemin: 'L'équation χ^{v}arrah – lumière – vie rend enfin parfaitement clair et intelligible un passage de Bundahišn. Selon celui-ci, 164,13 sq. "la lune doit distribuer le χ^{v}arrah au monde; pendant quinze jours elle croît, pendant quinze elle décroît; c'est comme l'organe sexuel des mâles donnant, quand il croît, la semence aux femelles; ainsi également, la lune croît pendant quinze jours et distribue le bonheur aux êtres du monde matériel; elle décroît pendant quinze jours, pendant lesquels elle accepte les bonnes actions de ces êtres et les place dans le trésor de Dieu." '[96]

(c) Christology and understanding of the Eucharist in dissolution[97]

In connection with the denial of the incarnation by a section of his listeners, Shenoute moves directly to speak of the rejection of the general church understanding of the Eucharist (§§ 0347–55, 0367–83). We see a profound crisis in the life of faith and liturgical prayer in the abbot's surroundings: 'Instead there is among us a new godlessness, namely, that Mary did not conceive the Saviour and, moreover, that it is not his body and his blood that we receive' (§ 0367). It sounds like the intra-Catholic difficulties of the period of modernism when we read: 'Some [hold]

95. J. Duchesne-Guillemin, 'Le X^{v}AR∃NAH', in *AION.L* 5 (1963) (19–31), 25. On this see G. Gnoli, 'Aχ^{v}arχtεm χ^{v}arεno', in ibid., 295–98; on the whole see J. Duchesne-Guillemin, *La religion de l'Iran ancien*, Paris 1962, 308–54: 'La Cosmologie mazdéenne'.

96. J. Duchesne-Guillemin, 'Le X^{v}AR∃NAH', 30–31. With this we are very close to the Manichaean myths. On the Manichaean mythos on the origin of the plant, tree and animal world see K. Wegenast, art. 'Mani. Manichäer. Manichäismus', *Kl.Pauly* 3, 953–56, esp. 954.

97. On gnosis and sacrament (esp. the Eucharist) see H.-G. Gaffron, 'Studien zum koptischen Philippusevangelium unter besonderer Berücksichtigung der Sakramente', diss. Bonn 1969, 171–85 ('Eucharistie'). Also important: K. Koschorke, *Die Polemik der Gnostiker gegen das kirchliche Christentum*, Leiden 1978, 147–48. The Gnostics' reproach is that the church's understanding of the Eucharist confuses reality and image. In pneumatic monasticism there was more disagreement with the bishops' church over the Eucharist and its constant repetition (and ecclesiastical control) than over baptism. This assertion of Koschorke also fits our situation. – Cf. M. Krause, *Die Sakramente in der 'Exegese über die Seele'* (NHSt 7), Leiden 1975, 47–55. – P. du Bourguet, 'Entretien de Chenouté sur des problèmes de discipline ecclésiastique et de cosmologie', *BIFAO* 57 (1958) (99–142), trans. 118–19 ((§§ 1–3), on fasting before the celebration of the Eucharist.

further that the bread and the cup are not the body and blood of Christ but only a symbol' (§ 0348).[98] Bread and wine in the celebration of the Eucharist only 'signify' the body and blood of Christ; in the mysteries they do not become *soma* and *haima Christou*, as is nonetheless proclaimed in the words of institution and administration. Incensed, Shenoute reminds the doubters of the eucharistic speech at Capernaum (Jn 6,22–59) and Jesus' words of institution at the Last Supper. Such doubt violates the 'mystery in the spirit of the scripture' (§ 0352). This is all the worse when the doubter 'is a presbyter or a member of the clergy, whatever his position in the holy hierarchy may be' (§ 0354). This, incidentally, is an indication that the crisis encompasses not only Shenoute's monastery but also his broader surroundings, just as the above-mentioned letter of Patriarch Dioscorus to the abbot presupposes. Thus the denial of the real presence of Christ is in vogue here: 'It is not the body and not the blood of Christ' (ibid.).

Immediately the abbot thinks of the faithful, who in their 'unenlightened state' are the victims of such a denial. For unbelief in the real presence of Christ, of his body and his blood, means renunciation of Jesus himself and the Holy Spirit, whom God sent so that these gifts would become the body and blood of Christ (epiclesis!); it also means contempt

---

98. Orlandi's *simbolo* renders the Coptic Greek *typos*. Cf. Lampe, *PatrGrLex*, s.v., section D 3, Sp. 1419b: it can have (1) a negative meaning, i.e. *typos*, 'esp. in contrast to ἡ ἀλήθεια'; (2) a positive meaning: pattern, model, example (Lampe, l. c. E and F). – Both meanings successively in the use of the same word are found in Cyril of Alex., *Comm. in Matt.*, on Mt 26,27 (words over the cup): PG 72, 452C. *Typos* means first 'pattern, model' of the thanksgiving. But then negatively: *figura; ne figuram esse arbitreris ea quae videntur, sed arcana ratione aliqua transformari ab omnipotente Deo in corpus et sanguinem Christi vere oblata* (451C). – On the occurrence of *typos* in the NHC see F. Siegert, *Nag-Hammadi-Register* (= 26 [1982]), s.v. 'typos', pp. 314–15. For *Gos. Phil.* see J. É. Ménard, *L'évangile selon Philippe*, Paris 1967, Index, p. 256. Coming closest to the negative sense of *symbol* in reference to the Eucharist is the behaviour that had to be proscribed in the *Great Greek Renunciation Formula*: 'Anathema also to those who avoid the communion of the precious blood and body of Christ but pretend to accept them and in their place understand by them the words of Christ's teaching (*ta rhēmata tēs . . . didaskalias*), which, they say, he gave to the apostles, saying: "Take, eat, drink" ' (there is also a similar 'symbolic' understanding of baptism, which does not say more than the words of Christ, 'I am the living water' [Jn 4,7]). (See A. Adam, KlT 175, p. 102; PG 1, 1469). An interesting synthesis is offered by the Anaphora of Serapion of Thmuis (d. *c.* 362): before the consecration the bread and wine are *figura* of the body and blood of Christ, even after the recitation of the words of institution: 'Dopo le parole del Signore, il pane è ancora *grano disperso e riunito*, e il calice è ancora *immagine* (ὁμοίωμα αἵματος). In virtù dell' epiclesi invece i due elementi si cambiano in "Corpo del Verbo" e in "Sangue della Verità"'; see G. Giamberardini, *La consecrazione eucaristica nella Chiesa Copta* (AegC 1, 8), Cairo 1957, 60. Similarly, Serapion of Thmuis, *Anaphora*, in F. X. Funk, *Didascalia et Constitut. Ap.*, II, Paderborn 1905, 174; Athanasius, *Sermo ad baptiz.*: PG 26, 1325; Eutychius *Const.*: PG 86, 2401. This is genuine Egyptian tradition.

for the holy place and for the altar and for those who prostrate before it and receive these gifts in faith. Among those for whom the mysteries are merely a matter of bread and wine are unfortunately not only pagans but – 'and this is much worse – also some of us. They are worse than dogs and swine. Do we say perhaps that it is bread that we take? Or is it not a mystery in accordance with the scripture?' (§ 0352). This unbelief comes from lack of faith in the power of God as creator, 'that God can effect this and even more than this' (§ 0354); such an unbeliever is worse than animals and unclean spirits (§ 0353).

Frightening for the archimandrite is the realization that priests and monks can carry within them such a conflict of saying, on the one hand: 'This is my body, which is given for you for the forgiveness of sins, and this is my blood, which is poured out for many for the forgiveness of sins [and yet not believing in the real presence of this body and blood]' (§ 0355). With this the true mediation of salvation through the Eucharist falls. For mere bread and mere wine can cleanse no one of his or her sins or heal illnesses or become an eternal blessing. If that is your whole faith, to whom do you claim to pray? Who gives you his attention? 'If you do not accept the scripture on this [point], how can you maintain that you belong to Jesus, since you despise his holy body and his pure blood?' (§ 0369).

> Why do you receive the holy mysteries? Do you not find other bread to eat and wine to drink – as we have written elsewhere: 'hypocritical and truly false people, false Christians, who in name only are priests or monks or superiors (*archegos*) or fathers!' (§ 0370).

It is probably a matter of Gnostics, who boast about a 'false philosophy' and deceptively draw souls 'with the wisdom of the psychic world' (§ 0372). Perhaps this is a giving back of the reproach that the Gnostics directed against church Christians, whom they call 'psychics'. In reality they themselves fall for this psychic wisdom. The believers are, to be sure, confident 'that they are wise ones. In reality, however, a fatherhood of this kind and hierarchies of this kind [pneumatic psychics?] are suited to defile the hearts of many believers in many sanctuaries of Christ' (§ 0376). In short, the evil has already penetrated to a broad extent and through the spiritual leaders threatens to seize the believers.

In this connection Shenoute's exhortation also becomes interesting for the historian of liturgy, as we shall briefly indicate. Suddenly flowing into the sharp criticism of the conflict of these people, who are part laity and part clergy, are Greek words, which are apparently used in the distribution of the Eucharist: 'Cursed are those who receive it [the holy mystery] without faith and even more those who *confess* it [only] with the mouth and give it to others: σωμα χριστου, αιμα χριστου, but who deny that it is truly his body and his blood' (§ 0374).

Is it only a question here of *words of administration* in the distribution of the eucharistic gifts or of a *homology*? Indeed, Shenoute speaks of a 'confessing'. The words of administration can be understood on the part of the priest as well as on the part of the recipient as *protestatio fidei* and would thus have the function of a homology. The character of a homology is also underlined by the reference to 1 Cor 12,3 given in this context: 'It is not possible for someone to speak by the Holy Spirit who says that the body and blood of Christ are not the holy mystery. It is not possible for someone to say that the body and blood of Jesus Christ, the Son of God, are the holy mystery except by the Holy Spirit' (§ 0383).

We must also determine still more precisely how the following words to the conflicted priests are to be placed: 'Why do you not close your mouth, as I have already said before, when you call to the Lord: "The bread of blessing, the bread of purification and immortality and eternal life", and "the cup of immortality, the cup of the new covenant", and "this is my body", and "the blood of your only begotten Son Jesus Christ our Lord"?' (§ 0355). These words are spoken in Coptic in the exhortation, but they are without doubt quotations from the euchologion. What can we learn from this about the liturgy that Shenoute celebrated? The answer to this question cannot be attempted here, but on this see H. Engberding, 'Ein Problem der Homologia vor der Hl. Kommunion in der ägyptischen Liturgie', *OCP* 2 (1936), 145–54; O. H. E. Burmester, 'The Greek Kirugmata Versicles & Responses and Hymns in the Coptic Liturgy', ibid., 363–94.

The situation in the Coptic church of Upper Egypt and also of other regions in regard to the understanding of the Eucharist may be illustrated still somewhat further by two documents.

(1) Origen's writing on prayer contains a significant indication: 'But indeed only the influence of the Adversary, seeking to associate the most impious teachings with the name of Christ and the doctrine of the Son of God, could persuade certain men that they ought not to pray. The protagonists of this view are they who do away with all sense perception and practice neither baptism nor the Eucharist. They quibble about the Scripture . . .'[99] Does this not already include the radical denial of the bodily birth of Christ – even if it is a birth from the Virgin – as Shenoute must criticize it? One difference is considerable: Origen knows people who scorn even baptism and Eucharist. Shenoute's deniers of the (virgin) birth of Christ in the flesh can still take part in the Eucharist and even dispense it, yet in unbelief or with a 'symbolic' understanding. In reference to Origen, care is advisable here in the use of the terms *mystery* and *symbol*.[100]

(2) We can see a special variation in the *Gospel of Philip*. At first glance there seems to be much in agreement with the views and practices sought by Shenoute. 'The cup of blessing contains wine, contains water; it serves as *typos* of the blood over which thanks is given and is filled with the Holy Spirit. And it [the cup] belongs to the completely perfect human being. When we drink from it we receive the perfect human being.'[101] Gaffron adds: 'Among the Gnostics of the *Gos. Phil.* . . . the Eucharist is really celebrated as a festival. Bread and cup serve as *typoi* of Jesus' flesh and blood, and present in him in turn is the heavenly syzygy [i.e., the 'Logos' and the 'Holy Spirit'], which is shared by those who receive the bread and wine of the Eucharist.'[102] Thus we find here the word incriminated by Shenoute, *typos*, which does not, however, have the rationalistic sense that he imputes to his opponents. But is it an ecclesiastical understanding of the Eucharist? 'On closer examination this so ecclesiastical

---

99. Origenes, *De orat.*, V I: GCS Or. W. 2, p. 308,16–21; English: O'Meara, ACW 19, p. 27; see Jay, *Origen's Treatise on Prayer* (London 1954), 93–94.

100. See H. Crouzel, *Origène et la 'connaissance mystique'*, Bruges 1960, with his clarifications of the history of terminology, which are also important for what follows.

101. Cf. *Gos. Phil.* § 100: Ménard (Paris 1967), 94–95; comment., 218.

102. H.-G. Gaffron, op. cit., 180.

sounding text proves to be thoroughly gnostic, at least when one reads it in the context of the whole *Gos. Phil. Typos, pneuma hagion* and *teleios anthrōpos* and their arrangement acquire in the gnostic understanding a wholly different content. For those who take or receive the *teleios anthrōpos* thereby themselves become *teleios anthrōpos*; otherwise the whole process would have no meaning at all for the Gnostics' (Gaffron, p. 176).

In comparison to Shenoute's dissidents, we see yet another variation, namely, the faith of the *Gos. Phil.* 'that Christ also bore a *sarx* or *sōma*. But this *sarx* – this is how Philip seeks to help himself – was not the usual human *sarx* but the *alēthinē sarx*; our flesh, by contrast, is only a copy of this true flesh (cf. *Gos. Phil.* § 72 [= Ménard 81,34–37]). Mary was tainted by no "power" (§ 17 [= p. 55,27–28.31–32]); Christ was born from the Virgin (§ 83 [= p. 87,18–19]) and therefore bears a [*sōma*] *teleion* (§ 72 [= p. 81,33]). The Gnostic must gain this *sarx*, for without it there is no resurrection (§ 23 [pp. 57,26–59,19]). He receives it, however, in the Eucharist (ibid.). In the flesh and blood of Christ the syzygy Logos-Holy Spirit is mysteriously present in the form of bread and wine. Those who receive bread and wine attain with it this heavenly syzygy, that is, in the sense of §§ 44, 113: they join themselves with Logos and *pneuma*; they become Logos and *pneuma*. As such they have the ability to penetrate all things with this pneumatic substance, including their earthly body, which now is so to speak no longer earthly but heavenly' (Gaffron, p. 177). There is more religious substance in these Gnostics than in the rejecters of the presence of Christ in the Eucharist who are criticized by Shenoute.

4. Shenoute and Nestorius

The leader of the monks was not occupied with the christological discussion outside Egypt until his patriarch Cyril called him to participate in the Council of Ephesus (431). We have various documents for this.

(a) Shenoute's own report

In his writing *De modestia clericorum et magistratuum*[103] he mentions that he was pressured by Cyril and others to come to Alexandria in order to be appointed bishop. He stresses that he declined to accept the invitation in order to escape the (ecclesiastical and imperial) court life so desired by others. He had himself become familiar with this hustle and bustle 'when we were far away at the great gathering of the holy ecumenical council'.[104] He had fled from it, he says, and immediately obeyed only the call of the council and thus was the first to arrive at the site of the council, which Cyril himself had acknowledged before the other bishops at Ephesus. He also reports on his stay there in the writing *The Last Judgement*.[105] In the context of the Nestorian controversy he had reflected (*hoc indago et in hoc inquiro*) on what Mt 25,31ff. asserts about the identity

---

103. *Sinuthii Vita et Opera* III (= CSCO 96 [H. Wiesmann]), no. 15, pp. 15–18.

104. Sinuthius, *De modest. cler.*: CSCO 96, p. 16,29–30. In the context Shenoute's words recall the harsh criticism by Gregory of Nazianzus of the bishops' quarrels over rank at councils. See J. Barbel, *Gregor von Nazianz, Die fünf theologischen Reden* (Testimonia 3), Düsseldorf 1963, 18–19 (from ep. 130).

105. Sinuthius, *De iudicio finali*: CSCO 96 (V), no. 47, p. 127,14–21.

of the 'Son of Man' who, in accordance with the economy of salvation, comes again for judgement with him 'who is God and Son of God according to divinity'. Certainly he must have assumed with Cyril that Nestorius divided 'Son of Man' and 'Son of God' between two subjects or persons. Thus Shenoute supported the Alexandrian christological position. The catchword *theotokos* does not occur in this passage, but we find it in the already briefly mentioned christological catechesis in accordance with the Egyptian tradition present before Shenoute.[106] Otherwise the archimandrite mentions the third council in previously published texts only under the viewpoint of canonical law-giving, namely, that the Christmas festival is to be celebrated for two full days.[107] Finally, in a letter from the year 432 the stay in Ephesus is mentioned.[108]

(b) Shenoute's quotations from Nestorius[109]

A catechesis of Shenoute still to be discussed more closely does not expressly mention Ephesus but rather Nestorius as the denier of the divinity of Christ: 'Nestorius, who had also been given the name of bishop, whose tongue hung completely out of his mouth and who died in exile, said with some like-minded people: "she [i.e. Mary] who bore a competent (ΧΡΗϹΤΟϹ) man"; thus he compared Christ with Moses, David and others.'[110] The problem that led to the mention of Nestorius is christologically central and is given at the beginning of the Lefort catechesis:

> One day it happened – we had discussed the divinity of the Redeemer and that he made himself human and lived with human beings while he was completely God and Son of

---

106. See H.-F. Weiss, 'Zur Christologie des Schenute von Atripe', *BSAC* 20 (1969/70), 191; G. Giamberardini, *La Mediazione di Maria nella Chiesa Egiziana*, Cairo 1952, 6; idem, *La Teologia Assunzionista nella Chiesa Egiziana*, Jerusalem 1951, 124–25.

107. Sinuthius, *De synodo Ephesina*: CSCO 96 (V), no. 31, p. 54,5–6. See also *Le synaxaire alexandrin*, ed. J. Forget, CSCO 78 (V), 286–287 (Christmas on 28 and 29 Kīhak).

108. G. Zoega, *Catalogus cod. copt.*, Rome 1810, 459; E. Amélineau, *Oeuvres de Schenoudi. Texte copte et trad. franç.* I 3, pp. 365–441. J. Timbie, 'The State of Research on the Career of Shenoute of Atripe', in Pearson and Goehring, *Roots of Egyptian Christianity* (1986), 269–70, nevertheless doubts Shenoute's participation at the Council of Ephesus (431).

109. L. T. Lefort, 'Catéchèse Christologique de Chenoute', *ZÄS* 80 (1955), 40–55, with Coptic text and French trans. – H.-F. Weiss, 'Zur Christologie des Schenute von Atripe', *BSAC* 20 (1969/70), 177–209.

110. L. T. Lefort, p. 45,1–4.

God – that some of the crowd raised objections politely and without malice. They wondered about what they had heard . . .[111]

Thus we previously had only a few indications of the Nestorius problem in Shenoute. The Orlandi exhortation offers in §§ 0464–83 a more lengthy discussion of Nestorius, in which some of his main statements are given and criticized. We will present them first in the form in which Shenoute offers them and then will look for documentation from the writings of Nestorius.

At first it is not a matter of Nestorius alone. There are also other deniers of the divinity of Christ, probably in Shenoute's surroundings: 'Others say that he . . . is not God' (§ 0451). Various fragmentary words in §§ 0452–55 attest that Christ's divinity and humanity, his birth out of a woman and the entrance of the pre-existent One into the world were vigorously discussed. On these topics various opinions, probably also including gnostic ones, were presented. In §§ 0462–63 the pre-existence of Christ and his position as creator of the universe are clearly set forth. Then Shenoute concentrates on the chief opponent:

§ 0464: 'He, however, whom the prince of darkness shackled with his thoughts, Nestorius, this fox, who could never tolerate anything right, not even the synod that was held at Ephesus by blessed and godly bishops, does not believe that and says that Christ was a human being in whom God dwelled, and that the Logos entered him after he was born by Mary.'

§ 0465: 'Indeed, he said this: "Even if you search the whole scripture, the Old and the New [Testament], you will not find that it ever gives to him who was crucified [the name of] God." And also: "Christ said to his disciples: Touch me and see that the Spirit has neither nerves nor flesh, as you see that I have. Thus if he was a god" – he says – "would he not have said: Touch me and see that I am a Spirit and God?"'

§ 0469: 'And this other: "Eloi, Eloi, lema sabachthani" [Mt 27,46 par.], [on this] he said: "It is the flesh that cries to the divinity: Why have you forsaken me?" and "that the divinity ascended on high before he was nailed to the wood".'

§ 0470: 'He actually said in his letter: "Him who cries: My God, my God, why have you forsaken me? [Mt 27,46 par.], even him I worship with the divinity, because it had united with him."'

§ 0480: 'He also said: "Therefore one may not say that the Virgin bore a god" and "I will not say that the one is a god who was in the womb nine months, was suckled and slowly grew up." And he said: "It is written: Take the child and flee to Egypt [cf. Mt 2,13]; he did not say: Take God!"'

§ 0483: 'Numerous, by the way, are the blasphemies [that I do not cite], because I detest it and hate to repeat the words of this unclean one . . .'

What is the status of the archimandrite's information about Nestorius? Can these accusations be documented from the writings of the deposed bishop of Constantinople? We will briefly go through the individual paragraphs:

§ 0464: This pointed adoptionistic doctrine of indwelling was not advocated by Nestorius. In no way did he accept a (later) entrance of the Logos into the '[mere] human being' born by Mary. In his defence against the theopaschitism of the Arians and the Apollinarians ('God

---

111. L. T. Lefort, p. 43.

suffered') he fell into so strong a terminology of differentiation that he could be mis-interpreted in the sense of a 'separation' of the natures into two persons (cf. Nestorius, *On Heb* 3,1: Loofs, *Nestoriana*, p. 242,15–22). Shenoute intensified these weaknesses, as a comparison of the closing of § 0464 and Loofs, *Nestoriana*, p. 278,3–4 shows: 'God was the Logos, united to the human being and dwelling in him.'

§ 0465 a: On the theme 'crucified God' the closest Nestorius passage is from a speech in Marius Mercator: Loofs, *Nestoriana*, p. 269,14–28. How it is to be understood is shown in *JdChr*[3]I, p. 650.

§ 0465 b: In the presently known Nestorius texts Lk 24,39b appears only in the unauthentic counter-anathemas (cf. Loofs, *Nestoriana*, p. 216,15–17); Shenoute could, how-ever, have had an authentic one before him.

§ 0469: The first part of the quotation is in Severus of Antioch: 'That which said, God my God, why have you forsaken me? was human nature, O wise one' (Loofs, *Nestoriana*, p. 360, XIV). That is, Nestorius, still in the spirit of the old anti-Arianist and anti-Apollinarianist apologetic, did not want to let the cry of foresakenness on the cross be regarded as proof of diminished divinity or as *passio* of the Logos as Logos. With the same intention various Fathers had attributed the cry of foresakenness precisely to the *sarx* of Christ (cf. *JdChr* I[3], p. 468; *CCT* I[2], pp. 313–14). – What is said of the ascension of the divinity before the passion is old gnostic-docetic teaching, but not Nestorius.

§ 0470 is clearly recognizable, though not in a letter but rather in the speech against the *theotokos*, in which Nestorius disagrees with Apollinarius: it is not God who is killed, but the human being (according to Jn 8,40). On this very human being Nestorius wants to bestow adoration on the basis of union with the divinity (cf. Loofs, *Nestoriana*, pp. 259,16–260,6). Thus Shenoute's quotation is documented.

§ 0480: These are the well-attested difficulties of Nestorius with the so-called *communicatio idiomatum*; they are motivated by his opposition to Arians and Apollinarians (cf. *JdChr* I[3], pp. 647–52; *CCT* I[2], pp. 451–56; the emphasis on the wording of Mt 2,13 is found in Loofs, *Nestoriana*, pp. 246,13–15; 278,5–14).

The way in which Shenoute reproduces and rejects Nestorius shows the status of his Christology. As he himself finds the *communicatio idiomatum* in the scripture, he says in § 0471: 'The words of the apostle, however, refute his [Nestorius's] foolishness: "The Lord of glory is he who was crucified" [1 Cor 2,8b], and "You have killed the Author of life" [Acts 3,15]. But he did not say: "He is a human being who is united with God", but rather: "Since he was in the form of God, he became obedient unto death" [cf. Phil 2,6a, 8b].' The archimandrite then tries to show how one must understand theopaschite statements: if it says: 'God died', it means this: 'Not that the *nature* [ΦΥΟΙΟ] of the divinity died, but rather *he* in the flesh, as it is written: "Christ suffered according to the flesh" [cf. 1 Pt 4,1]. Yet the divinity is not separated from the body that hangs on the wood . . .' (§ 0472).

Thus Shenoute sensed the difference between *nature* and *subject*. The divine subject suffers in the human nature. But for this he does not use the whole oppositional pair, *hypostasis–physis*. Yet this was also the way that Nestorius sought. The archimandrite, as we can see from here, could have come to an understanding of 'two natures'. But with every distinction he, vis-à-vis Nestorius, urged unity in Christ. He explains it with the body–soul analogy:

§ 0473: 'If one for instance kills a person, does one then say: "A body was killed"? Does one not say that the whole person was killed, even if the soul does not die but only the body?' (Then follows the application to Christ. One would now expect:) 'Thus if Christ was killed only in regard to the body, then "God" was killed, because the Christ is inseparably God and human being.' Yet Shenoute stays with the strict application of the anthropological comparison to Christ and thereby misses what he wanted to say vis-à-vis Nestorius, even if in so doing he brings to expression something different, namely, his teaching of the soul of Christ:

(§ 0474) 'Thus the Lord also died in the flesh, whereas he was immortal in his entire soul. So said [the apostle]: "He participated in body and soul" ' (where what is meant is probably Heb 2,14: 'Since the children are people of flesh and blood, he also in like manner assumed flesh and blood . . .').

Let us remain briefly with the theme 'body–soul' in Christ. Following the just cited passage Shenoute also comes to the interpretation of the descent into hell (*amente*). Does this descent occur in the soul or according to the divinity? The former is probable but not completely certain: (§§ 0478–79) 'People who die leave their body on the bed of those who will bury them, and their soul goes to God. He [Christ] suffered death for us, the Lord Jesus; he left his body on the wood and went forth [in the soul?] to those who were in *amente* . . . Then he returned, let his body be raised on the third day and carried it with him into heaven. He went forth clothed in it in order to come again with it to judge the dead and the living, as he said: "When the Son of Man comes in his glory" [cf. Mt 24,30b].'

As Shenoute describes the resurrection, the ascension and the return of Christ, he seems nonetheless to emphasize only divinity and *sarx*. That is, the divine *pneuma* accomplishes the descent into *amente*, frees the souls there and awakens his own body . . . This corresponds entirely to that old Coptic *Descensus* fragment, which has a special place in the history of the *descensus*.[112]

---

112. See on this A. Shisha-Halevy, 'Unpublished Shenoutiana in the British Library', *Enchoria* 5 (1975) (53–108), 102, according to Brit. Lib. Or. 3581A f. 79, Copt.: p. 76; another version of the *Descensus* was published by E. A. Budge according to Cod. Mus. Brit. Or. 5001 (end of 7th cent.?): text in the translation of H. Quecke in A. Grillmeier, *Mit ihm und in ihm*, pp. 118–19; on the whole see J. Zandee, 'De Descensus ad Inferos bij de Kopten', *NTT* 9 (1954–1955), 158–74. – An express confession to the soul of Christ in the *Descensus* is found in H. G. E. White, *The Monasteries of the Wadi 'n Natrûn*. Part I, New York 1926, rpt. 1973, p. 13 (frag. 2, verso). That the Coptic church confesses to the soul of Christ was already established not only by Cyril, Dioscorus and Timothy Aelurus but also by a beautiful interpretation by C (= Nicaeno-Constantinopolitanum) (end of 13th cent.). See Ibn Sabâ', *La perle précieuse*, chap. 34: PO 16, p. 715: '*Et s'est fait homme*, c'est-à-dire que le corps pris de la Vierge Marie et grandissant par le pain et le vin, corps qui possède une âme véritable. [Ceci est dit] pour que l'on ne s'imagine pas que c'est un corps composé de chair et de sang, mais sans âme intelligente et raisonnable, car l'on n'est appelé homme que parce que l'on possède une âme douée de ces qualités.' We recall that Apollinarius did not want to allow the designation *human being* for Christ because he denied him a human spiritual soul. See A. Grillmeier, *JdChr* I³, p. 788. On confession to the soul of Christ in the Coptic church, see G. Giamberardini, 'La doctrine christologique des Coptes', *POC* 13 (1963) (211–20), 214.

All of this shows that while Shenoute made a certain contribution to the problems that at the time occupied Nestorius and the whole Eastern church, he still did not achieve a breakthrough. He stands on the level of the Cyrillian judgement in the case of Nestorius. He brings no complete clarity into the anthropological comparison and its application to Christ. With all of that, the new exhortation fits very well into the period between 431 and 451. § 0464 speaks of the teaching of Nestorius in the present, from which we could infer that he knows that his opponent is still alive. From the texts cited here one need not conclude that there were larger Nestorian groups in Thebaid. Along with Nestorius he no doubt also has Origenists in mind.

(c) Shenoute and Nestorius in legend

As is expected, the relationship Shenoute–Cyril–Ephesus was soon embellished with legendary features. Prominent here is Besa, the follower and successor of Shenoute in the White Monastery.[113] He tells of the meeting of his abbot with Nestorius in the council church at Ephesus. After the enthronement of the four Gospels 'the godless Nestorius, with a great exhibition of his pride and his impertinence, entered [the church]. He took away the four holy Gospels, laid them on the floor and sat down himself on the throne. My father Shenoute, however, at the sight of this deed of Nestorius, sprang quickly into the middle of the holy fathers, picked up the Gospels from the floor and with them struck the godless Nestorius on the chest. He said, "Do you want the Son of God to lie on the floor [i.e., in the form of the four Gospels] while you sit on the throne?"'[114] But Nestorius disputed the abbot's right to be at the council, since he was neither bishop nor archimandrite nor abbot but only a simple monk. Shenoute answered this by referring to his divine mission to unmask the heretic who denied the redeeming suffering of the only begotten Son of God. Then he announced to the heresiarch the punishment of God. Immediately the latter fell from his usurped throne and in the middle of the gathering became through obsession the prey of Satan. Afterward, with general acclamation, Shenoute was appointed archimandrite by Cyril.[115]

---

113. See the *Vita Bohairica* = CSCO 129 (V), Louvain 1951; cf. Chapter Two below.
114. *Sin. Vit. Boh.*, 128–29: CSCO 129, pp. 33,32–34,4.
115. Op. cit., 129–30: CSCO 129, p. 34,4–20.

The whole story is a legend, because Nestorius never appeared in St Mary's church before the gathering of bishops around Cyril.[116] It expresses well, however, the interpretation of the 'case of Nestorius' in Shenoutian and Coptic circles in general. At Ephesus it was a question of overcoming the dethronement of the teaching of the Gospels and the enthronement of the heresy of Nestorius, as it was seen by Cyril. The story of the obsession as punishment for the scandal of Nestorius was probably brought about through the designation of the deposed patriarch as the 'new Judas', who also imitated the old one in that Satan entered into him.[117]

Summary

The significance of the Shenoute exhortation edited by T. Orlandi for the clarification of the faith situation in the Coptic church of Upper Egypt in the time between the third and fourth councils can hardly be overestimated.

(1) In the new text we have perhaps the first proofs of knowledge of individual Nag Hammadi writings in the region of the Shenoutian and Pachomian monastic settlements. For what he calls 'apocrypha' Shenoute is probably referring to the catalogue of Apa Athanasius. Yet in the Easter festal letter of 367 this index does not cover everything that is

---

116. The fact that Nestorius did not appear at the Cyril synod was still known to Severus of Ashmunein, *Hist. Patr.*, cited by T. Orlandi, *Storia della Chiesa di Alessandria* II, Milan-Varese, 84. – Also legendary are the reports of several miraculous trips of Shenoute on a white cloud. The first journey was to Constantinople and back (*Sin. Vit. Boh.*, 54–63: CSCO 129, pp. 16–18). Emperor Theodosius II wanted to see the saint and speak to him. He wanted to be blessed by him. – On a second trip, which Shenoute undertook with other brothers to Constantinople, he performed a feeding miracle for his fellow travellers (CSCO 129, 76–79, pp. 21–22). – The most striking event is reported by Besa and Patriarch Benjamin I. It concerns the return trip from Ephesus, during which Shenoute is supposed to be proven as a prophet and man of the Spirit. He was hindered from boarding the ship either by the crew (Besa) or by a small boy (Benjamin I). After a prayer by Shenoute a white cloud appeared and carried him and his followers away *in raptus*. In the middle of the sea he is spotted by Cyril, who asks of him a blessing as the 'new Elijah' (CSCO 129, p. 7,20). Then Shenoute went quickly into his monastery. Cf. Besa: CSCO 129, 18, pp. 7,5–8,14; C. D. G. Müller, *Die Homilie über die Hochzeit zu Kana*, Heidelberg 1968, 291–94. Shenoute as the 'new Elijah' was already clothed with his mantle: *Sin. Vit. Boh.*, 7: CSCO 129, p. 3,30–31; p. 4,1–3; ibid., 10, p. 4,30, has talk of Elijah as *Israelis auriga* (cf. 2 Kings 2,12–14); Hymn III: CSCO 96 (V), p. 138, speaks therefore also of the cloud as the *currus Israelis*. – The above-mentioned journey to Emperor Theodosius II perhaps has as background a historical fact that is embellished to a legend. Cf. J. Leipoldt, *Schenute*: TU 25, pp. 90–91, with a fragment of a letter of Shenoute to an emperor, whether Theodosius II or Marcian (which is less likely); cf. on this *Sin. Vit. Boh.*, 54–67: CSCO 129, pp. 16–19.

117. Cf. ACO I 1, 2, p. 64; this is probably based on a combination of Lk 22,3 and Jn 13,27.

given here as apocryphal. So the subordinates of the abbot refer to 'another gospel outside the four Gospels and which the church has not condemned as heretical'. In addition, a title is given that is not known to the archimandrite: 'Gospel of Jesus Christ, the Son of God, begotten by the angels' (§ 0309). All this together means that despite the Athanasian prohibition, the reading of the apocrypha has by no means ceased. If the burial of the Nag Hammadi library can be connected with the publication of the Easter festal letter of 367 – which is not proven – then either there were other copies of these or other writings of this kind still in circulation or new collections were being made.

(2) Shenoute's exhortation teaches us that the Coptic church of Upper Egypt must struggle for the maintenance of orthodoxy on account of the wealth of problems that go far beyond the narrow realm of the Ephesian-Chalcedonian question and its solutions.

(3) Especially significant here is the discovery of a new phase of Origenism that does not lie along the line of Evagrius Ponticus. The boundary between this Origenism and a late Arianism and 'Nestorianism' is obviously fluid. The effect of these ideas on Shenoute's subordinates is a rationalist distancing from the sacramental life of the church.

(4) Although there were contacts with the Alexandrian church, the independent life of the Upper Egyptian communities of monks and Christians is nonetheless strongly in evidence. A faith history of the Coptic church that is limited purely to Alexandria must be regarded as inadequate. Yet again, the common developments must not be overlooked, also in regard to the appearance of docetic-gnostic groups in Alexandria, as Timothy Aelurus has shown us.

III. A SECOND CHRISTOLOGICAL CATECHESIS OF SHENOUTE

The last document that lets us know in more detail the Christology of the archimandrite was already made available to the public in 1955.[118]

Its theme is the divinity of Christ the incarnate One, who is entirely God and Son of God, although he became human and dwelled with humans. In it a dialogue develops with some hearers who are astonished

---

118. See L. T. Lefort, 'Catéchèse christologique de Chenoute', ZÄS 80 (1955), 40–45. The text was, however, already familiar to J. Leipoldt, *Schenute von Atripe*, TU 25, p. 46. It is not correct that in this sermon Nestorius is already called '*long since* dead'. On the catechesis see H.-F. Weiss, 'Zur Christologie des Schenute von Atripe', *BSAC* 20 (1969/70), 177–209.

by this message, and especially by the pre-existence of the Son before his birth from the Virgin. For the enlightenment of those perhaps still not sufficiently instructed in the Christian faith, the archimandrite answers with a series of testimonies to the pre-existence of Jesus.[119] He also refers to God's power as creator in the formation of humankind 'in his own image and likeness' (Gen 1,26) – a passage that we shall encounter in the monk Aphu as a *topos* of Coptic Christology or anthropology. One who could form humankind at all out of earth – thus Shenoute – could 'not be incapable of building his temple, the holy body, as he wanted it, in the womb of the one he praised more than all women on earth'. The following words deserve attention:

> Where could the earth [without the power of the Creator] find hand, foot, bodily shape, corporeality, head, shining hair, bright eyes, hearing ears, speaking mouth and tongue, sniffing nose, bones, flesh, nerves and all other marvellous members? All the more is this also the case for that one whom he loves, for that one whom he let become reality in Mary's womb. 'According to an economy' she is his mother, but according to the highest divinity [i.e., in regard to Christ as God] she is his maid.[120]

A similar specification of the corporeality of Christ is also contained, as already noted, in the letter of Patriarch Dioscorus, which he wrote from exile in Gangra to Secundianus(?) and which Timothy Aelurus also cites.[121] It probably concerns a *topos* of Alexandrian Christology, which could be employed both polemically and unpolemically with various partners. Does Shenoute have a priority here? This is rather improbable but not impossible. The present catechesis proceeds in a relatively unpolemical tone and addresses itself to the questioning listener, whereas Dioscorus and Timothy Aelurus confront Phantasiasts and 'Mani-chaeans', opponents who, it is true, also kept the archimandrite busy. It is noteworthy that the scriptural amalgam of Heb 2,17 and 4,15 (becoming like us in all things, except sin), which is so often quoted in such a context and which was actually quoted by the two patriarchs and by the Council of Chalcedon, does not appear in the Lefort catechesis (but rather in the same context in the Orlandi exhortation [§ 0476]). The main problem of the Lefort catechesis is not the fight against Docetism but against Nestorianism. The divine pre-existence of the one who had

---

119. Cited are Jn 8,56.58; 17,5; 1,10; 1,1–3; 1 Jn 1,1.2.3; Jn 8,42; Col 1,16.17; Jn 6,62; 1 Cor 10,4; Col 1,26; Eph 3,9; Gal 4,4.

120. Translation follows Lefort, op. cit., 44.

121. See R. Y. Ebied and L. R. Wickham, 'A Collection of Unpublished Syriac Letters of Timothy Aelurus', *JTS* 21 (1970) (321–69), 360.

true corporeality in every respect is what must be explained and sub-stantiated. An old argument appears here again: the reference to the plural in Gen 1,26: 'Let us make humankind in our image, according to our likeness.'[122] According to Shenoute, the Father is speaking here to his Son, to his holy, only begotten One:

> He did not say: 'I, I will form', in order not to exclude the Son at the creation; he also did not say: 'You, you form', in order not to place himself outside this activity.

For Shenoute this results in the communion of Father and Son in the work of the creation of humankind but also 'of heaven and earth, the sun, the moon, the stars, the ocean, the heaven of heavens and all of what they contain'.[123] We know what such an emphasis meant in the (gnostic) surroundings of the archimandrite.

It is interesting that Shenoute, on the basis of 'modest works of human art' (i.e., painted linens), claims to derive proof for faith in the 'birth of God from Mary'. Here we see an example of popular catechesis. With a few brothers the archimandrite goes through picture by picture, deciphers the inscriptions and then explains the correct incarnation doctrine: Mary gave birth to 'God' but 'according to the flesh', whereas according to his divinity he is the one who formed his own flesh in the womb of Mary. In this context comes the reference to Nestorius and his shameful death, which we have already discussed.[124] Thus the Lefort catechesis was written after 451, while the Orlandi exhortation offers every sign that it was extant before 449 or 451.

Other opponents of the true doctrine of the incarnation also appear: the Origenists. They are charged above all with the denial of the eucharistic presence of the body and blood of the Lord.

> 'These are certain people among us who say this, since their hearts were wounded by the chatterings of Origen. As far as I am concerned, I respond in this way to their stupidity: Is the one who made a human being out of earth incapable of making bread and wine become body and blood?' The comparison between the proof of God's power as Creator in the creation of humankind and in the Eucharist is further clarified but then closed with the words: 'All works of God are a question of faith; if you have faith, then you possess the fullness of the mystery; if you have no faith, you also have no hope in the mystery and in the Lord of the mystery . . . Truly blessed are those who follow the scriptures; those who follow them are in obedience to the Lord of the scriptures. Miracles of miracles are all his works, those that he called into reality since the beginnings of creation and those that he will realize at the end of the ages' (Lefort, p. 45).

In this catechesis is the entire Shenoute! The proof of the power of God in creation continues in the incarnation and in the Eucharist – a display of depth that the rationalism of his Origenists cannot match.

---

122. Cf. L. T. Lefort, op. cit., 44–45.
123. Ibid., p. 44.
124. Ibid., p. 45.

IV. *SODALIS DEI ET CHRISTI AMICUS*. A CLOSING REPORT ON SHENOUTE'S CHRISTOLOGY

In light of J. Leipoldt's undisputed competence, his well-known judgement of Shenoute's 'barren', inadequate and 'so to speak Christless piety'[125] was adopted without contradiction and indeed even intensified.[126] On the basis of the newly studied homilies or exhortations this judgement must be almost reversed. We are dealing not with a 'Christless' but, on the contrary, with an emphatically 'Christocentric' spirituality. It can be called 'barren' only if one does not look for the centre and wealth of Shenoute's piety and pastoral work. In short strokes we will try to sketch him summarily as *repraesentator Christi* in his monastic community and his church.

(a) A biblical Christocentrism

We read a significant statement in the *Vita Bohairica* of Besa: 'In the recitation of the scripture [called *meditatio*[127]] he shows Christ so persistently that his call and his teachings become sweet as honey in everyone's mouth.'[128] He read and recited the scripture in such a way that for him it talked about Christ alone and for him 'Christ' himself was the scope of the scripture. This found its expression in the above-cited Jesus prayers of the Orlandi exhortation, which we may regard as an important stage in the history of the Jesus prayer in general.[129] Besa can rightly put this saying in the mouth of his father in Christ: 'Not a word have I brought forth on my own without Christ placing it on my tongue.'[130] This saying sounds so strong that one can recognize in it the reason why mention of the Holy Spirit has receded. In reality the pneumatology is included therein, as individual texts will still show us. It is the Christ become Spirit who fills and inspires Shenoute.

---

125. See n. 4 above.

126. Thus in W. Schneemelcher, 'Von Markos bis Mohammed. Vom Werden und Vergehen einer Landeskirche', *EvTh* 8 (1948/49), 401: 'absolutely barren Christology'.

127. Cf. H. Bacht, *Das Vermächtnis des Ursprungs. Studien z. frühen Mönchtum* I, Würzburg 1972, excursus I: '"Meditatio" in den ältesten Mönchsquellen', 244–64. The *Sin. Vit. Boh.* has two passages: §§ 94 and 117: CSCO 129 (V), p. 26 and 31,25–26: *noctu memoriter recitantes.* – Also: *Letters and Sermons of Besa*, Fragm. 38, I, 6: CSCO 158, p. 121: Shenoute is called 'a man who has been filled with the *recitation of the scriptures* and the pains of Christ'.

128. *Sin. Vit. Boh.*, 11: CSCO 129 (V), p. 4,33–35.

129. For more detail see A. Grillmeier, 'Das "Gebet zu Jesus" und das "Jesus-Gebet". Eine neue Quelle zum "Jesus-Gebet" aus dem Weißen Kloster', in *After Chalcedon*, FS A. Van Roey (OLA 18), Louvain 1985, 187–202.

130. *Sin. Vit. Boh.*, 11: CSCO 129 (V), p. 5,4–6.

The biblical character of the Lefort catechesis stands out solidly in that it basically substantiates its pre-existence Christology through a series of testimonies from the scripture. The Orlandi catechesis also refers to the crucial scriptural passages. In it – as in the whole development of the ecclesiastical credo – a special significance is given to Mt 28,19 in connection with Rom 6,3 and other passages. Biblically, it is above all the fullness of the mysteries of the life of Jesus that are supposed to distinguish his image of Christ decidedly from gnostic and Manichaean docetic Christology. Also taken from the scripture is the early Christian theology of the names of Christ, which could be connected well with the Jesus prayer. According to the scripture Christ is designated 'brother of the virgin or of the bride or of her sister' and 'brother, bridegroom, virgin', all of which is probably taken from Song of Songs. 'Lord, sheep and shepherd, offering and high priest, vine, rock, day and sun, sword and lamb, first and last, Word and firstborn and God, who will judge the whole world and individuals according to their works.'[131] Striking is the frequent designation of Christ as 'king', which he is on the basis of his divinity.

Although Shenoute often refers to the Cappadocian trinitarian confession to the *three persons in one essence of God*, he is a long way from any discussion of the intratrinitarian life of God. He remains rather in the incarnational, salvation-economic context of God's self-revelation in the incarnate Son and Holy Spirit, for whom he also uses (in the sense of Gregory of Nazianzus in contrast to Basil) the Nicene *homoousios*.[132] The events of Jesus' life from conception to return as judge gain their meaning for salvation through anchoring in the hypostasis of the Logos, begotten by the Father. With bitterness he sees that his gnostic and Origenistic opponents dissolve this anchoring of the humanity of Christ and the humanity itself. In the Orlandi catechesis we can experience the superhuman strength with which Shenoute must fight in his area of influence against the dissolution of the church's kerygma. He deserves

---

131. Sinuth., *Ad philosoph. gentil.*: Op. III: CSCO 96 (V), no. 18, p. 33,19–26, with scriptural references. – On Christ as 'king and God' see Op. IV: CSCO 108 (V), no. 48, p. 3,13–32, with a beautiful passage about Christ the king, with whom we will also become kings. Now, of course, we belong to the *militia Christi regis et sumpto sibi fidei scuto* [Eph 6,16] *ad pugnae locum*[?] *profecti* (ibid., p. 3,34–35).

132. Shenoute speaks, according to §§ 0803, 0805, of the 'consubstantial Trinity', which presupposes the *homoousios* also for the Holy Spirit. He also mentions the objection of the Arians that this expression is not biblical, but against this he points to Jn 10,30 and Mt 28,19.

the sobriquet 'prophet' or the 'new Elijah' or another 'John the Baptist'.

The Christocentric position of the abbot found a hagiographic expression that is probably unique in the history of mysticism and spirituality of the first Christian centuries. About him, namely, a surprising number of visions of Christ are told. In the *Vita Bohairica*[133] we count about seven appearances of Christ described in detail. Certainly, Pachomius may have been the model here, which, however, was at the same time supposed to be surpassed. When the latter was harbouring the idea of becoming a monk, he – according to the testimony of the *Epistula Ammonis* – had discussions with Meletians and Marcionites, who sought to win him for their own communions. 'Through a dream vision he was instructed that he was to listen to the kerygma of Christ that is proclaimed in the church, in which he had received baptism. "The Christ who calls you is in Alexander, the bishop of Alexandria." '[134] It is not Christ himself who appears here; it is quite different with Shenoute, who was thereby raised

---

133. *Sin. Vit. Boh.*: CSCO 129 (V), (a)§§ 22–23: p. 8; (b) §§ 25–26: p. 9. Besa meets Shenoute in conversation with Jesus, who disappears. In answer to the question who the one who disappeared was, Shenoute says: It is the Lord Jesus Christ, who was with me to tell me secrets! – Yet in the Orlandi exhortation Shenoute, in the battle against the apocrypha, rejects such communications of 'secrets' or 'new revelations'. The scripture is sufficient! (c) §§ 70–72: pp. 19–20. This vision is significant for the relationship between charisma and office (Mt 16,19). (d) §§ 115–18: pp. 31–32. Also appearing are John the Baptist, Elijah and Elisha (Shenoute is a 'prophet'!). (e) §§ 121–24: p. 32,17–23 (see below). Also appearing are prophets, apostles and Paul (§§ 138–39: pp. 35–36). (f) Christ goes with Shenoute through the desert. In a dead man who is raised, an eyewitness to the presence of Mary with Jesus on the flight to Egypt is imagined at Shmin (§§ 154–60: pp. 39–40). The end of the wandering is a cell in which Christ spoke with Shenoute about 'great mysteries' (§ 160). (g) Shenoute had the last vision at his death (see n. 136 below). – The Arabic and Ethiopian reports of Shenoute's visions, which rest on Coptic tradition, actually claim to know of ten visions, but only three are offered, of which only two belong to the ten enumerated at the beginning. The third vision is about the heavenly church. See A. Grohmann, 'Die im Äthiopischen, Arabischen und Koptischen erhaltenen Visionen Apa Schenute's von Atripe. Text und Übersetzung', ZDMG 67 (1913), 187–267; 68 (1914), 1–46. See the overview in part I, pp. 206–7, as well as the discussion of the tradition on pp. 207–11 in reference to Shenoute.

134. See H. Bacht, *Das Vermächtnis des Ursprungs. Studien zum frühen Mönchtum II. Pachomius – Der Mann und sein Werk*, Würzburg 1983, 20–21. In the Adhortationes SS. Patrum (CPG 5570), no. 70: PL 73, 965D, is the story of a vision of Christ feigned by a demon, to which the old monk closed his eyes with the reasoning: 'I want to see Christ not here but in the next life.' The devil then disappeared. Evagrius, who lived in the Kellia, rejected any vision, be it of angels or of God, that was supposed to be communicated through the senses: 'Ne désire pas voir, dit-il, de façon sensible (*aisthētōs*) les anges, les puissances ou le Christ, pour ne pas devenir complètement fou, accueillir le loup au lieu du berger et adorer les démons, nos ennemis' (*De orat.*, 115: PG 79, 1192D–1193A) (under the name of Nilus). On the whole see A. Guillaumont, 'Les visions mystiques dans le monachisme orientale chrétien', in idem, *Aux origines du Monachisme chrétien*, Bégrolles en Mauges 1979, 136–47; the last quotation is on p. 145.

above Pachomius in the eyes of his monks.[135] It is not necessary to analyse the individual visions in detail. The archimandrite is supposed to be represented as a prophet and pneumatic filled with Christ. The *Vita Bohairica* strikes the hagiographic target exactly: 'Often he talked with the Lord Jesus Christ face to face', which means: Shenoute is the new Moses and law-giver for his community (cf. Ex 32,11; Num 12,8).[136] In some Shenoute hymns this is expressly stated: 'Shenoute . . . talked with Christ the King, as Moses the law-giver', as he is also praised because Christ has revealed to him the mysteries of the last days.[137] Finally the Lord comes with his angels, accompanied by patriarchs, prophets and saints, especially the holy fathers Psoi, Antonius and Pachomius. Over the dead man resounds a voice: 'O Shenoute, companion of God and friend of Christ (*sodalis Dei et Christi amicus*)'![138] The last admonition of the dying man, however, was: 'Do not miss the synaxis, the prayers and the fasting; rather, persist with them so that you may be companions of Christ'! A christological-trinitarian doxology closes this sketch of a 'friend of Christ'.[139]

It is significant that in all these visions Jesus appears as a human being. This spirituality is governed neither by the Docetism of the apocrypha combated by Shenoute nor by the *nous* Christology of Evagrius nor even by the Logos mysticism of Origen[140] but by the veneration of Christ as a human being! Thus these visions of Christ have a special assertive value

---

135. The motif of placing Shenoute among the great monastic founders or even above the others is often found. Cf. A. Grohmann, *ZDMG* 67 (1913), 237: Christ says to Shenoute: 'Truly I say to you, you will sit with the twelve on my right and judge all monks together with Antonius and Macarius.' Ibid., n. 22, refers to E. Amélineau, *Vie de Matthieu le Pauvre*, 734: according to this Shenoute is judge over all monks together with Antonius, Pachomius, Theodore, Petronius and Macarius. In the Arabian version of the *Vita* Shenoute is even called the fourteenth apostle. The Ethiopian Synaxarium, which is probably based on a Coptic model, says about Shenoute: 'He will cheer the hearts of all the elect, the saints, and the Son of God will often confer with him' – following the translation of A. Grohmann, art. cit., *ZDMG* 67 (1913), 190, according to I. Guidi, 'Le Synaxaire éthiopien II. Le mois de Hamlê', PO 7, p. 263,15f.

136. *Sin. Vit. Boh.*, 121: CSCO 129 (V), p. 32,17–23. The whole visionary life of Shenoute is indicated.

137. Hymn. I 3; IV 5: CSCO 96 (V), pp. 132, 139; I 9: ibid., 133: *Iesus Christus creator docuit te de mysterio his temporibus novissimis*.

138. *Sin. Vit. Boh.*, 188: CSCO 129 (V), 45; ibid., 182–90: 44–45.

139. Ibid., 180: CSCO 129 (V), p. 44.

140. An Ethiopian text cited by A. Grohmann, *ZDMG* 67 (1913), 191, names, among the greatest saints that the Ethiopian church venerates, after Shenoute also Euagris. Whether this means Evagrius of Pontus cannot be investigated here. – Dependence on Origen, especially for emphasis on the name *Jesus* and for name theology in general, may be linked with the rejection of Origen for other reasons. Cf. A. Grillmeier, *JdChr* I³, pp. 64–66.

for both Coptic and Ethiopian monasticism.[141] Shenoute more than others guarantees that the Coptic church precisely in its popular areas accepted no diminution of the reality of Christ's humanity. A. von Harnack's often-cited statement[142] that Shenoute has no Christology but a 'superstitious view that tolerated theologically only Monophysitism' is ingenious but an unjust distortion of the facts.

(b) A salvation-economic theology of the one history of creation and salvation
Vis-à-vis gnostic inclinations to accept a multitude of worlds and indeed even a doubling of the divine principle, to deny the unity of Old and New Testament, of 'higher' and 'lower history', to separate spirit and matter, to attain the return to the *pleroma* through the release of the spiritual from matter and not through bringing home the creation, we find here a theology that does justice both to *réalités terrestres* and to the primacy of the spirit. Notable is the fitting of the creator power of the one triune God into the picture of the world and history. The idea of creation is linked with the central events of redemption. Let us recall the emphasis on (1) the uniqueness of Creator and world; (2) the creation of humankind as the image of God in view of Christ; (3) the creator power of God in the conception of Christ in the womb of the Virgin, from whom is born the One who is to lead all people to the resurrection; (4) the creative effect of the eucharistic presence of Christ under the signs of bread and wine.

(c) A kerygmatic theology
Although many of his writings bear somewhat demanding titles, deliverance from the advance of the 'apocrypha', in which he includes all non-ecclesiastical writing, is to be sought not in speculative counterproposals but in the persistent proclamation of the baptismal faith. The preservation of the 'kerygma' in the unity of homily, catechesis and liturgy as given in the universal church also remained for Shenoute's monastery and community the deliverance from the *'polymorphos Gnosis'*. His Gnostics, to be sure, also know about this, but they interpret this kerygma in a consciously different way, especially in regard to Christ and the Eucharist.

---

141. See A. Grohmann, art. cit.
142. Cf. n. 4 above.

(d) A pre-Chalcedonian Christology in service to the patriarch Dioscorus
The kerygmatic character of his theology corresponds to the limited use
of technical theological language. In the presently known writings the
mia-physis formula does not appear, although Shenoute certainly knew
it.[143] Missing also is a more thorough christological discussion. In the
intensified, life-threatening crisis in the monasticism and church of
Upper Egypt between 431 and 451, it was a question of working out the
universal church's basic outline of faith in Christ and bringing it to bear.
Whether Shenoute was drawn into the battle over Chalcedon, and what
position he took, cannot be determined. It is true that he was invited to
the council, together with Paphnūte, the archimandrite of Tabennēse,
but because of an illness he could not answer this call.[144] To the extent
that he still adopted as his own the conviction of many monks that the
new council with its two-natures doctrine had defined Nestorianism, his
decision would clearly have been against it and for Dioscorus. This
indeed became more and more the position of the Alexandrian and
Coptic churches to the present day.[145] Probably some, but not all, of the
Pachomians, neighbours of the White Monastery, held to Chalcedon.[146]
Despite his veneration of Pachomius, on this issue Shenoute would likely

---

143. We find it in the Coptic lectionary for Holy Week in a homily of Ps.-Chrysostom.
See O. H. E. Burmester, 'The Homilies or Exhortations of the Holy Week Lectionary', *Mus*
45 (1932) (21–70), 65: 'And after He had risen from the dead, He raised His Flesh by the
power of His Divinity which is *a single Divine Nature with Him*.' In this lectionary there are
nine quotations from Shenoute texts (see p. 251 below).

144. Cf. J. Leipoldt, *Schenute*, TU 25, p. 90.

145. Cf. G. Giamberardini, 'La doctrine christologique des Coptes', *POC* 13 (1963),
211–20.

146. See M. Cramer and H. Bacht, 'Der antichalkedonische Aspekt im historisch-
biographischen Schrifttum der koptischen Monophysiten (6.–7. Jahrhundert)', in *Chalkedon*
II (314–38), 334. First, the Pachomians of Metanoia-Kanopos in the vicinity of Alexandria
were Chalcedonian. The opponents of Timothy Aelurus and Peter Mongus come from this
monastery. The Pachomian Paul Tabennesiotes as patriarch under Justinian becomes the
Chalcedonian restorer in 537. Outspoken opponents of Chalcedon in Justinian's time, on the
other hand, are Pachomians Abraham and Apollo of Pbôu, a place that already in the lifetime
of Pachomius became the capital of his monastic community. Called to Constantinople to
Emperor Justinian, the abbot Abraham refused to accept Chalcedon and was therefore
deposed as the head of his monastery. 'Returning to Egypt, Abraham entered Shenoute's
monastery in Atripe . . . where until the end of his life he peacefully occupied himself with
the copying of manuscripts' (op. cit., 335). Abraham probably did not look for refuge in a
monastery sympathetic to Chalcedon even if he did not want to be propagandistically active.
– The speech at the consecration of the great monastery of St Pachomius, which is ascribed
to Timothy Aelurus, is unauthentic. See CPG 5491; A. van Lantschoot, 'Allocution de
Timothée d'Alexandrie', *Mus* 47 (1934), 13–56. – See J. E. Goehring, 'Chalcedonian Power
Politics and the Demise of Pachomian Monasticism', *Occasional Papers of the Institute for
Antiquity and Christianity* 15 (1989), 1–20.

have held to his patriarch Dioscorus. This can be inferred from the above-mentioned letter of the patriarch to Shenoute, which reveals a strong relationship of confidence.

Excursus: On the wider Coptic-christological context of Shenoute's exhortation

We have a few additional sources that lead into the time of the (younger) Shenoute. Again the name of Origen plays a role. But the motifs of the struggle are different here.

(a) Anthropomorphism against Origenism in the 'Life of Aphu'[147]
In the desert in the vicinity of Oxyrhynchos around 395 a monk named Aphu lived together with his animals. In that year he went to the Easter festival in the church to hear the sermon. Read aloud was the Easter festal letter of Patriarch Theophilus of Alexandria, who at this time was still a follower of Origenism. To his astonishment the eremite heard a sentence 'that did not agree with the knowledge of the Holy Spirit'. It read: 'The humanity (*uomo*) that we bear is not the image of God.'[148] Struck by this, he set out for Alexandria, reached the patriarch and had the afore-mentioned Easter sermon read to him. He really heard the quoted words. The monk bravely disagreed. The patriarch pointed to the difficulty of recognizing this image of God in an Ethiopian, a cripple, a blind person. Quickly came the answer, namely, a reference to Gen 1,26–27 on the creation of humankind in the image and likeness of God. Theophilus claimed that this applied only to Adam himself (i.e., in the prelapsarian state), but not to his sons and descendants, whose misery Theophilus described very concretely, and then he concluded: 'I am afraid to say that

---

147. See W. Rossi, *I papiri copti del Museo Egizio di Torino (1887–92)*, vol. I, f. 3, pp. 5–22; E. Drioton, 'La discussion d'un moine anthropomorphite audien', *ROC* 20 (1915–17), 92–100, 113–28; G. Florovsky, 'Theophilus of Alexandria and Apa Aphu of Pemdje', in *Wolfson Jubilee Volume*, Jerusalem 1965, 275–310; T. Orlandi, 'Estratto dalla "Vita di Aphu"', in S. Felici (ed.), *Cristologia e catechesi patristica* 1, Rome 1980, 219–21, with a better translation than in Drioton. On anthropomorphism see G. van der Leeuw, art. 'Anthropomorphismus', *RAC* 1, 446–50. Since Augustine, *Haer.* 50: PL 42, 39, the Audians have been confused with the anthropomorphites (as still in Drioton). See H.-C. Puech, art. 'Audianer', *RAC* 1, 910–15.

148. T. Orlandi, art. cit., p. 219.

a sick or suffering person bears the image of the impassible and perfect God.'[149] But the monk said: it takes faith to recognize this image in people, just as one needs faith at the celebration of the holy Eucharist to recognize in bread and wine the body and blood of Christ.[150]

Two standpoints seemed to be mutually exclusive: (1) the assumption resting on literal exegesis that human beings have the right, on the basis of Gen 1,26–27 and Jas 3,9, to think of God in human terms because humankind, after all, was created in his image. Critics of Christianity like Celsus found fault with this 'anthropomorphism', which they say Christians adopted from the Jews, and they themselves felt greatly superior with their concept of God. (2) Already in the Old Testament, however, the other standpoint was emphasized: that one cannot and may not make an image of God. Pagan Greek and Christian theology expanded this idea – even to the rationalism and spiritualism of Evagrius, who under the name of Theophilus is probably under discussion here.[151] We see that through reference to 'faith', with which both the image of God in humankind and the real presence of Christ with flesh and blood in the Eucharist are accessible, the monk Aphu to some degree aptly overcomes, on the one hand, the crass anthropomorphism of other monks as well as, on the other, the anti-corporeal spiritualism of the Origenists. Although Shenoute mastered this problem above all through a sound anthropology and his conception of the body–soul unity, and although the quarrel with anthropomorphism plays no role in the texts known to us, he sees himself, nonetheless – as we have ascertained – confronted with strong rationalist tendencies that certainly also have to do with Origenism. After 399 Patriarch Theophilus turned away from Evagrianism and became its most vehement opponent. Thus Shenoute, in the context of his exhortation, could rather quote in detail the Easter festal letter of the year 401 and above all on the damnation of the doctrine of apocatastasis, the redemption of demons (for Origen, according to Shenoute, Christ is *daemonum quoque mediator*), the re-creation of mortal

---

149. Ibid., p. 220.
150. Ibid.
151. On Hellenistic intellectualism and rationalism in Origenistic monasticism see A. Favale, *Teofilo d'Alessandria (345 c.–412). Scritti, Vita e Dottrina*, Turin etc. 1958, 93ff.; A. Grillmeier, 'Markos Eremites und der Origenismus', in FS Marcel Richard III (TU 125, 1981) (253–83), 274–75.

bodies, although Christ has conquered death once and for all.[152] In a certain fragment of Shenoute's,[153] in a sentence closing the above line of thought, we read:

> Now let us leave the maliciousness of Origen and stay away from [books] that are called *apocrypha* . . . in accordance with all that we have said in this *exegesis* and [what is] in the writings of the blessed (*makarios*) archbishop Apa Theophilus.[154]

(b) Coptic Origenists against anthropomorphism

Without really knowing it, the history of Christology has had already since 1915 some important documents at its disposal, which had been well edited and translated but still not satisfactorily arranged even by A. Ehrhard. They can make a contribution by shedding some light on the turn of the fourth and fifth century. T. Orlandi takes a new path to the clarification of the history of tradition and theology of the collection of 'Agathonicus of Tarsus'.[155] This dossier will occupy us also for the post-Chalcedonian period, yet for the moment only with the 'catechesis' (thus T. Orlandi) of a Coptic monk. T. Orlandi would like to place him among the followers of Evagrius. This might be harder to prove. But certainly it concerns the problem of anthropomorphism, that is, the possibility of ascribing a human form to God. The position of 'Agathonicus' interests us above all in regard to Christology. Whereas in the text of the monk Aphu the problem of the likeness of God was solved without recourse to Christology (cf. Col 1,15–20), here reference to Christ is

---

152. Cf. Theophilus of Alex., *Osterfestbrief a. 401* = Jerome, ep. 96: Hilberg II: CSEL LV, 159–81; PL 22, 774–90; A. Favale, op. cit., 7–8. The long quotation is from Shenoute K 9206, P. 167 (after a gap); cf. W. E. Crum, *Der Papyruscodex saec. VI–VII der Phillippsbibliothek in Cheltenham. Koptische theologische Schriften. Mit einem Beitrag von A. Ehrhard* (SWGS 18), Strasbourg 1915, pp. XVII–XVIII, where it is more precisely described. Cf. § 6: PL 22, p. 778,1–31; § 9: p. 781,4 ss. and §§ 10–13 (end of col. 784,9) = CSEL LV, pp. 163,13–164,10; 167,27–172,28. – On the 'turning' of Patr. Theophilus from Origenism to relentless opposition see A. Favale, op. cit., 93–95, 105–15. Cf. Socrates, *HE* VI 7: Hussey II, pp. 676–82; Sozomen., *HE* VIII, 11: Bidez-Hansen (GCS 50), Berlin 1960, 363–64; PG 67, 1544C.

153. W. E. Crum, op. cit., p. XVIII.

154. When in this text Origen and the apocrypha are juxtaposed, this does not mean that the works of Origen are identical with the apocrypha.

155. On the following see T. Orlandi, 'Il Dossier copto di Agatonico di Tarso. Studio letterario e storico', in D. W. Young (ed.), *Studies presented to H. J. Polotsky*, Beacon Hill 1981, 269–99. Presupposed are the editorial and translating efforts of W. E. Crum and the interpretations of the texts by A. Ehrhard (1915). T. Orlandi comes to quite different results from those of Ehrhard. The codex is now in the Bibl. Bodmeriana of Cologny-Genève. Of the seven pieces, only two are relevant to the clarification of Shenoute's exhortation: no. 1, the *Fides Agathonici* on anthropomorphism; no. 7: *Apologia de incredulitate*. Agathonicus belongs to the side of the Origenists who spoke against anthropomorphism.

made immediately. We will follow the main idea of the 'confession of faith' that 'Agathonicus' presents:[156]

Although God is the Creator of all things above and below heaven, it would not be right to say: 'God is in this form', which would be a blasphemy against the divinity and a falling in with the archon of darkness. 'But it is right to think with integrity of the body (*sōma*) that Christ bore. But the divinity that united with the flesh (*sarx*) is inexpressible. The body (*sōma*) is called Christ, for the explanation of "Christ" is "the one who has been anointed".'[157] One must exclude the idea of thinking of the 'divinity' of Christ in some kind of form. 'For we believe of the Son that he is the Word of the Father; and [of] the Holy Spirit that he is his breath; [and we believe of] the Trinity (*trias*) of the same essence (*homoousios*) that it is incorporeal (*asōmatos*), without beginning and without end.'[158] To think of God in human form is not supported by Gen 1,26. One cannot conceive of the essence and form of the holy Trinity. It takes a special wisdom to understand the biblical statements of the 'eyes of God', etc. It is true that God in his omnipotence as Creator can assume various forms at will.[159] In this very variety lies the proof 'that they [i.e., the various examples of this from the Bible] do not restrict the divinity to a small, weak . . . being, in the manner of human beings, who do not change themselves out of their wretchedness'.[160]

'Agathonicus' seeks to solve the problem of God's taking form with reference to Christ in such a way that the corporeality and divinity of Christ are clearly distinguished. One can perceive a certain tendency towards a separation Christology that is typically Origenistic, as, in our view, the Opusculum XI of Marcus Eremita shows.[161] In our text, however, it is still subdued. Nevertheless, Origenistic traits are recognizable:

Thus those whose hearts are inspired at the time of their praying, they like to pray to the Son of God, who bears (*phorein*) the body (*sōma*) in which he saved humankind. For the Father is in the Son and the Son in the Father and in[?] the Holy Spirit . . . And the Word of the Father embodied himself in the Virgin as impassible (*apathēs*). He became passible (*pathētos*), however, of his own will, not through impotence. Of his own will he died, and on the third day he rose from the dead. He took the flesh (*sarx*) up into heaven, will also come in it in order to judge (*krinein*), and will judge everyone. It is this [flesh] that on the table mingles (*koinonein*) with the bread when it is blessed, as Paul said. And it is also his blood that mingles with the [wine] cup, after the latter becomes blood, as the priest proclaims aloud: Σῶμα καὶ αἷμα Χριστοῦ.[162]

We recall the role played by the question of prayer *to* Jesus in Origen and in the exhortation of Shenoute. The latter had to defend himself against

---

156. See the German translation in W. E. Crum, op. cit., pp. 76–81; Italian in T. Orlandi, in S. Felici (ed.), *Cristologia e catechesi patristica* 1, pp. 217–18.

157. W. E. Crum, op. cit., p. 77.

158. Ibid., p. 78.

159. See the almost identical texts from Tertullian and Ps.-Clem., *Hom.* 20, 6, 8 in A. Grillmeier, *JdChr* I³, p. 771, n. 6.

160. W. E. Crum, op. cit., p. 79.

161. See A. Grillmeier, *Markos Eremites* (TU 125), pp. 272–75.

162. W. E. Crum, op. cit., pp. 80–81.

massive Origenism in this respect. The same problem is discreetly indicated here. 'To pray to the Son' is so emphatically said here that it can only mean a reference to the pure divinity. This points to Evagrius. Can the 'one Christ' with divinity and corporeality be simply adored as such? The Coptic monk seems to have reservations. Therefore he also describes so clearly the relationship of Father, Son and Spirit, the three hypostases in one essence (*ousia*) of God.[163] In the incarnation he emphasizes that the Logos remained impassible, that death was adopted out of his own fullness of power, but only in the flesh. The Antiochenes could have affirmed all of this with no problem. Thus if Origenistic exegesis is also applied and the accent of the Christology rests clearly on the emphasis of the pure spiritual divinity, if finally a certain looseness is given to the unity in Christ, then an Evagrian spirit shines through; the main intention of the monk, however, lies in warding off the primitive anthropomorphism of unenlightened exegesis. Thus we are in the time of the archimandrite of the White Monastery, but we hear very little of the serious errors that are buzzing through the heads there.

(c) 'Agathonicus' between Christian Gnostics and Patriarch Theophilus/Shenoute?

It is a question of item no. 7 in the collection of 'Agathonicus', as T. Orlandi interprets it, of the 'Apologia . . . on Unbelief':[164]

> The end of the fourth century saw the last flourishing of the Egyptian gnostic circles, which are attested, for example, by the texts of Nag Hammadi. In these texts, which in the majority are related to a Christian and Jewish-Christian culture founded on the Bible, the return to pagan culture is based precisely on Plato and Homer . . . In the same period this type of polemic was also tackled by Shenoute, the main representative of southern Egyptian culture of Pachomian provenance. But he [Shenoute] stood decidedly on the side of the anti-Origenists and cited with visible satisfaction the important festal letter of Theophilus on the topic, while he combined this with long anti-gnostic observations. Our author [i.e., 'Agathonicus'] and his surroundings seem to us to be in the middle of the road between the Christian gnosticizing circles and the position of the hierarchy in Alexandria and of Shenoute.[165]

'Agathonicus' does not feel in agreement with the proceedings of Patriarch Theophilus against the Origenists and therefore in his strong temptations can find no comfort from the 'shepherd'; thus he takes part in the Gnostics' criticism of the hierarchy.[166] These sharp words may well

---

163. Ibid., p. 80; Copt.: p. 86.
164. 'Apologia of Agathonicus, Bishop of Tarsus in Cilicia Concerning Unbelief', Copt. in Crum, pp. 38,5–41,20; German, ibid., pp. 94–98; commentary: T. Orlandi, 'Il Dossier', pp. 288–91.
165. T. Orlandi, art. cit., p. 290.
166. Cf. W. E. Crum, op. cit., pp. 38–39 (Copt.), p. 95 (German).

also apply to the patriarch: 'If he does not answer in this way [as 'Agathonicus' does it], then he is not an archbishop or even a Christian.'[167] The following sentence could be directed against the Gnostics (and Manichaeans): 'Unbelief says: "There is no judgement (*krisis*), nor is there a resurrection." The scripture says: "Christ is risen, and we will rise with him." '[168] 'Agathonicus' is in agreement with Shenoute in the lament over 'Hellenization' when he asserts:

> For there is a crowd of Christians who have read the books [of the] Greeks (ἕλλην) and have [thereby] begun to wander in their thoughts (*logismos*), in that their hope (*elpis*) has become disappointment and they believe [in the] words of Homer and Socrates [and the] other Greeks, straying [from] the words of scripture, just like the [pagans]. For such [people] are no Christians. For in all these [things] [un]belief has [tested] us, and [the venerable] scripture has saved us.[169]

---

167. Ibid., p. 40,30–31 (Copt.); p. 97 (German).
168. Ibid., p. 97.
169. Ibid., p. 98.

CHAPTER TWO

IN THE LIGHT AND SHADOW OF THE MASTER: ARCHIMANDRITE BESA (d. after 474)

In the Christology of the disciple and successor of Shenoute in the leadership of the White Monastery we find nothing new in comparison with his great predecessor, unless something hidden emerges from the unedited larger part of his writings. Therefore we could quickly dispense with him if we did not see the disciple, like his teacher, burdened with similarly negative judgements regarding the position of Christ in his spirituality.[1] Thus, since for us it must be a matter of shedding light on this important issue, above all for ecumenical reasons, some clarifications are necessary. We have now already been brought into the time of the *Henoticon* of Emperor Zeno (474/475 and 476–491). It would be of great interest to know whether an interview that took place between the emperor and Besa[2] came before or after the publication of the *Henoticon* (482). Yet one can presume that the first part of the emperor's reign hardly allowed room for such a meeting. In the writings of Besa edited thus far, there is no trace of this document that is so significant for Egypt, nor of Chalcedonian problems in general. The most knowledgeable scholar of Besa's texts, K. H. Kuhn, attributes this gap to three things: (1) To the thoroughly pastoral and practical character of Besa's letters and admonitions, which are all occasional writings.[3] We also find no more discussion of the 'apocrypha', the Gnostics, Manichaeans and Origenists,

---

1. Thus in the research of K. H. Kuhn, 'A Fifth-Century Egyptian Abbot: I. Besa and His Background; II. Monastic Life in Besa's Day; III. Besa's Christianity', *JTS* 5 (1954), 36–48, 147–87; 6 (1955), 35–48. On the texts: idem, *Letters and Sermons of Besa*: CSCO 157 (T); 158 (V), Louvain 1956; idem, 'Another Besa Fragment', *Mus* 97 (1984), 25–28 (which concerns obedience to superiors).

2. See the documentation in K. H. Kuhn I, 38. According to legend, Hilaria, the daughter of Zeno, was a nun in Egypt; A. Guillaumont, *DSp* 2 (1953), 2273.

3. K. H. Kuhn III, *JTS* 6 (1955), 35.

which certainly would have evoked christological responses – always assuming that the still unedited fragments do not create contrary facts. (2) To the influences that were operative in Besa's life and work: Bible,[4] Shenoute himself[5] and his forefathers, such as Pgōl, Athanasius, Antonius and Pachomius, or in a word: tradition. (3) To the understanding of monasticism as a charismatic vocation with its moral and ascetic demands, which permeate everything in the texts edited thus far. At this point our question is the one also raised by K. H. Kuhn: What role do Christ and Christology play here? According to Kuhn, 'satanology' and 'demonology' receive a more positive accent[6] than the person of Christ. On this he makes some statements[7] that are astounding for us, who have our eyes on Shenoute as *socius Christi*: (1) There is no indication whatever that Christ and his redeeming work have found their proper place in Besa's thought. (2) In spite of all relations between human beings and the judging and merciful God, divine actions are not determined by the redeeming death and resurrection of Christ. The effects of Christ's work on God and on humankind and on the world are obviously totally unknown. (3) Although Besa has a glowing expectation of the last judgement, his eschatology, says Kuhn, is nonetheless devoid of Christocentricity. Especially missing are the hope of the transforming power of Christ's return and the knowledge of the relativization of all earthly values. (4) Because Christ is generally denied his proper place in Besa's theology, the monastic vocation does not come personally from Christ either. It represents 'a mode of life' that is pleasing to God in itself – that is, apparently without any relation to Christ – and is therefore to be recommended to all: 'The essential truth that not all men have the same vocation from Christ, seems to have been ignored.'[8] Finally, the lack of a strong Christology means, according to Kuhn, that the ethical teachings of Besa also have no centre: 'He shows but little awareness that apart from Christ's redemptive work the good life cannot be lived.'[9] Kuhn himself states that the deficiencies in such a theology are great, if this appraisal can be accepted.

It is precisely on this appraisal, however, that we would like to cast doubt, based first of all on methodological grounds and then on the

4. K. H. Kuhn I, *JTS* 5 (1954), 39–43.

5. Ibid., pp. 43–48.

6. K. H. Kuhn III, *JTS* 6 (1955), 37: 'Satanology and demonology form a substantial part of Besa's religion.'

7. K. H. Kuhn III, *JTS* 6 (1955), 46–48.

8. Ibid., p. 47.

9. Ibid., p. 48.

application of these grounds to a series of Besa's statements, which we want to analyse briefly. A few methodological notes: (1) Between Shenoute's and Besa's person and work there is a closer connection than is usually found in other master–follower relationships. Already initiated into his office during the last three years of Shenoute's life, the successor, according to the vita that he wrote, shows hardly any independence vis-à-vis the great model. This remains a living presence, like the sketch of a picture of a great master, which the follower can hardly expand with his own. Therefore Shenoute's Christocentrism also remains the fixed point that determines Besa's practical admonitions. It is not for nothing that we can point to the so-called 'christological' interpretation of the person of Shenoute himself in the visions of the vita. (2) Even if only a few christological texts are scattered around, their theological capacity is to be examined. Perhaps individual sentences can be accorded the significance of principles or axioms that are suited to lending a special quality to the ascetic-practical admonitions and raising them as a whole to a special level. (3) From the exhortations of Shenoute we know the significance in the White Monastery of the liturgical celebration, the synaxis, with its worship in word and sacrament. To remain close to it was one of the last admonitions of the dying leader, and this precisely *ut socii Christi sitis*.[10]

After these methodological remarks, let us look briefly at the points of substance in Kuhn's critique of Besa's Christology.

(a) Absence of Christ's redeeming work in Besa?

Fundamentally, we must note that instruction in the tradition of the Fathers, in the scripture and especially in the 'Gospels of Jesus Christ' are represented as the foundation of moral order for a fellowship of nuns placed under the archimandrite Besa.[11] In fragment 3, 'On the Punishment of Sinners', we read: 'But you, my beloved, building yourselves up in your most holy faith, praying in the Holy Spirit, keep yourselves in the love of God, looking for the mercy of our Lord Jesus Christ unto eternal [life].'[12] Here already we point to the significance of Christ for Besa's eschatology. – The nun Antinoe is admonished to stay away from useless quarrels. For 'they are harmful and destructive for the souls of those who desire their salvation and who love God and our Lord Jesus who gave himself a ransom for everyone and died for us, that he might redeem us from all lawlessness, and purify us for himself as a people specially his own, zealous for good works which God has prepared in order that we should walk in them.'[13]

---

10. *Sin. Vit. Boh.*, 180: CSCO 129 (V), p. 44,17.
11. Thus in frag. 21, II 6: CSCO 158, p. 57. Besa says that these things are not lacking. Failure comes from hardheartedness and prejudice.
12. Frag. 3, II 1: CSCO 158, p. 5.
13. Besa, *To Antinoe*, V 2: CSCO 158, p. 95.

(b) Ignorance of the effects of Christ's work on God, humankind and world?

In reply, we refer to the well-sketched teaching of the *imitation of Christ*, which is made therein the standard of the formation of the Christian life. In an admonition on 'obedience'[14] Besa quotes Ps.-Clement, *On Virginity* VII: 'Those who imitate Christ, imitate vigorously; and those who put on Christ vigorously, make Christ take *form* in them in all their life, in frame of mind, in speech, in behaviour, in deeds, in constancy, in love perfect towards God.'

'Imitation of Christ' is realized especially when it is a matter of enduring contempt. In this way one is made like the suffering Christ. This is Besa's word in a *Letter to the Nun Herai*, who suffers desolation from within and misjudgement and scorn from without, and is in danger of being untrue to her vocation. The means of salvation is looking to the suffering and scorned Christ (cf. 1 Pt 2,23 and 21), which will grant participation in the kingdom of heaven.[15] We note this reminder of the *imago Christi patientis*, which we find here in Coptic asceticism, and its eschatological perspective! – In frag. 5, 'On Faith, Penitence and Watchfulness' (I 2, p. 11) Christ is recalled as 'rock', from which all deliverance comes. In the same text Christ, the glorified Lord, is recommended as help on the day of tribulation and affliction (cf. ibid., II 1, p. 11).

(c) A Christless eschatology?

The just-mentioned text is already one answer to this question; an even more powerful one is contained in frag. 12, 'Reproofs and Monastic Rules' (IV 2, pp. 30–1), since reference is made to 'the King, the Lord of glory, Jesus, the Son of God', who upon his return will call into his glory those 'who walk in purity, and truth, and obedience in all things, and righteousness, and humility' to inherit the kingdom, which has been prepared for you since the founding of the world (Mt 25,34). Certainly, corresponding to the moral condition of those addressed, the seriousness of the idea of judgement stands in the foreground for Besa, but even here it is always motivated by the view of God and Christ and meant as an intermediate stage to glory with Christ.[16] Here Besa is in the tradition of the idea of

---

14. Frag. 10: *On Obedience* I 2: CSCO 158, p. 20, n. 2 with reference to L. T. Lefort, *Une citation copte de la Pseudo-clémentine 'De virginitate'* (BIFAO 30), pp. 509ff.; idem, *Les Pères Apostoliques en copte* (CSCO 135/136), Louvain 1952, 40 or 34. – The well-known orthodox theologian W. Lossky, in his study, *Essai sur la Théologie Mystique de l'Église d'Orient*, Paris 1944, maintained the thesis that the mysticism of the 'imitation of Christ' was known only in the West but was foreign to Eastern spirituality (p. 212). I. Hausherr subsequently showed the untenability of this idea: 'L'imitation de Jésus-Christ dans la spiritualité byzantine', in *Mélanges F. Cavallera*, Toulouse 1948, 230–59 (with an overview from the Apostolic Fathers through Maximus the Confessor to Nicholas Kabasilas). Hausherr had omitted Egyptian-Pachomian monasticism – a gap that H. Bacht filled in 'La loi du "retour aux sources" (De quelques aspects de l'idéal monastique pachômien)', *Revue Mabillon* 51 (1961), 6–25. Here Bacht goes into Pachomius, Horsiesius and Theodore, examining not only their texts with regard to the idea of the discipleship of Christ but also their Christology in general (pp. 7–13). Here we also see the nearness of Shenoute and his followers to the Pachomians.

15. Besa, *To Herai*, V 1–6: CSCO 158, pp. 99–100.

16. Frag. 17: *Admonitions to Sinners*, II 3: CSCO 158, p. 44; likewise, nuns are referred to the 'judgement-seat of Christ': frag. 18, IV 6, p. 50; the same admonition to fear before God and Christ the judge concerns nuns who destroy their fellowship: frag. 21, I 1–4, pp. 55–56; also monks who steal from the sick: frag. 24, III 7, p. 67; V 5, p. 69; in general those who violate God's commandments and the precepts of the Fathers: frag. 26, IV 1–2, p. 73; likewise in the admonition *To the Brethren on Maintaining Unity* = frag. 27, VI 2, pp. 79–80; ibid., XIII 3–5, pp. 85–86. Here all monastic life is related to the 'day of Christ' at the end of the world, likewise in *To Antinoe*: frag. 29, V 3, pp. 95–96.

judgement in the *Apophthegmata Patrum*.[17] In short, the archimandrite cannot conceive of a last judgement without Christ. Because it is always a question of the return of the glorified Lord, the shape of the new world and the new humankind naturally forms the background. A few examples may suffice: (a) Besa reminds the nun Herai what she is forfeiting through her unfaithfulness. Instead of the 'resting place' (*anapausis*; *katapausis*: Heb 4,3) in the kingdom of heaven, she will find the punishment of hell.[18] As of itself, the parable of the wise and foolish virgins occurs to the admonisher with its alternative final destinies (cf. CSCO 158, index, Mt 25,1 ss.). (b) With all the seriousness of the idea of judgement, there is no lack of enthusiastic words on the vocation to fellowship with the glorified Lord after the judgement, with reference to Mt 25,34. Besa must describe both: the desolation of eternal damnation and the fortune of those who have gone the way of faithfulness; this is especially clear in frag. 12: 'Reproofs and Monastic Rules'.[19]

(d) Salvation through asceticism?

Even if certainly not intended, it almost amounts to a reduction of the monastic life to a Stoic and Pelagian assessment of moral probation that is supposed to survive without the grace of God in Christ when K. H. Kuhn says: 'In early monasticism – and Besa is no exception here – asceticism has become a rule of life, the acceptance of which finally ensures salvation.'[20] In reality, Besa gives ample evidence that the monastic way of life has its fruit only from the Holy Spirit.[21] Even the 'personal vocation' is allegedly supposed to be missing.[22] By contrast, let us refer to the *Letter to Herai*, which caused Besa special concern: her name has already been written into the book of life – thus a sign of her 'election'. She is counted among the saints and the heavenly hosts – this by virtue of her vow in faith and in the knowledge of the Lord. Precisely this is what she has not maintained. She did not follow the counsels of God and must now taste the fruit of her way of life (Prov 1,24–31): 'For you did not believe God or hope for his salvation which he wrought with you.'[23] In this way Herai takes back what she vowed to the Lord Jesus.[24] Thus it is Christ 'who teaches us to direct our way and our heart towards heaven'.[25] Herai has to know that monastic communities are 'communities of the Lord'. Therefore one who enters them cannot leave them again with impunity, because one does not enter them without the call of the Lord. Indeed, it would be better not to join them than to betray the persistence 'and the holy commandment which was given to you'.[26] Thus Besa reminds a straying nun of her personal vocation by God in Christ, and in his conception such a vocation means a 'commandment', although the monastic life is not thereby represented as

---

17. See K. Schedl, 'Jesus Christus, sein Bild bei den Mönchen der Sketis', diss. Vienna 1942 (typescript that could not be consulted). According to the author's correspondence, 'The surprising result is that the Christ of the desert fathers is seen primarily as Christ the judge, which fits in well into the old Egyptian otherworldly ideas with the judgement of the dead.' For us, nonetheless, it is a question here of emphasizing the illuminating christological element in Besa, which in all the strictness required by the situation must not be mistaken.

18. Frag. 32, V 3, p. 105.

19. Frag. 12, IV 1–2, pp. 30–31.

20. K. H. Kuhn III, *JTS* 6 (1955), 47.

21. Cf. frag. 12, V 5–6, p. 31; frag. 36, II 2–3, pp. 114–15, etc. (indwelling of the Holy Spirit).

22. K. H. Kuhn III, *JTS* 6 (1955), 47: 'Moreover, the acceptance of the monastic yoke does not appear to be the result of a personal call from Christ but is rather a mode of life, thought to be *eo ipso* more acceptable to God, and therefore recommended to all.'

23. Besa, *To Herai*, VI 4, p. 107.

24. Ibid., VIII 3, p. 108.

25. Ibid., IV 3, p. 99 with reference to Lk 9,62.

26. Ibid., V 2, p. 105.

the only way to salvation. It was God who offered Herai a covenant with himself and turned it into reality ('he swore to you, he entered into a covenant with you and you became his').[27] Can one express more clearly the initiative and grace of God in the vocation to the monastic life than through the parallel between the covenant of God with Israel and the covenant between an individual person and the Lord, sealed by the vows in the monastic community?

Thus for ecumenical reasons it must be our special concern to correct wrong judgements on Shenoute and Besa and their monastic communities and to point to their explicit and implicit Christocentrism. We would, so to speak, rip the heart out of the body of the Coptic church and its piety if we spoke of an absence of Christ in such monastic communities, which are in no wise to be separated from the life of this church.[28] If there are those who, through the mosaic stones gathered here, still cannot recognize the image of Christ in the White Monastery, they might read the long prayer to 'our Lord Jesus Christ' and his Father which Besa composed on the occasion of a lengthy famine.[29] The monks cared for more than five or six thousand starving people in the vicinity of the monastery, buried 128 dead 'with the blessing of Christ Jesus', who gave the brothers the strength to serve the starving until the region was delivered from the catastrophe and all could return home to their villages. We know what the 'prayer to Jesus' meant in the tradition of Shenoute. His disciple also found expressed in it a great experience of life in dealing with suffering people, to whom he recommended looking to Jesus just as urgently as Shenoute had done in his prayers.

The few other known testimonies in Coptic literature for the period between 451 and 604 provide nothing for the content differentiation of the picture of Christ. It is a question mostly of traditional polemic, even if there is also interesting contemporary historical or cultural information.[30]

---

27. Ibid., V 6, p. 106.

28. On the connection between the monastic ideal and Christian perfection in general see A. Guillaumont, art., 'Copte (Littérature spirituelle)', *DSp* 2 (1953), 2273.

29. Frag. 16 ('On a famine'): CSCO 158, pp. 39–43.

30. See A. Grillmeier, *CCT* II/1, pp. 41–43, esp. under (b) (vii). These testimonies are analysed and evaluated in M. Cramer and H. Bacht, 'Der antichalkedonische Aspekt im historisch-biographischen Schrifttum der koptischen Monophysiten (6.–7. Jh.). Ein Beitrag zur Geschichte der Entstehung der monophysitischen Kirche Ägyptens', in *Chalkedon* II, 315–38, esp. 328ff. on Daniel of Scete (CPG 7363).

CHAPTER THREE

ON CHRISTOLOGY IN THE LITURGICAL PRAYER OF THE COPTIC CHURCH

The Coptic church's faith in Christ cannot be considered apart from its liturgical celebrations and prayers. Here Eucharist and worship are a more comprehensive *demonstratio fidei* than in other churches in which theological reflection has won a greater life of its own vis-à-vis worship. Indeed, we saw in Shenoute himself the close connection between faith and liturgical celebrations. A detailed presentation of liturgical Christology would also have the great advantage that it could make apparent the vertical and horizontal unity of the church from the view of Alexandria: in the vertical, because we are led back into the time of the undivided church before Chalcedon, for which the name of Hippolytus alone is sufficient guarantee;[1] in the horizontal, because the liturgical traditions bind together the churches from Rome to Constantinople, from Antioch through Jerusalem to Alexandria, even into the times of separation.

A special dividing line seemed to become visible at the linguistic boundary between Coptic and Greek in the liturgy. In regard to the post-Chalcedonian split, especially if it was seen to be extended into politics, one could be inclined to set up these equations: Greek = Melkite = Chalcedonian, and Coptic = anti-Chalcedonian. Here we had best leave the overloaded term *Monophysite* out of the picture. First, the Coptic church regarded itself absolutely as the legitimate heir of the church of St Athanasius and of Cyril the opponent of Nestorius. Here Greek also held an unsurrenderable position.[2] Hence the suggested

---

1. Cf. Altaner-Stuiber, *Patrologie* (⁹1980), § 22; E. Lanne, PO 28, p. 276!
2. See H. Brakmann, 'Zu den Fragmenten einer griechischen Basileios-Liturgie aus dem koptischen Makarioskloster', *OrChr* 66 (1982), 118–43; K. Treu, *Liturgische Traditionen in Ägypten* (on P.OXY 2782) (BBA 45), Berlin 1974, 50–51, n. 16; E. Hammerschmidt, 'Probleme der orientalischen Liturgiewissenschaft', *OstKSt* 10 (1961), 28–47; H. Quecke, 'Zukunftschancen bei der Erforschung der koptischen Liturgie', in R. Mcl. Wilson, *The Future of Coptic Studies* (Coptic Studies I), Leiden 1978, 164–96, here pp. 165–67.

equation cannot in any case be maintained.[3] The manuscript tradition itself shows overlappings. We have liturgical fragments in Greek[4] that are to be regarded as anti-Chalcedonian ('Monophysite') and represent a separate strand of tradition. Even the anti-Chalcedonians of Egypt have kept the Greek liturgical language, though to a lesser degree than the Melkites. This is true not only for the native liturgy of Mark, but also for the adopted liturgies of Basil and Gregory. The Copts separated from the imperial church preserved even in the Middle Ages the Greek and Coptic liturgical languages simultaneously, as shown by the newly discovered Kacmarcik Codex, first published in 1975.[5]

This intra-Egyptian language parallelism in the older liturgy has its historical background in the adoption of liturgical models from Syria and Byzantium, including Asia Minor (Apostolic Constitutions; liturgies of James, Chrysostom and the Byzantine liturgy of Basil), besides the Egyptian liturgy family of the fourth and fifth centuries (Serapion, Mark liturgy). In Egypt a special role was played by the Gregory anaphora from the group of Greek anaphoras of the Antiochene-Byzantine model. It in turn represents a connection between two anaphora types that could otherwise appear separated, namely, the anamnestic (given above all in Syria) and the epicletic type (Rome, Egypt, East Syria).[6]

---

3. See H. Engberding, 'Ein Problem der Homologia vor der hl. Kommunion in der ägyptischen Liturgie', *OCP* 2 (1936) (145–54), 149ff.; E. Renaudot, *Lit. Or. Coll.* 1, XCIIff.; 251–52, did not want to grant these equations validity even for the time around 750. Cf. A. Gerhards, *Die griechische Gregoriosanaphora. Ein Beitrag zur Geschichte des Eucharistischen Hochgebets* (LQF 65), Münster 1984, 14–18 (cited below as: *Gregoriosanaphora*).

4. See H. G. E. White, *The Monasteries of Wadi 'n Natrûn* I, New York 1926, 200–13: Greek text fragments of the Basil and Gregory liturgies. Also H. Engberding, art. cit., *OCP* 2 (1936), 147–48; H. Brakmann, art. cit., 121–23, on White and Engberding; A. Gerhards, *Gregoriosanaphora*, pp. 14–20.

5. See W. F. Macomber, 'The Greek Text of the Coptic Mass and of the Anaphoras of Basil and Gregory According to the Kacmarcik Codex', *OCP* 43 (1977), 308–34; idem, 'The Anaphora of Saint Mark according to the Kacmarcik Codex', *OCP* 45 (1979), 75–98; K. Samir, 'Le codex Kacmarcik et sa version arabe de la Liturgie alexandrine', *OCP* 44 (1978), 74–106; H. Brakmann, art. cit. (124–26), 125–26: 'The manuscript originally contained two equivalent copies of all three formulas of the mass that had become canonical for the Copts, the Basil, Gregory and Cyril/Mark liturgies, in the first part in Coptic, in the second in Greek, in each case with an accompanying Arabic translation.'

6. The various types are distinguished in A. Raes, 'Anaphorae Orientales', in Hänggi-Pahl, *PE*, III, pp. 97–415. On the following, besides Hänggi-Pahl, *PE*, pp. 134–41, see: (1) F. E. Brightman, *Liturgies Eastern and Western. I. Eastern Liturgies*, Oxford 1896; (2) E. Renaudot, *Liturgiarum Orientalium Collectio* I–II, Frankfurt ²1847; (3) C. A. Swainson, *The Greek Liturgies chiefly from original authorities*, Cambridge 1884; (4) E. Lodi, *Enchiridion Eucologicum Fontium Liturgicorum* (*EEuFL* [= BEL.S 15]), Rome 1979; idem, *EEuFL Clavis*

Besides the anaphoras that are contained in (1) the *Euchologium* and form its centre, we also want to examine other liturgical books, such as (2) the *Lectionaries* (but here only the lectionary for Holy Week), then (3) the '*Psalmody*' (of the year) with its odes, *theotokia* and *psalia*, and (4) the *Synaxarium*. This comprises only a part, and that incompletely. For the difficulties (above all for a non-Coptologist) are for the time being insurmountable. Many texts have still not been edited or translated. The chronology is largely uncertain. Our investigation, however, is limited to the patristic period and can at best recover old material in retrospect from later works (which will be especially important for the Ethiopian church).

1. The three leading anaphoras of the Egyptian liturgy

(a) The liturgy of Mark (Cyril)

Renaudot, *Lit. Or. Coll.* I, pp. 38–51, 120–48; Brightman, *Lit. Eastern and Western*, 144–88; *PE*, pp. 101–23; *EEuFL* nos. 542–50. – R. Coquin, 'L'Anaphore alexandrine de saint Marc', *Mus* 82 (1969), 307–56; W. F. Macomber, 'The Anaphora of Saint Mark according to the Kacmarcik Codex', *OCP* 45 (1979), 75–98; O. H. E. Burmester, 'The Greek Kirugmata, Versicles and Responses, and Hymns in the Coptic Liturgy', *OCP* 2 (1936), 363–94; H. Brakmann, *OrChr* 66 (1982), 125. Recently published: G. J. Cuming, *The Liturgy of St Mark* (OLA 234), Rome 1990 (edition and commentary) (not used here).

When the mss. come from Melkite churches (Egyptian, Sinaitic, Italo-Greek), there are many assimilations of the Mark liturgy to Byzantine anaphoras. The Copts have a Bohairic version of this anaphora, which often goes under the name of Cyril. Even after the separation of churches, the exchange between Melkite and Coptic mss. continued. Three Greek mss. are very old (fifth or fourth century). Cf. M. Andrieu and P. Collomp, 'Fragments sur papyrus de l'anaphore de saint Marc', *RevSR* 8 (1928) (489–515), 514: 'On peut, sans témérité, admettre que cette rédaction de l'anaphore de saint Marc était déjà en circulation au temps de saint Athanase.' Coquin, art. cit., strengthens the evidence through a comparison of the Renaudot and Brightman texts with the three oldest fragments (Strasbourg, BN et Universitaire Gr. 254; British Mus. papyrus 2037 E. F.; John Rylands Library of Manchester, parchm. no. 465). These three fragments offer us most of the Mark anaphora of Egypt of the fifth and sixth centuries. The tradition of the Greek-Melkite sources, the Bohairic translation and the three above-mentioned Greek fragments suffice, according to Coquin, pp. 312–13, to determine four versions or *états* of the anaphora:

(I.) Fifth–sixth or seventh century. – (II.) Revision that was used between the eighth and ninth centuries by Chalcedonians and anti-Chalcedonians. – (III.) Text of the Melkites in

---

Methodologica cum commentariis selectis, Bononiae 1979. Lodi has only a little on the Gregory anaphora. See also E. Lanne, 'Le Grand Euchologe du Monastère Blanc. Texte copte éd. avec trad. franç.': PO 28 (1958), 269–407. For additional lit. see A. Gerhards, *Gregoriosanaphora*, bibliography.

Egypt and southern Italy. – (IV.) The greatly Byzantinized Bohairic translation of the Coptic church.

Thus in the extant Mark liturgy we do not have the original redaction but a text that, according to its structure and content, is already developed. The John Rylands text shows that from the sixth century on, two epicleses were in use, of which the second, inspired by the epiclesis of the James anaphora, betrays that in Egypt a very realistic doctrine of the Eucharist was adopted (Coquin, *Mus* 82 [1969] 354–55). Also the doctrinal formulas on the Holy Spirit, in their common form around 381 in the East, appear in the Melkite form and in the Coptic translation of the Mark anaphora. We were also able to establish all this after 431 in Shenoute (Orlandi exhortation). Also to be noted for the Melkite and Bohairic texts is the penetration of the *timor reverentialis* before the *mysterium tremendum*, so typical of many Eastern liturgies. The author adheres to a purely kerygmatic explanation without any kind of theological digression – this in the *gratiarum actio*, the institution report and the anamnesis. Naturally, according to Coquin, with the change in theological climate, this made room for many interpolations in the Coptic and Greek texts of the Mark anaphora. Then, however, this contributed more and more to this anaphora being out of circulation. At the beginning of the fourteenth century its use was limited to the period between 27 November and 26 December of the Julian calendar. In summary:

'The "Christ-loving city" on the Nile not only was not able to decide the manifold rivalry between Alexandria and Antioch in its favour; beyond that it had to accept the fact that even in its own territory, in the city as in the patriarchate – and even in a prominent position, in the liturgy of the mass – the native worship traditions were repressed or even replaced by texts and rites that were Antiochene (in the narrower or broader sense). With the Melkites, who were true to Chalcedon and to the emperor, it is true that the Alexandrian Mark liturgy was not finally replaced by the Constantinopolitan books until the thirteenth century, but even earlier the inherited form succumbed to the influences of the James liturgy and then its "double first cousins", the Byzantine Basil and Chrysostom liturgies, to which it finally had to yield completely. Already considerably earlier, at the latest in the seventh and probably in or even before the sixth century, the Basil anaphora, which originated at the beginning of the fourth century in the sphere of influence of Antiochene euchologion, in its older form before undergoing a reworking by the later patron saint Basil of Caesarea (d. 379), gained entrance into the worship text repertoire of the anti-Chalcedon-minded churches of Egypt. The imported eucharistic prayer, not the native Mark anaphora, named by the Copts after Cyril I of Alexandria (d. 444), attained in this part of Egyptian Christianity even the position and importance of the standard eucharistic prayer' (H. Brakmann, *OrChr* 66 [1982], 118–19). These statements are of some significance for an ecumenical history of faith.

(b) The liturgy of Basil

Renaudot, *Lit. Or. Coll.* I, pp. 1–25. *PE*, pp. 230–43, 347–57 with lit.; *EEuFL* nos. 535–41; A. Renoux, 'L'anaphore Arménienne de saint Grégoire l'Illumateur', in *Eucharisties d'Orient et d'Occident* II (LO 47), Paris 1970, 83–108.

Here it is a question of the old Armenian anaphora of St Basil, which in the Armenian version closely approximates the Greek Basil liturgy in Alexandria.

The Basil anaphora originated in the sphere of influence of the Antiochene euchologion at the beginning of the fourth century, already before Basil (d. 379), to whom it was later ascribed. It was revised by Basil, as has been demonstrated by H. Engberding, *Das eucharistische Hochgebet der Basileiosliturgie* (Theol. d. christl. Ostens 1), Münster 1931. See B. Capelle, 'Les liturgies "basiliennes" et saint Basile', in I. Doresse and Dom E. Lanne, *Un témoin archaïque de la liturgie copte de S. Basile* (BiblMus 47), Louvain 1960, 45–74; H. Brakmann, art. cit., examines 10 of the 25 sheets that H. G. E. White discovered in 1920/21 in the Makarios monastery (Wadi 'n-Natrûn) and edited: *The Monasteries of the Wadi 'n Natrûn*, New York 1926, 202–13. All the texts are to be classified under the Greek Basil liturgy and not the Mark liturgy. 'Moreover, this removes any basis for the assumption that the traditional Alexandrian text was able at least to a limited extent to assert its position in the Coptic patriarchate as the normal form of the mass for an extended period' (Brakmann, op. cit., 143). Contrary to White, however, Brakmann proposes a new ordering of the analysed sheets. Thus the main form of the post-Chalcedonian Egyptian celebration of the Eucharist is the plenary form of the Basil liturgy. This was based on the foundation of a Syrian-Antiochene mass ceremony, which was expanded through revisions and expansions (anaphoric secondary prayers, priestly texts for the service of the word and celebration of the Eucharist).

(c) The liturgy of Gregory

Sources given and discussed in A. Gerhards, op. cit.

(a) Greek tradition: (aa) Cod. Paris. gr. 325. According to Renaudot I, XCIV–XCVIII, ascribed to the anti-Chalcedonian church because of a 'Monophysite insertion' in the homology before the communion. H. Engberding, *OCP* 2 (1936) (145–54), 146–47, wanted to assume Melkite provenance because of openness to Byzantine influences. Definitively against this is H. Brakmann, *OrChr* 66 (1982) (118–43), 124–25 with Renaudot. A. Gerhards adds further individual observations in the same direction. – (bb) The so-called Kacmarcik Codex. See W. F. Macomber, 'The Greek Text of the Coptic Mass and the Anaphoras of Basil and of Gregory According to the Kacmarcik Codex', *OCP* 43 (1977), 308–34.

(b) Arabic: K. Samir, 'La version arabe de la Liturgie alexandrine de saint Grégoire (codex Kacmarcik)', *OCP* 45 (1979), 308–58.

(c) Armenian: P. Ferhat (ed.), 'Denkmäler altarmenischer Meßliturgie I: Eine dem hl. Gregor von Nazianz zugeschriebene Liturgie', *OrChr* NS 1 (1911), 204–14.

(d) Coptic-Bohairic: E. Hammerschmidt (ed.), *Die koptische Gregoriosanaphora. Syrische und griechische Einflüsse auf eine ägyptische Liturgie* (BBA 8), 1957. – Coptic-Sahidic: H. Lietzmann, 'Sahidische Bruchstücke der Gregorios- und Kyrillosliturgie', *OrChr* NS 9 (1920), 1–19 (= H. L., *Kleine Schriften* III, Berlin 1962, 99–117).

Author of the liturgy of Gregory. A. Gerhards would not like simply to contradict the traditional attribution of the Gregory anaphora to Gregory of Nazianzus. Actually, he says, the anaphora contains many traits that speak for Gregory of Nazianzus as its author. Gerhards examines the internal criteria for this in the historical-theological part (pp. 104–65), but he also mentions stylistic peculiarities (e.g., the 'I–thou' style). To be noted is the investigation of H. Engberding, 'Die Kunstprosa des eucharistischen Hochgebets der griechischen Gregoriusliturgie', in Mullus, FS Th. Klauser (*JAC* Supp. 1, 1964), 100–10. With the eucharistic prayer in the euchologion of Serapion, the eighth book of the *Apostolic Constitutions*, the Gregory anaphora professes especially joyfully the use of rhythmic prose. While otherwise in eucharistic prayers the formulation of the content strives for a simple, kerygmatic style, as appears in the *Symbolum Apostolicum*, the redactor of the Gregory anaphora reaches the acme of the application of literary art forms: 'Not only the overflowing fullness and wealth of the forms assures him this place of distinction but even much more the genuine artistic talent that is revealed in everything and in each individual part' (Engberding, op. cit., 109). According to Gerhards there are commonalities between the Gregory anaphora and the sermons of Gregory of Nazianzus, who was bishop of Constantinople from 379 to 381. An origin of the anaphora around this time in Constantinople would be conceivable. A few peculiarities regarding the vocabulary used and the theological ideas, however, speak against Gregory of Nazianzus as the *final* redactor. Instead Gerhards makes two counter-proposals: (1) An anaphora going back to Gregory of Nazianzus received a final redaction by an author of the fifth century. Or (2) an author familiar with Gregory's style and theology wrote in his spirit a form to which he gave Gregory's name. Such an author could be Proclus of Constantinople (d. 446). 'Based on the dogmatic-historical evidence of our anaphora as well as its linguistic form, we run into Proclus again and again' (Gerhards, p. 246; see his 'Zusammenfassung und Ausblick', pp. 243ff.; here we follow the Greek-German text of Gerhards and his line count of 1–403).

2. The christological peculiarities of the three Egyptian eucharistic prayers[7]

(a) The addressing of Christ in the Gregory anaphora and in the other eucharistic prayers

This issue is already familiar to us from Shenoute. Based on his struggle against Origenists and Arians, he would probably have been able to join in the text coming from the north of the kingdom. Although the trinitarian introit of the Gregory anaphora, which is patterned after 2 Cor 13,13, consciously places the Father in initial position (2–6), the '*vere dignum et iustum est*' begins immediately with the address to the Son, 'the one true God' (17). Also the negative divine predicates often applied to God or the Father in Greek theology (inexpressible, invisible, unlimited, without origin, [eternal,] timeless, immeasurable, immutable, unfathomable)[8] (18–20) are apparently already true of the Son when he is seen as Logos. Yet in Origen's sense they would be an expression of the transcendence of the Father, who is simply 'the God'. But because the Logos-Son is introduced here immediately and perfectly smoothly as 'Creator of the universe', 'Redeemer of all', 'humanitarian'(!) (17), he is also to be considered the subject of the foregoing negative predicates. Naturally, in all of this the Son is not to be separated from the Father and Holy Spirit, as the trinitarian introit itself in vv. 2–5 shows. Thus everything is also still open for an application of the named predicates to the Father. The direction of the anaphora towards the Son, however, is more and more prominent. A. Gerhards finds the first unambiguous, if also indirectly indicated, 'christological colouring' of the anaphora in the

---

7. On the following: I.-H. Dalmais, 'Quelques grands thèmes théologiques des anaphores orientales', in *Eucharisties d'Orient et d'Occident* II (LO 47), Paris 1970, 179–95; H. Engberding, 'Das chalkedonische Christusbild und die Liturgien der monophysitischen Kirchengemeinschaften', in *Chalkedon* II, 697–733; I. Pahl, *Die Christologie der römischen Meßgebete mit korrigierter Schlußformel* (MThS.S 32), Munich 1966; J. Quasten, 'Der Wandel des liturgischen Christusbildes. Zur Erstlingsarbeit von J. A. Jungmann', in B. Fischer and H. B. Meyer (eds.), *J. A. Jungmann. Ein Leben für Liturgie und Kerygma*, Innsbruck 1975, 117–19; a good orientation is offered by B. Fischer, 'La place du Christ dans la Liturgie', in *Sacrements de Jésus-Christ* (Coll. 'Jésus et Jésus Christ', dirigée par J. Doré, 18), Paris 1983, 185–98; J. M. Sanchez Caro, 'Historia de la Salvación en la anáfora alejandrina de San Gregorio Nacianceno', *Salmanticenses* 24 (1977), 49–82; idem, 'Eucaristia e Historia de la Salvación. La Historia de la Salvación en las anáforas orientales' (diss. excerpts, Pont. Univ. Greg.), Salamanca 1977; C. Jones, G. Wainwright and E. Yarnold (eds.), *The Study of Liturgy*, London 1978; A. M. Triacca and A. Pistoia (eds.), *Le Christ dans la liturgie. Conférences Saint-Serge XXVIIe Semaine d'Études Liturgiques Paris, 24–28 Juin 1981* (BEL.S 20), Rome 1981. Here, however, there is no contribution to Coptic liturgy.

8. Cf. A. Buckel, *Die Gottesbezeichnungen in den Liturgien der Ostkirchen*, Würzburg 1938, 68–71; A. Gerhards, *Gregoriosanaphora*, p. 53, points out that the *agennetos* is missing here.

insertion of the Pauline 'powers', 'dominions', 'thrones' and 'authorities' (Eph 1,21; Col 1,16) into the anaphoric angelic praise, which seen from Paul's point of view can apply only to Christ.

The focusing of the anaphora on the Son of God becomes unambiguous, however, in the so-called Egyptian *Sanctus introduction* (38–52), in which the *Nicaenum* appears: 'You, Lord, who are true God of true God.' This confession receives its special accent in that it is linked in the Greek text directly with Ex 3,14: ὁ ὢν θεὲ κύριε ἀληθινὲ ἐκ θεοῦ ἀληθινοῦ (38). The vocative ὁ ὤν, as the LXX translates the name of Yahweh, becomes here the Logos predication, which is easily possible for the Greeks.[9] This prepares one for the fact that the Sanctus is also already applied to Christ. It is a matter of the Eucharist as praise of God, which is pronounced most powerfully in the Trishagion.[10] What is expressed directly in 38–52, however, is actually first a certain mediator function of Christ, yet one that goes here from 'above' to 'below': Christ is praised as one who brings us worthy praise of God, when he brings us human beings together with the choir of the incorporeal ones and 'has turned over to the earthly ones the hymn of praise of the seraphim' (or according to the Coptic text for vv. 43–44:) 'who has placed the choir of the incorporeal ones under human beings'. The function of Christ consists in turning over to human beings the Trishagion of Is 6,3, which belongs to the seraphim (ὁ τὴν τῶν σεραφὶμ τοῖς ἐπὶ γῆς παραδοὺς ὑμνωδίαν) (45). Here we have an indication of the role of Christ in the revelation of the Trinity. 'If the Logos-Christ is the mediator of every revelation, then the vision of Isaiah also goes back to him.'[11] Thus, although in vv. 38ff. ('You, Lord, who are true God of true God') the prayer address to Christ is maintained, the role of this Logos-Christ is described in such a way that he appears as the bringer of the revelation of the Trinity from above to below and at the same time as the founder of the true praise of the trinitarian God from below to above. This corresponds to the parabolic descending and ascending Johannine Christology. Thus we have here no 'Christomonism', no factual reduction of the doctrine of the Trinity to

---

9. Gregory of Naz., Or. 38, 19: 'The One who is becomes'; PG 36, 325C: ὁ ὢν γίνεται. Cf. the representation of Christ as angel in the Meteora monasteries, with a ὁ ὤν in the nimbus. See M. Werner, *Die Entstehung des christlichen Dogmas*, cover of the edition, Stuttgart 1959.

10. On the Trishagion in the Coptic church cf. M. Robertson, 'The Good Friday Trisagion of the Coptic Church', in *The 17th Internat. Byzant. Congress, Abstracts of Short Papers*, Washington DC 1986, p. 293.

11. A. Gerhards, p. 59 on vv. 44–45, with reference to John Chrysostom, *In 'Vidi Dominum'*, Hom. 1, 1: SC 277, p. 216, in n. 151.

Christology; rather, the praise of the Sanctus is for the One who connects God with human beings and human beings with God.

Now, before this *Sanctus* is introduced, we find an unexpected interpolation: in the so-called 'Syrian Sanctus introduction' (54–64), there is a further extension of the Sanctus from a *theologia* to an *oikonomia*. Not only is God's nature being praised, but our salvation! The hymn of the seraphim becomes the song of deliverance and victory for redemption. This leads to the christological significance of the Sanctus and the Benedictus (66–70), which is of special interest for the post-Chalcedonian discussion. The Trishagion of Is 6,3 was already expanded in Judaism: whereas in the vision of the prophet the glory of God filled only the earth, in *Greg.* 66–70 it encompasses heaven and earth.[12] Speaking of the filling of 'heaven' seems to divert attention from Christ. But the Gregory anaphora – alone among all Egyptian liturgies – adopts the hosanna already inserted into the liturgy in Syria (Mk 11,10: *Greg.* 68–70). Through the *hosanna benedictus*[13] (this according to Mt 21,9 with Ps 118[117],26) the Trishagion is further developed to the 'hymn of victory', which can now be clearly recognized as christological, and indeed through the (anamnestic) reference to the first and second coming of the Lord, which had already penetrated the realm of Semitic languages and is moreover prefigured by Rev 4,8: '. . . hosanna in the highest. Praised be the one who has come and who comes in the name of the Lord. Hosanna in the highest' (*Greg.* 68–70). The victorious King, Christ, makes his entrance into his church 'when he actualizes the past deeds of salvation'.[14] The fullness of the glory of God spreads in heaven and earth through Christ until the completion of history, until his coming again.

Now, since the Gregory anaphora is the celebrative form for Easter, Christmas and Epiphany in the Coptic church, A. Gerhards finds in this an indication of the *Sitz im Leben* of the direction of the Sanctus to Christ, which, however, can already be demonstrated in the Cappadocian liturgy of the third and fourth centuries. For these festivals of the Lord, especially Easter, are completely centred on Christ. Other eucharistic prayers conceive of the Sanctus in a christological-trinitarian way. The first testimony for this comes from Theodore

---

12. Cf. E. Kähler, *Studien zum Te Deum und zur Geschichte des 24. Psalms in der alten Kirche* (VEGL 10), Göttingen 1958, 19; D. Flusser, 'Sanctus und Gloria', in *Abraham unser Vater*, FS O. Michel, ed. by O. Betz et al., Tübingen 1963, 131; cited in A. Gerhards, *Gregoriosanaphora*, pp. 62–63; idem, 'Le phénomène du Sanctus adressé au Christ. Son origine, sa signification et sa persistance dans les anaphores de l'Église d'Orient', in *Le Christ dans la Liturgie*, 65–83.

13. E. Hammerschmidt, *Die koptische Gregoriosanaphora*, Berlin 1957, 118–20.

14. A. Gerhards, *Gregoriosanaphora*, p. 63 with n. 167.

of Mopsuestia (cf. *PE* 216). The James liturgy has the underlying schema of all texts conceived in a trinitarian manner, as A. Tarby demonstrates:[15]

A. You are holy . . .	Father, King of the ages
B. Holy also is your Son	Son
C. Holy also is your Spirit	Spirit
D. Holy are you,	Father, Author of the history of salvation

The Nazianzene bracketing of trinitarian doctrine and Christology made it possible for such a formal trinitarian outline to be restructured christologically without further ado, as can be discovered in the Gregory anaphora:

Title:

Holy, holy are you, Lord, and holy in all things	(71)
A. Towering light of your being	(72)
B. Inexpressible power of your wisdom	(73)
C. Immeasurable ocean of your love of humankind (*philanthropia*)	(74–75)
D. You, as humanitarian, have created me, a human being	(76)

Whereas the Sanctus formulas understood in a trinitarian way connect more with the name and are taken personally, in the *Greg.* the point of departure is, in a typical Greek fashion, the *one being* that the Logos has in common with the Father and the Holy Spirit through the *homoousia*. For the *Greg.* the participation of the Son in the one being of God is thus based on the possibility of interpreting the Sanctus christologically, similar to the way Shenoute also bases the prayer address to Christ on this. But in the James and Gregory anaphoras the *oikonomia*, the dynamic-personal aspect, is also based on the *holiness* of God, which is a *characteristic of being*. One can imagine that this anaphora may have been too abstract in the eyes of Shenoute and in general made theological demands that were too great for the Coptic province.

The Christocentrism of the Gregory anaphora becomes stronger in the *post-Sanctus* (71–146) and the *oratio oeconomiae* (76–140). It becomes all the more impressive as the theological perspectives that are developed before the recitation of the institution statement become more comprehensive. They are already summarily indicated in the transition from Sanctus to *oratio oeconomiae*: to be praised are the brilliance of being (*ousia*) of the Logos, the power of his wisdom, which are at work in creation and history, the ocean of *philanthropia* of the Logos in his incarnation. The outline of the *oratio oeconomiae* itself sufficiently indicates its theological goal:

76–86:	Creation
88–100:	Human beings: their election and their failure
102–11:	The salvific ordering of the divine mercy in the OT
113–32:	The incarnation and God's salvific action in the NT
134–40:	The completion of salvation in the death, resurrection, ascension and return of Christ

---

15. A. Tarby, *La prière eucharistique de l'Église de Jérusalem* (TheolHist 17), Paris 1972, 124.

Forgoing all technical theological terms, this artfully[16] constructed prayer develops the history of creation and its head, humankind (cf. Ps 8), and this from protology to eschatology. This history receives its unity and its completion in Christ, the incarnate Logos, and his destiny. Facing each other in this prayer are an 'I' that represents the church and a 'he', that is, the Logos, which, however, is taken as the incarnate One. The Gregory anaphora offers here its own version of the early Christian psalm prayer, in which the psalms are understood as *vox ecclesiae ad Christum*.[17] With A. Gerhards we call attention to an interesting ongoing influence of Phil 2,6: 'But I have captured for myself the verdict of death' (v. 100). Juxtaposed to this in v. 115 is: 'You did not regard equality with God as booty.' Here death is called the booty of the fall of human beings (ἥρπασα). In his *kenosis* Christ also forwent his immortality, which he does not want to grasp like booty (ἁρπαγμόν). In this way he turns the destiny of humankind around.[18]

In this Christocentric intensification we almost have a trinitarian modalism. That is, the title *Father* is applied to Christ (v. 104), which has a parallel in the Syrian-Antiochene anaphora of John of Bostra.[19] It would be wrong, however, to understand this transference of the Father title to Christ in an intratrinitarian way. Rather, this is a way to emphasize the significance of Christ for the economy of salvation. It consists, indeed, in making the Father present among us or showing God as Father in regard to us human beings and revealing his humanitarian nature.

In that the remembrance of the *oikonomia* already comprises the death, resurrection and return of Christ, the narrative of the institution is at first excluded. The Lord's Supper anamnesis receives a theological context that already comes into view 'through the extension of the *oratio oeconomiae* to eschatology with strong emphasis on the Pascha event'.[20] The transition to the institution statement (142–146) has the task of leading from the 'praising memory of the work of salvation' to the remembrance

16. H. Engberding, 'Die Kunstprosa des eucharistischen Hochgebets der griechischen Gregoriusliturgie', *JAC* Supp. 1 (1964), 102–4, 109–10.

17. B. Fischer, 'Zum Problem einer christlichen Interpretation der Psalmen', *TR* 67 (1971), 5–12; see A. Grillmeier, *JdChr* I³, pp. 93, 143.

18. A. Gerhards, *Gregoriosanaphora*, pp. 69–70 with n. 186.

19. Cf. *PE* 296; R. Cantalamessa, 'Il Cristo "padre" negli scritti del II.–III. sec.', *RSLR* 3 (1967), 1–27; V. Grossi, 'Il titulo cristologico "Padre" nell'antichità cristiana', *Aug* 16 (1976), 237–70; A. Ferrua, '*Qui Filius diceris et Pater inveniris*' (APARA.R XXXIII [1960/61]), Vatican City 1961, 209–24.

20. A. Gerhards, op. cit., p. 78.

of the Lord, the 'cultic anamnesis'. The transition is the key to the understanding of the Lord's Supper anamnesis: 'In the participation in Christ's body and blood the whole of the salvation effected by God through Christ becomes present sacramentally.'[21] The word *symbol* appears at this point, as in Shenoute. But the archimandrite would not be able to report a contradiction here. For the anaphora proceeds step by step:

Bread and wine are first 'symbols of my freedom' (τῆς ἐλευθερίας τὰ σύμβολα) (v. 142). They represent, namely, the salvific work of Christ 'for me'. With these symbols, however, something must then happen beyond my prosphora, and indeed through the words of Christ: 'I offer you the symbols of this, my freedom; to *your* words I ascribe the realization. You have transferred to me this mystical service; you have granted me participation in your flesh in bread and wine' (142–46). Given here is a connection between symbol and real participation in the flesh (and blood) of Christ that is acceptable even for Shenoute. But it is clear that in his exhortation analysed above he did not have in mind this interpretation of the Eucharist given by the Gregory anaphora. Also, if this eucharistic prayer in its final form goes back to Proclus, it can hardly have been known to Shenoute.

The Christ address in this anaphora is so consistently maintained that even the narrative of the institution is stylized in the 'thou' form of address (147–181). In everything it is a matter of a profiling of the position of Christ.[22]

The following anamnesis (183–194) encompasses in short sentences the events of Jesus' life from the incarnation[23] through the immediately mentioned 'life-giving death' to the 'second tremendous and glorious arrival from the heavens'. This goes beyond the bounds of the original scope of the anamnesis, which comprised the Pascha event. In terms of the Christology and the history of liturgy, it is extraordinarily striking that Christ is not only the focus of the anamnesis but also the recipient of the prosphora. 'This unusual idea comes from the fact that the offering

---

21. A. Gerhards, op. cit., p. 79.

22. An exact analysis and comparison with other anaphoras is given by A. Gerhards, *Gregoriosanaphora*, pp. 81–83. In this anaphora there is a noticeable tendency to harmonize the individual biblical Last Supper reports with one another. See *EEuFL*, pp. 532–44: *Textus collati Institutionis Eucharisticae.*

23. The incarnation is called by the word typical of Chrysostom: συγκατάβασις. Cf. S. Leanza, 'L'intervento di Dio nella storia secondo la dottrina crisostomica della condiscendenza divina', *Aug* 16 (1976), 125–34; K. Duchatelez, 'La "condescendance" divine et l'histoire de salut', *NRT* 95 (1973), 593–621; A. Gerhards, *Gregoriosanaphora*, pp. 84–85, nn. 247–48. Gerhards sees in the emphasis of the Gregory anaphora on *synkatabasis* its special interest not only in the work but also in the person of the redeemer.

formula (192–193) is attached to the anamnesis.'[24] Yet we find a narrative of the institution thus composed in various other areas of liturgy.[25] To explain this peculiarity A. Gerhards (chap. 10, 3.1) points out that the original addressee of the words of institution was not God (the Father) but – corresponding to all biblical reports of the meal – the church. The accommodation of the direction of address of the *institutio* to the anaphora is, accordingly, regarded as a later stage of development that was not yet reached in, for example, the anaphora of the *Traditio Apostolica*. Apparently the phenomenon is to be explained by the difference between two Last Supper traditions: (1) In the Semitic (East Syrian) language area the presence of Christ is seen as *personal*: Christ becomes the person faced and hence the addressee of prayer. The version of the Benedictus there points in this direction: 'Highly praised is the one who has come and who comes', which was adopted by the Gregory anaphora, but also by the James anaphora of Jerusalem. 'The Eucharist appears here as a new epiphany of the exalted Lord or, in the Gregory anaphora, as a renewal of the incarnation of the Logos.'[26] Thus one may with a certain correctness explain the addressing of Christ in the institution statement here on the basis of the peculiar nature of Semitic-personal, Jewish–Christian prayer, without having to resort to anti-Arian polemic. Different from this is (2) the *Hellenistic* view: the Eucharist is the sacramentally mediated presence of Christ's work of salvation in the eucharistic gifts, in which Christ appears as the mediator of divine grace. This interpretation makes possible a new evaluation of the addressing of Christ himself in the narrative of the institution. This also makes understandable the *realism* of the conception of the Eucharist in the Gregory anaphora. In the analysis of Shenoute's understanding of the Eucharist we were likewise able to observe the close nexus between an anti-docetic emphasis of the incarnation and a eucharistic realism. In this

---

24. A. Gerhards, *Gregoriosanaphora*, p. 85. Vv. 192–93 read: 'He calls out: We offer unto you what is yours from your gifts, for all, because of all and in all.' In n. 249 Gerhards notes that in the anamneses of some older anaphoras the offering formula is missing, e.g., in Pap. Dêr-Balyzeh (*PE* 126), in the Syrian Anaphora of the Twelve Apostles (PE 267) and in the East Syrian anaphora of Addai and Mari (*PE* 380). But all three texts are addressed to Christ! See A. Gerhards, op. cit., pp. 225ff.: institution report and anamnesis, where the strangeness of the 'Direction of address towards Christ' in the *institutio* is discussed.

25. Thus in the Coptic anaphora of the holy Evangelist Matthew, ed. by A. Kropp, *OrChr* 29 (1932) (111–25), 114–15; in a Coptic anaphora fragment, ed. by H. Quecke, *OCP* 39 (1973), 218–19; in the Ethiopian Anaphora *Athanasii Apostolici*: *PE* 183; in the Ethiopian anaphora of Jacob of Sarug: Euringer 89; in the Armenian Gregory anaphora: *PE* 329; in the Maronite anaphora of Peter (III): *PE* 413; in an *Anaphora Abrahae* (14th cent.). See A. Gerhards, op. cit., n. 1073.

26. A. Gerhards, op. cit., p. 228.

Shenoute recalls the creator power of God revealed in the epiclesis. Thus he would have been able to connect the Gregory anaphora with his views.[27] A difficulty arises, however, from the fact that the Syrian anaphoras, apart from the above-mentioned *Anaphora of the Twelve Apostles* and also the Gregory anaphora, connect with the address to Christ also the offering to Christ. Thus Christ is seen here as the recipient of the sacrifice, as this is already given in the East Syrian Apostles liturgy. J. A. Jungmann claimed to see there a reference to the Monophysites. But this intellectual connection is already older and points rather to anti-Arianism. Theophilus of Alexandria, the contemporary of Shenoute, calls Christ 'priest and sacrificial lamb, sacrificing and sacrificed, recipient and distributor'.[28] Certainly in such pointed texts the divinity of Christ is to be emphasized, and this at the expense of the salvation-economic view. Yet here again in a broader perspective a mediation of Christ becomes discernible: ultimately Christ is supposed to offer the petition and gift of the church to the Father. The humanity of Christ is included here.

(b) Epiclesis

The epiclesis[29] also belongs in the history of liturgical Christology, especially because of the distinction of a Logos and a Spirit epiclesis analogous to the other antithesis: creation through the Logos or creation as work of the Holy Spirit (or ultimately as *opus ad extra* attributed to Father, Son and Spirit in unity and diversity).

The Logos epiclesis means that the act of eucharistic sanctification or consecration is ascribed to the Logos as subject. From this comes the

---

27.. See pp. 203–07 above.

28. Theophilus of Alex., *In mysticam coenam* (inter op. Cyrilli) (CPG 2617): PG 77, 1029B; Ps.-Cyrill. Hier., *Hom. in occursum Domini* (CPG 3592): PG 33, 1193A: 'and he himself is the one who accepts the sacrifice'. Cf. R. Taft, *The Great Entrance* (OCA 200), Rome 1975, 132–34: the homily exhibits Alexandrian traits; according to others it belongs to Jerusalem but was not held until the middle of the fifth century by an unknown author. Ephraem Syr., *Sermo de D. N.*, according to E. Beck, 'Die Eucharistie bei Ephräm', *OrChr* 38 (1954) (41–67), 42.

29. Cf. G. Kretschmar, 'Abendmahlsfeier' I, *TRE* 1 (1977) (229–78), 260–62; W. Schneemelcher, 'Die Epiklese bei den griechischen Vätern', in *Die Anrufung des hl. Geistes im Abendmahl* (ÖR.B 31), Frankfurt 1977, 68–94; *Le Saint-Esprit dans la Liturgie*, ed. by A. M. Triacca and A. Pistoia, Rome 1977. The patristic precursors of the liturgical-pneumatological texts are treated by V. Saxer, 'Le Saint-Esprit dans les prières eucharistiques des premiers siècles', in S. Felici (ed.), *Spirito Santo e catechesi patristica* (BiblScRel 54), Rome 1983, 195–208. On the epiclesis, cf. ibid., 201–5. On the broader problems of the Egyptian epiclesis (doubling) see H. Quecke, 'Zukunftschancen bei der Erforschung der koptischen Liturgie', pp. 177–80.

analogy to the incarnation. Early Alexandrians and with them the Cappadocians subscribed to the so-called 'eucharistic incarnation principle' (J. Betz).[30] The Egyptian Logos epiclesis is found in the Serapion anaphora and in the anaphora of Jacob of Sarug. It is related here to the Christ invocations of the epicleses of the coming and the name in the *Acts of Thomas* and had its antecedents in the early Christian '*Maranatha*'. The coming epiclesis can serve as an invocation before Communion, as it does in the later Byzantine liturgy. In it Christ is addressed as the one who sits above with the Father and yet is invisibly present here (ἀοράτως παρών/συνών),[31] a saying that is also found in the Gregory anaphora: 'Now you yourself, Lord, transform the offered [gifts] with your voice; you, who yourself *are there* (αὐτὸς παρών), make this mystical service complete' (197–200). In his personal presence Christ is host and giver of the eucharistic meal.

In the analogy of incarnation and Eucharist we already have a starting-point for the connection of the Logos and the Spirit epicleses – especially if for the incarnation event we draw in the activity of the Holy Spirit according to Lk 1,35.[32] Another connection of both kinds is also given on the basis of the unexplained terminology of the so-called Spirit Christology,[33] especially for Syria: 'Since the incarnation, however, had always been described here in such a way that it was the divine Spirit who became bodily historical in Christ, the *ruha* corresponds . . . in Syria largely to the Logos of the Greeks.'[34] The history of the epiclesis has its part in the process of dogmatic history in that two things were involved: (1) the cleaning up of the terminology for the designation of the divinity of Christ, which could also be expressed with *pneuma*, and (2) the distinction of *Logos* and *Hagion Pneuma* as second and third hypostases in the one Godhead. After 381 there was a striving for greater clarity in language. If – as we have seen in Shenoute – the *homoousios* is given for Logos and Spirit on the one hand and on the other the trinitarian formula of the three hypostases in the one *ousia*, and if, further, the functions of Logos and Spirit are clearly separated theologically in the event of the

---

30. J. Betz, *Die Eucharistie in der Zeit der griechischen Väter* I/1, Freiburg 1955, 285–86; G. Kretschmar, art. 'Abendmahl' III/1, *TRE* 1 (59–89), 80; on J. Betz see W. Schneemelcher, art. cit., 87. Cf. Gregor Naz., Ep. 171: PG 37, 280C: with his word, the priest draws in the Logos. On the whole matter see also K. Gamber, 'Die Christus- und Geist-Epiklese in der frühen abendländischen Liturgie', in L. Lies (ed.), *Praesentia Christi*, FS J. Betz, Düsseldorf 1984, 131–50.

31. F. E. Brightman, *Eastern Liturgies*, p. 341.

32. A. Gerhards, *Gregoriosanaphora*, p. 232 with n. 1120.

33. Cf. A. Grillmeier, *JdChr* I[3], index, p. 826.

34. G. Kretschmar, art. 'Abendmahl' III/1, *TRE* 1, p. 68.

oikonomia, the Logos and the Spirit epicleses can be connected with each other without confusion. With this we understand the important section 197–208 in the Gregory anaphora. The already quoted vv. 197–200 continue thus:

> Accomplish for us yourself the remembrance of your service. Send yourself your Holy Spirit, so that he through his holy, good and glorious presence may consecrate these offered, venerable and holy gifts and transform them into the body and the blood of our redemption (201–208).[35]

In the Coptic church in Shenoute's time the Spirit epiclesis was already adopted, as the Orlandi exhortation shows: '. . . the Holy Spirit, whom God sent to them [bread and cup] so that they would become the body and blood of Christ' (§ 0350). This corresponds to Shenoute's teaching of the divine action in the conception of Christ, which is ascribed to the Holy Spirit by him and by the Cappadocians. The same is attested by the epicleses of the Basil and Mark anaphoras.[36]

3. Christological elements in some other Coptic anaphoras

(a) *From the 'Great Euchologion'*[37] *of the White Monastery.* It offers two fragments[38] from an anaphora of Patriarch Severus of Antioch, which bring us into direct contact with the post-Chalcedonian controversy.

From the prayer for the church.[39] It contains a clear reference to the 'heresy' that came into the church through Chalcedon:

---

35. A. Gerhards, pp. 234–35, gives two additional texts: Ps.-Ephraem, *Sermo in hebd. sanct.* 4, 4 according to E. Beck, 'Die Eucharistie bei Ephräm', *OrChr* 38 (1954) (41–67), 62: 'In the beginning our Lord Jesus took plain bread in his hands and blessed it, he designated it and consecrated it in the name of the Father and in the name of the Spirit[!] and broke it and passed it out to his disciples . . . He called the bread his living body and filled it with himself and with the Spirit.' Jacob of Sarug, according to B. D. Spinks, 'The Consecratory Epiclesis in the Anaphora of St James', *StudLit* 11 (1976) (19–38), 27: 'Together with the priest, the whole people ask the Father to send his Son so that he might come down and dwell in the sacrificial gift. And the Holy Spirit, his power, shines down into the bread and wine and consecrates it, and indeed makes it the body and blood.'

36. Basil anaphora: Renaudot, *Lit. Or. Coll.* I, pp. 15.67; Mark anaphora: 141. On the development of the epiclesis in the latter see R.-G. Coquin, 'L'anaphore alexandrine de Saint Marc', *Mus* 82 (1969) (307–56), 343–53; see also E. Lanne, 'Le Grand Euchologe du Monastère Blanc', PO 28, pp. 357,13–359,11.

37. According to E. Lanne, 'Le Grand Euchologe', PO 28, p. 273, the ms. comes approximately from the time of the tenth and eleventh centuries. It contains, according to Lanne, a much richer liturgy than that which is in use among the Copts today. 'Certaines des prières qu'il contient permettent d'établir plus facilement la filiation qui existe entre la liturgie alexandrine et la liturgie éthiopienne et de faire ressortir l'influence considérable exercée par le rite syrien sur le rite égyptien' (ibid., p. 275). This is confirmed by the mention of the baptism of Christ (cf. n. 43 below) and by the *descensus* text (traducianism).

38. Cf. Lanne, PO 28, p. 276.

39. See PO 28, pp. 313–23. Cf. Lanne, pp. 312–13, n.

Eliminate the filth of the heresies and do not allow your holy name to be besmirched by them among the nations (ἔθνος); also the heresy that has now been planted in the heart of your churches, cast it far away from them and do not forget to look upon your holy body (σῶμα), which they tear into scraps: but remember the whole remainder of the orthodox believers and do not forget your covenant (διαθήκη), for we have become very poor. Help us, God our Saviour (σωτήρ) for the glory of your name. For you alone really have the power to give a solution to those who have no solution.[40]

These words of the Thomas anaphora can also match the feeling of Severus and many anti-Chalcedonians regarding the split in the church, in which they, to be sure, had a considerable part in the view of the Chalcedonian opposition. The quoted words could be related to the time of the reform of Justin and Justinian (after 518). We must note that the 'kerygma' of the last judgement (Mt 25,34–36) also appears in this anaphora, as it indeed often does elsewhere in Coptic spirituality.[41]

In the fraction prayer of Severus we also find what is otherwise rare in the anaphoras, the christological primary formula with more discriminating terms:

God assumed flesh (σάρξ) without change by the Holy Spirit (πνεῦμα) in the holy *theotokos* Mary, this virgin who bore God; he was born by her; he became human without any modification or change or transformation; he became one with us according to the incorruptible, unknowable and immutable hypostasis (ὑπόστασις); it is this [the divine hypostasis] that was conceived in the – in every respect – holy womb of this holy (ἁγία) Mary.[42]

(b) *The mysteries of the life of Jesus*. In a prayer at the closing bow (*inclinatio finalis*) there is a detailed mention of the chief mysteries of Jesus' life that also mentions the baptism of Christ, which deserves our attention in regard to the Ethiopian tradition.[43]

(c) *A doxology of Hippolytus*. A further peculiarity of the euchologion from the White Monastery is a striking doxology of Hippolytus: '. . . the Holy Spirit in the holy catholic and apostolic church'.[44]

4. Christological peculiarities in the lectionaries

The lectionary of the Coptic church contains four parts: normal days, Lent, Holy Week, and Eastertide. A presentation of the Christology of these books with their patristic readings would have to examine the

---

40. PO 28, p. 315,2–14.
41. Ibid., p. 319,20–27. See also the 'Anaphora of St Matthew': PO 28, pp. 355,1–357,5. Also E. Lanne, op. cit., p. 277.
42. Ibid., p. 371,17–27.
43. Ibid., pp. 377,17–381,21; mention of the baptism of Christ, p. 379,7–10.
44. Ibid., p. 345,20–21; also p. 278, where further evidence is presented.

selection of texts, the text form and the authenticity before the christological content could be checked. The texts of Holy Week, which O. H. E. Burmester has made accessible,[45] will serve as an example.

According to the tradition of the Coptic church, the lectionary of Holy Week was compiled by Patriarch Gabriel II (1131–46) with the help of the monks of St Makarius. Later, more texts were added by Peter, bishop of Behnesa,[46] which for that very reason are not found in all mss. We will limit ourselves to the patristic texts.

Since the central period of the liturgical year is involved, we would expect a selection clearly centred on the salvific event. Yet we are to some extent disappointed. Reference to the celebrative mysteries is relatively weak, though we must note at this point that the office for this week includes extensive, intentionally selected scriptural readings. They precede the patristic readings!

Most (nine) of the readings for the period from Monday of Holy Week through Maundy Thursday are taken from Shenoute's exhortations. Then come eight excerpts from the sermons of St John Chrysostom (CPG 5154,8), which, however, are certainly partly unauthentic; then three from 'Athanasius' (Dubia: CPG 2188); one each from Abbot Constantine, Peter of Alexandria (Dubia: CPG 1662) and Severian of Gabala (unauthentic: CPG 4280 according to H. D. Altendorf). They are primarily admonitions to examination of conscience, conversion and penance. Only brief reference is given to baptism, grace and the Spirit of Christ. In this selection from the Fathers the event of foot-washing (beyond the scriptural reading) is only touched on, not actually discussed. With authentic and unauthentic Chrysostom texts the Eucharist is presented especially as *mysterium tremendum*. In the homily (no. 22) for Good Friday we have a noteworthy section on *Christ's descent into hell*. It is a relatively late text, since the human soul of Christ is so prominent.[47] For that very reason the text cannot belong to Chrysostom.[48]

> While I speak with you there comes to me the remembrance of the Lord of glory, our *Saviour* and God, and how He descended into Hell being one with the *rational soul* which He took from men, and made it all one *with* the Divine *Nature*. And He proclaimed the

45. See O. H. E. Burmester, *Le Lectionnaire de la Semaine Sainte* I–II (according to Br. L. Add. 5997): PO 24 (1933), 173–294; PO 25 (1935), 179–485. The scriptural pericopes used are easily perused in the tables: PO 25, 471–85; idem, 'The Homilies or Exhortations of the Holy Week Lectionary', *Mus* 45 (1932), 21–70.

46. See *Mus* 45 (1932), 21.

47. Cf. A. Grillmeier, 'Der Gottessohn im Totenreich', in idem, *Mit ihm und in ihm*, pp. 76–174, esp. pp. 158ff.

48. For in his genuine writings Chrysostom speaks only rarely of the soul of Christ and then only after his elevation to the see of Constantinople, according to C. Hay, 'St John Chrysostom and the Integrity of the Human Nature of Christ', *FrancStud* 19 (1959), 298–317; cf. *JdChr* I[3], pp. 610–14; CCT I[2], pp. 418–21. Also now a part of the history of the doctrine of the soul of Christ is M. Aubineau, *Un traité inédit de christologie de Sévérien de Gabala. In Centurionem et Contra Manichaeos et Apollinaristas. Exploitation par Sévère d'Antioche (519) et le Synode du Latran (649)* (Cahiers d'Orientalisme V), Geneva 1983, esp. II, nos. 24–34 (pp. 130–40). This text – like the passage on the *descensus* – also went under the name of Chrysostom.

good news to all other *souls* which were in that place where Death held them, on account of the first *transgression*, which cleaves to our *fleshly race* in that they had sinned. *Moreover*, He prepared for Himself the *regions* which are below the earth, being one and with a human *soul according* to the likeness of the souls which dwell there without a *body*. But His *soul* was a true God, and He broke the sting of Death until He crushed its thorn which pierced men. And He destroyed him who possessed that power of death, that is to say, the *Devil*, and He bound him and delivered him into the hand of every man who shall go to him, and He *took captive* Hell. He brought up with Him all the *souls* which slept until His descent into Hell, and *freed* them from the hand of Death and Hell, and bore them with Him on high. And after He had risen from the dead, He raised His *Flesh* by the power of His Divinity which is a single Divine *Nature* with Him. He is the King of Glory Who has gone before them to the exalted kingdom of His Divinity.[49]

In the history of the *descensus* texts, the present one, in addition to the strong emphasis on the human soul of Christ, is also noteworthy in that it apparently presupposes traducianism. One would hesitate to assume this here, were this teaching not to be found so prevalent later in Ethiopian sources, with which perhaps even a connection is possible (see below). The subordinate clause, 'which He took from men', speaks in the spirit of traducianism. Also notable is the massive emphasis on unity between divinity and the soul ('his soul was a true God'), which is finally emphasized at least by allusion through the *mia-physis* formula.

5. *The Book of Psalmody*

This comprises (1) four biblical odes (Ex 15,1–21; Ps 135; Dan 3,52–88; Pss 148–150); (2) the theotokia (hymns to Mary);[50] (3) the doxologies, that is, hymns of various content, which are used on individual days or at certain times of the church year. Also other hymns can be incorporated into the *Psalmody*, for example, the so-called *Psali*.[51] We will take up only

---

49. Burmester, 'Homilies', *Mus* 45 (1932), 64–65.

50. These theotokia, according to a thesis of Quecke, developed from specially composed responsorial verses to the New Testament canticles (Lk 1–2) (whereas in the Old Testament odes the refrain was taken from the biblical text itself): H. Quecke, *Untersuchungen zum koptischen Stundengebet*, Louvain 1970, pp. 205–19; cf. idem, *Zukunftschancen bei der Erforschung der kopt. Liturgie*, p. 182.

51. On the following see H. Malak, *Les livres liturgiques de l'Église Copte, Mél. Eug. Tisserant*, vol. III: *Orient Chrétien, Deuxième Partie* (ST 233), Vatican City 1964, 1–35. – On the liturgy of the hours: H. Quecke, *Dokumente zum koptischen Stundengebet* (ZDMG Suppl. 1, 1969), 392–402; idem, *Untersuchungen zum koptischen Stundengebet* (PIOL 3), Louvain 1970; on the *Psalmody*, ibid., 52–80. – On the biblical odes: H. Schneider, 'Die biblischen Oden im christlichen Altertum', *Bib* 30 (1949), 28–65; idem, 'Die biblischen Oden seit dem sechsten Jahrh., ibid., 239–72; also ibid., 433–52, 479–500. – On the theotokia: A. Mallon, 'Les théotokies ou office de la sainte Vierge dans le rite copte', *ROC* 9 (1904), 17–31; D. L. O'Leary, *The Daily Office and Theotokia of the Coptic Church*, London 1911; further studies by O'Leary in H. Quecke, *Untersuchungen*, p. XXVIII; S. Euringer, 'Der mutmaßliche Verfasser der koptischen Theotokien und des äthiopischen Weddâsê Mârjâm', *OrChr* NS 1 (1911), 215–26; M. Cramer, 'Zum Aufbau der koptischen Theotokie und des Difnars. Bemerkungen zur Hymnologie', in *Probleme der koptischen Literatur* (WB [H] 1968/1 [K 2]), pp. 197–223; eadem, *Koptische Liturgie. Eine Auswahl* (Sophia 11), Trier 1973; eadem, *Koptische Hymnologie in deutscher Übersetzung. Eine Auswahl aus saidischen und bohairischen Antiphonarien vom 9. Jahrhundert bis zur Gegenwart*, Wiesbaden 1969. – On the Difnar: D. L. O'Leary, *The*

individual traits of the Christology. They offer, to be sure, nothing new beyond what is already known. They are worth mentioning only in that they show how far the anti-Chalcedonian controversy had gained entrance into the prayer life of the Coptic church. The counterpart to this was offered by the liturgical books of the Chalcedonian churches. Because such traces are found relatively seldom, however, the common ground in christological convictions stands out rather powerfully. This corresponds to the particular kind of liturgical prayer, especially when it is very popularly oriented.

(a) *The mysteries of the life of Jesus in prayer form.* Reflection on the basic events of Jesus' life belongs not only in the eucharistic anaphoras but also in the prayer of the hours. As an example of a richer enumeration we lift up the *Psali Batos*, which belong to the Thursday theotokion.[52] From the pre-existence to the second coming of Christ, the main events of Jesus' life are made present in invocations, with the baptism of Christ already in second place. Also the 'doxology'[53] awakens the memory of this as it corresponds to the festival of Epiphany.

(b) *Christocentrism of the prayer of the hours.* The *Psali* in particular give testimony of a strong Christocentrism and the practice of direct prayer to Christ,[54] and this in numerous echoes of the OT psalms. The Coptic church was not satisfied with a 'christologization' of the OT psalms (through textual modifications or christological interpretation), in order thereby to permeate the canonical hours with the New Testament. It created for itself new prayers to Christ or long series of invocations to Christ.[55] Yet Brogi does not value the theological worth of these prayer series very highly and points out the many repetitions.[56]

Difnar (Antiphonarium) of the Coptic Church I–III, London 1926, 1928, 1930. – Especially important for the following: J. Muyser, *Maria's heerlijkheid in Egypte. Een studie der Koptische Maria-literatur* (only vol. I appeared), Louvain–Utrecht 1935. In his translation Muyser follows the Editio princeps of the theotokia by the catholic Coptic bishop 'Anba Rūphā'īl al-Tūkhī (Rome 1764). – In addition: M. Brogi, *La Santa Salmodia Annuale della Chiesa copta. Traduzione, introduzione e annotazione* (= SOC.Ae), Cairo 1962. Brogi translates according to the Coptic orthodox edition: *Il Libro della santa Salmodia dell'anno secondo l'ordine dei nostri Padri della Chiesa egiziana*, ed. by Sig. Claudio Labîb Bey, Cairo 1908, but consults other editions and mss., since Labîb omitted numerous elements (Brogi, op. cit., p. VI). – On the *Psali*: E. Lanne, 'La "prière de Jésus" dans la tradition égyptienne. Témoignage des psalies et des inscriptions', *Irén* 50 (1977), 163–203. – For important references for this section I am indebted to Hans Quecke, Rome.

52. Cf. M. Brogi, op. cit., p. 61.
53. M. Brogi, op. cit., pp. 138–39.
54. Cf. M. Brogi, op. cit., pp. 30–33: Psali Adam.
55. Cf. also E. Lanne, *Irén* 50 (1977), 163–203.
56. M. Brogi, op. cit., pp. XVIII–XXI.

(c) *More discriminating christological formulas in the liturgy of the hours?*
Liturgical celebration is not the appropriate place for polemic and
abstract reflection. It thrives on concrete Christology and the personal
consummation of the human-divine relationship, precisely as it corresponds to the Christian tradition. In fact, the Coptic orthodox liturgy is
not greatly burdened by theological conflict formulas, but they are not
lacking either. First we will look at the one-nature formula and its
counterpart, the formula of the two natures in the one hypostasis. The
liturgical books of the two confessions, Chalcedonian and anti-
Chalcedonian, do not fail to express their conviction regularly, even if
rarely. As an example we cite verse 6 of the Monday theotokion, which
in (a) and (b) is common to both confessions yet in (c) is typically
different:

Coptic-Orth. according to C. Labîb (in Brogi, p. 50; also in M. Cramer, *Kopt. Liturgien*, 16)	Coptic-Chalced. text according to Ṭukhi (in Muyser, pp. 102–3)

(a) He who is,
    Who was,
    Who has come
    And will come again,
    Jesus Christ, the LOGOS,
    Took on flesh,
    Without any change
    And became a complete human being.

(b) He did not pour himself out,
    Not mixed (ἀσύγχυτος),
    Also not divided (ἀδιαίρετος)
    In any way whatever after the union,

(c) But (He, the God-Logos) is	Yet God the Word has
One single nature (μία φύσις)	— (!)
One single hypostasis	One single hypostasis (ὑπόστασις)
One single *prosopon*	One single *prosopon* (πρόσωπον)
Of God the Logos.	And two natures (φύσις).

He appeared in the flesh
From the Virgin . . .[57]

The anti-Chalcedonian and Chalcedonian confessions stand side by side
in all clarity. In the difference in terminology and basic structure of the
Christ statements we recognize nonetheless the fundamental unity of
faith in the true incarnation in the tension of 'unmixed' and 'undivided'.

---

57. M. Brogi, op. cit., 50, translates no. 6b thus: 'Non aumentò nè si mescolò ne si divise
per nulla nelle nature dopo l'unione.' M. Cramer, l.c., 'He is not poured out'; J. Muyser, l.c.,
'Hij stortte Zich niet uit.' Whether the otherwise christologically attested ἐκχέω, ἐκκέχυται
(Gregory of Nyss., *C. Eunom.* I: Jaeger I, 224,15; PG 45, 464B) can correspond to this cannot
be determined.

For the maintenance of these two poles the one side demands the 'one-nature formula', the other the formula of the 'one hypostasis in two natures'. The same idea returns in more elegant form in the Wednesday theotokion (V):[58]

> Greetings, workplace (ἐργαστήριον) (Brogi: 'sede'; Muyser: 'burcht') of the undivided union in which the natures (φύσις) come together without mixing to one single hyposta-sis (ὑπόστασις).

(d) *Amplifying Cyrillian formulas*. One can easily find the entire formulary of Cyrillian Christology in the canonical hours of both confessions. Let us take the well-known formula, 'out of two, one' (ἐκ δύο εἷς). It can be used by both sides, since it came into use again through the neo-Chalcedonians after 451, although the fathers of Chalcedon had rejected this expression.[59] We cite two examples:

Sunday theotokion, tune: Adam, III (thus Muyser, pp. 80–81): 'Jesus Christ, our Lord, our God and our hope, is truly one *out of two and in two natures*, namely, out of the pure divinity without corruption, consubstantial with the Father, and out of the pure humanity without sexual coupling, of the same nature as we, according to the economy of salvation, which he took from you [Mary], the immaculate one, and with which he united hypostatically.' (Tukhi's text adds to the 'out of two natures' the Chalcedonian 'in two natures'.)

The same theotokion (according to Brogi, no. 2, pp. 34–35): 'One out of two, one holy divinity, which is indestructible, consubstantial with the Father, and one holy humanity, absolutely undefiled, consubstantial with us according to the economy.[60] That which he assumed in you, the immaculate one, and united with according to the hypostasis.'

Thursday theotokion, tune: Batos V (Brogi, p. 63; Muyser, p. 126): 'He is *one out of two natures*: the divinity and the humanity: the Magi worshipped him as such when they tacitly recognized his divinity.'

With Cyril[61] the Coptic liturgy also applied the image of the *burning bush* (Ex 3,1–5) to the incarnation, yet first to the union of divinity and humanity in Christ and then to the presence of the incarnate One in Mary: as the divinity did not burn up the human nature of Christ (thus the christological conception of Cyril), so also Mary is not injured by the

---

58. See Muyser, pp. 117–18; Brogi, p. 59, whose translation, however, seems less appropriate.

59. Cf. I. Ortiz de Urbina, 'Das Symbol von Chalkedon. Sein Text, sein Werden, seine dogmatische Bedeutung', in *Chalkedon* I, p. 396; A. Grillmeier, *CCT* II/2, p. 432.

60. This 'consubstantial with us' also contains, according to the Tuesday theotokion, no. 4, the confession to the spiritual soul in Christ. Cf. M. Brogi, op. cit., 55: 'Pienamente consostanziale a noi, ed ha un'anima intellettiva. Rimase Dio secondo il suo essere e divenne uomo perfetto.'

61. Cyril of Alex., *Hom. pasch.* (CPG 5240), 17: PG 77, 781C.

fire of Christ's divinity (thus the mariological conception contained in the Lôbsh Batos[62]).

(e) Even the vigorously disputed 'one of the Trinity [suffered, was born, etc.]'[63] is not missing. Thus the Thursday theotokion, no. 8, reads: 'One of the Trinity, consubstantial with the Father, regarded our lowliness.'[64] Or Mary is called the temple of the 'one of the Trinity'.[65]

Also an impressive example of the fondness for this formula is the following troparion, which served (nine times in all) as responsorial verse to the Magnificat and the Nunc Dimittis:

'One of the Trinity, the God-Logos Christ, assumed flesh without division in the Virgin Mary. He endured the cross. He was resurrected from the dead. He ascended to heaven. Come, let us worship him.'[66]

6. The Coptic synaxarion

More than a few observations on the position of Christology in Coptic liturgical life can be made on the basis of the *Synaxarium Alexandrinum*, which unfortunately has not yet experienced the same careful treatment and explanation as the synaxarion of the Ethiopian church (see below). We find in it, however, the needed information about the christological structure of the church year,[67] which makes no difference between orthodox and catholic Copts. The dividing elements result only (1) from the mentioning or ignoring of synods, which concerns above all Chalcedon, and (2) from the relatively frequent information on the festivals of saints who are among the disputants against Chalcedon:

---

62. In Brogi, pp. 65–66; Muyser, pp. 131–32. This mariological application of the image of the fire goes back to Ephraem the Syrian. For more detail cf. A. Grillmeier, 'Die Taufe Christi und die Taufe der Christen', in *Fides Sacramenti Sacramentum Fidei. Studies in honour of Pieter Smulders*, Assen 1981 (137–75), 161–62.

63. See A. Grillmeier, *CCT* II/2, pp. 317–43.

64. M. Brogi, op. cit., p. 65.

65. Thus in the Wednesday theotokion, no. 6 (Brogi, p. 60).

66. From the ms. M 574 of the Pierpont Morgan Libr. (end of 9th cent. in the Fayyum), p. 134,6–11, ed. in H. Quecke, *Untersuchungen*, p. 409. On the text of the Troparion: ibid. pp. 267–69.

67. See I. Forget, *Synaxarium Alexandrinum* I–II: CSCO 47–49, 67; N. Nilles, *Kalendarium Manuale utriusque Ecclesiae Orientalis et Occidentalis* I–II, Oeniponte 1879, 1881; on II, appendix, chap. II, pp. 637–59: *De anno ecclesiastico Coptorum*. According to this, seven *Festivitates maiores* are named: *Annuntiatio, Nativitas, Baptismus Christi, Fest. Olivarum, Resurrectio, Ascensio, Pentecostes*. Then there are *Festa minora: Circumcisio, Primum miraculum, Ingressus in templum, Coena Domini, Dominica Thomae* (= 1st Sunday after Easter); *Ingressus in Aegyptum, Transfiguratio*. Yet one must note here that the month Kiyahk as preparation for the celebration of Christmas and then the time of the 'forty days' before Easter must be added to the schedule (cf. M. Cramer, *Koptische Liturgien*, 10–11, 26–28). – One could also note the

Named, according to Forget I, are: Dioscorus (519), Severus of Antioch (520, 522, 525), Felix, Roman pope (because of the so-called Apollinarian forgeries!) (521); Acacius of Constantinople (as instigator of the Acacian schism) (522); John I of Alexandria (patriarch 496–505) with reference to Emperor Zeno (*Henoticon!*): 'Erat tunc temporis in urbe Constantinopoli imperator fidelis et sanctus, qui huic patri sancto pioque auctor fuit ut manum in *vicinas* regiones extenderet, indeque fides orthodoxa in universas Aegypti partes diffusa est' (Forget II, p. 102,8–12). Naturally, one must not leave out Timothy Aelurus, who is called the successor of Dioscorus (Forget II, p. 254).

Thus was the Coptic church remembered in the leading figures of its history. For them there are also individual *doxologies for the saints*, which in accordance with their hymnic character have a more powerful effect. We close with the typical doxology for Severus of Antioch:

> Solid leader, best fighter, victor in the battles, shining lamp! Herald of orthodoxy is the patriarch Severus, the master of the reasonable flock of Christ. Your right doctrines struck the heart of the heretics like a two-edged sword in the power of the Trinity . . . Ask the Lord for us, master of orthodoxy, Severus [with Dioscorus (which is a later addition)], that He forgive us our sins (doxology for Patriarch Abba Severus, Brogi, p. 106).

---

christological reference in the Coptic sacramental liturgy. Cf. C. Kopp, *Glaube und Sakramente der koptischen Kirche* (OC 25), Rome 1932, where, however, this does not happen. But see pp. 11–74: general information on the Coptic church. Instructive is the article of M. de Fenoyl, 'La liturgie eucharistique dans le rite copte', POC 7 (1957), 193–206; 8 (1958), 117–29. Further perspectives on the nature of prayer in the Coptic church are offered by G. Giamberardini, *La preghiera nella Chiesa Copta* (SOC.C 8), Cairo 1963, which distinguishes between private prayer, monastic prayer and liturgical prayer with the inclusion of individual christological texts.

PART THREE

THE 'CROSS OF CHRIST' OVER NUBIA

Only in recent decades, in the wake of the archaeological rescue work made necessary by the construction of the Aswan High Dam, have we had access to unexpectedly rich discoveries and new knowledge about the one thousand years of Christianity in the Sudan. The main phase of the Christianization of these broad lands is directly connected with the post-Chalcedonian religious policy under Emperor Justinian and his wife Theodora and their followers. Without the application of military force, Byzantium was able to establish in Africa beyond the imperial borders at the first cataract of the Nile a bridgehead of its religiously political influence, which was to last about as long as the Byzantine Empire itself. It is true that at present we have only a few testimonies of the content of the faith in Christ of the newly evangelized tribes on the Nile between Philae and Khartoum. Yet they convey several insights that are suited to clearing away some clichés that burden the presentation of post-Chalcedonian history. On the positive side, there are gains for the ecumenical concern that this presentation seeks to serve.

CHAPTER ONE

THE SILENT 'EREMITE MISSION' IN PRE-CHALCEDONIAN NUBIA[1]

In the traditional sense Nubia is understood as the lands in the Nile valley from the first cataract at Aswan to approximately present-day Khartoum

---

1. On the following: (1) general literature: J. Maspero, *Histoire des Patriarches d'Alexandrie*, Paris 1923; idem, 'Théodore de Philae', *RevHistRel* 59 (1909), 299–317; J. Kraus, *Die Anfänge des Christentums in Nubien*, Mödling 1930; republished in MWSt 2 (1931) (= Kraus I); idem, 'Neues zur Geschichte des christlichen Nubien', *NZM* 24 (1968), 241–57 (= Kraus II); U. Monneret de Villard, *Storia della Nubia cristiana* (OCA 118), Rome 1938; also E. Stein, 'Nubie chrétienne', *RHE* 36 (1940), 131–42; U. Monneret de Villard, *La Nubia medioevale* IV, Cairo 1935–57; G. Lanczkowski, 'Aethiopia', *JAC* 1 (1958), 134–53. II. Nubien (148–53) with bibl. B. Spuler, HO 1, 8, 2 (Leiden/Cologne 1961), 295–97; W. H. C. Frend, 'Nubia as an Outpost of Byzantine Cultural Influence', *ByzSlav* 29/2 (1968), 319–26; idem, *The Rise of the Monophysite Movement*, Cambridge 1972, 297–303; I. Engelhardt, *Mission und Politik in Byzanz. Ein Beitrag zur Strukturanalyse Byzantinischer Mission zur Zeit Justins und Justinians* (MiscByzMon 19), Munich 1974. – (2) Excavations and research: (a) *Nubia. Récentes recherches. Actes du Colloque Nubiologique International au Musée National de Varsovie 19–22 Juin 1972*, ed. K. Michałowski, Warsaw 1975, including: W. Y. Adams, 'The Twilight of Nubian Christianity', 11–17; E. Dinkler, 'Beobachtungen zur Ikonographie der nubischen Kunst', 22–30; C. D. G. Müller, 'Die nubische Literatur. Bestand und Eigenart', 93–100; P. van Moorsel, '"Bilder ohne Worte". Problems in Nubian Christian Iconography', 126–29; E. Dinkler, *Kunst und Geschichte Nubiens in christlicher Zeit. Ergebnisse und Probleme auf Grund der jüngsten Ausgrabungen*, Recklinghausen 1970, including: M. Krause, 'Zur Kirchen- und Theologiegeschichte Nubiens', 71–86; C. D. G. Müller, 'Deutsche Textfunde in Nubien', 245–58 (with plates); (b) *Études Nubiennes. Colloques de Chantilly 2–6 Juillet 1975*, Cairo 1978, including: W. H. C. Frend, 'The Greek Liturgical Papyri from the Cathedral at Q'asr Ibrim', 95; M. Krause, 'Bischof Johannes III von Faras und seine beiden Nachfolger. Noch einmal zum Problem eines Konfessionswechsels in Faras', 153–64; C. D. G. Müller, 'Grundzüge der Frömmigkeit in der nubischen Kirche', 209–24; (3) Individual studies: K. Michałowski, *Faras. Die Kathedrale aus dem Wüstensand*, Einsiedeln–Cologne 1967; J. Vantini, *The Excavations at Faras. A Contribution to the History of Christian Nubia*, Bologna 1970; idem, *Christianity in the Sudan*, Bologna 1981; M. Krause, 'Zur Kirchengeschichte Nubiens', in T. Hägg, *Nubian Culture Past and Present. Main Papers Presented at the Sixth International Conference for Nubian Studies in Uppsala, 11–16 August 1986*, Stockholm 1987, 293–308 (with summary in English).

at the confluence of the White Nile and the Blue Nile. The population was composed of 'a non-transparent multiplicity of tribes'.[2] In the sixth century the land consisted of three kingdoms: (1) to the north, between the first and third cataracts, the most significant of them: Nobatia or Maris with the capital Faras (Pachoras); (2) south of there Makuria (Arabic: Maqorrah) with the capital (Old) Dongola; (3) further south, with fluid boundaries, Aloa with the capital Soba in the area of present-day Khartoum. Between 650 and 710 the old kingdom of Nobatia was united with Makuria.[3]

Already before 451 – more precisely, even in the third and fourth centuries – Christianity advanced from Egypt towards Nubia through slow infiltration.[4] Yet one must not form exaggerated ideas of this. The most important missionary base still lay in Egypt, on the Nile island of Philae, the 'harbour of the kingdom of Nubia'.[5] According to a statement of Barhebraeus, which is unfortunately not supportable through sources, Christianity is supposed to have penetrated 'not only all of Egypt but also the Sudan and Nubia and Abyssinia' already by the end of the time of persecution.[6] Yet such a global testimony does not mean much. We are better informed by a Coptic text that was found in the outer wall of the monastery of St Mercurius at Edfu in a region that was the centre of Nubian culture until the eleventh century.[7] The monastery library also contained texts in Nubian and Greek. According to T. Orlandi, this allows the conclusion that it was a question of Nubian monks, because the libraries of purely Coptic-Egyptian monasteries contained no Greek codices. The codex presents the 'Histories of the Monks in the Egyptian Desert', written by Paphnutius. In it the *Vita Aaronis* is described in

---

2. Kraus II, p. 242.

3. M. Krause, 'Zur Kirchen- und Theologiegeschichte Nubiens', p. 71. U. Monneret de Villard, *Storia*, pp. 79ff., places this union less than two decades before 710 (date of the inscription of King Mercurius), probably 704. He designates 704/705 as a very significant year in Nubian history. Something definitive can be asserted only after further excavations, if possible (M. Krause).

4. See Kraus II, p. 242; I. Engelhardt, *Mission und Politik in Byzanz*, pp. 44–51; T. Orlandi, 'Un testo copto sulle origini del cristianesimo in Nubia', in *Études Nubiennes*, Chantilly 1975, 225–30.

5. Kraus I, p. 30, n. 111, according to Arabian sources; H. Munier, 'Le christianisme à Philae', *BSAC* 4 (1938), 42–43 with n. 1; idem, *Recueil des listes épiscopales de l'église copte*, Cairo 1943, 8–9.

6. Barhebraeus, *Hist. comp. dyn., arab.-latine*, ed. E. Pocockius, Oxford 1663, T.: p. 135, V.: p. 85.

7. See T. Orlandi, art. cit.

detail.[8] This text represents the only presently known written testimony that we have about earlier contacts between Christians and Nubians (and Blemmyes), apart from a reference by Cosmas Indicopleustes.[9] The monk Paphnutius traversed the 'southern region' (Maris) in search of eremites, to whom the first part of the writing is dedicated.[10] The geographical centre of the story here is Syene (= Aswan) on the eastern bank of the Nile, known for its syenite (Pliny). Between 425 and 450 the bishop of this city (and of the new Syene and the island Elephantine) wrote a communication to Emperor Theodosius II from which we discern that Nubians and Blemmyes are still an acute danger for the churches on the island of Philae.[11] In the second part of the story Paphnutius is guided by the eremite Pselusius to Isaac, the disciple of Aaron. The latter conceals himself on a little island of the first cataract and thus a little south of Philae. Now, Isaac first tells the history of the conversion of the island of Philae and of its bishops.[12] Then follows the life of Aaron[13] with many miracle stories, in which the topic is often the Nubians.[14] Thus a direct contact between Nubia and Egypt is arranged by the monks. The Christian life and piety of the Nubian church were more strongly shaped by such eremite monks than by the so-called 'official mission' of the sixth century.[15] They came not so much from the strictly Coptic Upper Egypt, or from the strongly Hellenized Lower Egypt, as from the Fayyum.[16] Yet the archimandrite Shenoute also seems to have made efforts from Upper Egypt to convert the Nubians and Blemmyes, yet without lasting success.[17]

---

8. See E. A. W. Budge, *Miscellaneous Coptic Texts in the Dialect of Upper Egypt*, London 1915, 445–93 (T), 984–1011 (V); excerpted in Kraus I, pp. 47–51; cf. M. Krause, art. cit., p. 75; F. F. Gadallah, 'The Egyptian Contribution to Nubian Christianity', in *Sudan Notes and Records* 40 (1959), 38–43; I. Engelhardt, op. cit., pp. 44–45.

9. Cosmas Ind., *Top. chr.* III, 66: Wolska-Conus, SC 141, p. 505, where the Nubians and Garamantes are mentioned.

10. E. A. W. Budge, op. cit., pp. 432–71 (Copt.), pp. 948–87 (Engl.).

11. Cf. H. Munier, 'Le christianisme à Philae', *BSAC* 4 (1938) (37–49), 43, on Shenoute.

12. Mentioned are Bishop Macedonius as the first bishop of Philae: Budge, (V), pp. 958–89; and his son Marcus, who as bishop took part in the Synod of Alexandria in 362: PG 26, 807–8; H. Munier, *Recueil des Listes Épiscopales d'Église Copte*, Cairo 1943, 8–9.

13. E. A. W. Budge, op. cit., pp. 471–95 (Copt.), pp. 986–1011 (Engl.).

14. T. Orlandi, art. cit., *Ét. Nub.* (1975), p. 227, n. 1.

15. Cf. C. D. G. Müller, 'Grundzüge der Frömmigkeit in der nubischen Kirche', in *Études Nubiennes*, Chantilly 1975 (209–24), 222–24.

16. Ibid., p. 223.

17. J. Leipoldt, *Schenute von Atripe*, Leipzig 1903, 21ff.; J. Barns, 'Shenute as a Historical Source', in *Actes du Xe congrès international des papyrologues Warschau-Krakau, 3.–9. Sept. 1961*, Warsaw–Kraków 1964, 151–59.

On the part of many archaeologists there was an inclination to draw a rather optimistic picture of the pre-Chalcedonian evangelization of Nubia. After the discovery of the oldest church of Faras by K. Michałowski, proof seemed to have been found for the presence of a relatively strong Christian community there already in the middle or end of the fifth century. The successful excavator also believed that he could date the so-called Southern Church from the same time.[18] Yet this assumption was called into question with strong arguments. According to P. Grossmann it is certain that the early datings can be supported neither for the oldest church nor for the palace nor for the Southern Church nor, finally, for the Rivergate Church.[19] There were, Grossmann says, probably modest beginnings of a Christianization of the land before the evangelization presented by John of Ephesus, and these can be demonstrated for individual places.[20] Yet greater successes are not to be assumed for the eremite mission through which the pre-Justinian Christianization of the land was introduced. In any case, they were probably not sufficient to enable the church of Faras under the eyes of the local pagan ruler 'to erect at the most prominent place in the city such a large church building – as the so-called Oldest Church below the cathedral is – and several further church buildings in other parts of the city'.[21] One thing is worth noting, however: the so-called silent eremite mission does not yet show the separation into confessions that marked the next phase. We have here a peculiar chapter of post-Chalcedonian missionary history.

---

18. Cf. K. Michałowski, *Faras – Die Kathedrale aus dem Wüstensand*, Einsiedeln–Cologne 1967, 48–49; on this see F. W. Deichmann, *ByzZ* 62 (1969), 110; K. Michałowski, *Das Wunder aus Faras. Ausstellungskatalog der Villa Hügel*, Essen 1969, 13; M. Krause, 'Zur Kirchen- und Theologiegeschichte Nubiens', pp. 73–74; these assumptions are very positively adopted by Kraus II, pp. 252–53.

19. P. Grossmann, 'Zur Datierung der frühen Kirchenanlagen aus Faras', *ByzZ* 64 (1971), 330–50.

20. For indications see ibid., p. 348, n. 163.

21. Ibid., pp. 348–49; I. Engelhardt, *Mission und Politik in Byzanz*, pp. 46–49.

CHAPTER TWO

THE 'OFFICIAL' EVANGELIZATION OF NUBIA IN THE SIXTH CENTURY

The forces responsible for the evangelization of Nubia are related to each other in a very complicated way. One must mention the imperial couple, Justinian and Theodora, as well as the Alexandrian patriarch Theodosius, living in Constantinople in exile.

1. The missionary expedition of the priest Julian (542–548)

Emperor Justinian had already forbidden the Isis cult in the temple of Philae in the year 535. In his commission the Persarmenian Narses destroyed the pagan shrines, had the priests arrested and transported the cult images to Constantinople.[22] The fact that the Nobatian neighbours did not resist this could be taken as a sign that Nobatia was receptive to the gospel.

Two Alexandrian clerics had come with Theodosius to the imperial city: the already very old Julian and the younger Longinus.[23] Presumably with the approval of Theodosius, Julian went to Empress Theodora and recommended to her evangelizing the people of the Nobatae, with the result that he himself was immediately appointed for this (around the year 542). Emperor Justinian was apprised of this, but according to John of Ephesus was unhappy that an opponent of Chalcedon had received this commission. So he arranged a special legation and wrote to 'his bishops' in Thebaid

---

22. On the Isis cult on the island of Philae and its end under Justinian cf. L. Kákosy, 'Das Ende des Heidentums in Ägypten', in *Graeco-Coptica*, ed. P. Nagel, Halle 1984 (61–76), 70–73.

23. On the following see John of Eph., *HE* IV 6–9, 49–53: CSCO 106 (V), 136–41, 175–83; Schönfelder, pp. 141–47, 180–88. A different translation is found in F. Altheim and R. Stiehl, *Die Araber in der Alten Welt* IV, Berlin–New York 1967, 319–33, which is cited here; cf. I. Engelhardt, *Mission und Politik in Byzanz*, pp. 52–56.

that they [the bishops] came and instructed them [the Nobatae] and that they planted there the name of the synod. And since then [or: already] he was also at work, and he quickly sent envoys ahead with gold and baptismal gowns and gifts for the king of that people and letters to the *dux* of Thebaid [asking] that the latter seek to help his [the emperor's] envoy and send him over to that people.[24]

The empress, however, 'zealous in her intelligence', wrote letters to the *dux* of Thebaid and turned them over to [a] Magistrianus. They talked of both legations. Yet Theodora gave the instruction: 'And look! I also send a blessed man, whose name is Julian. And I want this one, mine, to reach that people before that one of the emperor . . .'[25] Threatened with death if the command was refused, the *dux* obeyed the empress and held back Justinian's legation until Julian, together with Theodore, the bishop of Philae, reached the king of the Nobatae.

Already around 543 the kingdom of Nobatia officially accepted the Christian faith in its anti-Chalcedonian form, although King Silko seems not to have taken this step himself. The most important testimony for this adoption of faith is the Silko inscription known since 1820, that is, the Greek victory inscription of the Nobatian king Silko in the temple of Kalābsha (Talmis).[26] Since this ruler is designated *basiliskos* (*regulus*), it has been believed that one could assume an official relationship between him and Byzantium. This would then result in an ordering of various dates that affect the position of paganism and Christianity on the border between Egypt and Nobatia.[27]

In the year 453, still under Emperor Marcian, Florus, the governor of Upper Egypt, concluded a lasting peace treaty with the Blemmyes and Nubians. The object of the agreements was a concession of the Roman victor to both peoples, signed by the Christian general Maximus, to be able each year to hold a pilgrimage to the temple of Isis in Philae. Nevertheless, it was a great concession on the part of a Christian Roman when the wooden statue of the goddess was allowed to be picked up by ship in Philae and brought over the border to Nobatia, where one could

---

24. John of Eph., *HE* IV 6: CSCO 106, p. 137; Altheim-Stiehl, p. 320; Schönfelder, pp. 141–42.

25. John of Eph., *HE* IV 6: CSCO 106, pp. 137–38; Altheim-Stiehl, pp. 320–21; Schönfelder, p. 142. The arrival, ibid. IV 7: CSCO 106, pp. 138–39; Altheim-Stiehl, pp. 321–23; Schönfelder, pp. 143–44.

26. Greek-German in Kraus I, pp. 100–1, with explanation on pp. 101–9; Kraus II, p. 243, n. 10, where Kraus adopts the verdict of K. Michałowski, *Faras*, p. 28: 'Nothing indicates that Silko was a Christian, yet the writer was a not uneducated follower of the new religion.' Cf. I. Engelhardt, *Mission und Politik in Byzanz*, pp. 48–51, where the question of the relationship between Silko and Byzantium, particularly that of an alliance between the two, is discussed.

27. See I. Engelhardt, op. cit., pp. 46–51, which we follow.

question the idol as an oracle and then take it back again to Philae.[28] Thus the Isis cult of the Nobatae may have had a 'vital significance' (I. Engelhardt) around 453 and even into the time of Justinian. With the strenuous efforts of the emperor to eradicate paganism, the toleration of the cult of Philae must have seemed more and more unacceptable. To bring about the turning-point, the emperor seems to have played the Nobatae and Blemmyes off against one another.

> He caused the Nobatae – possibly with promises – to fight against the Blemmyes with Byzantine support. After the defeat [of the Nobatae] the action of Narses would then have taken place. The latter could then destroy the shrines on the island without encountering any resistance, since the goddess no longer had any defenders and the Nobatae, already under Christian influence, offered no resistance.[29]

Theodore, the bishop of Philae (525–578) would soon have been able to take advantage of the opportunity to transform the anteroom of the temple of Isis into a Christian church. This is attested by several inscriptions.[30] The terminating of the Isis cult and the freeing of the temple building for Christian worship must have seemed to the Christians of that time

> a far greater deed than the erection of a simple new building, which before the appropriation of the temple, moreover, could take place only with the indulgence of the pagan priesthood, which was likewise still present on the island, and its followers. At the same time, the first event means an act of overcoming paganism, and it was in fact followed by the general Christianization of Nubia.[31]

The evangelization began in the year 542 and already in 543 had achieved a considerable, even if still not thorough, success. John of Ephesus describes in detail that it was orientated 'against the synod', that is, Chalcedon:

> And immediately, when they [the Nobatae, after the reception of the gifts of honour and the numerous baptismal gowns] rejoiced, they dedicated their souls and denied all errors of their fathers and confessed the God of the Christians when they said: 'He alone is the true God, and there is no other besides him.' And after he [Julian] had given them [the Nobatae] much teaching and instruction, he let them know and taught them also in advance to the effect that 'because certain quarrels arose between the Christians because of the faith, the blessed Theodosios [the patriarch of Alexandria], when it was demanded of him that he accept [the decisions of the synod] and he did not obey, was driven from his see by the emperor; the empress, however, accepted him . . . and sent us to you so that

---

28. Sources in I. Engelhardt, op. cit., p. 46, n. 1.
29. Eadem, op. cit., p. 51, with reference to U. Monneret de Villard, *Storia*, p. 58.
30. Documentation in P. Grossmann, 'Überlegungen zum Grundriss der Ostkirche von Philae', *JAC* 13 (1970) (29–41), 40.
31. Ibid.

you also will follow the patriarch Theodosios and be baptized in his faith and follow his truth.'[32]

Certainly, even according to this report, the orderly baptismal catechesis was prominent. The newly converted were not immediately plied with the question of one or two natures in Christ. We can also document for Syria such reserve in similar circumstances. Nevertheless, Julian could not refrain – if this is not simply an addition of John the historian – from combining confessional propaganda with his catechesis. Surely the new Christians regarded themselves as bound to Theodosius, who was, of course, considered by Julian himself to be the real patriarch of Alexandria. This led naturally to inclusion of Nobatia in the Alexandrian anti-Chalcedonian obedience and succession. In any case, John of Ephesus rejoiced over the successful deception of the emperor by his spouse. Informed by Julian, the king of the Nobatae with his important officials received the imperial legates, accepted their gifts of honour, promised a reciprocal gift for the emperor, yet declared:

> We do not accept his faith, however. Rather, if we are deemed worthy to become Christians, we will follow Patriarch Theodosios, the one whom – in consequence of the wickedness of the emperor's faith, which he [Theodosios] did not want to accept – he [the emperor] drove out of his church and expelled. And if we flee from paganism and error, we also do not, on the other hand, accept falling victim to the wickedness of faith.[33]

Julian had brought the already aged bishop of Philae with him across the border. After three years of missionary work he himself returned to Constantinople and was received with great honours by Empress Theodora. He had turned the care of the Nobatae over to Theodore, who remained with the new converts until about 551. This ends the first phase of the official evangelizing of northern Nubia. It led to the success of the opponents of the fourth council. Besides the above-mentioned Silko inscription, a few other witnesses fill the large gaps in this history. In the same temple of Kalābsha in which Silko's victory was immortalized, shorter Coptic inscriptions have been found that are certainly Christian in origin. They want to tell future generations that a priest named Paul was the first Christian to pray in this temple and that he 'erected the cross' there – a motif that will engage us further. There is no reason not to regard this Paul as an anti-Chalcedonian Copt. But the mission caravan to which he belonged remains uncertain: that of Julian or only that of the following one under Bishop Longinus. Since he is

---

32. John of Eph., *HE* IV 7: CSCO 106, pp. 138–39; Altheim-Stiehl, pp. 321–22; Schönfelder, p. 143.

33. Ibid.: CSCO 106, p. 139; Altheim-Stiehl, p. 322; Schönfelder, pp. 143–44.

designated as priest, however, there is some probability that he is to be connected with Longinus.[34]

Another text has an even greater significance; this is the so-called Eirpanome inscription of Dendur (five hours further south of Kalābsha).[35] According to J. Maspero, it is to be dated 22 January 559,[36] the day of the consecration of the church of Dendur. Perhaps we have here the first example of the transformation of a pagan temple into a Christian house of God. It could well have remained relatively inconspicuous because it involved a temple consecrated to a private divinity. If around this time caution was still advisable in such undertakings, then this is a new indication that the construction of public churches there is to be placed in the sixth rather than the fourth century. For us this year of 559 is important for yet another reason: it says something about the position of Theodore of Philae for Nobatia. Apparently he accepted the responsibility for the new converts transferred to him by Julian, which he had for a lengthy period until the arrival of the new legate of Patriarch Theodosius, Bishop Longinus, and thus at least until 569.

2. The missionary expedition of Bishop Longinus (566–580)

Shortly before his death in the year 566 the ex-patriarch Theodosius designated his second companion Longinus as missionary for Nubia.[37] We are now beyond the Justinian era. Against the will of Justin II (565–578) the new envoy could escape only through flight into his mission territory. His activity unfolded in two periods.

(a) The mission of 569–575

The first catechumenate under Julian had apparently not been thorough. John of Ephesus concedes that Longinus had to start over from the beginning. The Nobatae were instructed 'anew'. Also, churches were

---

34. See J. Kraus I, p. 110; on p. 109 is the inscription, which Maspero was the first to translate and publish.

35. Text in Kraus I, pp. 111–12; M. Krause, 'Zur Kirchen- und Theologiegeschichte Nubiens', pp. 75–76 (evaluation). This inscription was later confirmed by the Greek Christian inscription of the Christian king Tokiltoeton on the fortress of Ikhmindi, which is probably also from the second half of the sixth century. Text and explanation in S. Donadoni, 'Un'epigrafe greco nubiana da Ikhmindi', in La Parola del Passato 69 (1959), 458–65.

36. J. Maspero, 'Théodore de Philae', RevHistRel 59 (1909) (299–317), 309.

37. Cf. here Theodos. Al., Mandat. prim. (CPG 7143): Doc. mon., CSCO 103, pp. 92–93. Paul of Antioch is commissioned by Theodosius to consecrate Longinus as bishop of the Nobatae.

built, an appropriate clergy designated and instruction given in all the ordinances of service and all the rules of Christianity.[38] A legation from the king of the Nobatae was to express gratitude to Justin II for the sending of Longinus:

> Even if we were Christians in name, we did not know what Christianity really is until Longinus came to us.[39]

After six years of activity the bishop let himself be drawn into the inner confusion of the anti-Chalcedonian party of Alexandria, which also set itself against him.[40] His opponents sought to separate him from the Nobatae.[41]

(b) The evangelization of the Alodaeans

In southern Nubia the Alodaeans in several legations requested the proclamation of the Christian message in their land. Longinus set out in that direction with a caravan, but the Makurites prevented him from passing through to the south. Only by extremely dangerous detours was he able to reach his goal and begin his successful work, whose duration is unknown.[42] It was typical of the time that Longinus encountered Julia-nist missionaries already in Aloa, who had come into the land from Axum.[43] In this way the north and the south of Nubia were won for Christianity in the anti-Chalcedonian mission. What about Makuria, which lies in between, and the Garamantes living west of there?

---

38. John of Eph., *HE* IV 8: CSCO 106, p. 140,15–17; Altheim-Stiehl, p. 324; Schön-felder, pp. 180–81.

39. Ibid.: CSCO 106, p. 140,24–26. The historian was 'often in their company' (Schön-felder, p. 181).

40. John of Eph., *HE* IV 49. Cf. J. Kraus I, pp. 148–51, with reference to W. A. Wigram, *The Separation of the Monophysites*, London 1923. This report of John of Ephesus is confirmed by an author who likewise knows that Longinus was called out of the distant land of the Nobatae for the patriarchal election of 575. See J. Chabot, *Documenta ad origines mono-physitarum illustrandas*, CSCO 103 (V), pp. 141–42; 192,23–26; 194,3–16; cf. E. W. Brooks, 'The Patriarch Paul of Antioch and the Alexandrine Schism of 575', *ByzZ* 30 (1929), 468–76; E. Honigmann, *Évêques et Évêchés*, pp. 226–29; I. Engelhardt, *Mission und Politik in Byzanz*, p. 65, n. 2.

41. John of Eph., *HE* IV 49–50: CSCO 106, pp. 175–78; Altheim-Stiehl, pp. 325–27; Schönfelder, pp. 180–82.

42. Ibid., IV 51–53: CSCO 106, pp. 178–83; Altheim-Stiehl, pp. 327–33; Schönfelder, pp. 183–88. Cf. Kraus I, pp. 153–56; II, pp. 243–48.

43. John of Eph., *HE* IV 53: CSCO 106, pp. 180,30–181,2; Altheim-Stiehl, p. 330; Schönfelder, pp. 185–86.

3. The Chalcedonian mission in the Middle Kingdom

At first it seems obvious that the evangelization of the named areas is to be traced back to Emperor Justinian himself.[44] Yet this is not easy to prove. John of Ephesus reports on the Makurites only in the context of describing the Alodaean mission: the king of the Makurites learned of the planned transit of missionaries towards the south and wanted to prevent it.[45] The motive is unclear: was the king of the Makurites reacting as a pagan against the Christian missionary or, as is often assumed, as a Chalcedonian against the 'Monophysites'? L. Duchesne believed that he had found the answer in the orthodox Goth from Spain, John of Biclar. From 567 to 576 John was in Constantinople and says in his chronicle for 569: 'Around this time the people of the Makurites accepted the faith of Christ (fidem Christi).'[46] According to the usual linguistic usage, fides Christi by itself seemed to mean the Chalcedonian faith. Yet the chronicler uses the expression supraconfessionally. For he also uses it to describe the conversion of the Monophysite Armenians.[47] Thus the testimony of John of Biclar offers no further help. The last resort remains the Annals of the Melkite patriarch Eutychius of Alexandria (933–940).[48] Yet here we immediately encounter serious reservations. Eutychius wrote 300 years after John of Ephesus and in such a polemical form that he challenges an anti-Chalcedonian counter-presentation by Severus ibn al-Muqaffaʿ, the bishop of Ashmunein (tenth century).[49] His report on the conversion of 'Nubia' is apparently in direct opposition to that of John of Ephesus. For we read in Eutychius that the 'Nubians' were first Melkites; only later – during the ninety-seven-year vacancy in the Melkite patriarchate of Alexandria (629–726) – were anti-Chalcedonian bishops sent to the 'Nubians' from Alexandria. Thus were the 'Jacobites' able to occupy all the churches of Egypt and Alexandria. The victory of the anti-Chalcedonians was more exactly fixed in the year 719. With this we

---

44. Detailed discussion in I. Engelhardt, *Mission und Politik in Byzanz*, pp. 67–71 (Makuria); pp. 71–73 (Garamantes).

45. John of Eph., *HE* IV 51: CSCO 106, pp. 178–79; Altheim-Stiehl, p. 328; Schön-felder, p. 183.

46. John of Biclar, *Chronica*: MGH AA, vol. 11, *Chron. min.*, ed. T. Mommsen, Berlin 1894, 212. See A. Grillmeier, *CCT* II/1, p. 33 (II.4.); L. Duchesne, *L'Église au VIᵉ siècle*, Paris 1925, 300, n. 1.

47. John of Biclar, op. cit., p. 211.

48. Eutychius of Alex., *Annales*: PG 111, pp. 1122–23. See A. Grillmeier, *CCT* II/1, p. 31 (2b). On the credibility of Eutychius cf. G. Graf, *Die christliche arabische Literatur bis zur fränkischen Zeit*, Freiburg 1905, 40; idem, *Geschichte der christlichen arabischen Literatur* II, 32–34; Kraus I, pp. 60–61, 89–90; I. Engelhardt, *Mission und Politik in Byzanz*, pp. 57–73.

49. Severus ibn al-Muqaffaʿ, *Hist. Patr.*: PO 1, pp. 403–23.

seem to be a long way from the presentation of John of Ephesus, which we have followed thus far.

Deciding against John of Ephesus and for Eutychius is above all U. Monneret de Villard:[50] The 'Nubians' were first Chalcedonians and only later became opponents of the council. Indeed, according to Monneret John betrays confessional narrowness and partiality. A support for this view of the original Chalcedonian evangelization of the 'Nubians' seemed to be provided by H. Junker. He had discovered that most of the Greek inscriptions on Nubian Christian gravestones contained the prayer of the dead from the *Euchologion Mega*,[51] a formula that, according to Junker, is typical of the Greek Orthodox but not of the Egyptian church. This seemed to establish that Nubia received its liturgy directly from Byzantium and accordingly through Chalcedonian missionaries and was thus itself Chalcedonian.[52] Yet H. Junker himself had to concede that the formula from the *Euchologion Mega* was in use in various anti-Chalcedonian churches, for example, in Egypt, Ethiopia and Armenia. It was found, moreover, already on the gravestones of the earliest period as well as on those of the late period.[53]

W. Y. Adams believed that he had found a further argument for a change of confession in Nubia in the eighth century. He ascertained that in this period the sanctuary (*haikal*) of the Nubian churches was enlarged and inferred a general shift from the Chalcedonian to the anti-Chalcedonian confession of faith.[54] M. Krause took a position against this thesis.[55] Although he also, while referring to G. Graf, believes that he must doubt the reliability of Eutychius – which, as we will see, is not necessary, at least in our case – he correctly emphasizes 'that the archaeological evidence can give no answer to the question whether worship in a church is celebrated according to the Monophysite or Dyophysite direction of faith, and indeed for the reason that until now it has not been demonstrated . . . that the theological difference has been manifested in various church types' (op. cit., p. 77). Certainly, confession and church meeting-place play a definite role in the post-Chalcedonian controversy. According to M.

---

50. U. Monneret de Villard, *Storia*, pp. 62–63, 158–60; idem, 'La chiesa melkita', *Aegyptus* 12 (1932), 309–16. Monneret believes he is able to make out Taphis (present-day Tāifā) in a list of Melkite episcopal sees, in that he identifies it with Tathis, which is mentioned in the list but not otherwise verifiable. Versus H.-G. Beck, *Kirche und Literatur*, p. 155: 'Here imagination seems to have outstripped every historical possibility.' Cf. I. Engelhardt, *Mission und Politik in Byzanz*, p. 61, n. 7.

51. Cf. J. Goar, *Euchologion sive rituale Graecum*, Venice 1730, 724.

52. H. Junker, 'Die christlichen Grabsteine Nubiens', *ZÄS* 60 (1925), 111–48. Junker's arguments were adopted by U. Monneret de Villard, *Storia*, pp. 61–62; K. Michałowski, *Faras*, pp. 90–91; Kraus II, p. 223. Against this liturgical-historical thesis is T. Lefort, in E. Stein, 'Nubie chrétienne', *RHE* 36 (1940), 138; M. Krause, 'Zur Kirchen- und Theologiegeschichte Nubiens', p. 83; H. Quecke, *Orientalia* 43 (1974) (135–41), 137–38, review of: S. Jakobielski, *Faras III. A History of the Bishopric of Pachoras on the Basis of Coptic Inscriptions*, Warsaw 1972.

53. Bibl. in I. Engelhardt, *Mission und Politik in Byzanz*, p. 63 with n. 8; ibid., pp. 63–64: 'If the prayer of the dead were as specifically Dyophysite as Junker asserts, then the transition of Nubia from the presumed original Dyophysitism, according to Junker, to Monophysitism would have to have brought with it a change in the gravestone formulas. Yet even today both the Melkite and Monophysite Copts use almost identical liturgical books' (with reference to T. Lefort).

54. See W. Y. Adams, 'Post Pharaonic Nubia in the Light of Archaeology I', *JEA* 51 (1965), 160–78; idem, 'The Architectural Evolution of the Nubian Church, 500–1400 A.D.', *JARCE* 4 (1965), 87–139. Adams abandoned this judgement.

55. M. Krause, 'Zur Kirchen- und Theologiegeschichte Nubiens', p. 76, n. 64.

Krause, W. Y. Adams, with his first assumption, could have appealed to the quarrel of Chalcedonians and anti-Chalcedonians over the possession of churches in the city of Menas under Michael I (764–768). More apt is an example that A. Guillaumont offers in his report on the excavations in the Kellia.[56]

According to the Council of Chalcedon (451) there were two churches in the Kellia, since the monks there were divided into two parties, pro and contra Chalcedon. We have knowledge of this not through the findings of excavations but through an *Apophthegma*, namely, Phokas 1 (PG 65, 432A-433A). Abba Phokas from the monastery of Abba The-ognius of Jerusalem stayed in the Kellia after 451 and tells of a young monk, Abba Jacob, whose bodily father was likewise a monk there and his spiritual leader. 'Now the Kellia have two churches: that of the orthodox [Chalcedonians], where he receives Communion, and that of the schismatics [anti-Chalcedonians]. Since Abba Jacob had the grace of humility, he was loved by all, both by those of the Church and by the schismatics (ἀποσχίσται). The orthodox said to him: "Be careful, Abba Jacob, that the schismatics do not deceive you and draw you into their community." The schismatics said the same thing to him: "Know this, Abba Jacob: when you have communion with the Dyophysites, you lose your soul, for they are Nestorians and falsify the truth"' (PG 65, 432AB). In his simplicity, Abba Jacob escaped this dilemma by fleeing to a cell lying outside the laura. He donned his death clothes (tunic, hood), as if in order to die. After forty days he saw a child full of joy coming to him. Jacob recognized the figure and told the Lord all his woes. The Lord spoke to him: 'There where you are, that is, with the Chalcedonians, there you are good.' Hardly had he heard these words when he found himself again before the doors of the holy church of the orthodox, the followers of the council (ibid., 432D-433A).

Nothing indicates that there had been a difference in the structure of the two churches. On the contrary: each of the two parties had to be careful to proclaim its loyalty to the tradition and introduce no innovations. In this regard the Chalcedonians had the greater burden of proof in Egypt, because the anti-Chalcedonians claimed for themselves 'loyalty to tradition'. In the two named churches the Eucharist was also celebrated, and certainly according to the same liturgy. What separates the monks is the conviction that participation in the opponents' eucharistic celebration brings not life but death, even if it may proceed exactly according to liturgical traditions. Indeed, we also saw with Shenoute that within the same communities and with the same eucharistic celebration, with no liturgical and architectural difference, there could be profound separation simply on the basis of the conviction with which one met the mysteries. The first manifestation of this difference was abstention from the common celebration. The lament over this is well known.[57] Thus as one could have in the Kellia two churches in the same area without requiring an architectural difference, so also one cannot, conversely, infer from successive architectural changes a change in the faith of the community of Faras. Nor can it be demonstrated that the symbolic content of the *haikal* was essentially

---

56. A. Guillaumont, 'Histoire du Site des Kellia d'après les documents écrits', in *Kellia I KOM 219 Fouilles exécutées en 1964 et 1965 sous la direction de F. Daumas et A. Guillaumont* (Fasc. I), Cairo 1969 (1–15), 8–9. See also R. Kasser, *Kellia. Topographie* (Rech. Suisses d'Archéol. Copte, vol. II), Geneva 1972, 55–59.

57. See A. Shisha-Halevy, 'Unpublished Shenoutiana in the British Library', *Enchoria* 5 (1975), 104: Shenoute lamented Satan's seduction, whose aim was 'that they should abandon their assemblies, as is the custom of some; and thus has every heresy seceded, since Adam, the first man, until today . . .' It is not for nothing that the archimandrite admonished at his death: 'Do not miss the synaxes, the prayers and fasting . . .': *Sin. Vit. Boh.* 180: CSCO 129, p. 44,16–17.

differently conceived for the two confessions.[58] M. Krause can exclude this by referring to the 'Order of the Priesthood' (chap. 21).[59] None of the here named thirteen differences between Copts and Melkites is sufficient to draw on the archaeological findings as the criterion for whether the faithful in a church were Mono- or Dyophysites. From our viewpoint it is significant that precisely in chapter 21 this Order of the Priesthood refers to Patriarch Theodosius I.[60]

The controversy over the historical reliability of the *Annals* of Eutychius for the question of a change of confession by the 'Nubians' was, in our opinion, already settled in the year 1940.[61] In an informative review of U. Monneret de Villard's work, *Storia della Nubia cristiana*, E. Stein also ascribes to Patriarch Eutychius a *notitia episcopatuum* of the Melkite patriarchate of Alexandria. This is known to us through a commentary of the Egyptian Yusif, written around 1316.[62] In it we find a narrowed usage of the name *Nubia*. It refers, namely, not to the three united kingdoms as we know them, but only to the Makurite part (Arabian *Maqorrah*, in contrast to the Nobatian part, which is called *Maris* here[63]). Now, the *Annals* of Eutychius have the same linguistic usage. The 'Nubians' here are the Makurites. The Melkite confession is ascribed to them alone. Nothing is said about Nobatia and Aloa. Thus John of Ephesus and Eutychius need not contradict each other.

---

58. One would have to consider to what extent the unchangeability of the altar area (*haikal*), as it is described and substantiated in the *Order of the Priesthood*, belongs so much to the general religious consciousness in Egypt and Nubia that even on this basis a change of its symbolic elements must be accepted as impossible. See J. Assfalg, *Die Ordnung des Priestertums. Ein altes liturgisches Handbuch der koptischen Kirche* (Publications du Centre d'Études Orientales de la Custodie Franciscaine de Terre-Sainte – Coptica 10), Cairo 1955, 79–86. The whole chapter points to the heavenly origin of the liturgical precepts – always with reference to the Old Testament. Again, it must have been important to the Melkites to show that they also wanted to preserve this heavenly tradition precisely for the *haikal*. Otherwise they would have put themselves in the wrong from the beginning.

59. M. Krause, 'Zur Kirchen- und Theologiegeschichte Nubiens', p. 78; J. Assfalg, op. cit., pp. 127–37. This *Order of the Priesthood* did not originate, it is true, until the first half of the thirteenth century. Yet the lack of a reference to differences in the arrangement of the *haikal* allows the conclusion that there were none of confessional significance.

60. J. Assfalg, op. cit., p. 127: 'As especially concerns the difference among them with regard to the union, namely the basic doctrine in which they disagree, the Copts who are the Jacobites – who follow the teaching of Jacob who received it from the father, Patriarch Abba Theodosios – believe of Christ that he is one single nature out of two natures, one single will out of two wills, one single person out of two persons.'

61. E. Stein, 'Nubie chrétienne', *RHE* 36 (1940) (131–42), 135.

62. Translated by H. Hilgenfeld, in H. Gelzer, 'Ungedruckte und wenig bekannte Bistümerverzeichnisse der orientalischen Kirche', *ByzZ* 2 (1893) (22–72), 36–37.

63. H. Gelzer, art. cit., p. 38.

CHAPTER THREE

THE FURTHER HISTORY OF CHRISTIAN NUBIA

Serious military events shaped the subsequent history of Nubia. In the year 616 the Sassanid Persian Chosroes II (590–628) conquered Egypt. According to the results of the excavation of Faras, he seems to have broken through to this city, but this cannot be definitely proved.[64] Of much greater consequence was the occupation of Egypt by the Arabs in the year 641,[65] with the following results:

(1) Externally there was a temporary ecclesiastical isolation of Alexandria and a definitive separation from Byzantium in terms of church politics. (2) The internal result, however, was a unification of the Nubians, who had previously been divided into three groups. This history begins with King Mercurius of Makuria (d. after 710) around the turn of the seventh to the eighth century. He forced the annexation of the northern kingdom of Nobatia into the middle kingdom.[66] Dongola was made the new common capital. For post-Chalcedonian history it is significant that Mercurius adopted the anti-Chalcedonian confession of the Nobatae – probably in connection with the installation of a corresponding leadership. Aloa, anti-Chalcedonian since Longinus, 'carried on its own rather vacillating politics in sometimes closer, sometimes looser association with the real Nubia'.[67] In any case, now began 'the real history of the united kingdom of Nubia' (Kraus). It is significant that this kingdom appears as an offshoot of the imperial ecclesiastical structure of the Byzantine Empire. Mercurius was celebrated by his bishops as the

---

64. See the overview of the further history of Nubia in K. Michałowski, *Faras*, pp. 31–39.

65. Ibid., pp. 31–32; U. Monneret de Villard, *Storia* (OCA 118), pp. 71–78.

66. K. Michałowski, op. cit., p. 32.

67. Kraus II, p. 245; U. Monneret de Villard, op. cit., pp. 147–57.

'new Constantine',[68] whom his actions seemed to resemble, especially in the transformation of old pharaonic temples into Christian churches or in the expansion of buildings that had become too small. The information from the middle of the eighth century to the effect that Nubian kings were at the same time ordained priests sounds curious but reliable. They were permitted to celebrate the liturgy, however, only as long as they had shed no blood. In the middle of the ninth century the heir to the throne, George, requested from the Alexandrian patriarch a collapsible portable altar, which he wanted to take with him on trips.[69] The son of Mercurius and two later successors renounced the throne and became monks.[70] Nevertheless, the kingdom of Nubia was able to survive eight hundred years in all. After the demise of the kingdom, the Christian church persisted for yet some time, but finally suffocated under the pressure of Islam.

We have devoted a relatively large space to Nubia, because here the buried past must again be awakened. If we already look ahead to Ethiopia, our eyes fall on a closed territory from Alexandria through Philae and Khartoum to the sources of the Blue Nile, which was united and anti-Chalcedonian under the leadership of the patriarch of Alexandria, and whose extent far exceeded the kingdom of Chalcedonian Byzantium. Apart from Alexandria, neither the Coptic nor the Nubian nor the Ethiopian territory stands in opposition to Byzantium, although the anti-Chalcedonian confession completely prevailed there.

---

68. U. Monneret de Villard, op. cit., p. 80, according to the 'Lives of the Patriarchs': PO 5, p. 140; Kraus II, p. 245. – It should be noted, however, that after the conquest of Egypt by the Arabs (640/641) no further proof is given for direct contacts between Nubia and the *court* of Constantinople. Yet Byzantine influence continued to spread even in the following period. Cf. W. H. C. Frend, 'Nubia as an Outpost of Byzantine Cultural Influence', *ByzSlav* 29/2 (1968) (319–26), 320: '. . . the imprint of Byzantium was preserved and even extended'. The resurrection of Byzantine power in the tenth and eleventh centuries and the simultaneous weakening of the Coptic church encouraged the Nubians to maintain further contacts beyond Egypt with Byzantium. Not until the 14th century did the influence of Byzantium yield to that of Islam. Then in the 15th century came the end of one-thousand-year-old Christian Nubia (ibid., p. 326). – Cf. W. Y. Adams, 'The Twilight of Nubian Christianity', in *Nubia. Récentes recherches*, Varsovie 1975, 11–17.

69. See John Diaconus in U. Monneret de Villard, *Storia*, p. 99.

70. Cf. Kraus II, p. 246. We should note that John of Nikiu may not be named as a witness to the developing Christianity in Nubia. Cf. Kraus I, pp. 77–82.

CHAPTER FOUR

IN SEARCH OF NUBIAN FAITH IN CHRIST

After the anti-Chalcedonian direction of the Nubian church was so strongly emphasized by John of Ephesus, one would expect that the post-Chalcedonian battle-cry, here *mia physis*, there *dyo physeis*, would be audible from all sides. Yet in the few text fragments that are presently available, silence rules.[71] Various observations suggest that the Nubian picture of Christ developed from the common material of the pre-Chalcedonian tradition in such a way that the post-Chalcedonian formulaic language could not become prominent here. Influential in this was the so-called eremite mission, whose content can probably be judged correctly according to the texts as we met them with the archimandrite Shenoute and shall soon meet again. Yet we are tempted, following John of Ephesus, to assign the deposed patriarch Theodosius the role of a repeatedly quoted church father not only for the mission but also for the theological writings of Nubia. But the tangible part of this is limited to the influence of a Michaelmas sermon of the patriarch.[72] The richest stimuli to reflect on Nubian Christology, however, are offered by the now-famous murals of Faras and by a longer known hymn of the cross. We want to look only briefly at both of these.[73]

---

71. On the textual discoveries in Nubia see C. D. G. Müller, 'Die nubische Literatur. Bestand und Eigenart', in *Nubia. Récentes Recherches*, Varsovie 1975, 93–100; idem, 'Deutsche Textfunde in Nubien', in E. Dinkler (ed.), *Kunst und Geschichte Nubiens in christlicher Zeit*, Recklinghausen 1970, 245–56 and tables (see below on liturgical texts).
72. See C. D. G. Müller, 'Grundzüge der Frömmigkeit in der nubischen Kirche', in *Études Nubiennes* (Colloques de Chantilly 1975), Cairo 1978, 209–24. The Michaelmas sermon is found in E. A. W. Budge, *Miscellaneous Coptic Texts in the Dialect of Upper Egypt*, London 1915, Copt.-Engl. trans. pp. 893–947; there is also a Bohairic version. Cf. C. D. G. Müller, 'Die alte koptische Predigt', diss. Heidelberg 1954, 100–1.
73. On Nubian archaeology and art cf. also M. Krause (ed.), *Nubische Studien. Tagungsakten der 5. internat. Konf. der Int. Soc. for Nubian Studies, Heidelberg 22.–25. Sept. 1982*, Mainz 1986.

1. The iconographic testimony

During the excavations that led to the discovery of the cathedral of Faras, in the narthex niche workers found an image of the *Eleusa* that originated in the tenure of Bishop John (997/998–1005) and thus at a relatively late time for us. In the arcade of the north vestibule they discovered a *Maria Galaktotrophusa* (*Maria lactans*), that was painted under John's successor, Bishop Marianus.[74]

A connection between the portrayal of the *Galaktotrophusa*, especially frequent in Egypt, and the role of Isis suckling Horus in late Egyptian iconography is pointedly formulated by P. O. Scholz: 'Manifested in the Hathor-Isis cult were the conceptions of fertility that were deeply rooted in the northeast African region and reached back into primeval history. From them there developed within the people over the course of centuries – probably even millennia – the archetype of a mother of god, which in its sacral function and significance could no longer be relinquished. This archetype of a mother of god, provided with new contents, was transferred to the *theotokos*, which for these reasons and in this sense became an integral component of Coptic church doctrine. This transference phenomenon probably in no small measure made possible the survival of Christianity in the Nile valley.'[75]

Yet if we ask about the *theological* sources of these representations, we will be referred not only to the post-Chalcedonian phase but already back to the time of the fourth and fifth centuries. An initial interpretation sought all too quickly to establish the historical-theological situation of these images. The two representations, it was said, could be explained only by the Chalcedonian and thus Dyophysite formula of faith. On the basis of this first assumption a manifold change of confession was also assumed, at least for Faras. The named images were believed to stand in clear opposition to the Christology and Mariology of the Coptic 'Monophysites'. The strong emphasis on the human seemed to require a Dyophysite background, an opinion that was supported above all by K. Wessel[76] and

---

74. See the reproductions in K. Michałowski, *Faras. Die Kathedrale aus dem Wüstensand*, Einsiedeln 1967, *Eleusa*: plate 24/25, pp. 91–92 and 106–7; *Galaktotrophusa*: 76, p. 91 and 153–54; P. van Moorsel, 'Die stillende Gottesmutter und die Monophysiten', in E. Dinkler (n. 1 above), 281–90.

75. P. O. Scholz, 'Bemerkungen zur Ikonologie der Theotokos', in T. Orlandi and F. Wisse (eds.), *Acts of the Second International Congress of Coptic Studies, Rome, 22–26 September 1980*, Rome 1985, pp. 323–38 (appended reproductions). Cf. P. van Moorsel, art. cit., p. 286; M. Tatić-Djurić, 'La Vierge Galaktotrophousa', in *The 17th Internat. Byzant. Congress. Abstracts of Short Papers, Washington, D.C., Aug. 3–8, 1986*, pp. 338–39.

76. See K. Wessel, 'Zur Ikonographie der koptischen Kunst', in idem (ed.), *Christentum am Nil*, Recklinghausen 1964 (233–39), 234.

adopted by the leading excavators of Faras.[77] Wessel wonders 'whether Bishop John of Faras – he died in the year 1006 – did not introduce Dyophysite doctrine with the reopening of the cathedral after its renovation, and his successors up to Bishop Jesu (or Josua), who died in 1169, were Dyophysites'. This interpretation is rightly rejected above all by M. Krause.[78] We will pass over this controversy in its detailed arguments, but would like to attempt to formulate a few observations that can contribute to the broader clarification.

(a) *The clichéd usage of the one- and two-nature formulas.* The confusion over the interpretation of the Faras murals was caused by the uncritical interpretation of the *mia-physis* formula in the sense of a so-to-speak self-evident real Monophysitism. The phenomenon is familiar enough to us. From our inquiry into the faith of the Coptic and Nubian Churches we learned that quarrels over the formulas were more an affair of the intellectuals than a concern of the first catechesis. The concrete consideration and defence of the economy of the incarnation and the presentation of the mysteries of the life of Jesus and their celebration in the liturgy stand in the foreground. The importance of this concrete Christology was brought vividly to our attention by Shenoute. In his eyes it is endangered from two sides: through a dualistic devaluation of the humanity of Christ but also through an Origenist-Nestorian separation of God and human being in Jesus of Nazareth. Participating in the defence against this double dissolution of the *mysterium Christi* were both the moderate Antiochenes and the Chalcedonians in union with moderate representatives of the *mia-physis* formula from Dioscorus and Timothy Aelurus to the ex-patriarch Theodosius.

(b) *Various motifs in the presentation of the Galaktotrophusa.* All too hastily, only *one* motif was sought in the Mary and Christ representations of Faras, namely, the defence against the 'Monophysitism' of the anti-Chalcedonian Nubians through their Bishop John. If we go back to the texts, another picture emerges.

---

77. Cf. S. Jakobielski, *Faras III: A History of the Bishopric of Pachoras on the Basis of Coptic Inscriptions*, Warsaw 1972. According to Jakobielski, at the end of the tenth century the bishops of Faras went over from Monophysitism to the Chalcedonian confession and after a good half century returned again to Monophysitism, in order after perhaps another half century to endorse orthodoxy again. On Jakobielski's arguments see H. Quecke, *Orientalia* 43 (1974), 135–41, esp. 136ff.; but see K. Michałowski, *Faras*, p. 92; also Kraus II, p. 253.

78. M. Krause, 'Zur Kirchen- und Theologiegeschichte Nubiens', pp. 80–83; idem, 'Bischof Johannes III von Faras und seine beiden Nachfolger. Noch einmal zum Problem eines Konfessionswechsel in Faras', in *Études Nubiennes* (Colloque de Chantilly 1975), Cairo 1978, 153–64.

(1) *Maria lactans* in an unpolemical, poetic view. A number of texts find expressed in the image of the 'nursing mother' the tremendous tension of the *kenosis* of the incarnation. The paradox of the incarnation is supposed to be made overt: there 'immortal God', here *parvoque lacte pastus est.*[79] Though the christological version of this tension is given here, it means mariologically the joining of mother and virgin in Mary.[80]

(2) The polemical theological background of the motif. Here it was overlooked that the appeal to *Maria lactans* could be made from two contrary positions: first, out of the necessity of emphasizing the reality of the incarnation against the Docetists, Marcionites and Manichaeans, and ultimately also in a certain regard vis-à-vis the so-called aphthartodocetists or Julianists and Gaianites, the opponents of Patriarch Theodosius; to the extent that the problem was already there in the fourth century, this also includes Athanasius and Cyril of Jerusalem.[81] If we look at Shenoute's energetic battle against the devaluation of the economy of the flesh by his gnostic Manichaean contemporaries in Thebaid, he would have included himself here without further ado. We are all the more surprised to find in him a completely different context for the *Galaktotrophusa*: namely, the denial by Nestorius of the so-called communication of idioms.

It is a question above all of § 0480: 'He [Nestorius] also said: "Therefore one may not say that the Virgin gave birth to a god" and "I will not say that the one who was in the womb nine months and was suckled and gradually grew up is a god" [cf. Lk 2,52].'

Shenoute answers this in § 0481: 'But what then is this that is written: "The Lord and God appeared to them" [Dt 31,15; 32,2; etc.]. What is the moment that he appears to human beings other than that when he was born out of the Virgin, as it is written: "Behold, a virgin will conceive and bear a son, and he will be called Emmanuel, which means: God is with us" [Is 7,14]. Hence *the one* whom the Virgin bore is God; therefore it is impossible not to be united on the fact that Mary gave birth to God, as our fathers said.'[82]

This text contains every problem that can arise regarding the presentation of the incarnation and the *Galaktotrophusa* of Faras.[83] To begin with, we ascertain a special closeness of Shenoute to Nubia: first in the mention

---

79. Thus Sedulius, *Hymnus* II, 23: CSEL 10, p. 164; this and other texts in P. van Moorsel, art. cit., pp. 284–85: Ephraem Syr., John Chrysostom, Amphilochius of Iconium, the Syrian Balai; in the West Augustine (beside Sedulius).

80. Thus in Athanasius, Jacob of Sarug; see van Moorsel, art. cit., pp. 283, 285. Cf. M. Tatić-Djurić, art. cit.

81. Athanasius, *Letter to Epictetus* (CPG 2095) 5: PG 26, 1057; Cyril of Jerus., *Fourth Catechesis* (CPG 3585), 9: PG 33, 468; Rupp-Reischel I, 100.

82. See Shenoute, *Contra Origenistas*: ed. Orlandi, §§ 0475–80.

83. Cf. C. D. G. Müller, 'Grundzüge der Frömmigkeit', pp. 213–16.

of the *lactatio* and then of the three young men in the fiery furnace.[84] This closeness does not rest on Shenoute alone. Thus we find *Maria lactans* five times in the monasteries of Bawit and Saqqara and four times in Sahidic manuscripts of lives of saints.[85] Special significance has to be accorded to the so-called *theotokia*, which often praise Mary as *Galaktotrophusa*.[86] We can simply exclude the idea that the mention or graphic representation of the *Galaktotrophusa* is based on opposition to the *mia-physis* formula, although the exhortation comes from the time after Ephesus (431). Till now we have not discovered this formula in the archimandrite. Two motives are possible for Shenoute's speaking of the *Galaktotrophusa*: (1) the danger that at this time still emanated from docetic Gnosis, Marcionites and Manichaeans, and which threatened to abolish the earthly history of Jesus; the reference to the humble childhood of Jesus would have spoken for itself; (2) the danger that in the Alexandrian view emanated from Nestorius, who endangered the union in Christ through his restrictive linguistic regulation vis-à-vis *theotokos* and other traditional assertions that corresponded to the law of the communication of idioms, for example: God was born of a virgin and nourished by milk. Thus we determine that the *Galaktotrophusa* in Shenoute can have and has two statements to make: confession to the human reality of Christ and confession to the true unity of God and human being in Christ. Now, which content is concretely expressed, say, in the *Maria lactans* of Faras can hardly be decided. Why should not both assertions be grasped by the viewer: the truth of the incarnation and the true divinity of the incarnate One?

Now, however, P. van Moorsel calls attention to a phenomenon in the iconography that could be connected with the anti-Nestorian interpretation of the *Galaktotrophusa*. This is the occurrence of double apse compositions, such as those that appear in chapel 42 in Bawit: above, a 'theophany of the *Trishagion*', below, a *Galaktotrophusa* between other saints: 'Below we see God's Son as he appeared among us as a human

---

84. Ibid., p. 215: in Egypt and in Nubia there was a twofold tradition of the names of the three young men.

85. See P. van Moorsel, 'Die stillende Gottesmutter und die Monophysiten', p. 282; on the mss. see M. Cramer, *Koptische Buchmalerei*, Recklinghausen 1964; information in van Moorsel, n. 6.

86. P. van Moorsel, art. cit., p. 282, where the older sources of this concept of *Maria lactans* are also cited (*Protoevangelium of James*, Athanasius, Cyril of Jerusalem, esp. Theodotus of Ancyra and Theophilus of Alexandria). On the legend of the origination of this image through Luke see J. Assfalg, *Die Ordnung des Priestertums*, Cairo 1955, 92–95.

being, but above we see him as he lives forever in glory.'[87] Van Moorsel also mentions a corresponding text in the *Psali Adam* (from the *theotokion* of the Sunday for the whole year):

> You are high above the cherubim, more honoured than the seraphim. You have given birth to God's Son, our God; we glorify him as God, and we worship him. The one who lives in the inaccessible light and shows his wonders is the one you suckled.[88]

In regard to Shenoute's exhortation, which occupies us here once again, we can discover at this point post-Ephesian-Alexandrian and Coptic piety as it was also practised in Nubia. The union of God and human being is expressed in this double apse composition in a very curious way. One could say that the communication of idioms so strongly in mind around Ephesus in 431 is represented graphically and most impressively. Because this communication of idioms was familiar and essential to Chalcedonians and anti-Chalcedonians alike, believers from both directions could understand such an image without further ado. Any Copt or Cyrillian contemplating the image could read his *mia-physis* formula into it, while followers of Chalcedon did not find it difficult to see their two-natures formula expressed there. In other words, the common faith in the incarnate God that precedes this formula quarrel is decisive here. Not even the apparent antithesis of the formulas can abolish it. If in these images of the *Maria lactans* or the *Eleusa* a renunciation of certain errors or heresies is to be sought – and this is absolutely possible – then the radical Phantasiasts and Docetists with their rejection of the humanity of Christ or the real Monophysites with their doctrine of mixing were affected just as much as the separation Christology of the 'Nestorians'. Since both were probably known in Upper Egypt, this knowledge could also pass over the border to Nubia, especially in connection with the liturgies that were usual in the Coptic church.

---

87. See P. van Moorsel, art. cit., p. 285. Van Moorsel points to an apse composition like that of the Pantokrator cave at Latmos in Asia Minor, which is dated in the 7th or 9th century: Christ sits on the throne surrounded by four creatures who hold books. On the Mandorla is written: 'Holy, holy, holy the Lord of hosts; heaven and earth are full of your glory'. And on the book is written again: 'Holy, holy, holy'. Under this picture, however, is a *Maria lactans*. Thus P. van Moorsel, 'The Coptic Apse-Composition and its Living Creatures', in *Études Nubiennes* (Colloque de Chantilly 1975), Cairo 1978 (325–33), 330, ibid. Illustration, pl. LXIII. In ibid., 331, the writer expresses an important recognition of the double apse composition among the Copts and Nubians: '. . . I conclude that the double-zonic apse composition of the Copts, which has been adopted by the Nubians, originates from the heavenly Throne-vision, as the Coptic liturgy, inspired by the Bible as it is, celebrates that.'

88. Quoted according to J. Muyser, *Maria's Heerlijkheid in Egypte. Een studie der Koptische Maria-literatuur* I, Louvain–Utrecht 1935, 155–56.

2. The liturgical testimony

Without having to refer back to written testimonies for liturgical texts, with the above-mentioned Coptic-Nubian apse composition we are already in the realm of liturgy. For the Sanctus theophanies are nothing but visual testimony of the close of the eucharistic prayer in the celebration of the mysteries. With the representation of this theophany in the six apses of Bawit we come back to the sixth century, since the high point of the quarrel is reached concerning the additions to the '*Trishagion*'.[89] The 'triple holy' applies to the enthroned Christ, completely in correspondence to other liturgies of the East.[90] In the described double composition, however, this is underlined by the representation of a heavenly 'throne vision' in the upper part of the apse. P. van Moorsel could convincingly demonstrate that the four creaturely beings are, according to Ezek 1,5–25 and Rev 4,6–8, not understood as symbols of the four evangelists, as in Irenaeus, but as throne assistants of God or Christ. They bear the chariot of God and sing the Sanctus high in heaven, as the latter is also done in worship by the church on earth.[91] Thus the sitting Mother of God with the child (in our double apse composition) is an earthly counterpart of the throne chariot above, and therefore we have an upper and a lower theophany. For this van Moorsel has an interesting text from Pseudo-Ephraem[92] that deserves to be quoted:

> Trembling the chariot of fire carries the Lord,
> weak knees carry Him and do not get burnt.
> Angels of fire carry Him devoutly
> but David's daughter carries Him on her lap.
> Cherubim carry Him and tremble
> Seraphim chant Him as three times Holy
> and are filled with fear.
> But Maria cherishes Him lovingly on her lap.

Corresponding to this is the Coptic *theotokion* for Friday: 'Inspired City, in which the Sublime lives, who sits enthroned on the chariot of the Cherubim.'[93] The rich apse compositions of Bawit and Faras, with their combination of Is 6,1–4; Ezek 1,4–16 and Rev 4,6–8 come from 'a well-balanced view of the Mystery of Christ and the role of the Mother of

---

89. A. Grillmeier, *CCT* II/2, pp. 253–59; cf. pp. 385–86 below.

90. Cf. A. Gerhards, *Gregoriosanaphora*, pp. 57ff., on vv. 38–52 of the Gregory anaphora.

91. P. van Moorsel, 'The Coptic Apse-Composition and its Living Creatures', in *Études Nubiennes* (Colloque de Chantilly 1975), pp. 329–30.

92. Ibid., p. 330, according to Ps.-Ephraem, ed. Lamy II, pp. 582–84.

93. Ibid., p. 330, with reference to J. Muyser, *Maria's heerlijkheid in Egypte*, pp. 134–35.

God in that Mystery'.[94] The reference to liturgy and to the Eucharist is uniquely emphasized in that these triple-holy theophanies are found only in the apses. Since only the enthroned Christ is represented, the triple holy is for him. This also establishes the relationship to the Coptic liturgy.[95] We do not need to go deeper into the extant remainder of the Nubian liturgy, since it apparently contains no newly created material but only older adoptions.[96]

3. Veneration of the cross in Nubia

Again we can begin with the newly discovered murals in Nubia. Connected with the triple Sanctus theophany of Abdallah Nirqi is a gemmed cross. In addition six further theophanies with the cross were found: five in Faras and one in Tamit.[97] Various things are notable about these seven representations. The figure of Christ gets smaller, but the cross is enlarged. Soon the triple holy disappears. Then comes the inscription CTAYROC (or CTAYROY) and also garlands and other decorations. The cross stands on a platform under which is the grave of Adam. Thus it is true that Christ, the four creatures and the cross remain as constants. But the relationships among them shift.

P. van Moorsel makes an interesting observation: in the church of Cheik in Tamit one finds the Sanctus theophany and the theophany with a cross together, both from the eleventh century. But the apse is reserved for the old Sanctus theophany; here and in the six other cases the theophany of the cross is banned from the apse and nave and moved to the side aisles.[98] There too it has no fixed place. Sometimes it is here, sometimes there, above all in connection with the portrayal of national saints. In any case, it is removed from the main liturgical space.

---

94. Ibid., p. 331.

95. Cf. P. van Moorsel, 'Une théophanie Nubienne', *RivArchCr* 42 (1968), 297–316.

96. On the sources see W. H. C. Frend, 'Greek Liturgical Documents from Q'asr Ibrim in Nubia', in *Atti del IX Congresso di archeologia cristiana, Roma, 21–27 Settembre 1975*, vol. II, Vatican City 1978, 295–306; idem, 'The Greek Liturgical Papyri from the Cathedral at Q'asr Ibrim', in *Études Nubiennes* (Colloque de Chantilly 1975), Cairo 1978, 95 (the Nubians were familiar with a liturgy in Greek); K. Gamber, 'Zur Liturgie Nubiens. Teile eines Eucharistiegebetes auf Fragmenten eines Pergamentblattes vermutlich des 10. Jahrhunderts', *OstKSt* 20 (1971), 185–88; H. Quecke, *Orientalia* 40 (1971), 308; W. H. C. Frend, P. Parsos, I. A. Muirhead and J. Zizioulas, *The Greek Liturgical Papyri from Qasr Ibrim* (Egypt Exploration Society Texts from Excavations), London 1981; W. H. C. Frend and G. Dragas, 'A Eucharistic Sequence from Q'asr Ibrim', *JAC* 30 (1987), 90–98 (an early version of the Mark liturgy seems to have been in use in the Nubian church until into the twelfth century).

97. P. van Moorsel, 'Une théophanie Nubienne', pp. 303–7.

98. Ibid., pp. 308–9.

Thus the theme of the cross becomes the object of the *devotio*, whose liturgical content is small. But the cross that becomes the focus is the cross as sign of victory.[99] That points to Jerusalem. It is true that here too the reference to Christ is lacking, yet this changes. While the Sanctus theophany serves the recognition of Christ as God, the soteriological and eschatological motifs now come to the fore. Prominent is Mt 24,30, the saying about the sign of the Son of Man which appears in the sky. In the Coptic and thus also in the Nubian church the idea of the return of Christ thereby receives outstanding significance. We have already encountered this idea many times in the development of this chapter.

Already in 1913 a *stauros* text from Nubia was edited and translated.[100] It was a homily or sermon that first offers a revelatory talk given by Jesus to his disciples on the Mount of Olives at the end of the forty days after Easter before the ascension (I–IV). Then Peter makes the request for the revelation of a special secret (IV–V), namely, of the cross of glory, because of which Jesus on his return for judgement will have the cross symbol with him. What the disciples have thus heard, they want to proclaim to the whole world. Behind this lies a special conception of the 'sign of the Son of Man' according to Mt 24,27, 30.

Jesus' revelatory talk (VIII–XV) begins with the reminder of the suffering on the cross with all the individual evil deeds that the 'cursed Jews'(!) did against Jesus with the suffering and crucifixion. Therefore he is coming again with his cross to reveal to them their folly (but cf. 1 Cor 1,23, where folly is charged to the Gentiles) and give back all curses on their head. The judgement takes place in the valley of Jehoshaphat (cf. Joel 4,2.12 [Heb.]). Here Jesus holds the cross in his right hand. The apocalyptic talk of Mt 24 is restyled on the sign of the cross: whoever believes in it whole-heartedly can receive its protection and live under it. Yet this faith must be tested in the feeding of the hungry (Mt 25,35) or in the writing of a book to honour the cross or in the erection of a cross in a church. After the separation of the righteous and the unrighteous, the cross will ascend in glory to heaven, and with it all who have believed in it. Through the power of the trophy of the cross, they escape judgement.

After this revelatory talk on the role of the cross in judgement comes the sending out of the disciples now with the commission (in variation from the sending saying of Mt 28,19) to preach the cross. The whole is concluded with an early Christian doxology (XVI–XVIII).

In forty-six verses (XIX–XXVII) with litany-like acclamations the cross is praised as the content of all the hopes of burdened humanity. Revealed here is the Nubian church's understanding 'of the participation of the cross in the salvation-history of Christ'.[101] In the foreground, however, stands faith in the connection of the sign of the cross with the return of Christ. This nexus is graphically represented in the cruciform architecture of the cathedral of Faras, yet with certain differences from the concept of the hymn of the cross. It is a question

---

99. Ibid., pp. 310–13.

100. See text and English translation in F. Ll. Griffith, *The Nubian Texts of the Christian Period* (*APAW.PH* 8), Berlin 1913, 41–53; German translation in E. Zyhlarz, *Grundzüge der nubischen Grammatik im christlichen Frühmittelalter* (AKM 18, 1), Leipzig 1928, 155–69. – E. Dinkler, 'Beobachtungen zur Ikonographie des Kreuzes in der nubischen Kunst', in *Nubia. Récentes Recherches*, Varsovie 1975, 22–30; C. D. G. Müller, 'Die nubische Literatur. Bestand und Eigenart', 93–100; Müller emphasizes that the hymn is designated as *cal*, which corresponds to the Coptic *logos*. This means a homily or sermon that is especially orientated towards biblical kerygmatic content. Although the hymn is not dated until the year 972/973, it contains old material.

101. E. Dinkler, art. cit., p. 25.

'of the return of Christ for the last judgement accompanied by the *Trishagion* of the four *zoa* and the cross that precedes it'.[102] We have already highlighted the special role of the idea of judgement in Coptic tradition, especially the *Apophthegmata Patrum*, and cited other testimonies for it (Emperor Anastasius I). But our *stauros* litany points to older testimonies that for the traditional core of the text (with the cross litany) definitely go back into the fourth and perhaps even into the third century.[103] Of special significance for Nubia, however, is the surrounding sermon and legend text with the handing over of a secret teaching to the apostles. E. Dinkler sees the topos of such instruction on the last things by the resurrected One already given in the second half of the second century by the *Epistola Apostolorum*, preserved in Coptic, the *Apocalypse of Peter* and the apocryphal *Gospel of Peter*.[104] What is special about the Nubian text is that it is no longer a question of the when and how of the return for judgement and for the general waking of the dead (cf. Mt 24,1–25,46) 'but of the special role that the *cross* plays in it, in order to follow with the question of what saving function the cross – as cult object – has or should have in the life of the Christian'.[105] The topic is not the return of the Judge himself into heaven together with the righteous but the ascent of the sign of the cross to heaven in glory (XIV). The believers follow it in order 'that they may inherit eternal life and the paradise of' eternity. Is there an anti-Jewish point where it says that Christ 'will not judge them according to the law, in any [matter] either in word or in deed, but the power of the glorious Cross shall save them and justify them' (XIV–XV)? E. Dinkler calls attention to a difference between a revelatory text and a 'litany'. The *litany* places the cross in the middle of the events of everyday earthly life in Nubia and Egypt: the dependence of the fellahin on the Nile flood, the manifold attacks by enemies from the desert, deliverance from death by drowning. We encountered similar things in the Jesus litany of Shenoute. The *revelatory talk* provides the 'theological framework'. It contains the reference to the future as the actual basis of the present (E. Dinkler). This reveals the echo of Johannine eschatology in Nubian piety of the cross. 'The historical cross is the past; the present power is the glorified, the doxological cross. In this way the Passion scenes recede in art [although they are not lacking]. Dominant is the idea of Easter and the Parousia, both symbolized in the cross.'[106]

The litany of the cross itself comes to a powerful close in the following words:

78. 'The cross is the *thing that makes alive* (Lebendigmacher), because it is God who hung upon it, so that he gave himself for us who are in need of peace . . .'

80. 'We will all receive through him the realization of life and peace . . .'

83. 'If we peacefully hold out [in hope], we will hear him say to us: "Come, you blessed ones of my Father; as heirs take possession of the kingdom, which already before the beginning of the world is determined to be yours!" – [at the time] when he will judge in righteousness according to the grace and philanthropy of our Lord Jesus Christ, whose is the glory together with the most good Father and the *one who makes alive* (Lebendigmacher), the

---

102. E. Dinkler, ibid., with reference to P. van Moorsel, 'Une théophanie nubienne', *RivArchCr* 42 (1968), 297–316. Dinkler, ibid., p. 29, emphasizes that a considerable number of the Nubian murals go back to antecedents, and thus specific Nubian sources for them are not at all to be expected. Also one must not, he says, see dogmatic theology as background for the hymnological and hagiological material, apart from biblical texts and liturgy. On the Coptic background see G. Giamberardini, *La Croce e il Crocifisso presso i Copti* (SOC.C 7), Cairo 1962, 47–100 (mostly later sources).

103. E. Dinkler, art. cit., p. 29.

104. Cf. A. Grillmeier, *JdChr* I³, p. 178.

105. E. Dinkler, art. cit., p. 30.

106. Ibid.

Holy Spirit, in one single figure (Zyhlarz: person) now and forever into eternity. Amen.'[107]

Instead of the colourless 'Comforter' that F. Ll. Griffith chooses for our § 78 (p. 51) and the 'ersehnenswert' ('worth longing for') marked by E. Zyhlarz himself with a question mark, C. D. G. Müller, after a philological investigation, employs the designation 'Lebendigmacher' ('one that makes alive'). Here it is first applied to the cross. The connection between cross–life–tree of life is known.[108] Then we can also easily explain why the same word appears in connection with the *Pneuma Hagion*, which brings to mind the *Nicaeno-Constantinopolitanum*.[109] In § 83 C. D. G. Müller also chooses the other designation of the Holy Spirit, which to be sure at the *Constantinopolitanum* in 381 was itself not yet inserted into the credo, but was discussed before and afterwards and finally generally received: the 'consubstantial' or *homoousios*! He finds it in the Nubian *dūrtū welkel*, which he would like to translate literally as 'a single figure'.

Thus Nubian piety has a noteworthy attachment to both Byzantine and Coptic theology, a connection that in its individual elements we also ascertained in Shenoute. For in him we found the expression *trias homoousios*, which encompasses Father, Son and Holy Spirit.

---

107. Text according to E. Zyhlarz, *Grundzüge*, pp. 165–67, with corrections by C. D. G. Müller. See here also F. LL. Griffith, *The Nubian Texts of the Christian Period*, Berlin 1913, 50–51, with reference to Schäfer and Schmidt, who have taken a parallel of 52 verses from a Ps.-Chrysostom text: *In venerabilem crucem sermo* (BHG[a] 446): PG 50, 815–20; see CPG 4525. A shorter form is given in one *sermo* that is ascribed to Ephraem Syr.: Assemani, BO 2, pp. 247B–258. Cf. CPG 3948 (*Sermo in pretiosam et vivificam*(!) *crucem . . .*).

108. Cf. G. Q. Rijners, *The Terminology of the Holy Cross in Early Christian Literature*, Nijmegen 1965, 20–21, 79. Lampe, *PatrGrLex* (1968), ζωοποιός 4 g; no. 5 (*pneuma*); ibid., σταυρός 6. The Nubian verb *dam*, 'make alive', occurs in the whole text (other than together with *pneuma*) another four times, each time in connection with the cross.

109. F. LL. Griffith, art. cit., 51,7; E. Zyhlarz, *Grundzüge*, p. 167 and elsewhere.

PART FOUR

CHRIST IN A NEW MESSIANIC KINGDOM
FAITH IN CHRIST IN ETHIOPIA

At the end of our long voyage of discovery upstream to the source of the Blue Nile in the Ethiopian highland[1] we encounter, contrary to expectation, christological traditions that bring to mind the great names of Alexandrian theology. We hear of a Byzantine emperor who wishes to implement Byzantine imperial church principles there beyond the borders of his empire. As the Nile flowed down, it repeatedly enticed merchants, conquerors and missionaries to move in the opposite direction, even beyond the Sudan, although up to now we hardly have any direct evidence of this. For the Ethiopian highland was more easily accessible for trade and culture, for military conquerors and for religious missionaries from the east, from the Red Sea. It also exercised a curious power of attraction that radiated as far as Arabia, Palestine and beyond to Syria and Mesopotamia. It was not for nothing that Mani already had his eyes on this region, which he included in the list of four empires that aroused his missionary interest: Babylon and Persia, the Roman Empire, the Empire of Silis (China?) and the Empire of the Auxumites.[2] It is not our task to present the history of Christian missions in Ethiopia. We will

---

1. Important for the following are: A. Dillmann, *Über die Anfänge des Axumitischen Reiches* (*AAWB.PH* 1878), Berlin 1879, 177–238; idem, *Zur Geschichte des Axumitischen Reiches im vierten bis sechsten Jahrhundert* (*AAWB.PH* 1880), Berlin 1881, 1–51; C. Troll, 'Die kultur-geographische Stellung und Eigenart des Hochlandes von Äthiopien zwischen dem Orient und Äquatorialafrika', in *ACIStEt*, pp. 29–44. Helpful in understanding the following is the observation of Troll, 31–32: according to its intellectual and religious culture, Ethiopia falls into three areas: (1) the central Christian highland; (2) the Muslim lowlands and border areas to the west, north and east; (3) the mostly pagan area of Galla and Sidamo, as well as Nilotic and negroid border tribes to the southwest. For an overview see: E. Hammerschmidt, art. 'Äthiopien', in *KlWbChrOr* (1975), 53–56; idem, *Äthiopien. Christliches Reich zwischen Gestern und Morgen*, Wiesbaden 1967, with bibl., pp. 165–70; F. Heyer, *Die Kirche Äthiopiens. Eine Bestandsaufnahme*, Berlin–New York 1971; idem, art. 'Äthiopien', in *TRE* 1 (1977), 572–96; G. Lanczkowski, 'Aethiopia', *JAC* 1 (1958), 134–53 with maps and bibl.; idem, art. 'Aethiopia', in RAC Suppl. 1 (1985), 94–134; A. S. Atiya, *A History of Eastern Christianity* I, London 1969, 146–66; O. Raineri, art. 'Etiopia', in *DPAC* I (1983), 1251–61; in 1992 the comprehensive article of H. Brakmann, 'Axomis (Aksum)', was published in RAC Suppl. 1 (1992), 718–810 (not used here).

2. Cf. Kephalaion 77: C. Schmidt, *Manichäische Handschriften der staatlichen Museen Berlin* I, 1–2: Kephalaia, Stuttgart 1940, chap. LXXVII, p. 189 (attributed to Mani).

presuppose[3] and only define in a sketchy way the historical framework of our presentation, noting the variety of influences and the resulting difficulty of developing a somewhat recognizable picture of Christ from the still not completely researched sources. Fortunately we must first deal with a relatively closed period, which is called the Axumite period of Abyssinian history. It covers the fourth or fifth to the seventh century.[4] Within this time we distinguish again two phases of the Christianization of the Axumite Empire.

---

3. See E. Hammerschmidt, 'Die Anfänge des Christentums in Äthiopien', *ZM* 38 (1954), 281–94; A. Dihle, *Umstrittene Daten. Untersuchungen zum Auftreten der Griechen am Roten Meer* (WAAFLNW 32), Cologne–Opladen 1965, II. Frumentios und Ezana, pp. 36–64; I. Engelhardt, *Mission und Politik in Byzanz*, 104–27; F. Thelamon, *Paiens et Chrétiens au IV* *siècle. L'apport de l' "Histoire ecclésiastique" de Rufin d'Aquilée*, Paris 1981, 37–83. The three last named authors argue with the research of F. Altheim and R. Stiehl: "Ēzānā von Aksūm', *Klio* 39 (1961), 234–48; F. Altheim, 'Die Zeitstellung 'Ēzānās von Aksum', in idem, *Geschichte der Hunnen* V, Berlin 1962, 157–80; also F. Altheim and R. Stiehl, *Die Araber in der Alten Welt* II, Berlin 1965, 284–97; IV, Berlin 1967, 272–78, 306–19, 502–14; V/1, Berlin 1968, 316–50; V/2, Berlin 1969, 166–98, 539–49; *Christentum am Roten Meer* I, Berlin 1971, 402–29, 465–71; R. Stiehl, 'Christliche Mission beiderseits des Roten Meeres', *Die Welt des Orients* 4 (1967), 109–27. – G. Rißße, *'Gott ist Christus, der Sohn der Maria'. Eine Studie zum Christusbild im Koran* (Begegnung Bd. 2), Bonn 1989, 82–85. – We must forgo presenting the pagan background and possible influence on Christian missions in Ethiopia and southern Arabia. On this see M. Höfner, 'Über sprachliche und kulturelle Beziehungen zwischen Südarabien und Äthiopien im Altertum', in *ACIStEt*, pp. 435–44, esp. pp. 442–44; eadem, 'Die vorislamischen Religionen Arabiens', in *Religionen der Menschheit*, ed. by Chr. M. Schröder, vol. 10/2 (1970), 234–402; J. Wellhausen, *Reste arabischen Heidentums*, 1st ed. 1887; reprint 1961. Very negative about Ethiopian Christianity (in its relationship to pagan influences) is the judgement of E. Kromrei, 'Glaubenslehre und Gebräuche der älteren abessinischen Kirche', inaugural diss., Leipzig 1895. Versus F. Heyer, *Die Kirche Äthiopiens. Eine Bestandsaufnahme*, Berlin–New York 1971, esp. 349–51. That rather relations with Judaism are given here is shown by Heyer, 187–211: 'Wallfahrten und Heilwesen', but esp. E. Ullendorff, *Ethiopia and the Bible*, London 1967, 79–82 ('Magic').

4. Cf. E. Hammerschmidt, art. 'Äthiopien', in *KlWbChrOr*, 55: 'This empire [of Axum] maintained relations with Byzantium and in the year 525 again reached to southern Arabia, which remained under Ethiopian sovereignty until 572. The spread of Islam in the seventh century brought to Ethiopia increased isolation and contributed to the fall of the Axumite Empire in the tenth century.'

CHAPTER ONE

THE INTRODUCTION OF CHRISTIANITY

South of the kingdoms of the Nobatae, the Makurites and the Alodaeans in the mountains of Habesh stretched a kingdom that was founded from Axum:

> In the first pre-Christian millennium there immigrated from southern Arabia Sabaean tribes, Semites, who were replenished again and again from Arabia. They became the real culture bearers, founded trade settlements and later the Empire of Axum in the region of Tigre (Ἀξουμῖται, Ἀξωμῖται, *Exomitae*). The decline of the kingdom of Meroe favoured the rise of Axum.[5]

Famous is the legend that the first king of Abyssinia was a son of Solomon and the queen of Sheba (1 Kings 10 and 2 Chr 9), namely, Menilek I. According to E. Hammerschmidt, the seed of this legend is to be found in the fact that Jewish missionaries converted native tribes to Judaism, whose descendants still live today in larger communities in Amhara and are called 'Falashas'.[6] The founding of Christian groups or churches is to be credited first to merchants and wandering missionaries, but then – as in the neighbouring Sudanese lands – to the native princes. At least this is the view of the Axumite chronicle, which, however, was not recorded until the fourteenth or fifteenth century:[7]

> And Saifa 'Arʿād fathered 'Abrehā and 'Aṣbehā, under whom Christianity came while they were in Axum. In those days there were still no Turks. The father of Salāmā [i.e.

---

5. E. Hammerschmidt, 'Die Anfänge', p. 285.

6. Ibid. with n. 23 and the reference to the Solomon legend in the book *Kebra Nagaśt* (= glory of the kings) from the time of the ʿAmda Ṣeyon (1314–44). – On the Falashas, ibid., 285.

7. The Ethiopian text has long been given 'no independent value as a historical source' (I. Engelhardt, op. cit., p. 128); cf. F. Thelamon, *Paiens et chrétiens au IVᵉ siècle*, Paris 1981, 42–44. Yet the Ethiopian sources experience a considerable appreciation in value in the thorough and detailed investigation of B. W. W. Dombrowski and F. A. Dombrowski, 'Frumentius/Abbā Salāmā: Zu den Nachrichten über die Anfänge des Christentums in Äthiopien', *OrChr* 68 (1984), 114–69. Beginning with the Ethiopian tradition, these authors develop a chronology (ibid., p. 131) (see below). Then they ascertain from the reports of the Greek and

Frumentius[8]] was a merchant; there came Salāmā with his father. Of the people of Ethiopia, however, some worshipped the dragon, but the others lived according to the law of the Torah. Afterwards the news of Jesus Christ converted them and did miracles before them. They believed and were baptized with Christian baptism. Their conversion took place, however, 340 years after the birth of Christ, and 'Abreḥā and 'Asbeḥā built [the church of] Axum.[9]

The first name 'Abreḥā is equated with the king ʿĒzānā, the second with Šeʿazānā, as the inscriptions of Axum attest.[10] According to some of these inscriptions (nos. 6, 8, 9 and 10), one must assume that ʿĒzānā at first had a penchant for paganism, that is, for polytheism. Then according to inscription no. 11 a new situation developed:[11] a plaque that is preserved in the small treasure room of the church of Zion, and originally was the back of a throne, attests to a clearly monotheistic faith in God. This 'one God' receives three designations that are often echoed and in part expanded with additions:

(1) 'Lord of heaven' (vv. 1, 5, 38, 39, 45, 46, 49, 52). This Lord of heaven is also 'victorious on earth over all beings' (v. 1); 'he created me [the king]' (v. 5); 'he helped me and gave me dominion' (v. 45); 'may he strengthen my dominion' (v. 46); 'who made me king' (v. 49), since he also 'is the Lord of earth, which carries it [the throne erected by the king]' (v. 50).

(2) 'Lord of the universe' (vv. 5 and 7).

(3) Finally comes the talk of the 'power of the Lord of the land' (vv. 14, 15, 33, 34).

Latin church historians in juxtaposition (pp. 147–54, summary: pp. 155–56) that the presumed historical core 'essentially agrees with the Ethiopian tradition' (ibid., p. 156) and supports the developed chronology. They come to the conclusion that the Ethiopian text represents 'an extremely valuable historical source, the most valuable of all traditions' (ibid., p. 165)!

8. On the meaning and equating of these names cf. B. W. W. Dombrowski and F. A. Dombrowski, art. cit., pp. 115–27.

9. E. Littmann (ed.), *Deutsche Aksum-Expedition* I, Berlin 1913, 51; quoted in E. Hammerschmidt, art. cit., 287. Almost the same text is found in a chronicle (after 1730): F. A. Dombrowski, *Ṭānāsee 106. Eine Chronik der Herrscher Äthiopiens* (ÄthFor 12 B), Wiesbaden 1983, pp. 146–47 (German). There (in distinction to the text in Littmann) only Abbā Salāmā is clearly characterized as the teacher of the message of Christ, and there the year is 333 instead of 340.

10. E. Littmann dealt with all the inscriptions found during the German Axum expedition in *Deutsche Aksum-Expedition*, vol. IV, Berlin 1913; E. Littmann re-edited the three main inscriptions in the anniversary publication of the Deutsche Akademie, *Miscellanea academica berolinensia*, Berlin 1950, 97–127: 'Äthiopische Inschriften'. This version with German translation is used here. Also for the new discovery of 1969: P. Anfray, A. Caquot and P. Nautin, 'Une nouvelle inscription grecque d'Ézana', *Journal de Savants*, Oct.–Dec. 1970, 260–74 (Greek text with French translation); E. Dinkler, 'König Ezana von Aksum und das Christentum. Ein Randproblem der Geschichte Nubiens', in *Ägypten und Kusch. Schriften zur Geschichte und Kultur des Alten Orients* (Mélanges F. Hintze, 13), Berlin 1977, 121–32 (from this comes the German translation of the inscription of 1969). See E. Hammerschmidt, *Äthiopien*, Wiesbaden 1967, 41; idem, 'Die Anfänge', *ZM* 38 (1954), 287–88.

11. Inscription 11 in E. Littmann (Berlin 1950), 114–27: III. 'Der Feldzug gegen die Nōbā und Kāsū'.

E. Littmann, for example, simply assumes that with these designations it is a question of predicates of the God of the Christians, that through additions and minor modifications ʿĒzānā reinterpreted old traditional formulas in such a way that Christians could no longer be offended by them. Yet the talk here is still not about the Christian Trinity, about Father, Son and Holy Spirit.[12] On this issue G. Lanczkowski holds that the text of the ʿĒzānā inscription clearly shows that the power of the Christian God should be presented as that of the Pantocrator and that the emphasis should be placed on confession to the first article of faith.[13] A. Dihle adds a new element: confession to the one and only God, which on many early Christian mission fields had to be prominent at first (as the antithesis of polytheism), is also 'plausible' for old southern Arabia and Axum in that 'here Christianity was competing with a strong Jewish mission'.[14]

The peculiarity of this inscription no. 11 does not become clear until it is placed beside a new one that was first discovered in 1969 and is clearly Nicaean and trinitarian:[15]

(1) In faith in God and in the power of the (2) Father and Son and Holy Spirit, in the one (3) who preserved my kingdom through faith in his Son (4) Jesus Christ, who helped me

12. Cf. G. Lanczkowski, 'Aethiopia', *JAC* 1 (1958), 57–60.

13. A. Dihle, *Umstrittene Daten*, pp. 57–60. The detailed comparison of the still pagan inscriptions with the (allegedly) Christian (no. 11) is made by A. Rahlfs, 'Zu den altabessi-nischen Königsinschriften', *OrChr* 6 (1916) (= II 6), 282–313. Rahlfs knows of later(!) inscriptions from the Christian period (in Littmann nos. 12 and 13) that begin with the trinitarian formula. He concedes that inscription 11, 'although it so often speaks of God, nowhere [contains] even the slightest reference to the Son and the Spirit' (300). This circumstance had moved A. Dillmann to venture the hypothesis that inscription no. 11 presupposes Jewish monotheism, although he then decides for the 'Christian' interpretation (*Über die Anfänge des Axumitischen Reiches*, 219). In addition to Littmann, the same solution is also advocated by Rahlfs. Yet for his comparisons between the 'pagan' inscriptions and inscription no. 11 he lacks precisely the trinitarian text of 1969, which clearly belongs to ʿĒzānā. Thus comparisons must be made beyond Rahlfs: the pagan inscriptions, the new one of 1969, and this in relation to no. 11 lying in between. G. Lanczkowski, 'Aethiopia', *JAC* 1 (1958), 144, sees too quickly already in inscription no. 11 the reference to the 'Pantocrator' and the 'confession to the first article of faith'. Totally erroneous is the assumption of F. Altheim and R. Stiehl, *Araber* IV, 275; *Araber* I 1, 336–38; V 2, 179; *Christentum am Roten Meer*, 417–18, 469–70, that in the cited inscription no. 11 the conversion of the king to Monophysitism is expressed, on the basis of which Altheim and Stiehl would like to shift the reign of ʿĒzānā into the second half of the fifth century. On the basis of the new comparative situation, the editors of the inscription of 1969 propose that the newest text be attributed to Bishop Frumentius, who thereby gave a new interpretation to the reign of ʿĒzānā. – It is impossible with C. Troll, art. cit., p. 31, to call the Christianity of Abyssinia of the first half of the fourth century 'Monophysite'. That is at least 150 years too early.

14. A. Dihle, *Umstrittene Daten*, p. 56.

15. See the text in P. Anfray, A. Caquot and P. Nautin, art. cit.; the text here follows the German text of E. Dinkler, 'König Ezana von Aksum', pp. 126–27.

(5) and always helps me, I, (6) Azanas, king of the Axumites and Ḥimyarites . . . (10) . . .
servant of Christ, thank the Lord my God; . . . (16) and has given me a great name through
his Son, (17) in whom I have believed, and for me he makes him (18) leader of my whole
kingdom on the basis of (19) faith in Christ according to his will and (20) through the
power of Christ; for he himself led (21) me, and in him I believe, and he became my leader
. . . (27b) And I rose in the power of God, Christ, in whom I (29) have believed, and he
led me [namely, in the victorious war against the Noba; cf. vv. 23ff.] . . .

In the light of this newly found inscription one would prefer not to
declare text no. 11 Christian. A twofold change of faith may perhaps be
hard to accept, but it cannot be excluded either. That is, if inscription no.
11 is 'monotheistic', which cannot be doubted, one must ask: What kind
of faith in the one God is this? There are definite indications for the idea
that before conversion to Christianity ʿĒzānā was first devoted to Jewish
monotheism and to Judaism in general. Nothing in inscription no. 11
requires going beyond the Jewish framework of faith in God. Conversion to Judaism in Axum is not improbable in the fourth century. As
already indicated, Jews had penetrated into pre-Christian Abyssinia and
probably also reached Nubia, Upper Egypt and beyond.[16]

We have another testimony about ʿĒzānā and Śeʿazānā and their
relationship to Christianity, namely, the letter of Emperor Constantius
II, which is preserved in the *Apologia* of St Athanasius to this very
emperor:[17]

In it Athanasius explains that now, already for the third time, reports have reached him that
the emperor, with the help of the ruler of Axum, wants to take Bishop Frumentius from his
seat to Alexandria to be ordained again there by the Arian-minded Bishop Georgius and that
only then may he be returned to his believers. If the bishop does not accept this [the reports
say], he must be regarded as a heretic. In this Constantius is clearly referring to the Constantinian imperial church principle, although Axum lay outside the governing power of the
ruler of Byzantium. He insinuates to the two *tyrannoi*, namely, that with them as with the
Romans 'one and the same church doctrine may reign' (PG 25, 636; SC 56, p. 125) – this
with the presupposition that only thus is God's good pleasure assured and the well-being of
the peoples guaranteed. The words of the emperor point in this direction: 'It is then [namely,
in case of the incorrigibility of Frumentius] to be feared that he [Frumentius] after his journey
to Axum will ruin you with reprehensible and godless talking and not only confuse and
disturb the churches, as well as blaspheme God, but also will *thereby* become an initiator of
ruin and destruction for your whole people' (PG 25, 637A; SC 56, p. 126).

The letter says nothing about which faith the emperor wishes from the addressees themselves. One can hardly suggest that he is perhaps speaking as an 'Arian' and thus wants to get

---

16. See A. Dihle, *Umstrittene Daten*, p. 56 with n. 59: 'Whether Judaism came to Abyssinia
from southern Arabia or from Upper Egypt is a question still to be clarified.' Cf. E.
Ullendorff, 'Hebraic-Jewish Elements in Abyssinia (Monophysite) Christology', *JSS* 1
(1956), 216–56.

17. Athanasius of Alex., *Apol. ad Constantium* (CPG 2129), 29, 31: PG 25, 631 and 636;
SC 56, 121 and 124/126. The letter of the emperor is from the years 356–357. Cf. F.
Thelamon, op. cit., p. 61.

the Arian confession accepted.[18] He himself had defended himself against the charge of being an Arian. For him it was presumably only a matter of tearing Frumentius and thus also the church of Axum away from Athanasian discipleship. The relationship of the two *tyrannoi* vis-à-vis this church remains in a certain neutrality.[19] The letter of Constantius probably contains an indication that the rulers of Axum are monotheistic, but none that they are already Christian.[20] The real testimony for the latter remains the inscription found in 1969.

These reports on the first expansion of the gospel in the Axumite kingdom, even with all the variations in detail and some gaps, are confirmed by Latin and Greek church historians.[21] From the reports of Rufinus and Gelasius, Socrates, Sozomenus and Theodoret one can 'ascertain a common core that essentially agrees with the Ethiopian tradition'.[22] In the Ethiopian Synaxarium, namely, one finds the following presentation of the 'Meropius – Aidesius – Frumentius history', which we reproduce here following the new translation of Dombrowski and Dombrowski:

> On this day, the 26th of Hamlē, *Abbā Salāmā* died, the revealer of the light . . ., bishop of Ethiopia, and thus reads his history:
> There came a man from Greece named *Mēropyos*, a senior of the wise, because he wanted to visit the land of Ethiopia, and with him were two boys of his family. One was named *Frēmenāṭos* and the other *Adesyos*, called *Sidrākos*. And he came by ship to the coast of the land of the *Agʿāzi* and saw all the beautiful things that his heart desired. When he wanted to return to his homeland, however, enemies arose against him and killed him and all who were with him. Only the two small boys survived. Residents of the region held them captive, taught them the craft of war and brought them as a gift to the king of Axum, whose name was *Ella Allādā*. Afterwards the king appointed *Adesyos* master of the household and *Frēmenāṭos* guardian of the laws and scribe of Axum. A short time later the king died and left behind a small son with his mother; the honoured foreigners looked after the government. And *Adesyos* and *Frēmenāṭos* remained and raised the child and

---

18. Cf. R. Farina, 'Religion und Politik des 4. Jahrhunderts in der Pars Orientis des Römischen Reiches', in FS G. Söll, Rome 1983 (85–96), 91.

19. J.-M. Szymusiak in SC 56, 125, incorrectly translated the words: 'en tais ekklesiais' as 'vos églises' (your churches) and the other 'Frumention ton episkopon' as '*votre évêque* Frum.' (*your* bishop Frum.). In reality ʿĒzānā is addressed only as a prince, who rules over a Christian people, who as such in the opinion of the emperor must fulfil certain conditions in order to participate in the welfare of heaven. As a 'monotheist', in any case, ʿĒzānā fulfilled the role of being the mediator of the divine will to his people, as understood in the 'Constantinian' fashion.

20. F. Thelamon, op. cit., pp. 78–79, points out the very vague designations for God that Constantius uses: Κρείττων and Θεός.

21. See Rufin., HE X 9: Mommsen-Schwartz, *Eusebius Werke* II (GCS), Leipzig 1908, 972–73; PL 21, 478–80; Sozomen., HE II 24: Bidez-Hansen (GCS 50), Berlin 1960, 82,3–84,4; Socrates, HE 19: Hussey I, 113–17; Theodoret, HE I 23: Parmentier (GCS 19), 73–74. According to Rufinus and the contemporary parallel reports in Sozomenus, Socrates and Theodoret it is certain that their knowledge of Frumentius as the bishop consecrated by Athanasius and sent to *India ulterior* can be related to the bishop of Ethiopia. Cf. here the juxtaposition of texts in B. W. W. Dombrowski and F. A. Dombrowski, art. cit., pp. 133–56, esp. the table on pp. 147–54.

22. B. W. W. Dombrowski and F. A. Dombrowski, art. cit., p. 156.

taught him the faith [*of Christ*] – may he be praised – in small steps. They built him a house of prayer and gathered to him children, whom they taught *Mazmur* and *Maḥlēt*. When this child reached a certain maturity, however, they bade him to let them move to their homeland. *Adesyos* went into the province of Ṭiros to see his parents. *Frēmenāṭos* went to Alexandria to Patriarch *Abbā Atnātyos* and met him in his new office. He reported to him everything that had happened to him and about the religion of the land of the *Aǵāzi* and how they believed in *Christ* – may he be praised – although they were without bishops and without priests. Then *Abbā Atnātyos* appointed *Frēmenāṭos* bishop of the land of the *Aǵāzi*, that is, Ethiopia, and sent him out with great honour. He returned to the land of the *Aǵāzi* when *Abrehā* and *Aṣbeḥa* were governing. He proclaimed salvation through Christ – may he be praised – in all parts of the land, and for this reason he was named *Abbā Salāmā*. After he had brought the population of Ethiopia to the faith, he departed in peace. Salvation, salvation through the praised Word, I say, as I exalt him and lift him up, the *Salāmā*, gate of mercy and of forgiveness. He let the shining of the light of Christ rise on this Ethiopia when darkness reigned over it.[23]

For good reasons one may begin with the following chronology for the evangelization of Ethiopia according to Dombrowski and Dombrowski:[24]

ca. 303:	imprisonment of the perhaps ten-year-old boys Frumentius and Aidesius
ca. 320:	Frumentius and Aidesius take over the regency and education of the (about ten-year-old) prince
ca. 328:	suspension and return home/journey to Athanasius
328/329:	Frumentius with Athanasius
ca. 330:	Frumentius again in Ethiopia
ca. 340/341 or 347/348:	One can speak of Ethiopia as a 'converted' land.
until ?:	continued Christianization until the death of Frumentius

Thus since 'all traditions agree that Christianity was finally introduced into Ethiopia under Abrehā and Aṣbeḥa [= ʿĒzānā and Śeʿazānā]',[25] one will no longer shift the winning of the Axumite kingdom and of King ʿĒzānā to the Christian faith into the fifth or even sixth century, despite the contrary efforts of F. Altheim and R. Stiehl. The inscription found in 1969 fits into the fourth century; there is no trace of Monophysitism. Even the difficulties that E. Dinkler, judging from some numismatic discoveries,[26] brought into the discussion are not a definitive objection. He believed, namely, that he had found representations of the symbol of

---

23. *Synaxaire éthiopien* II, *Hamlê*: ed. Guidi (PO 7), Paris 1911, [411]–[413]; new German translation: B. W. W. Dombrowski and F. A. Dombrowski, art. cit., pp. 116–19.

24. B. W. W. Dombrowski and F. A. Dombrowski, art. cit., p. 131.

25. Idem, art. cit., p. 162.

26. See the data in E. Dinkler, art. cit., pp. 129–31. He naturally demands proof 'that all texts that deal with Ezana can be confirmed as those of the fourth century' (ibid., 128). He believes it possible that the new Christian inscription from Axum was more the work of an Axumite 'Eusebius' than that of Frumentius (ibid., 129). Yet this critical attitude is already inspired by the assumption that the symbolism of a few Ezana coins would be difficult to fit into the second third of the fourth century (see next note).

the cross, which for him created the strongest doubt of the previous placing of the Christianization of Axum under King ʿĒzānā:

> The most unlikely history would have to be postulated if the Ezana/Ezanas/Azana coins were to be regarded as issued by King Ezana as a convert to the Christian faith: the symbol of the cross in the developed form with ends swinging out would have been designed and minted in Axum and would have to have made its way from there into the Mediterranean world. For such a postulate it is equally burdensome whether Ezana is already dated 320–330 or whether he is placed in the period 350–360 with Athanasius on the basis of the Constantius letter. Here would be a theological conception, namely, the summary of the Christian faith in the symbol of the cross anticipated as 'sign of victory', for which any historical context is lacking. Judged on the basis of the history of the iconography of the cross, the Ezana coins, when they show the symbol of the cross in the middle of the reverse side, can only be assigned to the fifth century.[27]

This very discovery – seeing here 'the summary of the Christian faith in the symbol of the cross as "sign of victory"' – is denied by M. R.-Alföldy, who seeks to investigate thoroughly the numismatic discoveries.[28]

---

27. Ibid., p. 132.

28. With her seminar M. Radnoti-Alföldy is working 'on a somewhat definitive new ordering of the Axumite coinage, which will be the basic presupposition for a chronology . . .' As an 'interim view' she offers by letter the following view: 'For me, more than one cross in the coin image can have only decorative character; if one wants to show the cross of Christ, one cannot insert three or four of them around the picture of the ruler or as separation of the legend. But it seems that even with the momentary uncertainty of the chronology, these crosses have replaced the elements of half moon and star, previously used in similarly multiple – that is, for me ornamental – fashion. Half moon and star are ornaments in the sense of the southern Arabian, pagan religion formerly common in Axum; the arrangement certainly brings to mind Sassanidic coins. In my view it is quite conceivable that this ornamentation is already to be understood as the use of Christian symbols – only they cannot represent *the* cross itself.' This communication is greatly appreciated.

CHAPTER TWO

THE MISSION OF THE 'NINE SAINTS'

A second phase of the evangelization of the kingdom of Axum leads into the reign of Emperor Justin I. The tradition here is, to be sure, purely Ethiopian and was not written down until the fourteenth or fifteenth century.[29] The Ethiopians now regard the so-called 'nine saints' as their actual church founders.[30] They are supposed to have all been monks and to have come to Ethiopia from various regions of the Roman Empire at the time of 'Ella 'Amīdā, that is, around the turn of the fifth to sixth century. Yet today the conviction prevails that the new missionaries came from Syria, as indicated by their names in the *Acta Pantaleonis*.[31] It is also indicated by the form of their asceticism. Their meeting with Pachomius is a legend that was invented solely to increase their authority.

According to the vitae the 'nine saints' evangelized, founded monasteries and translated the Holy Scriptures. The vita of Za-Mīkāʾēl 'Aragāwī relates 'that they and especially Za-Mīkāʾēl

29. See E. Carpentier, 'De S. Elesbaa rege et sanctis septem monachis in Aethiopia, commentarius historicus', ASS Octobris XII (Brussels 1867), 296–337; A. Dillmann, 'Zur Geschichte des Axumitischen Reiches im vierten bis sechsten Jahrhundert', *AAWB.PH* 1880 (1–51), 24–27. Dillmann, p. 26, holds that in the period after Chalcedon these monks, coming from Egypt(!) 'in part as persecuted and refugees, penetrated southward into the highland, which at that time was already populated by numerous Christians'. This assumption is improbable. Cf. E. Ullendorff, *Ethiopia and the Bible*, London 1968, 52. See also F. Heyer, *Die Kirche Äthiopiens*, Berlin 1971, 154–80; I. Engelhardt, *Mission und Politik in Byzanz*, pp. 128–34 with sources and bibliography.

30. The Ethiopic Synaxarium contains all nine names. See E. A. W. Budge, *The Book of the Saints of the Ethiopian Church. A Translation of the Ethiopic Synaxarium* I–IV, Cambridge 1928, I 155: Za-Mīkāʾēl 'Aragāwī; I 116–17: Pantaleōn; IV 1009–10: Garīmā (Yeshaq); III 944: Jafsē and Gūbā; III 688: 'Alēf; I 198: Yematā; I 299–300: Līqānos; II 505: Sehmā. See on this Iobi Ludolfi, *Historia Aethiopica sive Brevis & succincta descriptio Regni Habessinorum Quod vulgo male Presbyteri Iohannis vocatur*, Frankfurt-on-Main 1681; idem, *Ad suam Historiam Aethiopicam antehac editam Commentarius*, Frankfurt-on-Main 1691, vol. I.: book III, chap. III; also in vol. II, commentary: nos. 18–25.

31. *Acta Pantaleonis*, ed. C. Conti Rossini, Acta Yārēd et Pantalēwon: CSCO 27, Louvain 1904 (1955).

'Aragāwī converted many unbelievers and corrected and strengthened the faith of those who had already been converted by Abbā Salāmā'.[32] This is also a reference to the first mission, which was not yet governed by the antithesis for or against Chalcedon. 'For a correction of the faith would not have been necessary if 'Ēzānā had only so recently beforehand converted to the Christian faith of the Monophysite kind, as Altheim and Stiehl would like one to believe. . . . In the Greek and Syriac literature, after Frumentius and 'Ēzānā, the Ethiopian Church and its bishops are nowhere mentioned until towards the end of the fifth century. If one thinks of the dependence of the Church of Ethiopia on Alexandria, it is striking that in the frequent councils of the Alexandrian patriarchate the presence of a bishop from Ethiopia is never reported. That can hardly be blamed on travel conditions alone. Even in the Ethiopian diptychs and in the Ethiopian Synaxarium there are no significant ecclesiastical personalities named between 'Abrehā and 'Aṣbehā on the one hand and the "nine saints" on the other.'[33]

The 'nine saints' were successful. For Cosmas Indicopleustes expressly attests that at the beginning of the century 'Αξώμη τε καὶ πᾶσα ἡ περίχωρος were Christian.[34] According to the just-mentioned word of the correction of the faith in this second missionary wave, Ethiopia was won for the anti-Chalcedonian movement. Yet what is to be understood by this must then be worked out from the few sources. First, one must point out that at the time of Justin I and Justinian the Axumites were already so strong as Christians that they could appear as the powerful

32. See I. Guidi, *Il Gadla 'Aragāwī* (AANL.M Ser. 5, vol. II, 1), Rome 1895 (1–98), 38–39, cited in Engelhardt, *Mission und Politik in Byzanz*, pp. 132–33.

33. I. Engelhardt, *Mission und Politik in Byzanz*, p. 133. According to the vita of St Cyriacus by Cyril of Scythopolis, nevertheless, a monk Thomas is mentioned, who according to the *vita graeca* (Schwartz, *Kyrillos von Skythopolis*, pp. 225,27–226,3) was sent by the deacon Phidos to the archbishop of Alexandria to acquire the necessary ecclesiastical linen for the monastery of St Euthymius, which was under construction (479–482). Now, here the Georgian translation also knows that Thomas was simultaneously the bearer of letters from Patriarch Martyrius of Jerusalem (478–486) and was consecrated bishop for Abyssinia by Timothy II (Saloph.), the Melkite patriarch of Alexandria (460–475, 477–482). In the translation of G. Garitte: *Et accepit secum epistulas patriarchae Martyrii ad Alexandrinum patriar-cham; et ivit ut perficeret ministerium diaconatus sui. Et ut vidit patriarcha sanctum hunc, non latuit eum thesaurus qui erat in eo, et consecravit eum episcopum super Abyssiniorum terram; et ut intravit Thomas in terram Kusim in Abyssinia, gratiā quae erat apud eum splendidus, erexit ecclesias multas pro Christo; totam Aethiopiam illuminavit per virtutes suas; et erat cum eo pellis vestiaria sancti Euthymii; sicut fecit Elias Elisaeo, splendidi inter prophetas, ita faciebat per pellem signa multa sanctus Thomas.* Cf. G. Garitte, 'La version géorgienne de la Vie de S. Cyriaque par Cyrille de Scythopolis', *Mus* 75 (1962), 399–440; text above on p. 415; discussion on pp. 405–6. Yet while referring to E. Cerulli, G. Garitte noticed that in the Ethiopian literature known today, nothing is known of this Bishop Thomas. But Garitte supports the idea that Cyril of Scythopolis himself wrote this expansion of the Greek vita. 'La version géorgienne nous restitue ici un épisode authentique que nos manuscrits grecs ne connaissent pas et qui enrichit d'une donnée intéressante l'histoire, très pauvrement documentée, de l'Église éthiopienne au Ve siècle' (p. 406). If this assumption is correct, then around 480 Chalcedonian missionary work was introduced into Ethiopia and preceded the probably anti-Chalcedonian oriented work of the 'nine saints'. Nevertheless, it is curious that no memory of this remains in the Ethiopian literature. See E. Isaac, *Mus* 85 (1972), 246, n. 8.

34. Cosmas Ind., *Top. chr.* III, 66: SC 141, p. 505.

protector of Christianity in the southern lands on the opposite side of the Red Sea and were able to assert themselves for some time.[35]

---

35. A. Dillmann, *Zur Geschichte des Axumitischen Reiches im vierten bis sechsten Jahrhundert* (*AAWB.PH* 1880), Berlin 1881, 27.

CHAPTER THREE

AXUM AS THE FIRST CHRISTIAN KINGDOM OF NON-CHALCEDONIAN CONFESSION AND ITS CRUSADE INTO SOUTHERN ARABIA

After Christianity was established in the kingdom of Axum around the turn of the fifth to the sixth century, it was caught up in the current of anti-Chalcedonian propaganda emanating from Syria and Persia. Apart from important epigraphic discoveries, only the more recent literary-historical studies have produced the possibility of determining the role of Ethiopia in the whole Chalcedonian–anti-Chalcedonian movement between 451 and 600. Here our eyes are directed across the Red Sea to Arabia: first to its west coast and the city of Najrān, but then beyond into the land of culture on the Euphrates, even over the Tigris to Bēth Aršām and from there again back to Gbītā not far from the Golan Heights.

The persecution of the followers of Severus of Antioch by Emperor Justin I (518–527) and serious events in Arabia shook this region, and indeed all Christendom, and evoked a reaction, whose driving force was regarded to be Bishop *Simeon of Bēth-Aršām*. Beside Severus of Antioch and Philoxenus of Mabbug, he became one of the most zealous defenders of Syrian-Alexandrian Christology. His activity spread as far as Axum. Like Bernard in the Middle Ages, he became the preacher of a crusade, for which the Christian king of Axum was won. At the centre are reports on the massacre of thousands of Ethiopian and southern Arabian Christians by a king of Jewish faith in the kingdom of Ḥimyar. In order to understand the involvement of Abyssinia in these events we must briefly go into its relations with Arabia.[36]

---

36. See M. Höfner, 'Die Kultur des vorislamischen Südarabien', *ZDMG* 99 (1945–49), 15–28; J. Ryckmans, 'Le christianisme en Arabie du Sud préislamique', in *Atti del Convegno Internazionale sul tema: L'Oriente nella storia della civiltà*, ed. by Acc. Naz. Linc. a. CCCLXI–1964, Rome 1964, 413–53; N. Pigulewskaja, *Byzanz auf den Wegen nach Indien. Aus der Geschichte des byzantinischen Handels mit dem Orient vom 4. bis 6. Jahrhundert* (BBA 36), Berlin–

The Ḥimyarites had been in the southern mountain land of the
Arabian peninsula since the fifth century BC. In their expansion further
south (second century BC) they allied themselves with the Habasat (Abyssinians) against Saba and Haḍramawt. Their capital was Zafār. After the
appearance of internal difficulties in the third century AD Abyssinia was
able to build a strong bridgehead on the Arabian peninsula. In the year
335 King ʿĒzānā succeeded in occupying all of southern Arabia and
naming himself king of Ḥimyar and Saba. Yet in 378 southern Arabia
was able to free itself from this dominion and form a large kingdom.
Decisive for the religious culture of the land was the penetration of
Judaism, followed by Christian missionaries. Their leader at first was the
Arian Theophilus, called the 'Indian'. He was sent by Emperor Constantius II,[37] yet out of not only religious but also political motives. In
spite of the resistance of numerous Jews, whose presence is also attested
by Philostorgius, Theophilus was able to convert the ethnarch of the
Ḥimyarites. At his own cost the new convert built a church in Zafār,
likewise in Aden and in another large harbour city at the entrance to the
Persian Gulf, which was possibly Hormuz. Yet Christianity, which still
lacked a hierarchy, could not prevail against Judaism, which retained its
dominance in southern Arabia, as monotheistic royal inscriptions attest
(cf. Ryckmans below). Nonetheless, in the middle of the fifth century
Christianity gained a foothold in the oasis city of Najrān, which – lying
at the intersection of important caravan routes – connected southern
Arabia with central Arabia, Syria and Mesopotamia. According to John
Diakrinomenos, Emperor Anastasius I sent a bishop to the Ḥimyarites,[38]
who had participated in a manifold change of faith: first, adoption of the
Jewish religion, then – under Persian pressure – relapse into paganism.
The missionary of the emperor, however, was probably preceded by the

---

Amsterdam 1969, section III 3: 'Äthiopien und Ḥimyar im 5. und 6. Jahrhundert u. Z.',
211–71. In both writings one must note the new text conditions as worked out by I. Shahīd,
The Martyrs of Najran. New Documents (SubsHag 49), Brussels 1971. An overview for
understanding the following is offered by G. Riße, *'Gott ist Christus, der Sohn der Maria'. Eine
Studie zum Christusbild im Koran* (Begegnung vol. 2), Bonn 1989, pp. 63–82; cf. also C. D. G.
Müller, *Kirche und Mission unter den Arabern in vorislamischer Zeit* (SGV 249), Tübingen
1967.

37. Philostorgius, *HE* III 4–6: Bidez-Winkelmann (Berlin 1972), 32–34. Christianity in
Yemen, however, never had a comprehensive hierarchical organization. Cf. J. Ryckmans,
art. cit., p. 414.

38. See J. Diakrinomenos, in Theodorus Lector, *HE* Epit. 559: Hansen (Berlin 1971),
157; *Martyrium S. Arethae*: ed. by Carpentier, ASS Oct. X (Brussels 1869), 721–59; cf. on the
following: I. Shahīd, op. cit., p. 46; I. Engelhardt, *Mission und Politik in Byzanz*, pp. 28–31.
Letter G of Simeon of Bēth-Aršām, edited by I. Shahīd, reports in II C – III A (translation in
Shahīd, p. 46) of the consecration of Bishops Paul I and Paul II by Philoxenus.

bishop of Mabbug, Philoxenus, who consecrated the first bishops of Najrān.

A new chapter in the history of Christianity began when King Yūsuf 'As'ar Yat'ar,[39] a follower of Judaism, initiated a major action that affected various groups. According to the Ethiopian version of the *Martyrium Arethae* (§§ 2–3), the king first attacked the Ethiopian garrison that the Negus had left behind in the land; after it was annihilated, Yūsuf decided to destroy the Christian city of Najrān and its church. Thus the first was a bellicose action, the second a religious-political one. With this the Greek documents (§ 3) are in agreement. Yet the compiler of these documents then gave his imagination free reign and distinguished three phases of the persecution: (1) action against all *foreign* Christians in Yūsuf's kingdom, whether Greeks, Persians, Romans or Ethiopians; then (2) murder of all *native* Christians of his realm; finally (3) the annihilations of *Najrān* and the Christians there. In contrast to the *Martyrium Arethae* (of various versions), the *Book of the Ḥimyarites* (p. 4a) and a soon-to-be-mentioned letter of Bishop Simeon of Bēth-Aršām then include the military action against the Ethiopians in the actual religious persecution.

Only through more recent discoveries and the concomitant reclassification of other documents already known earlier has it become possible to comprehend to some extent from the religious side the reaction of the Christian world, in which the Chalcedonians and anti-Chalcedonians were one. But above the high ethos of the martyr reports, above the zeal of faith of a Simeon of Bēth-Aršām, above the religious conviction of King Kaleb, one must not forget the intertwining of trade and power interests with religious motives, which governed all groups, whether Byzantine, Ethiopian, Ḥimyarite or Persian. 'Crusade' and 'war of conquest' can be closely connected. Since in Najrān and Ẓafār it was the upper levels of society who had accepted Christianity, special relationships resulted – above all of the economic kind – with Ethiopia and with Byzantium. Between the activity of Ḥayyān the Elder, who lived already in the time of Yazdgard I (399–420) and had done much for the spread of Christianity in the land of the Ḥimyarites, and the Cushitic-

---

39. Three inscriptions attest this name. Cf. J. Ryckmans, 'Inscriptions sud-arabes, dixième série', *Mus* 66 (1953) (267–317), specifically Ry 507, pp. 284–95; Ry 508, pp. 295–303; A. Jamme, *Sabaean and Ḥasaean Inscriptions from Saudi-Arabia* (StSem 23), Rome 1966, 39–42 (Ja 1028). According to this last inscription the full name reads as given above. See I. Shahīd, op.

Ḥimyaritic wars (420–520), there had already been encounters between Christian, pagan and Jewish Ḥimyarites. The father of the martyr Ḥabsā from the clan of the mentioned Ḥayyān the Elder had already set fire to a synagogue in Najrān.[40] The colourfully woven carpet of interests on the Arabian peninsula is well described by N. Pigulewskaja:[41]

> Judaism played a certain role with the Ḥimyarites; the proselytes represented Jewish commercial interests; at the same time they strove to liberate themselves from the dominion of the Cushites, who were dependent on the Christian groups. Like orthodox Christianity, Monophysitism among the Ḥimyarites was also under Syrian-Arabian influences, which came in with the trade caravans from Syria and Mesopotamia, Edessa and Ḥīrtā. Of no less importance also was Ethiopia (*Book of the Ḥimyarites* 6a, CIV, chap. XXXIXf.; 5b, CIII, chap. XXV). Organizationally, the Ethiopian Church was under the patriarch of Alexandria, who appointed its clerics. Thus this other direction of influence in the southern Arabian regions went out from Alexandria and Axum. All these conditions and possibilities were considered and exploited by Constantinople, whose diplomacy strove to consolidate Byzantine commercial bases here (Malalas, 434). The Cushites and Romans were dependent on the Christian groups at the various levels of Ḥimyar society. The pagan and Jewish groups of Ḥimyarites sought to liberate themselves from Ethiopian influence, an effort actively supported by Iran, which strove to gain a solid foothold on the Arabian peninsula.

1. The new source situation

It is primarily a question of hagiographic documents, which, however, should be evaluated with regard to Christology and confessional history. The Arabian desert begins to live. A net of communications is spun, in the middle of which stands an anti-Chalcedonian bishop.

---

cit., pp. 260–68. The name Yūsuf, which the king, son of a Jewish woman from Nisibis, bore since his acceptance of the Jewish faith, was probably supposed to express his messianic ideas, to which the Christians of southern Arabia fell victim. His opponents, the Christians, gave him the nickname *Masruq* ('stolen' or 'robbed'). Cf. the Chronicle of Seʿert: A. Scher, PO 5, pp. 330–31. Yūsuf's mother was taken captive and bought by a ruler. He himself took part in the Jewish polemic against the resurrection of Christ, with the assertion that the body of Christ was stolen by the disciples (cf. Mt 28,13). The Christians answered with the counter-charge that it was not Christ but the king himself who was stolen (cf. Gen 40,15); cf. *Book of the Ḥimyarites* on the other names (13a). On the name Ḏū Nuwas see I. Shahīd, op. cit., pp. 264–66.

40. Cf. *B. Ḥimyar.* 32b: Moberg, p. CXXIII.

41. Cf. N. Pigulewskaja, *Byzanz auf den Wegen nach Indien*, p. 223. On the significance of Judaism in southern Arabia see also J. Ryckmans, 'Le christianisme en Arabie du Sud préislamique', 430–31, 446; C. D. G. Müller, 'Kirche und Mission unter den Arabern in vorislamischer Zeit', loc. cit.

(a) The writings of Bishop Simeon of Bēth-Aršām

(1) His letter to Simeon, abbot of Gabula (near Aleppo), on the end of the so-called Ḥimyarite blood witnesses (siglum S) (BHO 99–101). Syriac-Latin in I. S. Assemani, *Bibliotheca Orientalis* I, Rome 1719, 364–79; Syr.-Ital.: I. Guidi, La lettera di Simeone vescovo di Bēth-Aršām sopra i martiri omeriti, ARAccLinc s. III, Memorie della Cl. di Scienze morali etc., vol. VII, Rome 1881, 471–515; Syr. text: 501–15; reprint in I. Guidi, *Raccolta di scritti*, vol. I: *Oriente cristiano* I (Pubblicazioni dell'Istituto per l'Oriente), Rome 1945, 1–60. English translation by A. Jeffery, 'Letter giving an Account of the Himyarite Martyrs by Simeon, Bishop of the Persian Christians', in *The Moslem World* 36 (1946), 204–16. This letter also came into the third part of the chronicle of Ps.-Dionysius of Tell Maḥrē, who copied it from John of Ephesus, in abbreviated form also in Zacharias Rhetor cont., *HE* VIII 3: CSCO 88 (V), 43–50; see J.-B. Chabot, *Incerti auctoris Chronicon anonymum pseudo-Dionysianum vulgo dictum*: CSCO 104 (T), pp. 54–69, 111–12; there is a paraphrasing translation of this in N. Pigulewskaja, *Byzanz auf den Wegen nach Indien*, Berlin 1969, appendix II, pp. 325–35. S was sent from Ḥīra.

(2) In S reference is made to an earlier letter that Simeon wrote from Ramla (siglum R).

(3) In the year 1960 I. Shahīd discovered a new letter of Simeon in Syriac, of which there already existed a translation in Karshūni since 1733/34 within a larger hagiographic collection that was described in 1913 by G. Graf in *OrChr* NS III (1913), 311–27, without Simeon's letter as such coming to his attention. The new letter (siglum G) was written in July 519 and sent from Gbītā, the military camp of the anti-Chalcedonian Ghassanids. It tells of the martyrdom of women in southern Arabia, which must be placed already in the year 518. This report closes with the admonition to come to the aid of the oppressed Christians in the south. By comparing this letter G with S, I. Shahīd can make out the bishop of Bēth-Aršām as the author. Later than R and S, letter G is at the same time more comprehensive than either of the other two in themselves; it has the best literary structure of all. The new material that G contains vis-à-vis R and S is given by I. Shahīd, p. 122 (see also pp. 126–28).

Edition of the Syr. text with English translation in I. Shahīd, *The Martyrs of Najrān*, pp. III–XXXII or 43–64. Then come notes on the Syr. text and English translation (pp. 65–111) and finally in part III, 113–79, 'Arshamiana' with excellent analyses of all the writings of Simeon, but esp. of letter G, pp. 121–28.

(4) The *Book of the Ḥimyarites* (siglum B): already in the year 1963 Shahīd expressed the supposition that this famous book, which A. Moberg had discovered and edited, likewise had Simeon of Bēth-Aršām as its author: 'The Book of the Himyarites. Authorship and Authenticity', *Mus* 76 (1963), 349–62. Moberg, on the other hand, had attributed this book to Sergius, the bishop of Sergiopolis, a follower of Chalcedon. I. Guidi ascribed to this Sergius the yet-to-be-mentioned *Martyrium Arethae*. I. Shahīd was the first to recognize that letter S and the *Book of the Ḥimyarites* (B) must have the same author, which he now finds confirmed by the discovery of G. Shahīd can support his discovery with the comparison of S, B and G: 'Simeon's authorship of G has been established independently of B, just as Simeon's authorship of B had been argued for in 1963 independently of G. The present discussion (op. cit., pp. 132–39) then represents a confrontation of the two documents, G and B: this confrontation promotes the possibility of Simeon's authorship of B into a certainty' (op. cit., 132). See A. Moberg, *The Book of Himyarites. Fragments of a hitherto unknown Syriac Work*, Lund 1924.

With the attribution of the named letters and the *Book of the Ḥimyarites*, Simeon of Bēth-Aršām now takes shape as an agitator for southern Arabian Christians, and this, to be sure, is at the same time in the interest of the anti-Chalcedonian movement, which now has new martyrs. The vita that John of Ephesus wrote contains an unexpectedly rich confirmation. See E. W. Brooks, John of Ephesus, *Lives of the Eastern Saints*, PO 17, pp. 137–58: 'Next the Tenth History, of the Brave Warrior on behalf of the True Faith, Mar Simeon the Bishop, the Persian Debater'. Cf. I. Shahīd, op. cit., 159–79. John of Ephesus wrote *c.* 565 as head of the anti-Chalcedonian group in Constantinople. Simeon's activity comprised a quarter century.

Of this, the period between 520 and 540 falls into the time of the Chalcedonian reform under Justin I and Justinian. The key words for his life and work are given by John of Ephesus in the subtitle quoted above: he was a brave warrior for the faith especially in Persia against Nestorianism, under which he naturally classified Chalcedon, but also against Judaism, which was flourishing in southern Arabia. He also included Ethiopia directly in the anti-Chalcedonian discussion, as a section of the newly found letter G reveals: 'And in addition, there is being sent to your Holiness [the recipient of letter G] a copy of the *documents concerning the Faith* which have been written by the believing Cushites to the Orthodox Persians, together with a copy of the petition and the *discourse* which had been submitted by our humble person to the reverend AWFRFYS [Euprepios], the bishop of the Cushites, and to KLB [Caleb], their believing king, a copy of which we formerly sent to your Reverence' (see plate IX. B; translation in Shahīd, p. 63; also p. 222). These 'documents concerning the Faith' would naturally be highly significant for us but are unfortunately lost.

(b) The Martyrium Arethae

The *Martyrium Arethae* (*MA*), compared with letter G, cannot be considered the first source for the events in Ḥimyar but has, nonetheless, its own significance. For between the *MA* and the *Book of the Ḥimyarites* there is a similarity in structure. Thus from the various versions of the *MA* something can be inferred about the content of certain lost parts of B. Its importance is supported by the fact that Arabic and Ethiopian translations are extant.

(1) The Arabic version has survived in four mss.: Sinai cod. 428 and 443 (which follow the Greek version) and 469 and 535. Cod. 469 and 535 report that the settlement of the Jews in southern Arabia coincided with the destruction of the Temple in Jerusalem in the year 70, which could be important for the filling out of chap. II of B. The Arabic version represents a link between the various other versions. The *MA* had been translated from the Greek (or perhaps from Coptic or Syriac) into Arabic and from there into Ethiopic. The result was close contact between Syriac, Arabic, Coptic and Ethiopic literature (cf. I. Shahīd, op. cit., p. 194).

(2) The Ethiopic translation is especially significant for hagiography (King Kaleb). It is the source of the Ethiopian Synaxarium and for the Antiphonies. See Esteves Pereira, 'Historia dos Martyres de Nagran, Versao ethiopica', in *Quarto centenario do descobrimento da India*, Lisbon 1899. Ethiopic text, pp. 79–122.

(3) Greek text[42] with Latin translation ed. by E. Carpentier, 'Martyrium Sancti Arethae et Sociorum in civitate Negran (BHG 166)', in ASS, Octobris t. X (1861), pp. 721–59. A metaphrastic Greek version (BHG 167) by Symeon Metaphrastes is to be found in PG 115, 1249–89; another anonymous and somewhat older metaphrase (BHG 166z), presumably the model for the version of Symeon Metaphrastes,[43] has now been published by F. Halkin: 'Le martyre d'Aréthas et de ses compagnons himyarites', in idem, *Six inédits d'hagiologie byzantine* (SubsHag 74), Brussels 1987, 133–78; 134–57 (Greek); 157–78 (French). Now, it is clearly recognizable that the last two named versions (BHG 166z and 167) were composed by a terminologically schooled Chalcedonian; that edited by Carpentier (BHG 166), on the other

---

42. M. van Esbroeck, 'L'Éthiopie à l'époque de Justinien: S. Arethas de Neǧrān et s. Athanase de Clysma', in *IV Congr. Internaz. di Studi Etiopici*, ed. by Acc. Naz. Linc. a. 371, 1974, Rome 1974 (117–39), 119–20, provides 19 manuscripts of the Greek *Martyrium* (BHG 166).

43. A. Ehrhard, *Überlieferung und Bestand der hagiographischen und homiletischen Literatur der griechischen Kirche. Von den Anfängen bis zum Ende des 16. Jahrhunderts* I (TU 50), Leipzig 1937, p. 467 with n. 3.

hand, contains much more common formulations that are also acceptable to 'Monophysites'. We present the examples below.

The *MA* comes from the sixth century, between 529 and 597. Perhaps the *MA* is not an independent writing but part of a trilogy that would also include the *Leges Homeritarum* (BHG 706h) and the *Dialogus* (Disputatio BHG 706–706d), which is attributed to St Gregentius. Yet this assumption is in no way assured. According to I. Shahīd (op. cit., 203) the *MA* could have been written in Constantinople, where John of Ephesus resided, who, according to his own statement, inherited the manuscript legacy of Simeon of Bēth-Aršām (cf. PO 17, p. 158).

I. Shahīd (*Martyrs of Najrān*, 202ff.) believed he could show that the author of the *MA* was a Chalcedonian,[44] especially because he speaks of Emperor Justin differently from the sources attributed to Simeon of Bēth-Aršām. Justin's part in King Kaleb's undertaking is emphasized in detail, according to Shahīd; above all, in the *MA* the Byzantine emperor plays a major role in various critical situations and their being overcome: thus in the delegation to King Mundir, the ruler of the Lakhmids. He mentions Justin's letters to Patriarch Timothy III of Alexandria and to King Kaleb in Axum. Conversely, the writer also reports on the communication of King Kaleb to Emperor Justin on his success in Ḥimyar. Cf. §§ 25, 27, 38 of the *MA*. The role of the Byzantine fleet in Kaleb's undertaking is described in detail, esp. in the third part, for which the *MA* represents the only source. The Byzantine Chalcedonian colouring, which remains without polemical harshness, permeates the whole book, according to Shahīd; the *Book of the Ḥimyarites* passes over the role of Byzantium and Emperor Justin. Because of its conciliatory attitude, I. Shahīd would like to place the *MA* in the later period in the reign of Emperor Justinian, where he as a neo-Chalcedonian sought a balance between the parties. Yet out of such an atmosphere one could not succeed (according to Shahīd) in making Arethas and King Kaleb saints of the universal church.[45]

Through the investigations and editions of I. Shahīd a new starting position has been created with regard to sources relating to southern Arabia. In his works Shahīd offers rich data on the prehistory of relations between Byzantium and the Arabs: *Rome and the Arabs. A Prolegomenon to the Study of Byzantium and the Arabs* and *Byzantium and the Arabs in the Fourth Century* (Dumbarton Oaks Research Library and Collection), Washington DC 1984, also *Byzantium and the Arabs in the Fifth Century* (Dumbarton Oaks Research Library and Collection), Washington DC 1989 (here not yet evaluated). Important information on the sources of Ḥimyar history is given in N. Pigulewskaja, *Byzanz auf den Wegen nach Indien*, Berlin, Amsterdam 1969, 175–96. In the future even more attention will have to be given to the (Christian) Arabic sources, such as the Arab chronicler Tabarī (ed. M. A. Ibrahim, 2 vols., Cairo 1961). N. Pigulewskaja still uses the old edition (aṭ-Tabarī, *Annales quos scripsit Abu Djafar Mohammed Ibn Djarir At-Tabarī*, ed. M. J. de Goeje, 1st ser., 2, Leiden 1879–1901), while I. Shahīd already uses the new. On the whole, in the study of Ethiopian Christology the nearness of certain motifs (e.g., the position of Jesus' mother) to the early history of Islam (Koran) is striking. Cf. C. Schedl, *Muhammad und Jesus. Die christologisch relevanten Texte des*

---

44. In disagreement is L. Van Rompay, 'The Martyrs of Najran. Some Remarks on the Nature of the Sources', in J. Quaegebeur (ed.), *Studia Paulo Naster Oblata II. Orientalia Antiqua* (OLA 13), Louvain 1982, 301–9, who says that the Greek *Martyrium* still bears anti-Chalcedonian traits; at least, a non-Monophysite revision (if it occurred) was not radical. He advises using it with caution as a historical source.

45. *Synaxarium Eccl. Constantinop.* 159,14: 24 Oct.; *Martyrolog. Roman.* 24 Oct.: Feast of St Arethas; 27 Oct.: Feast of King Elesbaas, i.e., Kaleb.

Koran, Vienna-Freiburg-Basel 1978; G. Riße, *'Gott ist Christus, der Sohn der Maria'. Eine Studie zum Christusbild im Koran*, Bonn 1989.

2. The events

With all brevity let us consider the events that, according to the just-mentioned and other sources already known earlier, are important in describing the faith situation.

(a) The Conference of Ramla (520/521)[46]

After his coming to power (518), Emperor Justin suspended the payments to the Persians that had been granted them by Emperor Anastasius I (d. 518). In order to compel continuation, the Persians mobilized the troops of its vassal, the Lakhmid king Mundir III (503–554). In two successive campaigns these troops struck around 520/521 against the Byzantine imperial border. In order to re-establish peace, Emperor Justin sent a legation, which probably already towards the end of 520 or beginning of 521 met with King Mundir in Ramla, the latter's field camp southeast of his capital of Hīra. The legation was under the leadership of the reliable presbyter Abraham, the son of Euporus and the father of Nonnosus. He belonged to a whole 'dynasty' of interpreters and envoys 'who throughout three generations carried out diplomatic assignments from Byzantium. They were sent especially into the Near Eastern lands, to the small Arabian princes and sheiks, to Ethiopia and Iran. This time Abraham had the assignment of "moving him [Mundir] to make peace with the Christians under his dominion".'[47] Moreover, the envoy was supposed to effect the release of two of Justin's army leaders who had been taken captive. It is worthwhile to look briefly at the participants in this meeting in Ramla: coming with Abraham was Sergius, the (Chalcedonian) bishop of Ruṣāfa (Sergiopolis); he is mentioned by Simeon of Bēth-Aršām, the third significant man in the place, in his letter S. Simeon

---

46. On the conference of Ramla see I. Shahīd, 'Byzantino-Arabica. The Conference of Ramla, A.D. 524[?]', *JNES* 23 (1964), 115–31; idem, *The Martyrs of Najrān* (1971), pp. 114, 120–21, 240. Shahīd now calls into question his dating of 524. Ramla is to be placed earlier. Based on the *explicit* of letter G, the year of persecution in Ḥimyar is 518. The date in the letter that reads 523 is by a later hand. The end of 520 or beginning of 521 is probable for Ramla.

47. On Abraham, the father of Nonnosus and son of Euporus, see N. Pigulewskaja, op. cit., p. 238.

represents the anti-Chalcedonian party of Persia. He arrived in the camp at the latest at the beginning of 521. Also present from Persia was the presbyter Isaac, apocrisiarius of the 'orthodox' Christians and thus probably of the Chalcedonians. The subdeacon John Mandinus was probably assigned to him. The Nestorians of Persia were represented by Bishop Shilas.[48] About him the *Martyrium S. Arethae*[49] says that he came with a large crowd with the intention to dispute with the Roman (Byzantine) and Persian orthodox (Chalcedonians) and to contradict (ἀντιδογματίσαι) [them], and to please the Greeks (pagans) and Jews. Also coming with Mundir was a certain Ḥajjāj, Greek *Aggaios*, who is mentioned in the Nestorian chronicle of Seʿert.[50] He was no Nestorian but from either the Chalcedonian or anti-Chalcedonian followers. The designation *comes* in the *Martyrium S. Arethae* is not to be taken in the technical sense but to be translated simply as *companion*. He was erroneously regarded as the 'ethnarch' (commander) of the whole army camp. Functioning as such, rather, was Zayd ibn Ayyūb (Zayd, son of Job). He was Christian and probably the brave advocate of Christians before the Lakhmid king Mundir, as we shall immediately see. The Lakhmids were not yet Christians, but became such in the year 591 towards the end of their reign.[51]

Certain church historians seem to make Mundir a Christian and even a follower of Chalcedon. According to them, he was visited by envoys of Patriarch Severus of Antioch who wanted to win him to 'theopaschitism', that is, to the anti-Chalcedonian confession; this he clearly rejected. It is a question, however, of a confusion of names. Theodorus Lector, who is the topic here,[52] speaks of an Alamundaros, an otherwise unknown phylarch in the area of

---

48. *Historia Nestorianorum*: PO 7, pp. 135–38.
49. *Mart. Areth.* VI, 25: Carpentier, p. 742.
50. *Hist. Nest.*: PO 7, p. 143.
51. Assemani, *BO* III, 109.
52. Theodorus Lector, *HE* II 35, Epitome 513: Hansen 147, with nn. to 16–25. Cf. Theophanes, *Chronogr.* A. M. 6005: De Boor I, 159,19–160,1. Because I. Shahīd, op. cit., pp. 269–72, does not notice this, he has difficulties with the interpretation of the relationship of Mundir to Severus and to Christianity in general. On this see I. Guidi, 'Mundhir III. und die beiden monophysitischen Bischöfe', *ZDMG* 35 (1881), 142–46. Very useful in this connection is G. Rothstein, 'Die Dynastie der Laḥmiden in al-Ḥīra. Ein Versuch zur arabisch-persischen Geschichte zur Zeit der Sasaniden' (diss.), Teil I, Halle 1898; Teil II, Berlin 1899; B. Rubin, *Das Zeitalter Justinians*, vol. 1, Berlin 1960, 268–79: 'Arabische Satellitenstämme im Vorfeld der Grossmächte: Laḥmiden, Ghassaniden und die römische Limestradition'.

the Roman Limes; he must not be confused with Mundir III, who was decidedly hostile to Christians. Still, in the year 527 he had four hundred virgins from the church of Thomas in Emesa kidnapped and slaughtered as sacrifices to the Arabian goddess al-ʿUzzā.[53] Later he also sacrificed the son of the Ghassanid Arethas, his enemy, to the same gods (to Aphrodite).[54]

Thus the Ramla meeting was a model of the confessional and religious-political situation in the Greek – Persian – Arabian world, and it was even more so when during the conference pagan Arabs arrived and brought the first direct news of the events in Ḥimyar, together with a letter of King Yūsuf (Masruq) himself. In it he reported full of pride on his proceeding against the Christians of Najrān. The writing was part of a comprehensive action in which – in co-operation with the Persians, who included Nestorians – the Christian Byzantines and Ethiopians were to be robbed of their influence (religious and economic) on the Arabian peninsula. Therefore Christianity was supposed to disappear from Persia to Yemen. Yūsuf invited Mundir to accept the Jewish faith and promised him in return 'the weight of 3,000 dinari'.[55] Simeon reports in letter S that Mundir – before the troops in formation, among whom there were also Christians – read out Yūsuf's letter and then shouted at the Christians:

'Have you all heard what has happened? Deny Christ now, for I am not better than those kings who persecute the Christians.' (The letter of Simeon of Bēth-Aršām, which contains these words, continues:) 'A man from his army, a Christian, got excited and spoke bravely to the king: "We did not become Christians in your time in order to deny Christ." Mundir became enraged and spoke: "You dare to speak before me [in my presence]?" He said: "Out of reverence for God I am not afraid, and no one holds me back; for my sword is not shorter than the swords of the others, and I am not afraid to fight

---

53. Cf. Zacharias Rh. cont., *HE* VIII 5: CSCO 88 (V), 53; Hamilton-Brooks, pp. 206–7.

54. See Procop., *De bello Persico* II 28,13: Haury-Wirth I (1968), 284; O. Veh, *Prokop, Perserkriege*, Munich 1970, 407. See in ibid. the detailed drawing of the figure of Mundir in I 17: Haury-Wirth, 87–99; O. Veh, 122–26; from this, p. 125: 'Alamundaros [= Mundir] . . ., an enemy who for perhaps fifty years had the Romans on their knees. Beginning with the border areas of Egypt and reaching to Mesopotamia, he plundered the estates and stole everything that fell into his hands. When he came to houses, he left them in ashes; likewise, he turned people by the thousands into slaves and killed most of them without any consideration, while he sold the rest for a lot of money. But no one in the whole world dared to go against him.' All the more notable is the argument of the soldier with one probably of high rank, of whom Simeon reports. As already said, his name may have been Zayd ibn-Ayyūb.

55. *Mart. Areth.* VI, 25: Carpentier, p. 742.

until my death." Because of his lineage, his appearance and his fighting courage, Mundir
left him [unharmed].'[56]

What Simeon had learned here he passed on from the camp in Ramla in
the already mentioned, but lost, letter R. In letter S from Ḥīra (521) he
sought to mobilize public opinion among his fellow believers for a
crusade for the Christians of southern Arabia. There he had also heard of
the participation of the Jews of Tiberias in the proceedings in Ḥimyar.
The closing of letter S is directed towards anti-Chalcedonian clerics and
especially towards Patriarch Timothy III of Alexandria. This closing
probably also contained a list of greetings with the names of anti-
Chalcedonian bishops and abbots. It is no longer extant in S but is to be
found in John of Ephesus.[57]

> We bid your charity on whose support we depend, as well as the archimandrites and
> bishops, but especially the archbishop of Alexandria, to write to the king of the Ḥimyar-
> ites, so that he will write to the king of the Cushites. The latter should be ready to aid the
> Ḥimyarites. Also they should seize the high priests of the Jews in Tiberias, torment them
> and tell the Jewish king that he is to show understanding and stop the fighting and
> persecutions in the kingdom of the Ḥimyarites. For the rest, however, I ask forgiveness,
> for this is the task of the archbishops of the present day and the archimandrites of the
> believers.

According to the indications given in letters S and G, the persecution of
the Ḥimyarite and Arab Christians must fall in the first years of Justin's

---

56. See Assemani, BO I, 372–73; N. Pigulewskaja, Byzanz auf den Wegen nach Indien, p.
330. Mundir had to take into consideration the large group of Nestorian-Christian Ibad in
Ḥīra. Cf. G. Rothstein, 'Die Dynastie der Laḫmiden in al-Ḥīra' I, pp. 18–28. The Ibad (from
ibād, 'servant', 'slave', to expand: of God, or better, of Christ, that is, of the Messiah) were
composed of various influential Arab families and in al-Ḥīra had attached themselves to
Nestorian Christianity (on the list of bishops see ibid., 24). Christian ideas were transmitted
by them to Arabia in a special way. 'It was the intellectual elite of the bedouin, their poets,
who preferred to gather in al-Ḥīra (and at the likewise Christian court of the Ghassanids)'
(ibid., 25). Together with the Jews, they (the Ibad) were especially strong in the wine trade
and inns in Ḥīra, which attracted many bedouin: 'In the inns many things were told, naturally
also the biblical and extrabiblical Christian and Jewish legends' (ibid., 26). The written
language of the Ibad was Syriac; their everyday language Arabic. But in this very way,
according to Wellhausen, they could 'have substantially contributed to the formation of an
Arabic written language' (ibid., 27). See also I. Shahīd, 'Ramla', p. 125: from Ḥīra the
Nestorians, and later the Monophysites, penetrated Arabia.
57. Following the translation of N. Pigulewskaja, op. cit., p. 333. Incorporated into letter
S is the earlier letter of Simeon (R) that he had written from Ramla between 31 Jan. and 10
Feb. 521. Cf. I. Shahīd, The Martyrs of Najrān (1971), pp. 114–17, with the passages that
Shahīd assumes to be excerpts from R.

reign, that is, between 518 (assumption of power) and 520 (death of Vitalian).[58]

(b) Actions of Bishop Simeon of Bēth-Aršām

In order to help the persecuted Christians, Simeon turned first to the Ghassanids. These were mercenaries of the Byzantine emperor, but they belonged to the anti-Chalcedonian party. They had their camp in al-Jābiya (Gbītā) and thus on imperial soil. Simeon went there and requested the mercenaries to leave the imperial service and go to southern Arabia in order to aid the persecuted of Najrān.[59] Above all, his interest concerned the Ethiopian king, who could not stand aside and do nothing. We can overlook other addressees of his activity.

(c) The crusade of King Kaleb

We must distinguish between two invasions of Ethiopia into southern Arabia. The first was undertaken by a king who probably had not yet accepted the Christian faith but hoped to gain a foothold in southern Arabia for political and economic reasons. Nevertheless, a heavenly sign of the God of the Christians led the Negus to accept the Christian religion. This is attested by the title of chapter VI of the *Book of the Himyarites*, the rest of which is lost: 'Account telling the amazing sign which the Lord showed the Himyarites in the ranks of the Abyssinians'. Thus he was a new Constantine, who was moved by the sign to fulfil his

---

58. This is also indicated by the letter of Bishop Jacob of Sarug, which he directed towards the Himyarite Christians and which must have been written before 29 Nov. 521, the bishop's date of death, probably shortly after Simeon's letter G (July 519). See R. Schröter, 'Trostschreiben Jacob's von Sarug an die himyaritischen Christen', *ZDMG* 31 (1877), 360–405, 369–85; appendix: 'Hymnus des Joh. Psaltes', 400–5; S. M. Grill, *Jakob von Sarug, Ausgewählte Briefe* (Heiligenkreuzer Stud. no. 17), Heiligenkreuz 1971, 18. Letter, pp. 17–20. Jacob probably had received both letters of Simeon, S and G, and was moved by them to write his letter (Shahīd, op. cit., p. 240).

59. Simeon of Bēth-Aršām, Letter G, Pl. IXA: translation in Shahīd, p. 62, and commentary, p. 99; p. 102: '[Ghassanids] as mercenaries in the pay of Chalcedonian Byzantium'. Simeon's reasoning for his request reads: if these 'barbarians' (the Himyarites) have suffered so much for the faith, then it is only fitting for us 'to abandon [both our] wretched sheds and opulent residences and be with Christ in the fair mansions which [are prepared] for us in his Father's dwelling' (loc. cit., 62). Simeon had to express himself very carefully with this advice, because this action of his had to be interpreted by the Byzantines as high treason. He had also contacted the Lakhmids of al-Ḥīra and the Harithids of Najrān. See further Ismāʿīl R. Khalīdī, 'The Arab Kingdom of Ghassan. Its Origins, Rise and Fall', in *The Muslim World* 46 (1956), 193–206; important is I. Kawar, 'Ghassān and Byzantium: A New terminus a quo', in *Der Islam* 33 (1958), 232–55. – On al-Ḥīra see M. J. Kister, 'Al-Ḥīra. Some notes on its relations with Arabia', *Arabica* 15 (1968), 143–69.

promise to become a Christian in the event of victory over Ḥimyar.[60] The engagement of the now Christian king Kaleb is described in the *Book of the Ḥimyarites* XXXIX–XLIX.[61] The second invasion occurred soon after the first and was occasioned by the second act of persecution in Ḥimyar, which took place around 520. After the first victory the Ethiopian king had brought to the throne of Najrān a Christian with the name Maʿdī-Karib Yaʿfur. He seems to have installed Yūsuf as successor, since the latter had apparently placed himself on the side of the Christian party – so much that he was held to be a Christian. The name *Yūsuf* could indicate that he really was, and indeed even before the second invasion of the Ethiopians. Then, however, he turned against the Christians and arranged their persecution.[62] The second invasion is also attested above all by the *Martyrium S. Arethae*, which, however, presupposes the *Book of the Ḥimyarites*.[63] It reports that the Ethiopians landed in two places on the Arabian coast, also the victory over Yūsuf and occupation of the land, its Christianization and the construction of churches and finally the installation of a Christian king of Ḥimyar and the return of Kaleb to Ethiopia.[64]

It will reward us to pursue a little further with I. Shahīd the perspectives that opened up with the conference of Ramla:

(1) According to him, the Byzantine style of diplomacy, which made use of clerics, attests that since the Christianization of the Roman Empire in the fourth century religion had become the determining factor in the

---

60. Cf. Ps.-Dionys. of Tell Mahrē, *Chronicle*, in N. Pigulewskaja, op. cit., p. 326, together with pp. 228–29. The subject is King Kaleb.

61. See the titles in Moberg, p. CIX. For the extant text see ibid., pp. CXXXIV–CXLVI.

62. Simeon of Bēth-Aršām, Letter G, Pl. VI C; translation in Shahīd, p. 56; also p. 266. But when Shahīd assumes here that the *Book of the Ḥimyarites* calls Yūsuf himself a treacherous 'Judas' (in chap. XLVI, Syr., p. 53a; Engl., p. CXXXIX), that is an oversight. It is a question, rather, of remorseful Christians of Ḥimyar, who had become weak in the persecution and in a petition to King Kaleb had made known their readiness to do penance. They are compared in the text with Judas, but also with the remorseful Peter, who found forgiveness, although in the incomplete text it is not clear who expresses this comparison. Probably an excerpt from the answer or Kaleb's speech is used, which is an interesting testimony for the handling of ecclesiastical penance. The fall of King Yūsuf himself, however, is sufficiently attested, also through the Ethiopian version of the *Martyrium S. Arethae*, which calls him a 'renegade' (Shahīd, op. cit., pp. 266–67).

63. Cf. *Martyrium S. Arethae*, VII,29–IX,38: Carpentier, 747–58, with *Book of the Ḥimyarites*, chaps. 42–48: Moberg, pp. CXXXIV–CXLII. See the presentation of the campaign in N. Pigulewskaja, *Byzanz auf den Wegen nach Indien*, pp. 243–47.

64. Cf. I. Shahīd, op. cit., p. 214 and pp. 218–30 with a detailed analysis of sections 29–38 of *Martyrium S. Arethae*. In § 39 it is reported that King Kaleb renounced the throne and became a monk (Carpentier, pp. 758–59).

development of the Middle East. (2) Likewise, the interference of religious and political factors became a fact. The pious King Kaleb had a clear interest both in the Christianization of southern Arabia and in the securing of his sovereignty in this land. Likewise, even Chalcedonian Byzantium could not only tolerate but also support anti-Chalcedonian activity in southern Arabia in order to promote its political and economic interests. (3) Around the year 520 diplomatic missionary activity shows a continental radius that reached from Constantinople through Alexandria to Axum and Najrān, but likewise from the capital to Ctesiphon and on to lost Ramla. A Christian Ethiopia seems to have been the way of achieving what Augustus and Constantius II had tried to do in vain: to draw southern Arabia into the Roman sphere of influence. Yet this had a different appearance for Ethiopia. As once migration had reached from southern Arabia towards Axum, as is expressed in the *Monumentum Adulitanum*,[65] so now the movement went in the opposite direction. Ethiopia shares in the arrangement and division of the world just as much as Byzantium. Looking back from the perspective of a thousand years, the book *Kebra Nagast* describes this in chap. 117, which carries the title: 'Of the King of Rome and the King of Ethiopia'. We quote the crucial section:[66]

> And the king of Rome and the king of Ethiopia and the archbishop of Alexandria will give each other reciprocal information in order to annihilate them [the Jews]; since, namely, [even] the Romans are orthodox. They will arouse themselves to war in order to fight and annihilate the Jews, the enemies of God, the king of Rome the Ēnjā [Jews in Armenia] and the king of Ethiopia the Finehas [in southern Arabia]; they will devastate their land and build Christian churches there, and will butcher the kings of the Jews . . . Then the dominion of the Jews will be over, and the kingdom of Christ will prevail until the arrival of the Antichrist. Those kings, however, *Justinus*, the king of Rome, and *Kālēb*, the king of Ethiopia, will both meet in Jerusalem; their archbishops will arrange sacrifices; they will sacrifice and be in the love of one faith and present each other with mutual gifts and the greeting of peace, and they will *divide* the earth among themselves, beginning with Jerusalem's half, as we said at the very beginning of this document [see § 20].

In this view Kaleb and the king of Ḥimyar, the rulers of two kingdoms, are opposed like the faith of the New Testament and that of the Old Testament. With the victory of the king of Axum over Ḥimyar, Christianity seemed to be firmly installed in southern Arabia, and this all the more when lasting support from Axum, from Ghassan, and finally from Ḥīra could be regarded as assured. Yet the fall of Ḥimyar was ultimately

---

65. See Cosmas Ind., *Top. chr.* II, 54–65: SC 141, pp. 365–81; esp. 60–63: pp. 373–79. Also M. Höfner, 'Über sprachliche und kulturelle Beziehungen zwischen Südarabien und Äthiopien im Altertum', in *ACIStEt*, pp. 435–44.

66. See C. Bezold, *Kebra Nagast* = *ABAW.PP* 23 (Munich 1909) 136. See the description of the boundaries of Ethiopia in the *KN* § 92: Bezold, p. 98.

the Arabs' opportunity. A power that was pressing them was out of the way, 'and it was this Ethiopic rhythm introduced into the structure of Arabian history in the sixth century that deranged the hitherto familiar pattern of its evolution and created conditions which favoured the elevation of Makka to that position of dominance which set the stage for the mission of Muhammad and the rise of Islam'.[67]

3. The confession of Christ of the martyrs of Himyar

The named documents, especially the *Book of the Himyarites*, letter G of Simeon and the *Martyrium S. Arethae*, present themselves as a strong and surprisingly unified testimony to the faith in Christ in southern Arabia.

Yet in the *Martyrium S. Arethae* one must consider that the version of BHG 166 (ed. Carpentier) was revised in the (later) versions BHG 166z and 167 in theologically precise formulation for Chalcedonian readers (in some unknown place). That can be shown, for example, in the following confession of BHG 166:

'. . . the divine *oikonomia* that the God-Logos, who dwelled in the immaculate womb of the *theotokos*, united at his conception with a rational, ensouled body and became a perfect

---

67. See I. Shahīd, 'Ramla', p. 131. On Muhammad's relationship with the Christians of Najrān, see the detailed study of W. Schmucker, *Die christliche Minderheit von Naǧrān und die Problematik ihrer Beziehungen zum frühen Islam* (BOS 27/1 = *Studien zum Minderheitenproblem im Islam*, vol. 1, by T. Nagel, G.-R. Puin et al., ed. O. Spies), Bonn 1973, 183–281, pp. 187–88: 'The Muslim tradition is agreed that probably in the year 10 H, . . . among the known legations who paid Muhammad a courtesy visit in Medina, a Christian Najrānian delegation also came in . . . The majority of the reports about this speak . . . on the basis that soon after the arrival . . . a christological dispute took place.' According to Schmucker, this is to be seen in connection with Sura 3,59–61; cf. also C. Schedl, *Muhammed und Jesus*, Vienna–Freiburg–Basel 1978, 374–97, esp. 374–76. Yet the relationship between the encounter of Muhammad with the legation from Najrān and the Koran passage might represent a later construction (cf. Schmucker, pp. 192–94). Some of the Najrānians allegedly converted to Islam: cf. Ibn Ishaq, *Das Leben des Propheten*, translated from the Arabic (into German) by G. Rotter, Tübingen-Basel ²1979, 77, cited in G. Riße, op. cit., p. 89. – In any case, the result was a contract between the Christians of Najrān and the prophet, in which in return for appropriate contributions the following pledge of Muhammad was given: 'And the Nagranians with their followers enjoy the patronage of God and the protection of Muhammad for their person and their religion and their land and their possessions, for those present and those absent, for their churches and . . . services of worship – no bishop and no monk and no Vâqif will be forced to give up his status', according to Ibn Saʿd, *Sira*, chap. 1 ('Die Schreiben und Boten Muhammads'), no. 72: J. Wellhausen, *Skizzen und Vorarbeiten* IV, Berlin 1889, p. 132 (German trans., Arabic text at the end), from a writing of Muhammad to the inhabitants of Najrān. W. G. Greenslade, 'The Martyrs of Nejran', *The Moslem World* 22 (1932), 264–75, discusses the question of the relationship of Sura 85 of the Koran to the martyrs of Najrān; see esp. p. 272: 'The city [Nejran] was unquestionably treated with especial leniency by Mohammed in the time of his triumph. The delegation of Christians who came to Medina in the "year of the deputations" were given more favorable terms than any other Christian Arabs, and were in fact the only Christians in Arabia who were allowed not only to practice their religion but to bring up their children as Christians.' Whether Sura 85 really alludes to Najrān is left open by Greenslade.

human being, one and the same capable of suffering like us in everything, except sin. And in his flesh we ascertain suffering and in his divinity power.'[68] This is a statement that corresponds throughout to Severan theology, but that can also be endorsed by a Chalcedonian.

Instead of this, the two Chalcedonian metaphrases bring an anti-Nestorian demarcation: against Nestorius 'they confess Christ as perfect God and perfect human being, two natures joined together (συνάπτω) unmixed in one hypostasis'[69] – that is, a purely Chalcedonian confession that no miaphysite endorses! The definition of Chalcedon is quoted here, which Carpentier, Annotata o, p. 744, also noted.

All the current faith orientations tried to get in: Chalcedonians, anti-Chalcedonians and even the Nestorians from Persia. The appearance of a king who had returned to Judaism was able both to move the Christians of Ḥimyar to an early-Christian-like confession to Christ and to lead divided Christendom, whether Chalcedonian or anti-Chalcedonian, beyond their differences in belief. And if the Christian soldiers of Mundir III were supposed to have been Nestorians, then we also find with them – in regard to the king's demand of apostasy – the same courage of faith as in southern Arabia. The separating formulas, whether Chalcedonian, anti-Chalcedonian or Nestorian, do not in any case appear directly in the confessions of the martyrs or of soldiers. The tensions between the parties are only indirectly indicated.

(a) Christocentrism

In all three of the just-mentioned sources it is exclusively a question of confession to Christ, provoked by the repeatedly made demand of King Yūsuf and also Mundir to deny Christ, confess him as merely human and scorn the cross. Even in southern Arabia – to mention it only briefly – the *signum crucis* plays a special role, whether as a scandal for the Jews or as the sign of a confessor for the Christians. The tattooing of the sign of the cross on the arms of believers is expressly mentioned. They want thereby to let the incoming Abyssinians know that they are Christians in order not to be killed. We recall the practices of the Copts, which are in use even today, and the piety of the cross in Nubia.[70]

---

68. *Mart. Areth.*, chap. VI, 26: Carpentier, pp. 742–43.

69. Halkin, SubsHag 74, p. 150 (end of no. 14); likewise Symeon Metaphr., chap. XXVI: PG 115, 1280B.

70. See the *Book of the Ḥimyarites*, p. 49b: Moberg, p. CXXXVIII. N. Pigulewskaja, *Byzanz auf den Wegen nach Indien*, refers to Turkish tribes in central Asia who had accepted Christianity. In the same sixth century they were likewise familiar with the tattooing of the cross, 'which the mothers placed on their children's foreheads' (248). A testimony for this is Theophylactus Simocatta, *Historiae* V 10,13–15: De Boor and P. Wirth, Stuttgart 1972, 208.

(b) Yūsuf's demand on the Christians

In the named sources we almost always find the same demand on the Christians to renounce their faith. We offer examples from the *Book of the Ḥimyarites* and the *Martyrium Arethae*.

'. . . listen to my words and deny Jesus Christ, the son of Mary, because he was of mankind and a mortal as all men; and spit upon this cross and be Jews with us, and ye shall live . . . ye worship a mortal man, who, being of mankind, yet said about himself, that he was the son of God, the Merciful (Raḥmānā). And in this very time his false doctrine has been manifest, and all lands understand that he was a man and not God'[71] (then comes a reference to the 'Romans', who now, after they had gone astray with regard to Christ, know better than others what they have to believe about him).

The 'Romans', according to the statement of Masruq, which the *Martyrium Arethae* reproduces, also recognized that 'our fathers in Jerusalem, as priests and teachers of the law, crucified him as a human being; they scourged and scorned him as a blasphemer of God and through a shameful death put to death a *human being*, not God . . . Why then do you go astray and follow this man? You are no better than the Nestorians,[72] who are among you to this day and who say: "We do not believe him to be God but a prophet of God." '[73]

This reference to the 'Nestorians' does not need to be without historical background. For the Jews of Ḥimyar regarded the Nestorians in Persia and elsewhere as their allies. For during the siege of Zafār by Yūsuf, the latter sent two men to the citizens of the city with the commission to persuade them to surrender. They were called KWNB and ʿAbdullah. It was said of them that they were Christians in 'name' only, which probably identified them as Nestorians.[74] The brave protest from the troops of King Mundir against his demand to deny Christ has shown us, however, that there were also differentiations for Nestorians.

(c) The confession of the martyrs

Often in our sources there is a reference to the '*bona confessio*' of 1 Tim 6,12. The martyrs of Ḥimyar participate in the 'good confession' that Jesus Christ made before Pilate. We offer a few examples of how this was specifically said:

---

71. *Book of the Ḥimyarites*, chap. 13: Moberg, p. CIX. Cf. also chap. 21: Moberg, p. CXXIV; chap. 22, Moberg, p. CXXIX infra.

72. L. Van Rompay, art. cit., OLA 13, pp. 303–4 with n. 17, chooses the reading here: 'than those Romans who are called Nestorians'; this means, he says, Chalcedonian Byzantines who in 'Monophysite' interpretation are called Nestorians; cf. also Van Rompay, p. 306 (on Carpentier, p. 742).

73. *Mart. Areth.*, chap. II, 6: Carpentier, p. 728.

74. *Book of the Ḥimyarites*, chap. 7: Moberg, p. CV; letter G, Plate II a: Shahīd, op. cit., 44 with 171/172 and 213, where one reads: (in the *Book of the Ḥimyarites*) it 'is implied that the Nestorians have allied themselves with the Ḥimyaritic king against the non-Nestorian Christians'. What he says, however, on pp. 270–72 on Mundir's relationship to Nestorianism requires correction by G. C. Hansen, *Theodoros Anagnostes, Kirchengeschichte*, Berlin 1971, 147, n.

(1) The confession of the women of Najrān: 'God forbid that we should deny our Lord and our God, Jesus Christ. For He is God and the Maker of all things, and He has saved us from eternal death. And God forbid that we should spit on His Cross or that we should treat it with contempt, for by it He has prepared for us redemption from all error.'[75] The Christians also confess their confidence that God will overcome Judaism and transform its synagogues into churches. They also trust in the growth of Christianity through their death, a variation of the *sanguis martyrum, semen christianorum*.[76]

(2) In the *Martyrium Arethae* the confessions of martyrs in individual cases are 'theologized', that is, freighted with implicit answers to unsettled controversies, whether between Christians and Jews or between Chalcedonians and anti-Chalcedonians. Thus, vis-à-vis the Jews, belief in the 'trinitarian God' comes out stronger: 'We were taught, O king, to revere and worship the almighty God and his Word, through which everything was made, and his Holy Spirit, who makes everything alive; we are not introducing several gods; we know no diminution of the monarchia but [only] one Divinity in three persons.[77] We teach that there is only one power and worship it, which our fathers Abraham and Jacob, Moses, Aaron, Samuel and all prophets have taught.'[78]

This is clearly aimed at the Jews' reproach against the trinitarian faith of the church that it abolishes monotheism. Old Testament testimonies to the Christian faith are consciously invoked.

(3) Another situation is given in the following text, which alludes to the discussion of the 'unus ex Trinitate [passus, crucifixus est]': (The confessor says:) 'Jesus, however, whom you [i.e., the Jewish persecutor] have slandered, is one of the Trinity, the God-Logos, incarnate in recent time for our salvation from the Holy Spirit and Mary.'[79] The fact that the disputed formula 'one of the Trinity' is employed here allows us to infer neither the author's 'Monophysitism' nor the neo-Chalcedonianism of the Justinian period. This formula is also found, incidentally, in the two Chalcedonian metaphrases (BHG 166z and 167).[80]

The just-cited (general) confession to the incarnation is missing in the Chalcedonian metaphrases; there is instead a rejection of the position of the Nestorians, 'who boldly tear the human being inseparably and hypostatically united with the God-Logos away from the divine hypostasis of the Logos and have invented the God-Logos appearing in flesh as a mere human being with his own hypostasis (*idiohypostaton*!)'.[81] This is polished technical language (*idiohypostaton* may go back to Leontius of Jerusalem![82]).

---

75. *Book of the Ḥimyarites*, chap. 20: Moberg, p. CXVIII; cf. CXX; chap. 21: p. CXXV; chap. 22: p. CXXVII, where the martyr Ruhm says: 'For He is God, Son of God, Creator of the worlds.'

76. Cf. *Book of the Ḥimyarites*, chap. 21: Moberg, p. CXXIII.

77. *The Anonymous Metaphrase* (BHG 166z), ed. by Halkin, SubsHag 74, p. 136 (no. 3), speaks here in a somewhat more differentiated way in Basilian terminology: 'one unseparated nature dividing into three *prosopa*'; likewise Symeon Metaphr., chap. IV: PG 115, 1253B.

78. *Mart. Areth.*, chap. I, 3: Carpentier, p. 723: *Nos edocti sumus, o rex, venerari et adorare Deum omnipotentem et Verbum eius, per quod omnia facta sunt, et Spiritum Sanctum eius, qui omnia vivificat; non deos plures invehentes, neque imminutionem monarchiae cognoscentes, sed unam Deitatem in tribus personis (en trisin hypostasesi). Eamdem unicam potestatem veneramur et adoramus, quam patres nostri Abraham et Isaac et Jacob, Moyses, Aaron, Samuel et prophetae omnes venerati sunt.* Cf. also chap. IV, 16: Carpentier, p. 735 with echoes of the *Nicaenum*.

79. *Mart. Areth.*, chap. II, 7: Carpentier, p. 728.

80. Halkin, SubsHag 74, p. 139 (no. 6); Symeon Metaphr., chap. X, PG 115, 1260A.

81. Halkin, SubsHag 74, p. 139 (no. 5); in Symeon Metaphr., chap. IX, PG 115, 1257C except for minor variations of the same text.

82. Lampe, *PatrGrLex*, s.n., p. 666; cf. A. Grillmeier, *CCT* II/2, pp. 283–85.

On the whole, the relatively numerous confessional formulas of our sources are quite simply formulated. They are direct answers to provocation by the Jewish persecutor-king. They reproduce the common faith that binds Chalcedonians and anti-Chalcedonians. Apparently Simeon of Bēth-Aršām forbore to work in his anti-Chalcedonian points with full trenchancy, though the fact that he and the martyrs belonged to the non-Chalcedonian community of faith is sufficiently clear.[83]

---

83. Through the use of certain characterizations, 'believing', 'orthodox' for the non-Chalcedonians. Cf. I. Shahīd, *The Martyrs of Najrān*, pp. 105–6: 'Although the Ethiopians shared with the writer [Simeon] the same doctrinal persuasion, i.e. Monophysitism, the adjective used to describe them is "believing", while the adjective used to describe the Persians [the author] is "orthodox"; this is accountable: the Ethiopians, or the Christians among them, were Monophysites, but not so the Persian Christians, most of whom were Nestorians. The writer thus wanted to narrow down the denotation of "Persians" by the qualifying word "orthodox", which to him and to his correspondent meant "Monophysite" ... Simeon was the orthodox Persian *par excellence*, whose efforts in behalf of spreading Monophysitism earned him the title "the Persian disputant".'

CHAPTER FOUR

THE RELIGIOUS-CULTURAL BACKGROUND OF ETHIOPIAN CHRISTIAN FAITH

In addition to the external presuppositions of the particular form of faith in Christ in Ethiopia during the Axum period, which is of primary interest for us, there are inner religious–intellectual preconditions, which are nothing but the consequences of the external prior history described above. We see three important components of Ethiopian Christian faith.

1. Jewish influences

E. Ullendorff has presented an investigation that pursues a more comprehensive purpose than is required in our context. It sketches the Hebraic-Jewish elements in Abyssinian Christianity as a whole.[1] The result for him is the determination that one must speak of a Jewish-Christian civilization in the kingdom of Axum:

> The doctrinal position of the Ethiopian national Church was always unenviable, caught as it was between the deeply rooted Judaic customs of the country and the necessity to maintain its theological prestige as a truly Christian body.[2]

---

1. E. Ullendorff, 'Hebraic-Jewish Elements in Abyssinian (Monophysite) Christianity', *JSS* 1 (1956), 216–56. He calls this study a prolegomena to a more comprehensive investigation. A continuation is already found in his work: *Ethiopia and the Bible. The Schweich Lectures of the British Academy 1967*, London 1968. An extensive source for what follows is Iobi Ludolfi, *Historia Aethiopica sive Brevis & succincta descriptio Regni Habessinorum Quod vulgo male Presbyteri Iohannis vocatur*, vol. I, Frankfurt-on-Main 1681; vol. II, *Commentarius*, 1691. Ludolfus drew much information from an Abba Gregory and was thereby also led astray in individual cases.
2. E. Ullendorff, *Ethiopia and the Bible*, p. 107.

It will suffice to name briefly the phenomena of the Old Testament-Jewish influence.[3]

(a) The Ethiopian church and its liturgical apparatus

After the model of the Jewish temple, the Ethiopian churches are basically divided into three parts. We find the rectangular 'holy of holies' (*maqdas*) and surrounding it the round *qeddest*, where the believers receive the Eucharist (*qodeš* of the tabernacle and *hēkāl* of the temple); in the 'holy of holies', which only the serving clergy may enter, stands the altar, on which is the *tābot*, the Ark of the Covenant. For according to the conviction of the Ethiopians, the 'genuine Ark of the Covenant' is preserved in Axum. The churches around the land have only imitations, which are mostly limited to the contents of the Ark, namely, the tablets of the law (cf. Dt 10,1−5; 1 Kings 8,9; Heb 9,4), which as *pars pro toto* are then also called *tābot* and are consecrated by the bishop (similar to the Latin altar stone).[4] The liturgy begins in a small hut, which is called 'Bethlehem' and usually stands beside the church. There, before the celebration of the liturgy, the bread is prepared with prayer and recitation of psalms.[5]

(b) The liturgical cycle of feasts

The church year also remains in part under Jewish influence, for example, in the new year's feast (on the first of Maskaram = 29 August in the Julian calendar, 11 September in the Gregorian), in which an animal is sacrificed by the head of the family. The feast of the discovery of the cross (17 Maskaram = 14 September Julian, 27 September Gregorian) as a Christian feast has a background of pagan and Jewish rites (connection between the Jewish new year feast and *yōm kippūr*). A peculiarly Jewish-Christian content is found in the feast of baptism (11 Ter = 6 January Julian, 19 January Gregorian), which is among the biggest feasts of the Ethiopian church. On this day the waters are blessed; the believers submerge in it as a renewal of baptismal grace and remembrance of the baptism of Jesus. A feast of Christ's birth is celebrated on the 29th of each month.

---

3. This according to E. Hammerschmidt, 'Der Kult der äthiopischen Kirche', in F. Herrmann, *Symbolik der Religionen* X, *Symbolik des orthodoxen und orientalischen Christentums*, Stuttgart 1962, 214−33.

4. Ibid., pp. 216−17, where a more detailed description is given.

5. According to E. Hammerschmidt, op. cit., p. 218, this means that in the eucharistic celebration as a whole the entire *vita Christi* is reconstructed, from birth in Bethlehem to sacrificial death on Calvary.

In the Ethiopian church the 'Sabbath' is also maintained. The observance of the Sabbath and of Sunday is enjoined by the Ethiopic *Didascalia* (chap. 38).[6] It was correctly pointed out that in early Christianity both the Sabbath and the Christian Sunday stood side by side as religious days, and this survived in the Ethiopian church. This is a special testimony to the influence of the Old Testament.[7] The accent, however, lies mostly on the 'Christian Sabbath', that is, our Sunday. Thus the late Athanasius anaphora praises the 'holy Sabbath of the Christians'.[8] The fact that the Sabbath is even personified points in a special way to Jewish influence, although the trinitarian faith is consciously emphasized when in § 105 this anaphora reads:

> O over this day, which is enlightening like the Father, outstanding like the Son and steadfast like the Holy Spirit! O you holy Christian Sabbath day, plead for us and put in a good word for us with the *Lord* our God . . . in all eternity.[9]

The 'Christian Sabbath' is not pre-eminent everywhere. There may be a certain equality: 'The northern tradition, in the actual homeland of the Semiticized Axumites, has without exception preserved the Jewish elements more faithfully than the southern sphere, which moderated and dissolved these elements.'[10] Especially the 'Kirchenordnung' (ecclesiastical discipline) of King Zar'a Yā'qob (1434–68) sought to achieve the equating of the Jewish Sabbath and the Christian Sunday. His addresses and decrees, which he as 'shepherd placed by God over the flock of God'(!) had promulgated to his spiritual and secular subjects, are collected in the Maṣḥafa Berhān (= Book of the Light). But at the centre of this book, which claims to lead to the proper adoration of God and Christ, stands Christ, the 'light of the world and of human beings'. With

---

6. Cf. E. Hammerschmidt, *Stellung und Bedeutung des Sabbats in Äthiopien* (Studia Delitzschiana 7), Stuttgart 1963; J. M. Harden, *The Ethiopic Didascalia*, London–New York 1920, 178–82; E. Ullendorff, *Ethiopia and the Bible*, pp. 109–13.

7. E. Ullendorff, op. cit., p. 111: 'Yet the closer approximation to Old Testament practice and its enduring importance in Ethiopia represent a singular phenomenon which has to be evaluated in association with the Judaic elements from South Arabia which had crossed the Red Sea in the early centuries of the first millenium A.D.'

8. See S. Euringer, 'Die äthiopische Anaphora des hl. Athanasius', *OrChr* 24 (1927) (243–98), § 105, p. 285; § 116, p. 287. The Athanasius liturgy is a Sunday liturgy: ibid., p. 243.

9. S. Euringer, loc. cit., p. 285; cf. § 116, p. 287.

10. E. Hammerschmidt, *Stellung und Bedeutung des Sabbats in Äthiopien*, Stuttgart 1963, 22.

these decrees the king only adopted old traditions rather than introducing new ones, as E. Ullendorff has shown.[11] For the Sabbath they
distinguish the following:

the eucharistic liturgy, consisting of pre-anaphora and anaphora;
the rite of veneration of the cross in the sixth hour of the day;
the agape celebration in the evening of the Sabbath.[12]

The Sabbath question was finally dealt with also in the controversy
between the Ethiopians and Latin missionaries of the modern period and
led to the important (for us) *Confessio Claudii* (King Claudius = Galāw-
dēwos, 1540–59). Its first part (*Confessio* §§ 1–5) is an exposition of the
anti-Chalcedonian faith;[13] in the second part (§§ 7–15) the customs of the
Ethiopian Church are defended.[14] In it Claudius distanced himself from
the Jewish celebration of the Sabbath and especially emphasized the
significance of Sunday.[15]

(c) Circumcision and other observances

From the Pauline viewpoint the greatest accommodation to Judaism
seems to be given in circumcision (*gezrat*). It is the general practice and is
considered obligatory, although in the *Fetḥa Nagast* (Legislation of the
Kings, chap. 51) the opposite is declared.[16] Is it a matter of the actual

---

11. Ibid., pp. 21–35. See C. Conti Rossini col concorso di L. Ricci, *Il Libro della Luce del
Negus Zaŕa Yāqob* (Maṣḥafa Berhān) I, T and V: CSCO 250/251; II, T and V: CSCO
261/262. See, e.g., T. I, 3rd Sabb. 7[h]: CSCO 251, pp. 51–52: the Sabbath observation is not
against the abolition of the law by Christ, for the name of Jesus begins with *J* = the number
10. So the Ten Commandments are still valid, and they include the commandment to keep
the Sabbath holy.

12. E. Hammerschmidt, op. cit., p. 35, who on pp. 29–30 notes that in various
determinations or in the permitted and proscribed activities, as well as in the liturgical rubrics,
a distance from the Old Testament and Talmudic Judaism is recognizable. The book Maṣḥafa
Berhān, in defending the observance of the Sabbath, appeals to the *Didascalia*, then to the so-
called Kidān, i.e., the Ethiopic version of the *Testamentum DNJChr* (see E. Hammerschmidt,
pp. 39–47).

13. See in I. Ludolf, *Commentarius* II 6,29 = 237–38; E. Hammerschmidt, op. cit., pp.
48–54.

14. I. Ludolf, *Commentarius* II 6,29 = 240–41.

15. See the excerpt in E. Hammerschmidt, op. cit., p. 51 (with explanation, 51–54): 'In
regard to our celebration of the Sabbath day, however, we do not celebrate it like the Jews,
who crucified Christ, saying: "His blood be on us and on our children . . ." But we celebrate
it by presenting the offering on it and holding the agape, as our fathers the apostles bade in the
Didascalia. We do not celebrate it as Sunday, which is the new day [cit. Ps 118,24]. For on it
our Lord Jesus Christ rose and on it the Holy Spirit descended on the apostles in the [Lord's
Supper] room of Zion and on it he [Christ] became a human being in the womb of holy
Mary, Virgin at all times, and on it he will come again to reward the righteous and punish
sinners.'

16. Cf. E. Hammerschmidt, 'Der Kult der äthiopischen Kirche', in *Symbolik der Religionen*
X, p. 230; P. Tzadua, *The Fetha Nagast, the Law of the Kings*, Addis Ababa 1968.

carrying out of the Jewish law? This is expressly rejected in the *Confessio Claudii*. Circumcision is considered local custom and a purely human practice.[17]

(d) The Jewish Targum in the Ethiopian Tergum

The adoption of Jewish theological method, the Targum, in Ethiopian schooling is perhaps the strongest and most persistent among the previously named factors of Jewish influence. The role of the Tergum is described as follows by an expert on Ethiopia:[18]

> In the higher schools of the Mashaf the method of the Tergum is used to lay the biblical and patristic foundation of orthodox faith, to accomplish monastic education and to reckon the calendar. Dogmatic work does not contain the element of creative speculation and system formation, as is characteristic of the West, but is performed in interpretation of patristic writings. The Tergum [. . .], literally 'explanation', has to translate the ecclesiastically received literature of Ethiopian orthodoxy, which is composed in the sacral language, Ge'ez, into the present-day [Amharic] vernacular, that is, to make this literature understandable in the circle of scholars, determine its meaning and reveal it to the people of the church not involved in Ge'ez education. It is a question of an act of spiritual nourishment of the whole church from the heritage of scripture and tradition. The whole corpus of Tergum-worthy literature comprises over eight hundred books in use in the church . . . The Tergum presents only traditional text interpretation, never new personal interpretations of the teacher . . . The dogmatic conflicts within Ethiopian orthodoxy have always grown out of mutually opposing Tergum schools.

The connection with Judaism is all the more effective the more one may infer from the 'sameness of name, essence and method' of Tergum and

---

17. *Confessio Claudii*, in I. Ludolfus, *Commentarius*, pp. 237–41; p. 240: *Quod vero attinet rationem* circumcisionis, *non utique circumcidimur sicut Iudaei, quia nos scimus verba doctrinae Pauli, fontis sapientiae, qui dicit* . . . [cit. Gal 5,6; 1 Cor 7,18]. *Omnes libri doctrinae Pauli sunt apud nos, et docent nos de circumcisione et de praeputio. Verum circumcisio est apud nos secundum consuetudinem regionis, sicut incisio faciei in Aethiopia et Nubia; et sicut perforatio auris apud Indos. Id autem quod facimus, non [fit] ad observandas leges Mosaicas, sed tantum propter morem humanum.* The king expressly emphasizes: *Mea vero Religio et Religio Presbyterorum Doctorum, qui docent iussu meo in ambitu regni mei, talis est, ut neque recedant a via Evangelii, neque a doctrina Patris nostri Pauli, sive ad dextram sive ad sinistram* (p. 241). Cf. along with *Fetha Nagast* chap. 51 esp. Mashafa Berhãn T. I, reading for 2nd Sun. 6[h]: CSCO 251, pp. 90–97 with detailed defence of circumcision for both sexes, which it says was also still valid in the NT – this with reference to Abraham.

18. See F. Heyer, *Die Kirche Äthiopiens*, Berlin–New York 1971, 132 and 140–41. In the Ethiopian Church there are four disciplines for education: Belui (OT), Haddis (NT), Liqawent (patristic literature, together with interpretation of the books of the law) and Manakosat (monastic literature). Although all biblical, patristic and post-patristic writings have the same status, in practice selections are made, according to Heyer. Prominent are Matthew and John; from the OT, Psalms, the christologically interpreted Song of Songs and Isaiah. Cf. S. Euringer, *Die Auffassung des Hohenliedes bei den Abessiniern*, Leipzig 1900. For patristics a key position is held by: Mashafa Manakosat, which today, however, has greatly receded; also the *Qẽrellos* and *Hãymãnota Abaw*. It should be noted that the Mashafa Milãd, edited by H. Wendt (see below), is unknown among the clergy today. The Apocrypha are used in the Tergum in order to state biblical reports more precisely (Heyer, p. 136).

Targum that a historical connection also exists. For the Ethiopian Christian Tergum teachers also place the beginnings of their interpretive art in the pre-Christian period of Axum. According to some teachers, it begins already with Enoch(!); he already translated the revelations he received into all languages, and Job was the next one to do the same. They say that at the meeting between Solomon and the queen of Sheba at the beginning of Ethiopian history the priest Zadok handed over the nineteen books of the Old Testament in existence at that time and thus made their translation possible. Other teachers regarded Christ as the creator of the Tergum, and this was connected with the instruction of his apostles. F. Heyer[19] believes it quite possible to place the Tergum already in the pre-Christian period of Axum, specifically with the tribes believing according to the Old Testament: 'The formal similarities are too striking not to cause one to conceive of the Tergum as the direct continuation of the Targum.'[20] It is typical of Abyssinia, however, that the Alexandrian allegorical method of interpretation was adopted, not least of all in order to remove the Old Testament and Apocrypha from strict Judaic interpretation. A further development of the Judaic Targum is also involved in the fact that the Tergum includes New Testament and patristic writings (*Hāymānota Abaw!*).

The Falashas

Under the name of the 'Falashas' Ethiopia acquired a special problem. Through Jewish immigration from Arabia there arose a stronger Jewish religious stratum with its special traditions, and it ultimately drew individual tribes under its influence. Among them the strongest group are the Fälaša, who today, however, are no longer very widespread (between 15,000 and 60,000?). Ethnologically they belong to the Ägäw and are thus Cushites but have adopted a Judaizing form of religion. They live scattered in the regions east, west and north of Lake Tana. Their Bible is the Old Testament (Pentateuch) and the book of *Jubilees*, adopted from the Christians. Unknown to them, however, are the Mishnah and Talmud. Their cult is a curious mixture of pagan, Jewish and Christian beliefs and ceremonies. Their monasticism clearly distinguishes them from the Jews. But they also stand completely outside the anti-Chalcedonian tradition. E. Ullendorff understands the Falashas as descendants of the groups in the Axumite kingdom who resisted conversion to Christianity.[21] Thus one cannot group them with Jewish Christians. For this would require, in the first place, acceptance of Jesus Christ. Thus it is also probable that the effective bearers of Hebraic elements, rites and

19. F. Heyer, op. cit., pp. 143–45.

20. Ibid., p. 144.

21. See E. Ullendorff, *Ethiopia and the Bible*, London 1967, 115–18; idem, 'Hebraic-Jewish Elements in Abyssinian (Monophysite) Christianity', *JSS* 1 (1956), 216–56; E. Hammerschmidt, *Äthiopien*, Wiesbaden 1967, 50–51 ('Die Fälaša').

forms became those Jews in Abyssinia who accepted Christianity and brought their tradition into the Abyssinian church.[22]

Thus, though we can establish that nowhere else has such a strong synthesis between Judaism and Christianity arisen as in Ethiopia, various unanswered questions still remain: (1) In what way did it originate? (2) What is it like, that is, what degree of integration – if we can speak of this at all – has this combination achieved?

There are two answers to the first question. Some assume a double conversion of smaller or larger groups of Axumites: first from paganism to Judaism, then from there to Christianity. Others say that the real connecting link between Hebraic-Jewish and Christian is an already previously created Jewish-Christian synthesis. E. Isaac would like to recommend the latter explanation and offers the following reasons:[23]

(1) In the Ethiopian church it is believed that Matthew and Bartholomew and other early Christians came out of Judaism to Ethiopia and proclaimed the gospel there.[24]

(2) Jewish-Christian elements came in when the Axumites dominated South Arabia and Yemen (esp. under King Kaleb). 'These Jewish Christians accepted the authority of Mosaic law and, when they could, frequented the Temple in Jerusalem. They retained circumcision, the Sabbath, and the dietary laws. There is no doubt that most of the practices of the Ethiopian church are remarkably close to those of the early Jewish Christians, so that almost every aspect of the strong Hebraic-Jewish ingredient in Ethiopian Christianity can find its explanation on the basis of their influence.'[25]

(3) Aramaic-speaking Jewish Christians played a much larger role than Hellenistic-Jewish Christians in the creation and shaping of Ethiopian Christendom. Here E. Isaac points to the linguistic research of H. J. Polotsky, according to which Syrian Christians were responsible for the fact that certain expressions came into Ge'ez, the classical language of Ethiopian literature.[26] Yet with E. Ullendorff we must make a more careful distinction here. In a follow-up of H. J. Polotsky, he examined 35 Hebrew and Aramaic loanwords in Ge'ez.[27] Of

---

22. E. Ullendorff, *Ethiopia and the Bible*, p. 117: 'Their socalled Judaism is merely the reflexion of those Hebraic and Judaic practices and beliefs which were implanted on parts of south-west Arabia in the first post-Christian centuries and subsequently brought into Abessinia.' The Falashas can be regarded as the living testimony of the Judaized civilization of southern Arabian immigrants in Ethiopia: 'Like their Christian fellow Ethiopians, the Falashas are stubborn adherents to fossilized Hebraic-Jewish beliefs, practices, and customs which were transplanted from South Arabia into the Horn of Africa and which may here be studied in the authentic surroundings and atmosphere of a semitized country' (ibid., 118). But cf. F. Heyer, *Die Kirche Äthiopiens*, pp. 220–27, esp. p. 225: 'Since 1951 (Ethiopian calendar) the Falashas have been caught up in change. At the initiative of a capable priest many have attached themselves to Ethiopian Christianity.' On the state of the Ethiopian church today see the recently founded journal *Maedot* ('Passover') 1 (1983), 6–8 (editorial).

23. Cf. E. Isaac, 'An Obscure Component in Ethiopian Church History. An examination of various theories pertaining to the problem of the origin and nature of Ethiopian Christianity', *Mus* 85 (1972), 225–58.

24. Cf. *KN* § 95: Bezold, p. 102.

25. E. Isaac, art. cit., p. 236.

26. See H. J. Polotsky, 'Aramaic, Syriac, and Ge'ez', *JSS* 9 (1964), 1–10.

27. Cf. E. Ullendorff, *Ethiopia and the Bible*, pp. 119–25, esp. pp. 124–25.

these, 15 are clearly of Jewish-Aramaic origin; 16 are 'dialectically neutral'. Only 4 are characteristically Syriac and distinguishably Christian in meaning (and thus not actually 'Jewish Christian', as one must conclude against E. Isaac). This confirms Polotsky's view that the overwhelming majority of these words are derived from Jewish-Aramaic and belong to the *pre-Christian* Jewish leaven in Ethiopia. The Syriac-transmitted loanwords must be attributed to a later linguistic layer. E. Ullendorff concludes from this: 'The great majority of Aramaic loanwords thus belongs to the homogeneous group of Jewish notions introduced into Ethiopia by Judaized immigrants from south-west Arabia. The dialectal pattern conforms closely to cultural distribution: the Jewish Aramaic words, while predominantly of a religious type, also include some notions of a more general kind. The small Syriac minority, on the other hand, is confined to narrowly Christian religious terminology.'[28]

Thus we gain a sufficiently clear picture, which agrees with what we know from the Axumite inscriptions. We are dealing first with an immigration of followers of the Jewish faith who themselves were ethnic Jews. They could also have come (say, as merchants) via South Arabia.[29] Then, however, we must assume a heavier influx of Judaized Arabs from the south-western part of the Arabian peninsula. These immigrants brought with them the religious forms of Judaism that were common in South Arabia and went beyond those of the first named groups. For in Axum we find traces of the South Arabian pantheon.[30] Only then was there an influx of Syrians, who brought Christian elements of the kind that no longer came from an early Jewish Christianity but already from the time of the Chalcedonian controversies (cf. the nine saints).

With this we can come to a responsible conclusion in the matter of how our question about the origin of a 'Jewish-Christian' synthesis in Ethiopia is to be answered. E. Ullendorff[31] is of the well-founded opinion that the Abyssinian Jews who were converted to Christianity were the effective bearers of Hebraic elements, rites and forms as they were received in the Ethiopian church.

Nevertheless, in order to support his thesis of the Syrian Jewish-Christian origin of the Ethiopian form of Christianity, E. Isaac still appeals to the Axum inscriptions of the ʿĒzānā period. Yet he argues with the state of discoveries before 1969 and hence must reach outdated conclusions. If the above cited inscription no. 11 probably speaks of Jewish monotheism but not of Jesus, E. Isaac interprets this not, say, as Jewish monotheism but as the Jewish-Christian

28. Ibid., p. 125; cf. M. Höfner, 'Über sprachliche und kulturelle Beziehungen zwischen Südarabien und Äthiopien im Altertum', in *ACIStEt*, pp. 435–44, esp. pp. 439ff.

29. Cf. E. Ullendorff, 'Hebraic-Jewish Elements', p. 223: 'It has already been mentioned that among the South Arabian immigrants into the Aksumite Empire there must have been some Jews. It is not likely that they entered the country as a compact community, a complete tribal *golah*, but they probably came in small groups together with their non-Jewish fellow-merchants and settlers.'

30. See M. Höfner, art. cit., pp. 442–44; eadem, 'Die vorislamischen Religionen Arabiens', in C. M. Schröder (ed.), *Religionen der Menschheit*, vol. 10/2 (1970); J. Wellhausen, *Reste arabischen Heidentums* (1st ed. 1887; rpt. 1961).

31. E. Ullendorff, *JSS* 1 (1956), 227.

faith, which out of opposition to the Jews must likewise put the accent on monotheism. Even Frumentius is claimed for this purpose, though he, as a follower of the champion of the *Nicaenum*, St Athanasius, was a decided representative of the *Nicaenum*.[32] And does genuine Jewish Christianity not include confessing faith in the Son of God? In any case, however, the inscription found in 1969 thwarts any attempt to call Frumentius a Jewish-Christian missionary.

2. Cyrillian-Alexandrian influences

E. Isaac was too quick to remove the Alexandrian components from the history of the Christian faith in Ethiopia. Even if it must be conceded that the Arabian-Jewish-Syrian bearers of religious convictions are preeminent and the gospel led more from the east over the Red Sea than from Nubia into the Ethiopian highland, we still learn, surprisingly, that it is precisely Alexandria that conveyed the soundest foundation of Ethiopian Christology and theology; and this was done not so much through the living word as through an Alexandrian collection of great value, the so-called *Qērellos*, a collection that was named after Cyril of Alexandria (d. 444). We have it now in an excellent edition and with a German translation, which we owe to B. M. Weischer:

First part of the collection

I   1. Der Prosphonetikos 'Über den rechten Glauben' des Kyrillos von Alexandrien an Theo-dosios II. (Afrikanistische Forschungen 7), Glückstadt 1973, now also in a revision of the translation of O. Bardenhewer by Weischer, in *Schriften der Kirchenväter* 8 (ed. N. Brox), Munich 1984, 12–66.

II   2. Der Prosphonetikos 'Über den rechten Glauben' des Kyrillos von Alexandrien an Arkadia und Marina (ÄthFor 31), Wiesbaden 1992.

III   3. Der Dialog 'Daß Christus einer ist' des Kyrillos von Alexandrien (ÄthFor 2), Wiesbaden 1977.

IV   1. Homilien und Briefe zum Konzil von Ephesos (ÄthFor 4), Wiesbaden 1979: nos. 4–18 of the collection.

Second part of the collection

IV   2. Traktate des Epiphanios von Cypern und des Proklos von Kyzikos (ÄthFor 6), Wiesbaden 1979: nos. 19–21 of the collection.

IV   3. Traktate des Severianos von Gabala, Gregorios Thaumaturgos und Kyrillos von Alexandrien (ÄthFor 7), Wiesbaden 1980: nos. 22–25 of the collection.

Third part: Final tractate

= nos. 26–29: 'Traktat über Melchisedech, Über die 318 Bischöfe von Nikaia, Über die Geburt und das Leben Christi, Glaubenstraktat mit antihäretischem Anhang': Weischer, 'Die äthiopischen Psalmen- und Qērlosfragmente in Erevan/Armenien', *OrChr* 53 (1969), 113–58.

---

32. Cf. E. Isaac, *Mus* 85 (1972), 240, 242–43.

The actual collection on the Council of Ephesus (431) is composed of Weischer I–IV 1, with nos. 1–18. IV 2 and 3 (nos. 19–25) represent a theological expansion of the original collection, which, however, comes from the same Alexandrian store as nos. 1–18. Of these IV 2 (nos. 19–21) were perhaps already added in Alexandria. It contains documents from the time before the Nestorian controversy (before 429). With the exception of no. 21 (Proclus), which is christological, nos. 19 and 20 deal with the trinitarian mystery. Some homilies still exist only in the Ethiopic language, although they were given at the Council of Ephesus. The Greek originals were presumably lost. Nos. 1–25 are directly brought from the Greek into Geʾez and thus belong to the Axumite period of literature (fourth/fifth to seventh century). The ʿFinal Tractateʾ (nos. 26–29), thus named by Weischer, was probably not translated from the Arabic and attached to the expanded collection until the thirteenth or fourteenth century; on this cf. the corrections and expansions in Qērellos III, 245–46. In an appendix to Qērellos IV 2, pp. 89–108, Weischer also gives the Ethiopian text with German translation of Epiphanius, Ankyrōtos 118 and 119, which is of special significance for the history of dogma: the Ethiopic text, namely, reproduces the original Greek text. The symbol that Epiphanius added there was the Nicaean symbol. The present-day Greek text reproduces the *Nicaeno-Constantinopolitanum*. With this, old disputed issues are finally resolved. See also B. M. Weischer, ʿDas christologische Florilegium in Qērellos IIʾ, *OrChr* 64 (1980), 109–35; idem., ʿDie christologische Terminologie des Cyrill von Alexandrien im Äthiopischenʾ, in W. Hoenerbach (ed.), *Der Orient in der Forschung*, FS O. Spies, Wiesbaden 1967, 733–41.

For the further direct influence of the work of Cyril in Ethiopia we have indications from the Ethiopic translation of the Song of Songs. This is all the more significant since the *Canticum Canticorum* can be made responsible in a special way for the fact that the biblical symbolism of the Old Testament could be so well-developed in Ethiopian theology and poetry.

In the study of the Ethiopian translation of the Song of Songs (Cant.), which was made from the Greek text and not from Arabic or Coptic or Syriac, Euringer[33] knew from the analysis of Ethiopian readings and comparison with entirely or partially extant commentaries on the Cant. that

(1) the Ethiopian translator in the interpretation of the Cant. is directly or indirectly a descendant of Hippolytus and Origen;[34]

(2) the direct channel to Ethiopia was probably the Cant. commentary of Cyril, who knew the above-mentioned commentaries and adopted from them the allegorical interpretation of the Cant. (as Christ/church). Cyril's commentary is extant only in fragments;[35]

(3) the Abyssinians also knew the interpretation of the whole Cant. as concerning Mary.[36] Testifying to this are also the commentaries of S. Euringer on the various long mariological poems (see below) and of A. Grohmann, *Äthiopische Marienhymnen*, Leipzig 1919, 6–36 (overview of Ethiopian mariological literature). Christology is largely connected with this.[37]

---

33. S. Euringer, *Die Auffassung des Hohenliedes bei den Abessiniern. Ein historisch-exegetischer Versuch*, Leipzig 1900.

34. Ibid., p. 31.

35. Ibid.; Cyril of Alex., *Fragm. in Cant. Canticorum* (CPG 5205, 4): PG 69, 1277–93.

36. S. Euringer, op. cit., pp. 35–44.

37. Cf. ibid., p. 36.

3. Syrian influences

For this we have the already introduced names of Simeon of Bēth-Aršām, Philoxenus of Mabbug and Jacob of Sarug. Then comes Severus of Antioch, among others, in the time of the mission of the nine saints. To be named in the fourth century are Ephraem the Syrian and then above all the *Constitutiones Apostolorum* (*CAp*) (CPG 1730), whose first six books are assimilated in the Ethiopian *Didascalia* (CPG 1738).[38] This relationship is especially significant because the author of the *CAp* is identical with the forger of the Ignatius letters and the author of a Job commentary. He advocates the Christology of Eusebius of Emesa, as well as an Arianism.[39] We will establish that the Ethiopian *Didascalia* brings important corrections to the reworking of the *CAp*. With this, only a few connections between Syria and Egypt have been demonstrated.[40]

We must also note a hypothesis of E. Cerulli. He suggests a special relationship between Ethiopia and *Edessa*:

During the reign of the Zaguè dynasty, the capital of Ethiopia was renamed after King Lalibelà, who was honoured as a saint, after earlier being called Rohà, as can be demonstrated from documents. Rohà (Orhay), however, was the Syrian name of the city that was renamed under the Seleucids as Edessa. Why was Rohà also the name of the capital in Ethiopia? E. Cerulli thinks it was the influence of the Abgar legend, which is also found in Ethiopic (Aqāryos negusa Rohà), and the charm that the apocryphal correspondence of Abgar with Jesus was able to exercise on the Ethiopian ruler.[41]

4. Translations from Arabic

There were special transmissions of writings to the Ethiopian Church through translations from Arabic,[42] above all, three Syriac works of the sixth century, which are still in use today as *Books of the Monks* (Masâhefta

---

38. Easy to use in the translation of J. M. Harden, *The Ethiopic Didascalia*, London–New York 1920.

39. Cf. D. Hagedorn, *Der Hiobkommentar des Arianers Julian* (PTSt 14), 1973; A. Grillmeier, *JdChr* I³, pp. 457–59.

40. Also to be noted is the work – not available to me – of R. Beylot, *Le Testamentum Domini éthiopien. Édition critique: texte éthiopien établi d'après sept manuscrits et traduction française*, Louvain 1984. See now W. Witakowski, 'Syrian Influences in Ethiopian Culture', *Orientalia Suecana* 38–39 (1989–90), 191–202 (not used here).

41. See E. Cerulli, *Storia della Letteratura Etiopica*, ²1961, 35–37; S. Grébaut, 'Les relations entre Abgar et Jésus', *ROC* 21 (1918–19), 73–87 (trans. 190–203); 88–91 (trans. 253–55).

42. Cf. E. Cerulli, op. cit., chap. IX, pp. 189–90.

manakuosât): namely, two writings of John Saba and the 'Tractate on Asceticism' of Isaac of Nineveh (Mâr Yeshak). The collection also contains the translation of 'Questions on the Monk's Life' of Philoxenus of Mabbug.[43] On further translations from Arabic, cf. CPG 1730 and 1732.

---

43. Cf. A. de Halleux, *Philoxène de Mabbog. Sa vie, ses écrits, sa théologie*, Louvain 1963, 291–93.

CHAPTER FIVE

FAITH IN CHRIST IN THE
ETHIOPIAN CHURCH

───────

After what we have said thus far one must expect a disparate structure of christological ideas and doctrines. Will there be an integration, especially of the Judaic and Greek elements? Do we have here perhaps an opportunity to observe Jewish Christianity in a special form – even a special form of faith in Christ? Thus we will ask first about the Jewish-Christian and then the Greek elements in Ethiopian Christology.[1]

───────

1. The development of Ethiopian Christology – according to the state of the sources known at the time – is presented by: (1) M. da Abiy-Addiʾ (Aielè Tekle-Haymanot), *La dottrina della Chiesa Etiopica Dissidente sull'unione ipostatica* (OCA 147), Rome 1956. This work is an excerpt from a larger work with the same title (Rome 1956), which was not used here. Its tendency is to set as late as possible the Ethiopian church's falling in with the anti-Chalcedonian position (cf. chap. 2, pp. 23–36), namely, in the 16th and 17th centuries. The particular nature of the theological foundation in the 6th century is completely passed over. The split from Rome was, according to P. Mario, the result of being separated from the West by the Muslims and the Alexandrian patriarchs. Therefore their Christology remained in a pre-Chalcedonian state. The author wants, among other things, to limit himself to the Ethiopian sources, which causes him to miss entirely the relationships with Syria. – (2) Tesfaghi Uqbit, *Current Christological Positions of Ethiopian Orthodox Theologians* (OCA 196), Rome 1973. In this work the various phases of the christological discussion in Ethiopia are presented in every detail: he goes only briefly into the time of Zarʾa Yāʿqob (1434–68) but thoroughly into (a) the 16th and 17th centuries: pp. 49–71; (b) the 18th and 19th centuries: pp. 72–108; (c) the christological controversy of today: pp. 111–82. Missing, however, from the good information about the more recent development is the embedding in the genesis of Ethiopian Christianity on the basis of Judaism and Alexandrian-Syrian influences. – (3) Further – yet very late – texts are offered by Yakob Beyene, *L'unzione di Cristo nella teologia etiopica. Contributo di ricerca su nuovi documenti etiopici inediti* (OCA 215), Rome 1981. 1. Document A: 'Origine della questione dell'unzione di Cristo', pp. 28–41 (end of 17th to beginning of 18th cent.); 2. Document B, pp. 51–199, written in 1875. It deals with the three schools on the theme of the anointment of Christ: I. Kārrā ('Coltello', plur. Kārroč); II. Qebāt ('Unzione', plur. Qebātoč); III. Ṣaggā Leǧ ('Figlio della Grazia', plur. Ṣaggā Leǧoč). The *opusculum* defends position III. – Beyene makes many references to the work *Hāymānota Abaw*. 'Fides Patrum' (cf. op. cit., p. 23, n. 51, which refers to the revision of the patristic texts by the later theologians, which is seen especially in the Cyril texts. The result in some cases

1. Jewish and Jewish-Christian motifs in Ethiopian Christology

The first theme that emerges from the sources is the Messiah title and its significance for the image of Christ. In the whole sacral state church of Ethiopia[2] it also plays the role that is assumed by the Logos idea in the Eusebian-Constantinian understanding of the imperial church (the emperor as the representative of the Logos on earth). This messianic leitmotiv has different variations, which in a special way are suited to connect the Ethiopian Middle Ages with the old tradition of the Axum period.

(a) Translatio Regni Messianici

Given here is the first element that acquires christological significance, namely, the legend of the queen of Sheba and her connection with Solomon (cf. 1 Kings 10,1–13 par.; Mt 12,42; Lk 11,31). It became the foundation of the Ethiopian royal ideology. The Abyssinians understand

---

is the opposite of the genuine Cyril, especially with regard to the interpretation of the anointment). For this work also the recourse to the *Qērellos* would have been necessary. – (4) Kachali Alemu, Η ΧΡΙΣΤΟΛΟΓΙΑ ΤΩΝ ΑΙΘΙΟΠΙΚΩΝ ΑΝΑΦΟΡΩΝ ΕΝ ΣΧΕΣΕΙ ΠΡΟΣ ΤΟ ΔΟΓΜΑ ΤΗΣ ΧΑΛΚΗΔΟΝΟΣ, Thessalonica 1977. The work tests the Ethiopian anaphoras on their relationship to Chalcedon. With this the Greek conciliar formula becomes prominent. – Important for the christological question in the 15th century (Zarʾa Yāʿqob!) is: K. Wendt, 'Die theologischen Auseinandersetzungen in der äthiopischen Kirche zur Zeit der Reformen des XV. Jahrhunderts', *ACIStEt*, pp. 137–46. It concerns the reform writings of the period 1464–68: (a) *Book of Light* = Maṣḥafa Berhān, T. I–II, ed. by C. Conti Rossini col concorso di L. Ricci = T. I: CSCO 250 and 251; T. II: CSCO 261, 262 (Louvain 1964–65); Liber Nativitatis = Maṣḥafa Milād, and Liber Trinitatis = Maṣḥafa Sellāsē, T and V by K. Wendt: CSCO 221, 222, and 235, 236 (Louvain 1962–63). Still unedited are the *Book of Essence* (Maṣḥafa Bāhrey), the *Book of the Preservation of the Mystery* (Maṣḥafa Taʾāqbo Mestir). This is very much to be regretted, since K. Wendt says: 'On the basis of the last work of this complex of writings one can perhaps best justify and most generally undertake a monograph study of their underlying theological discussions in the Monophysite church of Ethiopia' (137). According to Wendt in these named writings four overlapping layers are to be distinguished: (1) synodal records; (2) file material (theses turned over to synods and symbol-like summarized discussion results); (3) royal decrees and ordinances; (4) catechetical-homiletical pieces, which show the whole to be a sermon collection (Wendt, op. cit., pp. 138–39).

2. The self-consciousness of the ruler is expressed in the Maṣḥafa Berhān (*Book of the Light*) T. II, B. III (reading for the 3rd Sunday, 6th hour): CSCO 262 (V), p. 20,1–4: 'E voi, popolo cristiano, fate come vi abbiamo commandato, perché il Signore ha costituito noi pastore sopra di voi, me Zarʾa Yāʿqob, il cui nome regale è Quaṣṭanṭinos, perché voi siete le pecore del gregge di Cristo.' The ruler also designates the kings as 'envoys' of God or as bearers of the messianic dignity (ibid., line 13). The appeal to Constantine is expressed in his name.

themselves as *däk' ik'ä 'Esra'el*, 'Israel's children'.[3] They are convinced that they have inherited from Israel the legitimate claim of being the chosen people of God, which is a variant of the universal church idea that Christians are 'Verus Israel', as M. Simon showed in his famous book of the same title – whence also Axum's claim to be the possessor and 'guardian' of the Ark of the Covenant with the tablets of the law. Connected with this is the tradition that the Axumite clergy is of Aaronite origin.[4] The Ethiopian rulers, on the other hand, had to work themselves up into the role of the kings of Israel.[5] Especially in the *Kebra Nagast* (*KN*) it was seen as a duty to support the claims of the royal house as the continuation of the Solomonic dynasty, which could happen only through an appeal to the Old Testament.[6] Brought in as proof here is the idea that through its disbelief of Christ, the Son of God, and his crucifixion, Israel lost its calling (did the Ethiopians not read Rom 9–11?).[7] The idea of a *Translatio Regni Messianici* is logically extended from Zion

---

3. On the royal legend and royal ideology in Ethiopia cf. *Kebra Nagast* (*KN*) §§ 21–40: Bezold, pp. 10–32. The recording of this legend did not take place until between 1314 and 1322. Soon after 1208 an Armenian writer of Arabic, Abū Ṣāliḥ, attests to the spread of such stories in Ethiopia. See M. Rodinson, 'Sur la question des "influences juives" en Éthiopie: "Ethiopian Studies"', *JSS* 9 (1964) (11–19), 15. – On the self-understanding of the people cf. also Maṣḥafa Berhān T. I, B. I: CSCO 251 (V), p. 10: the believing sons of Ethiopia are to make a covenant with Christ, as Moses had the sons of Israel enter a covenant with the Lord on Mount Horeb. How Ethiopian *poetic art* sees the unity of the two testaments while utilizing the canonical books, the Apocrypha and secular historical works is shown by the song 'Der Weise der Weisen': Ethiopic in A. Dillmann, *Chrestomathia aethiopica*, Leipzig 1866, 108–31; German by S. Euringer, 'Ṭabiba Ṭabibân', *OrChr* 31 (1934), 240–60.

4. Cf. E. Ullendorff, 'Hebraic-Jewish Elements in Abyssinian (Monophysite) Christianity', *JSS* 1 (1956), 226–27.

5. With this went the strong philosemitic assertion that 'all kings of the earth are descendants of Shem', C. Bezold, *KN*, 'Einleitung', p. XXXIX.

6. E. Ullendorff, *Ethiopia and the Bible*, London 1967, 75–77, refers to the dissertation of D. A. Hubbard, deposited at St Andrews University in 1956, in which the literary sources of the *KN* are thoroughly researched, and says on pp. 76/77: 'Hubbard (op. cit., pp. 14ff.) has called the Old Testament the primary source of *K.N*.' In it we find developed according to a strategic plan: 'The Sheba cycle, the *tabot* cycle, the voluminous concatenations of prophecies beginning with chapter 102, the numerous typological interpretations – are all rooted in the Old Testament.' The connecting of prophetic word and 'type' is early Christian (cf., e.g., Melito of Sardis!). The ratio of quotations from Old and New Testament in the *KN* is 5:1 (art. cit., 78). See also D. A. Hubbard, diss., p. 112: 'There can be little doubt that the Ethiopians were acquainted with substantial portions of the O.T. before they knew anything about the N.T. This early deposit of O.T. material on Ethiopian soil is reflected in the vast preponderance of O.T. quotations and references, especially in the collections of O.T. commandments.' In the detailed scripture readings in the Ethiopian worship service, which encompassed the entire OT and NT, *law* and prophecy had pre-eminence (E. Ullendorff, art. cit., 98).

7. *KN*, § 95: Bezold, pp. 101–2. It is typical for Ethiopia that the Jews were also reproached for having rejected not only Jesus but also his mother. Cf. *Das Maṣḥafa Milād*

to Axum. Both the residence and the *pignora* of the messianic kingdom, the 'ark of the law and the covenant, which he made into a seat of grace out of mercy towards the children of humankind',[8] are now in Axum.

With regard to the Jews, however, this proof concentrated again and again on the Messiahship of Jesus of Nazareth and his recognition as the Son of God. The goal of the criticism was not Jewish observance: on the contrary, it belonged to the proof of the transference of the kingdom! The explanation of the name of the central figure of the Solomon legend already leads to Christ: Solomon means Christ.[9] Then, however, the Pentateuch and the prophets of the OT are discussed in order to demonstrate Jesus' rank as messianic king and Son of God.[10] The *KN* sketches a genealogy of the Redeemer in the image of the pearl that was hidden in Adam's body before the creation of Eve and wandered a predesignated path through the generations to the fulfilment of the ages.[11] Linked with the history of this pearl, which ultimately is Christ, is the story of the

---

(trans. by K. Wendt), CSCO 222, p. 30: 'Therefore it was over for the enemies of Mary, the house of Israel, the Hebrews (through invasion of the enemies of Israel: Babylonians, Greeks, Romans).' The awareness of being heirs of the promise of the OT, through the acceptance of faith in Christ and the Trinity, then also required the *christological interpretation* of the OT. Here the Ethiopians have their own parallels to the universal church's christological interpretation of Psalms (cf. A. Grillmeier, *JdChr* I³, pp. 93, 143 with reference to B. Fischer). The text was extensively rewritten. See the *Psalter of Christ* (*Mazmura Krestos*), a Christian adaptation of the Psalms of David, which serves as the daily lectionary of the Ethiopian church. Cf. E. Cerulli, 'The "KALILAH WA-DIMNAH" and the Ethiopic "Book of Barlaam and Josaphat" (British Museum Ms. Or. 534)', *JSS* 9 (1964), 75–99. On pp. 76–77 Cerulli gives the English translation of Pss 1–2 of the *Psalter of Christ*.

8. *KN*, § 95: Bezold, p. 102 and his 'Einleitung', pp. XXXIX–XLI.

9. *KN*, § 66: Bezold, p. 62: '"Solomon", namely, in the secret language, in the interpretation of prophecy, means Christ.' Ibid., 63: 'Solomon, however, the king, the son of David, the king and prophet, was also himself a king and prophet, and in wisdom about Christ and the Christian church he prophesied many parables, wrote four prophetic books and was reckoned with Abraham, Isaac and Jacob and his father David in heaven.' Cf. 'Die Marienharfe' XVII, 36: S. Euringer, *OrChr* 25 (1928), 87,35–38.

10. On the Pentateuch see *KN* §§ 96–98: Bezold, pp. 103–10; § 105 (Abraham): Bezold, pp. 120–21. For the proof of the messianic rank of Christ see *KN* § 66: Bezold, pp. 62–63; § 69: ibid., pp. 68–69; § 106: ibid., pp. 121–25; § 107: ibid., pp. 125–27 under the utilization of the Ethiopian *Ascensio Isaiae*. – The *Anaphora of the 318 Orthodox* § 5 praises God the Father as the 'Father of the unique One, Father of the Lord, Father of the Messiah' (cf. S. Euringer, *ZSem* 4 [1926], 266).

11. *KN* § 68: Bezold, pp. 65–68; see also the 'Einleitung', pp. XL–XLI. A clear overview of the topic 'pearl' is given by E. Cerulli, *Storia*, ²1961, pp. 52–53, n. 1. The pearl can mean: (a) the Redeemer (from Clement of Alex. to Ephraem the Syrian); this interpretation came to the Ethiopian church through the *Physiologus*: the priceless pearl is Christ, the Sun of righteousness. It is found later in the disseminated Anaphora of Mary. She is the 'case' of this pearl; cf. S. Euringer, *OrChr* 34 (1937), 255; (b) the human soul; thus in Gnosticism but also in Syriac literature from Jacob of Sarug to the 'Hymn of the Soul' in the *Acts of Thomas*. For

cross[12] and of Mary, the mother of the Messiah and Son of God. Christ, the cross and Mary are considered the three means of the realization of redemption, even if not on the same level.[13]

King Zarʾa Yāʿqob (1434–68) also made every effort in his works to defend Jesus' messianic status as Son of God, and this naturally against the Jews.

> The discussion with the Jews takes place naturally on the basis of the Septuagint. Beyond this there is also appeal to the ancient Jewish apocryphal writings such as *Jubilees* and *Enoch*, which are common to the two partners. Yet the authority of *Enoch* is still disputed by both sides [it is supposed to be canonized by synodal decision] . . . Scriptural understanding, however, culminates in the question of the Messiah. The more the Jews refuse to recognize him in Jesus Christ, the more Christocentrically the Old Testament is interpreted on the Christian side. For this the book of *Enoch* was especially well suited. For the Christians it is above all a question of the historicity of Christ within God's plan of salvation, which from the beginning was temporally determined and proclaimed by the prophets. By contrast, the Jews reject any idea of history related to this and refer to the 'rise of the morning star' into the realm of the ever repeating, ahistorical course of nature, or the appearance of the Messiah as well as the end of the world in an unknown distance.

---

this meaning Cerulli finds no instances among the Ethiopians. On the occurrence of this 'pearl theory' and its meaning, a great deal is offered by S. Euringer, 'Das Hohelied des "Bundes der Erbarmung" ', *OrChr* 35 (1938) (71–107), 85–97. As a special motif Euringer picks out: 'In their opposition to the "enemies of Mary", the so-called Stephanites, and in their striving, on the basis of their Monophysite position, to bring the Mother of God as close to God as possible, at least individual theologians sought to form the conception and birth of Mary as much as possible like that of her divine Son and in this employed a speculation in which the "pearl" plays the main role and which one can therefore simply call the "pearl theory" ' (p. 86). In the 'Life of St Anne' the 'pearl' is interpreted entirely mariologically. Mary's body, or the cell of her future body, was created at the same time with Adam, hence *before Eve* and *before the first sin*. Then follows the migration of this pearl from Adam to Anne, the mother of Mary (text in Euringer, op. cit., p. 87). On the basis of the 'pearl theory' Euringer interprets very insightfully the frequently appearing title 'Virgin in two respects'. It asserts 'virginity' and 'sinlessness' (cf. art. cit., pp. 93–94). The occurrence of the image and theory of the 'pearl' is given more completely than in Euringer, art. cit., p. 91, in A. Grohmann, *Äthiopische Marienhymnen* (*ASAW* XXXIII, 4), Leipzig 1919, 378–79. The pearl speculation is interpreted *mariologically* and completely carried through in the 'Life of St Anne'; it is briefly addressed in the hymn 'Akkōnū Beʿesī and other hymns. Grohmann also gives patristic sources. On the lineage of Mary, the 'mother of the Messiah'(!) see also: 'Marienharfe' XXVI, §§ 96–107: S. Euringer, *OrChr* 25 (1928), 103–4; ibid., XXX, § 42: p. 263: Mary 'mother of the pearl'.

12. In the more christological interpretation of the 'pearl' in the *KN* its way is so directed that it leads to Jesus' death on the cross. This is a variation of the theme of Western Christology that asks whether Christ would have become a human being even if Adam had not fallen and redemption through the cross had not been necessary. The author of the *KN* does not speculate about this, but rather begins with the fact of the cross. See, however, the *Praedestinatio Christi* in the *Qalēmantōs* (n. 45 below).

13. Cf. C. Bezold, *KN*, p. 67, n. 12: 'The three means of redemption are Christ, the Virgin Mary and the cross. Abyssinian theologians assumed that both the Virgin and the cross were due veneration, since both were dwelling places of Christ.' In *KN* § 68 (Bezold, 65) Mary receives the title 'our Redemptress Mary'.

Like the Arians before them, they bring onto the field the long disputed Prov 8,22 passage according to which 'Wisdom was created by God' . . .[14]

As David and Solomon were messianic kings, and as the Abyssinian rulers are their heirs, so the Ethiopian church also understands itself as the messianic people of God, which is still expressed in, for example, the very late Athanasius anaphora:[15]

> What are we talking and chatting about there, like a harp without a soul? Rather, as Christians who are anointed by the grace of the *Lord* and truly messianic [i.e., anointed], we want to strive and hasten, to step up and compete, so that we may move from glory to glory.

(b) Jesus the 'anointed One'

Linked with such strong emphasis on the messianic status of Jesus of Nazareth is *vi tituli* (Aram.: *mᵉšīḥā*; Heb.: *hammāsiaḥ*; Eth.: *qebù*), the idea of anointment. It is true that this topic did not become acute in Ethiopia until the seventeenth century, and then in such a way that the result was the formation of theological schools that were mutually and fiercely combatant. Its introduction into Ethiopian tradition, however, lies significantly earlier and can be demonstrably placed in the period around 500–525, even if it did not become fully appreciated at the time.

(aa) Patristic discussion: Qērellos – Philoxenus of Mabbug

A first and indeed basic discussion is produced already by the *Qērellos* in the first three Cyril writings: (1) the *prosphonetikos* 'On Right Faith' to Theodosius II; (2) the *prosphonetikos* 'On Right Faith' to Arcadia and Marina; (3) the dialogue 'That Christ is One', and especially in the third. Therefore we can limit ourselves to this dialogue and refer only briefly to the first two writings. Through the two *prosphonetikoi* from the period shortly before Ephesus and from the dialogue, Cyril's last anti-Nestorian writing, a sufficient familiarity of Ethiopian theology with the idea of the 'anointment of Christ' is guaranteed. It receives, precisely in the third writing of the *Qērellos*, an alarming function, when it is used by Palladius

---

14. Cf. K. Wendt, 'Die theologischen Auseinandersetzungen', p. 142. Of the *c.* 30 passages from the book of *Enoch* that are offered in Wendt's index in CSCO 236, p. 95, most refer to Christ. Then come numerous passages from the book of *Jubilees*: ibid., 95–96, and many passages from 4 Ezra (ibid., 94).

15. See S. Euringer, 'Die äthiopische Anaphora des hl. Athanasius', *OrChr* 24 (1927), 257. – J. M. Harden, *The Anaphoras of the Ethiopic Liturgy*, London 1928, did not translate the passage. On pp. 289–91 Euringer offers a good commentary with a reference to I. Guidi, *La chiesa abissina e la chiesa russa*, Rome 1890, 606–7.

(in some mss. 'Hermeias'), Cyril's discussion partner, to introduce and 'substantiate' the Nestorian interpretation of the person of Christ:[16]

> Palladius: Yes, they say, only one who comes from woman and from David's seed can be called Christ because of the anointment, since he is anointed with the Spirit. – *Yet Christ means 'anointed One'* [which, according to Weischer, is an 'explanatory addition' in the Ethiopic]. – The divine Logos, however, as far as its nature [is concerned], requires no anointment *in its nature* [the italicized words again are an Ethiopic addition], for according to his nature he is holy. The name Christ means anointment, *that is, Messiah* [italicized words only in Ethiopic].

The question of the anointment of Christ already appears here as a Nestorian difficulty, that is, as a possible objection to the Cyrillian conception of Christ's unity of person. There can be no 'anointment' in the divine nature of Christ (but cf. Justin and Origen), but only with regard to the 'human being' Jesus of Nazareth, who in this very way becomes the Christ. But does this not introduce the dreaded division in Christ? 'Logos' and 'Christ' are – so urged Palladius in essence – 'two': two subjects, two persons. If the *Logos* as such were anointed, then an anointment would also be fitting for the Father and the Holy Spirit (§ 33,2). Other names with which the Son is named in the scripture, such as *Lord, light, life,* etc., can also be applied to Father and Spirit as an expression of the one essence, but not the name *Christ*. That means that one cannot say that the Logos is the Christ (§ 34,3)! Hence one must distinguish between the Logos and the one who is 'from David's seed'. Only he can be said to be the 'Christ'. This conjures up the ghost of a second, purely human hypostasis in Christ. In order radically to chase away this ghost, Cyril greatly narrows his doctrine of the anointment.

The patriarch attributes the title 'Christ' to the 'Logos', the 'only begotten', yet with the restriction that he receives it only 'with the marks of the incarnation, for the anointment is spoken of openly for those who comprehend that he was anointed at his incarnation and is thus named [i.e., as the anointed One]' (cf. Acts 10,38) (§ 35,1). Thus in order not to jeopardize the unity of the one Christ through the doctrine of the anointment, Cyril wants nothing to stand between the assuming Logos and the assumed humanity: no messianic gifts, no 'created grace' (thus the scholastics), but only the 'uncreated grace' that the *Logos* is for the united humanity. Therefore the anointment is accomplished exclusively in the incarnation of the Son (§ 35,2). Only the incarnation makes it possible to speak of anointment at all (§ 35,2 and 3 with reference to Heb 2,11–12; Ps 45,7–8). 'He is called Christ, that is, the anointed One, if we may also know after our consideration that he received no anointment in

---

16. See B. M. Weischer, *Qērellos* III (1977), §§ 32,2–35,4, pp. 73–79.

his divine nature, since the Logos is really God' (§ 35,4). In the immediately following words the *ultima ratio* of the whole dialogue is revealed:
if we understand the anointment, say, as Nestorius did, 'how could we
otherwise believe that *Christ is one* as Son and as Lord . . .'? (ibid.).[17]
Thus, on the one hand, Cyril stands against Justin and Origen, who
know a pre-cosmic anointment of the Logos, which is given with the
proceeding of the Logos from the Father, that is, with the reception of
the divine essence, however the two may have understood this.[18] On the
other hand, he stands against the Antiochenes, who want to have the true
humanity of Christ clearly come into being with reference to the messianic anointment: there can be no *'mia physis* in the incarnate Logos',
because as a human being he is the recipient of grace! He makes no
reference, however, to the older Syrian Christology, which attributes a
special role to the baptism of Jesus and the anointment by the Spirit (see
below). The assumption of a birth of the Messiah in the baptism in the
Jordan is for Cyril no longer a point open to discussion. For Cyril joins
Logos and humanity so closely together in the incarnate One that there
is no longer any place for a lasting impartation of grace by the Spirit to
inhere in the humanity as such. The 'Logos' as such lays claim to the term
anointment for itself.[19]

More lengthy comments on the name of Christ and on 'anointment'
are also found in Philoxenus of Mabbug, who can be demonstrated as a
source for Ethiopian Christology. We have already followed his trail as
far as Najrān in Arabia, the contact point with the Ethiopians. We will
briefly summarize an analysis that he gives in the second letter to the
monastery of Beit Gaugal.[20] It concerns the question: If there is only one
Son in Jesus Christ, then we must ask the Nestorians: Who is the bearer
of this title of Son? If it is the God-Logos, then that is right. If they say,
however, that the Son is the 'Christ', then they are deceived! For they
then mean by this 'Son' 'the Christ', and indeed one who has earned the
grace to be called Son. In contrast to this, however, it must be established
that the God-Logos – that is, the one who according to *nature* is the true

---

17. It should be noted that the word *one* is not in the Greek text but was probably in the
Syriac version with which the Ethiopic agrees. Cf. B. M. Weischer, *Qērellos* III, p. 79, n.
16.

18. For more detail see A. Grillmeier, *JdChr* I³, pp. 70–71 and 269.

19. In order to reach an overall judgement here we would have to investigate Cyril's
whole christological pneumatology.

20. Syr. text and French translation by A. de Halleux, 'La deuxième lettre de Philoxène
aux monastères du Beit Gaugal', *Mus* 96 (1983), 5–79.

Son – is called 'Christ', yet only according to the *oikonomia*. This emphasis, 'according to the *oikonomia*', is typical of Philoxenus. The name *Christ* depends on the historical event of the incarnation, even if it befits only the Logos as subject (§ 30). Is there still enough room here to define the true essence of the anointment on the basis of *pneuma* and not only on the basis of the Logos?

According to Philoxenus, 'Christ' is the one who is anointed with us for the *oikonomia* of his *kenosis* (Acts 10,38; Phil 2,7; the connecting of these two scriptures is to be noted for later). In what Christ has from the Father he needs no anointment. He needs it only in what he has become for us and with us (§ 31). Here he is anointed 'as we, so that we ourselves, in his anointment for us, receive purification in his baptism' (§ 31). In the cited *Qērellos* discussion Cyril himself would not have gone so far. But does Philoxenus say much more than the patriarch? Even for him Christ 'himself', as a human being, did not receive through the anointment of the Spirit anything that he had not had already through the unity with his divinity. He too steers attention immediately away from a 'reception' by Christ himself. Everything happening with him is only a passing through, for our sakes, in his *oikonomia* 'for us': *kenosis*, birth, growing up, fasting and praying, everything up until his resurrection, including anointment by the Spirit 'for us'(!) (§§ 30–31, pp. 53–55). For proof one is referred to the voice of the Father (Mt 3,17). The last subject of all statements on the Spirit (such as Is 61,1 = Lk 4,18; Mt 12,48; 4,1; Lk 2,52; 1 Tim 3,16; Jn 3,31–32; 1,30) is the pre-existent hypostasis of the Logos. To make the human nature of Christ himself for itself and for its own sake – even if ultimately then really for us – into the receiving, lasting organ of anointment is too much even for the bishop of Mabbug. This would already yield 'two sons'. But how can the hypostasis of the Son receive through anointment something that it did not have already beforehand on the basis of the God-nature? The answer: The voice of the Father is directed towards the crowd and John in order to attest to them what Christ secretly already is![21] Also in the wilderness, in battle against Satan (Mt 4,1ff.), Christ does not actually need the help of the Spirit; rather, this is only supposed to show that the Spirit is in him. And he is in the Spirit because of the equality of nature (§ 33, p. 56). Even in order to drive out

---

21. Ibid., p. 55. 'Et ce n'est pas un autre (qui) fut appelé le Fils bien aimé par le Père, mais (c'est) Dieu le Verbe; (et ceci), non (parce) qu'il n'est pas le Fils auparavant aussi, mais pour indiquer par une voix publique à la foule et à Jean sa naissance cachée. Et c'est celui-là qui fut indiqué par la voix qui reçut l'Esprit; (et ceci) non (parce) qu'il avait en rien besoin de lui pour (en) être aidé, mais pour le distinguer, entre lui et le Baptiste, devant les foules qui se tenaient (là), car c'est lui (qui fut) appelé le Fils bien-aimé, et non point Jean.'

the evil spirits (Mt 12,28) he does not need any extra help from the Spirit that he did not already have beforehand in himself. Here again is a reference to the consubstantiality between Son and Spirit. Whenever Jesus gives the Spirit, he gives out of his own supply (§ 34, pp. 56–7). Also 1 Tim 3,16 and Rom 1,3 are not to be understood as the giving of a present to Christ as a human being for his own sake, not as a gift remaining in him. It is only a matter of the 'revelation' of a hidden mystery to the outside world.[22]

(bb) The 'anointment' in the Ethiopian theology of the late Middle Ages and the modern period

Through the Qērellos and through Philoxenus of Mabbug the way was probably prepared for the theme of the anointment to be treated over the centuries in a uniquely forceful way in the history of the Christian theology of Ethiopia. This certainly could happen only on the foundation of Old Testament and Judaism that is typical of Ethiopia. Now, initially, we certainly stand before uncharted territory on the theological map. According to the documentation known up until today, we hear again of 'anointment' for the first time after the sixth century through writings that originated during the reform activity of King Zarʾa Yāʿqob in the years 1464–68. Then, however, several rulers and synods are occupied with this topic into the nineteenth century.[23] We will look only at typical phases, especially in consideration of how far the Qērellos and Philoxenus or patristic sources in general have become influential.

(1) In the Maṣḥafa Milād

The anointment in the messianic-eschatological sense is the topic especially in the passionately anti-Jewish reading II of the Maṣḥafa Milād.[24]

In connection with Dan 9,26–27 the end of the anointment is announced for Israel. 'After sixty-two weeks the anointment will be over' (Dan 9,26). Kingship, priesthood, prophecy will come to an end. Not only the Jews will fail to hear this message but also 'Christian people' who abandon the 'perfect gift' (= the flesh and blood of our Saviour) and run after those 'who are driven out of their homeland' (p. 25). Thus, as in other lands, so also

---

22. Cf. A. Grillmeier, 'Die Taufe Christi und die Taufe der Christen', in *Fides Sacramenti-Sacramentum Fidei*, FS P. Smulders, Assen 1981, 142–44, 158. How much Philoxenus differs from the early Syrian doctrine of the baptism of Christ is seen in G. Winkler, 'Ein bedeutsamer Zusammenhang zwischen der Erkenntnis und Ruhe in Mt 11,27–29 und dem Ruhen des Geistes auf Jesus am Jordan. Eine Analyse zur Geist-Christologie in syrischen und armenischen Quellen', *Mus* 96 (1983), 267–326; see ibid., chap. VI.

23. Cf. F. A. Dombrowski, *Ṭānāsee 106: Eine Chronik der Herrscher Äthiopiens* (ÄthFor 12 B), Wiesbaden 1983, 290–95: 'Zur Auseinandersetzung zwischen Qebāṭočč und Tawāḥdowočč'.

24. Maṣḥafa Milād, II (reading on 29th of Ṭerr): Wendt, CSCO 222, pp. 23–36.

in Ethiopia Judaism exerts a strong attraction for Christians. But that is the wrong choice. For 'we Christians . . . say: after the captivity there was no more oil of the kingship and no more oil of the priesthood . . . until Christ, the King of glory, the Son of the pure Mary' (p. 26).

In the third reading, however, this end of the anointment is again emphasized, but at the same time how it is now brought to an end – that is, to completion – in Christ is explained.

> Dan 9,24 says: 'Something most holy is to be anointed.' 'But the most holy is Christ. "He is to be anointed" [ibid.] means, however: he is to put on the flesh of Mary. Hear, O Jew, who should the most holy be other than the Son of God? For one does not name something created most holy. But the most holy is Christ, the Son of Mary, who is more holy than the heavenly watchmen and earthly bearers of the Spirit. He is worshipped and praised and with his Father and his Holy Spirit thanked by all creatures, for ever and ever, amen and amen, so be it!'[25]

Altogether in Cyril's sense, anointment is explained here as identical with the event of the incarnation. The reference to the book of *Jubilees*[26] gives the whole matter a typically Jewish-Christian eschatological context. We get the impression that the anointment of the Holy Spirit is at first not directly shared with Christ, for he cannot actually be the recipient, since he has everything in the Logos. Rather, Mary conveys the anointment of the Spirit to the flesh of Christ. This is indicated in various passages by reading XIII of part II of the Maṣḥafa Milād for the festival of the birth of Christ on the 29th of Ṭeqemt (4 Nov.). We cite an especially clear one:

> See here, O Christian: Mary was also created. After the Comforter united with her flesh and with her soul, she bore God, our Lord Jesus Christ. Therefore the scriptures also say that he became a human being from the Holy Spirit and out of Mary, the blessed Virgin. The Comforter dwelled upon her in special measure, strengthened and purified her, so that with her flesh she could bear the frightful fiery flame . . . 'He who anointed me' is what is said of the flesh of Mary, which the Saviour has put on, and of his incarnation by the Holy Spirit and of his anointment with the Holy Spirit.[27]

We close with a verse from the ʿArganōna dengel, the office of Mary and at the same time the most important work of Ethiopic sacral literature, which the Armenian George, under commission from Zarʾa Yāʿqob, wrote in the year 1440, and in which we again discover a reference to the Qērellos:

> [To Jesus as king of kings] Thus you are the anointing oil, but what is anointed, your flesh, is the high priest and king of kings Jesus Christ, for Christ means anointed one, as Cyril explained.[28]

---

25. Ibid. (reading on 29th of Yakkāttit), pp. 45–46.
26. Ibid., p. 46.
27. Maṣḥafa Milād, T. II: CSCO 236, pp. 61,33–62,18.
28. In A. Grohmann, Äthiopische Marienhymnen (ASAW 33, 4), Leipzig 1919, 316.

In all these texts the anointment of Christ with the Holy Spirit is already shifted to the incarnation. This moves the baptism of Christ into the background.

(2) A church history text

With the seventeenth century we find ourselves already in the period when the topic of 'anointment' and its realization led to deep-seated controversies in the Ethiopian church. With the text from a 'Church History of Abyssinia', edited and translated by I. Guidi, we are initially in the time of King Susneos (1607–32).[29] It is the first quarrel over the topic of the anointment.

In the discussion reference is made to such scriptural passages as Jn 3,34, 35; 1,16; Heb 1,8, 9; Lk 4,18; Acts 4,27 and others. We understand the *first thesis* right away if we keep the *Qērellos* in mind: 'The union of the divinity [with the humanity] in him [Christ] takes the place of the anointment of his humanity' (Guidi, p. 11). The antithesis reads: 'The Father is the anointer, the Son the anointed, the Holy Spirit the anointment' (which in Greek would read: χρίστης, χριστός, χρίσμα). The two parties took their quarrel to King Susneos, who was currently involved in undertaking a campaign against the Gāllā. Therefore he postponed the deciding of this question of faith until his return. The first party, however, was forbidden to teach the people that the anointment of Christ consists *only* in the uniting of the divinity with his humanity and not in anything *else* and not in another, different act (Guidi, p. 11). After the victorious return of the king, a council was held in the year 1622/23. Like the first party, the second also held to its view but formulated it thus: 'Christ was anointed in his flesh with the Holy Spirit when he became a human being.' The disputants both presented their proof from the scripture, but also from the collection *Hāymānota Abaw*.[30] The decision of the king read:

'In truth, the anointment of our Lord and Redeemer Jesus Christ is the grace of the Holy Spirit, which was given to him in his humanity, and indeed in the moment of the uniting of the humanity with the divinity. While in his divinity he is like the Father and the Holy Spirit and gives grace to all, in his humanity he received grace in order to give grace to the sons of Adam, his brothers. The grace that he received from the Holy Spirit, however, was without measure . . .' (the opposite of this was the case with the prophets and apostles, with reference to Jn 3,34, 35) (Guidi, p. 12).

We know that only the first-named party had accepted the position of Cyril or of Philoxenus of Mabbug, whereas the second held a teaching that accepted, beyond the union of divinity and humanity, a *grace of the*

---

29. See I. Guidi, *Di due frammenti relativi alla storia di Abissinia*, Rome 1893; idem, 'Uno squarcio della Storia Ecclesiastica di Abissinia', *Bessarione* 8 (1900/01), 10–25; idem, art. 'Abyssinie (Église de)', in *DHGE* 1 (1912), 217–20. See T. Uqbit, *Current Christological Positions*, pp. 49–71, esp. pp. 58–64. The information in the above text is from Guidi, *Bessarione*.

30. *Hāymānota Abaw*, 'The Faith of the Fathers', is a collection of patristic texts on the Trinity, the incarnation and the nature of Christ, which was assembled in Arabic around the year 1078 (*Itirāf al-abā* = confession of the fathers) and translated into Ethiopic in the 16th century. See the analysis and bibl. in E. Hammerschmidt, *Äthiopische Handschriften vom Ṭānāsee* 1, Verz. Or. HssD XX 1 (1973), 110–14 (Ṭānāsee 11); ibid., XX 2 (1977), 82–86 (Ṭānāsee 73); 112–15 (Ṭānāsee 90).

Spirit in Christ, the recipient of which was his human nature – and indeed in all fullness – for the brothers of Christ. It is probable that we have here, via Portuguese missionaries, the expression of Western, Chalcedonian ideas.[31]

(3) 'The Mirror of Insight'[32]

This writing was composed in the years 1621–22. In the third chapter it also speaks of the anointment in connection with an interpretation of the death of Jesus Christ and of his person. The text is especially interesting because it refers to the *Qērellos* and more specifically of Cyril's dialogue, 'That Christ is One'. Therefore we quote some excerpts:[33]

> This is the mystery of the death of our Lord: while he was alive in his divinity, he suffered death in his flesh; while on the one hand his divinity was not ready for [i.e., refrained from] working miracles [namely, to prevent Jesus' death], on the other hand his humanity never stopped accepting suffering. Rather, he achieved both [refraining from miracles, acceptance of suffering] with *one* will, *one* accord and in *one* nature [substance, *bāhrey*] and *one* person, who was anointed by the Holy Spirit and was called Messiah, that is, Christ; Cyril declared this in the 37th Dissertatio, when he said: 'Because Christ means "anointed one"'[34] . . . As far as the anointment is concerned, it is by the Holy Spirit.

Then follows a series of statements on the anointment of Christ: the divinity of Christ itself is the anointment of his humanity [cf. Cyril]; again: humanity became the anointment for the divinity. And again: the uniting of the humanity and the divinity in Christ is called anointment [cf. Cyril]. Finally: Christ was anointed in the Jordan River when the Holy Spirit descended upon him. Then it says, surprisingly:

> But these are all errors. His anointment took place in the womb of the Virgin, and the ointment on him was the Holy Spirit. Thus the name 'anointment' for his incarnation is

---

31. See T. Uqbit, *Current Christological Positions*, pp. 49–56. On the origin of the theme of anointment in Ethiopian theology cf. F. A. Dombrowski, *Ṭānāsee 106*, pp. 290–95, esp. p. 291, where the question of Western influence is discussed.

32. *Mashēta Lebbunā* ('specchio dell'Intelligenza'), Ethiopic with Ital. trans. by E. Cerulli, ST 204 (1960), 139–60, 163–86. Cf. E. Hammerschmidt, *Äthiop. Hss vom Ṭānāsee* (Verz. Or. HssD XX 1), 198–99.

33. E. Cerulli, *Specchio dell'intelligenza*, ST 204, pp. 184–86.

34. Ibid., p. 184. This 37th Diss. can be nothing other than *Qērellos* III 3, p. 79, § 35,2: 'Obviously, the name *Christ*, that is, "anointed one", is not appropriate for the only begotten One.' That the *Qērellos* is thereby cited is seen from the fact that the apposition indicated here occurs only in the Ethiopic. Cf. also *Qērellos* II 2 = Cyril of Alex., *Ad Reginas* XIII: PG 76, 1220 C (here 1219C–1222A:) *Nos autem ita sentire aut loqui nequaquam didicimus: quandoquidem tunc primum Verbum Jesu Christi appellationem sortitum dicimus, cum factum est caro; siquidem [Verbum] ob id Christus vocatur, quia exsultationis oleo, hoc est Spiritu sancto, a Deo Patre inunctum est. Quod autem inunctio illa assumptae humanitatis ratione illi conveniat, id apud recte sentientes in quaestionem non venit: nam si Dei Verbum Deus est, nulla utique unctione indiget. Nec ullus unquam docuit Dei Verbum Spiritu suo inunctum aut sanctificatum esse, quasi is secundum naturam ab illo sit diversus, superior et excellentior . . .*

to be translated as 'staying' (*permanenza*),[35] because [the Holy Spirit] remained on him. [Quotation from 2 Cor 8,9: 'For you know the grace of our Lord Jesus Christ, that though he was rich, yet for your sakes he became poor, so that by his poverty you might become rich.'] And this is the beginning of his 'poverty': that he received the Holy Spirit, although both [the Son and the Holy Spirit] are nevertheless consubstantial [so that a reception or being given is actually impossible]. But out of love for us he assumed it, according to Paul's statement: so that we might become rich through his poverty. He [Christ] is [however] full of the Holy Spirit [in distinction to every other blessing by the Spirit], since the Holy Spirit is his life.

Then follow as proof Acts 10,38; 2,22; 4,27; Lk 4,18; also a quotation from Severus of Antioch and his letter to Patriarch Theodosius of Alexandria:[36] 'The Spirit that in my essence is my Spirit remained over me, and I was therefore called Messiah'; then we apparently have a free quotation from the *Qērellos*, the mentioned dialogue of Cyril with Palladius: 'The Creator of the angels was anointed.'[37] Finally a testimony of 'St Cyriacus' is given. This Cyriacus is to be equated with Ḥeryāqos, the metropolitan of Behnasā in middle Egypt.[38] He sees the relationship to the Trinity expressed directly in the name *Christ*, as we find it already in I. Guidi, p. 11, namely, to the Father as the anointer, to the Son as the anointed and to the Holy Spirit as the anointment. But the anointment is in the incarnate One already from the conception to the ascension into heaven – not for the enrichment of this Christ himself but only for us.

(4) A new phase in the dispute

Under King Fāsiladas (1632–67) the controversy over anointment broke out again.[39] 'Heretics' from Goggiam said: 'Through the anointment Christ became the natural Son of God.'[40] In his thirty-third year of governing the king called a council with the whole clergy of Dabra Libanos. The new idea was clarified as follows:

---

35. On the meaning of this word *permanenza* see G. Winkler, art. cit., *Mus* 96 (1983), 295–97. The reading for Jn 1,32, *et permansit super eum* (instead of *requievit*), which is presupposed here, is probably adopted from the Syriac – a new indication of the dependence of Ethiopia on the Syrians.

36. Severus Ant., *Ep. syn. ad Theodos. ep. Alex.* (CPG 7070 [8]): Chabot, CSCO 103, p. 11,11–14; reproduced here according to E. Cerulli, ST 204, p. 185 with n. 6, which refers to *Hāymānota Abaw*, Cod. Paris Aeth. 111, fol. 76 r, c. 1.

37. In this form the quotation is not to be found. Yet in the very section on the anointment it is stated: that Christ is one, Christ called 'King and Lord of hosts' (§ 34,2). The context of the dialogue yields the essence of the cited quotation.

38. Cf. S. Euringer, 'Die Äthiopische Anaphora unserer Herrin Maria', *OrChr* 34 (1937), 68–69; E. Hammerschmidt, *Studies in the Ethiopic Anaphoras*, Berlin 1961, 17.

39. Cf. T. Uqbit, *Current Christological Positions*, pp. 64, 77. – G. Haile, *The Faith of the Unctionists in the Ethiopian Church* (Haymanot Mäsihawit), CSCO 517 (T), 518 (V), Louvain 1990, offers now a text (with Italian trans.) presenting according to Haile (CSCO 518, p. XI, cf. ibid., 32) 'the actual decision' of an ecclesiastical council on the unction in the presence of King Fāsiladas (on 23 June 1655).

40. I. Guidi, *Bessarione* 8 (1900/01), 15.

When the Logos united to himself the flesh, he became poor; he emptied himself [Phil 2,7], and he lacked his divine riches; but then he was anointed with the Holy Spirit, was exalted and became the natural Son of God; that is our belief.[41]

This was declared heresy by the scholar Adam of Emferāz, and the counter-position was set out:

When the Word united to himself the flesh, he became poor but still remained rich in his divinity; and when we say: he was poor but in the body, we are not calling him poor in regard to the riches of his divine nature and the first eternal procreation; rather, we say: he put on a flesh that was deprived of the honour of the Holy Spirit, the honour [namely] that God had given to Adam when he was placed in paradise, and therefore he [Christ] would have been [deprived] of the spiritual procreation that Adam had lost through his sin, if he had not been anointed in his body with the anointment of the Holy Spirit. He was hallowed as a human being in his humanity and gave this procreation back to his honour, and became Son of grace in the womb, as Paul wrote in his letter to the Romans: 'And he showed that he is the Son of God through his power and his Holy Spirit' [Rom 1,4 according to the Ethiopic Vulgate]; and for a similar reason he was called the second Adam [cf. 1 Cor 15,45].[42]

Again a significant step was taken beyond Cyril and the anti-Chalcedonian teaching, yet in a way that was not inconceivable even for a Chalcedonian. Although there were, namely, also Western theologians who assumed a double sonship in Christ (natural sonship by virtue of procreation from the Father and an 'adoptive' one on the basis of the blessing by the Holy Spirit in his humanity), there was, nonetheless, the generally pervasive teaching that there is only *one* sonship in Christ, the divine, which in consequence of the *communicatio idiomatum* must also be asserted of the incarnate One. This agrees, however, with the assumption of blessing of Jesus by the Spirit in his humanity, in his human intellectuality, his understanding and his will, for the fulfilment of his messianic task. While Adam of Emferāz correctly rejected the *kenosis* of the 'heretics' from Goggiam, his own solution remained unclear. Obviously, Christ would only be in the *kenosis* by having to be without the grace of the Spirit, not by having simply assumed humanity, as Phil 2,7 presupposes. Also strange is the idea that through the blessing by the Spirit Christ was placed into the paradisaical state of Adam before sin. What does this mean?

To answer this question we may turn to the interesting text that E. Cerulli edited and translated as an appendix to the small writing *Storia dei*

---

41. I. Guidi, art. cit., p. 16.
42. Ibid.

quattro concili or *Mazgaba Hāymānot* ('Il Tesoro della Fede').[43] It presents a protology and a christological anthropology that are typical of Ethiopia and point to Jewish or Jewish-Christian ideas.

Chapter [on Jesus' food in his earthly life]

On Christ, who fulfilled the law of human existence while he was in the divinity, and on the food that he ate before the crucifixion. [The question] is this: As Adam ate when he was in Eden, before he had eaten the forbidden fruit, and as [God] at one time (*anticamente*) ate in his divinity in Abraham's house [cf. Gen 18,1–33] and as Christ, after the resurrection from the dead, ate a piece of a broiled fish and a honey cake [cf. Lk 24,42], so he ate [before the crucifixion] and fulfilled the whole law of human existence, with the sole exception of sin. But the event of the emptying of the stomach and of urine did in fact not exist in him. Since he was not born of human seed, he was immune to such a birth and thus also immune to the emptying of the stomach and of urine.

And as our Lady Mary was free from male contact, she was also immune to concupiscence and the monthly regularity of women. And as Eve was before the guilt, when the Lord had not yet cursed her [cf. Gen 2,23–25], so was our Lady Mary until her departure from this world. Therefore we call her: 'She who eradicated the curse.'

Thus Christ put on the flesh of Adam, as it was pure flesh before the first sin, because the Holy Spirit purified our Lady Mary when Gabriel said to her: 'The Holy Spirit will come upon you' [Lk 1,35]. Therefore Christ had no emptying of the body or urine. Thus when he had hunger like us, [he had it not] out of necessity but out of [free] will; and when he had thirst, then not out of necessity but out of his will; and when he became tired, then not out of necessity but out of his will, whose purpose was to be with us. Thus St Paul said: 'Since, therefore, the children are together in flesh and blood, so he joined them' [Heb 2,14]. Regarding the emptying of the body and urine, however, these things were not in Adam before his expulsion from Eden. Rather [not until] the Lord said to him: 'In the sweat of your brow shall you eat your bread' and then said to him: 'May the earth be cursed for your work!' [Gen 3,17]; and with this curse Adam received the emptying of the stomach and urine. And the word of the curse also came to Eve, saying: 'You will give birth with pain and have bleeding each month' [cf. Gen 3,16]. And so she suffered in procreation, in menstruation and in giving birth; by contrast, Christ the Lord, the second Adam, and our Lady Mary, the second Eve, crushed and annihilated the curse. Understand this; do not mix with the godless; and whoever has no brain will not understand this.

One probably thinks immediately of 'Docetism', or the doctrine of the apparent body of Jesus. But this would be a misjudgement. Jesus' body has reality, but it is a reality that corresponds to the first Adam in the condition before the fall in paradise. Jesus is above the laws of the vital acts by virtue of the virginal conception from Mary. It is not out of the question that this conception was already latent in the above quoted words of the scholar Adam of Emferāz. Perhaps more important are two other ideas:

---

43. See E. Cerulli, ST 204 (1960), 100–1. This very text is also given by Y. Beyene, *L'unzione di Cristo nella teologia etiopica* (OCA 215), Rome 1981, pp. 202–3, n. 212, in his own translation without further information on the ms.

(1) The aphthartodocetist whom Leontius of Byzantium fought[44] or his friends apparently assumed that bodily purity was already given also to the mother of Jesus from the moment of conception of the Son through the Holy Spirit. In their simplicity, however, they did not notice the absurdity that a *(corpus) incorruptibile* cannot conceive and give birth. If, moreover, it is already 'pure', the body of Mary must also be 'immortal' and would thus become the cause of our immortality in place of Christ.

(2) The closest relationship to the ideas set forth in the Cerulli text are probably found in the teaching of the original state in the Ethiopian Pseudo-Clementines, in the so-called *Qalēmentos*. It also shows well the connection between teaching of the original state, Mariology and Christology. Thus we find in book II:

> 'Those who dwell there [in paradise] do not need to eat and drink. In this place there is no cold and no heat. Because of the sweetness of [its] perfume, the fragrance spreading in paradise takes all desire for eating and drinking . . .' (chap. VIII 5; similarly 8: freedom from sickness and suffering). – (Chap. II: connection between original state, Christology, Mariology) 'O Peter [says Jesus], if I had not become a human being, the world would not have been created [at all]. O Peter, if I had not assumed flesh of the blessed [Virgin] Mary, I would have created neither Adam nor heaven nor earth . . . O Peter, if the blessed Virgin should not have existed, I would not have created Eve.'[45]

The connection of ideas is probably to be found in the Jewish-Christian milieu.

---

44. Cf. Leont. Byz., CNE: PG 86, 1325C–1329C. See A. Grillmeier, *CCT* II/2, pp. 213–29. We have already encountered the idea of being above bodily needs in regard to the person of Christ in Clement of Alexandria, *Strom.* III 7, 59,3, where reference is made to its gnostic origin. Cf. A. Grillmeier, *JdChr* I³, p. 266; *CCT* I², p. 138; on the Gnostics see A. Orbe, *Cristología gnóstica* I, Madrid 1976, pp. 396–403.

45. See *Qalēmentos*, II. B., chap. VIII 5: trans. by S. Grébaut, *ROC* 17 (1912), 343–44; II. B., chap. II, ibid., 250. On this work, which was written in Arabic by a Christian in Egypt around 750–60, see A. Dillmann, 'Bericht über das Aethiopische Buch Clementinischer Schriften', *NGWG* 1858, 185–226; F. Nau, art. 'Clémentins', *DTC* 3/1, col. 217. Also to be compared is the book of *Jubilees* 3,9–16: O. S. Wintermute, in J. H. Charlesworth (ed.), *The Old Testament Pseudepigrapha* II, Garden City, NY 1985, 59. – Thus in order to understand the Cerulli text we do not have to turn back to Julian of Halicarnassus, which seems obvious. Julian, like Severus of Antioch, assumes that Christ really ate and drank and had a genuinely vital life. What he rejects is this: on account of this 'vitality' one may not call Christ's body 'corruptible' (φθαρτός). Cf. R. Draguet, *Julien d'Halicarnasse et sa controverse avec Sévère d'Antioche sur l'incorruptibilité du corps du Christ*, Louvain 1924, 152, n. 4 with reference to frag. 13 and 99, pp. 48* and 67*.

That Christ in his virginal conception had a body similar to Adam's *before the fall* is expressed in two favourite texts: (1) in *KN* § 96: Bezold, pp. 104–5, it says of Mary, the bearer

(5) The conflict under King Yoḥannes

A third phase of the dispute around the anointment of Christ came under the successor of Fāsiladas, under King Yoḥannes (d. 1682).[46] Those condemned by his father wanted again to get their teaching accepted. A council, to which the Abuna with his Ečāgē, his highest administrator, was called, was supposed to decide.

The people of Goggiam around Akāla Krestos asserted again that through the anointment Christ became the natural Son of the Father. The monks from Dabra Libanos, on the other hand, said: through the *unio* Christ became the natural Son of the Father, but through the

---

of God: 'She was born without blemish: for he created her pure, without defilement. And she accomplished her task without marriage and without coitus. She bore in a *heavenly body* a king; he was born from her and renewed life through the purity of his body; he killed death with his pure body and arose without corruption . . .' – (2) In the 'Ethiopian Anaphora of Our Lady Mary', specifically in § 34 in the application of the image of weaving and the loom to Mary: 'You are a loom, for from you Emmanuel has put on the inexplicable dress of the flesh: he made the *original flesh of Adam* his warp [the series of threads running lengthwise in a loom], but his weft [threads running crossways] was his flesh and his shuttle the Word itself, Jesus Christ, his weaver's beam the overshadowing of the most high God from above and his weaver the Holy Spirit.' Cf. S. Euringer, 'Die Äthiopische Anaphora Unserer Herrin', *OrChr* 34 (1937), 76–77. In the commentary, p. 94, Euringer calls attention to the homily *De Laudibus S. Mariae* of Patr. Proclus of Constantinople, which was incorporated into the *Qērellos* (cf. *Qērellos* IV 2 [1979], 64–86). In Weischer's translation (p. 67) we read: 'She is the frightening dress with which the garment of his miraculous incarnation is covered, whose maker is the Holy Spirit and whose weavers are the shadows of the power from on high, and whose threads [or weave] is *Adam's body from the beginning* and whose warp of the weave is the pure flesh from the Virgin and whose weaver's reed is the grace of him who clothes himself and whose artist is the Logos, who stands in obedience to his Father.' Obviously, the Ethiopian translator has unclearly reproduced the text of Proclus. The Greek text can be translated thus (following Euringer, p. 94): 'Mary . . . the frightful loom (ἱστός) of the salvation event; on it was woven in unspeakable manner the dress of the union [namely, of the two natures]: the weaver (ἱστουργός) was the Holy Spirit, the spinner (ἔριθος) the overshadowing power from on high, the wool (ἔριον) the *original skin of Adam* (τὸ ἀρχαῖον τοῦ Ἀδὰμ κώδιον), the weft (κρόκη) the spotless flesh of the [holy] Virgin, the shuttle (κερκίς) the immeasurable grace of the bearer[?], the artist (τεχνίτης) the Logos who jumped in through the hearing.' One detail from these three texts is notable: according to the anaphora the flesh of Christ is the 'original', that is, probably paradisaical, supralapsarian flesh of Adam. The same interpretation is adopted by the translator of the *Qērellos*: 'Adam's body from the beginning'. By contrast, the reference to the 'skin' of Adam in the Greek text of Proclus probably means Adam *after* the fall (Gen 3,21). If this interpretation is correct, then the above-cited text of Cerulli, the anaphora of Our Lady Mary and Proclus in the translation of the *Qērellos* agree that they assume for Christ a body that corresponds to Adam's body before the fall. Different is the Greek Proclus. Also different are 'Die beiden gewöhnlichen äthiopischen Gregorius-Anaphoren', ed. O. Löfgren, trans. by S. Euringer (OC 30/2), Rome 1933, 89: '. . . the Word became flesh and dwelled among us and hid itself from us. He dressed himself with *corruptible* flesh and made it incorruptible. In this flesh God, who cannot be scourged, was scourged.'

46. Cf. T. Uqbit, op. cit., p. 78: 'Johannes . . . backed the "unctionists" in a synod where the speakers were Akale-Christos for the Goggiamese and Nicolaos for the Debre-Libanos. The conclusion of this was that the Goggiamese were persecuted.'

unctio the first born of the whole creation (or of all believers) (cf. Col 1,15b). The latter gained the approval of the king.[47] The controversy also continued under the two successors of King Yohannes. In the year 1721 King David III took the side of those who asserted that through the *unctio* Christ became the natural Son of the Father. He had their teaching proclaimed everywhere. The opposing party was not able to prevail at a called council and therefore betook themselves to Abuna Krestodolu and asked him about his teaching. He proclaimed: 'The faith of Alexandria(!) is that through the *unio* Christ is the only begotten Son of the Father, consubstantial with the Father; through the *unctio*, however, he is *masih*, anointed One, Messiah and the first born of the whole creation. This I too believe.'[48]

Thus something that Cyril had sought to suppress was proclaimed as 'Alexandrian' faith. The decision of King Susneos was also designated as such.[49] Some of the Ethiopian theologians thus broke through the narrow boundaries drawn by Cyril and Philoxenus and professed a doctrine that seemingly any follower of Chalcedon also could and had to defend: that in his human nature Jesus is the recipient and bearer of the Holy Spirit and his messianic gifts. The 'History of the Four Councils' or the 'Treasury of Faith', a work originating under King Claudius between 1555 and 1559, says briefly:

> He was in the womb of the Virgin Mary, our Lady . . . he nourished himself like the children and grew. *He became strong in the Holy Spirit* and became a youth precisely as a human being. He fulfilled the whole law of human beings [of human existence], with the sole exception of sin.[50]

Yet in this context much comes to light that could unbalance Ethiopian Christology: (1) with the interest in the teaching of the original state of Adam and Eve – an interest that certainly came from Jewish sources – the main effect of the anointment was declared to be the re-establishment in Christ of the original state of the human body (lack of desire, being above human vital needs); (2) the effect of the anointment with the Holy Spirit is shifted to Mary, in whom bodily and spiritual gifts were already assumed that were similar to those re-established to the original state in the body of Jesus born from her. Thus the main effect of the anointment is a physical, bodily one and is already realized in Mary in anticipation of Christ. It should be noted that this interpretation of the anointment of the Spirit is suited to letting the baptism of Jesus as a Spirit event take a secondary position behind the conception in Mary. Here the Ethiopian original-state doctrine or protology has gained its independence. That in this connection the *mia-physis* formula is never called in, other than with

---

47. I. Guidi, art. cit., p. 18.
48. I. Guidi, art. cit., p. 20.
49. I. Guidi, art. cit., p. 14.
50. Following the Ital. text of E. Cerulli in ST 204, p. 71.

Julian of Halicarnassus, indicates the strength of Jewish and Jewish–Christian ideas.

(c) The baptism of Jesus in the Jordan

An old theme in Jewish-Christian theology – again probably entering Ethiopian Christology through the Syrian route – is the baptism scene (Mt 3,13–17; Mk 1,9–11; Lk 3,21–22; also Jn 1,32–34).[51] Can we here again turn back to the dialogue, 'That Christ is One', to explain the power of this theme in Ethiopian Christology? Yet we notice immediately that in the just-named dialogue (Qērellos III) none of the gospel baptismal passages is cited.[52] Also, in other writings Cyril has a difficult time with the interpretation of the baptism of Jesus. Yet caution must be exercised in passing judgement on the treatment of the topic in his Matthew and Luke commentaries, since they are only incompletely preserved.[53] Nevertheless, the Luke commentary in the Syrian tradition reveals the patriarch's position with sufficient clarity.[54] But his John commentary speaks even more clearly, especially on Jn 1,32–34.[55] Already here he explains the descent of the Holy Spirit as he will later explain the anointment in Qērellos III (i.e., in the named dialogue). He wants to take away from the Antiochenes any ground for reading out of the interpretation of the baptism of Christ a 'receiving subject' in Christ that is not identical with the 'Logos'. So first the consubstantiality of the Holy Spirit with the Logos is emphasized, with the result that the *pneuma* could not give anything to the baptized One that he did not already have. The unity between the Logos and the humanity of Christ is so narrowly conceived that any enrichment or impartation of grace in Christ threatens to become an improvement of the Logos himself. Therefore Cyril

---

51. See here A. Grillmeier, *JdChr* I³, Index: Jesus Chr. I 2 c.

52. See B. M. Weischer, *Qērellos* III (ÄthFor 2), Index, p. 249.

53. Cf. CPG 5206–8.

54. See R. M. Tonneau, *S. Cyrilli Alexandrini Commentarii in Lucam*, Pars prior, Hom. 10, CSCO 140 (V) (Louvain 1953) 10–11: *Praeterea dicit etiam descendisse super eum Spiritum de caelo. Num in Verbum Dei nudum et sine carne dicunt descendisse Spiritum Sanctum? Num datorem Spiritus participem Spiritus sui proprii perhibent? Aut potius illud dicunt: Cum humanitus receperit Spiritum, divinitus baptizat in Spiritu Sancto? Est enim ipse unus et unicus, etiam vere Filius Dei et Patris. Beatus enim Baptista, qui a Deo edoctus erat, dicit 'Ego vidi et testimonium perhibui quia hic est Filius Dei'* (Jn 1,34). Cyril does not succeed in making sufficiently clear the role of the humanity of Christ as recipient of the Spirit in the baptism. He immediately turns again to the divinity. On Matthew cf. PG 72, 372 (nothing on Jesus' baptism); J. Reuss, *Matthäus-Kommentare aus der griechischen Kirche* (TU 61), Berlin 1957 (153–269), frag. 29, p. 162 on Mt 3,16: the Spirit is not mentioned.

55. Cyril of Alex. on Jn 1,32.33: P. E. Pusey, *Cyrilli Archiepiscopi Al. in D. Joannis Evangelium* I, Oxford 1872, 174–90.

immediately guides attention from Christ to the human race to be blessed: Christ receives the grace of the Spirit not for himself but for us out of the salvation-economic intention of God (οἰκονομικῶς . . . διὰ τὴν τῆς ἀνθρωπότητος χρείαν).[56] The *pneuma* himself also assumes vis-à-vis Christ the figure of humility and gentleness, namely, that of the dove, in order to show *luce clarius* that it brings no elevation of existence to the baptized One.[57] Unfortunately Cyril fails to leave room here for a christological pneumatology. The messianic status of Jesus, which must also be possible in a Logos Christology, can no longer experience an enlightening substantiation. The pneumatic equipping of the human being Jesus, so important an element of the image of Christ, must necessarily come up short.

Thus Cyril cannot have contributed anything to the fact that in Ethiopian theology and liturgy the baptism of Christ has a special position. We need not look long for a possible source of the stimulation. Philoxenus of Mabbug, though substantially in agreement with Cyril of Alexandria in the interpretation of the baptism of Christ, can jump in here with the extant fragments of his commentaries on Matthew and Luke. For in them he devotes a relatively large space to the baptism of Christ.[58] His commentary on the prologue of John also mentions the baptismal event. In the enumeration of the mysteries of Jesus' life, whose significance for baptismal instruction he emphasizes, the baptism of Christ is expressly named, though here with an explicit monastic spiritual intention:[59]

> And he obeyed John as a prophet, and without needing it, he was also baptized by him with the rest of the Jews. And he was led by the Spirit into the wilderness and he was

---

56. Ibid., Pusey I, p. 190,3–4.

57. Thus in the John commentary (loc. cit.) Cyril already has a connection of Mt 11,29b (ὅτι πραΰς εἰμι) with the description of the remaining or resting of the Spirit 'in the figure of the most gentle animal' over Jesus at the baptism (Jn 1,32), yet in a significant departure from and expansion of the same connection in Syriac and Armenian sources. See Pusey I, pp. 189,15–190,4: in this humble figure the *pneuma* is like the one who said: 'Learn from me, because I am gentle and humble' (189,18–21). Cf. for the Syr. and Arm. sources: G. Winkler, 'Ein bedeutsamer Zusammenhang zwischen der Erkenntnis und Ruhe in Mt 11,27–29 und dem Ruhen des Geistes auf Jesus am Jordan', *Mus* 96 (1983), 267–326, esp. 302ff.

58. See J. W. Watt, *Philoxenus of Mabbug. Fragments of the Commentary on Matthew and Luke* (CSCO 392 [T], 393 [V]), Louvain 1978. On the following see A. Grillmeier, 'Die Taufe Christi und die Taufe der Christen', op. cit., pp. 137–75.

59. See Philoxène de Mabbog, *Commentaire du prologue johannique* (Ms. Br. Mus. Add. 14,534), édité et traduit par A. de Halleux (CSCO 380 [T], 381 [V]), Louvain 1977. Here according to (V), p. 158.

tempted by the devil, and in three struggles at the same time he overcame the passions as well as the demons.

Besides this mention of the baptism in an enumeration in the style of the *regula fidei*, we also find it in a text that already plays the role of a *symbolum*, even if a private one, in his letter to Emperor Zeno.[60] In it we read:

> We confess . . . He was baptized by John in the Jordan [Lk 3,21–22], and the Father testified that He is His Beloved Son. I recognize the Trinity in the Jordan: the Father Who speaks; the Son Who is baptized; and the Holy Ghost Who shows . . . The One Whom I have seen in baptism, I have acknowledged in the womb [of the Virgin], and the One Whom I have found in the womb, I contemplate stretched on the Cross. One of the Trinity was in the womb; one of the Trinity in baptism; one of the Trinity on the Cross.

Thus, in contrast to Cyril of Alexandria, Philoxenus is not afraid to speak of the baptism of Christ in detail and even to include it in the *symbolum*. Yet we must note that here too, in the fragmentarily extant explications of the baptismal scene according to Matthew and Luke, he avoids two things: (1) even mentioning in any way adoptionist initiatives of the older Syrian Christology; (2) simply assuming an enrichment of Christ, not even of his humanity, through the Spirit or gifts of the Spirit. It is true that even for him a new beginning in Christ himself is given with the baptism of Jesus. Philoxenus first looks back to the eternal 'primordial beginning', the birth of the Son from the bosom of the Father. Also a new beginning, however, was the existence of the Logos as human embryo in the Virgin, his entrance by human birth into the world. But this earthly life of Jesus was marked at first by a restriction, namely, by the subjection to the law that Christ adopted with circumcision. With the baptism, however, something new comes: Jesus overcomes the law; he is revealed as the 'firstborn' (cf. Col 1,15) and as a 'new human being'. The baptism is a turning-point in the history of salvation. Now it is no longer a matter of the fulfilment of the 'law' but of testifying to the fact that with the revelation of the Trinity the fulfilment of the law has come. Jesus

---

60. See A. A. Vaschalde, *Three Letters of Philoxenus*, Rome 1902, C. The Letter to Emperor Zeno (pp. 118–26), 122–23. The baptism of Christ is also treated in the part of *Liber Heraclidis* that Luise Abramowski has attributed to one Ps.-Nestorius, who argued with Philoxenus; see L. Abramowski, 'Ps.-Nestorius und Philoxenus von Mabbug', *ZKG* 77 (1966), 122–25; F. Nau, *Le Livre d'Héraclide de Damas*, Paris 1910, nos. 71–72, pp. 61–63.

takes over the 'new service of the Spirit'. He stands in the new order of the Spirit, which will shape his whole earthly life from the walk into the wilderness until the ascension into heaven. It is true that another birth occurs here. The Lord emerges again from a 'womb', but now not only in his own reality but with the body of the church. Thus the real winner through this blessing by the Spirit in the baptism is not Christ himself but the church. The Christ spiritually born in the baptism can become the head of the church and also the founder of a new discipleship. For Jesus goes from the Jordan into the wilderness to battle Satan. The new way of life of the perfect discipleship of Christ is introduced.[61]

Although Philoxenus with his firm Christology from above can only with abhorrence think of older Syrian representatives of a baptismal adoptionism, the fact of the baptism of Christ still holds a very important place in his theology and above all also in his proclamation, that is, in the *symbolum* and in the *regula fidei*. Therefore he takes seriously other models of the Syrian tradition.[62] But because this place in the *symbolum* has until now been demonstrable only for Syria and in dependence on it in Armenia, any appearance of the baptism of Christ in Ethiopian *symbola* or comparable texts can only be explained on that basis. We now turn to the position of the baptism of Christ in the Ethiopian church, in its theology and piety.

(aa) The baptism of Jesus in Ethiopian formulas of faith
We find a first formulation in the *Book of the Light* (Maṣḥafa Berhān) of the negus Zarʾa Yāʿqob (1434–68). The king orders the distribution of the holy Eucharist to people who have no 'spiritual father' and to foreigners. The priest must first require of them the confession of faith, which in its brevity is interesting:

> I am neither Jew nor Gentile nor a heretic; I believe in the Father, the Son and the Holy Spirit; I believe in the birth of Christ out of Mary, who is twofold a Virgin, *in his baptism*,

---

61. Cf. A. Grillmeier, art. cit., pp. 146–56.
62. See G. Winkler, 'Zur frühchristlichen Tauftradition in Syrien und Armenien unter Einbezug der Taufe Jesu', *OstKSt* 27 (1978), 281–306; eadem, 'Eine bemerkenswerte Stelle im armenischen Glaubensbekenntnis: Credimus in Sanctum Spiritum qui descendit in Jordanem proclamavit missum', *OrChr* 63 (1979), 130–62; eadem, *Das armenische Initiationsrituale. Entwicklungsgeschichtliche und liturgievergleichende Untersuchung der Quellen des 3. bis 10. Jahrhunderts* (OCA 217), Rome 1982; also eadem, *Mus* 96 (1983), 302–18.

his crucifixion, his resurrection, his ascension and his new coming. For all this my witness is this church.[63]

As the next formula of confession we have the famous *Confessio Claudii* (1540–58; Ludolf: 1541–59),[64] which was written in the year 1555 or more likely 1558. Claudius appeals to the 'kings of the Israelites' as his predecessors:

> We believe in one God and in his only begotten Son Jesus Christ, who is his Word and his Might, his Counsellor and his Wisdom. He was with him before the world was created. At the end of days, however, he came to us, yet not so as to abandon the throne of his divinity: he became a human being through the Holy Spirit out of the holy Virgin Mary; and he was *baptized in the Jordan at the age of thirty years*; and he was a perfect human being (*et baptizatus fuit in Jordane trigesimo anno; et erat vir perfectus*); he was hung on the cross in the days of Pontius Pilate. He suffered, died and was buried and rose on the third day. Then on the fortieth day he ascended with glory into heaven and sits at the right hand of his Father. And he will come again in glory to judge the living and the dead, and of his kingdom there will be no end.
>
> We believe in the Holy Spirit, the Lord and Giver of life, who went out from the Father. And we believe in the one baptism, the forgiveness of sins. And we hope for the resurrection of the dead and the coming life in eternity. Amen.

When this creed emphasizes that the incarnation is not a giving up of the divinity, then that could be an indication that already in the sixteenth century the way was prepared among the Ethiopians for the *kenosis* doctrine that then in the seventeenth century under King Fāsiladas (1632–67) was taught by Eur Za-Jyasūs or Za-Jyasūs the blind from the party of the Qebātoč.[65] With the words 'he was a perfect human being' we are perhaps referred to the anti-Apollinarian and anti-Eutychian polemic that found expression in the Chalcedonian confession to the 'perfection' of Christ's human existence with body and soul. It is more

---

63. Cf. C. Conti Rossini, *Il Libro della Luce del Negus Zaŕa Yāqob (Maṣḥafa Berhān)* (CSCO 251, T. I, B. I), p. 30,15–23. – Ibid. in B. II, p. 71,3–35, a longer text from the Ethiopic *Didascalia* is cited (Harden, pp. 178–79) in which the Negus so to speak holds the *regula fidei* to be the substance of his catechesis in the *Book of the Light*. Expressly mentioned in it is the baptism of Christ, which he 'as a human being' received 'while he was God' (lines 10–12)! Here again we have a Syrian testimony to the baptism of Christ! – For further references to the baptism of Christ by the same emperor see K. Wendt, *Das Maṣḥafa Milād (Liber Nativitatis)* (CSCO 222 [V]), T. I, reading 2, p. 27,8–9; (CSCO 236 [V]), T. II, reading 13, p. 59,9–18 (baptism of Jesus as witness to the Trinity).

64. Text in Eth. and Latin in Ludolf, *Historia Aethiopica* vol. II (1691), N. XXIX: *Confessio fidei Claudii Regis Aethiopiae*, pp. 237–41; here p. 238.

65. See on this the already mentioned excursus 1 in F. A. Dombrowski, *Ṭānāsee 106*, pp. 290–95.

likely, however, that this alludes already to the theme of the re-establishment of the 'perfect human being' in the impartation of grace to Christ by the Spirit. For there is obviously a close connection between the baptism of Jesus and this confession, which otherwise had not previously existed in patristic writings except in the Syrian tradition, to which we could already make multiple references. In Jesus the protological-soteriological significance of baptism is revealed: the first-born, the new Adam, the perfect man,[66] which in Philoxenus together with other Syrians becomes the emphatic recommendation of the monastic ideal. The baptism of Christ has an important place! In Christ it means the return to the original state.

(bb) The baptism of Jesus in Ethiopian anaphoras

A mention of the baptism of Christ in the symbol of faith can be equated with the emphasis in anaphoras in either the anamnesis or the epiclesis. We find relatively numerous references. Thus the 'Anaphora of St James, the Brother of the Lord'[67] places side by side the descent of the Holy Spirit 'in the form of a dove on our Lord Jesus Christ at the Jordan River' and 'over his holy apostles in the form of a tongue of fire'. And this descent is supposed to become effective again in the Eucharist! In the 'little' Cyril anaphora we read: 'In the thirtieth year he [the Lord] stood in the middle of the Jordan in order to complete the incarnation', and indeed through the 'third birth', that is, the anointment through the Holy Spirit to *primogenitus omnis creaturae*.[68] The Ethiopian Epiphanius anaphora, by contrast, emphasizes the rebirth out of sin.[69] Further testimonies to the meaning of Christ's baptism in the Ethiopian church are

---

66. Cf. also the 'Mirror of Insight', chap. III: E. Cerulli, *Scritti Teologici Etiopici* (ST 204), p. 179. Here it is emphasized, on the one hand, that Christ was born as *Uomo completo* but, on the other, it speaks of *perfetta Umanità*, which is realized in virginal conception and birth in and from Mary. Then reference is made to the *mia physis* of Christ (p. 180). Cf. the above-cited text on the food of Jesus! – The baptism of Jesus and its significance for Adam(!) is also referred to in the *Qalēmentos* T. I, chap. VII 4: *ROC* 6 (1911), 174. Cf. also *ROC* 22 (1920–21), 113.

67. See S. Euringer, 'Die Anaphora des hl. Jakobus, des Bruders des Herrn', *OrChr* 4 (1914), 11 (epiclesis).

68. See O. Löfgren and S. Euringer, 'Die beiden aethiopischen Anaphoren "des heiligen Cyrillus, Patriarchen von Alexandrien"', *ZSem* 9 (1933/34) (44–86), 46, with comm., 51.

69. See S. Euringer, 'Die äthiopische Anaphora des hl. Epiphanius, Bischofs der Insel Cypern', *OrChr* 23 (1927), 113.

'The Ethiopian Dioscorus Anaphora'[70] and that of St Athanasius.[71] Obviously the baptism of Christ received a stronger accent in the Ethiopian liturgy than in the Syrian anaphoras, in which out of nineteen formulas there are only three that mention the baptism of Christ.[72]

Thus we cannot overlook the fact that not only Ethiopian theology but also liturgy and piety are shaped in a special way by the *mysterium* of the baptism of Christ. In addition there is its position in the whole church year, which in significance towers above Christmas (Leddat) and Christ's circumcision (Gezrat).[73] Nothing less than a broadening and deepening of the baptism theme is represented by the regarding of baptism as a 'new birth' (of Christ, of the believers), which was probably also influenced by or adopted from Syria. Considered christologically, this soon demands a listing of a variable kind: (1) birth from the Father before time (with an anti-Arian pointedness); (2) birth from Mary; (3) the new birth from baptism. This ordering could be variously interpreted. In consequence of Philoxenus of Mabbug and other Syrians, with baptism and the journey into the wilderness Jesus became free from life under the law, which precisely means birth for life from the Spirit. On this Philoxenus of Mabbug builds the typical Syrian doctrine of perfection.[74] The Ethiopians adopt such suggestions but deal more freely with them. They speak now of a twofold,[75] now of a threefold birth, but by the latter they mean

---

70. See O. Löfgren and S. Euringer, 'Die äthiopische Dioscorus-Anaphora', *Le Monde Oriental* 26/27 (1932/33) (229–55), 245.

71. See S. Euringer, 'Die äthiopische Anaphora des hl. Athanasius', *OrChr* 24 (1927), 277. In the Ethiopian Anaphora of Our Lady Mary, which S. Euringer has edited according to the *editio princeps* of 1548, in § 23 a confession to the Trinity and esp. to the divinity of the Holy Spirit is connected with the reference to baptism and Pentecost. See *Katholik* 96 (1916), 255; on p. 258 baptism by John and temptation are mentioned. This is not found in the edition according to the 16th cent. Vatican ms. in *OrChr* 34 (1937), 63–102, 248–62.

72. See *Anaphorae Syriacae* II, f. 3, Rome 1973: H. G. Codrington, *Anaphora Caelestini Romani*, p. 255 (dependent on the Basil and Gregory liturgies) (date: *c*. 614); ibid., J. M. Sauget, *Anaphora S. Petri Apostoli Tertia*, p. 291: all the mysteries of Jesus' life with the baptism. – Ibid., A. Raes, *Anaphora S. Thomae Apostoli* (12th cent.?), 'Anamnesis', p. 341.

73. Cf. Fr. Heyer, *Die Kirche Äthiopiens*, Berlin–New York 1971, 86.

74. See A. Grillmeier, 'Die Taufe Christi und die Taufe der Christen', pp. 143, 168–70 with references to further investigations (G. Winkler, S. Brock, W. Strothmann, etc.). Philoxenus already had predecessors, e.g., Clement of Alex., Aphrahat (6th instruction), Makarios/Symeon, John of Apamea, but esp. Ephraem, *Hymn. de Ecclesia* XXXVI,3: E. Beck, CSCO 198/199, Louvain 1960, 90–91 (Syr.); 88 (trans.).

75. See the great hymn of praise to the birth from the Father (first birth) and the birth from the Virgin (second birth) in 'Marienharfe' XXXI, §§ 72–78: S. Euringer, *OrChr* 25 (1928), 97–98.

either events for Christ or for the believers.[76] Through the connection of anointment–baptism–new birth, the Ethiopians understood how to develop a messianic Christology that is more differentiated than that of the Syrians.

(d) Names and numbers

In Ethiopian theology the knowledge and interpretation of names,[77] especially the names of angels, is an old legacy from Judaism and Jewish-Christian magic literature.[78] Words of gnostic origin cannot be established. The fact that magic formulas could acquire such a meaning is associated by W. H. Worrell with the serious dangers to human life in the regions there. Yet it is a question here not only of magic but also of language-symbolic interpretations that could gain value as theological assertions. We will highlight only details that concern Christology.

(aa) Solomon-Jesus: This connection is already familiar to us from the *KN. Solomon* read backwards produces secret words for Jesus with various transformations, such as *Nemlos* (as basic form), *Nemlosāwi, Neblosāwi, Mēlos, Mēlyos, Mēdyos, Lamēlos, Malālyos, Milālyos, Malayālos, Malālis*.[79] In

---

76. See E. Hammerschmidt, *Äthiopien*, Wiesbaden 1967, 114: 'Later the monks of Däbrä Libanos developed the doctrine of the "three births" (*sost ledät*): (1) the *generatio aeterna*, through which the Logos is the *unigenitus* of the Father; (2) the *nativitas ex Virgine*, through which he is *primogenitus*, and (3) the *nativitas per unctionem Spiritus Sancti*, through which he is *primogenitus omnis creaturae*. The strict unctionists (who were then called Karročč) set this view over against the conception of the "two births" (*hulätt ledät*): (1) the *aeterna* from the Father and (2) that from the Virgin.' On the threefold birth of Christians: 'Äth. Anaphora d. hl. Athanasius', § 31: S. Euringer, *OrChr* 24 (1927), 259 (baptism–Eucharist–repentance with reference to the Jordan).

77. See A. Grillmeier, *JdChr* I³, 144–47; *CCT* I², 41–44; on the name *Jesus*, ibid., pp. 62–68 and 96–107, respectively.

78. Cf. W. H. Worrell, 'Studien zum abessinischen Zauberwesen', *ZAss* 23 (1909), 149–83; 24 (1910), 59–96; 29 (1914/15), 85–141; S. Strelcyn, *Prières magiques éthiopiennes pour délier les charmes* (Rocznik Orientalistyczny 18), Warsaw 1955; idem, 'La magie éthiopienne', in *ACIStEt*, pp. 147–65; esp. p. 150: 'les noms magiques du Christ' (names of the divine essence, expressed by Solomon; names of the nails of the cross); S. Euringer, 'Das Netz Salomons', *ZSem* 6 (1928), 77–100, 179–99, 301–14; 7 (1929), 68–85, 82–83: an alphabetized list of the occurring names and magic words; J. Tubiana, 'A propos du "Livre des Mystères du Ciel et de la Terre"', in *ACIStEt*, pp. 403–8; according to E. Cerulli (ibid., 409), this book is part of the literature that was inspired by late Gnosticism, a development that is to be observed especially in northern Ethiopia in the 14th cent. Cf. also E. Ullendorff, *Ethiopia and the Bible*, London 1968, 79–82.

79. Cf. O. Löfgren and S. Euringer, 'Die beiden äthiopischen Anaphoren des hl. Cyrillus', *ZSem* 9 (1933/34), 84.

the form *Mēlos*, with the meaning of 'sword of fire', 'Solomon–Christ' has also penetrated individual anaphoras.[80]

(bb) The name *Jesus* and its number symbolism: Typical above all is the number symbolism connected with the Yud, the first letter of the name *Jesus*. Yud has the numeric value of 10. This connection is found already in the *Didascalia Apostolorum* from the third century and is rather detailed in the extant Syriac version, chap. 26.[81] It concerns the question of the validity of the law, following the words of the Sermon on the Mount: 'Do not think that I have come to abolish the law or the prophets; I have come to fulfil' (Mt 5,17.18–20). A solution to the problem was found when the law is narrowed to the 'ten sayings', that is, the Ten Commandments (Ex 34,28; Dt 4,13), and the 'second legislation' after the worshipping of the golden calf is contrasted with it:

> The *Law* therefore is indissoluble, but the *second legislation* is temporary, and is dissoluble. Now the Law is the ten utterings and the judgements.[82]

The imperishability of the latter is founded on Mt 5,18 and its salvific power assured by the fact that the connection with the name *Jesus* is established through a number game: the first letter, the Yud, means ten. This number is the symbol of totality.[83] This interpretation is adopted from the *Didascalia* into the *Constitutiones Apostolorum* (*CAp*) (4th cent.),[84] and through its incorporation into the *Didascalia Aethiopica* it enters the tradition of the Ethiopian church.[85] In the fifteenth century the writings of Zar'a Yā'qob adopt this symbolism, several times with reference to the *Didascalia*, especially in substantiation of the Sabbath

---

80. See the epiclesis in the Anaphora of Jacob of Sarug, § 35, OC 33, p. 95, quoted in Löfgren/Euringer, art. cit., p. 83: '. . . may Mēlos be dispatched, that fearful sword of fire, and appear over this bread and cup and complete this Eucharist'!

81. See A. Vööbus, *The Didascalia Apostolorum in Syriac* II (CSCO 408 [V]), chap. XXV, p. 223,14–17: 'Indeed, you know that He gave a simple and pure and holy law of life, wherein our Saviour set His name. Indeed, [when] He spoke the ten utterings, He pointed out Jesus – for Ten represents Yud but Yud is the beginning of the name of Jesus.' See op. cit., I: CSCO 402 (V), chap. IX, p. 99 = Harden, *The Ethiopic Didascalia*, 47–48.

82. Op. cit. II, chap. XXVI: CSCO 408, p. 224,13–15; on the meaning of the Ten Commandments cf. *KN*, § 42: Bezold, 34–36.

83. See J. de Fraine, art. 'Zahl', in *Bibel-Lexikon*, ed. H. Haag (Einsiedeln, etc. ²1968), cols. 1917–20.

84. *CAp* II 26: Funk I, pp. 102–3.

85. *Did. aeth.*, ch. VIII: Harden, p. 48: 'The beginning of the name of Jesus is iota, by number, ten. Hear, O thou Holy Church, the Congregation of people which hath been founded on iota, which was manifested in the law, and hath kept the faith, and believed in our Lord Jesus Christ, and been a guide to the knowledge of the word iota, and hath stood fast in the perfection of His glory.' Thus it gives the relationship between Jesus, the law (represented by the Ten Commandments) and the church, which is built on the knowledge of this iota.

commandment, the third of the ten sayings (commandments).[86] It belongs to the indissoluble part of the law! To destroy the Sabbath means to destroy the name *Jesus* and thus the *mysterium* of the Trinity, indeed one's own Christianism.[87] The king himself continues to utilize this number symbolism more than his own sources do. He relates the 'ten sayings' to the Son as *the* Word and can thus hold up Jesus as the content of the Decalogue, which is itself a summary of the Pentateuch.[88] This is far from all magic, which is expressly fought in the Maṣḥafa Berhān.[89]

The theme 'name of Jesus = law' has its mariological version. Mary, the mother of Jesus, is often called tabernacle, holy of holies, Ark of the Covenant, in which the tablets of the law, the sign of the covenant, namely, Jesus, are preserved. Therefore Mary is called 'bearer of the Ten Commandments'.[90] Cf. the hymn 'Akkōnū Beʿesī, V.XXV: 'Temple of the Torah, Mary, and gospel structure that the Paraclete visited'.[91] Cf. also the 'Marienharfe' XVII, 38: 'Mary the second dwelling, the holy of holies',[92] which refers to the Ethiopian church building; further: Mary = tablets of the law and of the covenant, on which the ten sayings stand, written with the fingers of Sabaoth.[93]

(cc) Jesus the 'beginning': This name means the continuation of the name theology of the first centuries.[94] The history of influence of Gen 1,1; Jn 1,1 and Col 1,15 continues. The book *KN* devotes considerable attention to this title.

In § 102 (Bezold, 115) Ps 109(110),3 and Gen 1,1 are interpreted christologically: 'Note now: "in the beginning" means: through Christ; the "beginning" means Christ.' Then

---

86. *Inter alia*, Maṣḥafa Berhān, T. I, B. I, reading for 1st Sabb.: CSCO 251 (V), p. 9; ibid., reading for 2nd Sabb.: CSCO 251, pp. 30–31; cf. also pp. 33, 36; likewise Maṣḥafa Milād (Liber Nativitatis), T. I, reading on the 29th of Genbot: CSCO 222 (V), pp. 84–87.

87. Maṣḥafa Berhān, T. I, B. I: CSCO 251, pp. 32,21–33,15.

88. Ibid., reading for 2nd Sabb.: CSCO 251, p. 34,25–27: 'Con quel suo verbo, che è il Figlio suo, pronunciò il Padre le dieci Parole mentre tutto il popolo sentiva.' L. Ricci on this, ibid., n. 4: 'Il giuoco dell'equazione voce = parola = verbo = comandamento è permesso nell'etiopico dall'uso di un unico termine, *qāl* "voce, parola", che esprime quelle nozioni.'

89. According to W. H. Worrell, art. cit., p. 164, the name *Jesus* is adapted to ancient magic. The Negus, however, is pursuing not a magical but a theological purpose here. He is, rather, fighting against magic. Cf. Maṣḥafa Berhān, T. I, B. II, reading for 1st Sun.: CSCO 251 (V), p. 64,1–5: 'Questo Libro della Luce tratta della abolizione delle pratiche magiche, che si facevano nel paese d'Etiopia, ed insegna il culto unico del Signore, senza alcuna intrusione di altri culti nè per computo di stelle nè per guida di uccelli.' Thus it goes against horoscopes and augury. A good picture of the occurrence of magic and the defence against it is offered by 'Die Marienharfe' XII, 44: S. Euringer, OrChr 25/26 (1928/29), 89–90.

90. A. Grohmann, *Äthiopische Marienhymnen* (*ASAW* 33, 4), Leipzig 1919, 125 (CVI), with commentary, pp. 279–80, and numerous patristic sources and parallels.

91. Op. cit., p. 349; commentary, p. 374.

92. S. Euringer, *OrChr* 25/26 (1928/29), 88.

93. Ibid., XXVII, 6, p. 251. Ibid., XXXVI, 61 and 66: pp. 268–69; ibid., XLIII, 49: OrChr 27 (1930), 213–14. Cf. in the prayer of the hours 'Gateway of Light' 2–3: PO 33, p. 279.

94. See A. Grillmeier, *JdChr* I³, 148–50; *CCT* I², 45.

follow 1 Jn 1,1–2; Acts 1,1; Mk 1,1 in the translation: 'The beginning of the gospel is Jesus Christ, the Son of God; this means: Christ was the promise for the prophets and apostles, and we have shared his grace' (ibid.). To be noted is the reference to the creation power of God, which is not typically Jewish.

Also Christ as 'beginning' provides the nexus to the 'virginal conception', which in Ethiopian piety receives an extraordinarily strong accent. It is understood as the creative act of God. Thus in the Maṣḥafa Berhān T. II, B. III, reading for 3rd Sun., h. 6: CSCO 262 (V), p. 22,14–22. Here Prov 8,22 is withdrawn from the Jews and Arians, in that it is interpreted not as the creation of the pre-existent One but as the origin of Christ's human nature in Mary. Do we have here a Christian tradition that was adopted into the Koran, Sura 3,45–48?

3,45:   *At that time the angels spoke:*
O Mary, Allah proclaims to you a word from himself:
his name is Messiah 'Isā, Son of Mary.

47:      *She spoke:*
My LORD, where am I supposed to get a child,
since a man does not touch me!
He spoke:
So be it! Allah does what he will!
When he has decided on a work,
he says to it, 'Let it be', and it is . . .'[95]

(e) The mysticism of the symbols

Inspired by the Bible – and here especially by the Song of Songs,[96] which is interpreted in an Alexandrian, allegorical manner – the Ethiopian church shows a special fondness for symbols and pictures, whose number is hardly to be grasped. They were interpreted more lyrically and mystically than strictly rationally. We present only a few examples:

(aa) The symbol of the fire: The point of contact appearing again and again is the vision of Moses on Mount Horeb (Ex 3,2–3). The *KN* has Moses say: 'I saw a thornbush on Mount Sinai, which consuming fire did not burn up.' This fire is either unapproachable divinity itself or the divinity of the Son, which is united with human flesh, symbolized by the wood of the thornbush. This image is found in Cyril, Nestorius and Babai the Great.[97] It is typical of the *KN* that this image is immediately interpreted in a christological-mariological way. In Cyril the fire of the divinity permeates the human nature of Christ. Now the divine fire (= the God conceived in the womb of the mother) is placed over against Mary herself: 'The interpretation of this fire is the divinity, the Son of God. The wood of the thornbush, however, which burns while its leaves are not scorched, is Mary' (*KN* § 96: Bezold, p. 105). A typical carrying out of this motif is seen in the Ethiopian *Song of Songs Commentary*

---

95. Cf. C. Schedl, *Muhammad und Jesus*, Vienna–Freiburg–Basel 1978, p. 422 with 425–26.

96. Cf. S. Euringer, *Die Auffassung des Hohenliedes bei den Abessiniern*, Leipzig 1900. To the dependence on the OT is added the Syrian influence. See R. Murray, *Symbols of Church and Kingdom. A Study in Early Syriac Tradition*, Cambridge 1975, 159–204; already utilized in vol. I of this work. See the index there.

97. See Cyril of Alex., *Hom. pasch.* 17: PG 77, 781C; *Quod unus est Christus*, 55, 2: *Qērellos* III, p. 111; Nestorius, *Liber Heraclidis*, Bedjan 234–35; Nau, 141; Babai the Great in L. I. Scipioni, *Ricerche sulla cristologia del 'Libro di Eraclide' di Nestorio* (Paradosis 11), Fribourg 1956, 149.

according to some codices in Berlin and London on SS 2,8–9: 'The Logos, the Son, my brother, leapt between the mountains. Bent down, he looks through the net and sees through the window. He unites the burning beauty of his divinity with *your* flesh [and thus not so much with his own flesh!]. Mary, since we have found confidence through him, we name you the wood of the fiery litter [ark].'[98]

One example from *poetry*, the 'Flower Song', V.XXIII:[99] 'Your miracle, Mariam, was proclaimed in the Torah / When you made a covenant with the Divinity, thornbush, / You whom Moses, the archprophet, saw. / Shade me with your branches, green tree! / May your blossom, the fire [which means Christ], burn up the thorn[shrub] of my sin.' Cf. also *KN*, § 97: Bezold, p. 106, which speaks of Christ the 'fiery coal' for which Mary represents the smokebox.

The testimony of the *anaphoras*: The symbolism of the 'fire of the divinity' in the womb of Mary leads here to the Eucharist as the *tremendum mysterium*. This is the topic, for example, in the 'Great Cyril Anaphora',[100] which in § 27 speaks of Mēlos, the blazing fire. This is naturally a good image for the epiclesis; the Eucharist itself becomes the fiery coal that the believers must accept into themselves in a worthy manner (§§ 29, 30). – 'The Anaphora of our Lady Mary' has the same connection of fire–Mary–Eucharist.[101] – 'The Anaphora of the Holy Evangelist John':[102] 'There dwells in the daughter of the flesh the one who sits enthroned over the cherubim; the consuming fire clothes itself with flesh, and the fine Spirit shrouds itself with a body.'

The 'Marienharfe' ('Argānona Weddāsē), which overflows with images, says in § 37: 'Rejoice, O thornshrub, you who bear the terrible fiery flame.'[103] We close with the Maṣḥafa Berhān:[104] 'But Mary . . . is great and worthy of honour, since her womb did not burn up with the fire of the divinity, which she bore for nine months . . .' It was different for Mount Sinai, which with its trees and rocks was consumed by fire.

(bb) Similarly abundant is the *light symbolism* that the Maṣḥafa Berhān has produced on the special theme: 'Book of the Light because Christ is called light' (cf. Jn 8,12; 12,36) (CSCO 251, p. 9 and p. 63). Immediately the christological symbol is also extended mariologically, as in the 'Marienharfe' § 8: 'O tent of the light'; § 11: 'O Virgin, tent of the light, cover of the lightning of the glory of the only begotten of Sabaoth.'[105]

Thus 'light' and 'fire', adopted from the Old and New Testaments, are the favourite symbols of the divinity and of deification. Earthly fire is only the point of departure. '. . . it is explorable and measurable. Therefore it would not be right if we wanted to compare the fire of the divinity with the earthly explorable and measurable fire.'[106] The symbol appears here in place of the abstract concept in order to express the unity of the divinity: 'The Father

---

98. S. Euringer, *Die Auffassung des Hohenliedes bei den Abessiniern*, Leipzig 1900, 36, with further explanations: the *window* refers to the revelation of the Logos by the prophets, the *net* to the preaching of the apostles.

99. A. Grohmann, *Äth. Marienhymnen*, p. 77.

100. O. Löfgren and S. Euringer, *ZSem* 9 (1933/34), pp. 56–58.

101. S. Euringer, *Katholik* 96 (1916), § 21, p. 254; § 32, pp. 256–57; § 36, p. 258; § 54, p. 264: the believer receives 'not earthly bread but the fire of the divinity'.

102. S. Euringer, OC 33, 1 (Rome 1934), § 36, p. 27.

103. S. Euringer, *OrChr* 27 (1930), 211.

104. Maṣḥafa Berhān, T. I, B. I, reading for 2nd Sabb. 7^h: CSCO 251, p. 38,24–26.

105. S. Euringer, *OrChr* 27 (1930), 203–4.

106. S. Euringer, 'Die äth. Anaphora unserer Herrin Maria', § 21, *Katholik* 96 (1916), 254.

is fire, the Son is fire and the Holy Spirit is fire: the fire of life that [comes] from empyreum is one.'[107]

(cc) An especially favourite image is Christ the 'pilot of the soul'. It is formed as a prayer to Christ that is prayed after communion in all celebrations of the Eucharist.[108] The image is also familiar to the Coptic liturgy.[109] Here it can also be related to the everyday life of people who know themselves under the protection of Christ. Yet it is understood in the context of Christ as lamb and doctor and this more from the viewpoint of salvation.[110] The image is broadened mariologically and ecclesiologically, in the 'Marienharfe' XXX, 32: 'Ship [= Mary] that the wave does not reach: the pilot on it is Jesus Christ, who steers the world out of the surf of sin by means of the rudder [?] of his holy gospel; but the captain of the ship is the Father, who is over all, and the calmer of the seas is the power of the [Holy] Spirit, who protects the ship of virginity, so that it will not founder!'[111] Perhaps we should think here of the *navis ecclesiae*, whose type is Mary.

Thus this image of the 'pilot of the soul' can be established here for Syria, Egypt and Ethiopia. So what E. Lanne says about the 'Great Euchologium of the White Monastery' may be especially true of this image: 'Certain prayers that contain it allow one especially easily to substantiate the filiation that exists between the Alexandrian and Ethiopian liturgies and to stress the considerable influence exerted by the Syrian rite on the Egyptian.'[112]

(f) Retrospective

The result of this overview of the variations of messianism in Ethiopian Christology and piety is sufficiently assured: we have here an expression of Christian tradition in Jewish-Christian form that had not otherwise existed in the universal church and which has persisted until today.

(1) Unusually strong is the continuity with the Old Testament in the self-understanding of one's history and in the origin and mission above all of the messianic kingdom. Being *verus Israel* is what the Christians of

---

107. Ibid., § 29, p. 256, where still more images are added and followed by the *Nicaenum*.

108. See: O. Löfgren and S. Euringer, 'Die "große" Cyrillus-Anaphora', *ZSem* 9 (1933/34), § 41, p. 73 (text); p. 86 (commentary); 'Epiphanius-Anaphora', § 79: S. Euringer, *OrChr* 23 (1927), 133 with 140; J. M. Harden, *The Anaphoras of the Ethiopic Liturgy*, London 1928, 66: 'Pilot of the soul, Guide of the righteous, and Glory of the saints'. Harden refers to the *Testamentum Domini*, ed. Rahmani, p. 49.

109. See E. Lanne, 'Le grand euchologe du Monastère Blanc', PO 28, 377: 'Si je t'appelle nautonnier, c'est que tu es le pilote (κυβερνήτης) de ceux qui naviguent (πλεῖν) sur mer (θάλασσα) et sur les fleuves . . .'

110. Cf. ibid., p. 373,23.

111. S. Euringer, *OrChr* 25/26 (1928/29), 259.

112. E. Lanne, PO 28, p. 275.

Ethiopia sought to realize, not only in the faith, in observance, in worship, but also in their culture.

(2) Pushing to the foreground in teaching and proclamation are christological themes that can only be understood as the ongoing influence of Jewish-Christian initiatives, such as, especially, the emphasis on 'anointment' and 'baptism'.

(3) How far the formation of the church year is affected by this will have to be discussed later. Here we recall only the special position of the baptism in the Jordan, which again also results in certain relationships with the Koran.[113] It is not for nothing that even the saints of the Old Testament are so often mentioned in texts and celebrated liturgically.[114]

(4) Also peculiarly determined by the Old Testament is the veneration of the mother of Jesus, the Messiah, in which the virginity receives an unusually strong accent (which again also creates a connection with Islam).[115] The theme of the virginity of the conception and birth of Jesus in and from Mary is related to the motif of the original state of humankind in paradise and its re-establishment, a theme that was very familiar to Judaism. In the KN the biblical succession of generations leads first to Mary, as the image of the 'pearl' shows (§ 68), and the descent from David is especially stressed (§ 71). What in the universal church is the theme of 'Mary, type of the church' becomes in Ethiopia 'Mary, the image of the heavenly Zion' (§ 95: Bezold, p. 102). The connection 'Mary–church' is effusively celebrated in the 'Marienharfe' VIII, §§ 51–56.[116] When the 'Marienharfe' XXXVI, 58 says: 'O net [= Mary] that gathers up the family of fish, those are the souls of the saints, the community of the three names',[117] then the last designation contains good early-church ecclesiology. Thus what in the universal church is the antithesis Adam : Christ becomes here the juxtaposition Adam/Eve : Mary: 'Adam was formed in order to bring you as fruit, and Eve was

---

113. Cf. M. Borch-Jensen, 'An Ethiopian View of the Qūr'ān and Christ', *The Muslim World* 43 (1953), 173–76.

114. Cf. Maṣhafa Berhān, T. II, B. III, reading for 3rd Sun., h. 6: CSCO 262 (V), p. 27, where first only the saints of the OT, then the apostles are mentioned; New Testament saints in T. II, B. V, reading for 4th Sun.: CSCO 262, pp. 62–63.

115. On the position of the mother of Jesus in the Koran, cf. C. Schedl, *Muhammad und Jesus*, Vienna–Freiburg–Basel 1978, 175–206, 398–426; G. Riße, *'Gott ist Christus, der Sohn der Maria'*, Bonn 1989, 16, 176–77, 197.

116. S. Euringer, *OrChr* 24 (1927), 139–41, which again is very well based on the OT; cf. ibid., XLIV, 80–82: *OrChr* 27 (1930), 225.

117. *OrChr* 25/26 (1928/29), 267.

created in order to bear you.'[118] Yet ultimately this line is also brought to a christological end.[119]

Though in some places here valuable dogmatic connections and patristically proven motifs may have been touched, the concrete implementation is for us today largely unacceptable.

2. Limitations

(a) Jewish-Christian – and yet Christology from above

The test by example of genuinely Jewish-Christian theology seems to be the presence of a 'Christology from below' or a purely functional Christology in which one asks not about the essence but only about the duties, the role of Jesus of Nazareth. Now if the Ethiopian church exhibits a Judaization going beyond the usual extent, the question arises: Can we also observe within its Christology the struggle between a Christology 'from below' and one 'from above', or between a functional interpretation of Christ and one that asks about the essence of Jesus Christ? With the lack of sources for the Axum period, this question is hard to answer. We have also determined that the beginning of Ethiopian theology already presupposes the acceptance of the *Nicaenum*. Yet one of its oldest sources, the *Constitutiones Apostolorum* (*CAp*), was written by an Arian who is at the same time also the author of the Ps.-Ignatian writings and a Job commentary.[120] The first six books of the *CAp* are assimilated by the *Didascalia aethiopica* and are again an adaptation of the *Didascalia* (CPG 1738) (3rd cent.).[121] Thus in this way Ethiopia came in contact with a Christology from the fourth century that still advocated a subordination of the Son under the Father, although his procreation (in contrast to the Arian creation) is accepted. Based on this subordination, it was easy to advocate a functional Christology whose concepts could immediately be understood by Jewish Christians. Opportunity for this was given, since Julian wanted to substantiate christologically the subordination of the deacon under the bishop:[122]

> As, namely, Christ does nothing without the Father (cf. Jn 5,19), so also the deacon not without the bishop; and as the Son is *dependent* (ὑπόχρεως) on the Father, so also every

---

118. 'Marienharfe' IX, § 57: *OrChr* 24 (1927), 338.

119. Ibid., §§ 64–65, p. 341, where the adoption of OT images approaches the boundaries of good taste. On Eve–Mary see also *KN*, § 96: Bezold, pp. 104–5.

120. See p. 334 above.

121. See J. M. Harden, *The Ethiopic Didascalia*, London–New York 1920, 'Introduction', pp. XV–XVII.

122. See *CAp* II 30: Funk I, p. 113,4–8.

deacon on the bishop; and as the Son is the angel and prophet of the Father, so also the deacon is the angel and prophet of the bishop.

The connection of 'dependence' of the Son with two functions known from earlier Christology, those of the angel and of the prophet, makes the passage explosive. The Ethiopian or even an earlier (Coptic or Arabic) translator has nothing to consider in this passage with regard to the names. But one may perhaps see a mild correction in the fact that the subordination of the Son under the Father is less severely expressed than in the Greek text.[123] One could mention here the so heatedly disputed Pauline formulation in 1 Cor 15,28. Clearly, however, corrections were made elsewhere that removed some ambiguities of the *CAp*, and did so in the spirit of the *Nicaenum* (regarding the Son) and the Cappadocians (regarding the divinity of the Holy Spirit). We cite some passages as proof that the Ethiopian translators critically verified their models.

In *CAp* II 27,5: Funk I, p. 107,14–15 we read: 'Now if *the Christ* does not glorify himself without the Father, how can a man being by himself take the priesthood to himself . . . ?' The Ethiopian says: 'But if Christ glorified not Himself without the Father, *who is equal with Him* . . .' He inserts nothing less than the confession to the *homoousios*, which in the Greek index of the *CAp* in Funk is missing!

In *CAp* II 47,2: Funk I, p. 143,18–19 we read: 'And how [the Christian] in judgement has the *anointed One of God* as supporter and legal advisor . . .' – In the Ethiopian *Didascalia* this becomes: 'For with you in the court of judgement is Christ *the Son of God*' (chap. X: Harden, p. 66).

In *CAp* II 55,2: Funk I, p. 157,1–3 we read: 'We are honoured [with James the brother of the Lord] to be witnesses *of his return.*' – In the Ethiopian *Didascalia* this becomes: 'We are they to whom He hath granted that we should be witnesses concerning *His Son our Lord Jesus Christ*' (chap. XII: Harden, p. 72).

In *CAp* III 17,4: Funk I, p. 213,1–4 the topic is the Trinity in the understanding of a pneumatomachian, as Julian appears to be. After the Father and Christ, the only begotten God, the beloved Son and Lord of Glory are named, we read: 'The Holy *Pneuma*, the Paraclete, who is sent *by Christ* and *taught by him* and proclaimed him . . .' In the *Didascalia* this confession of the Spirit becomes: 'and the Paraclete is the Spirit of truth who was sent *by the Father* to teach all things' (thus greatly abbreviated and above all changed in the sense that the Spirit is sent *by the Father*, which in the dispute against the pneumatomachians is the proof for the divinity of the Holy Spirit and equality with the Son; see *Didascalia*, chap. XVII: Harden, p. 96).

---

123. This is shown by the *Did. aeth.*, chap. VIII–IX: Harden, p. 52, where the just-cited text of the *CAp* is treated thus: 'As Christ did nothing without the Father, in like manner let the deacon do nothing without the counsel of the bishop. Also there is *nothing* that the Son *doeth without the Father*, and as the Son is *subject to His Father*, in like manner let the deacon be subject to the bishop. [Chap. IX:] Even as the Son is the good pleasure of the Father, and His angel of counsel and His prophet, in like manner is the deacon the messenger and prophet of the bishop.' The 'dependence' of the Son on the Father is moderated here. On the titles 'prophet, apostle, high priest' see Cyril of Alex., *Quod unus est Christus* (= *Qērellos* III), §§ 85,4–88,1: pp. 155–59.

An important text for the christological position of the *CAp* is no longer understood in the Ethiopian *Didascalia*, because while it was important for the fourth century, it was superseded for the translators or revisors of the *CAp*. It is a matter, namely, of the question of the soul of Christ, which Julian does not assume and wants to dismiss with a strange argument. In *CAp* XXVI,2: Funk I, pp. 367,46–369,4 we read: 'Some of them, however, advocate another impiety: they imagine that the Lord is a mere human being (ψιλὸν ἄνθρωπον), since they hold that he consists of soul and body.' This agrees completely with the teaching of the Ps.-Ignatians.[124] To understand Jesus Christ as a being composed of a human soul and a body means for Julian to make of him a 'mere human being'. In his eyes this would be to discard the transcendence of Christ, even if it might still be understood in a subordinationist manner. In chap. XXXIII the Ethiopian *Didascalia* goes into *CAp* VI,26 and defends itself against various christological errors, especially against a separation Christology: '. . . and who believe not in Christ the Son of God, and separate[?] His birth in the flesh, and blaspheme against His sufferings in the flesh, and revile His cross, and mock at His death, and believe not in His resurrection, and make void His generation from the Father, before the whole creation [from here on the translator abbreviates, but it remains clear that the above-mentioned rejection of the soul of Christ remains recognizable] [and say, (that in Him) are flesh *and soul* and *not the Godhead*]' (Harden, op. cit., pp. 162–63).

The position of the Ethiopian *Didascalia* is clear: it confesses the true divinity of Christ and of the Holy Spirit; it assumes a human soul in Jesus Christ, which is otherwise also the tradition of the Ethiopian church.[125]

Thus the investigation shows that Ethiopian Christology is able to establish a synthesis between an interpretation of Christ with Old Testament-Jewish categories – and this with unusual strength – and a clear Nicaean Christology from above.

---

124. Cf. A. Grillmeier, *JdChr* I[3], 458; *CCT* I[2], 306.

125. For the teaching of the soul of Christ see *Qērellos* III, § 31,1: p. 73; § 74,2: p. 133; § 102,2: p. 185. To the *Qērellos* belong especially the two important documents of the union of 433 with the uniting symbol, in which the wholeness of the humanity of Christ is expressly confessed, which then went into the definition of Chalcedon. Cf. *Qērellos* IV, 1: doc. XIV,3, pp. 150–51; doc. XV,6, pp. 162–63. The uniting formula of 433 is found (in excerpt) also in the *Hāymānota Abaw*. Cf. B. M. Weischer, op. cit., pp. 171–77. – Also found in later documents is the express confession to the soul of Christ; thus: (1) in the Eth. Athanasius liturgy (epiclesis), § 101: S. Euringer, *OrChr* 24 (1927), 283: 'But none of us when he eats this bread may hold that he eats only the flesh without the blood and without the Spirit [= soul]; and none of us when he drinks this cup may hold that he drinks only the blood without the flesh and without the Spirit; rather, the flesh and the blood and the Spirit are one, as also his divinity with his humanity is one, namely, the Lord our God.' – (2) Ethiopian Anaphora of Our Lady Mary, § 42: S. Euringer, *Katholik* 96 (1916), 258. – (3) Several texts are also in E. Cerulli, *Scritti teologici etiopici dei secoli XVI–XVII*, II (ST 204), Vatican City 1960, 92–98. In these also, however, so-called traducianism is related to the soul of Christ (96: the soul of Christ taken out of the soul of the mother and from Adam. For only in this way could the soul of Christ in the descension also save the soul of Adam; this is an application of the universal church principle: *Quod non est assumptum, non est sanatum*). The 'Mirror of Insight', chap. III (Cerulli, op. cit., 179) calls Christ 'uomo completo' and emphasizes that 'Egli solo è perfetta Umanità ed Egli solo è perfetta Divinità, que nacque da Nostra Signora Maria . . . in una Persona ed una natura' (179–80).

(b) Nearness to and distance from Judaism

The profound Judaization of the Ethiopian church is repeatedly connected with a marking of the distance from Judaism. For the Abyssinian kingdom is the heir of Israel on account of the latter's guilty condemnation because of its rejection and execution of the true Messiah. So the Ethiopian people are now the 'people of God', but the Jews are rejected: 'For our Lord came, but they did not believe in him and did not accept his teaching; and therefore they have lost their salvation.'[126] Especially the kings Zar'a Yā'qob and Claudius were at pains to limit the validity of the Jewish law (reduction to the Ten Commandments!), and this with express reference to Paul's doctrine of salvation. The criticism of Israel's behaviour can even lead to vigorous anti-Jewish attacks, for example, in the Maṣḥafa Milād.[127] Here we almost find the picture of the Ahasver, the eternal Jew, who according to Dan 9,27 is given to destruction 'until the end of the world, without aim'.[128]

3. Relationship to universal church Christology, its terminology and systematic representation

In the fourth century Ethiopia had the Christian faith preached into its largely Jewish religious culture, but at first clearly from the loftiness of the Nicaean image of God and Christ. Vouching for this are the name Frumentius and his connection with Athanasius. The Syrians stayed with and strengthened this line. The guarantee for this development is, however, above all the *Qērellos*. It is also due to this extensive collection that the anti-Chalcedonian polemic remained in the background. Ethiopian Christology built at first on the state of the doctrine as it is represented by the Ephesian Cyril. It is true that the *mia-physis* formula, exalted later as the anti-Chalcedonian symbol, is already found in this *Qērellos*,[129] but it did not yet initiate any dispute. 'A comparison of the Greek and Ethiopian terms also shows that to this day the Ethiopian church stands on the foundations of Cyrillian Christology.'[130] Where it suffers is in the poverty of theological concepts and the lack of a methodology for theological

---

126. *Did. aeth.*, chap. XXIX: Harden, p. 127; cf. the whole of chap. V of the *CAp* in Harden, pp. 107–36.

127. Maṣḥafa Milād, T. II, reading VIII: CSCO 236, pp. 1–7.

128. Ibid., T. I, reading II: CSCO 222, p. 25 and the whole text on pp. 23–36 and the following readings.

129. On the *mia-physis* formula in the various Cyrillian documents of the *Qērellos* see the references in B. M. Weischer, *Qērellos* III, p. 25; ibid., p. 109.

130. Idem, *Qērellos* III, p. 27. Thus the starting-point of Ethiopian Christology is pre-Chalcedonian, not anti-Chalcedonian.

reflection. The Tergum remains dominant. Only with the later translations from the Arabic does the theological language grow in
comprehensiveness.[131] But the theological themes of Jewish-Christian
origin already developed here lead beyond the conceptual language
connected with the *mia-physis* formula.

Nevertheless, there was in various respects more and more a thematic
contact between Ethiopia and the (above all Greek-speaking) Eastern
church.

(a) Negative

The Ethiopian teachers adopted without any revision the universal
church catalogue of heresies and were thereby confronted with the
corresponding theological topics. The witness to this is the Maṣḥafā
mesṭīr, which represents the first work of apologetics in Ethiopia. It is a
catalogue of twenty-seven heresies, whose author, George of Saglā, gives
an often brief description of each and then attempts a refutation.[132] He
distances himself from pre-Ephesian heretics and heresies, such as Origen, Sabellius, Arius (Arians), Macedonius, Photinus – that is, from those
who in his opinion were related to the *Nicaenum*. Then, however,
everything was listed as christological heresy that could in some way or
other be classified as such, for example, Mani, naturally Eutyches, Apollinarius of Laodicea, but also Severus of Antioch and Theodosius of
Alexandria, the recognized masters of the Alexandrian church. Is the
author of this work thus a Julianist, or have Chalcedonian and anti-

---

131. See the adopted concepts in Weischer, op. cit., p. 28. The fact that they are not yet
found in the *Qērellos* indicates its great age.

132. G. Colin is preparing a full edition of this work, as he announces in his art.: 'La notice
sur Nestorius du *Maṣḥafa Mesṭīr* de Georges de Saglā (Traduction)', *OCP* 50 (1984), 107–25;
cf. p. 109, n. 9; on all the writings of George of Saglā: G. Colin, *Vie de Georges de Saglā*
(CSCO 493), Louvain 1987, pp. X–XI. On the content of the Maṣḥafa mesṭīr see E.
Hammerschmidt, *Äthiopische Handschriften vom Ṭānāsee*, vol. XX, 1, Wiesbaden 1973,
123–25. The translation of the text on Nestorius, however, is based at the moment on only
one ms.: Paris BN, ms. 113 du fonds éthiopien, fols. 37va to 52vb. In the text we make some
references to this translation. Characterizing the entire work is Colin, OCP 50 (1984), p. 109:
'Comme beaucoup d'autres écrits théologiques éthiopiens, le *Maṣḥafa Mesṭīr* constitue moins
un exposé dogmatique en règle qu'une réfutation des opinions contraires à celles de son
auteur, en matière trinitaire et christologique notamment. Il ne faut toutefois pas entendre ce
terme de réfutation en un sens pas trop rigoureux et technique; il s'agit bien plutôt, en
général, d'un amoncellement de citations scripturaires jugées suffisamment démonstratives
pour confondre l'auteur de l'hérésie qui, lui-même, est accablé des invectives souvent les plus
violentes.' – Meanwhile, Part I (with Ital. trans.) of the Maṣḥafa mesṭīr was edited by Y.
Beyene, *Giyorgis di Saglā. Il Libro del Mistero (Maṣḥafa Mesṭīr)* I, CSCO 515 (T), 516 (V),
Louvain 1990; the text on Nestorius: pp. 72–104 (Ethiop.), pp. 44–62 (Ital.).

Chalcedonian heretic catalogues been mixed? The information is often very inexact or misunderstood and is enlarged by extensive legends; this is now made quite accessible by G. Colin with the text on Nestorius:

The deposed Nestorius is credited with the teaching that Christ is nothing more than one of the prophets and is Son of God only out of 'grace'. From this comes the reproach of a 'two-sons doctrine'. He allegedly learned this from the bishops Tāsrōs and Dīdrōs. By this nothing else is to be understood but Diodore of Tarsus. In order to illustrate the *scandalum* of the denial of the *theotokos* title for Mary, the 'Book of Secrets' offers a legend that belongs in the *genus litterarium* of heresiological pornography. As in other Ethiopian sources, it is first reported of John Chrysostom, yet in him with the intention of proving his veneration of the mother-of-God title. In Nestorius it becomes a demonstration of his disdain for it. In this regard the following words are attributed to him:

'Anathème [soit] celui qui croit que le Seigneur est né d'une femme par ce corps! Maudit celui qui croit que le Seigneur a été porté dans une matrice génitrice et qu'il a eu le sort des nourrissons selon qu'il a été alimenté par le lait des mamelles et selon toute la façon d'être de la parturition des femmes!'[133] This comes close to Mani's denial of the incarnation, as we encountered it earlier.[134]

The Emperor Marcian became a follower of the teaching of Nestorius after the latter's death(!) and wanted to hold a council to reinforce his impiety: 'But God did not allow him to do as he wanted and hastened the decline of Nestorius'![135]

Nonetheless, the writer knows of the Council of Chalcedon. Naturally, it stands with Pope Leo on the side of Nestorius.[136] Also named as opponents of the true doctrine of the incarnation, however, are Apollinarius, Eutyches and John Philoponus.

(b) Positive

The counterpart to the effective authorities is first given once again by the *Qērellos* through the florilegia offered therein[137] and the selection of homilies and tractates. This explains a relatively broad contact with the

---

133. G. Colin, art. cit., p. 111.

134. See above p. 195 and *CCT* II/1, pp. 181–86.

135. G. Colin, art. cit., p. 114.

136. Cf. L. Guerrier and S. Grébaut, 'Le Fragment anti-chalcédonien du Mashafa Meśtīr', *Aethiops* 3 (1930), 1–4, 17–20. The most detailed anti-Chalcedonian text is 'La storia dei Quattro Concili ed altri opuscoli monofisiti', in E. Cerulli, ST 204, pp. 76–98; in ibid., 98–100, is a catalogue of heresies, each with an antithesis. Again named are Apollinarius, John Philoponus, Macedonius and Eutyches.

137. Cf. B. M. Weischer, 'Das christologische Florilegium in Qērellos II', *OrChr* 64 (1980), 109–35. According to Weischer, 109, §§ 9–18 are 'a significant florilegium of the statements of nine known theologians and church fathers of the fourth and fifth centuries' on christological questions. Some of them have also gone into the large florilegium *Hāymānota Abaw*.

Greek tradition. A later collection of the 'Faith of the Fathers' (*Hāymānota Abaw*) was able to go much further.[138] The Ethiopian translation is based on an Arabic model that is rather literally reproduced, the *I'tirāf al-abā'* (confession of the fathers), originating in the year 1078. This Arabic version presupposes a Coptic (Sahidic) text, which, however, is itself a poor, free translation from the Greek. The whole is a collection on the doctrines of the Trinity and the incarnation, which are chronologically arranged.[139] The breadth of information is described by B. M. Weischer:

> Appearing as authorities are first the apostles (*Didascalia*) and alleged students of the apostles (Irenaeus, Attikos of Constantinople, Dionysios), then theologians of the third and fourth centuries, including Apollinarian texts under the name of Athanasius and the popes Julius and Felix, then the famous Alexandrian theologians Theophilus, Cyril, Theodosius, also Severus of Antioch and Jacob of Sarūg and finally letters and writings of the Coptic and Syrian Patriarchs up to Christodoulos of Alexandria (1050–78) . . . The excerpts of the works of Cyril of Alexandria are, to be sure, numerous (52 pieces), but often rather fragmentary' (only the larger works such as Thesaurus, Dialogue on the Trinity and letters are utilized; by contrast, few of the homilies).[140]

This also made accessible to the Ethiopians the *Laetentur* letter of Cyril (in excerpt) with the formula of union of 433. Yet the Ethiopian version of this formula in the *Hāymānota Abaw*, in contrast to the *Qērellos*,[141] contains a tendentious modification of the Arabic model. It concerns Cyril's sentence: δύο γὰρ φύσεων ἕνωσις γέγονεν ('the uniting of two natures took place'). Into Ethiopic via Arabic this became: 'and the two natures became one in the uniting'.[142] Such modifications, however, were isolated cases. Above all, the *Qērellos* remained protected from them. From conciliar sources the Nicaeno-Constantinopolitan creed is offered in the 'Faith of the Fathers' with other materials from the *Nicaenum* (no. 11 in Hammerschmidt). The Western church is represented by no text; the papal names of the Apollinarian forgeries cannot be counted.

---

138. See on this E. Hammerschmidt, *Äthiopische Handschriften*, XX,1, Wiesbaden 1973, 196–98; XX,2, Wiesbaden 1977, 82–86. On the determination of the excerpts from the individual authors, who also include the Apollinarian forgers, see A. Dillmann, *Catalogus codicum manuscriptorum qui in Museo Britannico asservantur* III, London 1847, 113–19.

139. See A. Grillmeier, *CCT* II/1, p. 70.

140. B. M. Weischer, *Qērellos* IV 1 (= ÄthFor 4), p. 172.

141. B. M. Weischer, *Qērellos* IV 1, pp. 148, 150.

142. Ibid., p. 173.

The position on the first four councils can best be read from the Mazgaba Hāymānot, the 'Treasury of the Faith'.[143] The picture of the Fourth Council is purely polemical and totally distorted. Marcian as well as Leo I and with them the whole council of 'teachers of foolishness' are considered Nestorians. In spite of their great number (737) they could not validate their claim as 'continuatori' of the 318 fathers of Nicaea to teach the right faith. Also condemned, however, is Eutyches, who is alleged to have taught: 'The body of Christ was immaterial and did not suffer pain like our body.'[144] The hero of this book is Dioscorus! The failure of the fathers of Chalcedon consisted in becoming victims of the excommunication of Cyril and the Council of Ephesus, which they say forbade the composition of a new symbol. But in the eyes of the author the wrong symbol was made not by the fathers of 451 but Nestorius, who formulated: 'There were two persons in Christ: the Son of our Lady Mary and the Son of God, who became one through synthesis (Annäherung, accostamento)!'[145] Out of fear of the excommunication threatened by Cyril, the synod members did not dare reject this sentence. But they themselves would have contaminated Cyril with Nestorius through their formula of the one person in two natures. Also put forth as a false doctrine of Chalcedon is the statement that the humanity in Christ is lower than the divinity.[146] At the council, it says, Dioscorus defended the true faith against Pope Leo but was mistreated and finally banned to the island(!) of Gangra, where he died.[147]

(c) Ethiopia and the conceptual language of the universal church

The blame for misunderstandings such as those just described is borne by the lack of an exact theological language and a conceptual clarification. The Ethiopists who have something to say here offer little hope of a

---

143. See E. Cerulli, *Scritti Teologici Etiopici dei Secoli XVI–XVII*, II: *La Storia dei Quattro Concili ed altri opuscoli monofisiti* (ST 204), Vatican City 1960; on Chalcedon see 76–98 (V).

144. Ibid., pp. 76–77.

145. Ibid., p. 77.

146. Ibid., pp. 76–77.

147. Ibid., p. 80. On this it reads: 'Questo è il motivo della nostra separazione dai Melchiti, che sono gli Europei . . . Noi invece fummo detti Giacobiti perchè fu nostro dottore Giacomo Baradeo discepolo del savio Dioscoro.' The knowledge of the story is very spotty and inexact. The designation of Gangra as an island is found in the Alexandrian Synaxarium. Cf. J. Forget, *Synaxarium Alexandrinum* I, p. 8.

solution to the difficulties.[148] We can only point to the description of the situation by E. Hammerschmidt:[149]

> The problem here lay in the indefiniteness of the Ethiopian expressions, since none of the words available for the translation of Greek terms into Ge'ez were as definite and clear in their meaning through centuries-long discussions as were the Greek counterparts. In terms of the history of dogma, the main difficulty of Ethiopian Christology lies in the unclear delineation of the terms *baḥrey* and *hellawē*, which both render the Greek *physis*. In the understanding of the Ethiopians, however, *baḥrey* has not so much the meaning *natura* as rather *natura subsistens* or *persona*. The situation is similar with *hellawē*, which is perhaps the least clear concept in Ethiopian theology. Hence also the unwillingness of the Ethiopians to concede two *baḥreyat* (plural of *baḥrey*) in Christ, since in their eyes this would result in Nestorianism. In consequence of this uncertainty they speak of *äḥädu* (= one) *baḥrey* in Christ. If the divinity or humanity in Christ is designated, both words receive an addition: *mäläkot* (= divinity) or *śega* (= Greek *sarx*) or *śegawē* (= incarnation).

The relatedness to the universal church is based on the fact that the Ethiopian church received its supporting framework from the faith as it prevailed in Alexandria, Antioch, Byzantium and Rome between the *Nicaenum* (325) and the *Ephesinum* (431). The compilation of the documents of the *Qērellos* shows that with all the individual Jewish-Christian motifs, in particular the messianism of this sacral kingdom, the overall picture of faith is shaped by the two basic Christian doctrines, the confession to the triune God and to the incarnation of God in Christ. Many individual proofs of this can be offered. Even without using terminology or concepts to the same degree as the Greeks in order to get

---

148. Cf. B. M. Weischer, 'Die christologische Terminologie des Cyrill von Alexandrien im Äthiopischen', in W. Hoenerbach (ed.), *Der Orient in der Forschung*, FS O. Spies, Wiesbaden 1967, 733–41; idem, Indices in *Qērellos* III and IV,1–3; E. Hammerschmidt, 'Ursprung philosophisch-theologischer Termini und deren Übernahme in die altkirchliche Theologie', *OstKSt* 8 (1959), 202–20; idem, 'Zur Christologie der äthiopischen Kirche', *OstKSt* 13 (1964), 203–7 (review of M. da Abiy-Addi', *La dottrina della chiesa etiopica dissidente sull'unione ipostatica* [OCA 147], Rome 1956); idem, *Äthiopien*, Wiesbaden 1967, 112–15; T. Uqbit, *Current Christological Positions of Ethiopian Orthodox Theologians*, pp. 21–48.

149. E. Hammerschmidt, *Äthiopien* (1967), 112, with reference to E. Cerulli, *La littérature éthiopienne dans l'histoire de la culture médiévale* = Annuaire de l'Institut de Philologie et d'Histoire Orientales et Slaves 14 (1954/57), 20–23. According to Hammerschmidt the terms *hellawē* and *baḥrey* in the beginning were not used at the same time and side by side. 'We owe the knowledge of the contexts to E. Cerulli, who showed that one first went back to the verb *hälläwä* (= be, exist) and used the *nomen actionis hellawē* formed from it to render the Greek *physis*. That seems to have been the oldest way of translating, since it is already found in the Qērlos. It is characteristic of the varying terminology, however, that even in the Qērlos in two places the translation with "person" is suggested' (op. cit., 112–13). Later the Greek *physis* was rendered *baḥrey*, although this means etymologically: 'belonging to the ocean', and lexicographically means 'pearl'. For how it came to this development, see ibid., 113. – For the Ethiopian form of the *mia-physis* formula see B. M. Weischer, 'Das christologische Florilegium in Qērellos II', *OrChr* 64 (1980), 115, n. 5. – Cf. now J. Lössl, 'One as the Same. Elements of an Ethiopian Christology', *OstKSt* 42 (1993), 288–302.

a grip on the problem of distinguishing person and nature in the Trinity and incarnation, Ethiopian theology still had the possibility of representing in the image of God both the unity and the diversity in such a way that even the incarnation could be comprehended on the one hand as the common creative work of the Father, the Son and the Spirit, and on the other hand as belonging to the Son alone. The 'Book of the Birth' (Mashafa Milād) draws here an image of the belonging together of *theologia* and *oikonomia*, as was characteristic of all other churches:[150]

> The Father in his form, in his image and in his person put on no flesh. Also the Holy Spirit in his form, in his image and in his person put on no flesh. Only the Son in his form, in his image and in his person put on flesh from Mary, twofold Virgin. But we interpret for you through the power of the Spirit of Jesus Christ: when he speaks of the body of Jesus Christ as that of the Holy Spirit, then he means by this the Holy Spirit that rests upon him, and that he became a human being by the Holy Spirit and from Mary, the blessed Virgin.

This framework of faith, despite individual upheavals such as that caused by the Stephanites,[151] was strong enough to bear a synthesis of Jewish-Christian and Greek-Christian elements, and this in a shaping that we do not otherwise find. Here, with all the peculiarities of individual currents within the Ethiopian church, we can ascertain a substantial unity with the universal church. A particular point of attack has at times been offered by the Ethiopian liturgy, into which we still must briefly go.

---

150. Mashafa Milād, T. II, reading for 29th Teqemt: CSCO 236, pp. 60–61.

151. See ibid., T. I, reading for 29th Tāhsās: CSCO 222, p. 12; Taddesse Tamrat, 'Some Notes on the Fifteenth Century Stephanite "Heresy" in the Ethiopian Church (14th and 15th Centuries)', in *Rassegna di studi etiopici (Roma)* 22 (1966), 103–15. It is a question of a heretical movement founded by Istefanos in Gunda Gundie. In 1454 King Zar'a Yā'qob destroyed their main monastery and wanted to cripple their worship by taking away the Tabotat. Because of the suspicion of heresy they could no longer find a bishop for the ordination of priests. Therefore they chose twelve ordination candidates by lot and sent them to Jerusalem for ordination as priests. Cf. F. Heyer, *Die Kirche Äthiopiens*, Berlin–New York 1971, 282–83.

CHAPTER SIX

THE POSITION OF JESUS IN THE WORSHIP AND PRAYER OF THE ETHIOPIAN CHURCH

With the peculiar nature of the Ethiopian church, a greater significance is probably attached to worship and to public and private prayer than elsewhere, where scholarly theology and reflection dominate over popular preaching and liturgical celebration. Therefore the quest for the image of Christ in the liturgical and extra-liturgical religious life of the Ethiopian church is of special importance.[1]

1. Christ in the structure of the church year

With the strong Jewish traditions in Ethiopia the suspicion may arise that they also shape the cycle of religious feasts, since culture and cult are very closely connected here. If the Jewish Sabbath could be kept beside the Christian Sunday, we must ask whether perhaps the Jewish Pascha or Jewish customs in general persist alongside the Christian Easter feast and Christian practices. The answers to these questions would require quite concrete knowledge of Ethiopian life, as is offered by the study of F. Heyer often referred to in this book. At this point we can present only partial information.

---

1. On the following see J. A. Jungmann, *Die Stellung Christi im liturgischen Gebet*, 40–51; H. Engberding, 'Das chalkedonische Christusbild und die Liturgien der monophysitischen Kirchengemeinschaften', in *Chalkedon* II (697–733), 708–14; E. Hammerschmidt, *Studies in the Ethiopic Anaphoras* (BBA 25 [1961]), 2nd revised edition (ÄthFor 25), Stuttgart 1987, not cited here; K. Alemu, Η ΧΡΙΣΤΟΛΟΓΙΑ ΤΩΝ ΑΙΘΙΟΠΙΚΩΝ ΑΝΑΦΟΡΩΝ ΕΝ ΣΧΕΣΕΙ ΠΡΟΣ ΤΟ ΔΟΓΜΑ ΤΗΣ ΧΑΛΚΗΔΟΝΟΣ, Thessalonica 1977 (cited here: K. Alemu, *Die Christologie der äthiopischen Anaphoren im Verhältnis zum Dogma von Chalcedon*). – The texts of the individual anaphoras are registered in E. Hammerschmidt, op. cit., 13–36, esp. 35–36, as well as ibid. under S. Euringer in the Bibliography. Convenient editions: J. M. Harden, *The Anaphoras of the Ethiopic Liturgy*, London 1928 (unfortunately sometimes abbreviated); A. Hänggi and I. Pahl, *Prex Eucharistica* (SpicFrib 12 [1968]), 142–203 (11 anaph. in Lat. trans.).

The Ethiopian church has nine main church feasts and a number of secondary celebrations.[2] The main feasts are all feasts of the Lord. The count varies, naturally, depending on whether Holy Week, which counts as one of the main feasts, is separated from the Easter celebration or not. Also the feast of the baptism of the Lord and the Cana miracle can form *one* celebration or *two*. In any case, the church year is clearly christologically structured:

First division	Second division
1. Incarnation of the Son of God (proclamation)	Incarnation (1)
2. Holy Week (*one* feast)	Holy Week with Easter (2)
3. Resurrection	
4. Feast of the apostle Thomas (Easter Tuesday)	Feast of the apostle Thomas (3)
5. Ascension	Ascension (4)
6. Parāqlitos/Pentecost	Pentecost (5)
7. Dabra Tābor	Transfiguration (6)
8. Birth of our Lord	Birth of our Lord (7)
9. Baptism of our Lord and miracle at Cana	Baptism of our Lord (8)
	Miracle at Cana (9)

In addition there are a few secondary feasts that for their part are again related to Christ: elevation of the cross, feeding miracle, feast of Simeon (= presentation in the Temple), discovery of the cross.

Thus from the main feasts a thoroughly christological structure of the Ethiopian church year is perceivable, provided that other strata do not cover it over. Hence the Ethiopian church has an unusually strong Marian piety, as well as a cult of angels inspired by Judaism and a special veneration of the saints.

There are four groups of Marian feasts: (1) for the realization of the Marian life; (2) for honouring a Marian saying; (3) in remembrance of 'Marian miracles'; (4) feasts relating to a holy place. In all, the church calendar knows fourteen such celebrations.[3]

The feasts of the saints are strictly limited to figures of the first centuries, the time of the united church, and to saints of the Coptic church and Ethiopian saints registered in the Synaxarium. Strongly represented are Old Testament persons (patriarchs, prophets, kings), the 'nine saints' we already know, the national saints from the kings, the apostles Peter and Paul, John Chrysostom and some others. On the whole, this calendar seems hardly survey-able.[4] Thus it is very possible that the veneration of angels and saints holds a position of inordinately high importance in the life of Ethiopian Christians, apart from the superstitious distortion of such veneration, against which the reform of King Zarʾa Yāʿqob emphatically fought.

---

2. See B. Velat, *Études sur le Meʿerāf. Commun de l'Office divin Éthiopien* (PO 33), pp. 21–37: 'Calendrier liturgique Éthiopien'.

3. Ibid., pp. 25–26: 'Fêtes mariales'. See the excellent study of G. Nollet, 'Le culte de Marie en Éthiopie', in *Maria*, edited by H. du Manoir, t. I, 363–413. Very useful is A. Grohmann, *Äthiopische Marienhymnen*, Leipzig 1919, 6–36: 'Übersicht über die äthiopische mariologische Literatur' (sources!).

4. B. Velat, PO 33, pp. 27–29. Cf. R.-G. Coquin, 'Le synaxaire éthiopien: note codicologique sur le ms. Paris B. N. d'Abbadie 66–66bis', *AnBoll* 102 (1984), 49–59.

2. The alleged Monophysitism of the Ethiopian anaphoras

For its liturgical prayer the Ethiopian church has at its disposal a multiplicity of anaphoras, which are not all of equal worth.[5] Also, the nexus with Egypt and Antioch is to be noted.[6] The oldest anaphora used in the liturgy, the 'Anaphora of the Apostles', is identical with the anaphora of the 'Egyptian Church Order',[7] which in turn leads to the 'Ethiopian Anaphora of Our Lord Jesus Christ'[8] and to the 'Testament of Our Lord Jesus Christ'.[9] This rooting in the common liturgical tradition encompassing East and West cannot be valued highly enough. The development of the Ethiopian anaphora, which could build on this good ground, was, however, not always fortunate. For broad stretches, according to H. Engberding, the understanding of the original sense of the first part of the anaphora, the eucharistic prayer, disappeared: 'The concern was no longer to praise God in the multiplicity of his arrangements for salvation; rather, some special object was selected and made the sole theme of the eucharistic prayer',[10] for example, praise of the Christian Sabbath (Sunday) in the anaphora of St Athanasius.[11] No room was left here for the praise of 'any kind of salvific deed of Christ'.

As much as certain aberrations are to be lamented here, it is still unjust to assume therein a Monophysitism and to make this responsible for abortive developments, a criticism expressed especially by J. A. Jungmann but also retracted by him.[12]

J. A. Jungmann begins with the observation that in the course of history the so-called mediator formula (*per Dominum nostrum Jesum Christum*) has been transformed into a prayer to Christ. He also seeks the cause of this in the Ethiopian church (1) in anti-Arianism and (2) in

---

5. See E. Hammerschmidt, *Studies*, pp. 13–36; J. M. Harden, *The Anaphoras of the Ethiopic Liturgy*, pp. 1–29.

6. See the references in A. Hänggi and I. Pahl, *Prex Eucharistica* (1968), 142–43. Included in the Antiochene type are the Anaphora Jacobi and the Anaphora Basilii; the Egyptian review includes the Anaphora of the Apostles, the Anaphora of Our Lord Jesus Christ and the Anaphora of Mark the Evangelist; the remaining texts represent a type peculiar to the Ethiopian church (besides the 11 in Hänggi/Pahl, also the Gregory Anaphora I–II, Anaphora of Jacob of Sarug and the Anaphora Cyrilli II³). A special peculiarity are the theological proclamations before and after the Sanctus (Praeconium I and II with two themes, the *oratio theologica* and the *oratio christologica*), which E. Hammerschmidt analyses in detail.

7. See J. M. Harden, *The Anaphoras of the Ethiopic Liturgy*, 31–50; G. Horner, *The Statutes of the Apostles*, London 1904, 139–43; H. Duensing, *Der aethiopische Text der Kirchenordnung des Hippolyt* (*AGWG.PH* 3. F., 32), Göttingen 1946, 21–25.

8. See E. Hammerschmidt, *Studies*, pp. 72–75.

9. See ibid., the foldout page with overview.

10. Cf. H. Engberding, 'Das chalkedonische Christusbild', in *Chalkedon* II, p. 708.

11. See S. Euringer, 'Die äthiopische Anaphora des hl. Athanasius', *OrChr* 24 (1927), 243–98.

12. J. A. Jungmann, *Die Stellung Christi im liturgischen Gebet*, Münster ²1962, 40–51.

an alleged evaporation of the humanity of Christ in consequence of the church's Monophysitism. Also S. Euringer made such judgements in his commentaries on the anaphoras, without letting himself be corrected by the texts. According to Jungmann, only the Anaphora of the Apostles maintained the 'liturgical treasures' from the patristic period. A negative grade is given especially to the 'Anaphora of John Chrysostom' and the 'Anaphora of Our Lady Mary'.[13] In both liturgies God the Father and Christ would strongly 'flow into each other', according to Jungmann (op. cit., p. 48). With this, he says, the divinity of Christ moves very much into the foreground, to the detriment of the humanity; and this also explains why Mary is appealed to as advocate before Christ, while 'he [i.e., Christ] himself, however, nowhere appears as mediator of our prayers – apart from the unharmoniously employed doxology of Hippolytus' (ibid.). Yet it sounds very vague when we read: 'Now, although in all these peculiarities no heretical confession is in any way yet included, the Monophysite idea that lets the humanity of our Lord sink into his divinity still offers here the most obvious explanation for this development' (ibid.). H. Engberding dismissed this unjustified conclusion, using quotations from the Anaphora of Mary itself and then from the 'Anaphora of St John the Evangelist' and the 'Anaphora of Jacob of Sarug'.[14]

Yet regarding the Chrysostom anaphora, Jungmann must concede that the familiar way of addressing Christ, used in the Sanctus, first appears at the very end of the long Preface. Then it does not resume until after the long anamnesis. In this, however, the passion of Christ is considered in detail up to his ascension. Finally it reads: 'With his body, together with the power of the divinity, he went towards heaven to the earlier state of his being' (op. cit., p. 45). Here one cannot speak of a 'sinking of the humanity into the divinity'. Nevertheless, it means a very unfortunate shift in accent when in the 'Anaphora of Mary' the 'by far largest part of its actual prayers [are] directed to Mary' (op. cit., p. 46). Yet here too Jungmann must admit 'that in this whole panegyric Mary appears in no way as an isolated entity; rather, her status is wholly derived from her position in the history of salvation' (op. cit., p. 47). Certainly there is also gross ineptitude when the redactor of the anaphora mixes the familiar form of address to Christ with the mediator formula. The two schemata of addressing prayer to God and to Christ simply makes a muddle (op. cit., p. 48).[15]

Thus, with all the drop from the intellectual height of the older anaphoras, one must not accuse the Ethiopian church of 'Monophysitism'. Certainly in an extra-liturgical text we have observed a pronounced onesidedness in the sense that the corporeality of both Christ and his mother are seen in the state of Adam and Eve before the fall. Yet even this does not mean that Monophysite influences have been at work here. Rather, one can ascertain that an apocryphal original-state teaching of Jewish

13. See J. M. Harden, op. cit., pp. 86–93 (Chrysost.); pp. 67–71 (Anaphora of Our Lady Mary); S. Euringer, Katholik 93 I (1913), 406–14 (Chrysost.); idem, OrChr 34 (1937), 63–102, 248–62 (O. L. Mary); Hänggi/Pahl, pp. 189–93 (Chrysost.); pp. 160–67 (O. L. Mary); see O. Raineri, Atti di Habta Māryām († 1497) e di Iyāsu († 1508), santi monaci etiopici, (OLA 235), Rome 1990, 111–15 with n. 2, p. 113.

14. H. Engberding, art. cit., pp. 708–10.

15. See A. Gerhards, 'Le phénomène du Sanctus adressé au Christ, son origine, sa signification et sa persistance dans les Anaphores de l'Église d'Orient', in Le Christ dans la Liturgie (= Conf. Saint-Serge 1980), Rome 1981 (65–83), 66–67, with reference to P. Prigent, Apocalypse et Liturgie, Neuchâtel 1964, 46–76.

origin has had its influence. In the Ethiopian Gregory Anaphora, more-over, we find a recognizable rejection of the teaching of Julian of Halicarnassus on the incorruptibility of the flesh of Christ:[16]

> . . . In the beginning was the Word; the Word was the Word of God; the Word became flesh and dwelt among us and concealed himself before us. He clothed himself with mortal(!) flesh and made it immortal. In this flesh God, who cannot be scourged, was scourged' (there follows a vivid sketch of all the mistreatment of Christ).

This text is dependent on the 'Mystagogia', that is, chap. 28 of *Testamentum Domini nostri Jesu Christi*,[17] which is translated into Ethiopic in the 'Teaching of the Mysteries' § 12:

> Cum itaque induit corruptibilem carnem, qui incorruptibilis est, incorruptibilem effecit carnem, quae sub morte erat: per hoc ostendit typum incorruptibilitatis in carne, quam induit Adae, qui mortuus erat, quo typo abolita fuerunt, quae erant corrupta.[18]

The 'Teaching of the Mysteries' reproduces this text as follows: 'He who is incorruptible put on flesh, which is corruptible. He made mortal flesh incorruptible; [he,] who through this type of the flesh of Adam, who was not mortal, showed immortality; through which type that which is corruptible was destroyed.'[19]

On the entrance to the *mystagogia* it is already said of Christ: *Ipse est, qui Adam iam mortuum induit, eumque vivificavit, qui ascendit ad coelum*[20] (He is the one who put on Adam, already in the state of death [i.e., his body in the state after the fall], who put life into him, who has ascended into heaven). Here the Ethiopian translator did not quite get it right when he said: 'He who put on Adam lived dying, who has ascended into heaven after he had subjected himself to death.'[21]

In the manner in which the teaching of Julian of Halicarnassus is rejected lies a new proof that in the Ethiopian liturgy there is no absorption of Jesus' humanity in the divinity, and this is also true because detailed references are to be found to the mysteries of the life of Jesus from conception in Mary to the cross, to descent into Sheol and to the ascension into heaven.[22]

---

16. Here according to O. Löfgren and S. Euringer, *Die beiden gewöhnlichen äthiopischen Gregorius-Anaphoren* § 18 (OC 30, 2), Rome 1933, 88–89. Cf. also the 'Marienharfe' XLIV,67: S. Euringer, *OrChr* 27 (1930), 221,26–33.

17. Cf. CPG 1743; I. E. Rahmani, *Testamentum Domini nostri Jesu Christi*, Moguntiae 1899, 59–67; E. Hammerschmidt, *Äthiopische liturgische Texte der Bodleian Library in Oxford* (VIOF 38), Berlin 1960, 39–72; French trans. by B. Velat, PO 33, pp. 215–17; see F. X. Funk, *Das Testament unseres Herrn und die verwandten Schriften* (FCLDG II, 1–2), Mainz 1901, 299–303.

18. *Test. Domini nostri Jesu Christi*, I, 28: Rahmani, p. 61.

19. E. Hammerschmidt, op. cit., p. 59; PO 33, p. 216.

20. Rahmani, p. 59.

21. E. Hammerschmidt, op. cit., p. 49.

22. 'Lehre der Geheimnisse', chap. 3–5: E. Hammerschmidt, *Äthiopische liturgische Texte*, pp. 61–71 with commentary; PO 33, pp. 216–17; Rahmani, op. cit., pp. 63–64.

Let us close with the words of the 'Teaching of the Mysteries', which sketch the magnificent horizon within which the celebration of the Eucharist by the believers is supposed to be carried out:

> He is the incomprehensible thought of the Father; he is the wisdom of the Father; he is his power; he is his right hand; he is his counsel; he is his thought, in that he is now the hand of the arm of the Father [§ 6]. When we believe in his faith [= faith in him], we humbly confess that he is the light, the fount of redemption, the refuge, the help and the teacher, who defends us, who rewards, who accepts, our strong fortress. He is the shepherd, the door of the gate, the way of life, the healing, the food, the drink, the judge.[23]

3. Chalcedonian–anti-Chalcedonian conceptual language in the liturgy?

In the flood of prayers with their language of symbols and images, the conceptual terms of the age of the christological controversies are hardly to be discovered.[24] It is true that we find the expressions *person*, *hypostasis* and *nature*, but only when faith in the triune God is the topic and not in the christological context.[25] Here again we see the rootedness of the Ethiopian church in the fourth century, since in the Greek-Alexandrian-Syrian sphere the formula of the triad in the person or hypostasis and the unity of essence had already been adopted. Such confessional formulas had also become innate in the faith of the community.

It is different with the christological language as it was used around 451 and afterwards in heated controversies. It has correctly been pointed out that with the *Qērellos* more of a pre- than a post-Chalcedonian way of speaking was adopted (B. M. Weischer). Thus in the anaphoras the Chalcedonian controversy plays hardly a role in regard to 'one' or 'two natures'. Still, we encounter a trace in the form in which the *Sanctus* is formulated in various anaphoras or in other prayer texts. This recalls the controversy around Peter the Fuller and the theopaschite formula.[26] We ask first, however, whether the triple holy in the Ethiopian liturgy is to be interpreted in a christological or trinitarian fashion or in regard to another name.

---

23. Ibid., chap. 1, §§ 6–7: Hammerschmidt, p. 51; PO 33, p. 215; Rahmani, op. cit., p. 61.

24. See K. Alemu, *Die Christologie der äthiopischen Anaphoren*, pp. 296 and 298.

25. One example in O. Löfgren and S. Euringer, 'Die beiden aethiopischen Anaphoren des hl. Cyrillus', *ZSem* 9 (1933/34) (trans.) § 32, p. 69: 'Three hypostases and one God; three persons and one appearance; three names and one essence.' – It can be different in the prayer of the hours. Cf. B. Velat, PO 33: in the 'Prières Mariales' I 6, p. 285, there is an abbreviated *mia-physis* formula: 'Le Fils unique n'a pas été changé, ni dissocié dans toutes ses oeuvres, mais est un aspect, *une nature*, une divinité du Verbe du Seigneur' (emphasis added).

26. Cf. A. Gerhards, 'Le phénomène du Sanctus', pp. 69–77.

(1) In regard to the Father: The Little Cyril Anaphora: 'Holy, holy, holy are you, O Lord, Father of our Lord and our Saviour Jesus Christ.'[27] – This probably also applies to the Large Cyril Anaphora: 'Holy, holy, holy [are you], God Sabaoth, completely filling the heavens and the earth with the holiness of your glory.'[28] For in §§ 5–6 the Father is addressed (pp. 57–58). Likewise in the Epiphanius Anaphora,[29] where the Father is praised as the Creator who sends his *Son* (§ 33), to whom the triple holy therefore applies (§ 24).

(2) In regard to the Trinity: The Anaphora of St James[30] probably understands *God Sabaoth* as the Trinity, since in § 3 a further trinitarian development is immediately given, but from the salvation-economical viewpoint! The salvation-economical Trinity is meant by the triple holy in the Anaphora of Our Lady Mary: 'Holy is God the Father, who is well pleased with you [Mary]; holy is the only Son, who dwelled in your womb; holy is the Paraclete, who strengthened you.'[31]

(3) In regard to Christ: The Ethiopian Anaphora of St John Chrysostom, whose departure from the liturgical development and tradition of the East is emphasized, has in § 19: 'Holy, holy, holy are you truly, Jesus Christ, who are called holy by the mouths of all and who give to all your saints in your goodness, that they may become holy where His holiness is, which cannot be destroyed and which never passes away.'[32]

Probably directed towards Christ but integrated with the Trinity is the triple holy of priest and people in the Ethiopian Gregory Anaphora: 'Holy, holy, holy is the Lord Sabaoth, perfectly filling the heavens and the earth with the holiness of your(!) glory.'[33]

We distinguish the *Sanctus* from the so-called *Trishagion* ("Αγιος ὁ θεός κτλ.), which could be understood in a trinitarian way but may also have been made identifiable through addenda as related to Christ. We find the classical Trishagion expanded in theopaschite fashion in the Ethiopian anaphora of 'the 318 orthodox believers':[34]

The seraphim and the cherubim call and say: 'Holy God! Holy strong One, but not [strong] through the strength of arrogance! Holy living One, immortal One, who died out of love for humankind.'

Without doubt we have an imitation of the classical Sanctus expanded in a theopaschite manner, which here, however, is clearly related to Christ (mention of his *kenosis* and his death).

Similar is the Ethiopian 'Dioscorus Anaphora': 'Holy, holy, holy is the *Lord in his Triad!* Although he himself was a ruler, he showed his lowliness as a servant.'[35] Probably the 'Lord in his Triad' is nothing other than the *unus ex Trinitate (crucifixus est)* in an Ethiopian transformation.

---

27. O. Löfgren and S. Euringer, *ZSem* 9 (1933/34), 45, § 6.

28. Loc. cit., p. 57, § 4.

29. *OrChr* 23 (1927), 107–9, §§ 22–24.

30. *OrChr* NS 4 (1914), 5, § 2.

31. *OrChr* 34 (1937), 77, § 30.

32. S. Euringer, *Katholik* 93 I (1913), 410.

33. O. Löfgren and S. Euringer, OC 30,2, Rome 1933, 123, § 5; on the integration of the economy of salvation and the Trinity see esp. § 7.

34. S. Euringer, *ZSem* 4 (1926), 271.

35. O. Löfgren and S. Euringer, *Le Monde Oriental* 26/27 (1932/33), 245.

As the most beautiful example of Ethiopian additions to the Trishagion, when it is understood as related to Christ, we can offer the following verses from the preface of the 'Liturgy of the Apostles':[36]

> Holy God, holy mighty, holy living immortal,
>   who was born of Mary the holy virgin,
> have mercy upon us, O Lord.
> Holy God, holy mighty, holy living immortal,
>   who was baptized in Jordan and was hung on the tree
> of the cross,
> have mercy upon us, O Lord.
> Holy God, holy mighty, holy living immortal,
>   who rose from the dead the third day,
> ascended with glory into heaven and sat down at the right
>   hand of his Father,
>   shall come again with glory to judge the quick and the dead,
> have mercy upon us, O Lord.
> Glory be to the Father, glory be to the Son,
> glory be to the Holy Ghost,
>   both now and ever and world without end.
> Amen and amen: so be it, so be it.

Let us add here the question of controversial formulas in other religious texts. They flow in without polemic and appear seldom:

The *mia-physis* formula: It is found in the 'Marienharfe' §17: 'O extremely wonderful harmony of fire [divinity] and water [humanity] in *one* essence'.[37] Here we see the shimmer of Ethiopian terminology (see above p. 372, n. 129).

The *unus ex trinitate* in variations: 'But Mary bore the One from the Trinity and concealed him in her womb.'[38] – In the 'Flower Song' v. XVII we read: 'You who for us would have the One sprout from the Triad';[39] in the Weddāsē Maryam IV,9: 'For she became the *shrine* for One out of the holy Triad.'[40] – The Coptic theotokia: 'For she became the *temple* of the One out of the Triad'; 'She will be a *tower* for the One out of the Triad.' In the hymn 'Ed 'enta re'eya, verse 7,1–2, we read: 'One person out of the holy Triad put on your body and became a human being.'

The connection with Mariology no doubt favoured the reshaping of the theopaschite formula into the connection of the incarnation and *unus ex trinitate*. Here too, however, one could already go back to Syrian models, as Philoxenus of Mabbug showed us in his letter to Emperor Zeno (cited above on p. 357, n. 60).

---

36. F. E. Brightman, *Liturgies*, p. 218; see also E. Hammerschmidt, *Studies*, pp. 50–53 ('The Pre-Anaphora'), here p. 52.

37. S. Euringer, *OrChr* 24 (1927), 129.

38. Maṣḥafa Milād, T. II, chap. XIII: CSCO 236, p. 75,18–19.

39. Cf. A. Grohmann, *Äthiopische Marienhymnen*, p. 75; for explanation pp. 178–79, where still further examples are given.

40. Cf. A. Grohmann, op. cit., p. 16.

4. Christ in the priestly prayer of the hours

The picture thus far developed of the position of Christ in the liturgy is also abundantly confirmed by the prayer of the hours of the Ethiopian church. Hence it will suffice to give only a few examples, since in our view the *horologion* has been researched in excellent fashion.[41]

The Christian people of Ethiopia to a striking extent take part in the prayer of the hours of the church, even if privately or within the families. There are a considerable number of appropriate books, in manuscript or printed, that attest to the general practice of the hours among the people. Nevertheless, when we speak of 'priestly prayer', we are referring to those parts of the prayer of the hours which, in the course of the *officium*, may be spoken only by the priests.

Going under the name *Kidān za-naghe* (testament of the morning) is one of the most important prayers of considerable length that the Ethiopians say every day in private, but which also has an important place in the official liturgy. It consists of several parts:

(1) the Trishagion, whose text we already know from the 'Liturgy of the Apostles';

(2) from three Kidān (testaments): (a) the Kidān of midnight, (b) the Kidān of the morning, (c) the Kidān of the evening. Since each of these prayers is in turn subdivided into three such Kidān, the result is nine prayers, which are each preceded by the Trishagion.[42]

The doctrinal content of these nine Kidān has undergone a thorough analysis,[43] which again produced the same picture as in the anaphoras: B. Velat established that it is difficult to designate the persons of the Trinity to whom individual ones of the nine Kidān are directed. Regarded from a doctrinal standpoint, most can address either the Father or the Son. But in some this distinction can be made.[44] The result is a picture that shows the Christocentrism of these prayers: 'The Kidan prefer to address the Word of God that became a human being. Hence the Christology is also much more detailed than the doctrine concerning the Father' (ibid.).

Throughout there is a Christology 'from above' or with emphasis on the divinity (Christ as Word of God, wisdom and knowledge of the Father, begotten from eternity, God of light, Proclaimer of the invisible, Revealer of the mysteries of God). Therefore the creator-power of Christ in all spheres of being is praised (ibid., 168).

The incarnate One, by contrast, is presented as the mortal One, but also as the Healer and Comforter of people. His activity as Redeemer gives us reconciliation with the Father, the eternal light, freedom from slavery and sin and death.

B. Velat stresses that praise and glorification in the Kidān are very richly represented, but intercessory prayer only very modestly, and in this the spiritual concern is prominent (ibid.). Here a modern liberation theology is in the far distance. Yet the temporal concerns of a tormented people is richly expressed in other offices.[45]

---

41. See B. Velat, *Études sur le Méeráf. Commun de l'office divin éthiopien. Introduction, trad. française, commentaire liturgique et musical* (PO 33), Paris 1966; idem, *Soma Deggua. Antiphonaire du Carême. Quatre premières semaines* (PO 32), Paris 1966. H. Quecke, *Untersuchungen zum koptischen Stundengebet*, Louvain 1970, indicates repeatedly the dependence of the Ethiopian prayer of the hours on the Coptic.

42. B. Velat, PO 33, p. 162.

43. Idem, op. cit., pp. 166–74.

44. Ibid., p. 167.

45. Cf. chap. III, 'Supplications', PO 33, pp. 187–209.

5. An example of extra-liturgical prayer to Christ

As significant testimony of private prayer, there are two litanies in the tradition, a shorter and a longer one, which address Christ exclusively. They are noteworthy in that according to E. Hammerschmidt, in the whole realm of the Eastern churches there are no litany-like prayers *outside* the prayers of supplication contained in the liturgy books.[46] It is highly probable that this is 'a unique phenomenon in the area of Eastern prayer texts'. In addition to the two litanies of Christ there is a litany of Mary, which, however, again contains a reference to Christ in every invocation.[47]

All three prayers show a great veneration of the Passion of Christ or of the compassion of the mother of Christ in the style of the Western *Stabat Mater*. Especially the second litany is of theological value. It connects all the events of Jesus' life, from his exit from heaven to his ascension and his coming again in glory, with the *propter nostram salutem* of the creed:

(1) O you who for our sake came down from heaven, hear us, our God and our Redeemer, O Christ (op. cit., 21).

(41) O you who will come again in glory to judge the living and the dead, hear us, our God and our Redeemer, O Christ.

(42) The hope of all ends of the earth, Jesus Christ, because of your flesh, which was offered for sinners, make pure our prayer, our petition, our plea (op. cit., 25).

---

46. Text and trans. by E. Hammerschmidt, *Äthiopische liturgische Texte der Bodleian Library*: (1) Christ Litany: 16–19 (33 invocations); (2) Christ Litany: 20–25 (43 invocations). This litany 'has been published in an even longer and in part different form by Grébaut with French translation' (ibid., 13, with reference to *Aethiopica* 3 [1935], 13–19: 'Litanies de Jésus-Christ'). According to E. Hammerschmidt, *Äthiopische Handschriften vom Ṭānāsee* 1, p. 118, this second litany was later inserted into the 'Book of the Eucharistic Liturgy'.

47. E. Hammerschmidt, *Äthiopische liturgische Texte*, 28–35 (litany of Mary with 48 invocations).

FINAL REFLECTIONS

With the examination of the development of post-Chalcedonian faith in Christ in the patriarchate of Alexandria, in the Sudan and in Ethiopia up to southern Arabia, we are touching important missionary areas of Christianity. The christological contribution of the region on the Nile between 451 and the appearance of Muhammad is to be characterized with few key words. With Ethiopia, for reasons of substance and practicality, we went beyond the given temporal framework.

1. Alexandria, the 'Christ-loving City'[48]

With this frequently used predicate Severus of Antioch wants to express the anti-Chalcedonian orthodoxy of this city. On the whole, it owes its theological weight in the christological discussion on Ephesus (431) and Chalcedon (451) and the related division to the three great names Cyril (d. 444), Severus of Antioch (d. 538) and Theodosius (d. 566). With the dominance of the theological initiatives of these three men, an essentially moderate Christology prevailed in Alexandria and Egypt; against the exaggerations of the Julianists and Gaianites, it left the earthly Jesus his full rights and rejected all docetic-aphthartic leanings. Yet here, in our opinion, one must consider the fact that in the miaphysite initiative, in regard to both the formula and the real interpretation of the person of Christ, certain prejudices were applied and misinterpretations suggested, which again and again led to schisms. Besides the Julianists or Gaianites, powerful groupings were represented by the tritheists (and their splinter groups), the Agnoetes and finally the Damianites, in addition to whom a large number of smaller schismatic (or heretical) groupings existed, with whom both Chalcedonian and anti-Chalcedonian patriarchs had to deal (cf., e.g., our discussions on Eulogius or Damian). Timothy Aelurus and Peter Mongus had indeed already had to fight against extremists. It is the

---

48. Cf. Severus of Ant., *Epistulae* (CPG 7070 [1]), Brooks, *SL* II (I 53, 56, IV 3, V 8), pp. 151, 169, 257, 320: 'the great Christ-loving city of the Alexandrines'; (II 3, V 15), pp. 216.357: 'the great Christ-loving city of Alexander'. Also Theodos. of Alex., *Mandat. alt.*: 'christophilae civitatis Alexandrinorum' (Doc. mon., CSCO 103, p. 95,2–3).

sixth century, however, that offers in Alexandria an impressive picture when patriarchal authority sometimes either could not prevail ('anarchy') or shut itself off in the form of mutually competing patriarchs – which in Syria was commented on with mockery and scorn with these words: 'It was necessary in Antioch to appoint two patriarchs, as there were in Alexandria at the same time three patriarchs besides the one of the synodites [i.e., Chalcedonians].'[49]

Speculative initiatives can be made out only in Alexandria: among the patriarchs on the Chalcedonian side in Eulogius – even if his contribution may be quite a bit smaller than was for a long time assumed – and on the anti-Chalcedonian side in Theodosius and, among the scholars, above all in John Philoponus. Yet the Chalcedonians managed at most to achieve the success of personal respect. The *mia-physis* Christology finally prevailed for the most part in the hierarchy, in popular faith and among the monks.

With regard to conceptual language, for the Alexandrian anti-Chalcedonians *hypostasis* and *physis* in the doctrine of the incarnation ('*oikonomia*') continued to remain synonymous (in contrast to the doctrine of the Trinity), and this mostly without reflection. John Philoponus employed his whole Aristotelian schooling to offer to his confession a philosophical justification in the equating of particular nature and hypostasis. With logical consistency his initiative on the doctrine of the Trinity led, nonetheless, to theoretical tritheism, and further groupings split off over his doctrine.

Of great significance was the intensified application of the concept of *energeia* to the interpretation of unity in Christ. Cyril was the starting-point of this new emphasis in the interpretation of the miracles of Christ, but Severus gave the *mia energeia* in Christ a greater function for the explanation of the *henosis* in Christ (in order thus to suppress especially the temptation to aphthartism). Patriarch Theodosius clearly maintained this prominence in the Agnoete dispute. The confession of *mia energeia* now clearly belonged to the foundation of the miaphysite confession. In this, however, with all the recognition of Christ's soul in the picture of Christ, the intellectual activity of the humanity of Christ could not come into its own. A stronger awareness of the problem was developed here only by Philoponus, who acknowledged the intellectual activity (at least) as an instrument of the Logos. But the underlying anthropological

---

49. John of Eph., *HE* IV 44: Brooks, CSCO 106, p. 171: 'sicut Alexandriae etiam tres praeter patriarcham Synoditarum'.

initiative is not easy to discern with him; with others it is lacking altogether.

No one ventured to think of a natural, autonomous – though peculiar to the Logos-subject – intellectual human cognition or activity of Christ, because it seemed to be necessarily connected with Nestorianism. A takeover of the passion that is borne by free human decision and yet peculiar to the divine subject and bearer of human nature was even less conceivable, as even the Logos as Logos had to give 'permission'.

2. The Archimandrite Shenoute and his christological significance

In the environment of this younger contemporary of Cyril we were able to ascertain a proclamation almost completely free from the dispute over the one or the two natures. The simple kerygma and plain Jesus piety stand at the centre. In him no progress in the conceptual language or analysis and thus in christological speculation is recognizable. Through the utilization of texts newly made available, we were able to clear away the old ingrained suspicion that the monastic father subscribed to a 'Christ-less, barren piety'. On the contrary, in his writings a strong Christocentrism can be made out. He also belongs in the history of the Jesus prayer. Around him, however, 'the wilderness was alive', even if this was other than he would have wished it. The new exhortation *Contra Origenistas* reveals a downright frightening view of the gnostic, Marcionite, Manichaean and Origenist endangerment of the Christian faith and monastic life in the middle and upper Nile up to the imperial boundary. The observations that result for us from the newly edited letters of Patriarch Timothy Aelurus to Alexandria (and Constantinople) have also been confirmed by Shenoute's admonition for the monasteries and churches of the upper Nile in the same period.

3. Nubia

On the basis of excavations in connection with the erection of the Aswan High Dam, this early Christian kingdom was able to become the object of intensive research, which not just incidentally also produced valuable christological results. Because of the activity of Patriarch Theodosius (d. 566) and the imperial couple Justinian and Theodora, sixth-century Nubia belongs in the history of the Chalcedonian–anti-Chalcedonian struggle. Through it, faith in Christ was established in the Sudan for approximately one millennium.

4. Ethiopia

The kingdom of Axum, in which the proclamation of the gospel began already in the fourth century, belongs to the most peculiar and varied of ecclesiastical formations. In this land, as nowhere else, in the building up of the Christian life of faith, of ritual and customs, the result was a mixture of universal-church traditions and striking idiosyncrasies, of Hellenistic-Alexandrian, Jewish, Arabic and Byzantine influences. Here are a theology and a piety in which in individual cases Mariology receives such pre-eminence that even a eucharistic anaphora is styled in Marian fashion! Was a Jewish-Christian church developed here that deserves this name more than in other patriarchates? How seriously may one value the claim of a messianic kingdom as religious heir? What a curious vision, to feel oneself to be a parallel to the Byzantine God-empire and to regard the city of Jerusalem as the common centre for both empires, so to speak as an 'open city' of the *orbis christianus*!

Cyril, the 'father of dogmas', did not survive only in Alexandria and Egypt. In a peculiar way he was also already present very early in Ethiopia, especially through the so-called *Qērellos*, the translation into Ethiopic of the collection of Cyrillian and other writings now sufficiently available to us. To it Ethiopian theology and spirituality may owe – to mention only this – the theme of anointment, which also, unfortunately, unleashed centuries-long disagreement. It will be the task of scholarship to research more thoroughly Cyril's teaching of anointment and his pneumatology in general and to compare them with Ethiopian doctrinal history and spirituality.

SELECTED BIBLIOGRAPHY

Abramowski, L., 'Ein Text des Johannes Chrysostomus über die Auferstehung in den Belegsammlungen des Timotheus Älurus', in C. Laga et al. (eds.), *After Chalcedon* (OLA 18), Louvain 1985, 1–10.

Accademia Nazionale dei Lincei, *Convegno Internazionale. Passaggio dal mondo antico al medio evo da Teodosio a san Gregorio Magno*, Rome, 25–28 May 1977 (= Atti dei Convegni Lincei 45, Rome 1980).

Alemu, K., Η ΧΡΙΣΤΟΛΟΓΙΑ ΤΩΝ ΑΙΘΙΟΠΙΚΩΝ ΑΝΑΦΟΡΩΝ ΕΝ ΣΧΕΣΕΙ ΠΡΟΣ ΤΟ ΔΟΓΜΑ ΤΗΣ ΧΑΛΚΗΔΟΝΟΣ (The Christology of the Ethiopian Anaphoras in Relation to the Dogma of Chalcedon), Thessalonica 1977.

Allen, P., *Evagrius Scholasticus the Church Historian* (SpicSLov 41), Louvain 1981.

Ananian, P., 'L'opuscolo di Eutichio patriarca di Costantinopoli sulla "Distinzione della natura e persona"', in *Armeniaca*, Venice 1969, 316–82.

Anfray, P., A. Caquot and P. Nautin, 'Une nouvelle inscription grecque d'Ézana', *Journal de Savants* (Oct.–Dec. 1970), 260–74.

Assfalg, J., *Die Ordnung des Priestertums. Ein altes liturgisches Handbuch der koptischen Kirche* (Publications du Centre d'Études Orientales de la Custodie Franciscaine de Terre-Sainte-Coptica 1), Cairo 1955.

Atiya, A. S., *A History of Eastern Christianity* I, London 1968.

Bacht, H., 'Die Rolle des orientalischen Mönchtums in den kirchenpolitischen Auseinandersetzungen um Chalkedon (431–519)', in *Chalkedon* II, 193–314.

— 'Christusgemeinschaft. Der theologische Gehalt der frühesten ägyptischen Mönchsdokumente', in *Praesentia Christi*, FS J. Betz, ed. L. Lies, Düsseldorf 1984, 444–55.

Bethune-Baker, J. F., *Nestorius and his Teaching*, Cambridge 1908.

Beyene, Y., *L'unzione di Cristo nella teologia etiopica. Contributo di ricerca su nuovi documenti etiopici inediti* (OCA 215), Rome 1981.

Bezold, C., *Kebra Nagast. Die Herrlichkeit der Könige. Nach den Handschriften in Berlin, London, Oxford und Paris* (*ABAW.PP* 23), Munich 1909.

Bianchi, U., 'Polemiche gnostiche e anti-gnostiche sul Dio dell'Antico Testamento', *Aug* 22 (1982), 35–51.

— 'Le gnosticisme et les origines du Christianisme', in *Gnosticisme et monde hellénistique*, ed. J. Ries et al., Louvain 1982, 211–35.

Böhm, W., *Johannes Philoponus. Grammatikos von Alexandrien (6. Jh. n. Chr.). Christliche Naturwissenschaft im Ausklang der Antike, Vorläufer der modernen Physik, Wissenschaft und Bibel. Ausgewählte Schriften*, Munich–Paderborn–Vienna 1967.

Brakmann, H., 'Zu den Fragmenten einer griechischen Basileios-Liturgie aus dem koptischen Makarioskloster', *OrChr* 66 (1982), 118–43.

Brightman, F. E., *Liturgies Eastern and Western* I: *Eastern Liturgies*, Oxford 1896.

Brogi, M., *La Santa Salmodia Annuale della Chiesa copta. Traduzione, introduzione e annotazione* (= *SOC.Ae*), Cairo 1962.

Brooks, E. W., 'The Patriarch Paul of Antioch and the Alexandrine Schism of 575', *ByzZ* 30 (1929), 468–76.

Budge, E. A. W., *Miscellaneous Coptic Texts in the Dialect of Upper Egypt*, London 1915, 445–93 (T), 984–1011 (V).

— *The Book of the Saints of the Ethiopian Church. A Translation of the Ethiopic Synaxarium* I–IV, Cambridge 1928.

Cameron, Alan, 'Wandering Poets. A Literary Movement in Byzantine Egypt', *Historia* 14 (1965), 470–509.

Camplani, A., *Le lettere festali di Atanasio di Alessandria. Studio storico-critico* (= CMCL), Rome 1989.

Carpentier, E., 'Martyrium Sancti Arethae et Sociorum in civitate Negran' (BHG 166), in ASS Octobris X, 1861, 721–59.

Cavallera, F., 'Le dossier patristique de Timothée Aelure', *BLE* 4/1 (1909), 342–59.

Cerulli, E., *Scritti Teologici Etiopici dei Secoli XVI–XVII* II: *La Storia dei Quattro Concili ed altri opuscoli monofisiti* (ST 204), Vatican City 1960.

— *Storia della letteratura etiopica*, Milan ²1961.

Chabot, J. B., *Chronique de Michel le Syrien. Patriarche jacobite d'Antioche (1166–1199). Éditée pour la première fois et traduite en français* II, Paris 1901, Brussels ²1963; IV (Syriac text), Paris 1910, Brussels ²1963.

— *Synodicon Orientale*, Paris 1902.

— *Documenta ad origines monophysitarum illustrandas*, CSCO 17 (T), Louvain 1908, ²1952; 103 (V), Louvain 1933, ²1952.

Chronicon anonymum ad annum 846 pertinens, ed. E. W. Brooks and J.-B. Chabot, in *Chronica Minora,* CSCO Syr. 3, 4, Paris 1903.

Colpe, C., 'Häretische Patriarchen bei Eutychios', *JAC* 14 (1971), 48–60.

Coquin, R., 'L'Anaphore alexandrine de saint Marc', *Mus* 82 (1969), 307–56.

Cramer, M., *Das christlich-koptische Ägypten einst und heute. Eine Orientierung*, Wiesbaden 1959.

Cramer, M., and H. Bacht, 'Der antichalkedonische Aspekt im historisch-biographischen Schrifttum der koptischen Monophysiten (6.–7. Jh.). Ein Beitrag zur Geschichte der Entstehung der monophysitischen Kirche Ägyptens', in *Chalkedon* II, 315–38.

Crouzel, H., *Théologie de l'image de Dieu chez Origène*, Paris 1955.

Cyril of Alexandria. Select Letters, ed. and trans. by L. R. Wickham, Oxford 1983.

Demicheli, A. M., 'La politica religiosa di Giustiniano in Egitto. Riflessi sulla chiesa egiziana della legislazione ecclesiastica giustinianea', *Aegyptus* 63 (1983), 217–57.

Dihle, A., *Umstrittene Daten. Untersuchungen zum Auftreten der Griechen am Roten Meer* (WAAFLNW 32), Cologne–Opladen 1965.

Dillmann, A., 'Über die Anfänge des Axumitischen Reiches', *AAWB.PH* 1878, Berlin 1879, 177–238.

— 'Zur Geschichte des Axumitischen Reiches im vierten bis sechsten Jahrhundert', *AAWB.PH* 1880, Berlin 1881, 1–51.

Dinkler, E., 'König Ezana von Aksum und das Christentum. Ein Randproblem der Geschichte Nubiens', in *Ägypten und Kusch. Schriften zur Geschichte und Kultur des Alten Orients* (Mélanges F. Hintze) 13, Berlin 1977, 121–32.

Dombrowski, F. A., *Ṭānāsee 106: Eine Chronik der Herrscher Äthiopiens* (ÄthFor 12B), Wiesbaden 1983.

Dombrowski, W. W., and F. A. Dombrowski, 'Frumentius/Abbā Salāmā: Zu den Nachrichten über die Anfänge des Christentums in Äthiopien', *OrChr* 68 (1984), 114–69.

Ebener, D., *Nonnos. Werke in zwei Bänden. Leben und Taten des Dionysos I–XXXII* (vol. I), *Leben und Taten des Dionysos XXXIII–XLVIII. Nachdichtung des Johannesevangeliums* (vol. II) (= Bibl. d. Antike, Greek series), Berlin–Weimar 1985.

Ebied, R. Y., A. Van Roey and L. R. Wickham, *Peter of Callinicum. Anti-Tritheist Dossier* (OLA 10), Louvain 1981.

Ebied, R. Y., and L. R. Wickham, 'A Collection of Unpublished Syriac Letters of Timothy Aelurus', *JTS* 21 (1970), 321–69.

— 'Timothy Aelurus: Against the Definition of the Council of Chalcedon', in C. Laga et al. (eds.), *After Chalcedon* (OLA 18), Louvain 1985, 115–66.

Engberding, H., 'Das chalkedonische Christusbild und die Liturgien der monophysitischen Kirchengemeinschaften', in *Chalkedon* II, 697–733.

Engelhardt, I., *Mission und Politik in Byzanz. Ein Beitrag zur Strukturanalyse byzantinischer Mission zur Zeit Justins und Justinians* (MiscByzMon 19), Munich 1974.

Euringer, S., 'Die Marienharfe (ʾArgānona weddāse). Nach der Ausgabe von Pontus Leander übersetzt', *OrChr* 24 (1927), 120–45, 338–55; 25/26 (1928/29), 79–108, 248–78; 27 (1930), 202–31; 28 (1931), 60–89, 209–39.

— 'Die Äthiopische Anaphora Unserer Herrin', *OrChr* 34 (1937), 63–102, 248–62.

Evagrius Scholasticus, *The Ecclesiastical History of Evagrius with the Scholia*, edited with introduction, critical notes and indices by J. Bidez and L. Parmentier, Amsterdam 1964.

Fedalto, G. *Hierarchia Ecclesiastica Orientalis. Series episcoporum ecclesiarum christianarum orientalium* I: *Patriarchatus Constantinopolitanus;* II: *Patriarchatus Alexandrinus, Antiochenus, Hierosolymitanus*, Padua 1988.

Felici, S., *Cristologia e catechesi patristica* 1 (BiblScRel 31), Rome 1980.

Frandsen, P. J., and E. Richter Aerøe, 'Shenoute: A Bibliography', in D. W. Young (ed.), *Studies in Honor of J. J. Polotsky*, East Gloucester, Mass. 1981, 147–76.

Frend, W. H. C., *The Rise of the Monophysite Movement*, Cambridge 1972.

Gaffron, H.-G., *Studien zum koptischen Philippusevangelium unter besonderer Berücksichtigung der Sakramente*, diss., Bonn 1969.

Gerhards, A., 'Le phénomène du Sanctus adressé au Christ. Son origine, sa signification et sa persistance dans les Anaphores de l'église d'Orient', in A. M. Triacca and A. Pistoia (eds.), *Le Christ dans la liturgie*, Rome 1981, 65–83.

— *Die griechische Gregoriosanaphora. Ein Beitrag zur Geschichte des Eucharistischen Hochgebets* (LQF 65), Münster 1984.

Ghedini, G., 'Luci nuove dai papiri sullo scisma meleziano e il monachismo in Egitto', in *La Scuola Catt.*, series 6, vol. 6, 1925, 261–80.

Giamberardini, G., 'La doctrine christologique des Coptes', *POC* 13 (1963), 211–20.

Golega, J., *Studien über die Evangeliendichtung des Nonnos von Panopolis* (BSHT 15), Breslau 1930.

Goubert, P., 'Patriarches d'Antioche et d'Alexandrie contemporains de S. Grégoire le Grand. Notes de prosopographie byzantine', *RevÉtByz* 25 (1967), 65–76.

Griffith, F. Ll., 'The Nubian Texts of the Christian Period', *APAW.PH* 8, Berlin 1913, 41–53.

Grillmeier, A., 'Markos Eremites und der Origenismus. Versuch einer Neudeutung von Op. XI', in F. Paschke (ed., in co-operation with J. Dummer, J. Irmscher and K. Treu), *Überlieferungsgeschichtliche Untersuchungen*, FS Marcel Richard III (TU 125), Berlin 1981, 253–83.

— 'Die Taufe Christi und die Taufe der Christen. Zur Tauftheologie des Philoxenus von Mabbug und ihrer Bedeutung für die christliche Spiritualität', in *Fides Sacramenti – Sacramentum Fidei*, FS P. Smulders, Assen 1981, 137–75.

— 'La "peste d'Origène". Soucis du patriarche d'Alexandrie dus à l'apparition d'origénistes en Haute Égypte (444–451)', in ΑΛΕΞΑΝΔΡΙΝΑ, Mél. Cl. Mondésert, Paris 1987, 221–37.

Grimm, G., H. Heinen and E. Winter, *Alexandrien. Kulturbegegnungen dreier Jahrtausende im Schmelztiegel einer mediterranen Großstadt* (Aegyptiaca Treverensia 1), Mainz 1981.

Grohmann, A., 'Die im Äthiopischen, Arabischen und Koptischen erhaltenen Visionen Apa Schenute's von Atripe. Text und Übersetzung I', *ZDMG* 67 (1913), 187–267; II. 'Die arabische Homilie des Cyrillus', *ZDMG* 68 (1914), 1–46.

— *Äthiopische Marienhymnen* (*ASAW* 33/4), Leipzig 1919.

Guidi, I., 'Uno squarcio della Storia Ecclesiastica di Abissinia', *Bessarione* 8 (1900/1), 10–25.

Guillaumont, A., art. 'Copte (Littérature spirituelle)', *DSp* 2, 1953, 2266–78.

— 'Une inscription copte sur la "Prière de Jésus"', in *Aux origines du monachisme chrétien*, Bégrolles en Mauge 1979, 168–83.

Haardt, R., *Die Gnosis. Wesen und Zeugnisse*, Salzburg 1967.

Hagedorn, U. and D. (eds.), *Olympiodor, Diakon von Alexandria. Kommentar zu Hiob* (PTSt 24), Berlin–New York 1984.

Hammerschmidt, E., 'Die Anfänge des Christentums in Äthiopien', *ZM* 38 (1954), 281–94.

— 'Äthiopische liturgische Texte der Bodleian Library in Oxford', *VIOF* 38 (1960), 39–72.

— *Studies in the Ethiopic Anaphoras* (BBA 25), 1961; 2nd revised edition (ÄthFor 25), Stuttgart 1987.

— 'Der Kult der äthiopischen Kirche', in F. Herrmann, *Symbolik der Religionen* 10, *Symbolik des orthodoxen und orientalischen Christentums*, Stuttgart 1962, 214–33.

— *Stellung und Bedeutung des Sabbats in Äthiopien* (Studia Delitzschiana 7), Stuttgart 1963.

— *Äthiopische Handschriften vom Ṭānāsee* 1: *Reisebericht und Beschreibung der Handschriften in dem Kloster des heiligen Gabriel auf der Insel Kebran* (Verzeichnis der orientalischen Handschriften in Deutschland XX/1), Wiesbaden 1973.

Hänggi, A., and I. Pahl, *Prex Eucharistica. Textus e variis liturgiis antiquioribus selecti* (SpicFrib 12), Fribourg 1968.

Harden, J. M., *The Ethiopic Didascalia*, London–New York 1920.

— *The Anaphoras of the Ethiopic Liturgy*, London 1928.

Hedrick, C. W., 'Gnostic Proclivities in the Greek Life of Pachomius and the Sitz im Leben of the Nag Hammadi Library', *NovTest* 22 (1980), 78–94.

Hefele, C. J., and H. Leclercq, *Histoire des conciles d'après les documents originaux* II/2, Paris 1908.

Helmer, S., *Der Neuchalkedonismus*, Bonn 1962.

Hermann, T., 'Johannes Philoponus als Monophysit', *ZNW* 29 (1930), 209–64.

Heussi, K., *Der Ursprung des Mönchtums*, Tübingen 1936.

Heyer, F., *Die Kirche Äthiopiens*, Berlin–New York 1971.

Höfner, M., 'Die Kultur des vorislamischen Südarabien', *ZDMG* 99 (1945–49), 15–28.

— 'Über sprachliche und kulturelle Beziehungen zwischen Südarabien und Äthiopien im Altertum', in *ACIStEt*, 435–44.

Honigmann, E., *Évêques et Évêchés monophysites d'Asie antérieure au VIᵉ siècle* (CSCO 127), Louvain 1951.

Inglisian, V., 'Chalkedon und die armenische Kirche', in *Chalkedon* II, 361–417.

Isaac, E., 'An Obscure Component in Ethiopian Church History. An examination of various theories pertaining to the problem of the origin and nature of Ethiopian Christianity', *Mus* 85 (1972), 225–58.

Jakobielski, S., *Faras III. A History of the Bishopric of Pachoras on the Basis of Coptic Inscriptions*, Warsaw 1972.

John of Damascus, see B. Kotter.

Johnson, D. W., 'Further Fragments of a Coptic History of the Church', *Enchoria* 6 (1976), 7–17.

— 'Coptic Reactions to Gnosticism and Manichaeism', *Mus* 100 (1987), 199–209.

Jugie, M., art. 'Gaianites', *DTC* 9 (1915), 999–1002.

— art. 'Gaianite (la controverse) et la passibilité du corps de Jésus-Christ', *DTC* 9 (1915), 1002–23.

Jülicher, A., 'Die Liste der alexandrinischen Patriarchen im 6. und 7. Jahrhundert', in *Festgabe Karl Müller*, Tübingen 1922, 7–23.

Jungmann, J. A., *Die Stellung Christi im liturgischen Gebet* (LQF 19/20), Münster ²1962.

Koenen, L., 'Manichäische Mission und Klöster in Ägypten', in G. Grimm, H. Heinen and E. Winter (eds.), *Das römisch-byzantinische Ägypten* (Aegyptiaca Treverensia 2), Mainz 1983, 93–108.

Kotter, B., *Die Schriften des Johannes von Damaskos*, ed. Byz. Institut d. Abtei Scheyern, II. *Expositio fidei* (PTSt 12), Berlin–New York 1973.

— IV. *Liber de haeresibus. Opera polemica* (PTSt 22), Berlin–New York 1981.

Kraus, J., *Die Anfänge des Christentums in Nubien*, Mödling 1930 (reprint: MWSt 2, 1931) (= Kraus I).

— 'Neues zur Geschichte des christlichen Nubien', *NZM* 24 (1968), 241–57 (= Kraus II).

Krause, M., 'Zur Kirchen- und Theologiegeschichte Nubiens', in E. Dinkler, *Kunst und Geschichte Nubiens in christlicher Zeit. Ergebnisse und Probleme auf Grund der jüngsten Ausgrabungen*, Recklinghausen 1970, 71–86.

— 'Koptische Literatur', *LexÄg* III (1980), 694–728.

Krause, M., and P. Labib, *Die drei Versionen des Apokryphon des Johannes* (ADAI.K 1), Wiesbaden 1962.

Krüger, G., *Monophysitische Streitigkeiten im Zusammenhange mit der Reichspolitik*, Jena 1884.

Kuhn, K. H., 'A Fifth-Century Egyptian Abbot: I. Besa and His Background'; II. 'Monastic Life in Besa's Day'; 'III. Besa's Christianity', *JTS* 5 (1954), 36–48; 147–87; 6 (1955), 35–48.

Laga, C., J. A. Munitiz and L. van Rompay (eds.), *After Chalcedon. Studies in Theology and Church History. Offered to Prof. A. Van Roey for His Seventieth Birthday* (OLA 18), Louvain 1985.

Lanne, E., 'Le Grand Euchologe du Monastère Blanc. Texte copte éd. avec trad. franç.', PO 28 (1958), 269–407.

Lebon, J., 'La christologie de Timothée Aelure . . . d'après les sources syriaques inédites', *RHE* 9 (1908), 677–702.

— *Le monophysisme sévérien*, Louvain 1909 (= Lebon I).

— 'La christologie du monophysisme syrien', in *Chalkedon* I, 425–580 (= Lebon II).

Leclercq, H., art. 'Kosmas Indicopleustès', *DACL* 8/1, Paris 1928, 820–49.

Lefort, L. T., 'Catéchèse Christologique de Chenoute', *ZÄS* 80 (1955), 40–55.

Leipoldt, J., *Schenute von Atripe und die Entstehung des national ägyptischen Christentums* (TU 25/1), Leipzig 1903.

Le Quien, M., *Oriens Christianus* II, Paris 1740, Graz 1958.

Lietzmann, H., *Apollinaris von Laodicea und seine Schule*, Tübingen 1904.

Lieu, S. N. C., *Manichaeism in the Later Roman Empire and Medieval China. A Historical Survey*, Manchester 1985.

— 'Some Themes in Later Roman Anti-Manichaean Polemics', I, *BJRL* 68 (1985/86), 434–69; II, *BJRL* 69 (1986/87), 235–75.

Livrea, E., *Nonno di Panopoli. Parafrasi del Vangelo di S. Giovanni. Canto XVIII, Introduzione, testo critico, traduzione e commentario*, Naples 1989.

Lodi, E., *Enchiridion Euchologicum Fontium Liturgicorum (EEuFL)* (BEL.S 15), Rome 1979.

Löfgren, O., and S. Euringer, 'Die beiden aethiopischen Anaphoren "des heiligen Cyrillus, Patriarchen von Alexandrien" ', *ZSem* 9 (1933/34), 44–86.

Loofs, F., *Nestoriana. Die Fragmente des Nestorius*, Halle 1905.

Ludolfus, I., *Historia Aethiopica sive Brevis & succincta descriptio Regni Habessinorum Quod vulgo male Presbyteri Iohannis vocatur*, Frankfurt/Main 1681.

— *Ad suam Historiam Aethiopicam antehac editam Commentarius*, Frankfurt/Main 1691.

Macomber, W. F., 'The Greek Text of the Coptic Mass and of the Anaphoras of Basil and Gregory According to the Kacmarcik Codex', *OCP* 43, 1977, 308–34.

— 'The Anaphora of Saint Mark according to the Kacmarcik Codex', *OCP* 45, 1979, 75–98.

Martin, H., *La controverse trithéite dans l'Empire Byzantin au VIe siècle*, diss. Louvain.

— 'Jean Philopon et la controverse trithéite du VI° siècle' (*StudPat* 5 = TU 80), 1962, 519–25.

Maspero, J., *Histoire des Patriarches d'Alexandrie depuis la mort de l'empereur Anastase jusqu'à la réconciliation des églises jacobites (518–616)*, Paris 1923.

Meyerhof, M., 'Von Alexandrien nach Bagdad. Ein Beitrag zur Geschichte des philosophischen und medizinischen Unterrichts bei den Arabern', *SPAW* 1930, 389–429.

Michałowski, K., *Faras – Die Kathedrale aus dem Wüstensand*, Einsiedeln–Cologne 1967.

Michel le Syrien, see J. B. Chabot.

Moberg, A., *The Book of Himyarites. Fragments of a hitherto unknown Syriac Work*, Lund 1924.

Monneret de Villard, U., *Storia della Nubia cristiana* (OCA 118), Rome 1938.

Moorsel, P. van, 'Une théophanie Nubienne', *RivArchCr* 42 (1968), 297–316.

— 'The Coptic Apse-Composition and its Living Creatures', in *Études Nubiennes* (= Colloques de Chantilly 1975), Cairo 1978, 325–33.

Müller, C. D. G., 'Benjamin I. 38. Patriarch von Alexandrien', *Mus* 69 (1956), 313–40.

— *Kirche und Mission unter den Arabern in vorislamischer Zeit* (SGV 249), Tübingen 1967.

— *Die Homilie über die Hochzeit zu Kana und weitere Schriften des Patriarchen Benjamin I. von Alexandrien* (*AHAW.PH* 1968/1), Heidelberg 1968.

— 'Der Stand der Forschungen über Benjamin I., den 38. Patriarchen von Alexandrien', *ZDMG* Supp. 1, 2, Wiesbaden 1969, 404–10.

— 'Grundzüge der Frömmigkeit in der nubischen Kirche', in *Études Nubiennes* (= Colloques de Chantilly 1975), Cairo 1978, 209–24.

— 'Damian, Papst und Patriarch von Alexandrien', *OrChr* 70 (1986), 118–42.

Muyser, J., *Maria's Heerlijkheid in Egypte. Een studie der Koptische Maria-literatur* I, Louvain–Utrecht 1935.

Nagel, P., *Probleme der koptischen Literatur* (WB [H] 1968/1, [K 2]), Halle 1968.

Nau, F., 'Histoire de Dioscore, Patriarche d'Alexandrie, écrite par son disciple Théopiste', *JA* 10/1 (1903), 241–310.

Orbe, A., *Cristología gnóstica* I, II, Madrid 1976.

— 'Gli Apocrifi cristiani a Nag Hammadi', *Aug* 23 (1983), 83–109.

Orlandi, T., *Storia della Chiesa di Alessandria II, Testo copto, traduzione e commento.* Vol II: *Da Teofilo a Timoteo II* (= *Testi e documenti per lo studio dell'antichità XXXI*), Milan–Varese 1970.

— 'Un testo copto sulle origini del cristianesimo in Nubia', in *Études Nubiennes* (= Colloques de Chantilly 1975), Cairo 1978, 225–30.

— 'Il *Dossier* copto di Agatonico di Tarso. Studio letterario e storico', in D. W. Young (ed.), *Studies presented to H. J. Polotsky*, Beacon Hill 1981, 269–99.

— 'Gli Apocrifi copti', *Aug* 23 (1983), 57–71.

— (ed.), *Shenute. Contra Origenistas. Testo con introduzione e traduzione* (= CMCL), Rome 1985.

— art. 'Koptische Kirche', *TRE* 19 (1989), 595–607.

Pearson, B. A., and J. E. Goehring (eds.), *The Roots of Egyptian Christianity*, Philadelphia 1986.

Perrone, L., *La chiesa di Palestina e le controversie cristologiche*, Brescia 1980.

Pigulewskaja, N., *Byzanz auf den Wegen nach Indien. Aus der Geschichte des byzantinischen Handels mit dem Orient vom 4. bis 6. Jahrhundert* (BBA 36), Berlin–Amsterdam 1969.

Preller, A. H., *Quaestiones Nonnianae desumptae e Paraphrasi Sancti Evangelii Johannei*, cap. XVIII–XIV, Nijmegen 1918.

Pusey, P. E., *S. P. N. Cyrilli archiepiscopi Alexandrini in D. Ioannis euangelium*, 3 vols., Oxford 1872.

Quecke, H., *Untersuchungen zum koptischen Stundengebet* (PIOL 3), Louvain 1970.

— 'Zukunftschancen bei der Erforschung der koptischen Liturgie', in R. Mcl. Wilson, *The Future of Coptic Studies* (Coptic Studies I), Leiden 1978, 164–96.

Renaudot, E., *Liturgiarum Orientalium Collectio* I–II, Frankfurt ²1847.

Reuss, J., 'Der Exeget Ammonius und die Fragmente seines Matthäus- und Johannes-Kommentars', *Bib* 22 (1941), 13–20.

— 'Der Presbyter Ammonius von Alexandrien und sein Kommentar zum Johannes-Evangelium', *Bib* 44 (1963), 159–70.

— *Johanneskommentare aus der griechischen Kirche* (TU 89), Berlin 1966.

Richard, M., 'Les florilèges diphysites du Vᵉ et du VIᵉ siècle', in *Chalkedon* I, 721–48 (= Op. Min. I, no. 3).

Riggi, C., *Epifanio contro Mani*, Rome 1967.

Riße, G., *'Gott ist Christus, der Sohn der Maria'. Eine Studie zum Christusbild im Koran* (= *Begegnung*, vol. 2), Bonn 1989.

Rondeau, M.-J., *Les commentaires patristiques du Psautier (IIIᵉ–Vᵉ siècles)*, vol. 1: *Les travaux des pères grecs et latins sur le Psautier. Recherches et Bilan* (OCA 219), Rome 1982.

— vol. 2: *Exégèse prosopologique et théologie* (OCA 220), Rome 1985.

Rothstein, G., *Die Dynastie der Lahmiden in al-Ḥira. Ein Versuch zur arabisch-persischen Geschichte zur Zeit der Sasaniden*, Teil I, diss. Halle 1898; Teil II, Berlin 1899.

Rucker, I., 'Cyrillus von Alexandrien und Timotheos Aelurus in der alten armenischen Christenheit', *HandAm* 11–12 (1927), 699–714.

Rudolph, K., *Die Gnosis*, Göttingen 1977.

Ryckmans, J., 'Le christianisme en Arabie du Sud préislamique', in *Atti del Convegno Internazionale sul tema: L'Oriente nella storia della civiltà*, ed. AccNazLinc a. CCCLXI–1964, Rome 1964, 413–53.

Saffrey, H.-D., 'Le chrétien Jean Philopon et la survivance de l'école d'Alexandrie au VIᵉ siècle', *RevÉtGrec* 67 (1954), 396–410.

Sambursky, S., *Das physikalische Weltbild der Antike*, Zurich–Stuttgart 1965.

Sanda, A., *Opuscula Monophysitica Ioannis Philoponi*, Beirut 1930.

Schedl, C., *Muhammad und Jesus. Die christologisch relevanten Texte des Koran*, Vienna–Freiburg–Basel 1978.

Schneemelcher, W., 'Die Epiklese bei den griechischen Vätern', in *Die Anrufung des hl. Geistes im Abendmahl* (ÖR.B 31), Frankfurt 1977, 68–94.

Schönfelder, J. M., 'Die Tritheiten', in idem, *Die Kirchen-Geschichte des Johannes von Ephesus. Aus dem Syrischen übersetzt*, Munich 1862, 267–311.

Schwartz, E., *Codex Vaticanus gr. 1431* (*ABAW.PH* XXXII 6), Munich 1927.

— *Drei dogmatische Schriften Justinians* (*ABAW.PH* 18), Munich 1939.

— *Vigiliusbriefe* (*SBAW* 1940, 2), Munich 1940.

Sedlar, J. W., *India and the Greek World*, Totowa, New Jersey 1980.

Shahīd, I., 'Byzantino-Arabica. The Conference of Ramla, A.D. 524[?]', *JNES* 23 (1964), 115–31.

— *The Martyrs of Najran. New Documents* (SubsHag 49), Brussels 1971.

Sieben, H. J., *Die Konzilsidee der Alten Kirche*, Paderborn–Munich–Vienna–Zurich 1979.

Sorabji, R. R. K., *Time, Creation and the Continuum. Theories in Antiquity and the Early Middle Ages*, London 1983.

— art. 'Johannes Philoponus', *TRE* 17 (1987), 144–50.

— (ed.), *Philoponus and the Rejection of Aristotelian Science*, London 1987.

Stein, E., *Geschichte des spätrömischen Reiches* I, Vienna 1928; revised French edition: *Histoire du Bas-empire*, ed. J.-R. Palanque, I, Bruges 1959; II, Paris–Brussels–Amsterdam 1949.

Studer, B., 'Consubstantialis Patri, Consubstantialis Matri. Une antithèse christologique chez Léon le Grand', *RevÉtAug* 18 (1972), 87–115.

Ter-Mekerttschian, K. and E. Ter-Minassiantz, *Timotheus Älurus' des Patriarchen von Alexandrien Widerlegung der auf der Synode zu Chalcedon festgesetzten Lehre*, Leipzig 1908.

Thelamon, F., *Paiens et Chrétiens au IVe siècle. L'apport de l' 'Histoire ecclésiastique' de Rufin d'Aquilée*, Paris 1981.

Theodorus Lector, *Historia Ecclesiastica*, ed. G. C. Hansen, GSC, Berlin 1971.

Theophanes, *Chronographia*, ed. C. de Boor, 2 vols., Lipsiae 1883–85.

Thompson, H., 'Dioscorus und Shenoute', in *Recueil . . . J.-Fr. Champollion* (BEHE 234), 1922, 367–76.

Till, W., *Die gnostischen Schriften des Papyrus Berolinensis 8502* (TU 60), Berlin 1955.

Triacca, A. M. and A. Pistoia (eds.), *Le Christ dans la liturgie. Conférences Saint-Serge XXVIIe Semaine d'Études Liturgiques Paris, 24–28 Juin 1981* (BEL.S 20), Rome 1981.

Troll, C., 'Die kulturgeographische Stellung und Eigenart des Hochlandes von Äthiopien zwischen dem Orient und Äquatorialafrika', in *ACIStEt*, 29–44.

Ullendorff, E., 'Hebraic-Jewish Elements in Abyssinian (Monophysite) Christianity', *JSS* 1 (1956), 216–56.

— *Ethiopia and the Bible*, London 1967.

Unione Academica Nazionale, *Coptic Bibliography* 1–4 (= CMCL), Rome 1989.

Uqbit, T., *Current Christological Positions of Ethiopian Orthodox Theologians* (OCA 196), Rome 1973.

Van Roey, A., 'Fragments antiariens de Jean Philopon', *OLP* 10 (1979), 237–50.

— 'Les fragments trithéites de Jean Philopon', *OLP* 11 (1980), 135–63.

— 'La controverse trithéite depuis la condamnation de Conon et Eugène jusqu'à la conversion de l'évêque Elie', in *Von Kanaan bis Kerala*, FS J. P. M. van der Ploeg, Kevelaer–Neukirchen–Vluyn 1982, 487–97.

— 'Théodose d'Alexandrie dans les manuscrits syriaques de la British Library', in J. Quaegebeur (ed.), *Studia Paulo Naster Oblata II Orientalia Antiqua* (OLA 13), Louvain 1982, 287–99.

— 'Un traité cononite contre la doctrine de Jean Philopon sur la résurrection', in ΑΝΤΙΔΩΡΟΝ. *Hommage à M. Geerard pour célébrer l'achèvement de la Clavis Patrum Graecorum* I, Wetteren 1984, 123–39.

— 'La controverse trithéite jusqu'à l'excommunication de Conon et d'Eugène (557–569)', *OLP* 16 (1985), 141–65.

Van Rompay, L., 'The Martyrs of Najran. Some Remarks on the Nature of the Sources', in J. Quaegebeur (ed.), *Studia Paulo Naster Oblata II. Orientalia Antiqua* (OLA 13), Louvain 1982, 301–9.

Veilleux, A., 'Monachisme et Gnose. Première partie: Le cénobitisme pachômien et la Bibliothèque Copte de Nag Hammadi', *CollCist* 46 (1984), 239–58.

Velat, B., *Études sur le Me̩eṟāf. Commun de l'office divin éthiopien. Introduction, trad. française, commentaire liturgique et musical* (PO 33), Paris 1966.

Vergote, J., 'L'expansion du manichéisme en Égypte', in *After Chalcedon*, FS A. Van Roey (OLA 18), Louvain 1985, 471–78.

Villey, A., *Alexandre de Lycopolis. Contre la doctrine de Mani* (Sources gnostiques et manichéennes 2), Paris 1985.

Weischer, B. M., 'Die äthiopischen Psalmen- und Qērlosfragmente in Erevan/ Armenien', *OrChr* 53 (1969), 113–58.

— *Qērellos* I (Afrikanist. Forsch. 7), Glückstadt 1973.

— *Qērellos* II/2 (ÄthFor 31), Wiesbaden 1992.

— *Qērellos* III (ÄthFor 2), Wiesbaden 1977.

— *Qērellos* IV/1 (ÄthFor 4), Wiesbaden 1979.

— *Qērellos* IV/2 (ÄthFor 6), Wiesbaden 1979.

— *Qērellos* IV/3 (ÄthFor 7), Wiesbaden 1980.

Weiss, H.-F., 'Zur Christologie des Schenute von Atripe', *BSAC* 20 (1969/70), 177–209.

Wellhausen, J., *Reste arabischen Heidentums*, 1887, reprint 1961.

Wendt, K., 'Die theologischen Auseinandersetzungen in der äthiopischen Kirche zur Zeit der Reformen des XV. Jahrhunderts', in *ACIStEt*, 137–46.

Wiles, M., 'ΟΜΟΟΥΣΙΟΣ ΗΜΙΝ', *JTS* 16 (1965), 454–61.

Winkelmann, F., 'Ägypten und Byzanz vor der arabischen Eroberung', *ByzSlav* 40 (1979), 161–82.

— *Die östlichen Kirchen in der Epoche der christologischen Auseinandersetzungen (5.–7. Jh.)* (Kirchengeschichte in Einzeldarstellungen I/6), Berlin ³1980.

— 'Die Stellung Ägyptens im oströmisch-byzantinischen Reich', in P. Nagel (ed.), *Griechen und Kopten im byzantinischen Ägypten* (WB [H] 1984/48 [I 29]), Halle 1984, 11–35.

Winkler, G., 'Ein bedeutsamer Zusammenhang zwischen der Erkenntnis und Ruhe in Mt 11,27–29 und dem Ruhen des Geistes auf Jesus am Jordan. Eine Analyse zur Geist-Christologie in syrischen und armenischen Quellen', *Mus* 96 (1983), 267–326.

Wipszycka, E., 'Les confréries dans la vie religieuse de l'Égypte chrétienne', in *Proc. of the XIIth Internat. Congress of Papyrology*, Toronto 1970, 511–25.

— 'La christianisation de l'Égypte aux IVᵉ–VIᵉ siècles', *Aegyptus* 68 (1988), 125–27.

Wolska, W., *La topographie chrétienne de Cosmas Indicopleustès. Théologie et Science au VIᵉ siècle*, Paris 1962.

Wolska-Conus, W., *Cosmas Indicopleustès. Topographie chrétienne, I–IV, V, VI–XII* (SC 141, 159, 197), Paris 1968, 1970, 1973.

Worrell, W. H., 'Studien zum abessinischen Zauberwesen', *ZAss* 23 (1909), 149–83; 24 (1910), 59–96; 29 (1914/15), 85–141.

Zacharias Rhetor, *The Syriac Chronicle known as that of Zachariah of Mitylene*, trans. F. J. Hamilton and E. W. Brooks, London 1899.

— *Historia Ecclesiastica*, ed. E. W. Brooks, CSCO Syr. 3, 6, Paris–Louvain 1921–24.

Zaehner, R. C., *Zurvan. A Zoroastrian Dilemma*, Oxford 1955.

Zyhlarz, E., *Grundzüge der nubischen Grammatik im christlichen Frühmittelalter* (AKM 18/1), Leipzig 1928, 155–69.

INDEXES

(by T. Hainthaler)

1. Biblical References

OLD TESTAMENT

NEW TESTAMENT

2. Words in Ancient Languages

3. Ancient Authors

4. Modern Authors

5. Subjects

Acephali 80
activity 34, 58–9, 76, 127–8
  two a. 34, 59, 61, 76
Adam–Christ 152, 157–8, 350–2
Aden 306
adoptionism 209, 357
Ag'azi 299, 300
Agnoetes 43, 49, 66, 69, 74, 76, 79, 390
Agranites 45
Alexandria *passim*
  Academy, school of A. 90, 101, 107–8, 112
  allegorization 104, 329, 365
Aloa 264, 272, 276, 277
Alodaeans 272–3, 295
anamnesis *see* liturgy
anaphora 236–50, 253, 337, 379, 381–2, 384,
    387, 392
  see also liturgy
  Abrahae 246
  of Addai and Mari (Syr.) 246
  of the Apostles (Eth.) 381–2
  of Athanasius (Eth.) 246, 341, 361–2, 381
  of Basili 381
  of Cyril (Eth.) 360, 362, 367, 381, 384, 385
  of Dioscorus (Eth.) 361, 385
  of Epiphanius (Eth.) 360, 367, 385
  of Gregory (Greek) *see* Liturgy
  of Gregory (Armen.) 246; (Eth.) 246, 353,
    381, 383, 385
  of Jacob of Sarug (Eth.) 246, 248, 363,
    381–2
  of James 381
  of James (Eth.) 360, 385
  of John the Evangelist (Eth.) 366, 382
  of John of Bostra (Syr.) 244
  of John Chrysostom (Eth.) 382, 385
  of Mark the Evangelist 381
  of Our Lady Mary (Eth.) 339, 349, 353, 361,
    366, 371, 382, 385
  of our Lord Jesus Christ (Eth.) 381
  of Matthew (Copt.) 246, 250
  of Peter (Maronite) 246
  of the Serapion of Thmuis 204, 248
  of Severus of Antioch (Copt.) 249
  Timothy A. 43–4
  Thomas A. (Copt.) 250
  of the 318 Orthodox Believers (Eth.) 339, 385
  of the Twelve Apostles (Syr.) 246-7
anathematisms
  of Constantinople II (553) 113, 151
  of Cyril 55–6, 72, 74, 87
Angelites 78
angels 182–4, 190, 192–4, 196–7, 199, 214,
    219–20, 349, 362, 365, 370
  cult 380
anointment of Christ 336–7, 341–50, 353–5,
    360, 362, 368, 392
anthropological paradigm 67–8, 211–12
anthropology 127–9, 390–1 (John Philop.);
    153–4, 161 (Cosmas Ind.); 199 (Origen);
    197–9, 215, 224 (Shenoute); 201 (Mani);
    351 (Ethiop.)
anthropomorphism 223-7
anti-Chalcedonians 2, 4, 7, 9, 10–12, 15, 31, 38,
    42–3, 53–6, 64, 71, 76, 81–2, 86–7, 100,
    103, 118–19, 235–6, 239, 253–4, 268,
    270, 272–4, 277–9, 281, 303, 305,
    308–13, 315–16, 318, 320, 323, 327, 329,
    336, 350, 372, 374, 384, 389–91
  divisions 18–24, 63, 66, 71, 74–5, 77–81,
    389–90
Antichrist 11, 21, 318
Antinoe 177–8
Antioch 41, 65, 74, 77, 81, 104, 147, 183, 227,
    235, 238, 281, 343, 355, 377, 381, 390
anti-Roman 113–14
aphtharsia (of the body of Christ) 44, 50, 129
aphthartodocetism 47, 282, 352
apocatastasis 224
apocrypha 170, 173, 175, 180–2, 189–90, 193,
    196, 201, 213–14, 219–21, 225, 229, 288,
    328–9, 334, 338, 340, 382